Civil War Veterans

of

Winnebago County Wisconsin

Volume 2
I–T

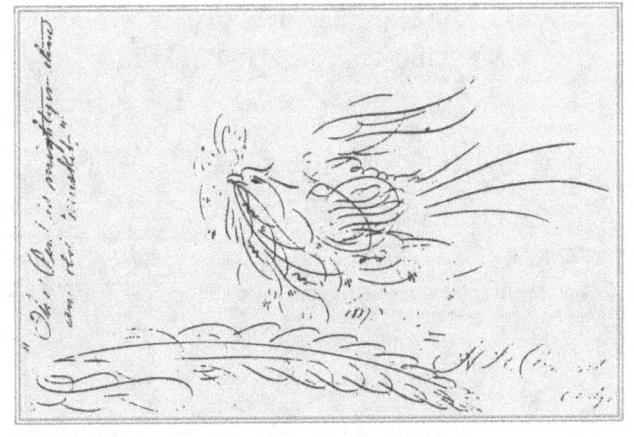

David A. Langkau

Heritage Books
2012

HERITAGE BOOKS
AN IMPRINT OF HERITAGE BOOKS, INC.

Books, CDs, and more—Worldwide

For our listing of thousands of titles see our website
at
www.HeritageBooks.com

Published 2012 by
HERITAGE BOOKS, INC.
Publishing Division
100 Railroad Ave. #104
Westminster, Maryland 21157

Copyright © 1994 David A. Langkau

Other Heritage Books by the author:
Civil War Veterans of Winnebago County, Wisconsin: Volume 1, A–H
Civil War Veterans of Winnebago County, Wisconsin: Volume 2, I–T

— Publisher's Notice —
This book starts with page 379.

All rights reserved. No part of this book may be reproduced or transmitted in any form or by any means, electronic or mechanical, including photocopying, recording or by any information storage and retrieval system without written permission from the author, except for the inclusion of brief quotations in a review.

International Standard Book Numbers
Paperbound: 978-0-7884-0035-3
Clothbound: 978-0-7884-9421-5

CIVIL WAR VETERANS OF WINNEBAGO COUNTY, WISCONSIN

Volume 2
I - T

DEDICATION

This volume is dedicated to the anonymous donor who generously provided a matching grant of $5 million in 1992 for an expansion and remodelling project at the Oshkosh Public Library. Library patrons will soon have greater access to the many research and historical holdings which have previously been in closed storage. Much of the information contained in these volumes was obtained from the closed collection holdings of the Oshkosh Public Library and many of these will also be available to the public.

Thank You!

INGEBRETHAM, Guttorm - Pvt., Co. B, 7th Regt., Wis. Vol. Inf.
Guttorm resided at Utica and enlisted there on Mar. 1, 1865. He was assigned as above and was mustered out on July 3, 1865.
{ROV}

INGLESON, Nels - Pvt., Co. A, 48th Regt., Wis. Vol. Inf.
Nels was born circa 1830 at Norway. He was listed in the 1860 federal census as a laborer residing in the town of Winneconne. Also listed was his wife, Malina, who was born circa 1832 at Norway. Nels resided at Winneconne and enlisted there on Feb. 6, 1865. He was assigned as above. Nels contracted a disease and died on Aug. 13, 1865 at Ft. Scott, Kansas.
{US 1860; ROV}

INGRAHAM, Eleazer S. - Pvt., Co. B, 37th Regt., Wis. Vol. Inf.
Eleazer resided at Oshkosh and enlisted there on Mar. 26, 1864. He was assigned as above and was wounded on June 17, 1864 at Petersburg, Virginia. Eleazer was mustered out on July 27, 1865.
{ROV}

ISKENIUS, Franz - Pvt., Co. E, 9th Regt., Wis. Vol. Inf.
Franz resided at Oshkosh and enlisted there on Sept. 5, 1861. He was assigned as above and was discharged on May 22, 1862.
{ROV}

ISQUCHAPIT, John - Pvt., Co. B, 21st Regt., Wis. Vol. Inf.
John resided at Winneconne and enlisted there on Feb. 6, 1864. He was assigned as above and was wounded at Dallas, Georgia. John was discharged on May 18, 1865 due to a disability.
{ROV}

JACKET, Victor - Pvt., Co. D, 12th Regt., Wis. Vol. Inf.
Victor resided at Benton, Lafayette County and enlisted there on Oct. 12, 1864. He was assigned as above and was mustered out on July 16, 1865. Victor was not found in the veteran section of the 1885 Wisconsin State census. He was listed in that section of the 1895 state census at P.O. Oshkosh and was not found in that part of the 1905 state census.
{WC-V 1885, 1895, 1905; ROV}

JACKMAN, Monroe Wesley - Pvt., Co. B, 21st Regt., Wis. Vol. Inf.
Wesley was born circa 1843 at Pennsylvania. He was a son of Cyrus and Sary Caroline Jackman. Cyrus was born circa 1808 at Vermont and Sary was born circa 1814 at New York. Cyrus was listed in the 1860 federal census as a laborer residing in the first ward of the city of Oshkosh. Listed with him were his wife and two children, Wesley and Frances Ella, who was born circa 1853 at New York. Monroe resided at Oshkosh and enlisted there on Aug. 11, 1862. He was assigned as above and was wounded at Resaca, Georgia. Monroe died from those wounds on May 30, 1864. Caroline, his mother, was listed in 1883 at P.O. Oshkosh and receiving a mother's pension of $8 per month since Mar. 1882.
{US 1860; ROV; LOP-1883}

JACKSON, Albert P. - Pvt., Co. G, 9th Regt., Vermont Vol. Inf.
Albert was born on Dec. 10, 1837 at Orange, Vermont. He enlisted on June 6, 1862 and was assigned as above. Albert was struck on the head by a piece of a rebel shell in the fight at Harper's Ferry, Virginia. He was listed in 1883 at P.O. Menasha and receiving a pension of $2.66 per month for chronic diarrhea and a disease of the lungs. He was listed as above in the veteran section of the 1885, 1895 and 1905 Wisconsin State census at P.O. Menasha. Albert was listed in the 1890 federal census as residing in the city of Menasha. He provided his service dates as having been from June 6, 1862 to Feb. 16, 1866. Albert was listed in 1905 as retired and residing at 517 Milwaukee Street in Menasha. A. Ellsworth, Goldie M. and L. Ray Jackson were then residing with him. Albert died on Mar. 5, 1920 at Menahsa. He was survived by his wife, sons A.E. Jackson of Milwaukee and Lyman R. Jackson of Menasha, and his daughter, Mrs. D.H. Timmerman, also of Menasha.
{US 1890; WC-V 1885, 1895, 1905; B-1905; LOP-1883; 21-33rd}

JACKSON, Andrew - Pvt., Co. D, 21st Regt., Wis. Vol. Inf.
Andrew was born in Nov. 1840 in the town of Bristol, Kenosha County. He was a son of Andrew B. and Mary A. (Bassett) Jackson and a brother to E. Gilbert of a following sketch. Both of his parents were natives of Connecticut. The parents were married at New Haven and then came west to Wisconsin in 1836, settling at Kenosha County. The family removed to Appleton, Outagamie County in 1856. Andrew B. was appointed in 1861 to the position of register of the United States Land Office at Menasha. He later removed to Evanston, Illinois where he died on Mar. 28, 1878. Mary A. survived him. She was residing at Merrill, Lincoln County in 1889. Andrew remained at Appleton, where he was a student at Lawrence University. He enlisted there on Aug. 15, 1862. Andrew was assigned as above and was wounded on May 14, 1864 at Resaca, Georgia. He received a rifle ball in the left thigh, which caused his confinement in a hospital until August of that year. Andrew was commissioned as 2nd Lieutenant of Co. D, 42nd Regt., Wis. Vol. Inf. on July 29, 1864 and was appointed as Regimental Quartermaster, which position he held until he was mustered out on June 20, 1865 at Madison, Wisconsin. He provided his residence as Menasha when he was commissioned. Andrew soon relocated to Oshkosh and began the study of law. He was admitted to the bar and practiced that profession for two years. Andrew was then married on Aug. 29, 1869 to Rebecca E. Doe. She was born at Eldersville, Pennsylvania and was a daughter of William H. and Elizabeth Doe. Andrew and Rebecca had the following children: Carl D., moved to Pelham Manor, New York; Grace; Rufus D.; Ralph D.; and an infant. Ralph and the infant died prior to 1889. Andrew moved to Rogers Park, a suburb of Chicago, and was engaged with his father in the purchase, improvement and sale of property in that area. He returned to Oshkosh in 1879. Andrew was listed in 1883 at P.O. Oshkosh. He was receiving pension #67,965 of $4 per month for a wound to his left thigh. Andrew was listed in the 1890 federal census as residing in the city of Oshkosh. He was listed in 1905 as a dealer in lumber and residing at 109 Church Street in Oshkosh. Grace, his daughter, was then residing with him. Andrew died in 1907. Rebecca died at Oshkosh on May 29, 1929. She was survived by one son, Carl Jackson. She was buried with Andrew in Oshkosh at Riverside Cemetery.
{US 1890; ROV; LOP-1883; Randall p.39; B-1905; ODN 30 May 1929}

JACKSON, E. Gilbert - Pvt., Co. D, 41st Regt., Wis. Vol. Inf.
Gilbert was born on May 31, 1838 at Bristol, Kenosha County. He was a son of Andrew

JACKSON, E. Gilbert (cont.)
B. and Mary A. (Bassett) Jackson and a brother of Andrew from a previous sketch. Gilbert attended the common schools of Racine County. He entered Lawrence University at Appleton, Outagamie County in 1854. He pursued his studies there until 1859 and at the same time he completed a course of civil engineering. He engaged in that position for a brief time and then, in 1861, he worked as an assistant to his father at the United States Land Office in Menasha. Gilbert enlisted at Menasha in June 1861. He was assigned as a Private, Co. E, 6th Regt., Wis. Vol. Inf. In Jan. 1862 he became ill and he was discharged due to that disability. As soon as his health improved, Gilbert returned to his position at the Land Office. He was married in Jan. 1864 to Eliza Mitchell. She was a daughter of Thomas Mitchell from Kaukauna, Outagamie County. They had one son, Harvey G. Jackson. Gilbert remained at the Land Office until May 1864, when he enlisted as above and was commissioned as 1st Lieutenant on June 9, 1864. Gilbert was mustered out on Sept. 23, 1864 at the end of his term of enlistment. He returned to his position in the Land Office but the following year he turned his attention to dealing in pine timber lands. He resided variously at Menasha, Marinette, and Oshkosh in Wisconsin and at Evanston, Illinois. He located in Oshkosh in 1882. Gilbert was listed in the veteran section of the 1885 Wisconsin State census at P.O. Oshkosh. He was listed in 1888 as a member of GAR Post #241 at Oshkosh. He was listed in the 1890 federal census as residing in the town of Oshkosh at P.O. Oshkosh. He was listed in 1905 as residing at the Athearn Hotel in the city of Oshkosh. Gilbert died in 1917. Eliza, his wife, died in 1930. Both are buried in the Menasha Section of Oak Hill Cemetery.
{US 1890; WC-V 1885; ROV; Randall p.39-40; B-1905; Cem. records}

JACKSON, Heman B. - 2nd Lt., Co. E, 2nd Regt., Wis. Vol. Inf.
Heman was born circa 1838 at Ohio. His obituary provided his birth as July 24, 1837 at Naperville, Illinois. He studied law and then removed to Oshkosh in April 1859 as a young practicing attorney. He was listed in the 1860 federal census as a lawyer residing with the family of James Freeman in the first ward of the city of Oshkosh. Heman resided at Oshkosh and enlisted there on Apr. 21, 1861. He was assigned as a Private in the above company and he was commissioned as 2nd Lieutenant of that company on Apr. 23, 1861. Heman resigned his commission on Aug. 5, 1861 due to a disability. He was married in Winnebago County on May 14, 1862 to Annette L. Harwood. Heman was listed in 1868 as a partner in the firm of Jackson & Halsey and residing at 12 High Street in Oshkosh. That firm was responsible for building of the Grand Opera House in Oshkosh. Heman was listed in the veteran section of the 1885 Wisconsin State census at P.O. Oshkosh. He was listed in 1888 as a member of GAR Post #241 at Oshkosh. Heman was listed in the 1890 federal census as residing in the town of Oshkosh at P.O. Oshkosh. He was listed in an 1899 article by Col. Harshaw as residing at Chicago, Illinois. Andrew died of a cerebral hemorrhage at his home in San Diego, California on Apr. 26, 1924. Annette had died some five or six years earlier, also at San Diego. She and Heman had four children: Jessie, married to Alan Cook, died prior to 1924; Lulu, married to Arthur Procter Smith of New York; Isadora, married to Charles Drain of Chicago; and Heman Harwood Jackson of San Diego.
{US 1860, 1890; WC-V 1885; WCMR v.1, p.230, #1281; ODN 07 May 1899; T-1868} {ROV; ODN 26 Apr 1924; ODN 28 Apr 1924}

JACKSON, James - Pvt., Co. C, 43rd Regt., Wis. Vol. Inf.
James resided at Utica and enlisted there on Aug. 13, 1864. He was assigned as above and was mustered out on June 24, 1865.
{ROV}

JACKSON, Lewis - Pvt., Co. I, 3rd Regt., Wis. Vol. Inf.
Lewis resided at Utica and was drafted there on Sept. 30, 1864. He was assigned as above and was mustered out on June 9, 1865.
{ROV}

JACKSON, Robert W. - 1st Lt., Co. C, 21st Regt., Wis. Vol. Inf.
Robert was born circa 1842 at Wisconsin. He was a son of Joseph and Emeline T. (Wight) Jackson. Joseph was born on Sept. 2, 1812 at Killagavanah, County Monaghan, Ireland and was a son of Robert and Anna (Stuart) Jackson. Emeline was born circa 1812 at Cayuga County, New York. Joseph came to this country with his parents in 1817. They settled at Lewis County, New York. Robert died there and Anna removed to Oshkosh for a time and then settled with her daughter Jane, wife of Dr. Charles Hastings, at Muscatine, Iowa. Joseph removed to Green Bay, Brown County in 1838. There he met his future wife. She removed with her father to Oshkosh on Mar. 1, 1838 and Joseph followed them there. A week later they were married in the first ceremony among white people to be performed in Winnebago County. Joseph was unsettled and moved several times between Green Bay, Kenosha and Oshkosh. He owned large tracts in what is now the northeast side of the city of Oshkosh, including much of what is now the downtown area. He was listed in the 1850 census as the Recorder at the Land Office and residing in the town of Winnebago. Joseph was listed in the 1860 federal census as a farmer residing in the second ward of the city of Oshkosh. Listed with him were his wife and the following children: Robert W.; Joseph H., born circa 1845, later resided at Creighton, Nebraska; Electa, born circa 1848, later to marry a Mr. Rhodes and reside at Denver, Colorado; Helen M., born in 1850, later the wife of Dr. W.A. Gordon of Oshkosh; George W., born circa 1854, later to reside at Sacramento, California; and Martha Virginia, born circa 1858, resided at Oshkosh. Joseph died on May 31, 1881 at Oshkosh. Robert resided at Oshkosh and enlisted there on Aug. 11, 1862. He was assigned as above and was promoted to 1st Sergeant in that company. Robert was commissioned as 2nd Lieutenant of that company on Oct. 9, 1862 and was taken prisoner at Chickamauga, Georgia. He was promoted to 1st Lieutenant on Feb. 20, 1863. He then resigned his commission on Apr. 17, 1865. Robert was listed in 1888 as a member of GAR Post #81 at Shawano, Shawano County. He was still residing there in 1895.
{US 1850, 1860; ROV; CBR-FRV 1165-6}

JACKSON, Samuel B. - 1st Lt., Co. K, 20th Regt., Wis. Vol. Inf.
Samuel was born circa 1821 at New Hampshire. Abigail, his wife, was born circa 1822 at Maine. Samuel was listed in the 1860 federal census as a shoemaker residing in the third ward of the city of Oshkosh. Also residing with him were his wife and the following children: Mary, born circa 1849 at Nova Scotia; and Charles, born circa 1853 at Maine. Residing with the family was Nancy Cheney, who was born circa 1793 at Maine. Samuel resided at Oshkosh and was commissioned as 2nd Lieutenant in the above company on Aug. 20, 1862. He was promoted to 1st Lieutenant on Feb. 27, 1863 and was mustered out on July 14, 1865. Samuel was listed in 1868 as a carpenter residing at 53 Tenth Street in the city of Oshkosh. Mary E. Jackson, an assistant

JACKSON, Samuel B. (cont.)
teacher, was boarding at that same residence.
{US 1860; ROV; T-1868}

JACOBS, Francis - Pvt., Co. C, 46th Regt., Wis. Vol. Inf.
Francis resided at Neenah and enlisted there on Feb. 13, 1865. He was assigned as above and was mustered out on Sept. 27, 1865. Francis was listed in the 1890 federal census as residing in the city of Neenah. Frank was listed in 1905 as the engineer at Stranges and residing at 316 Clark Street in Neenah. Residing with him then were Alice, Frank Jr. and George Jacobs. Frank was listed that same year with Eva, his wife, as residing at the Wisconsin Veterans' Home at King. A Franz Jacobs was listed in the 1910 federal census at King but it is not known if they are the same person.
{US 1890; ROV; B-1905; GAR 40th}

JACOBS, John Frederick - Pvt., Co. I, 43rd Regt., Wis. Vol. Inf.
John Frederick E. Jacobs was a son of Henry and Mary (Wockner) Jacobs and a brother of William from a following sketch. John was married on Dec. 21, 1860 in Winnebago County to Magdalena Busk. He resided at Neenah and enlisted there on Aug. 30, 1864. He was assigned as above and was mustered out on June 24, 1865. John was listed in the veteran section of the 1885, 1895 and 1905 Wisconsin State census at P.O. Neenah. He was listed in the 1890 federal census as residing in the city of Neenah and suffering the effects of rheumatism as a result of his military service. John was a brother-in-law of Henry Deitz from a previous sketch.
{US 1890; WC-V 1885, 1895, 1905; WCMR v.1, p.210, #1127; SCA 1:299-300; ROV}

JACOBS, William C. - Sgt., 12th Batt., Wis. Lt. Art.
William was born on Oct. 23, 1843 at Schwerin, Mecklenburg, Prussia. He was a son of Henry and Mary (Wockner) Jacobs. William attended the common schools of his native land until he came to this country with his parents in 1856. They landed at New York and then located in Wisconsin at Grand Chute, Outagamie County. There William attended school and was engaged at farming until he enlisted at Appleton, Outagamie County on Jan. 4, 1862. He was assigned as above and he re-enlisted at the end of his term. William was promoted to Corporal and then Sergeant in that company. He was mustered out on June 7, 1865. William returned to Wisconsin and settled at Neenah, where he learned the trade of a cooper. He was married there on Nov. 8, 1865 to Charlotte Roseann Hulce. She was born in New York and was a daughter of Edgar M. Hulce, the subject of a previous sketch. On Feb. 1, 1883 William began a grocer's establishment on the "Island" at Neenah. William was listed in the veteran section of the 1885 and 1895 Wisconsin State census at P.O. Neenah. He was listed in the 1890 federal census as residing in Neenah. He was not found in the veteran section of the 1905 state census. William was a brother of John F. Jacobs from a previous sketch. Henry, their father was 90 years of age on May 25, 1888 and was then living with son John at Neenah.
{US 1890; WC-V 1885, 1895, 1905; WCMR v.1, p.284, #1720; SCA 1:299-300; ROV}

JACOBSON, Eric Peter - Pvt., Co. C, 44th Regt., Wis. Vol. Inf.
Eric resided at Iola, Waupaca County and he enlisted there on Nov. 1, 1864. He was assigned as above and was mustered out on Aug. 28, 1865. Eric was listed in the veteran section of the 1885 Wisconsin State census at P.O. Iola, Waupaca County. He was listed

JACOBSON, Eric Peter (cont.)
in the 1890 federal census at Iola. He was listed in the veteran section of the 1895 state census at P.O. Oshkosh and was not found in that part of the 1905 state census.
{US 1890; WC-V 1885, 1895, 1905; ROV}

JAEGER, Gustavus - 2nd Lt., Co. I, 21st Regt., Wis. Vol. Inf.
Gustavus resided at Neenah and enlisted there on Aug. 13, 1862. He was assigned as above and was promoted to Corporal and then Sergeant in that company. Gustav was promoted to 1st Sergeant on Jan. 8, 1863. He was commissioned as 2nd Lieutenant in that company on Apr. 25, 1863 and was wounded at Chickamauga, Georgia on Sept. 20, 1863. He was mustered out on June 8, 1865.
{ROV; Lawson p.831, 833}

JAGER, Theodore - 2nd Lt., Co. F, 19th Regt., Wis. Vol. Inf.
Theodore resided at Winneconne and enlisted there on Jan. 30, 1862. He was assigned as above and was promoted to 1st Sergeant in that company. He was commissioned as 2nd Lieutenant of that company on Apr. 6, 1863 and was dismissed from the service on May 24, 1864. Theodore was listed in the veteran section of the 1885 and 1895 Wisconsin State census at P.O. Winneconne and was not found in that part of the 1905 state census. He was listed in the 1890 federal census as residing in the village of Winneconne. His name was alternately spelled as Yaeger.
{US 1890; WC-V 1885, 1895, 1905; ROV}

JAGERSON, Andrew - Sgt., Co. G, 3rd Regt., Wis. Vol. Inf.
Andrew was born circa 1841 at Norway. His parents were also natives of that country. Andrew resided at Neenah and enlisted there on Apr. 20, 1861. He was assigned as above and he re-enlisted at the end of his 3-month term. Andrew was promoted to Corporal and then Sergeant in that company. He was taken prisoner on May 25, 1862 and was wounded on May 25, 1864. Andrew was transferred to the Veteran Reserve Corps on Mar. 12, 1865 and was discharged on Aug. 19, 1865 due to a disability. He was married in Winnebago County on Dec. 3, 1865 to Cornelia Rugge. He was listed in 1883 at P.O. Neenah and was then receiving a pension of $4 per month for the loss of the index finger on his right hand. Andrew was listed in the veteran section of the 1885 and 1895 Wisconsin State census at P.O. Neenah. He was listed in the 1890 federal census as residing in the city of Neenah. Andrew was listed in the veteran section of the 1905 state census as a resident at the Wisconsin Veterans' Home at King. He was listed in the 1910 federal census as residing at King. He had been married once for 44 years. His wife was not listed with him.
{US 1890, 1910; WC-V 1885, 1895, 1905; WCMR v.1, p.290, #1768; LOP-1883; ROV} {GAR 40th}

JAMES, Edwin - Sgt., Co. A, 50th Regt., Wis. Vol. Inf.
Edwin resided at Rushford and he enlisted there on Feb. 1, 1865. He was assigned as above and was promoted to Sergeant in that company. Edwin was then mustered out on June 12, 1866 at the end of his term of enlistment.
{ROV}

JAMES, George H. - Pvt., 13th Batt., Wis. Lt. Art.
George resided at Beloit, Rock County and enlisted there on Dec. 12, 1863. He was

JAMES, George H. (cont.)
assigned as above and was mustered out on July 20, 1865. George was listed in the veteran section of the 1885 Wisconsin State census at P.O. Menasha.
{WC-V 1885; ROV}

JAMESON, Louis - Pvt., Co. G, 1st (3 yr.) Regt., Wis. Vol. Inf.
Louis resided at Oshkosh and enlisted there on Sept. 12, 1861. He was assigned as above and was wounded at Chickamauga, Georgia. Louis was discharged on Jan. 6, 1864 due to a disability.
{ROV}

JANES, H.M. - Pvt., Co. G, 12th Regt., Wis. Vol. Inf.?
He was listed as above in the veteran section of the 1885 Wisconsin State census at P.O. Neenah. He was not found in the records of that company.
{WC-V 1885}

JANNEE, Charles - Pvt., Co. B, 3rd Regt., Wis. Cav.
Charles was born circa 1832 at Belgium. He was a brother of Louis from a following sketch. Charles was listed (Jenne) in the 1860 federal census as a farmer residing in the town of Winneconne. Listed with him was his wife, Julia, who was born circa 1832 at Wisconsin. Also listed were the following children: Laura, born circa 1856 at Wisconsin; and Mary, born in 1860 at Wisconsin. Charles listed his residence as Butte des Morts when he enlisted on Dec. 24, 1861. He was assigned as above and was then mustered out on Feb. 14, 1865 at the end of his term of enlistment.
{US 1860; ROV}

JANNEE, Louis - Pvt., Co. B, 3rd Regt., Wis. Cav.
Louis was born circa 1834 at Belgium. He was a brother of Charles from a previous sketch. Louis was listed in the 1860 federal census as residing with Charles and his family in the town of Winneconne. He listed his residence as Oshkosh when he enlisted on Dec. 7, 1861. He was assigned as above and re-enlisted at the end of his term. Louis was transferred to Co. B, 3rd (reorg.) Regt., Wis. Cav. on Feb. 1, 1865. He was then mustered out on Sept. 8, 1865.
{US 1860; ROV}

JAQUES, John J. - Pvt., Co. F, 22nd Regt., Wis. Vol. Inf.
John resided at Racine, Racine County and he enlisted there on Sept. 2, 1862. He was assigned as above and was mustered out on June 12, 1865. William and Henry Jaques were members of that same company. John was not found in the veteran section of the 1885 Wisconsin State census. He was listed in that section of the 1895 state census at P.O. Oshkosh and in that part of the 1905 state census at P.O. Sawyer, Door County.
{WC-V 1885, 1895, 1905; ROV}

JAQUIER, Peter F. - Pvt., Co. B, 21st Regt., Wis. Vol. Inf.
Peter resided at Nekimi and enlisted there on Feb. 29, 1864. He was assigned as above and was transferred as unassigned to the 3rd Regt., Wis. Vol. Inf. on June 8, 1865. Peter was mustered out on July 14, 1865. Jennie R., a daughter of P.F. and M.M. Jaquier, died on Oct. 26, 1874 at age 14 years, 5 months and 3 days. She is buried in

JAQUIER, Peter F. (cont.)
the town of Winneconne at Bell Cemetery.
{ROV; Cem. records}

JARVIS, Edward - Pvt., 8th Batt., Wis. Lt. Art.
Edward resided at Menasha and enlisted there on Feb. 11, 1864. He was assigned as above and was mustered out on Aug. 10, 1865.
{ROV}

JARVIS, George - Pvt., Co. D, 41st Regt., Wis. Vol. Inf.
George resided at Menasha and he enlisted there on May 9, 1864. He was assigned as above and was mustered out on Sept. 23, 1864 at the end of his term of enlistment. George and Mary, his wife, had a daughter Elva who was born in Menasha on Nov. 14, 1876. George died circa 1877.
{ROV; Lawson p.840; WCBR v.2, p.17, #7}

JARVIS, George W. - Pvt., Co. C, 14th Regt., Wis. Vol. Inf.
George was born circa 1820 at Ohio. Ann, his wife, was born circa 1830, also at Ohio. They were listed in the 1860 federal census as residing on a farm in the town of Poygan. Listed with them were two sons: George, born circa 1856 at Illinois; and Henry, born circa 1857 at Wisconsin. George resided at Poygan and enlisted there on Sept. 20, 1861. He was assigned as above and was discharged on June 20, 1862 due to a disability.
{US 1860; ROV}

JAY, James M. - Pvt., Co. G, 3rd Regt., Wis. Vol. Inf.
James was born in 1837. He listed his residence as Neenah when he enlisted there on May 4, 1861. He was assigned as above and was mustered out on July 14, 1864 at the end of his term of enlistment. Harriet, wife of James, was born in 1866 and died in 1914. James also died in 1914. Both are buried at Rural Cemetery in the town of Dayton, Waupaca County.
{ROV; Cem. records}

JEFFERSON, Henry - Pvt., Co. G, 49th Regt., New York Vol. Inf.
Henry was listed in the 1890 federal census as residing in the town of Menasha at P.O. Neenah. He listed his unit designation as Pvt., Co. G, 48th Regt., N.Y. Vol. Inf. He was listed as a member of the 49th Regt., N.Y. Vol. Inf. in the veteran section of the 1895 Wisconsin State census at P.O. Neenah. He was listed in that section of the 1905 state census at P.O. Neenah as having been assigned to Co. C, 48th Regt., N.Y. Vol. Inf. Henry was listed in 1905 as a laborer residing in section 21 of the town of Menasha at P.O. Neenah.
{US 1890; WC-V 1895, 1905; B-1905}

JEFFRIES, Edward - Pvt., Co. D, 41st Regt., Wis. Vol. Inf.
Edward resided at Menasha and enlisted there on May 21, 1864. He was assigned as above and was mustered out on Sept. 23, 1864 at the end of his term of enlistment. Edward was listed (Jeffers) in the veteran section of the 1885 Wisconsin State census at P.O. Menasha. He was listed in that section of the 1895 state census at P.O. Menasha and was not found in that part of the 1905 state census.
{WC-V 1885, 1895, 1905; ROV}

JENKINS, Charles H. - Pvt., Co. C, 46th Regt., Wis. Vol. Inf.
Charles was born circa 1846 at New York. He was listed in the 1860 federal census as residing with the family of W.H. Cusick in the town of Omro at P.O. Oshkosh. Charles listed his residence as Algoma and he enlisted there on Feb. 3, 1865. He was assigned as above and was then mustered out on Sept. 27, 1865.
{US 1860; ROV}

JENKINS, Edward - Seaman, "Juliet," Gunboat Service, U.S. Navy.
Edward was born circa 1839 at Wales. He was a son of Mary Jenkins. She was born circa 1807 at Wales. Edward was listed in the 1860 federal census as a sailor residing in the village of Neenah. Listed with him were his mother and a brother, Richard, who was born circa 1845 at Wales. Edward enlisted on Aug. 17, 1864 and was assigned to the Naval Gunboat Service. He was assigned to the Gunboat "Juliet." Edward was listed as above in the veteran section of the 1895 Wisconsin State census at P.O. Neenah.
{US 1860; WC-V 1895; Lawson p.840-1}

JENKINS, Henry I. - Pvt., Co. F, 18th Regt., Wis. Vol. Inf.
Henry resided at Oshkosh and enlisted there on Dec. 7, 1861. He was assigned as above and was wounded at Shiloh, Tennessee. Henry died of those wounds on June 14, 1862 at Keokuk, Iowa.
{ROV}

JENKINS, Henry John - Pvt., Co. C, 10th Regt., Wis. Vol. Inf.
Henry resided at Menasha and he enlisted there on Sept. 19, 1861. He was assigned as above and was discharged on Sept. 22, 1862 due to a disability. Henry re-enlisted at Menasha on Jan. 4, 1864 and was assigned as Private, Co. D, 21st Regt., Wis. Vol. Inf. He was transferred as unassigned to the 3rd Regt., Wis. Vol. Inf. on June 8, 1865 and was mustered out on July 18, 1865. Henry was married to Rickey Koffman on Oct. 9, 1865 in Winnebago County.
{ROV; WCMR v.1, p.288, #1747}

JENKINS, James Howard - 2nd Lt., Co. B, 21st Regt., Wis. Vol. Inf.
James was born on Jan. 19, 1840/Jan. 24, 1841 at Bangor, Penobscot County, Maine. He was a son of Capt. and Mrs. James Jenkins and he was a descendant of John Jenkins who settled at Scituate, Massachusetts in 1640. James went to Boston at age 8 years and he grew up there. In the first month of the war James enrolled as a Private in Co. A, Boston Lt. Inf. At the end of his first three-month term, he enlisted in Co. A, 12th Regt., Mass. Vol. Inf., and on the organization of that company he was promoted to Sergeant. He was later promoted to Orderly Sergeant and then Sergeant Major in that company. James listed his residence as Oshkosh, Wisconsin when he accepted the commission as a 2nd Lieutenant of Co. B, 21st Regt., Wis. Vol. Inf. on Aug. 7, 1862. He was promoted to Adjutant of that regiment on Feb. 4, 1863 and was taken prisoner at Chickamauga, Georgia on Sept. 20, 1863. He was imprisoned for 18 months variously in the rebel prisons at Libby, Danville, Macon, Savannah, Charleston, Columbia and Raleigh. James resigned his commission on Mar. 24, 1865. While in service, his parents had removed to Oshkosh. Howard removed to Oshkosh after the war and was married there to Mary Lawrence Turnbull. She was born Oct. 31, 1837 at Hartford, Connecticut and was a daughter of Rev. Robert Turnbull. James, the father, was listed in 1868 as the proprietor of Jenkins & Co. and residing at 15 Jefferson Avenue in Oshkosh.

JENKINS, James Howard (cont.)
Howard was involved in many business interests at Oshkosh, including the Oshkosh Trunk Company and J. & G. Overall Company. J&G was then to become the Oshkosh Overall Company, the predecessor to Oshkosh B'Gosh. He helped to form the first circulating library in Oshkosh and, after the Sawyer/Harris gift which created the Oshkosh Public Library, Howard served as a director until several years prior to his death. Howard was listed in 1883 at P.O. Oshkosh and receiving a pension of $8.50 per month since May 1882 for an injury to his abdomen. He was listed in the veteran section of the 1885, 1895 and 1905 Wisconsin State census at P.O. Oshkosh. James was listed in 1888 as a member of GAR Post #241 at Oshkosh. He was listed in 1905 as involved in many business ventures and was residing at 80 Washington Street in Oshkosh. Son James Jr. was then residing at that same address. James was listed in 1920 as residing at Oshkosh. He died of heart trouble at Oshkosh on Oct. 18, 1922. He was survived by two daughters, Dr. Hester Jenkins of Skidmore, Saratoga Springs, New York and Mrs. Arthur D. Lancaster of Chicago, and son James Jenkins Jr. residing at Springfield, Massachusetts. Another daughter, Lillie, had been married on Aug. 30, 1876 to William Day of Boston, Massachusetts.
{US 1890; WC-V 1885, 1895, 1905; ROV; T-1868; SCA 1:148-9; 21-33rd; B-1905}
{ODN 11 Nov 1921; ODN 18 Oct 1922; OmJ 07 Sep 1876}

JENKINS, Martin L. - 1st Sgt., Co. C, 10th Regt., Wis. Vol. Inf.
Martin resided at Menasha and enlisted there on Sept. 12, 1861. He was assigned as above and was promoted to Corporal, Sergeant and then 1st Sergeant in that company. Martin was wounded at Chickamauga, Georgia and again at Stone River, Georgia. He was mustered out on Nov. 3, 1864.
{ROV}

JENKINS, William F. - Pvt., Co. C, 10th Regt., Wis. Vol. Inf.
William resided at Menasha and enlisted there on Sept. 23, 1861. He was assigned as above and was taken prisoner in the battle at Chickamauga, Georgia. William died in the rebel prison at Richmond, Virginia on Nov. 9, 1863.
{ROV}

JENKS, Isaac R. - Pvt., Co. G, 33rd Regt., Wis. Vol. Inf.
Isaac resided at Utica and enlisted there on Jan. 4, 1864. He was assigned as above and was transferred to Co. G, 11th Regt., Wis. Vol. Inf. on July 22, 1865. He was mustered out on Sept. 4, 1865.
{ROV}

JENKYNS, Ivan - Cpl., Co. C, 1st Regt., Wis. Hvy. Art.
Ivan was born on Apr. 12, 1832 at County Essex, England, a son of Richard E. and Eliza Ann (Piper) Jenkyns. The father was born in England and the mother was born in the East Indies. Richard and Eliza had the following children: Louisa; William; Richard; Sarah; Ann; Phoebe; Margaret; Charles; Sabina; Martha; and Ivan. Richard died in England and then, in 1851, Eliza came to America with William, Martha, Louisa, Charles and Ivan. They came to Winnebago County in that same year and Eliza died there in 1857. Ivan enlisted at Neenah on Sept. 28, 1863. He was assigned as above and was promoted to Corporal in that company. He was mustered out on Sept. 21, 1865. Ivan was listed in the veteran section of the 1885 Wisconsin State census at P.O.

JENKYNS, Ivan (cont.)
Oshkosh. He was listed in the 1890 federal census as residing in the town of Vinland at P.O. Oshkosh. He was listed in the veteran section of the 1895 and 1905 state census at P.O. Neenah.
{US 1890; WC-V 1885, 1895, 1905; ROV; Randall p.53}

JENKYNS, William Henry - Sgt., Co. C, 1st Regt., Wis. Hvy. Art.
William was born on Mar. 23, 1842 at County Essex, England. He was a son of William and Susan (Smith) Jenkyns. Both parents were born in England. They were parents of the following children: Nancy; Margaret; Elizabeth; William H.; Kate; Sarah; and Richard. The mother died in England and William brought his family to America soon thereafter. They settled in Winnebago County and William died there in 1880. William H. resided at Neenah and enlisted there on Sept. 2, 1863. He was assigned as above and was promoted to Corporal and then Sergeant in that company. He was mustered out on Sept. 21, 1865. William returned to Winnebago County and commenced farming. He was married there on Dec. 25, 1865 to Orline Haron. She was a daughter of Thomas and Catherine Haron. Orlin died on Apr. 12, 1878 at age 34 years and 11 months. She left two children: Carrie E.; and Kittie L. William was married second, in 1878, to Ida V. Payne. She was born in 1860 and was a daughter of E. and Mary Payne. William and Ida had three children: Richard; Mamie; and Daisy. William was listed in the veteran section of the 1885, 1895 and 1905 Wisconsin State census at P.O. Neenah. He was listed in the 1890 federal census as residing in the town of Vinland at P.O. Neenah and suffering from kidney trouble. William died in 1914 and Ida died in 1942. He is buried with both wives in the town of Vinland at Brooks Cemetery.
{US 1890; WC-V 1885, 1895, 1905; WCMR v.1, p.292, #1781; Cem. records; ROV} {Randall p.53}

JENNERJOHN, Christian - Pvt., Co. D, 51st Regt., Wis. Vol. Inf.
Christian resided at Menasha and enlisted there on Mar. 4, 1865. He was assigned as above. Christian died on Aug. 3, 1865 at Benton Barracks, Missouri.
{ROV}

JEWETT, John H. - Cpl., Co. C, 10th Regt., Wis. Vol. Inf.
John resided at Menasha and enlisted there on Nov. 16, 1861. He was assigned as above and was promoted to Corporal and then Sergeant in that company. John was killed on Sept. 19, 1863 at Chickamauga, Georgia.
{ROV; Lawson p.811}

JOHNS, Andrew - Pvt., Co. D, 21st Regt., Wis. Vol. Inf.
Andrew resided at Menasha and enlisted there on Dec. 17, 1863. He was assigned as above. Andrew contracted a disease and died on Aug. 6, 1864 at Vining's Station, Georgia.
{ROV}

JOHNSON, Aaron E. - Pvt., Co. C, 14th Regt., Wis. Vol. Inf.
Aaron was born circa 1847 at Indiana. He was a son of William and Catharine Johnson. William was born circa 1804 at New York and Catharine was born circa 1828 at New Jersey. They were listed in the 1860 federal census as residing on a farm in the town of Poygan. Listed with them were son Anson and daughter Margaret, who was born circa

JOHNSON, Aaron E. (cont.)
1842 at Indiana. Aaron listed his residence as Poygan when he enlisted on Feb. 22, 1864. He was assigned as above and was then mustered out on Oct. 9, 1865. Aaron was married in Winnebago County on May 20, 1865 to Amelia Vader/Vetter.
{US 1860; ROV; WCMR v.1, p.279, #1674}

JOHNSON, Ansel J. - Pvt., Co. B, 3rd Regt., Wis. Cav.
Ansel was born circa 1844 at Vermont. He was listed in the 1860 federal census as a farm laborer residing with the family of Morris Mantor in the town of Winneconne. Ansel listed his residence as Oshkosh when he enlisted on Aug. 2, 1862. He was assigned as above and was listed as having deserted on Jan. 30, 1863.
{US 1860; ROV}

JOHNSON, Charles E. - Pvt., Co. F, 18th Regt., Wis. Vol. Inf.
Charles was born circa 1845 at New York. He was listed in the 1860 federal census as residing with the family of John Noble in the town of Rushford at P.O. Eureka. Charles resided at Rushford and enlisted there on Jan. 18, 1864. He was assigned as above and was wounded at Allatoona, Georgia. Charles died of those wounds on Oct. 8, 1864 at Allatoona.
{US 1860; ROV}

JOHNSON, Charles M. - Cpl., Co. C, 14th Regt., Wis. Vol. Inf.
Charles resided at Winneconne and enlisted there on Sept. 11, 1861. He re-enlisted at the end of his term and was promoted to Corporal in that company. Charles was then wounded at Vicksburg, Mississippi and was mustered out on Oct. 9, 1865. He was listed in 1883 at P.O. Winneconne and receiving a pension of $2 per month since Dec. 1880 for a wound to his left shoulder. He was listed in the veteran section of the 1885, 1895 and 1905 Wisconsin State census at P.O. Winneconne. Charles was listed in the 1890 federal census as residing in the village of Winneconne. He was listed in 1905 as residing on E. Water Street near E. Main Street in Winneconne.
{US 1890; WC-V 1885, 1895, 1905; ROV; LOP-1883; B-1905}

JOHNSON, Christian - Pvt., Co. H, 1st Regt., Wis. Hvy. Art.
Christian was born Mar. 16, 1823 at Norway. He emigrated to America in 1845 and settled at Racine County, Wisconsin. He then moved to Winnebago County in 1846 and settled on a farm in section 21 of the town of Clayton. He soon purchased a farm in section 8 of the same town. Christian was married in 1847 to Pernella Christopherson. She was born in 1817 at Norway. They had four children, including Charles J., who was born on Dec. 3, 1848 at Wisconsin. Christian was listed in the 1860 federal census as residing on a farm in the town of Clayton at P.O. Neenah. He resided at Clayton and enlisted there on Aug. 31, 1864. He was assigned as above and was then mustered out at Ft. Lyons, Virginia on June 26, 1865. Christian died on May 1, 1888. Pernella was listed in 1889 as residing with son Charles. She died on June 16, 1890 at age 73 years. Christian and Pernella are buried in Winchester at Grace Lutheran Cemetery.
{US 1860; ROV; Randall p.18; Cem. records}

JOHNSON, Cornelius W. - Pvt., Co. A, 21st Regt., Wis. Vol. Inf.
Cornelius was born on May 26, 1846 at Canistata, Oswego County, New York. He came to Wisconsin with his parents in 1855 and settled at Fond du Lac, Fond du Lac County.

JOHNSON, Cornelius W. (cont.)
He worked on the logging boats on Lake Winnebago as a lad. Cornelius resided at Fond du Lac when he enlisted on Feb. 2, 1864. He was assigned as above and was taken prisoner on Mar. 25, 1865 while on a foraging expedition in North Carolina. He was carried off to Richmond, Virginia. The morning after his arrival at that place, the city of Richmond surrendered and he was set free. Cornelius was transferred as unassigned to the 3rd Regt., Wis. Vol. Inf. on June 8, 1865 but was listed in the records of that regiment as having been mustered out on May 11, 1865. He returned to Fond du Lac and for several years was the harbor master there. Cornelius was married at Fond du Lac on July 22, 1865 to Clarissa Worden of Sheboygan County and they had three children. Prior to 1889, the wife and children had all died. He was married second in 1878 to Mary Bollar of Dodge County. Cornelius and Mary had three children. He spent one season on the upper Mississippi River and then moved to Oshkosh in 1879. Cornelius was credited with having saved thirteen lives on Lake Winnebago and the Fox River. He was listed in 1883 at P.O. Winneconne and receiving a pension of $4 per month since Dec. 1881 for chronic diarrhea. Cornelius was listed in the veteran section of the 1885, 1895 and 1895 Wisconsin State census at P.O. Winneconne. He was listed in 1888 as a member of GAR Post #241 at Oshkosh. He was listed in the 1890 federal census as residing in the village of Winneconne. Cornelius was listed in 1905 as a game warden residing on the corner of E. Water Street and Fremont Street in Winneconne. Son Thomas A. was residing with him. Cornelius died there on Aug. 25, 1920. He was survived by his widow, son Edward, and daughter Mrs. John Schano. Cornelius was buried at Winneconne.
{US 1890; WC-V 1885, 1895, 1905; ROV; LOP-1883; Randall p.55; 21-33rd; B-1905}

JOHNSON, D. Ozias - 1st Sgt., Co. F, 32nd Regt., Wis. Vol. Inf.
Ozias resided at Green Bay, Brown County and enlisted there on Aug. 15, 1862. He was assigned as above and was promoted to Sergeant and then 1st Sergeant in that company. He was mustered out on June 12, 1865. Ozias was listed in the veteran section of the 1885 Wisconsin State census at P.O. Wrightstown, Brown County. He was listed in the 1890 federal census as residing in the city of Oshkosh. Ozias was listed in the veteran section of the 1895 and 1905 state census at P.O. Oshkosh. He was listed in 1905 as a millwright residing at 37 Saratoga Avenue in Oshkosh. Arthur A. and Lena L. Johnson were then residing with him.
{US 1890; WC-V 1885, 1895, 1905; ROV; B-1905}

JOHNSON, Erastus H. - Pvt., Co. I, 21st Regt., Wis. Vol. Inf.
Erastus was born circa 1840 at New York, a son of Luther and Amanda Johnson. Both parents were natives of New York, the father born there circa 1804 and the mother born circa 1807. They were listed in the 1860 federal census as residing with their family in the town of Omro. Erastus resided at Omro and enlisted there on Aug. 11, 1862. He was assigned as above and was wounded on July 2, 1864 at Kenesaw Mountain, Georgia. He was mustered out on June 8, 1865. Erastus was married in Winnebago County on Mar. 15, 1866 to Lucretia Barker.
{US 1860; WCMR v.10, p.67, #839; ROV; Lawson p.833}

JOHNSON, Haken E. - Pvt., Co. C, 2nd Regt., California Cav.
Haken was listed as above in the veteran section of the 1885 Wisconsin State census at

JOHNSON, Haken E. (cont.)
P.O. Utica.
{WC-V 1885}

JOHNSON, Halvor - Pvt., Co. A, 47th Regt., Wis. Vol. Inf.
Halvor was born on June 24, 1833 at Norway. Anna, his wife, was also born at Norway on Feb. 29, 1840. Halvor was listed in the 1860 federal census as residing on a farm in the town of Winchester. Listed with him were his wife and a daughter, Juliann, who was born circa 1857 at Wisconsin. Also listed there were his brothers, John and Ole, who are subjects of following sketches. Halvor resided at Winchester and enlisted there on Feb. 10, 1865. He was assigned as above and was mustered out on Sept. 4, 1865. Halvor was listed in the veteran section of the 1885 and 1895 Wisconsin State census at P.O. Winchester. He was listed in the 1890 federal census as residing in the town of Winchester at P.O. Winchester and he was listed in the veteran section of the 1905 state census at P.O. Larsen. Halvor and Anna were listed in 1905 as residing on 120 acres of section 25 in the town of Winchester. Son Elmer B. was then residing with them. Anna died on June 23, 1908 and Halvor died on Mar. 22, 1926. They are buried with several of their children in the town of Winchester at Grace Lutheran Cemetery.
{US 1860, 1890; WC-V 1885, 1895, 1905; ROV; B-1905; Cem. records}

JOHNSON, Harvey L. - Pvt., Co. C, 1st Regt., Wis. Cav.
Harvey enlisted on Sept. 1, 1861 and was assigned as above. He was discharged in Oct. 1862. Harvey was not found in the veteran section of the 1885 or 1895 Wisconsin State census. He was listed in the that section of the 1905 state census at P.O. Omro. Harvey was listed in that year as a bridge tender residing on Mill Street in the village of Omro. He is buried with a simple military marker on the GAR plot at Omro Cemetery, Pelton's Addition, Section C, plot 18.
{WC-V 1885, 1895, 1905; ROV; B-1905; Cem. records}

JOHNSON, Henry Hanse - Pvt., Co. B, 49th Regt., Wis. Vol. Inf.
Henry was born on Apr. 14, 1821 in Denmark. He was a son of Johan Titlo and Anna (Hanson) Markman. His parents died while he was young. At age 27 years Henry left his homeland and came to America. He settled for three years at Racine County, Wisconsin. In 1852 he moved to Winnebago County and purchased land in the town of Winchester, where he settled in 1854. He was married at Milwaukee, Milwaukee County in 1854 to Jacobina Christina Jacobson. She was born on Feb. 18, 1823 in Denmark. They had four children: Peter William, born circa 1855 at Wisconsin; Henry, died on Nov. 19, 1873 at age 15 years, 11 months and 15 days; Julius E., born in 1860 at Wisconsin; and Anna M., born in 1861, died in 1942. Henry was listed with his family in the 1860 federal census as residing on a farm in the town of Winchester. He enlisted at Winchester on Feb. 21, 1865. He was assigned as above and was mustered out on Nov. 1, 1865. Henry was listed in the veteran section of the 1885 and 1895 Wisconsin State census at P.O. Winchester. He was listed in the 1890 federal census as residing in the town of Winchester at P.O. Winchester and he was not found in the veteran section of the 1905 state census. Jacobina died on Sept. 2, 1891. Henry's marker shows that he died on Dec. 17, 1878 but it is more likely 1898 as he was not listed as deceased in his biography during 1889. He is buried with his wife and two of their children in the town of Clayton at Royer Cemetery.
{US 1860, 1890; WC-V 1885, 1895, 1905; Randall p.54; Cem. records; ROV}

JOHNSON, Israel - Pvt., Co. D, 31st Regt., Wis. Vol. Inf.
Israel resided at Utica and enlisted there on Aug. 15, 1862. He was assigned as above and was transferred to the Veteran Reserve Corps on Mar. 15, 1864. Israel was then discharged due to a disability on May 27, 1865.
{ROV}

JOHNSON, John - Cpl., Co. F, 46th Regt., Wis. Vol. Inf.
John was born circa 1836 at New York. He was listed in the 1860 federal census as a farm laborer residing with Byron Olcott in the town of Oshkosh. John listed his residence as Oshkosh when he enlisted there on Feb. 14, 1865. He was assigned as above and was promoted to Corporal in that company. John was mustered out on Sept. 27, 1865.
{US 1860; ROV}

JOHNSON, John L. - Pvt., Co. A, 47th Regt., Wis. Vol. Inf.
John was born Aug. 25, 1835 at Norway. He was a brother of Halver and Ole Johnson from other sketches. John was listed in the 1860 federal census as residing with his brothers and their families in the town of Winchester. He enlisted there on Feb. 10, 1865. He was assigned as above and was mustered out on Sept. 4, 1865. John was listed in the veteran section of the 1885 and 1895 Wisconsin State census at P.O. Winchester. He was listed in the 1890 federal census as residing in the town of Winchester at P.O. Winchester and he was listed in the veteran section of the 1905 state census at P.O. Larsen. John died on Aug. 21, 1909. He is buried with a daughter in the town of Winchester at Grace Lutheran Cemetery.
{US 1860, 1890; WC-V 1885, 1895, 1905; ROV; Cem. records}

JOHNSON, John S. - Pvt., Co. C, 14th Regt., Wis. Vol. Inf.
John was born on Dec. 23, 1813 at England. Ann, his wife, was born on Sept. 10, 1819 at Ireland. They were listed in the 1860 federal census as residing in the town of Omro. Listed with them were two sons, George and Walter. George was born circa 1846 and Walter was born circa 1848, both in Wisconsin. John resided at Omro and enlisted there on Feb. 5, 1864. He was assigned as above and was mustered out on Oct. 9, 1865. John was listed in the veteran section of the 1885 and 1895 Wisconsin State census at P.O. Omro. He was listed in the 1890 federal census as residing in the village of Omro. John then provided information that he had suffered an injury to his collarbone in a railroad accident. Ann died on Dec. 16, 1878 and John died on Dec. 20, 1901. Both are buried at Omro Cemetery, Original Section, plot 8. Several members of their family are also buried on that plot.
{US 1860, 1890; WC-V 1885, 1895; ROV; Cem. records}

JOHNSON, Nelson - Pvt., Co. B, 3rd Regt., Wis. Cav.
Nelson resided at Oshkosh and enlisted there on Aug. 2, 1862. He was assigned as above. Nelson contracted a disease and died on Dec. 6, 1862 at Ft. Leavenworth, Kansas.
{ROV}

JOHNSON, Ole - Pvt., Co. I, 21st Regt., Wis. Vol. Inf.
Ole resided at Neenah and enlisted on Aug. 14, 1862. He was assigned as above and was

JOHNSON, Ole (cont.)
discharged on Feb. 26, 1863 due to a disability.
{ROV}

JOHNSON, Ole B. - Pvt., Co. A, 47th Regt., Wis. Vol. Inf.?
Ole was born on June 11, 1820 (1860 census shows circa 1832) at Norway. Betsy B., his wife, was born on Aug. 12, 1830 (1860 census shows 1834) at Norway. Ole was listed in the 1860 census as residing with his brothers in the town of Winchester. Halver and John are subjects of previous sketches. Ole was listed as above in the veteran section of the 1885 Wisconsin State census at P.O. Winchester. He was not found in the records of that company. Ole was listed in the 1890 federal census as residing in the town of Winchester at P.O. Winchester. He was then listed as Private, Co. A, 49th Regt., Wis. Vol. Inf. He provided his service dates as having been from Feb. 10, 1865 to Nov. 24, 1865. He also provided that his discharged had been through a hospital due to rheumatism. Ole died on Oct. 25, 1903 and Betsy died on June 12, 1913. Both are buried with members of their family in Winchester at Grace Lutheran Cemetery.
{US 1860, 1890; WC-V 1885; Cem. records; ROV}

JOHNSON, Orange - Pvt., Co. C, 14th Regt., Wis. Vol. Inf.
Orange was born circa 1830/4 at New York/Indiana. He was married on Sept. 23, 1855 in Winnebago County to Rebecca Brown. She was born circa 1834 at New York. They were listed in the 1860 federal census as residing on a farm in the town of Omro. Listed with them were two sons, Orange and James. Orange was born circa 1856 and James was born circa 1859, both at Wisconsin. The father resided at Poygan and enlisted there on Feb. 20, 1864. He was assigned as above and was wounded at Lovejoy's Station. He was discharged on July 16, 1865 due to a disability. Orange was listed in the 1910 federal census as residing at the Wisconsin Veterans' Home at King. Pernellia, his wife of 29 years, was residing with him. She was listed as his second wife. She was born circa 1834 at New York. Her father was born in that same state and her mother was a native of New Hampshire. Pernellia had six children, four then living.
{US 1860, 1910; ROV; WCMR v.1, p.159, #719}

JOHNSON, Peter O. - Pvt., Co. B, 49th Regt., Wis. Vol. Inf.
Peter was born on June 15, 1826 in the town of Toten, Odegaarden, Norway. He was a son of Johann and Bertha Johnson. They had twelve children, only four of whom reached maturity. Peter emigrated to America in 1846 and in 1847 he settled on a farm in the town of Winchester. He was married in fall 1850 to Ingeburg Jensen, a native of Norway. They had three children: Betsey, born circa 1853; John, born circa 1855; and James, born circa 1856. Ingeburg died on Apr. 30, 1856. One of the children died prior to 1889. He was married second in 1858 to Oline Johnson, also a native of Norway. She was born on Nov. 25, 1829. They had one child, Petrine O., who died on Aug. 11, 1872 at age 3 months and 25 days. Oline died on Apr. 16, 1872. Peter was listed in the 1860 federal census as residing on a farm in the town of Winchester. He enlisted at Winchester on Feb. 21, 1865. He was assigned as above and was discharged on Aug. 23, 1865 at St. Louis, Missouri due to a disability. Peter was married third in 1873 to Agnette Lund. She was born on July 4, 1843 and was also a native of Norway. They had one child. Peter was listed in the veteran section of the 1885 and 1895 Wisconsin State census at P.O. Winchester. He was listed in the 1890 federal census as residing in the town of Winchester at P.O. Winchester and he was listed in the veteran section of

JOHNSON, Peter O. (cont.)
the 1905 state census at P.O. Larsen. Peter and Agnetta were listed in 1905 as residing with Julius M. Johnson in section 12 of the town of Winchester. Agnette died Nov. 22, 1907 and Peter died on Aug. 19, 1913. He is buried with all three wives in the town of Winchester at Grace Lutheran Cemetery.
{US 1860, 1890; WC-V 1885, 1895, 1905; ROV; Randall p.55; Cem. records; B-1905}

JOHNSON, Rufus R. - Pvt., Co. A, 21st Regt., Wis. Vol. Inf.
Rufus was born on May 26, 1844 near Ft. Brewington, Onondaga County, New York. He removed to Wisconsin in 1855 with his parents and settled at Friendship, Fond du Lac County. They soon removed to the city of Fond du Lac. Rufus enlisted on Aug. 12, 1862 and was assigned as above. He was mustered out on June 8, 1865. Cornelius and William Johnson were members of that same company. Rufus removed to West Union, Iowa in 1870 and remained there for fifteen years. He then returned to Wisconsin and settled at Winneconne. Rufus was married in Feb. 1884 to Sarah A. Stevens. He was listed as above in the veteran section of the 1885 Wisconsin State census at P.O. Winneconne. Rufus was listed in the veteran section of the 1895 state census at P.O. Winneconne as having been assigned to Co. B of the same regiment. He was listed in 1920 as still residing at Winneconne. Rufus died there on Feb. 27, 1927. He was survived by his widow, daughter Mrs. H.A. Cross of Sioux City, Iowa, son Oscar of Racine, Wisconsin and son William of Peoria, Illinois. Rufus was buried in the Winneconne Village Cemetery.
{WC-V 1885, 1895; ROV; 21-33rd; 21-40th}

JOHNSON, Servitus Louis - Pvt., Co. K, 104th Regt., New York Vol. Inf.
Servitus was born circa 1844 at Vermont. He was listed as above in the veteran section of the 1885 and 1895 Wisconsin State census at P.O. Menasha. He was listed as Louis S. Johnson in the 1890 federal census and residing in the town of Menasha at P.O. Menasha. Louis was listed in 1905 as residing at the Wisconsin Veterans' Home at King. Flora, his wife, was residing there with him. Records from the home showed that Louis had served in the army for 44 months. He was listed in the 1910 federal census as residng at King. Flora, his wife of 41 years, was born circa 1837 at Vermont. Each had only been married once and they had no children.
{US 1890, 1910; WC-V 1885, 1895; GAR 40th}

JOHNSON, Thomas W. - Lt., Co. E, 1st Regt., Wis. Cav.
Thomas was born circa 1838 at New Hampshire. He was listed in the 1860 federal census as a physician residing with Lathrop Hull in the town of Winneconne at P.O. Butte des Morts. Thomas enlisted at Butte des Morts and he was commissioned as 2nd Lieutenant of the above company on Oct. 2, 1861. He was taken prisoner at Bloomfield, Missouri. Thomas was transferred as 1st Assistant Surgeon to the 6th Regt., Missouri Cav. on Jan. 1, 1863.
{US 1860; ROV}

JOHNSON, William - Pvt., Co. D, 32nd Regt., Wis. Vol. Inf.
William resided at Oshkosh and enlisted there on Aug. 18, 1862. He was assigned as above and was listed as having deserted on Oct. 7, 1862.
{ROV}

JOHNSON, William - Pvt., Co. E, 18th Regt., Wis. Vol. Inf.
William resided at Utica and enlisted there on Mar. 7, 1862. He was assigned as above and he re-enlisted in that same comppany at the end of his first term. William was taken prisoner at Altoona, Alabama was then mustered out on May 11, 1865.
{ROV}

JOHNSON, William W. - Pvt., Co. I, 21st Regt., Wis. Vol. Inf.
William resided at Menasha and enlisted there on Aug. 11, 1862. He was assigned as above. William was killed on Oct. 8, 1862 at Chaplin Hills, Kentucky.
{ROV; OWN 16 Oct 1862}

JONES, Alonzo A. - Pvt., Co. A, 48th Regt., Wis. Vol. Inf.
Alonzo was born circa 1821 at New York. He was listed in the 1860 federal census as a laborer residing in the town of Omro. Listed with him was Laura, his wife. She was born circa 1832 at Massachusetts. Henry, their son, was born circa 1857 at Wisconsin. Alonzo resided at Omro and enlisted there on Jan. 17, 1865. He was assigned as above and was mustered out on Dec. 30, 1865. Alonzo was listed as a member of GAR Post #10 at Oshkosh in 1888.
{US 1860; ROV}

JONES, Augustus S. - Pvt., Co. B, 21st Regt., Wis. Vol. Inf.
Augustus was born in 1844 at Maine. He was a son of Lyman S. and Eleanor Jones and a brother of Francis, George Washington and Hiram Jones from other sketches. His sister, Mary E. Jones, was married to John Cowling, the subject of a previous sketch. Lyman was born circa 1807 at Maine. Eleanor was born circa 1815 in that same state. They were listed in the 1850 federal census as residing in the town of Winnebago. They then had the following children: Andrew J., born circa 1833; Silas, born circa 1834; Joel, born circa 1835; Hiram; Francis; Augustus S.; Benjamin, born circa 1844; and Mary E., born circa 1848. All of the children were listed as having been born in Maine. Lyman was listed in the 1860 federal census as residing on a farm in the town of Algoma. He then had these additional children: Rachel, born circa 1853; William, born circa 1855; and Charles, born circa 1858. Lyman died on Feb. 1, 1876 at age 69 years, 2 months and 11 days. Rachel C., another daughter, died on Aug. 2, 1873 at age 20 years, 1 month and 24 days. Electa M., wife of Augustus, was born in 1852. Augustus resided at Algoma and he enlisted there on Aug. 11, 1862. He was assigned as above and was discharged on Mar. 31, 1863 due to a disability. Augustus re-enlisted on Feb. 14, 1865 and was assigned as Private, Co. D, 49th Regt., Wis. Vol. Inf. He was mustered out on Nov. 1, 1865. Augustus was mustered in to GAR Post #10 at Oshkosh on Jan. 15, 1885. He was listed in the 1890 federal census as residing in the city of Oshkosh. He was listed in the veteran section of the 1895 and 1905 Wisconsin State census at P.O. Oshkosh. He was listed in 1905 as residing at 213 W. Lincoln Avenue in Oshkosh. Augustus was listed in 1920 as residing at Oshkosh. He was listed in 1927 as residing at 130 Cherry Street in Oshkosh. Electa died in 1924 and Augustus died in 1929. Both are buried in the town of Algoma at Ellenwood Cemetery, Section A. George W. Jones, his brother, is buried on that same plot. Lyman, daughter Rachel, daughter Mary Cowling and her husband John Cowling are all buried in that same cemetery.
{US 1850, 1860, 1890; WC-V 1895, 1905; ROV; ROV; 21-33rd; 21-40th; B-1905}
{SCA 1:190-1; Cem. records}

JONES, Charles - Pvt., Co. D, 8th Regt., Wis. Vol. Inf.
Charles was born circa 1830 at Wales. He was married to Lydia Phillips on Oct. 2, 1852 in Winnebago County. She was born circa 1833 at Wales and was a daughter of Daniel and Sophia Phillips. Both of her parents were also natives of Wales and both were born circa 1795. Charles and Lydia were listed in the 1860 federal census as residing in the town of Nekimi. They then had two daughters. Jane was born circa 1854 at Wisconsin and Phoebe was born in 1860 at Wisconsin. Daniel and Sophia Phillips were residing on an adjoining farm. Charles resided at Nekimi and enlisted there on Jan. 25, 1864. He was assigned as above. Charles died at Nashville, Tennessee on Jan. 4, 1865 at age 35 years. Phebe, a daughter of Charles & L. Jones, died on Mar. 24, 1881 at age 20 years, 11 months and 28 days. She is buried with Charles in the town of Nekimi at Salem Baptist Cemetery.
{US 1860; ROV; WCMR v.1, p.137, #538; Cem. records}

JONES, Charles H. - Cpl., Co. D, 41st Regt., Wis. Vol. Inf.
Charles was born on Apr. 13, 1845 at East Randolph, Orange County, Vermont, a son of Daniel and Clarissa (Hibbard) Jones. Both parents were natives of Vermont. Daniel removed with his family to Wisconsin in 1851 and they settled in Winnebago County at Menasha. Charles received a good education, studied for a year at Lawrence University at Appleton and then taught school for a year. He enlisted at Menasha on May 2, 1864. He was assigned as above and was promoted to Corporal in that company. Charles was mustered out on Sept. 23, 1864 at the end of his term of enlistment. He returned to Menasha and was engaged as a foreman in the sawing department of his father's spoke and hub factory. Charles worked there for a year and then attended a year at Ripon College. He moved between Menasha, Menominee in Dunn County and Minneapolis. Charles settled at Menominee in 1879 and formed the partnership of Ramsay & Jones. He was married on June 25, 1872 to Frances M. Tobey. She was born in New York and was a daughter of Gibbs and Harriet (Finch) Tobey, also natives of New York. Charles was residing at Menominee in 1888.
{ROV; SCA 1:431-2}

JONES, Charles W. - Pvt., Co. E, 52nd Regt., Wis. Vol. Inf.
Charles resided at Neenah and enlisted there on Mar. 14, 1865. He was assigned as above and was mustered out on July 28, 1865.
{ROV}

JONES, Christopher W. - Pvt., Co. B, 3rd Regt., Wis. Vol. Inf.?
Christopher was born on Dec. 25, 1825. Susan Talbot, his wife, was born on July 26, 1824. Christopher was listed in 1883 at P.O. Waukau and receiving a pension of $2 per month since May 1880 for the dislocation of his left shoulder. He was listed as such in the veteran section of the 1885 Wisconsin State census at P.O. Waukau. He was not identified in the records of that company. Christopher died on Sept. 21, 1888. There is no death date on the marker for his wife. He is buried with two daughters in the town of Rushford at Waukau Cemetery.
{WC-V 1885; LOP-1883; Cem. records}

JONES, Daniel A. - Petty Officer, "Siren," U.S. Navy.
Daniel was born on Mar. 26, 1842/3 at Brady's Bend, Pennsylvania. He was a son of William E. and Phoebe (Phillips) Jones, both natives of Wales. Each came here early

JONES, Daniel A. (cont.)
in life and they were married in this country. They removed to Wisconsin in 1865 at settled at Oshkosh for three years. They then removed to Clark County and purchased a farm there. William died there in 1884 at the age 74 years and Phoebe died there on Jan. 23, 1892 at age 65 years. Daniel was taken at age 3 to Ohio, where he lived with his grandparents. His grandfather brought him to Wisconsin three years later and they settled on a farm in the town of Nekimi. Daniel received a limited education in the town schools. After leaving school he moved to Oshkosh and worked for a year at the old gang saw mill and then learned the trade of a mechanical engineer. Daniel returned to Pennsylvania in 1861 and worked there for a year. In spring of 1862 he took a trip to Ohio and enlisted in the United States service as a brigade teamster. After four months in that capacity he returned to Oshkosh. Daniel enlisted at Oshkosh in 1864 and was assigned as a fireman to the "Siren" of the U.S. Navy. After about six months he was promoted to Petty Officer and he maintained that rank until he was discharged at Mound City, Illinois. He again returned to Oshkosh. Daniel was married at Omro in 1868 to Margaret Snowden. Daniel's grandfather was one of the first blacksmiths in the county and Daniel learned that trade from him. Daniel worked at that trade occasionally as a journeyman until 1874, when he entered into his own business on the south side of Oshkosh. Daniel and Margaret had five children: Frederick Simeon; Addie May, later a teacher in Milwaukee; William E.; Daniel A. Jr.; and Albert E. Jones. Margaret died at Oshkosh on May 6, 1879 at age 32 years, 7 months and 8 days. She had been severely injured by a lamp explosion. Daniel was married again in 1886 to Mrs. Elizabeth (Iverson) Gee, the widow of Frank Gee. Daniel was listed as above in the 1890 federal census and residing in Oshkosh. He then provided his service dates as having been from Aug. 18, 1864 to June 15, 1865. Daniel was listed as above in the veteran section of the 1895 and 1905 Wisconsin State census at P.O. Oshkosh. He was listed in 1905 as a horseshoer and manufacturer residing at 49 Jefferson Street in Oshkosh. He died on Apr. 12, 1923. Elizabeth was born in 1854 and died in 1938. Daniel is buried with both wives in the town of Algoma at Ellenwood Cemetery.
{US 1890; WC-V 1895, 1905; CBR-FRV 1082-3; B-1905; Cem. records}

JONES, David O. - Chaplin, U.S. Army.
David was born on Dec. 21, 1821 at Caernarvonshire, Wales. He was appointed as a Chaplin-at-Large during the Civil War and was stationed at Beaufort, S.C. David was listed in 1883 at P.O. Oshkosh. He was receiving a pension of $17 per month since Mar. 1882 for rheumatism as a result of his military service. He was a Methodist Minister at Oshkosh. David died at Oshkosh on May 26, 1886.
{LOP-1883; OWN 27 May 1886}

JONES, Edward - Sgt., Co. K, 11th Regt., Wis. Vol. Inf.
Edward resided at Winchester and enlisted there on Sept. 19, 1861. He was assigned as above and was promoted to Corporal and then Sergeant in that company. Edward was wounded at Vicksburg, Mississippi and was mustered out on Sept. 4, 1865.
{ROV}

JONES, Francis - Sgt., Co. B, 21st Regt., Wis. Vol. Inf.
Francis was born circa 1840 at Maine. He was a son of Lyman S. and Eleanor Jones and a brother of Augustus, Hiram and George Jones of other sketches. Francis resided at Algoma and he enlisted there on Aug. 11, 1862. He was assigned as above and was

JONES, Francis (cont.)
promoted to Corporal and then Sergeant in that company. Francis was taken prisoner at Chickamauga, Georgia and was then mustered out on May 30, 1865. He was married in Winnebago County on June 4, 1865 to Barbary Seigle.
{US 1850, 1860; ROV; SCA 1:190-1; WCMR v.1, p.275, #1644}

JONES, Fred - Pvt., Co. H, 27th Regt., Illinois Vol. Inf.
Fred was listed as above in the veteran section of the 1885 Wisconsin State census at P.O. Oshkosh.
{WC-V 1885}

JONES, George Washington - Pvt., Co. B, 21st Regt., Wis. Vol. Inf.
George was born on Sept. 29, 1841 at Maine. He was a son of Lyman S. and Eleanor Jones and a brother of Augustus, Francis and Hiram Jones of other sketches. He enlisted on Aug. 11, 1862 and was assigned as above. He was discharged on Nov. 24, 1862 due to a disability. George then re-enlisted at Algoma on Feb. 14, 1865 and he was assigned as a Private to Co. D, 49th Regt., Wis. Vol. Inf. He was promoted to Sergeant in that company and was then mustered out on Nov. 1, 1865. Renna, a daughter of George and E.M. Jones, died on July 28, 1885 at age 15 years, 6 months and 22 days. George died on Oct. 6, 1871. Both are buried in the town of Algoma at Ellenwood Cemetery, Section A. Augustus S., his brother, is buried on that same plot.
{US 1850, 1860; SCA 1:190-1; Cem. records; ROV}

JONES, Henry M. - Pvt., Co. D, 5th Regt., U.S. Cav.
Henry was listed as above in the 1890 federal census as residing in the city of Neenah. He provided his service dates as having been from May 1862 to Oct. 1865.
{US 1890}

JONES, Hiram - Pvt., Co. B, 21st Regt., Wis. Vol. Inf.
Hiram was born circa 1838 at Maine. He was a son of Lyman S. and Eleanor Jones and a brother of Augustus, Francis and George of other sketches. Hiram resided at Algoma and enlisted there on Aug. 13, 1862. He was assigned as above and was discharged on Nov. 24, 1862 due to a disability. Hiram died on Dec. 9, 1862 at age 25 years, 2 months and 25 days. Eleanor, his mother, died on Jan. 29, 1872 at age 55 years, 1 month and 27 days. Both are buried, along with other family members, in the town of Algoma at Ellenwood Cemetery, Section B.
{US 1860; ROV; Cem. records; SCA 1:190-1}

JONES, John - Pvt., Co. B, 3rd Regt., Wis. Cav.
John resided at Oshkosh and enlisted there on Dec. 16, 1861. He was assigned as a saddler with the above company and was mustered out on Feb. 14, 1865 at the end of his term of enlistment.
{ROV}

JONES, Morris - 1st Sgt., Co. K, 17th Regt., Connecticut Vol. Inf.
Morris was born on Aug. 4, 1844 at New York City. He was a son of Morris and Lydia Jones. The father was a dry goods merchant on the "Bowery" before removing to Cazenovia, New York with his family in 1851. Morris Jr. attended the academy there until 16 years of age. He went to Bridgeport, Connecticut in summer of 1860 to work

JONES, Morris (cont.)
in a dry goods store for a man formerly associated with the senior Morris at New York City. Morris enlisted at Bridgeport on Aug. 12, 1862 and was assigned as above. He was mustered out at Hilton Head, South Carolina on July 9, 1865. Morris returned to Cazenovia to reside with his mother. His father had died by then. Morris removed to Wisconsin in fall of 1865 and settled at Oshkosh with his brother, D.M. Jones. Both, along with brother E.R. Jones and an uncle, Mr. Watts, engaged in the dry goods business at Oshkosh. Morris was listed in 1868 as a partner in the firm of Watts & Jones Bros. and residing at 35 High Street in Oshkosh. At about that time Mr. Watts retired and the Jones brothers continued in the business. Morris was married to Sally J. Weed on Oct. 8, 1873. The great fire of 1875 burned out the Jones Brothers & Co. D.M. Jones withdrew from the company at that time and the other brothers rebuilt the business. Morris was listed in 1888 as a member of GAR Post #10 at Oshkosh. He was listed as above in the 1890 federal census as residing in Oshkosh. Morris was listed as above in the veteran section of the 1895 Wisconsin State census at P.O. Oshkosh. Morris died on Sept. 25, 1897 at Oshkosh. He was survived by his widow and three children: Mrs. Elizabeth S. Bell; Morris Phillip Jones; and Wade Jones. He was also survived by the following: Lydia Jones, his mother, of Oshkosh; a sister, Mrs. Charles H. Clark of Cedar Rapids, Iowa; a sister, Mrs. T.R. Morgan of Oshkosh; a brother, D.M. Jones of Pasadena, California; and a brother, Charles I. Jones. His brother, E.R. Jones, died on Aug. 15, 1897 at Oshkosh. Sally, his widow, was listed in 1905 as residing at 33 Franklin Avenue in Oshkosh. Son Morris P. was then residing with her. Lydia, mother of Morris, was listed in that same year as residing at 32 Franklin Avenue in Oshkosh.
 {US 1890; WC-V 1895; T-1868; B-1905; OWN 02 Oct 1897}

JONES, Robert - Pvt., Co. K, 11th Regt., Wis. Vol. Inf.
Robert was born circa 1835 at Wales. He was a son of John E. Jones. John was listed in the 1850 federal census as a hotel keeper in the town of Neenah. He was born circa 1802 at Wales. John had been in Wisconsin for at least two years. Caroline, his youngest daughter, was born there circa 1848. Robert was listed in the 1860 federal census as residing in the village of Neenah. Listed with him were brothers and sisters: Caroline; Emma, born circa 1851; John, born circa 1853; William, born circa 1856; and Mary, born circa 1858. Also listed was a Tina Jones, born circa 1825 at England. Robert enlisted at Neenah on Sept. 17, 1861. He was assigned as above and was then discharged on June 29, 1862 due to a disability.
 {US 1850, 1860; ROV}

JONES, Thomas - Cpl., Co. B, 44th Regt., Wis. Vol. Inf.
Thomas was born in 1842/3 at Wales. He was a son of John and Mary Jones. Both parents were natives of Wales, the father born there circa 1810 and the mother born circa 1800. John was one of the first settlers of the town of Nekimi, having entered 480 acres in 1847. He was listed in the 1860 federal census as residing on that farm. Listed with him were his wife and the following children: John Jr., born circa 1835; Mary A., born circa 1840; and Thomas. Thomas received a common school education and worked on the farm with his parents. He listed his residence as Wayne, Washington County when he enlisted on Sept. 28, 1864. He was assigned as above and was promoted to Corporal in that company. Thomas was then mustered out on July 2, 1865 at Paducah, Kentucky. He was listed in the veteran section of the 1885 and 1895 Wisconsin State census at P.O. Nekimi and was listed in that section of the 1905 state census at P.O.

JONES, Thomas (cont.)
Oshkosh. Thomas was listed in the 1890 federal census as residing in the town of Nekimi at P.O. Nekimi. He was listed in 1905 as residing on 120 acres of section 21 in the town of Nekimi. Jefferson, Milton, John and Lizzie Jones were all residing with him. His marker lists his date of birth as having been Dec. 25, 1831. Thomas died on Sept. 4, 1921. Mary Ann, his wife, was born on Mar. 4, 1853 and died Apr. 14, 1930. Thomas Jefferson Jones, a son, was born on Mar. 6, 1877 and died on July 17, 1951. All three are buried in the town of Nekimi at Bethesda Welsh Cemetery.
{US 1860, 1890; WC-V 1885, 1895, 1905; ROV; Randall p.27; Cem. records; B-1905}

JONES, William H. - Pvt., Co. G, 21st Regt., Wis. Vol. Inf.
William resided at Scandinavia, Waupaca County and enlisted on Mar. 8, 1864. He was assigned as above and was taken prisoner on Apr. 14, 1865. He was transferred as unassigned to the 3rd Regt., Wis. Vol. Inf. on June 8, 1865 and was mustered out on July 18, 1865. William was not found in the veteran section of the 1885 or 1895 Wisconsin State census. Carrie M., his widow, was listed in the 1890 federal census as residing at 290 Main Street in the city of Oshkosh, yet William was listed in the veteran section of the 1905 state census at P.O. Neenah.
{US 1890; WC-V 1885, 1895, 1905; ROV}

JONES, William H. II - Pvt., Co. K, 4th Regt., Wis. Cav.
William was born in Feb. 1838 at New York. His father was born in Wales and his mother was a native of Scotland. William resided at Brillion, Calumet County and enlisted on Apr. 24, 1861. He was assigned as above and was discharged on Jan. 31, 1863 due to a disability. William was listed in the veteran section of the 1885 Wisconsin State census at P.O. Brillion. He was listed in the 1890 federal census as residing in the village of Omro. He was listed in the veteran section of the 1895 state census at P.O. Omro. William was listed in the 1900 federal census as single and residing at the Wisconsin Veterans' Home at King. He was listed in the veteran section of the 1905 state census at King.
{US 1890, 1900; WC-V 1885, 1895, 1905; ROV; GAR 40th}

JORDAN, Albertus - Pvt., Co. K, 5th (reorg.) Regt., Wis. Vol. Inf.
Albertus resided at Rushford and enlisted there on Aug. 25, 1864. He was assigned as above and was mustered out on June 20, 1865.
{ROV}

JORDAN, John A. - Sgt., Co. B, 21st Regt., Wis. Vol. Inf.
John resided at Oshkosh and enlisted on Aug. 13, 1862. He was assigned as above and was promoted to Sergeant in that company. John was taken prisoner at Chickamauga, Georgia. He died on Feb. 28, 1864 while in the rebel prison at Danville, Virginia.
{ROV}

JORDAN, William H. - Sgt., Co. B, 21st Regt., Wis. Vol. Inf.
William resided at Oshkosh and enlisted there on Aug. 15, 1862. He was assigned as above and was promoted to Sergeant in that company. William was taken prisoner at Nolansville, Tennessee. He was then discharged on Feb. 13, 1863 due to a disability. He was not found in the veteran section of the 1885 Wisconsin State census. William was listed in that section of the 1895 state census at P.O. Clayton as having been assigned to

JORDAN, William H. (cont.)
Co. I, 20th Regt., Wis. Vol. Inf. He was not found in that part of the 1905 state census.
{WC-V 1885, 1895, 1905; ROV}

JOSLIN, Thomas - Pvt., Co. F, 18th Regt., Wis. Vol. Inf.
Thomas was a native of Rhode Island. He learned the blacksmith trade there at an early age. He was married at Winstead, Rhode Island to Eliza Moses. During their residence at that place they had three children, Sarah, Mary and Phronia. Thomas removed with his family to Wisconsin in 1845 and settled near the city of Oshkosh. His last child, Thomas H., was born there on July 13, 1849. Thomas then moved with his family to Waushara County in 1855 and continued in his blacksmith trade. He enlisted at Omro on Oct. 19, 1861 and was assigned as above. He was discharged on Nov. 27, 1862 due to a disability. Thomas was buried with a simple military marker in the town of Marion, Waushara County at Marr Cemetery. His wife survived him and resided with her son at Marion.
{ROV; PBA-GL& p.600-1; Cem. records}

JOSLYN, Eugene S. - Sgt., Co. C, 15th Regt., Maine Vol. Inf.
Eugene was listed as above in the veteran section of the 1895 Wisconsin State census at P.O. Oshkosh. He was listed in 1905 as residing at 250 Algoma Street in the city of Oshkosh.
{WC-V 1895; B-1905}

JOYCE, Patrick - Pvt., Co. C, 21st Regt., Wis. Vol. Inf.
Patrick resided at Nekimi and enlisted there on Aug. 21, 1862. He was assigned as above and was detailed to the Pioneer Corps on Mar. 14, 1863. He was then transferred as an Artificer to the 1st Regt., U.S. Veteran Volunteer Engineers on July 18, 1864. Patrick was mustered out on June 30, 1865. He was listed in the veteran section of the 1885 and 1895 Wisconsin State census at P.O. Nekimi. Patrick was listed in the 1890 federal census as residing in the town of Nekimi at P.O. Nekimi. He had suffered wounds to his left thigh and left arm. Patrick was listed in the veteran section of the 1905 state census at P.O. Oshkosh. He was listed in 1905 as residing at 176 Cherry Avenue in the city of Oshkosh. Son Walter was then residing with him. Joyce Joyce, his widow, was listed in 1920 as residing at Long Beach, California.
{US 1890; WC-V 1885, 1895, 1905; 21-33rd; B-1905; OWN 07 May 1863; ROV}

JUNEAU, Andrew - Pvt., Co. I, 1st Regt., Michigan Vol. Inf.
Andrew was married in Winnebago County on Jan. 27, 1868 to Amelia Bashow. He was listed as above in the veteran section of the 1885 Wisconsin State census at P.O. Menasha. He was listed in 1905 as a resident at the Wisconsin Veterans' Home at King. Emily, his wife, was residing there with him.
{WC-V 1885; WCMR v.1, p.367, #2231; GAR 40th}

JUST, Christian - Pvt., Co. M, 4th Regt., Wis. Cav.
Christian resided at Columbus, Columbia County and enlisted there on Feb. 25, 1864. He was assigned as above and he was then transferred to Co. B of the same regiment on Aug. 23, 1865. Christian was mustered out on May 28, 1866. He was listed in the veteran section of the 1885 Wisconsin State census at P.O. Neenah. Christian was listed

JUST, Christian (cont.)
in the 1890 federal census as residing in the city of Neenah.
{US 1890; WC-V 1885; ROV}

JUVE, Sauren H. - Pvt., Co. K, 3rd Regt., Wis. Vol. Inf.?
Sauren was listed as above in the veteran section of the 1885 Wisconsin State census at P.O. Winchester. He was not found in the records of that company.
{WC-V 1885}

KAEMPF, William - Pvt., Co. C, 46th Regt., Wis. Vol. Inf.
William resided at Oshkosh and enlisted there on Jan. 31, 1865. He was assigned as above and was mustered out on Sept. 27, 1865.
{ROV}

KAIME, G.S. - Pvt., Co. H, 48th Regt., Wis. Vol. Inf.?
He was listed as above in the veteran section of the 1885 Wisconsin State census at P.O. Oshkosh. He was not found in the records of that company.
{WC-V 1885}

KANE, John - Pvt., Co. A, 38th Regt., Wis. Vol. Inf.
John was born in Oshkosh and was a son of Patrick Kane. He removed with his parents to Menasha about 1850. John listed his residence as Neenah when he enlisted there on Mar. 23, 1864. He was assigned as above and was mustered out on July 26, 1865. John was listed as having served a total of nine years and six months in the U.S. Army. He then returned to Menasha. John became ill and spent most of his last five years at the National Soldiers' Home at Wood. He died there on Dec. 10, 1891. John was returned to Menasha for burial.
{ROV; OWN 17 Dec 1891}

KEATY, William - Pvt., Co. D, 32nd Regt., Wis. Vol. Inf.
William resided at Green Bay, Brown County and enlisted there on Nov. 25, 1863. He was assigned as above and was then transferred as a Private to Co. D, 16th Regt., Wis. Vol. Inf. William was mustered out on July 12, 1865. He listed his residence as Oshkosh when he was transferred.
{ROV}

KEELER, Charles - Pvt., Co. D, 92nd Regt., Illinois Vol. Inf.
Charles was listed in the 1890 federal census as residing in the city of Oshkosh at 35 Mt. Vernon Street. He then provided his unit designation as above and his service dates as having been from Aug. 25, 1862 to Jan. 21, 1865. He also listed that he was suffering from catarrh as a result of his military service. Charles was also listed as such in the veteran section of the 1895 Wisconsin State census at P.O. Oshkosh.
{US 1890; WC-V 1895}

KEENAN, Michael - Pvt., Co. C, 21st Regt., Wis. Vol. Inf.
Michael resided at Black Wolf and enlisted there on Aug. 21, 1862. He was assigned as above and was wounded at Chickamauga, Georgia. Michael was then mustered out on June 8, 1865.
{ROV}

KEENE, Albert F. - Pvt., Co. C, 1st Regt., Wis. Hvy. Art.
Albert was born circa 1846 at Maine. Both of his parents were natives of that state. Albert resided at Omro and enlisted there on Sept. 15, 1863. He was assigned as above and was mustered out on July 29, 1865. Albert was married in Winnebago County on July 5, 1873 to Amelia Wiseman. He was listed in the veteran section of the 1885 Wisconsin State census at P.O. Stetsonville, Taylor County. Albert was listed in the 1910 federal census as residing at the Wisconsin Veterans' Home at King. Nancy, his wife of 28 years, was residing with him. It was the second married for each. She was born circa 1852 at New York and both of her parents were natives of that state.
{US 1910; WC-V 1885; WCMR v.1, p.584, #3965; ROV}

KEENE, John C. - Pvt., Co. C, 53rd Regt., Wis. Vol. Inf.
John resided at Utica and enlisted there on Mar. 10, 1865. He was assigned as above and that company was then transferred to Co. K, 51st Regt., Wis. Vol. Inf. under orders dated June 10, 1865. The transfer was completed on June 30, 1865 at Ft. Leavenworth, Kansas and the regiment returned to Madison, Wisconsin on Aug. 1, 1865. John was listed as having been mustered out on July 15, 1865.
{ROV}

KEES, William H. - Capt., Co. G, 5th Regt., Wis. Vol. Inf.
William resided at Berlin, Green Lake County and enlisted there on Apr. 18, 1861. He was assigned as above and was then promoted to Sergeant in that company. William was commissioned as 2nd Lieutenant in that company on Dec. 23, 1862 and he was promoted to 1st Lieutenant on May 4, 1863. He was promoted to Captain on June 17, 1864 and was mustered out on July 30, 1864 at the end of his term of enlistment. William was a charter member in 1866 of GAR Post #4 at Berlin, Green Lake County. He was listed in the veteran section of the 1885 Wisconsin State census at P.O. Oshkosh. He was listed in the 1890 federal census as residing in the city of Oshkosh.
{US 1890; WC-V 1885; ROV}

KEIFFER, Peter - Pvt., Co. C, 1st Regt., Wis. Hvy. Art.
Peter resided at Neenah and enlisted there on Sept. 8, 1863. He was assigned as above and was mustered out on May 29, 1865.
{ROV}

KELLETT, Anthony - Pvt., Co. B, 3rd Regt., Wis. Vol. Inf.
Anthony was born circa 1841 at New York, a son of George and Margaret Kellett and a brother to John and Robert of following sketches. George was born on Jan. 15, 1817 at New York and died on Feb. 9, 1900. Margaret was born on Apr. 12, 1827 at New York and died on Sept. 9, 1894. George was a son of Robert and Nancy Kellett. Nancy was born in Ireland and died on Mar. 14, 1863 at age 86 years. George was listed in the 1860 federal census as residing on a farm in the town of Oshkosh. Listed with him were his mother, his wife, and the following children: Elizabeth, born circa 1838; Anthony; Robert; John; James, born circa 1859; Lucinda, born circa 1853; and Egbert, born circa 1854. The two youngest children were born in Wisconsin and the others were born in New York. Margaret Ann, another daughter, was born circa 1836 at New York. She was married in Oshkosh to Franklin S. Brown, subject of a previous sketch. Anthony listed his residence as Oshkosh when he enlisted on June 15, 1861. He was assigned as above and was then mustered out on June 29, 1864 at the end of his term of enlistment.

KELLETT, Anthony (cont.)
Anthony died on Feb. 1, 1872 at age 31 years, 4 months and 3 days. He is buried with his parents, his grandmother and other members of the family in the town of Vinland at Brooks Cemetery.
{US 1860; ROV; Cem. records; Family Research files of the author}

KELLETT, John B. - Cpl., Co. B, 21st Regt., Wis. Vol. Inf.
John was born circa 1845 at New York. He was a son of George and Margaret Kellett and a brother to Anthony and Robert of other sketches. John listed his residence as Oshkosh when he enlisted on Aug. 11, 1862. He was assigned as above and was then promoted to Corporal in that company. John was taken prisoner at Chickamauga, Georgia. He was imprisoned for a time in early 1864 at Danville, Virginia. He died of intermittent fever on July 27, 1864 while in prison at Andersonville, Georgia. John was buried at Andersonville in grave #4133.
{US 1860; ROV; OWN 04 Feb 1864}

KELLETT, Robert - Pvt., Co. B, 21st Regt., Wis. Vol. Inf.
Robert was born circa 1843 at New York. He was a son of George and Margaret Kellett and a brother of Anthony and John from previous sketches. Robert listed his residence as Oshkosh when he enlisted on Aug. 11, 1862. He was assigned as a wagoner with the above company and was discharged on Jan. 10, 1863. Robert was married to Eliza J. Fowler. They had a daughter, unnamed at registration, who was born in Oshkosh on July 18, 1880. Robert was listed in the veteran section of the 1885, 1895 and 1905 Wisconsin State census at P.O. Oshkosh. He was listed in 1888 as a member of GAR Post #10 at Oshkosh. He was listed in the 1890 federal census as residing in the city of Oshkosh and suffering from vericose veins.
{US 1860, 1890; WC-V 1885, 1895, 1905; ROV; WCMR v.3, p.2, #10}

KELLEY, James - Pvt., Co. D, 9th Regt., New York Vol. Inf.
James was listed as above in the veteran section of the 1885 Wisconsin State census at P.O. Oshkosh.
{WC-V 1885}

KELLEY, Michael - Pvt., Co. A, 4th Regt., New York Vol. Inf.
Michael was listed as such in the veteran section of the 1885 Wisconsin State census at P.O. Neenah.
{WC-V 1885}

KELLEY, Patrick - Pvt., Co. C, 45th Regt., Wis. Vol. Inf.
Patrick resided at Utica and enlisted there on Feb. 23, 1865. He was assigned as above and was mustered out on July 17, 1865.
{ROV}

KELLOGG, Hollis W. - Pvt., Co. I, 21st Regt., Wis. Vol. Inf.
Hollis resided at Neenah and enlisted there on Aug. 14, 1862. He was assigned as above. Hollis was taken prisoner at Perryville. He was paroled and was awaiting exchange at Camp Lew Wallace near Columbus, Ohio on Oct. 29, 1862. He was then wounded at Chickamauga and again at Resaca, Georgia. Hollis died on June 22, 1864 at Nashville,

KELLOGG, Hollis W. (cont.)
Tennessee due to the wounds he received at Resaca.
{ROV; OWN 13 Nov 1862}

KELLOGG, Lewis M. - 1st Lt., 5th Regt., U.S. Infantry.
Lewis was listed in 1888 as a member of GAR Post #133 at Appleton, Outagamie County. Marah G., his widow, was listed in the 1890 federal census as residing in the city of Neenah. She listed his unit designation as above and provided that he had died from a shell wound to the head. She was listed as Maria L. in 1905 and was residing at 118 Church Street in the city of Oshkosh.
{US 1890; B-1905}

KELLOGG, Oscar A. - Pvt., Co. E, 1st Regt., Wis. Hvy. Art.
Oscar resided at Johnstown, Rock County and enlisted there on Aug. 26, 1864. He was assigned as above and was mustered out on June 26, 1865. Oscar was listed in the veteran section of the 1885 Wisconsin State census at P.O. Poygan.
{WC-V 1885; ROV}

KELLY, Patrick - Pvt., Co. C, 48th Regt., Wis. Vol. Inf.
Patrick resided at Winneconne and enlisted there on Feb. 8, 1865. He was assigned as above and was mustered out on Mar. 24, 1866.
{ROV}

KELM, Franz - Pvt., Co. C, 9th Regt., Wis. Vol. Inf.
Franz resided at Oshkosh and enlisted there on Oct. 9, 1861. He was assigned as above and was transferred to Co. A of the same regiment on Jan. 1, 1864. Franz was mustered out on Dec. 3, 1864 at the end of his term of enlistment.
{ROV}

KELSCH, Peter - Pvt., Co. K, 4th Regt., Wis. Cav.?
Peter was listed in the 1890 federal census as residing in the city of Oshkosh. He provided information that he was a Private in Co. A, 11th Regt., Wis. Vol. Inf. and also a Private in Co. K, of the Veteran Reserve Corps. He provided his dates of service as having been from Sept. 8, 1861 to Sept. 27, 1864. He added that he had received a gunshot wound to his left leg. Peter was listed in the veteran section of the 1895 Wisconsin State census at P.O. Oshkosh, then as a veteran of Co. K, 4th Regt., Wis. Cav. He was not found in the records of that company. Peter was listed in 1905 as a cooper for the Cook & Brown Co. and residing at 56 Oxford Street in Oshkosh. Bessie, Sylvia and Mabel Kelsch were then residing at that same address.
{US 1890; WC-V 1895; B-1905}

KELSEY, Curtis - Pvt., Co. C, 21st Regt., Wis. Vol. Inf.
Curtis resided at Oshkosh and enlisted there on Aug. 18, 1862. He was reported to have deserted when the regiment was going forward into the action at Chaplin Hills, Kentucky on Oct. 8, 1862. He was transferred to the Mississippi Marine Brigade on Dec. 21, 1862.
{ROV; OWN 07 May 1863}

KELSEY, Frank - Pvt., Co. K, 1st Regt., New York Lt. Art.
Frank was listed as above in the 1890 federal census and residing in the city of Oshkosh.

KELSEY, Frank (cont.)
He provided information that he had been discharged on June 20, 1865.
{US 1890}

KELSEY, George W. - Pvt., Co. ?, 131st Regt., New York Vol. Inf.
George was listed as above in the veteran section of the 1905 Wisconsin State census at P.O. Algoma.
{WC-V 1905}

KENDALL, Edward - Pvt., Co. D, 37th Regt., Illinois Vol. Inf.
Edward was listed in the 1890 federal census as residing in the city of Oshkosh at 262 Main Street. He then provided his unit designation as above and his dates of service as having been from Aug. 15, 1861 to May 15, 1866. Edward added that he had received a wound to the head and that he had been scalded on his left leg between the knee and foot while in the service.
{US 1890}

KENFIELD, Alonzo - Pvt., Co. C, 46th Regt., Wis. Vol. Inf.
Alonzo was born in 1827. He was a son of Selah and Parthena Kenfield. Selah was born on Apr. 20, 1804 and died on Mar. 31, 1885. Parthena was born on Nov. 13, 1808 at New York and died in the town of Algoma on Apr. 3, 1894, survived by two sons and four daughters. They removed to Winnebago County in 1846. Alonzo listed his residence as Algoma and enlisted there on Feb. 14, 1865. He was assigned as above and was mustered out on Oct. 28, 1865. Alonzo was married to Sabrina P. Scott. They had a son, unnamed at birth, who was born in Oshkosh on Jan. 13, 1881. Another son, Arthur Lee, was born in Algoma on Sept. 21, 1882. Alonzo was listed in the veteran section of the 1885 Wisconsin State census at P.O. Oshkosh. He was listed in the 1890 federal census as residing in the town of Algoma at P.O. Oshkosh. Alonzo died in 1891. He is buried with his parents in the town of Algoma at Ellenwood Cemetery, Section B. Other members of their family are buried on that same plot.
{US 1890; WC-V 1885; OWN 07 Apr 1894; WCBR v.3, p.43, #258; Cem. records} {WCBR v.3, p.70, #419; ROV}

KENFIELD, Orsamus - Pvt., Co. C, 53rd Regt., Wis. Vol. Inf.
Orsamus resided at Black Wolf and enlisted there on Mar. 1, 1865. He was assigned as above. Most of that company was transferred to Co. K, 51st Regt., Wis. Vol. Inf. under orders dated June 10, 1865. The transfer was completed on June 30, 1865 at Ft. Leavenworth, Kansas. The regiment returned to Madison, Wisconsin on Aug. 1, 1865 and was mustered out by companies, with the last being mustered out on Aug. 30, 1865.
{ROV}

KENISTON, Eli W. - Pvt., Co. G, 3rd (reorg.) Regt., Wis. Cav.
Eli resided at Winneconne and enlisted there on Feb. 25, 1864. He was assigned as above and was mustered out on Oct. 27, 1865.
{ROV}

KENNAN, George Jr. - Pvt., Co. I, 21st Regt., Wis. Vol. Inf.
George was born circa 1832 at Vermont and was a son of George and Mary Kennan. The parents were natives of Vermont, the father born there circa 1796 and the mother

KENNAN, George Jr. (cont.)
born circa 1801. They were listed in the 1860 federal census as residing on a farm in the town of Menasha. George Jr. was married in Winnebago County on Dec. 1, 1859 to Ada Montgomery. She was born circa 1839 at Ohio. George and Ada were listed in the 1860 federal census as residing in the village of Neenah. He listed his residence as Menasha when he enlisted on Aug. 9, 1862. He was assigned as above and was then discharged on June 5, 1863 due to a disability.
{US 1860; ROV; WCMR v.1, p.197, #1017}

KENNEDY, Frank P. - Pvt., Co. E, 48th Regt., Wis. Vol. Inf.
Frank was born on Nov. 11, 1846 at Conshohocken, Montgomery County, Pennsylvania. He was a son of Michael and Elizabeth (McKean) Kennedy. Michael was a native of County Tipperary, Ireland and came to America when 18 years old. Elizabeth came to this country with her father when she was 4 years old. Michael removed with his family in 1850 and settled in Wisconsin on a farm near Neosho, Dodge County. Frank listed his residence as Oshkosh when he enlisted on Feb. 25, 1865. He was assigned as above and was mustered out on Dec. 30, 1865 at Ft. Leavenworth, Kansas. He returned to Neosho and managed his father's farm for two years. After another year he removed to Appleton, Outagamie County. Frank managed a farm there for two years and then was engaged in the manufacturing of shoes. He moved several times for short periods but kept returning to Appleton. He eventually removed and settled at Antigo, Langlade County. Frank was married on Oct. 28, 1873 to Nora E. Hafner. She was born in Neenah. They had a family of six children: Elizabeth; John; Alice; Mary; Matherine; and Margaret, died at age 3 months. James Kennedy, subject of a following sketch, was a brother of Frank.
{ROV; SCA 1:330-1}

KENNEDY, James - Pvt., Co. C, 1st Regt., Wis. Hvy. Art.
James was a son of Michael and Elizabeth (McKean) Kennedy and a brother of Frank P. from a previous sketch. James listed his residence as Neenah when he enlisted as above on Aug. 17, 1863. He was then a deserter from the 57th Regt., Ill. Vol. Inf. James returned to his original unit on Oct. 27, 1863. The biography of his brother lists that he was taken prisoner and paroled while a member of the 57th Regt., Ill. Vol. Inf. James then went to Neenah to visit a sister and, while there, he enlisted in the 1st Regt., Wis. Hvy. Art. After he returned to his former command he was not heard from again.
{ROV; SCA 1:330-1}

KENNEDY, William R. - Capt., Co. C, 46th Regt., Wis. Vol. Inf.
William was born on Dec. 6, 1830 at Somerset County, New Jersey, a son of William and Euphemia (Reading) Kennedy. Both parents were natives of New Jersey. William Sr. was a son of Henry Kennedy, a native of Scotland. Euphemia was born circa 1810 and was a daughter of Daniel K. and Jane (Kennedy) Reading. Euphemia died circa 1850 at New Jersey and William brought his children to Wisconsin in 1851. Daughter Jane was married to Luther M. Hayes, subject of a previous sketch. She was listed in 1895 as his widow and as residing at New York City. William was engaged in a grocery business with his son, William R. at Oshkosh. The father died there in 1868 at age 70 years. William R. was educated in the schools of Somerset County. He read law at the office of Hugo M. Gaston at Somerville, New Jersey. He came to Wisconsin in Apr. 1851. William was admitted to the bar at Milwaukee and in July of that same year he

KENNEDY, William R. (cont.)
came to Oshkosh to establish himself in his profession. William returned to Utica, New York and he was married there to Matilda T. Nellis on Sept. 18, 1855. She was a native of Utica and was born there circa 1834. William was listed in the 1860 federal census as a lawyer residing in the first ward of the city of Oshkosh. Listed with him were his wife, his father and his sister Jane E.R. Kennedy. Also listed were two children of William and Matilda: Mary Emma, born circa 1857 at Wisconsin; and William, born circa 1858 at Wisconsin. William was residing at Oshkosh when he helped form the above company. He enlisted in 1864 and was commissioned as 2nd Lieutenant of that company on Jan. 3, 1865. He was promoted to Captain on Feb. 17, 1865. William was detached as the Provost Marshal for the District of Northern Alabama from June 16, 1865 through Sept. 17, 1865. He was then mustered out on Sept. 27, 1865 at Nashville, Tennessee. William and Matilda had three children: Mary E., a teacher at Oshkosh; William N., resided at Berkeley, California; and Reading, resided at Minnesota. William was listed in 1868 as a lawyer residing at 10 Jackson Street in Oshkosh. His father and sister were also residing at that address. William was not found in the veteran section of the 1885 Wisconsin State census. He was listed in the 1890 federal census as residing in Oshkosh. William was listed in the veteran section of the 1895 state census at P.O. Oshkosh and was not found in that section of the 1905 state census. He was listed in 1905 as retired and residing at 222 Jackson Street in Oshkosh. Dora and Mary E. Kennedy were then residing at that same address.
{US 1860, 1890; WC-V 1885, 1905; T-1868; CBR-FRV 1150-1; Randall p.40; B-1905} {ROV; OWC 26 Sep 1855}

KEPE, Charles - Seaman, "Ohio," U.S. Navy.
Charles was listed as above in the veteran section of the 1895 Wisconsin State census at P.O. Oshkosh.
{WC-V 1895}

KERSTELL, Frederick - Pvt., Co. D, 2nd Regt., Wis. Vol. Inf.
Frederick resided at Watertown, Jefferson County and enlisted there on May 22, 1861. He was assigned as above and was taken prisoner at Gainesville. Fred was wounded at Gettysburg, Pennsylvania and was then transferred to the Veteran Reserve Corps on Nov. 15, 1863. His name was listed as Kouster when he was transferred. Fred was listed in the 1890 federal census as residing in the town of Poy Sippi, Waushara County at P.O. Auroraville. He then provided that he had received a gunshot wound to his left arm. Fred was listed in the veteran section of the 1895 Wisconsin State census at Poysippi. He was listed in that section of the 1905 state census at P.O. Omro. He was listed that year as a farmer residing on Quarter Street in the village of Omro. Fred was born in 1838 and died in 1906. His wife, Elizabeth, was born in 1846 and died in 1918. Both are buried at Omro Cemetery, Pelton's Addition, Section C, plot 28.
{US 1890; WC-V 1895, 1905; ROV; B-1905; Cem. records}

KETTELL, William M. - Cpl., Co. D, 41st Regt., Wis. Vol. Inf.
William was born on Feb. 21, 1842 at Stephentown, Rensselaer County, New York. He was a son of William and Fanny (Merchant) Kettell. They removed with their family to Wisconsin in 1861 and settled at Menasha. William enlisted there on May 3, 1864. He was assigned as above and was promoted to Corporal in that company. William was mustered out on Sept. 23, 1864 at the end of his term of enlistment. He returned to

KETTELL, William M. (cont.)
Menasha and then removed to Peshtigo, Oconto County in 1869. He was married to Harriet Delong, a daughter of Lawrence and Elonore (McClelland) Delong. William and Harriet had four children: Fannie; Lee; Waldo; and Sherman. Two nephews of Harriet, Henry and Jewett Brown, served in Wisconsin regiments during the war. William was listed in 1888 as residing at Peshtigo. He was also listed as having died in Washington.
{ROV; SCA 1:401; Lawson p.840}

KETTO, John T. - Pvt., Co. G, 3rd Regt., Wis. Vol. Inf.
John resided at Neenah and enlisted there on Apr. 20, 1861. He was assigned as above. John was discharged, date not listed, due to a disability.
{ROV}

KEVILL, Jesse - Cpl., Co. D, 49th Regt., Wis. Vol. Inf.
Jesse was born circa 1830 at England. Elisabeth, his wife, was born circa 1831 at England. They were listed (Keevil) in the 1860 federal census as residing on a farm in the town of Winchester. Listed with them were the following children: Jane, born circa 1855 at England; David, born circa 1857 at Wisconsin; and Henry, born in 1859 at Wisconsin. Jesse resided at Winchester and he enlisted there on Feb. 14, 1865. He was assigned as above and was promoted to Corporal in that company. Jesse was mustered out on Nov. 1, 1865. He was listed in the veteran section of the 1885 Wisconsin State census at P.O. Winchester. He was listed in the 1890 federal census as residing in the town of Winchester at P.O. Winchester. Jesse was listed (Kuvil) in the veteran section of the 1895 state census at P.O. Neenah and was listed in that part of the 1905 state census at P.O. Neenah. He was listed in 1905 as retired and residing at 230 Center Street in the city of Neenah.
{US 1860, 1890; WC-V 1885, 1895, 1905; ROV; B-1905}

KEYES, Charles A. - 2nd Lt., Co. G, 42nd Regt., Wis. Vol. Inf.
Charles resided at Lake Mills, Jefferson County and enlisted there on Oct. 25, 1861. He was assigned as Private, Co. D, 16th Regt., Wis. Vol. Inf. and was then promoted to Corporal in that company. Charles was transferred to Co. E of the same regiment on Nov. 1, 1862. He was commissioned as 2nd Lieutenant of Co. G, 42nd Regt., Wis. Vol. Inf. on Aug. 24, 1864 but was not mustered at that rank. Charles was listed as absent without leave when the regiment was mustered out on June 20, 1865. He was listed in the veteran section of the 1885 Wisconsin State census at P.O. Oshkosh.
{WC-V 1885; ROV}

KEYES, George H. - Pvt., Co. D, 41st Regt., Wis. Vol. Inf.
George was born on Apr. 13, 1845 at Wisconsin, a son of Abel and Mary E. Keyes. Abel was born on Mar. 25, 1822 at Vermont and was a son of Capt. Joseph and Olive Keyes. Joseph was born in 1795 and died on Sept. 17, 1874. Olive was born in 1800 and died on Feb. 10, 1878. Mary, wife of Abel, was born circa 1827 at New York. Abel was listed in the 1850 census as a miller residing in the town of Neenah. Also listed were his wife and the following children: George; Edward E., born circa 1847; and Frank A., born circa 1848. All three children were born in Wisconsin. Abel was listed in the 1860 federal census as a real estate dealer residing in the second ward of the village of Menasha. Another son, Frederick, had been born circa 1851 at Wisconsin. George resided at Menasha and enlisted there on May 16, 1864. He was assigned as above and

KEYES, George H. (cont.)
was mustered out on Sept. 23, 1864 at the end of his term of enlistment. George was married to Emma M. Thatcher. She was born in 1847 and died Mar. 7, 1917. George died on Mar. 6, 1935. He is buried with his wife, father, grand-parents and others of their family in the Menasha Section of Oak Hill Cemetery.
{US 1850, 1860; ROV; Cem. records}

KEYES, Oliver A. - Pvt., Co. B, 34th Regt., New Jersey Vol. Inf.
Oliver was born circa 1831 at Vermont. He was listed in the 1860 federal census as a chair maker residing in the first ward of the village of Menasha. Sarah, his wife, was born circa 1833 at New York. Arthur, a son, was born in 1860 at Wisconsin. Oliver was listed in the 1890 federal census as residing in Menasha. He then listed his unit designation as above and his service dates as having been from Feb. 10, 1865 to Aug. 15, 1865. Oliver died on June 9, 1906. He is buried in the Menasha Section of Oak Hill Cemetery.
{US 1860; 1890; Cem. records}

KEYES, Oliver B. - Pvt., 6th Regt., Wis. Vol. Inf.
Oliver resided at Menasha and enlisted there on July 16, 1861. He was assigned as a musician in the band of that regiment. Oliver was listed in the veteran section of the 1885 Wisconsin State census at P.O. Menasha. His unit at that time was listed as the 51st Regt., Wis. Vol. Inf. This is probably the same person as in the preceeding sketch.
{WC-V 1885; ROV}

KIENAST, Samuel - Cpl., Co. B, 3rd Regt., Wis. Cav.
Samuel was born circa 1839 at Prussia. He was a son of Samuel and Dorothea Kienast. The parents were also natives of Prussia, the father born there circa 1795 and the mother born circa 1792. They were listed in the 1860 federal census as residing on a farm in the town of Vinland. Listed with them were the following children: Samuel; Dorothea, born circa 1840; Auguste, born circa 1843; Wilhelm, born circa 1846; and Gustav, born circa 1846. All of the children were born in Prussia. Samuel listed his residence as at Oshkosh when he enlisted on Dec. 2, 1861. He was assigned as above and was then promoted to Corporal in that company. Samuel was listed as having deserted on June 11, 1862.
{US 1860; ROV}

KIERBERGER, George F. - Pvt., Co. B, 3rd Regt., Wis. Cav.
George resided at Menasha and enlisted there on Dec. 27, 1861. He was assigned as a bugler with the above company. George re-enlisted at the end of his term and was then transferred to Co. B, 3rd (reorg.) Regt., Wis. Cav. on Feb. 1, 1865. He was mustered out on Sept. 8, 1865. George was listed in the 1890 federal census as residing in the town of Dupont, Waupaca County at P.O. Marion. He reported then that he suffered from diarrhea during his military service.
{US 1890; ROV}

KILBORN, George A. - Cpl., Co. C, 21st Regt., Wis. Vol. Inf.
George resided at Oshkosh and enlisted there on Aug. 14, 1862. He was assigned as above and was promoted to Corporal in that company. George contracted a disease and died on Mar. 3, 1863 at Murfreesboro, Tennessee. Military records provide the year of

KILBORN, George A. (cont.)
death as 1865 but he was reported dead in an 1863 newspaper item.
{ROV; OWN 07 May 1863}

KIMBALL, Alonzo B. - Pvt., Co. G, 3rd (reorg.) Regt., Wis. Cav.
Alonzo was born circa 1847 at Canada. He was a son of Albert and Emily Kimball and a brother of William from a following sketch. The parents were both natives of New York, Albert born there circa 1827 and Emily born circa 1828. Albert was listed in the 1860 federal census as a carpenter residing in the town of Omro. Listed with him were his wife and the following children: Alonzo; William; Frederick, born circa 1854 at Wisconsin; and Katie, born circa 1857 at Wisconsin. Alonzo listed his residence as Omro when he enlisted on Feb. 22, 1864. He was assigned as above and was mustered out on Oct. 27, 1865. When brother William died in 1920, Alonzo was reported to be residing in Missouri.
{US 1860; ROV; ODN 27 May 1920}

KIMBALL, W.K. - Pvt., Co. F, 43rd Regt., Wis. Vol. Inf.?
He was listed as such in the veteran section of the 1895 Wisconsin State census at P.O. Oshkosh. He was not found in the records of that company.
{WC-V 1895}

KIMBALL, William W. - Pvt., Co. A, 17th Regt., Wis. Vol. Inf.
William was born in 1850 at Beaver Dam, Dodge County, Wisconsin. He was a son of Albert and Emily Kimball. His parents removed to Omro in 1853. William struck out on his own at age 11 when he hired out on a farm for the summers and attended school in Omro during the winter terms. William listed his residence as Belle Plaine, Shawano County when he enlisted on Oct. 17, 1864. He was assigned as above and was mustered out on July 14, 1865. William returned to Omro and purchased a home there for his mother. He worked on boats during the summer and attended Omro High School during the winter terms. William attended the normal school at Whitewater, Walworth County during 1868. From 1869 to 1874 he worked as a harness maker in summer and taught school in various districts during the winter terms. He taught at a rural school in the town of Poygan and then was appointed as assistant principal of the Omro High School. William was married in 1870 to Clara "Carrie" Cole of Beaver Dam. He took charge of the schools at Eureka in 1874 and remained in that position until 1878. He was then elected as the Winnebago County Superintendent of Schools and held that position for ten years. William and Carrie had a son, William Walter, who was born in Eureka on Aug. 12, 1881. William was listed in the veteran section of the 1885 Wisconsin State census at P.O. Omro. He was elected as clerk of courts in 1888, assumed that office in Jan. 1889 and remained in that position for four years. After retiring from office, William studied law in the office of Phillips & Hicks at Oshkosh and became a partner in that firm. William was listed in the 1890 federal census as residing in the city of Oshkosh. He was listed in the veteran section of the 1895 state census at P.O. Oshkosh. William was listed in 1905 as an attorney residing at 37 E. Irving Street in Oshkosh. Son William Jr. was then residing with him. William retired from his law practice in 1910 and then devoted much of his energy in managing the property and interests of the Elizabeth Batchelder Davis orphanage. William died on Feb. 26, 1920. His obituary states that he died on May 26, 1920. Clara, his wife, was born in 1848 and died in 1915. William is buried with his wife and parents at Omro Cemetery, Olin's

KIMBALL, William W. (cont.)
Addition, Section C, plot 19. He was survived by sons William and Frank, who resided on the family farm at Omro.
{US 1860, 1890; WC-V 1885, 1895; OWN 13 Oct 1894; ODN 27 May 1920; B-1905} {ROV; Cem. records; WCBR v.3, p.37, #218}

KINCAID, Isaac L. - Pvt., Co. H, 43rd Regt., New York Vol. Inf.
Isaac had a son, unnamed at registration, who was born in Oshkosh on Apr. 9, 1882. He was listed as above in the veteran section of the 1885 Wisconsin State census at P.O. Oshkosh. He was listed in that section of the 1895 state census at P.O. Oshkosh as having been assigned as a Private to Co. H, 15th Regt., Maine Vol. Inf. Isaac was listed in 1905 as an employee of the Morgan Co. and residing at 245 Seventh Street in the city of Oshkosh. Roy Kincaid was then residing at that same address.
{WC-V 1885, 1895; WCBR v.3, p.75, #450; B-1905}

KING, Adelphus - Pvt., Co. H, 16th Regt., New York Vol. Inf.
Adelphus was listed as above in the veteran section of the 1885 Wisconsin State census at P.O. Winneconne.
{WC-V 1885}

KING, Delos G. - Sgt., Co. B, 3rd Regt., Wis. Cav.
Delos resided at Oshkosh and enlisted there on Dec. 9, 1861. He was assigned as above and was promoted to Corporal and then Sergeant in that company. Delos was promoted to Regimental Quartermaster on July 1, 1864. He was mustered out on Feb. 14, 1865.
{ROV}

KING, George Y. - 1st Sgt., Co. K, 20th Regt., Wis. Vol. Inf.
George was born circa 1835 at New York. He was listed in the 1860 federal census as an engineer residing with the family of Oscar Watts in the second ward of the city of Oshkosh. George enlisted at Oshkosh on Aug. 12, 1862. He was assigned as above and was promoted to Sergeant and then 1st Sergeant in that company. George was mustered out on July 14, 1865. He was listed in 1868 as an engineer residing at 23 Eighth Street in Oshkosh.
{US 1860; ROV; T-1868}

KING, Martin - Pvt., Co. G, 3rd (reorg.) Regt., Wis. Cav.
Martin resided at Oshkosh and enlisted there on Jan. 16, 1864. He was assigned as above and was mustered out on Oct. 27, 1865.
{ROV}

KINGLAND, Ole T. - Pvt., Co. K, 3rd Regt., Wis. Vol. Inf.?
Ole was listed as above in the veteran section of the 1895 Wisconsin State census at P.O. Utica. He was not found in the records of that company.
{WC-V 1895}

KINGLAND, T.T. - Pvt., Co. H, 15th Regt., Wis. Vol. Inf.?
He was listed as above in the veteran section of the 1885 and 1895 Wisconsin State census at P.O. Utica. He was not found in the records of that company.
{WC-V 1885, 1895}

KINSLER, John - Pvt., Co. B, 3rd Regt., Wis. Vol. Inf.
John resided at Oshkosh and enlisted there on Apr. 19, 1861. He was assigned as above and was wounded at Winchester, Virginia. While home on furlough, John was married in Winnebago County on Oct. 5, 1863 to Alice Cowling. After returning to his unit, John was wounded again at Chancellorsville, Virginia. He was mustered out on June 29, 1864 at the end of his term of enlistment. He was listed (Kingsley) in the veteran section of the 1885 Wisconsin State census at P.O. Oshkosh. John was listed in 1888 as a member of GAR Post #241 at Oshkosh. He was listed in the 1890 federal census as residing in the town of Oshkosh at P.O. Oshkosh. He had worked on a farm for Tom Wall and was then engaged in 1879 as a teamster for the Cook & Brown Lime Co. at Oshkosh. John suffered from lung problems since his military service. He died as a result of those problems on Apr. 2, 1891 at age 54 years. John was survived by his wife and eleven children.
{US 1890; ROV; OWN 02 Apr 1891; WCMR v.1, p.245, #1406}

KINSLEY, Benjamin F. - Pvt., Co. B, 3rd (reorg.) Regt., Wis. Cav.
Benjamin resided at Oshkosh and enlisted there on Aug. 22, 1864. He was assigned as above and was mustered out on June 19, 1865.
{ROV}

KINSLEY, George - Sgt., Co. F, 18th Regt., Wis. Vol. Inf.
George was born in 1829 at Vermont. He was married to Martha Coats on June 21, 1859 in Winnebago County. She was born circa 1836 at Vermont. George was listed in the 1860 federal census as a shoemaker residing in the town of Rushford at P.O. Eureka. Listed with him and his wife was Emma Coates, a sister of Martha. She was born circa 1838 at Vermont. George resided at Eureka and enlisted there on Nov. 26, 1861. He was assigned as above and was promoted to Sergeant in that company. He was discharged on July 15, 1862. George was listed in the veteran section of the 1885, 1895 and 1905 Wisconsin State census at P.O. Eureka. Charlotte R., his wife, was born in 1828 and died in 1858. Martha A., his second wife, was born in 1835 and died in 1902. George E., a son, was born in 1851 and died in 1855. Elmer, another son, was born in 1856 and died in 1859. George was listed in 1905 as residing in the village of Eureka. He died in 1919. He is buried with both wives and both sons in the town of Rushford at Eureka Cemetery.
{US 1860; WC-V 1885, 1895, 1905; Cem. records; WCMR v.1, p.181, #893; ROV}
{B-1905}

KINTZ, Jacob - Pvt., Co. F, 17th Regt., Pennsylvania Vol. Inf.
Jacob was born circa 1826 at Germany. His parents were natives of that country. Jacob emigrated to the United States in 1850. He was listed as above in the 1890 federal census as residing in the town of Leon, Waushara County at P.O. Pine River. Jacob then reported that he had suffered a rupture during his service. Conrad Kintz, veteran of Co. B, 88th Regt., Penn. Vol. Inf. was also residing there, as was a George Kintz, veteran of Co. K, 46th Regt., Wis. Vol. Inf. Jacob was listed as above in the veteran section of the 1905 Wisconsin State census at P.O. Oshkosh. He was listed in 1905 as retired and residing at 255 Oak Street in the city of Oshkosh. That same year Jacob was accepted as a resident at the Wisconsin Veterans' Home at King. He was listed there as a veteran of Co. F, 2nd Regt., Penn. Cav. with 34 months of service. Jacob was listed

KINTZ, Jacob (cont.)
in the 1910 federal census as a widower residing at King.
{US 1890; 1910; WC-V 1905; B-1905; GAR 40th}

KIRBY, John - Civil War Veteran?
John was listed in 1883 at P.O. Neenah. He was then receiving pension #84,870 of $4 per month for a wound to his abdomen. John was not found in the index to the Roster of Wisconsin Volunteers.
{LOP-1883}

KIRKHAM, David - Pvt., Co. B, 22nd Regt., Wis. Vol. Inf.?
David was listed as such in the veteran section of the 1885 Wisconsin State census at P.O. Oshkosh. He was not found in the records of that company.
{WC-V 1885}

KIRKLAND, Edward T. - 1st Sgt., Co. H, 21st Regt., Wis. Vol. Inf.
Edward resided at Oshkosh and enlisted there on Aug. 12, 1862. He was assigned as above and was then promoted to 1st Sergeant in that company. Edward was killed on Oct. 8, 1862 at Chaplin Hills, Kentucky.
{ROV}

KITTELSEN, Hans - Cpl., Co. C, 1st Regt., Wis. Hvy. Art.
Hans resided at Winchester and enlisted there on Sept. 21, 1861. He was assigned as a Private, Co. K, 11th Regt., Wis. Vol. Inf. and was discharged on Dec. 6, 1862 due to a disability. Hans re-enlisted on Sept. 5, 1863 and was accepted as a veteran recruit in Co. C, 1st Regt., Wis. Hvy. Art. He was promoted to Corporal in that company and was mustered out on Sept. 21, 1865.
{ROV}

KITTLESON, Ole Jr. - Pvt., Co. H, 1st Regt., Wis. Hvy. Art.
Ole resided at Ft. Howard, Brown County and enlisted there on Aug. 29, 1864. He was assigned as a musician in the above company and was mustered out on June 26, 1865. Ole was listed in the veteran section of the 1885 and 1895 Wisconsin State census at P.O. Winchester.
{WC-V 1885, 1895; ROV}

KITTLESON, Ole Sr. - Pvt., Co. H, 1st Regt., Wis. Hvy. Art.
Ole resided at Winchester and enlisted there on Aug. 31, 1864. He was assigned as a musician in the above company and was mustered out on June 26, 1865. Ole was listed in the veteran section of the 1885 Wisconsin State census at P.O. Winchester. He was listed in the 1890 federal census as residing at P.O. Winchester.
{US 1890; WC-V 1885; ROV}

KLEBER, Christian - Pvt., Co. C, 21st Regt., Wis. Vol. Inf.?
Christian was born circa 1834 at Bavaria. He was listed in the 1860 federal census as a farmer residing in the town of Winneconne. Catharine, his wife, was born circa 1840 at Dormstadt. John, their son, was born circa 1859 at Wisconsin. Christian was listed as above in the veteran section of the 1885 Wisconsin State census at P.O. Poygan. He was not found in the records of that company. Christian was listed in the 1890 federal

KLEBER, Christian (cont.)
census as residing in the town of Poygan at P.O. Winneconne. He provided his unit designation as Co. C, 22nd Regt., Wis. Vol. Inf. and his service dates as having been from Feb. 27, 1865 to May 17, 1865. Christian was listed in the veteran section of the 1895 state census at P.O. Winneconne. He was then listed as a veteran of Co. G, 22nd Regt., Wis. Vol. Inf. Elizabeth, widow of Christian, was listed in 1905 as residing with John Bersch in section 24 of the town of Poygan. John was born circa 1836 at Hessen. He had been listed with Christian and his family in the 1860 federal census.
{US 1860, 1890; WC-V 1885, 1895; B-1905}

KLEIBERG, Ferdinand - Pvt., Co. F, 19th Regt., Wis. Vol. Inf.
Ferdinand was born on Oct. 1, 1838 in the kingdom of Prussia. He was a son of Peter and Christina Kleberg. The father was a native of Prussia and resided in the town of Winchester. The mother was a native of that same country and died there. They had five children, three of whom died in Prussia at young ages. Peter was then married to Wilhelmina Dreger. They had two children before emigrating to America in 1855. They came to Wisconsin and settled in the town of Winchester, where their third child was born. Ferdinand was raised on farms and received a good education. He worked for his father until age 20 and then worked as a farm laborer. Ferdinand resided at Winchester and enlisted on Feb. 11, 1864. He was assigned as above and was then transferred to Co. C of the same regiment on May 1, 1865. Ferdinand was mustered out on Aug. 9, 1865. He returned to Winnebago County and was again engaged as a farm laborer. Ferdinand was married in Winnebago County on Nov. 30, 1866 to Emilie Henriette Friedrike (Schroeder) Schroeder. She was born at Prussia on Sept. 25, 1847 and was a daughter of John and Fredericka Schroeder. They came to America in 1857 and settled in Winnebago County in 1860. Ferdinand was able to purchase his own farm in Waupaca County in 1867. He and Emeline had the following children: Julia, died prior to 1889; Albert H.; Cecilia E.; Emma M.; Edmund F.; Esther E.; and Martin F. Ferdinand moved back to Winchester in 1876, where he then owned a farm of 143 acres. He was listed in the veteran section of the 1885 and 1895 Wisconsin State census at P.O. Winchester and in that section of the 1905 state census at P.O. Larsen. Ferdinand was listed in the 1890 federal census as residing in the town of Winchester at P.O. Winchester. He was listed in 1905 as residing on 127 acres of section 3 in the town of Winchester. Sons Edmund and Martin were then listed as residing with Ferdinand.
{US 1860, 1890; WC-V 1885, 1895, 1905; ROV; Randall p.54; B-1905}

KLINKE, Rasmus H. - Pvt., Co. I, 21st Regt., Wis. Vol. Inf.
Rasmus was born circa 1838. He resided at Neenah and enlisted there on Aug. 13, 1862. He was assigned as above and was transferred to the Veteran Reserve Corps on Apr. 6, 1864. Rasmus was married in Winnebago County on Feb. 16, 1866 to Sophia Shaft. He was listed in the veteran section of the 1885 Wisconsin State census at P.O. Neenah. He was listed (Klinke) in the 1890 federal census as residing in the city of Neenah. He then provided that he was mustered out on Aug. 19, 1865. Rasmus died from the effects of being run over by a fire engine as he was assisting in taking it to the scene of a fire at Neenah on Sept. 15, 1893. Sophia, widow of Rasmus, was listed in 1905 as residing at 104 Main Street in Neenah. Arthur, Frank A., Fred and George Klinke were listed as residing at that same address.
{US 1890; WC-V 1885; WCMR v.1, p.292, #1784; OWN 23 Sep 1893; B-1905; ROV}

KLOCK, Isaac C. - Cpl., Co. C, 35th Regt., Wis. Vol. Inf.
Sarah Colista, widow of Isaac, was listed in the 1890 federal census as residing in the town of Neenah at P.O. Neenah. She then provided his unit designation as above and his service dates as having been from Feb. 15, 1864 to Mar. 15, 1866. Sarah was a daughter of John R. Wheeler from a following sketch. Isaac died in 1886 and was survived also by one child. Colista was listed in 1905 as residing at 117 Third Avenue in the city of Neenah.
{US 1890; SCA 1:450; B-1905}

KLOHN, Julius H. - Pvt., Co. I, 47th Regt., Wis. Vol. Inf.
Julius was listed in the 1890 federal census as residing in the town of Nepeuskun at P.O. Waukau. He then provided his unit designation as above and his service dates as having been from Feb. 7, 1865 to Sept. 11, 1865.
{US 1890}

KLUTH, John - Pvt., Co. C, 53rd Regt., Wis. Vol. Inf.
John was born circa 1823 at Mecklenberg. He was listed in the 1860 federal census as residing on a farm in the town of Nekimi at P.O. Oshkosh. Sophia, his wife, was born circa 1823 at Mecklenberg. John Jr., their son, was born circa 1852, also at Mecklenberg. John listed his residence as Menasha when he enlisted on Mar. 10, 1865. He was assigned as above and was mustered out on June 9, 1865. John died on Nov. 7, 1878 at age 55 years and 1 month. He is buried in the town of Nekimi at Salem Baptist Cemetery.
{US 1860; ROV; Cem. records}

KNAGGS, Charles - Pvt., Co. B, 21st Regt., Wis. Vol. Inf.
Charles was born circa 1845 at Wisconsin, a son of James and Mathilda Knaggs and a brother of James from a following sketch. The father was one of the earliest settlers of this part of Wisconsin. He operated Knagg's ferry, with a point in what is now Rainbow Park in Oshkosh and the opposite being across the Fox River where James had his home. That land is now a part of Riverside Cemetery in Oshkosh. Mathilda was born circa 1811 at Canada. She was listed in the 1860 federal census as residing on the farm of son Moses Knaggs and his family in the town of Oshkosh. Also listed with them were her sons James and Charles. Charles enlisted at Oshkosh on Jan. 26, 1864. He was assigned as above. Charles contracted a disease and died on Oct. 1, 1864 at Nashville, Tennessee. Mathilda was listed in 1883 at P.O. Oshkosh and receiving a mother's pension of $8 per month.
{US 1860; ROV; LOP-1883}

KNAGGS, James - Pvt., Co. D, 1st (3 yr.) Regt., Wis. Vol. Inf.
James was born circa 1836 at Wisconsin. He was a son of James Knaggs and a brother of Charles from a previous sketch. The father died prior to 1855 and, in 1859, his widow sold some of the family property to the city of Oshkosh for the expansion of Riverside Cemetery. She died on Jan. 29, 1884. James resided at Oshkosh and he was drafted there on Nov. 23, 1863. He was assigned as above and was then transferred to Co. F, 21st Regt., Wis. Vol. Inf. on Sept. 19, 1864. He was transferred to Co. F, 3rd Regt., Wis. Vol. Inf. on June 8, 1865 and was mustered out on July 18, 1865. James was listed in the veteran section of the 1885 Wisconsin State census at P.O. Oshkosh. He was listed in the 1890 federal census as residing in the city of Oshkosh. James is

KNAGGS, James (cont.)
buried with a simple military marker in Oshkosh at Riverside Cemetery, GAR plot, east row, #22 from the south.
{US 1860, 1890; WC-V 1885; ODZ 06 Apr 1859; ODN 01 Feb 1884; Cem. records} {OWC 09 May 1855; ROV}

KNAPP, Charles - Pvt., Co. I, 21st Regt., Wis. Vol. Inf.
Charles resided at Rushford and enlisted there on Aug. 11, 1862. He was assigned as above. Charles contracted a disease and died on Nov. 25, 1862 at Bowling Green, Kentucky.
{ROV}

KNAPP, Gilbert - Pvt., Co. I, 32nd Regt., Wis. Vol. Inf.
Gilbert resided at Medina, Outagamie County and enlisted there on Aug. 21, 1862. He was assigned as above and was mustered out on June 12, 1865. Gilbert was listed in the veteran section of the 1885 Wisconsin State census at P.O. Leeman, Outagamie County. He was listed in that section of the 1895 and 1905 state census at P.O. Omro. Gilbert was buried with a simple military marker. Abigail, his wife, was born on Aug. 9, 1830 and died on May 26, 1890. Both are buried in the town of Hortonia, Outagamie County at Hortonville Cemetery.
{WC-V 1885, 1895, 1905; ROV; Cem. records}

KNAPP, John - Cpl., Co. B, 85th Regt., New York Vol. Inf.
John was listed as above in the veteran section of the 1905 Wisconsin State census at P.O. Neenah.
{WC-V 1905}

KNAPP, Loring B. - Cpl., Co. G, 3rd Regt., Wis. Vol. Inf.
Loring resided at Menasha and enlisted there on Apr. 20, 1861. He was assigned as above and was promoted to Corporal in that company. Loring was then discharged on July 15, 1862 due to a disability.
{ROV; Lawson p.807}

KNAPP, Miles - Pvt., Co. C, 14th Regt., Wis. Vol. Inf.
Miles resided at Omro and enlisted there on Oct. 11, 1861. He was assigned as above and was discharged by orders dated May 10, 1862. Miles then re-enlisted on Feb. 21, 1865 and was assigned as a Private, Co. H, 49th Regt., Wis. Vol. Inf. He was mustered out on Aug. 31, 1865. Miles was listed in the veteran section of the 1885 Wisconsin State census at P.O. Knapp, Dunn County.
{WC-V 1885; ROV}

KNAPP, Oscar F. - Pvt., Co. B, 4th Regt., Wis. Vol. Inf.
Oscar was born circa 1837 at Painesville, Ohio. He was a son of Hosea and Laura Knapp. Hosea was born circa 1796 at New York and Laura was born circa 1804 at Vermont. They removed with their family to Wisconsin two years after Oscar was born and resided for nine years at Lake Geneva, Walworth County. They then removed to Winnebago County and settled near Omro. Hosea and Laura were listed in the 1860 federal census as residing on a farm in the town of Rushford at P.O. Omro. Listed with them were sons Oscar and Rufus. Rufus was born circa 1846 at Wisconsin. Oscar

KNAPP, Oscar F. (cont.)
resided at Omro and enlisted there on May 20, 1861. He was assigned as above and was discharged on Feb. 24, 1863 after having contracted typhoid fever. Oscar re-enlisted in the same company on Feb. 29, 1864 and was then mustered out on Sept. 15, 1865. He returned home and was married on Feb. 7, 1868 to Anna Noland of Cassville, Grant County. Oscar was not found in the veteran section of the 1885 Wisconsin State census. He was listed in that section of the 1895 state census at P.O. Attica, Green County and he was listed in that part of the 1905 state census at P.O. Omro. Oscar then removed with his family to Chehalis, Washington circa 1905. He died there after five years on June 23, 1911 and was buried there in the Masonic Cemetery. Oscar was survived by his wife and six children: Mrs. Carrie Compton of Omro; Orrie Knapp of Aberdeen, Washington; Leslie, Fred and Blanche Knapp and Mrs. Angie Fallon, all of Chehalis.
{US 1860; WC-V 1885, 1895, 1905; ROV; OmJ 13 Jul 1911}

KNIGHT, James M. - Pvt., Co. C, 46th Regt., Wis. Vol. Inf.
James resided at Oshkosh and enlisted there on Feb. 8, 1865. He was assigned as above and was mustered out on Oct. 7, 1865.
{ROV}

KNISELEY, Benjamin T. - Pvt., Co. C, 21st Regt., Wis. Vol. Inf.
Benjamin was born circa 1844 at Ohio. He was a son of Abram and Catherine Kniseley and a brother of George from a following sketch. Abram was born circa 1806 at Ohio and Catherine was born circa 1808 at Pennsylvania. They were listed in the 1860 federal census as residing on a farm in the town of Oshkosh. Listed with them then were the following children: George; Mary, born circa 1843; Benjamin; Thomas, born circa 1846; Alpha, born circa 1848; and Franklin, born circa 1850. All of the children were born in Ohio. Benjamin enlisted at Oshkosh on Aug. 12, 1862. He was assigned as above and was wounded and taken prisoner at Chaplin Hills, Kentucky on Oct. 8, 1862. He was paroled on the field that same day. Benjamin was discharged on May 17, 1863.
{US 1860; ROV; OWN 07 May 1863}

KNISELEY, George W. - Pvt., Co. F, 11th Regt., Wis. Vol. Inf.
George was born circa 1840 at Ohio. He was a son of Abram and Catherine Kniseley and a brother of Benjamin from a previous sketch. George resided at Oshkosh and enlisted there on Sept. 27, 1861. He was assigned as above and was wounded at Port Gibson, Louisiana. George died from those wounds on Sept. 6, 1863 at Milliken's Bend, Louisiana.
{US 1860; ROV}

KNOFSKER, Reuben M. - Pvt., Co. B, 21st Regt., Wis. Vol. Inf.
Reuben was born circa 1843 at Ohio, a son of Martin and Elizabeth Knofsker. Both parents were natives of Pennsylvania, the father born there circa 1810 and the mother born circa 1812. They were listed in the 1860 federal census as residing on a farm in the town of Vinland. Listed with them were the following children: Louise, born circa 1838; George, born circa 1840; Reuben; Emeline, born circa 1846; Ludwig, born circa 1850; Leonard, born circa 1853; and Francesca, born circa 1856. The youngest daughter was born in Wisconsin and the other children were all born in Ohio. Reuben resided at Vinland and enlisted there on Aug. 20, 1862. He was assigned as above. Prior to leaving the area with his unit, Reuben was married on Sept. 9, 1862 to Mary Jane

KNOFSKER, Reuben M. (cont.)
Pryne. Reuben contracted a disease and died on Nov. 16, 1862 at Louisville, Kentucky.
{US 1860; ROV; WCMR v.1, p.229, #1280}

KNOLL, William R. - Pvt., Co. K, 5th (reorg.) Regt., Wis. Vol. Inf.
William was born on Feb. 13, 1826 in the province of Ontario, Canada. He was a son of Henry and Jane (McEnty) Knoll. Henry was a native of New York, born there circa 1790, and was a son of Henry Knoll from Germany. Jane was born circa 1802 at Canada and was a daughter of James McEnty, a native of Scotland. James served as a British soldier in the battle during which Gen. Braddock was defeated and killed. During the American Revolution he served in the Continental Army. Henry and Jane were married at New York and then removed to Canada. They had nine children, including the subject of this sketch. In 1846 they moved their family back to the United States and settled in Wisconsin at Fond du Lac, Fond du Lac County. In 1848 they removed to a farm in the town of Rushford. Henry and Jane were listed in the 1860 federal census as residing on a farm in the town of Rushford at P.O. Omro. Listed with them were the following children: Eliza, born circa 1836 at New York; Matilda, born circa 1838 at New York; Francis, born circa 1841 at New York, and George, born circa 1844 at Ohio. Both parents died at Rushford, Henry in 1869 and Jane in 1880. Henry, father of Henry, also died there in 1856. All three are buried in the town of Rushford at Rushford Cemetery. William settled on a farm in the town of Poygan in 1854. He was married in 1856 to Mary Elizabeth Foster. She was born in Feb. 1838 at New York and was a daughter of Warren and Abigail (Cleves) Foster. She came to Wisconsin with her parents in 1852. William enlisted at Cottage Grove, Dane County on Sept. 15, 1864 and was assigned as above. He was mustered out on June 8, 1865. William and Mary had six children: Abigail Jane; Melissa Ann; William Henry; Hattie Belle; Dora M.; and one other. William was listed in 1883 at P.O. Omro. He had been receiving a pension of $4 per month since Sept. 1880 for a disease of the eyes. He was listed in the veteran section of the 1885 Wisconsin State census at P.O. Poygan and in that section of the 1895 state census at P.O. Omro. He was listed in the 1890 federal census as residing in the town of Poygan at P.O. Omro. William then listed that he had lost his sight due to the explosion of a shell on Feb. 6, 1865. Mary died at Poygan on Nov. 26, 1888 at age 47 years, 8 months and 28 days. William died on May 22, 1903. Both are buried in the town of Poygan at Oak Hill Cemetery. Their daughters Dora M. and Melissa A. Knoll are buried on that same plot.
{US 1860, 1890; WC-V 1885, 1895; LOP-1883; Randall p.50; Cem. records; ROV}

KNUDSON, Torger - Pvt., Co. H, 1st Regt., Wis. Hvy. Art.
Torger was born circa 1838 at Norway. He was a son of Knute Torgerson and Betsy Ostenson/Austin. Betsy was born circa 1804 at Norway. Torger came to this country with his parents in 1854. They first settled at Wisconsin in Dane County. Torger was listed in the 1860 federal census as residing on a farm in the town of Winchester. Listed with him were his mother and the following of her children: Isabel, born circa 1841; Austin, born circa 1843; Cornelia, born circa 1846; Swen, born circa 1848; and Kittle, born circa 1851. All of her children were born in Norway. Torger enlisted on Aug. 31, 1864 at Winchester. He was assigned as above and was mustered out on July 10, 1865. Torger was listed in the veteran section of the 1885 and 1895 Wisconsin State census at P.O. Winchester. He was listed in the 1890 federal census as residing in the town of Winchester at P.O. Winchester. Torger was then listed as suffering from chronic

KNUDSON, Torger (cont.)
diarrhea and typhoid fever. At that time Torger had been bed-ridden for 18 years. He was not found in the veteran section of the 1905 state census.
{US 1860, 1890; WC-V 1885, 1895, 1905; ROV; CBR-FRV p.1080-1}

KOEHN, Seigfried - Pvt., Co. F, 19th Regt., Wis. Vol. Inf.
Siegfried was born on Nov. 26, 1840. He resided at Oshkosh and he enlisted there on Feb. 4, 1862. Seigfried was assigned as above and was wounded on May 13, 1864. He was mustered out on Apr. 29, 1865 at the end of his term of enlistment. He was married in Winnebago County on Aug. 22, 1866 to Julia W. Retzack. She was born on May 4, 1847. Siegfried was listed in 1883 at P.O. Oshkosh as receiving a pension of $3 per month for a wound to his left hand. He was listed in the veteran section of the 1885 Wisconsin State census at P.O. Oshkosh. He was listed in the 1890 federal census as residing in the city of Oshkosh. Seigfried was listed (Charles) in that section of the 1895 state census at P.O. Oshkosh and in that part of the 1905 state census (Charles Kuehn) at P.O. Oshkosh. He died on Aug. 3, 1916. Julia died on Sept. 23, 1934. Edward W., a son, was born on Mar. 18, 1887 and died Jan. 6, 1958. All three are buried in the town of Algoma at Peace Lutheran Cemetery.
{US 1890; WC-V 1885, 1895, 1905; LOP-1883; WCMR v.1, p.305, #1884*; ROV} {Cem. records}

KOELSCH, Christian - Pvt., Co. E, 6th Regt., Wis. Vol. Inf.
Christian resided at Harrison and was drafted there on Oct. 3, 1864. He was assigned as above and was mustered out on July 14, 1865. Christian was listed (Kelsh) in the veteran section of the 1885 Wisconsin State census at P.O. Neenah. He was listed in that section of the 1895 state census at P.O. Neenah. Christian was listed in 1905 as the poor commissioner and residing at 125 W. Columbian Avenue in the city of Neenah.
{WC-V 1885, 1895; ROV; B-1905}

KOENIG, Thomas - Pvt., Co. E, 1st Regt., Wis. Vol. Inf.
Thomas was residing at Milwaukee, Milwaukee County when he was drafted on Nov. 11, 1863 and was assigned as above. He was transferred to Co. H, 21st Regt., Wis. Vol. Inf. on Sept. 19, 1864. He was then transferred as unassigned to the 3rd Regt., Wis. Vol. Inf. on June 8, 1865 and was absent sick when that regiment was mustered out July 18, 1865. Thomas listed his residence as Omro when he was transferred to the 3rd Regt.
{ROV}

KOHLER, Herman - Pvt., Co. F, 19th Regt., Wis. Vol. Inf.
Herman was born circa 1833 at Germany. He was listed in the 1860 federal census as residing with the family of James Clark in the town of Winchester. Herman resided at Winchester and enlisted there on Jan. 26, 1862. He was assigned as above and was mustered out on Apr. 29, 1865 at the end of his term of enlistment.
{US 1860; ROV}

KOHNKE, John - Pvt., Co. I, 21st Regt., Wis. Vol. Inf.
John resided at Neenah and enlisted there on Aug. 28, 1862. He was assigned as above. John contracted a disease and died on May 7, 1863 at Nashville, Tennessee.
{ROV}

KOLB, John - Pvt., 12th Batt., Wis. Lt. Art.
John resided at Eureka and enlisted there on Jan. 15, 1862. He was assigned as above and he re-enlisted in the same company at the end of his term. John was mustered out on June 7, 1865.
{ROV}

KOPITZKE, George - Pvt., Co. I, 37th Regt., Wis. Vol. Inf.
George was born circa 1829 at Prussia. He was listed (Kepetskey) in the 1860 federal census as residing on a farm in the town of Orihula at P.O. Fremont. Wilhelmina, his wife, was born circa 1824 at Prussia. They had a son, John, who was born circa 1853 at Prussia. George resided at Wolf River and was drafted there on Nov. 22, 1864. He was assigned as above and was mustered out on July 27, 1865.
{US 1860; ROV}

KOSSBERG, August - Pvt., Co. F, 19th Regt., Wis. Vol. Inf.
August resided at Oshkosh and enlisted there on Jan. 17, 1862. He was assigned as above and was then discharged due to a disability on May 13, 1863. August was listed (Kasberg) in the veteran section of the 1885 Wisconsin State census at P.O. Oshkosh.
{WC-V 1885; ROV}

KOTTE, Christian - Pvt., Co. C, 53rd Regt., Wis. Vol. Inf.
Christian was born in 1827/30 at Hanover, Germany. He was a son of Theodore and Mary Kotte. Christian was raised in his native country. He emigrated about 1852 and settled in this country at New York. Three years later he removed to Wisconsin, where he worked for hire for seven years. Christian married Anna M. Schelling in 1858. She was born in 1829 at Prussia and was a daughter of John Schelling. Christian was listed in the 1860 federal census as residing on a farm in the town of Nekimi. Listed with him were his wife and a daughter, Anna, who was born in 1860 at Wisconsin. Christian purchased a farm in the town of Nekimi in 1862. He listed his residence as Menasha when he enlisted on Mar. 9, 1865. He was assigned as above and was mustered out on June 6, 1865. Christian was listed in the veteran section of the 1885 Wisconsin State census at P.O. Nekimi. He was listed in the 1890 federal census as residing in the town of Nekimi at P.O. Oshkosh. He was listed in the veteran section of the 1895 state census at P.O. Oshkosh. Christian and Anna had six children, including: Henry; Frank; John; and Paulina. Mary, his widow, was listed in 1905 as residing on 80 acres of section 22 in the town of Nekimi.
{US 1860, 1890; WC-V 1885, 1895; B-1905; ROV; Randall p.27}

KPRULL, - Civil War Veteran?
Mary, his widow, was listed in the 1890 federal census as residing in the town of Menasha at P.O. Menasha. No other information was provided.
{US 1890}

KRAFT, Lewis - Sgt., Co. F, 50th Regt., Wis. Vol. Inf.
Lewis resided at Oshkosh and enlisted there on Mar. 1, 1865. He was assigned as above and was promoted to Sergeant in that company. Lewis was mustered out on June 14, 1866 at the end of his term of enlistment.
{ROV}

KRAKE, Delos W. - Cpl., Co. A, 1st (3 yr.) Regt., Wis. Vol. Inf.
Delos resided at Oshkosh and enlisted there on Oct. 21, 1861. He was assigned as above and was promoted to Corporal in that company. Delos was mustered out Oct. 13, 1864 at the end of his term of enlistment. He was married in Winnebago County on Oct. 22, 1865 to Polly Jane Strate.
{ROV; WCMR v.1, p.283, #1709}

KRAMER, John - Pvt., Co. B, 38th Regt., Wis. Vol. Inf.
John resided at Oshkosh and enlisted there on Aug. 24, 1864. He was assigned as above and was mustered out on June 2, 1865. John was listed in 1905 as a resident at the Wisconsin Veterans' Home at King. He had been received there from Prentice, Pierce County.
{ROV; GAR 40th}

KRAMER, Joseph - Pvt., Co. C, 9th Regt., Wis. Vol. Inf.
Joseph was born on Feb. 29, 1816. He resided at Oshkosh and enlisted on Sept. 6, 1861. He was assigned as above and was then transferred to Co. F of the same regiment on Aug. 1, 1862. He was mustered out on Dec. 3, 1864 at the end of his term of enlistment. Joseph was listed in the veteran section of the 1885 and 1895 Wisconsin State census at P.O. Omro. He was listed in the 1890 federal census as residing in the village of Omro. Joseph listed that he had suffered a rupture during his military service. He died at Omro on Dec. 25, 1901 and is buried at Omro Cemetery, Pelton's Addition, Section C, plot 24. It appears that several of his children were buried on that same plot.
{US 1890; WC-V 1885, 1895; ROV; Cem. records}

KRAMER, Michael - Pvt., Co. B, 38th Regt., Wis. Vol. Inf.
Michael resided at Oshkosh and enlisted there on Aug. 9, 1864. He was assigned as above and was mustered out on June 2, 1865.
{ROV}

KREMER, John - Pvt., U.S. Marine Corps.
John was listed in the 1890 federal census as residing at 284 Otter Street in the city of Oshkosh. He then provided his designation as above and that the information that he was assigned to the East Port during his enlistment. John provided his service dates as having been from May 15, 1863 to Dec. 12, 1863 and that he had been discharged on a surgeon's certificate.
{US 1890}

KRENKE, Charles - Pvt., Co. H, 37th Regt., Wis. Vol. Inf.
Charles was born circa 1828 at Prussia. Harriet, his wife, was born circa 1828, also at Prussia. They had a son, August, who was born in Prussia circa 1856 and a daughter, Ernestina, who was born in Wisconsin circa 1857. They were listed in the 1860 federal census as residing on a farm in the town of Orihula at P.O. Fremont. Charles was drafted at Wolf River on Nov. 5, 1864. He was assigned as above and was mustered out on July 27, 1865. Carl was listed in the 1890 federal census as residing in the town of Wolf River at P.O. Orihula.
{US 1860, 1890; ROV}

KROLL, John C. - Pvt., Co. C, 46th Regt., Wis. Vol. Inf.
John was born on Dec. 11, 1831 at Usezneudorf, Prussia. He was a son of Martin and Elizabeth (Hardin) Kroll. John emigrated to this country and settled at Wisconsin in Winnebago County. He was married to Wilhelmina Frederich at Oshkosh on July 23, 1856. She was born on Mar. 5, 1835 at Prussia. John was listed in the 1860 federal census as a laborer residing in the third ward of the city of Oshkosh. Listed with him were his wife and two children, Ameline, born circa 1857, and Auguste, born circa 1859. John resided at Oshkosh and enlisted there on Feb. 14, 1865. He was assigned as above and was mustered out on Sept. 27, 1865 at Nashville, Tennessee. John had been stricken with both body flux and hemmerhoids which had him hospitalized for four weeks during his military service. He returned to Oshkosh after his discharge and tried to recover his health. Being unable to work hard, he sold his land at Oshkosh and moved to a farm near New London, Waupaca County in the same year as his discharge. He managed his farm for five years, when he was again stricken with the same ailments that he suffered in the army. He was forced to give up the farm. John then was engaged as a carpenter. He and Wilhelmina had the following children: Sophie, born on Oct. 18, 1857; Augusta A.O., born on July 29, 1859, died on Apr. 29, 1863 at Oshkosh and was buried there; Henrietta M., born July 16, 1861; William R., born on June 21, 1863; and Wilhelmina L., born on Apr. 21, 1865. John was residing at New London in 1888 and was listed then as a member of GAR Post #46. John died at his home on Apr. 8, 1926 and Wilhelmine died on Dec. 25, 1928. Both are buried at Waupaca County in the town of Mukwa at Floral Hill Cemetery. William C. Kroll, a brother of John, is buried with his family in that same cemetery. He was also a veteran of the Civil War.
{US 1860; ROV; SCA 1:476; Cem. records; WCMR v.1, p.97, #400}

KRUCK, John Jacob - Pvt., Co. C, 46th Regt., Wis. Vol. Inf.
John was married in Winnebago County on Apr. 13, 1863 to Rose Pohl. He resided at Oshkosh and enlisted there on Feb. 3, 1865. He was assigned as above and was then mustered out on Sept. 27, 1865.
{ROV; WCMR v.1, p.250, #1442}

KRUEGER, August - Pvt., Co. K, 11th Regt., Wis. Vol. Inf.
August was born on Feb. 2, 1830. He resided at Winchester and he enlisted there on Oct. 16, 1861. He was assigned as above and he re-enlisted in that same company at the end of his term. He was mustered out on Sept. 4, 1865. August was listed in the veteran section of the 1885 Wisconsin State census at P.O. Zittau. He was listed in that section of the 1895 state census at P.O. Winchester and was not found in that part of the 1905 state census. August died on June 8, 1898. Louise, his wife, was born on Sept. 14, 1848 and died on Nov. 11, 1928. Heinrich H.G., a son, was born on Dec. 23, 1884 and died on June 7, 1890. All three are buried in the town of Winchester at St. Johannes Cemetery.
{WC-V 1885, 1895, 1905; ROV; Cem. records}

KRUEGER, Ferdinand - Pvt., Co. K, 37th Regt., Wis. Vol. Inf.
Frederica, widow of Ferdinand, was listed in the 1890 federal census as residing at 21 Cross Street in the city of Oshkosh. She provided his unit designation as above. She added that he had suffered from diseases of the kidneys and liver.
{US 1890}

KRUEGER, William - Pvt., Co. K, 11th Regt., Wis. Vol. Inf.
William listed his residence as the town of Caledonia, Waupaca County when he enlisted on Oct. 1, 1861. He was assigned as above and was wounded at Vicksburg, Mississippi. He was mustered out on Nov. 18, 1864 at the end of his term of enlistment. William was listed in 1883 at P.O. Oshkosh and receiving a pension of $8 per month for wounds to both hips. He was listed in the veteran section of the 1885, 1895 and 1905 Wisconsin State census at P.O. Oshkosh. William was listed in the 1890 federal census as residing at 376 Ceape Street in the city of Oshkosh. He then listed that he had been discharged on a surgeon's certificate. William was listed in 1905 as residing at 376 Ceape Street in Oshkosh. William F. Krueger was then listed at the same address.
{US 1890; WC-V 1885, 1895, 1905; ROV; LOP-1883; B-1905}

KRUEGER, William - Pvt., Co. C, 10th Regt., Wis. Vol. Inf.
William resided at Menasha and enlisted there on Sept. 3, 1861. He was assigned as above and was discharged on Mar. 7, 1863 due to an illness. William died in 1865 at Menasha.
{ROV; Lawson p.813}

KUHN, P. - Seaman, "Juliet," Gunboat Service, U.S. Navy.
He enlisted on Aug. 17, 1864 in the Naval Gunboat Service and was assigned to the Gunboat "Juliet."
{Lawson p.840-1}

KUHN, S. - Civil War Veteran?
He was listed in 1888 as a member of GAR Post #241 at Oshkosh.
{SCA}

KUSCHE, August Julius - Cpl., Co. C, 46th Regt., Wis. Vol. Inf.
August was born circa 1840. He resided at Oshkosh and enlisted there on Feb. 14, 1865. He was assigned as above and was promoted to Corporal in that company. He was then mustered out on Sept. 27, 1865. August was married in Winnebago County on July 26, 1866 to I.A.P. Riemenschneider. He was listed in 1868 as a setter residing at 44 Tenth Street in the city of Oshkosh. He was listed in the veteran section of the 1885 Wisconsin State census at P.O. Oshkosh. He was listed in 1888 as a member of GAR Post #241 at Oshkosh. August was listed in the 1890 federal census as residing in Oshkosh. He was a member of the Kusche Bros., who manufactured lime in their kiln south of the Main Street bridge on the river front. August died on Mar. 1, 1892 at Oshkosh due to a heart ailment. He was survived by a wife, two sons and one daughter. His widow, Augusta, was listed in 1905 as residing at 242 Tenth Street in Oshkosh. Albert W. and Carlton J. Kusche were then listed as residing with her.
{US 1890; WC-V 1885; ROV; T-1868; WCMR v.1, p.305, #1885; OWN 03 Mar 1892}
{B-1905}

KUSCHE, John G.H. - Pvt., Co. C, 46th Regt., Wis. Vol. Inf.
John emigrated from Germany and settled at Oshkosh in 1854. He was married to Anna Koschwitz on May 16, 1856 in Winnebago County. She was born circa 1829 at Prussia. John was listed in the 1860 federal census as a laborer residing in the third ward of the city of Oshkosh. He resided at Oshkosh and enlisted there on Feb. 14, 1865. He was assigned as above and was mustered out on Sept. 27, 1865. John returned to Oshkosh

KUSCHE, John G.H. (cont.)
and remained there until 1879. He had been engaged in operation of a lime kiln which he eventually sold to his brothers. He then purchased a farm in the town of Algoma three miles west of Oshkosh. John was listed in the veteran section of the 1885 Wisconsin State census at P.O. Oshkosh. He died of heart disease in the town of Algoma on Feb. 19, 1888. John was survived by his father, his wife, son Reinhold and daughter Mrs. Everett Clark. He was buried in a rural cemetery near his farm. Anna C., his widow, was listed in the 1890 federal census as residing in the town of Algoma at P.O. Oshkosh. Son Reinhold, born in 1857, then resided on his father's farm.
{US 1860, 1890; WC-V 1885; B-1905; Randall p.16; WCMR v.1, p.92, #383; ROV}
{OWN 23 Feb 1888}

LABORDE, Ambrose - see Ambrose L. Clark

LaBORDE, George D. - Pvt., Co. D, 1st Regt., Wis. Cav.
George was born circa 1838 at Wisconsin. He was a son of Luke and Louisa LaBorde and a brother of Louis from a following sketch. Luke was born circa 1809 in the Michigan Territory and Louisa was born there circa 1811. They were listed in the 1860 federal census as residing on a farm in the town of Rushford at P.O. Delhi. Listed with them were the following children: Frederick, born circa 1835; George; Harriet, born circa 1840; Louis; Jane, born circa 1850; Alexander, born circa 1852; Henry, born circa 1854; and William, born circa 1856. All of the children were listed as having been born in Wisconsin. George resided at Delhi and enlisted there on Aug. 20, 1861. He was assigned as above and was promoted to Corporal in that company. George was then mustered out on July 19, 1865. He was one of the few from Winnebago County to share in the bounty for the capture of Jefferson Davis. George is buried with a simple military marker in the town of Poygan at St. Thomas Cemetery.
{US 1860; ROV; Lawson p.843; Cem. records}

LaBORDE, Louis - Seaman, "Juliet," Gunboat Service, U.S. Navy.
Louis was a son of Luke and Louise LaBorde and a brother of George from a previous sketch. He was listed in the 1860 federal census as residing with his parents and their family in the town of Rushford at P.O. Delhi. Luke died on Dec. 21, 1868 at age 58 years. Louise died on Mar. 8, 1877 at age 63 years. Louis was at some time married to Mary Quandt. They had a stillborn son born Sept. 5, 1881 in the town of Rushford. Louis was listed as above in the veteran section of the 1890 federal census as residing in the town of Rushford at P.O. Eureka. He was suffering from a kidney disease. Louis was listed as above in the veteran section of the 1895 Wisconsin State census at P.O. Eureka and in that section of the 1905 state census at P.O. Omro. He was listed in 1905 as a carpenter residing on 5 acres of section 23 in the town of Rushford. Residing with him were Belle, his wife, and Grace and John LaBorde. Louis was buried with a simple military marker at the side of his parents in the town of Rushford at Delhi Cemetery.
{US 1890; WC-V 1895, 1905; Cem. records; B-1905; WCBR v.3, p.37, #221}

LACEY, Alonzo H. - Cpl., Co. F, 18th Regt., Wis. Vol. Inf.
Alonzo resided at Oshkosh and enlisted there on Nov. 25, 1861. He was assigned as above and was promoted to Corporal in that company. Alonzo was listed as having deserted.
{ROV}

LADD, George M. - Pvt., 8th Batt., Wis. Lt. Art.
George was born circa 1842 at New Hampshire. He was a son of Joseph and Charity Ladd. Joseph was born circa 1799 at Vermont and Charity was born circa 1804 at New Hampshire. They were listed in the 1860 federal census as residing on a farm in the town of Menasha. Listed with them were the following children: Christopher, born circa 1830 at Vermont; William, born circa 1838 at New Hampshire; and George. George enlisted at Menasha on Jan. 28, 1864. He was assigned as above and was mustered out on Aug. 10, 1865.
{US 1860; ROV}

LADD, Malcomb E. - Pvt., Co. I, 21st Regt., Wis. Vol. Inf.
Malcomb resided at Menasha and enlisted there on Aug. 18, 1862. He was assigned as above. Malcomb contracted a disease and died Nov. 29, 1862 at Louisville, Kentucky.
{ROV}

LADD, Moses - Pvt., Co. B, 21st Regt., Wis. Vol. Inf.
Moses was born circa 1827 at Wisconsin. Mary, his wife, was born circa 1832, also at Wisconsin. Both were listed in the 1860 federal census as Indians residing on a farm in the town of Winneconne. Listed with them were the following children: Elizabeth, born circa 1852; Yuno, born circa 1853; Samuel, born circa 1856; Charles, born circa 1858; and Moses, born in 1860. All of the children were born in Wisconsin. Moses enlisted at Winneconne on Aug. 15, 1862. He was assigned as above and was mustered out on June 8, 1865. Moses was listed in the veteran section of the 1885 Wisconsin State census at P.O. Winneconne. He died May 30, 1920 while residing at the Wisconsin Veterans' Home at King. Moses was buried there in the lot of the 21st Regiment.
{US 1860; WC-V 1885; ROV; 21-33rd}

LADD, Peter J. - Seaman, "Juliet," Gunboat Service, U.S. Navy.
Peter was born circa 1847 at New York. He was listed in the 1860 federal census as residing with the family of William Kelsey in the village of Neenah. Also residing there were Sarah and Mary Ladd. Peter enlisted on Aug. 17, 1864 and was assigned to the Naval Gunboat Service. He was trained on the "Great Lakes" at Chicago and was then assigned to the gunboat "Juliet." Peter was listed in 1905 as residing at 230 E. Doty Avenue in the city of Neenah. He was listed in the 1910 federal census as a widower residing at the Wisconsin Veterans' Home at King. Peter had been married for 36 years.
{US 1860, 1910; Lawson p.840-1; B-1905}

LaDOW, James - Asst. Surg., 32nd Regt., Wis. Vol. Inf.
James was married in Winnebago County on Oct. 19, 1855 to Adelaide Teal. He resided at Oshkosh and was commissioned as 1st Assistant Surgeon of the above regiment on Sept. 9, 1862. He resigned his commission on Jan. 17, 1863.
{ROV; WCMR v.1, p.81, #348}

LAIB, William C. - Pvt., Co. B, 37th Regt., Wis. Vol. Inf.
William resided at Oshkosh and enlisted there on Mar. 29, 1864. He was assigned as above and was mustered out on July 27, 1865.
{ROV}

LAIDLOW, William E. - Pvt., Co. F, 18th Regt., Wis. Vol. Inf.
William resided at Rushford and enlisted there on Jan. 27, 1864. He was assigned as above and was taken prisoner at Allatoona, Georgia. William was then mustered out on June 14, 1865.
{ROV}

LAKE, Ira S. - Pvt., Co. E, 1st (3 yr.) Regt., Wis. Vol. Inf.
Ira was born in 1835 at New York. He was married to Delcina Clemons in Winnebago County on Jan. 18, 1858. She was born on Feb. 16, 1840 at New York. Ira was listed in the 1860 federal census as residing in the town of Algoma. He had a daughter, Flora, who was born in 1858 at Wisconsin. Also residing with them at that time was Celia Clemens, a sister to Delcina. Ira resided at Omro and was drafted there on Nov. 24, 1863. He was assigned as above and was transferred to Co. H, 21st Regt., Wis. Vol. Inf. on Sept. 19, 1864. He was again transferred as unassigned to the 3rd Regt., Wis. Vol. Inf. on June 8, 1865 and was mustered out on June 23, 1865. Ira was listed in the veteran section of the 1885 Wisconsin State census at P.O. Antigo, Langlade County. He was listed in 1888 as a member of GAR Post #78 at Antigo. Ira was listed in the veteran section of the 1895 state census at P.O. Sheboygan, Sheboygan County. He was listed in that part of the 1905 state census at P.O. Omro. Ira was listed in 1905 as a mason residing on Johnson Street at the corner of Maple Street in the village of Omro. He was buried with a simple military marker. His wife, Delcina, died on May 25, 1910. Both are buried in the town of Omro at Omro Junction Cemetery.
{US 1860; WC-V 1885, 1895, 1905; ROV; B-1905; WCMR v.1, p.167, #781*}
{Cem. records}

LAKE, Israel S. - Pvt., Co. B, 3rd Regt., Wis. Vol. Inf.
Israel was born circa 1843 at New York. He was a son of Henry and Nancy Lake and a brother of Levi from a following sketch. Henry was born circa 1811 at New York and Nancy was born circa 1813 in that same state. Henry was listed in the 1860 federal census as a farmer residing in the fifth ward of the city of Oshkosh. Residing with him were his wife and the following children: William, born circa 1838; Levi; Israel; Nancy, born circa 1849; and Martin, born circa 1850. All of the children were born in New York. Israel resided at Oshkosh and enlisted there on Aug. 23, 1864. He was assigned as above and was transferred to Co. B, 3rd (reorg.) Regt., Wis. Vol. Inf. on Feb. 1, 1865. Israel was mustered out on June 19, 1865. He was married in Winnebago County on Apr. 3, 1866 to Huldah (Lisco) Dunn. She was the widow of Alvin Dunn from a previous sketch. Nancy, mother of Israel, was listed in 1883 at P.O. Omro. She had been receiving a mother's pension of $8 per month since May 1881. Israel was listed in the 1910 federal census as residing at the Wisconsin Veterans' Home at King. Carrie, his wife of 36 years, was residing there with him. That was her first marriage and his second. She was born circa 1859 at Wisconsin. Her father was a native of Wisconsin and her mother was born in Ohio. Carrie had 9 children, 7 then living.
{US 1860, 1910; ROV; WCMR v.1, p.305, #1881; LOP-1883}

LAKE, Levi C. - Pvt., Co. C, 21st Regt., Wis. Vol. Inf.
Levi was born circa 1840 at New York. He was a son of Henry and Nancy Lake and a brother of Israel from a previous sketch. Levi resided at Oshkosh and enlisted there on Aug. 13, 1862. He was assigned as above and was wounded at Chaplin Hills, Kentucky on Oct. 8, 1862. A ball passed through one shoulder and his other arm was completely

LAKE, Levi C. (cont.)
shot off. Levi died of those wounds on Nov. 5, 1862 at Perryville, Kentucky.
{US 1860; ROV; 21-33rd; OWN 07 May 1863}

LAKE, Warren W. - Cpl., Co. A, 38th Regt., Wis. Vol. Inf.
Warren resided at Oshkosh and enlisted there on Mar. 31, 1864. He was assigned as above and was promoted to Corporal in that company. He was then mustered out on July 26, 1865. Warren was listed in the veteran section of the 1885 Wisconsin State census at P.O. Oshkosh. He was listed in 1888 as being a member of GAR Post #10 at Oshkosh. He was listed in the 1890 federal census as residing in the town of Algoma at P.O. Oshkosh. Warren was then receiving a pension of $12 per month. He reported that he had been sick most of the time since his discharge.
{US 1890; WC-V 1885; ROV}

LALLEY, Phillip - Pvt., Co. F, 1st Regt., Wis. Hvy. Art.
Phillip was a son of Martin and Margaret Lalley. The father died on June 20, 1860 at age 47 years and 6 months. Margaret died on Jan. 29, 1894 at age 60 years and 9 months. A son, James, died on May 23, 1890 at age 31 years. Phillip resided at Utica and enlisted there on Sept. 5, 1864. He was assigned as above and was discharged on Apr. 27, 1865 due to a disability. Phillip died on Nov. 22, 1865 at age 21 years and 3 months. He is buried with his brother and parents in the town of Poygan at St. Thomas Cemetery.
{ROV; Cem. records}

LAMB, Edward P. - Cpl., Co. F, 18th Regt., Wis. Vol. Inf.
Edward resided at Oshkosh and enlisted there on Feb. 5, 1862. He was assigned as above and was promoted to Corporal in that company. Edward was then mustered out on Apr. 9, 1865 at the end of his term of enlistment.
{ROV}

LAMBERT, Charles W. - Pvt., Co. D, 1st Regt., Minnesota Cav.
Charles was listed in 1888 as a member of GAR Post #10 at Oshkosh. He was listed in the 1890 federal census as residing in the city of Oshkosh. Charles then provided his unit designation as above and his service dates as having been from Oct. 23, 1862 to Nov. 3, 1863. Charles was listed as above in the veteran section of the 1895 Wisconsin State census at P.O. Oshkosh. Matilda, his widow, was listed in 1905 as residing at 25 Walnut Street in Oshkosh. Charles may also be the C.W. Lampart from a following sketch.
{US 1890; WC-V 1895; B-1905}

LAMONDER, John - Pvt., Co. K, 14th Regt., Wis. Vol. Inf.
John resided at Oshkosh and enlisted on Jan. 4, 1865. He was assigned as above and was wounded at Spanish Fort, Alabama. John was mustered out on Sept. 16, 1865.
{ROV}

LAMONT, Charles A. - Pvt., Co. B, 3rd Regt., Wis. Cav.
Charles resided at Oshkosh and enlisted there on Nov. 16, 1861. He was assigned as above and was mustered out on Feb. 14, 1865 at the end of his term of enlistment.
{ROV}

LAMORE, Amos - Pvt., Co. C, 46th Regt., Wis. Vol. Inf.
Amos was born circa 1823 at Canada. Cylinde, his wife, was born circa 1829, also at Canada. They were listed in the 1860 federal census as residing on a farm in the town of Oshkosh. Listed with them were the following children: Olive, born circa 1851; Joseph, born circa 1853; Napoleon, born circa 1855; Catherine, born circa 1858; and Cylinde, born circa 1859. The three youngest children were born in Wisconsin and the others were born in New York. Amos resided at Winneconne and he enlisted there on Feb. 6, 1865. He was assigned as above and was mustered out on Sept. 27, 1865.
{US 1860; ROV}

LAMPART, C.W. - Pvt., Co. D, 7th Regt., Wis. Vol. Inf.?
He was listed as such in the veteran section of the 1885 Wisconsin State census at P.O. Oshkosh but was not found in the records of that company. He may possibly be C.W. Lambert from a previous sketch.
{WC-V 1885}

LAMPERT, Casmer D. - Pvt., Co. C, 6th Regt., Wis. Vol. Inf.
Casmer resided at Clayton and was drafted there on Sept. 30, 1864. He was assigned as above and was mustered out on June 6, 1865.
{ROV}

LAMPHRER, Henry C. - Civil War veteran.
Henry was a veteran of the civil war, unit designation unknown. Stated in his obituary is the information that he enlisted on Jan. 28, 1864 and was discharged on Sept. 20, 1865. He resided at Waupaca County until about 1919 and he then moved to Omro. Henry died at Omro on May 15, 1924. He was survived by his wife and two daughters, Mrs. B. Hom of Waupaca and Mrs. P.H. Morrow of Auroraville.
{ODN 16 May 1924}

LAMPMAN, Isaac - Pvt., Co. K, 1st Regt., Wis. Cav.
Isaac resided at Oshkosh and enlisted there on Oct. 17, 1861. He was assigned as above and was listed as having deserted on Nov. 15, 1863.
{ROV}

LANCE, Samuel W. - Pvt., Co. D, 1st Regt., New York Vet. Vol. Inf.
Samuel was listed as above in the veteran section of the 1905 Wisconsin State census at P.O. Oshkosh.
{WC-V 1905}

LANDGOOD, Andrew S. - Pvt., 8th Batt., Wis. Lt. Art.
Andrew resided at Menasha and enlisted there on Jan. 31, 1862. He was assigned as above and was listed as having deserted on Mar. 17, 1862.
{ROV}

LANDRY, Michael - Pvt., 2nd Regt., Wis. Cav.
Michael resided at Oshkosh and enlisted there on Sept. 1, 1864. He was not listed as having been assigned to any company within this regiment and no other information was provided.
{ROV}

LANE, Edwin W. - Pvt., Co. C, 21st Regt., Wis. Vol. Inf.
Edwin was married in Winnebago County on July 10, 1852 to Emma Barber. He listed his residence as Omro when he enlisted on Aug. 14, 1862. He was assigned as above and was discharged on Apr. 8, 1863 due to a disability. He was listed in 1868 as boarding at 97 Doty Street in the city of Oshkosh. That was then the residence of Rufus W.V. Lane. Edwin was married again to Mary Barrow in Winnebago County on May 31, 1869. He was listed in 1888 as a member of GAR Post #81 at Shawano, Shawano County. He was listed in the veteran section of the 1895 and 1905 Wisconsin State census at P.O. Regina, Shawano County.
{WC-V 1895, 1905; WCMR v.1, p.133, #507; WCMR v.1, p.422, #2674; ROV; SCA} {T-1868}

LANE, Joseph - Pvt., Co. B, 18th Regt., Kentucky Vol. Inf.
Joseph was listed as above in the veteran section of the 1905 Wisconsin State census at P.O. Clayton.
{WC-V 1905}

LANE, Nelson - Cpl., Co. B, 3rd Regt., Wis. Vol. Inf.
Nelson was born circa 1824 at New York. Almira, his wife, was born circa 1831, also at New York. Nelson was listed in the 1860 federal census as a laborer residing in the third ward of the city of Oshkosh. Residing with him were his wife and the following children: Herman, born circa 1850; Alice, born circa 1852; Delia, born circa 1857; and Carrie, born circa 1858. The older children were born in New York and the youngest was born in Wisconsin. Also residing with them was Elizabeth, a sister of Nelson. She was born circa 1845 at New York. Nelson resided at Oshkosh and he enlisted there on Apr. 22, 1861. He was assigned as above and was then promoted to Corporal in that company. Nelson was wounded on June 9, 1863 and he was mustered out on June 29, 1864 at the end of his term of enlistment.
{US 1860; ROV}

LANE, Oliver C. - Pvt., Co. I, 1st Regt., Wis. Hvy. Art.
Oliver resided at Menasha and enlisted there on Sept. 26, 1864. He was assigned as above and was mustered out June 26, 1865.
{ROV}

LANE, Samuel - Pvt., Co. K, 11th Regt., Wis. Vol. Inf.
Samuel was married in Winnebago County on Dec. 8, 1856 to Margaret Dubois. He resided at Oshkosh and enlisted there on Sept. 19, 1861. Samuel was assigned as above and was discharged on Nov. 18, 1862 due to a disability.
{ROV; WCMR v.1, p.102, #423}

LANE, Theron W. - Lt., Co. D, 1st Regt., Wis. Cav.
Theron resided at Utica and enlisted there on Sept. 18, 1861. He was assigned as above and was promoted to Sergeant and then 1st Sergeant in that company. Theron was commissioned as 2nd Lieutenant of that company on Jan. 6, 1865 and was mustered out on July 19, 1865.
{ROV}

LANE, William - Pvt., Co. H, 21st Regt., Wis. Vol. Inf.
William resided at Vinland and enlisted there on Nov. 16, 1864. He was assigned as above and was transferred to Co. H, 3rd Regt., Wis. Vol. Inf. on June 8, 1865. William was mustered out on July 18, 1865.
{ROV}

LANGE, Charles - Pvt., Co. E, 32nd Regt., Wis. Vol. Inf.
Charles resided at Oshkosh and enlisted there on Nov. 28, 1863. He was assigned as above and was transferred to Co. E, 16th Regt., Wis. Vol. Inf. on June 4, 1865. Charles was mustered out on July 12, 1865. He was listed in 1868 as a mill man residing at 87 Elm Street in the city of Oshkosh. Charles was listed in 1905 as working for the Morgan Company and residing at 221 Oregon Street in Oshkosh. Residing with him were Alma, Charles Jr., Edward and Emma Lange.
{ROV; T-1868; B-1905}

LANGHURST, William H. - Pvt., Co. K, 50th Regt., Wis. Vol. Inf.
William resided at Watertown, Jefferson County and he enlisted there on Jan. 30, 1865. He was mustered out on June 14, 1866 at the end of his term of enlistment. William was listed in the 1885 census at P.O. Neenah. Johannah, his widow, was listed in the 1890 federal census as residing in the city of Neenah.
{US 1890; WC-V 1885; ROV}

LANGLOTZ, George - Pvt., Co. C, 11th Regt., Massachusetts Vol. Inf.
George was listed in 1883 at P.O. Menasha and receiving a pension of $24 per month for paralysis. He was listed as above in the veteran section of the 1885 Wisconsin State census at P.O. Menasha. George died on Sept. 13, 1901. He is buried in the Menasha section of Oak Hill Cemetery. Lena, his widow, was listed in 1905 as residing at 415 Nassau Street in the city of Menasha. George, John and Minnie Langlotz were residing with her.
{WC-V 1885; LOP-1883; Cem. records; B-1905}

LANGNER, Charles - Pvt., Co. D, 50th Regt., Wis. Vol. Inf.
Charles resided at Lowville, Columbia County and he enlisted there on Feb. 10, 1865. He was assigned as above and was mustered out on June 12, 1866 at the end of his term of enlistment. Charles was listed in the veteran section of the 1885 and 1895 Wisconsin State census at P.O. Neenah. He was listed in 1905, with wife Olga, as residing on 120 acres of section 24 in the town of Clayton. Charles A., Edna and Minnie Langner were also residing with him.
{WC-V 1885, 1895; ROV; B-1905}

LANNEN, Patrick - Cpl., Co. H, 31st Regt., Wis. Vol. Inf.
Patrick resided at Milwaukee, Milwaukee County. He enlisted in Co. F, 31st Regt., Wis. Vol. Inf. and was then transferred to Co. H of the same regiment on Oct. 2, 1862. He was promoted to Corporal in that company and was then returned to Co. F on Jan. 1, 1863. Patrick was mustered out on July 8, 1865. He was listed in 1868 as a mason boarding at 8 Alley Street in the city of Oshkosh. Patrick was not found in the veteran section of the 1885 Wisconsin State census. He was listed in 1888 as a member of GAR Post #10 at Oshkosh. He was listed in the 1890 federal census as residing in Oshkosh. He was listed in the veteran section of the 1895 state census at P.O. Oshkosh

LANNEN, Patrick (cont.)
and was not found in that part of the 1905 state census.
{US 1890; WC-V 1885, 1895, 1905; ROV; T-1868}

LANSING, Abram B. - Pvt., Co. E, 5th (reorg.) Regt., Wis. Vol. Inf.
Abram was born on Apr. 26, 1822 at Madison County, New York. He was a son of Cornelius and Katie (Pease) Lansing and father of Willard from a following sketch. Cornelius was a veteran of the War of 1812. Garrett Lansing, his father, was a veteran of the American Revolution. Abram was married on on Sept. 15, 1841 to Mary Ann Knickerbocker of Cazenovia, New York. Her grandfather, Bartholomew Knickerbocker and two of his sons, Harry and Stephen, were also veterans of the Revolutionary War. Abram removed with his family to Wisconsin in 1856. He was residing at Oshkosh when he enlisted on Aug. 25, 1864. He was assigned as above and was discharged on May 17, 1865 due to a disability. Abram resumed his occupation as a papermaker in Appleton, Outagamie County after the war. He and Mary had five children: Willard, subject of a following sketch; Cyrus M., drowned at age 14 years; Augusta Marion; William Andrew; and Lucy D. Lansing. Abram was listed in 1888 as a member of GAR Post #133 at Appleton. Mary, his widow, was listed in the 1890 federal census as residing in the city of Appleton.
{US 1890; ROV; SCA 1:675}

LANSING, Willard Augustus - Pvt., Co. E, 5th (reorg.) Regt., Wis. Vol. Inf.
Willard was a son of Abram Lansing from a previous sketch. He listed his residence as Oshkosh when he enlisted there on Aug. 16, 1864. He was assigned as above and was slightly wounded at Little Sailor's Creek before being mustered out on July 3, 1865. Willard was married to Eliza Bauchers. They had a daughter, Helen, who was born in Neenah on Apr. 1, 1883. Willard was listed in 1883 at P.O. Neenah and receiving a pension of $8 per month since Oct. 1880 for a contusion on his left side and residual diseases of the lungs and kidneys. He was listed in the veteran section of the 1885 and 1895 Wisconsin State census at P.O. Neenah. Willard was listed in the 1890 federal census as residing in the city of Neenah and suffering from a gunshot wound and diabetes. He was not found in the veteran section of the 1905 state census.
{US 1890; WC-V 1885, 1895, 1905; SCA 1:675; WCBR v.3, p.108, #645; ROV}
{LOP-1883}

LAPHAM, Andrew Jackson - Cpl., Co. D, 32nd Regt., Wis. Vol. Inf.
Andrew was born circa 1827 at New York. Jane, his wife, was born circa 1836 at England. Andrew was listed in the 1860 federal census as a steamboat captain residing in the second ward of the city of Oshkosh. Residing with him were his wife and the following children: Josephine, born circa 1854; Anna Jane, born circa 1856; and Lillian, born circa 1858. All three children were born in Wisconsin. Andrew resided at Oshkosh and enlisted there on Nov. 21, 1863. He was assigned as above and was promoted to Corporal in that company. Andrew was commissioned 2nd Lieutenant of that company on Apr. 20, 1865 but was not mustered at that rank. He was transferred to Co. D, 16th (reorg.) Regt., Wis. Vol. Inf. on June 4, 1865 and was mustered out on July 12, 1865. Andrew was listed in 1868 as residing at 24 Jefferson Avenue in the city of Oshkosh.
{US 1860; ROV; T-1868}

LARIMORE, James Calvin - Pvt., Co. B, 3rd Regt., Wis. Vol. Inf.
James was born circa 1841 at Pennsylvania. He was a son of Robert and Margarette Larimore, both natives of that same state. He was also a brother of John from a following sketch. Robert was born circa 1798 and Margarette was born circa 1812. Both were listed in the 1850 federal census as residing in the town of Winnebago. With them were the following children: Charles, born circa 1832; Rachael, born circa 1836; Nancy A., born circa 1840; James C., John; Hugh A., born circa 1844; Mary C., born circa 1846; and Susan A., born circa 1848. All of the children were listed as being born in Pennsylvania. The parents were listed in the 1860 census as residing on a farm in the town of Oshkosh. They then had two additional children, Robert, born circa 1852, and Ella, born circa 1855. James was listed as residing at home with his parents and he was listed again as a laborer on the farm of Stephen Bowron. James resided at Oshkosh and enlisted there on Apr. 21, 1861. He was assigned as above. James was killed in action when shot in the neck on Aug. 9, 1862 at Cedar Mountain, Virginia.
{US 1850, 1860; ROV; OWN 21 Aug 1862}

LARIMORE, John - Pvt., Co. B, 3rd Regt., Wis. Vol. Inf.
John was born circa 1843 at Pennsylvania. He was a son of Robert and Margarette Larimore and a brother of James from a previous sketch. John was listed in the 1860 census both as residing at home with his parents and as a farm laborer residing with Stephen Bowron. He resided at Oshkosh and enlisted there on Apr. 22, 1861. He was assigned as above and was discharged by orders dated Oct. 25, 1862.
{US 1850, 1860; ROV}

LARISH, W.T. - Civil War veteran?
He was listed in 1888 as a member of GAR Post #10 at Oshkosh.
{SCA}

LARKEE, John - 1st Sgt., Co. B, 15th Regt., Wis. Vol. Inf.
John resided at Neenah and he enlisted there on Oct. 21, 1861. He was assigned as above and was promoted to 1st Sergeant in that company. John was then discharged on Nov. 14, 1862 due to a disability.
{ROV}

LARRABEE, Julius A. - Cpl., Co. D, 1st Regt., Wis. Cav.
Julius resided at Nepeuskun and enlisted there on Sept. 1, 1861. He was assigned as above and was promoted to Corporal in that company. Julius was then mustered out on July 19, 1865. He was listed in 1888 as a member of GAR Post #199 at Ripon, Fond du Lac County.
{ROV; SCA}

LARSEN, Syvert - Pvt., Co. D, 15th Regt., Wis. Vol. Inf.
Syvert resided at Neenah and enlisted there on Nov. 5, 1861. He was assigned as above and was taken prisoner at Stone River. Syvert was mustered out on Feb. 13, 1865.
{ROV}

LARSON, Gunder - Cpl., Co. D, 32nd Regt., Wis. Vol. Inf.
Gunder was born on July 15, 1831 near the city of Arendahl, Norway. He was a son of Torger and Anna (Gunderson) Larsen. They had a family of four sons and two

LARSON, Gunder (cont.)
daughters. Gunder left home at age 18 years and emigrated to New York City, where he landed on Aug. 16, 1849. In the next month he moved west and settled at Fond du Lac, Fond du Lac County. In early 1850 his parents came to this country and they joined Gunder at Fond du Lac in July of that year. In August the family removed to Winnebago County. Gunder was married on Apr. 4, 1857 to Mary Jane Rogers. She was born on May 7, 1839 at Oswego County, New York and was a daughter of Samuel and Mary (Enos) Rogers. She came to Winnebago County with her parents in 1846. Gunder and Mary were listed in the 1860 federal census as residing on a farm in the town of Winchester. Julius Larson, a brother of Gunder, was also residing with them. Gunder resided at Winchester and enlisted there on Aug. 21, 1862. He was assigned as above and was promoted to Corporal in that company. He was then mustered out on June 12, 1865. Gunder and Mary had five children: Samuel Webster, born on Sept. 12, 1859; Adina Louisa, born on Oct. 6, 1861; Elmer DeGraat, born on Oct. 3, 1866, died prior to 1889; Florence Edith, born on Aug. 27, 1875; and Arthur Tecumseh, born on Apr. 5, 1879. All of the children were born in the town of Winchester. Gunder was listed in the veteran section of the 1885 and 1895 Wisconsin State census at P.O. Winchester. He was listed in the 1890 federal census as residing in the town of Winchester at P.O. Winchester. Gunder was listed in the veteran section of the 1905 Wisconsin State census at P.O. Larsen. He and his wife were listed in 1905 as residing on 1 acre of section 19 in the town of Winchester at the village of Larsen.

{US 1860, 1890; WC-V 1885, 1895, 1905; ROV; Randall p.54; WCBR v.3, p.7, #37}
{B-1905; WCBR v.3, p.7, #38; WCBR v.3, p.7, #39; WCBR v.3, p.7, #40}
{WCBR v.3, p.7, #41}

LARSON, Lars - Pvt., Co. A, 47th Regt., Wis. Vol. Inf.
Lars was born on Mar. 6, 1828. Betsy, his wife, was born on July 19, 1832. Lars resided at Winchester and enlisted there on Feb. 10, 1865. He was assigned as above and was mustered out on Sept. 4, 1865. Lars was listed in the veteran section of the 1885 Wisconsin State census at P.O. Winchester. He was listed in the 1890 federal census as residing in the town of Winchester at P.O. Winchester. Betsy died there on Feb. 4, 1894. Lars died on Aug. 29, 1900. A daughter, Clara, was born in 1862 and died in 1902. All three are buried in the town of Winchester at Grace Lutheran Cemetery.

{US 1890; WC-V 1885; ROV; Cem. records}

LARUE, Joseph W. - Pvt., Co. A, 3rd Regt., Wis. Cav.
Joseph resided at Oshkosh and enlisted there on Dec. 18, 1863. He was assigned as above and was transferred to Co. K, 3rd (reorg.) Regt., Wis. Cav. on Mar. 23, 1865. Joseph was mustered out on Sept. 29, 1865.
{ROV}

LASSNA, Anthony - Pvt., Co. H, 30th Regt., Wis. Vol. Inf.
Anthony resided at Eureka and enlisted there on Oct. 6, 1863. He was assigned as above and was mustered out on Sept. 20, 1865. Anthony was listed in the 1890 federal census as residing in the town of Rushford at P.O. Eureka. He was suffering from measles that had settled inside.

{US 1890; ROV}

LATHROP, Oscar - Pvt., Co. G, 30th Regt., Wis. Vol. Inf.
Oscar resided at Wautoma, Waushara County and enlisted there on Aug. 21, 1862. He was assigned as above and was mustered out on Sept. 20, 1865. Oscar was listed in the veteran section of the 1885 Wisconsin State census at P.O. Eureka. He is buried with a simple military marker in the town of Rushford at Eureka Cemetery.
{WC-V 1885; ROV; Cem. records}

LAUDON, Wilhelm - Pvt., Co. C, 9th Regt., Wis. Vol. Inf.
Wilhelm resided at Oshkosh and enlisted there on Sept. 24, 1861. He was assigned as above and he re-enlisted in that same company at the end of his first term. He was transferred to Co. A, 9th (reorg.) Regt., Wis. Vol. Inf. and he was then mustered out on Jan. 30, 1866.
{ROV}

LAUTENBACH, Frederick E. - Pvt., Co. D, 52nd Regt., Wis. Vol. Inf.
Fred was born on Jan. 5, 1824. Karoline, his wife, was born June 27, 1831. Frederick resided at Oshkosh and enlisted there on Mar. 4, 1865. He was assigned as above and was mustered out on July 28, 1865. Frederick was not found in the veteran section of the 1885 Wisconsin State census. He was listed in the 1890 federal census as residing in the town of Wolf River at P.O. Orihula and suffering from rheumatism. He was listed in the veteran section of the 1895 state census at P.O. Orihula. Frederick was listed in the 1905 state census at P.O. Fremont, Waupaca County. He was then show as residing with his wife on 160 acres of section 20 in the town of Wolf River at P.O. Fremont. Sons August W. (with wife Matilda) and Adolph (with wife Laura) were then residing with Fred. He died on Jan. 29, 1908 and Karoline died on Aug. 3, 1916. They had at least one other son, Albert H., who was born on Aug. 31, 1865 and died on Aug. 31, 1890. Son Adolph E. was born on June 4, 1871 and died on Apr. 3, 1933. Fred, Karoline, both sons and daughter-in-law Eleanor are all buried in the town of Wolf River at Wolf River Cemetery.
{US 1890; WC-V 1885, 1895, 1905; ROV; B-1905; Cem. records}

LAW, John - Pvt., Co. E, 42nd Regt., Wis. Vol. Inf.
John resided at Oshkosh and enlisted there on Aug. 20, 1864. He was assigned as above and was listed as having deserted on Sept. 17, 1864.
{ROV}

LAW, Robert - Cpl., Co. K, 1st Regt., Wis. Hvy. Art.
Robert resided at Milwaukee, Milwaukee County and he enlisted there on Sept. 19, 1864. He was assigned as above and was promoted to Corporal in that company. He was then mustered out on June 26, 1865. Robert was listed in the veteran section of the 1885, 1895 and 1905 Wisconsin State census at P.O. Neenah. He was listed in the 1890 federal census as residing in the city of Neenah. He was listed in 1905 as a millwright residing at 123 Bond Street in Neenah. Daughters Ella M. and Jessie Law were then residing with him. Robert was listed in 1920 as residing at that same address.
{US 1890; WC-V 1885, 1895, 1905; ROV; 21-33rd; B-1905}

LAWRENCE, Albert M. - Pvt., Co. K, 4th Regt., Wis. Cav.
Albert resided at Rantoul, Calumet County and enlisted there on June 8, 1861. He was assigned as above. Albert contracted a disease and he died on Aug. 29, 1863 at Baton

LAWRENCE, Albert M. (cont.)
Rouge, Louisiana. Diantha, widow of Albert, was listed in 1883 at P.O. Menasha and receiving a widow's pension of $8 per month. She was listed in the 1890 federal census as residing in the city of Menasha. Diantha A. was listed in 1905 as residing at 354 Broad Street in Menasha.
{US 1890; ROV; LOP-1883; B-1905}

LAWRENCE, Frank H. - Pvt., Co. G, 5th Regt., Maine Vol. Inf.
Frank was born on Dec. 16, 1847. He was a son of William D. and Nancy A. (Pool) Lawrence. Both were natives of Maine and were of English descent. William was born on May 28, 1811 and was a son of William Lawrence, also a native of Maine. Nancy was born on May 22, 1817 and was a daughter of William and Lydia (Burnham) Pool, both also natives of Maine. William D. and Nancy had the following children: Anna L.; William D.; Lizzie P.; Harriet L.; Mattie H.; Maggie; and Frank H. Lawrence. Frank spend his youth in the city of Calais, Maine and received a common school education. He enlisted on Jan. 7, 1865 and was assigned as above. He received an honorable discharge at Augusta, Maine on July 6, 1865. Frank returned home and, at age 19 years, he came with his father and brother to Oshkosh. Frank made his home in the town of Algoma with the exception of two years residing in Chippewa County and five years at Menominee County, Michigan. He was engaged in lumbering and logging. Frank was married on Oct. 22, 1879 to Cornelia S. Bradley. She was born on May 8, 1856 at Connetville, Pennsylvania and was a daughter of Christopher C. and Margaret (Mayher) Bradley. In Sept. 1884 Frank engaged in a grocery partnership with H.C. Sawtell. They remained in that business for four years. Frank and Cornelia had at least two children: Clara B., born on Sept. 17, 1880, died on Aug. 21, 1883; and Ross G., born on Apr. 2, 1886. Frank was listed as above in the veteran section of the 1885 Wisconsin State census at P.O. Oshkosh.
{WC-V 1885; Randall p.40; WCBR v.3, p.32, #192}

LAWRENCE, Harlow J. - Pvt., Co. K, 21st Regt., Maine Vol. Inf.
Harlow was listed as a member of the 21st Regt., Wis. Vol. Inf. in the veteran section of the 1885 Wisconsin State census at P.O. Oshkosh. He was listed in the 1890 federal census as residing in the city of Oshkosh. He listed that he had served two enlistments. The first was as a Private in Co. K, 12th Regt., Maine Vol. Inf. from Oct. 23, 1861 to Dec. 21, 1863. His second enlistment was in Co. D of that same regiment from Jan. 1, 1864 to Apr. 18, 1866. Harlow was married to Ella McKinzie. They had a stilborn son at Oshkosh on Mar. 29, 1877. Harlow was listed in the veteran section of the 1895 Wisconsin State census at P.O. Oshkosh. He was listed in that section of the 1905 state census at P.O. Oshkosh. Harlow was listed in 1905 as a laborer at the Paine Lumber Co. and residing at 29 Graham Street in Oshkosh. Adelaide, Harry, Winifred and Wallace Lawrence were then residing with Harlow.
{US 1890; WC-V 1885, 1895, 1905; B-1905; WCBR v.2, p.60, #136}

LAWRENZ, John - Pvt., Co. B, 37th Regt., Wis. Vol. Inf.
John resided at Oshkosh and enlisted there on Mar. 31, 1864. He was assigned as above and was wounded at Petersburg, Virginia on July 30, 1864. As a result of those wounds, his leg was amputated and John was discharged on Apr. 20, 1865 due to wounds.
{ROV}

LAWSON, Henry L. - Pvt., Co. A, 23rd Regt., New York Vol. Inf.
Henry came to Winnebago County about 1860. He was married in Winnebago County on Feb. 18, 1868 to Rosemond Stone. He was listed as above in the veteran section of the 1885 Wisconsin State census at P.O. Oshkosh. Henry died in Oshkosh in April 1887. He was buried there in Riverside Cemetery.
{WC-V 1885, 1905; WCMR v.1, p.366, #2225; OWN 14 Apr 1887}

LEACH, Harvey W. - Pvt., Co. A, 2nd Regt., Illinois Vol. Inf.
Harvey was born on Apr. 9, 1830 at Oswego County, New York. He removed west with his parents in 1850 and settled in the village of Waukau, where they operated a hotel for several years. Harvey was educated in civil engineering and mechanics. He was the superintendent for the construction of various mills in the county. He did the same for other parts of Wisconsin and in Minnesota, Illinois and Missouri. Harvey was the assessor for the town of Rushford in 1868 and was elected as surveyor of Winnebago County in 1872. About that time he moved into the city of Oshkosh. He is noted for having engineered many early maps of the county. Harvey was listed as above in the veteran section of the 1895 Wisconsin State census at P.O. Oshkosh. He was not found in that section of the 1905 state census. Harvey was listed in 1905 as a civil engineer and the Winnebago County Surveyor. He was then residing on the southwest corner of State and Otter Streets in the city of Oshkosh. Harvey died in Oshkosh on Jan. 17, 1916. He had been a patient at the Alexian Brothers Hospital on Jackson Street for the previous five years. He had been involved in an accident in 1908. Harvey had been tangled in a rope and was dragged by an automobile for some distance, injuring his head and spine. He was survived by a brother, Frank Leach of Minneapolis, Minnesota, a nephew, Erik Eriksen of Hermiston, Oregon, and three nieces, one at Chicago and two at Kewaunee, Wisconsin. Harvey was buried at Waukau Cemetery.
{WC-V 1895, 1905; B-1905; ODN 18 Jan 1916}

LEACH, Jonas H. - Pvt., Co. E, 2nd Regt., Wis. Vol. Inf.
Jonas resided at Oshkosh and enlisted there on Apr. 21, 1861. He was assigned as above and was wounded at the first battle of Bull Run, Virginia. Jonas was then discharged on Dec. 14, 1863 due to a disability. He was listed as having died prior to May 1899 when Col. Harshaw presented his roster of Co. E.
{ROV; ODN 07 May 1899}

LEACH, William - Sgt., Co. B, 3rd Regt., Wis. Vol. Inf.
William was born circa 1824 at Vermont, a son of Waterman and Tryphena Leach. Waterman was born circa 1791 at Massachusetts and Tryphena was born circa 1798 at Vermont. William was married in Winnebago County on Mar. 29, 1854 to Mary Quinn. They were listed in the 1860 federal census as residing on a farm in the town of Algoma. With them was William, their son. He was born circa 1857 at Wisconsin. Waterman and Tryphena resided on the adjoining farm. William resided at Oshkosh and enlisted on Apr. 19, 1861. He was assigned as above and was promoted to Sergeant in that company. He was taken prisoner and died on July 18, 1862 at Lynchburg, Virginia.
{US 1860; ROV; WCMR v.1, p.150, #642}

LEACHMAN, Frederick - Pvt., Co. F, 21st Regt., Wis. Vol. Inf.
Frederick was born circa 1844 at England. He was listed in the 1860 federal census as residing with the family of Sidney Shufelt on a farm in the town of Poygan. Frederick

LEACHMAN, Frederick (cont.)
enlisted at Poygan on Aug. 14, 1862 and was assigned as above. He was killed in action on Oct. 8, 1862 at Chaplin Hills, Kentucky.
{US 1860; ROV}

LEE, Jefferson R. - Pvt., Co. D, 41st Regt., Wis. Vol. Inf.
Jefferson resided at Oshkosh and enlisted there on May 18, 1864. He was assigned as above and was listed as absent sick when that regiment was mustered out. Jefferson died in Sept. 1864 at Chicago, Illinois.
{ROV; Lawson p.840}

LEE, Orlando A. - Pvt., Co. C, 46th Regt., Wis. Vol. Inf.
Orlando resided at Omro and enlisted there on Jan. 30, 1865. He was assigned as above and was mustered out on Sept. 27, 1865. Orlando was listed in the veteran section of the 1885 Wisconsin State census (Ole A.) at P.O. Winchester. He was not found in that section of the 1895 state census and he was listed in that part of the 1905 state census at P.O. Winneconne.
{WC-V 1885, 1895, 1905; ROV}

LEE, Richard - Pvt., Co. D, 49th Regt., Wis. Vol. Inf.
Richard was born circa 1821 at England. Jane, his wife, was born circa 1824, also at England. They were listed in the 1860 federal census as residing on a farm in the town of Winneconne. Listed with them were the following children: Mary, born circa 1848; Thomas, born circa 1851; Elisabeth, born circa 1853; John, born circa 1857; and Ellen, born circa 1859. Mary was born in New York and the other children were born in Wisconsin. Richard resided at Winneconne and enlisted there on Feb. 14, 1865. He was assigned as above and was mustered out on Nov. 1, 1865. Richard was listed in the veteran section of the 1885 Wisconsin State census at P.O. Winneconne. Jane, his wife, was born at Hampton, England and died on Aug. 26, 1880 at age 57 years. Richard is buried with a simple military marker. Both are buried in the town of Winneconne at Bell Cemetery.
{US 1860; WC-V 1885; ROV; Cem. records}

LEE, Thomas - Pvt., Co. F, 32nd Regt., Wis. Vol. Inf.
Thomas resided at Rushford and enlisted there on Nov. 26, 1863. He was assigned as above and was transferred to Co. F, 16th (reorg.) Regt., Wis. Vol. Inf. on June 4, 1865. He was not found in the records of that company or regiment. Thomas was married to Eliza Sutherland. They had a daughter, unnamed at registration, who was born in Rushford on Nov. 8, 1880. Sarah, widow of Thomas, was listed in the 1890 federal census as residing in the town of Rushford at P.O. Eureka. She provided that Thomas had been mustered out on July 12, 1865.
{US 1890; ROV; WCBR v.3, p.21, #122}

LeFEVRE, George Hubert - Cpl., Co. K, 5th (reorg.) Regt., Wis. Vol. Inf.
George was born on Aug. 22, 1842 at Madison, Dane County, Wisconsin. He was a son of David and Mary Ann (Dousman) LeFevre. David's father was a native of France. He emigrated with his family and settled at LaPrairie, about 9 miles from Montreal, Canada, where both he and his wife died. David was born in Canada circa 1812 and was a farmer like his father. He was married at Mackinac to Mary Ann, a daughter of

LeFEVRE, George Hubert (cont.)
John and Rosalia (LaBorde) Dousman of Green Bay, Brown County. She was born on Aug. 5, 1815 at Michigan and was an instructor and an interpretor in an Indian school at Keshena, Shawano County. David and Mary Ann had nine children: David L., born on Mar. 9, 1840 at Michigan, married Nellie Chamberlain, died Feb. 13, 1911; George H.; Elizabeth, born circa 1846; Wallace W., born in 1849, died in 1920; Katie, born circa 1849; John G., born in 1852, died in 1930; Jennie, born in 1852, died in 1925; Rosalind, born on Mar. 31, 1855, died Feb. 29, 1888; and Eugene R., born circa 1858. All of the children except David were born in Wisconsin. Mary Ann died on Apr. 1, 1892. David survived her and resided with son Wallace at Tustin, Waushara County. George was raised on his father's farm near Madison. David and Mary were listed in the 1860 federal census as residing with their family in the town of Rushford at P.O. Eureka. George was listed there with them and he enlisted there on Aug. 25, 1864. He was assigned as above and was promoted to Corporal in that company. George was mustered out on June 20, 1865 at Hall's Hill, Virginia. He returned home to Rushford. George was married in Winnebago County on Jan. 13, 1866 to Elizabeth Haner. She was born on Oct. 3, 1844 at New York and was a daughter of Ellis Haner of Eureka. George farmed at Rushford for two years and then moved to Winneconne, where he ran a steamboat freight line for six years and did contract work for railroads. He then entered into employment with Thomas Wall. George was listed in 1883 as residing at P.O. Winneconne, where he was receiving a pension of $3 per month since Nov. 1881 for an injury to his abdomen. He was listed in the veteran section of the 1885 Wisconsin state census at P.O. Winneconne. He was listed in the 1890 federal census as residing in the village of Winneconne. George removed to New London, Waupaca County in 1891. In the fall of 1892 he moved to Shiocton, Outagamie County. There he built a house and an office, along with a steam sawmill. George and Elizabeth had two daughters: Maude, married Walter Oakes of Winneconne; and Ollie A. LeFevre. George was listed in the veteran section of the 1905 state census at P.O. Shiocton. Mary Ann and several of her children are buried in the town of Rushford at Eureka Cemetery.
{US 1860, 1890; WC-V 1885, 1905; LOP-1883; CBR-FRV p.522-3; Cem. records}
{Randall p.55; ROV}

LEGEAR, William - Sgt., Co. B, 15th Regt., Michigan Vol. Inf.
William (Legarre) was listed as above in the veteran section of the 1885 and 1895 Wisconsin State census at P.O. Oshkosh. He was listed in the 1890 federal census as residing at 43 E. Irving Avenue in the city of Oshkosh. He was suffering from a hernia and a nervous affection. Kate, his widow, was listed in 1905 as residing at that same address.
{US 1890; WC-V 1885, 1895; B-1905}

LEICHER, Jacob - Pvt., Co. F, 19th Regt., Wis. Vol. Inf.
Jacob was born circa 1828 at Bavaria. He was listed in the 1860 federal census as a tailor residing with the family of Jacob Spies in the town of Winneconne. Jacob enlisted at Winneconne on Feb. 11, 1862. He was assigned as above and was mustered out on Apr. 29, 1865 at the end of his term of enlistment. Jacob was listed (Lucher) in the veteran section of the 1885 Wisconsin State census at P.O. Winneconne. He was listed in 1905 as a city marshall and deputy sheriff residing on Williams Street in the village of Winneconne.
{US 1860; WC-V 1885; ROV; B-1905}

LEIDENBERG, William - Pvt., Co. A, 48th Regt., Wis. Vol. Inf.
William was born on Mar. 9, 1829 at Prussia. He was one of three sons of Gottlieb and Sophia (Reimer) Leidenberg. William emigrated to America in 1856 and he then moved to Winnebago County, where he settled in 1857. He was married there in 1858 to Elizabeth Spies. She was born circa 1830 at Dormstadt. They were listed (Lightenberg) in the 1860 federal census as residing on a farm in the town of Winneconne. Listed with them was a son, Julius, who was born in 1859 at Wisconsin. They later had two other children, Delia and Dora. William resided at Winneconne and enlisted there on Feb. 6, 1865. He was assigned as above and was mustered out on Dec. 30, 1865. William was listed in the veteran section of the 1885 Wisconsin State census at P.O. Winneconne. He was listed in the 1890 federal census as residing in the village of Winneconne. William died on his farm near Winneconne on Mar. 25, 1892. Elizabeth was listed as his widow in 1905. She was then residing on 80 acres of section 19 in the town of Winneconne.
{US 1860, 1890; WC-V 1885; Randall p.55; ROV; B-1905; OWN 30 Mar 1892}

LEIRMAN, John - Pvt., Co. G, 3rd (reorg.) Regt., Wis. Cav.
John resided at Oshkosh and enlisted there on Nov. 27, 1863. He was assigned as above and was mustered out on Oct. 27, 1865.
{ROV}

LEMKE, August - Pvt., Co. I, 3rd Regt., Wis. Cav.
August resided at Vinland and enlisted there on Aug. 8, 1864. He was assigned as above and was transferred to Co. E, 3rd (reorg.) Regt., Wis. Cav. on Feb. 1, 1865. August was mustered out on Sept. 8, 1865. He was married in Winnebago County on Nov. 10, 1865 to Emma Hirsh.
{ROV; WCMR v.1, p.285, #1721}

LENT, Lyman F. - Pvt., Co. E, 42nd Regt., Wis. Vol. Inf.
Lyman resided at Oshkosh and enlisted there on Sept. 7, 1864. He was assigned as above and was mustered out on June 20, 1865.
{ROV}

LENT, Ward - Pvt., Co. G, 3rd (reorg.) Regt., Wis. Cav.
Ward was born circa 1827 at New York. Angeline, his wife, was born circa 1828 in that same state. Both were listed in the 1850 federal census as residing on a farm in the town of Vinland. With them were the following children: Charles W., born circa 1846; and Alice A., born circa 1848. Both children were listed as having been born in Wisconsin. Ward resided at Winchester and enlisted on Feb. 22, 1864. He was then listed as a veteran recruit and he was assigned as above. Ward was mustered out Oct. 27, 1865.
{US 1850; ROV}

LEONARD, William T. - Pvt., Co. G, 3rd Regt., Wis. Vol. Inf.
William was born circa 1837 at Massachusetts. His parents were natives of that state. William resided at Menasha and enlisted there on Apr. 20, 1861. He was assigned as above and was wounded on Sept. 17, 1862. William was wounded again on May 3, 1863 and then was mustered out on June 29, 1864 at the end of his term of enlistment. He was listed in 1905 as a resident at the Wisconsin Veterans' Home at King. William was listed in the 1910 federal census as residing at King. He had been married twice, the second being for 33 years. His wife's name was not listed but she had also been married

LEONARD, William T. (cont.)
twice. She was born circa 1847 at New York. Both of her parents were born in Vermont. She had three children, two still living in 1910.
{US 1910; ROV; GAR 40th}

LEROY, Benjamin - Pvt., Co. D, 51st Regt., Wis. Vol. Inf.
Benjamin resided at Appleton, Outagamie County and enlisted there on Feb. 28, 1865. He was assigned as above and was then mustered out on Aug. 29, 1865. He was not found in the veteran section of the 1885 Wisconsin state census but was found in the 1890 federal census as residing in the city of Neenah. Benjamin was listed in the veteran section of the 1895 and 1905 state census at P.O. Neenah. He was listed in 1905 as a watchman at the Bergstrom Paper Co. and residing at 527 Maple Street in Neenah. Delia, Elizabeth and Frank Leroy were then residing at that same address.
{US 1890; WC-V 1885, 1895, 1905; ROV; B-1905}

LEROY, Frank - Pvt., Co. K, 11th Regt., Wis. Vol. Inf.
Frank resided at Greenville, Outagamie County and enlisted there on Apr. 14, 1864. He was assigned as above and was listed as absent sick when that regiment was mustered out on Sept. 4, 1865. Frank was listed in the veteran section of the 1885 Wisconsin State census at P.O. Omro.
{WC-V 1885; ROV}

LESTER, Benjamin H. - Pvt., Co. C, 6th Regt., Wis. Vol. Inf.
Benjamin resided at Utica and was drafted there on Mar. 20, 1865. He was assigned as above and was mustered out on July 14, 1865.
{ROV}

LESTER, Oscar D. - Pvt., Co. I, 6th Regt., Wis. Vol. Inf.
Oscar resided at Utica and was drafted there on Oct. 29, 1864. He was assigned as above and was mustered out on July 14, 1865.
{ROV}

LESTER, Richard - 1st Sgt., Co. E, 2nd Regt., Wis. Vol. Inf.
Richard resided at Oshkosh and enlisted there on Apr. 21, 1861. He was assigned as above and was promoted to 1st Sergeant in that company. He was wounded at the first battle of Bull Run, Virginia. Richard was mustered out on June 28, 1864 at the end of his term of enlistment. He was listed as having died prior to May 1999 when Col. Harshaw presented his roster of Co. E.
{ROV; ODN 07 May 1899}

LESTER, Sebastian - Pvt., Co. D, 8th Regt., Wis. Vol. Inf.
Sebastian resided at Omro and enlisted on Dec. 5, 1863. He was assigned as above and was transferred to the Veteran Reserve Corps on Jan. 7, 1865. Sebastian was mustered out on May 20, 1865.
{ROV}

LETT, Henry G. - Pvt., Co. D, 8th Regt., Wis. Vol. Inf.
Henry resided at Algoma and enlisted there on Feb. 29, 1864. He was assigned as above and was mustered out on Sept. 5, 1865.
{ROV}

LETT, Thomas - Pvt., Co. E, 5th (reorg.) Regt., Wis. Vol. Inf.
Thomas was born on Nov. 28, 1849 at Canada, a son of Robert and Mary Lett. Thomas received a common school education in Canada. The family came to Wisconsin in 1860 and settled in the city of Oshkosh. Thomas was listed in the 1860 federal census as a native of Wisconsin, then residing with the family of his brother William in the fifth ward of Oshkosh. William is the subject of a following sketch. Thomas resided at Algoma and enlisted there on Sept. 13, 1864. He was assigned as above and was wounded at Cedar Creek, Virginia. Thomas was mustered out on June 20, 1865. He returned to Oshkosh, finished his education, and entered the lumbering business. Thomas was married on Sept. 28, 1871 to Marion B. Fletcher. She was born on Nov. 17, 1851 and was a daughter of David J. and Perlina (Bush) Fletcher. David was born on July 28, 1826 at Canandaigua, New York. He was married at Steuben County, New York on Apr. 9, 1846 to Perlina, daughter of Jacob and Betsy (Odell) Bush. Perlina was born on Nov. 28, 1829. David came to Wisconsin in 1848 and first settled in the town of Nekimi. He removed to Oshkosh in 1862 and died there on Jan. 22, 1887. David and Perlina had the following: Henry, born on Feb. 9, 1847; Isaac, born on Oct. 9, 1849; Marion B., born on Nov. 17, 1851; Leonard, born on Mar. 11, 1857; and Adelbert, born on Feb. 17, 1864. Thomas and Marion Lett had the following children: Edna, born on Dec. 27, 1873, married William J. Leland of Oshkosh; Arthur J., born on Jan. 8, 1878; Jennie May, born on June 30, 1880; Mamie, born on June 15, 1883; Dorothy, born on July 16, 1888; and Phoebe, born on Jan. 18, 1893. Thomas was listed in the veteran section of the 1885 Wisconsin State census at P.O. Oshkosh. He was listed in the 1890 federal census as residing in the city of Oshkosh. He then provided information that he had suffered a gunshot wound to his leg. Thomas was not found in the veteran section of the 1895 state census and was listed in that part of the 1905 census at P.O. Oshkosh. He was listed in 1905 as the senior member of Lett & Son, dealers in lumber and logs at Oshkosh. Thomas was then residing at 242 W. Algoma Street in Oshkosh. J.A., Marion, Dorothy and Phebe Lett were then residing with him.
{US 1860, 1890; WC-V 1885, 1895, 1905; ROV; CBR-FRV p.1213-4; B-1905}
{WCBR v.3, p.2, #12}

LETT, William H. - Pvt., Co. A, 2nd Regt., Wis. Cav.
William was born circa 1836 at England. Ann, his wife, was born circa 1826 at Maine. They were listed in the 1860 federal census as residing in the fifth ward of the city of Oshkosh. They then had a son, Charles, born circa 1857 at Wisconsin and a daughter, Ida, born circa 1859 at Wisconsin. Also listed with them was Thomas Lett, brother of William and subject of a previous sketch. William enlisted at Oshkosh on Sept. 1, 1864. He was assigned as above and was mustered out on June 12, 1865.
{US 1860; ROV}

LEWIS, Charles O. - Pvt., Co. K, 44th Regt., Wis. Vol. Inf.
Charles was born in July 1841 at New York. His father was a native of Wales and his mother was born in New York. Charles resided at Randolph, Dodge County and enlisted there on Feb. 4, 1865. He was assigned as above and was mustered out on Aug. 28, 1865. Charles was not found in the veteran section of the 1885 Wisconsin State census. He was listed in 1888 as a member of GAR Post #10 at Oshkosh. He was listed in the 1890 federal census as residing in the city of Oshkosh. Charles was listed in the veteran section of the 1895 state census at P.O. Oshkosh. He was listed in the 1900 federal census as residing at the Wisconsin Veterans' Home at King. Hannah D., his wife of 34 years, was residing there with him. She was born in Jan. 1840 at New York. Both of her parents were natives of Vermont. Hannah had one child who died prior to 1900. Charles and Hannah were listed in the 1905 state census as residing at King.
{US 1890, 1900; WC-V 1885, 1895, 1905; ROV; GAR 40th}

LEWIS, E.A. - Civil War Veteran?
He was listed in 1888 as a member of GAR Post #10 at Oshkosh.
{SCA}

LEWIS, Hiram Jackson - Lt. Col., 52nd Regt., Wis. Vol. Inf.
Hiram was born circa 1832 at New York. He was listed in the 1860 federal census as a carpenter residing with Walter Bennett in the village of Neenah. Hiram resided at Neenah and he enlisted as a Private in Co. K, 11th Regt., Wis. Vol. Inf. He was commissioned as 1st Lieutenant of that company on July 22, 1861 and was then promoted to Captain on Nov. 2, 1861. Hiram was mustered out on Jan. 3, 1865. He was commissioned as Lt. Colonel of the 52nd Regt., Wis. Vol. Inf. on Feb. 24, 1865 and was mustered out on July 28, 1865. Hiram was married to Dollie Ingham Barnes in Winnebago County on Mar. 28, 1865. He died on Sept. 17, 1876 at Neenah. Hiram was the namesake of the GAR Post at Neenah. Dolly was residing in Neenah in 1880.
{US 1860; ROV; WCMR v.1, p.270, #1605; HN-1878; Lawson p.830}

LEWIS, James - Pvt., Co. B, 3rd Regt., Wis. Vol. Inf.
James was born circa 1840 at Wales. He was a son of John and Margaret Lewis and a brother of Thomas and Lewis Lewis from other sketches. Both parents were natives of Wales, the father born there circa 1812 and the mother born circa 1813. They were listed in the 1860 federal census as residing on a farm in the town of Utica at P.O. Fisk's Corners. Listed with them were the following children: Thomas; James; Sarah, born circa 1842 at Wales; Lewis; Anna, born circa 1850 at Wales; and William, born circa 1853 at New York. James resided at Nekimi and enlisted there on June 4, 1861. He was assigned as above and was wounded in the knee at Antietam, Maryland on Sept. 17, 1862. James was discharged on Oct. 25, 1862.
{US 1860; ROV; OWN 02 Oct 1862}

LEWIS, Lewis - Cpl., Co. C, 21st Regt., Wis. Vol. Inf.
Lewis was born circa 1844 at Wales. He was a son of John and Margaret Lewis and a brother of Thomas and James Lewis from other sketches. Lewis was listed in the 1860 federal census as residing with his parents and their family in the town of Utica at P.O. Fisk's Corners. He resided at Nekimi and enlisted on Aug. 14, 1862. He was assigned as above and was promoted to Corporal in that company. Lewis was mustered out on June 8, 1865. He then resided for some at Iowa. When his wife died there, Lewis

LEWIS, Lewis (cont.)
returned to Oshkosh. He was then married to Martha V. Bennett. Lewis suffered a mild stroke in early 1922. Both he and his wife died at Oshkosh on Feb. 11, 1923 when overcome by fumes from a gas heater in their home. Lewis was 79 and Martha was near 69 at that time. Lewis was survived by two sons, William Lewis of Sioux Rapids, Iowa and John H. Lewis and by three daughters, Mrs. Laura Leger of Spencer, Iowa, Miss Martha Thomas of Sioux Rapids, and Mrs. Jennie Phillips of Little Grove, Iowa. He was also survived by a brother, William Lewis, and a sister, Mrs. William B. Greenwood, both of Oshkosh. Martha was survived by her sister Jane Bennett of Oshkosh and brother Edward E. Bennett of Lincoln, Nebraska. She was preceded in death by a brother, R.E. Bennett, and a sister, Mrs. Sarah Edwards.
{US 1860; ROV; ODN 12 Feb 1923}

LEWIS, Thomas F. - Pvt., Co. D, 8th Regt., Wis. Vol. Inf.
Thomas was born circa 1837 at Wales. He was a son of John and Margaret Lewis and a brother of James and Lewis Lewis from other sketches. Thomas was listed in the 1860 federal census as residing with his parents and their family in the town of Utica at P.O. Fisk's Corners. He was also listed in that year as a farm laborer residing with David James in the town of Nekimi. Thomas resided at Nekimi and enlisted there on Jan. 25, 1864. He was assigned as above and was mustered out on Sept. 5, 1865. Thomas was married in Winnebago County on Apr. 28, 1866 to Margareth Williams.
{US 1860; ROV; WCMR v.1, p.298, #1829}

LEWIS, William - Pvt., Co. D, 13th Regt., Illinois Vol. Inf.
William (Louis) was listed as above in the veteran section of the 1885 Wisconsin State census at P.O. Oshkosh.
{WC-V 1885}

LEWIS, William - Pvt., Co. A, 43rd Regt., Wis. Vol. Inf.
William resided at Utica and enlisted there on Aug. 23, 1864. He was assigned as above and was mustered out on June 24, 1865.
{ROV}

LEWIS, Z.D. - Civil War Veteran?
Z.D. was born on Feb. 8, 1824 at Mooers, Clinton County, New York. He was a son of Miner and Chloe (Walker) Lewis. Z.D. removed to the western part of New York at age 16 years and remained there for 11 years. He worked at the tanner's trade for several years and then engaged in merchandise. Z.D. was burned out after about a year. He was married on Sept. 12, 1850 to Rebecca Horning. She was a daughter of Peter F. and Olive (Bailey) Horning. He then came west and settled at Weyauwega, Waupaca County. Z.D. remained there for about 13 years and then removed to the town of Omro. During the war he was the head carpenter for the Union Army while in the South. Z.D. and Rebecca had the following children: Addie, born on Jan. 20, 1857, died on Nov. 11, 1862; and Olin B., born on Mar. 12, 1861, married Della Barnett. Z.D. was listed in 1889 as residing on 160 acres in the town of Omro.
{Randall p.30}

LICK, John - Pvt., Co. C, 21st Regt., Wis. Vol. Inf.
John resided at Oshkosh and enlisted on Aug. 13, 1862. He was assigned as above and

LICK, John (cont.)
was wounded at Chaplin Hills, Kentucky in Oct. 1862. John was then discharged due to his wounds on Feb. 10, 1863. He was listed in 1883 at P.O. Oshkosh as having received a pension of $1 per month since Oct. 1880 for a wound to his right thigh. John was listed in the veteran section of the 1885 Wisconsin State census at P.O. Oshkosh. John was listed in 1888 as a member of GAR Post #241 at Oshkosh. He was listed in the 1890 federal census as residing in the city of Oshkosh. John was listed in the veteran section of the 1895 state census at P.O. Zion and in that section of the 1905 state census at P.O. Oshkosh. He was listed in 1905 as residing at 64 Eighteenth Street in Oshkosh. John was then employed at the meat market of son John Jr. He was listed in 1920 as a resident at the Wisconsin Veterans' Home at King.
{US 1890; WC-V 1885, 1895, 1905; ROV; LOP-1883; 21-33rd; B-1905}

LIDDLE, Albert - Pvt., Co. G, 3rd Regt., Wis. Vol. Inf.
Albert was born on Oct. 18, 1842 at Canada and he was a son of Francis and Mary (Cooley) Liddle. Albert resided at Rushford and enlisted there on Aug. 31, 1864. He was assigned as above and was mustered out on July 18, 1865. Albert was married to Helen. She was born in 1849. Albert was not found in the veteran section of the 1885 Wisconsin State census. He was listed in the 1890 federal census as residing in the village of Omro and suffering from chronic diarrhea. Albert was listed in the veteran section of the 1895 state census at P.O. Omro and was not found in that section of the 1905 state census. Helen died in 1919 and Albert died on Feb. 7, 1926. Both are buried at Oshkosh in Riverside Cemetery, block 157, lot 21. Albert was survived by seven children: Burt of Denver, Colorado; Jesse of Omro; Lewis and Roy, both of Oshkosh; Mrs. E.P. Stanton of Kenosha, Wisconsin; Mrs. Chris Peterson of Omro; and Mrs. R.W. Chipman of Oshkosh.
{US 1890; WC-V 1885, 1895, 1905; ROV; ODN 08 Feb 1926; ODN 11 Feb 1926}
{Cem. records; Family Research Files of the author}

LIDDLE, Harvey O. - Pvt., Co. G, 3rd Regt., Wis. Vol. Inf.
Harvey resided at Rushford and enlisted there on Aug. 31, 1864. He was assigned as above. Harvey contracted a disease and he was discharged for that reason on Dec. 29, 1864 at Savannah, Georgia. He died at Savannah on Jan. 18, 1865 at age 18 years and 4 months. He is buried in the town of Rushford at Eureka Cemetery. He is listed there as the son of J.R. and A.M. Liddle. J.R. is John Rensselaer and A.M. is Agnes Matilda (Knoll) Liddle. She cannot be the mother of Harvey as Agnes was only 8 years of age when Harvey was born and she married John R. in Winnebago County in 1861. They are buried on the same plot with Harvey. John R. Liddle died at Eureka on June 11, 1924.
{ROV; Randall p.51; Cem. records; Family Research Files of the author}
{ODN 12 Jun 1924}

LILLICRAP, Edward - Pvt., Co. B, 37th Regt., Wis. Vol. Inf.
Edward was born on Mar. 13, 1830 and his wife was born on Jan. 21, 1837. Edward resided at Bloomfield, Waushara County and was drafted there on Nov. 2, 1864. He was assigned as above and was mustered out on July 27, 1865. He had at least the following children: Richard, born on Sept. 14, 1866, died on Dec. 8, 1933; and Washington, born on Sept. 26, 1868, died on Oct. 22, 1880. Edward was listed in the veteran section of the 1885 and 1895 Wisconsin State census at P.O. Tustin, Waushara County. He was

LILLICRAP, Edward (cont.)
listed in the 1890 federal census as residing in the town of Bloomfield, Waushara County at P.O. Tustin. He was listed in the veteran section of the 1905 state census at P.O. Omro. Edward was listed in 1905 as residing on Waukau Road two houses west of Main Street in the village of Omro. Also listed at that address were Edith and Edna Lillicrap. Son Richard was residing in the next house west. Edward's wife died on Apr. 3, 1903 and Edward died on Mar. 4, 1909. They are buried together at Omro Cemetery, Pelton's Addition, Section C, plot 30.
{US 1890; WC-V 1885, 1895, 1905; ROV; B-1905; Cem. records}

LILLIE, Frank - Pvt., 2nd Batt., Ohio Lt. Art.
Frank was listed as above in the veteran section of the 1885 Wisconsin State census at P.O. Oshkosh.
{WC-V 1885}

LILLIE, Norman William - Cpl., Co. A, 21st Regt., Wis. Vol. Inf.
Norman was born on June 30, 1836 at Salem, Washington County, New York. He was a son of Aaron and Mary (Batchelder) Lillie, both natives of New York. Aaron removed with his family in 1836 and settled on a farm at West Dorset, Bennington County, Vermont. He was engaged there in farming for about 16 years. In about 1850 he brought his family to Wisconsin and settled on a government claim at Weyauwega, Waupaca County. Aaron eventually removed to Kansas and was residing there in 1888. Mary died in 1859. Norman was the second of ten children in the family. He resided at Royalton, Waupaca County and enlisted there on Dec. 3, 1863. Norman was assigned as Private, Co. K, 10th Regt., Wis. Vol. Inf. When the company was organized at Madison, Wisconsin he was assigned as a nurse. There he contracted erysipelas which led to the disabling of his right hand. Norman was treated at Harvey Hospital and then rejoined the regiment at Kenesaw Mountain, Georgia. He was transferred to Co. A, 21st Regt., Wis. Vol. Inf. on Nov. 4, 1864 at Marietta, Georgia and was promoted to Corporal in that company. Norman was taken prisoner at Rockingham, S.C. and was held for 26 days at Libby prison before being paroled and taken to Annapolis, Maryland. Norman was then transferred to St. Louis, Missouri and was sent home on a furlough. While at home he was transferred as unassigned to the 3rd Regt., Wis. Vol. Inf. and was mustered out on May 10, 1865. Norman returned to Weyauwega and resumed his farming interests. He was married to Eliza Jane Sherman and they had two daughters and three sons. He was listed in the veteran section of the 1885 Wisconsin State census at P.O. Weyauwega. Norman was listed in 1888 as a member of GAR Post #180 at Weyauwega. He was listed in the 1890 federal census as residing in the town of Royalton, Waupaca County. Norman provided that he had suffered from rheumatism during his military service. He was listed in the veteran section of the 1895 and 1905 state census at P.O. Oshkosh. Norman was listed in 1905 as retired and residing at 49 Monroe Avenue in the city of Oshkosh.
{US 1890; WC-V 1885, 1895, 1905; ROV; SCA 1:591-2; B-1905}

LILLIE, Peter Jens - Pvt., Co. G, 3rd Regt., Wis. Vol. Inf.
Peter resided at Neenah and enlisted there on Jan. 5, 1864. He was assigned as above. Peter was taken prisoner on Feb. 14, 1864 and was exchanged. He was mustered out on July 18, 1865.
{ROV; Lawson p.807}

LINDSAY, Ezekiel - Pvt., Co. I, 7th Regt., Wis. Vol. Inf.
Ezekiel was born on July 6, 1822 at Coburg, Canada. He was a son of John and Polly (Dewey) Lindsay. John was a veteran of the War of 1812 and his father, John, was a veteran of the American Revolution. Ezekiel was married on Jan. 9, 1842 at Elgin, Kane County, Illinois to Emuretta Barnes. They remained there until 1854, when Ezekiel brought his family to Wisconsin and settled in Jefferson County. He was engaged in farming at that place. Ezekiel enlisted at Bloomfield on Mar. 22, 1864. He was assigned as above and was wounded in the battle at Wilderness, Virginia on May 5, 1864. He received a minnie ball in his thigh and two bucksot in his body. James E. Casey, a comrade who enlisted with Ezekiel, was fatally wounded at his side. Ezekiel was taken prisoner and was held at a plantation until they were recaptured by Union forces in June. He was taken to Alexandria, Virginia and remained there until he was discharged on Oct. 15, 1864 due to his wounds. Ezekiel returned to Jefferson County and remained there until May 7, 1877. He then removed to Oshkosh, where he was engaged in real estate and other light work. He was listed in 1883 at P.O. Oshkosh, where he was receiving a pension of $31.25 per month for a wound to his left thigh and the results of that wound. The wound to his thigh had left him permanently mutilated and disabled. He was listed in the veteran section of the 1885 Wisconsin State census at P.O. Oshkosh. He was still residing at Oshkosh in 1888 when he was listed as a member of GAR Post #10, having been elected to that post on Mar. 12, 1885. His widow was listed in the 1890 federal census as residing in the city of Oshkosh. Ezekiel had eight children: Henry Bradley; Malvina; George Milford; William Sanford; Willard; Wallace Freeman; Emma D.; and Dora. Emma and Dora died before their father and are buried in Oshkosh at Riverside Cemetery.
{US 1890; WC-V 1885; ROV; LOP-1883; SCA 1:255-6}

LINDSLEY, George H. - Pvt., Co. K, 11th Regt., Wis. Vol. Inf.
George was born circa 1823 at New York. He was listed in the 1850 federal census as a lumber merchant residing in the town of Neenah. Margaret E., his wife, was born circa 1827, also at New York. They were residing with the family of his brother Charles H. Lindsley. George was married second in Winnebago County on Aug. 29, 1852 to Louisa A. Jones. She was born circa 1833 at New York. George was listed in the 1860 federal census as a teamster residing in the village of Neenah. He then listed that he was born circa 1830. Listed with him were the following sons: Aaron, born circa 1855; Leslie, born circa 1856; and Herbert, born circa 1858. George resided at Neenah and enlisted there on Sept. 17, 1861. He was assigned as above and was then transferred to the Veteran Reserve Corps on Sept. 4, 1863. George was listed (Lindsey) in the veteran section of the 1885 Wisconsin State census at P.O. Neenah.
{US 1850, 1860; WC-V 1885; ROV; WCMR v.1, p.135, #525}

LINK, August - Cpl., Co. C, 53rd Regt., Wis. Vol. Inf.
August was born in 1834 at Prussia, a son of Michael and Caroline Link. Michael was born circa 1797 at Prussia. He raised his family in his native country. At age 22 years August emigrated to America with his parents and settled on a farm in the town of Nekimi. August was married in 1858 to Amelia Thom. She was born in 1838 at Prussia. They were listed in the 1860 federal census as residing on a farm in the town of Nekimi. His father was then listed with him. They had seven children: Henry; Elizabeth; Lydia; Alma; and three that died prior to 1889. Son Gustav was born in 1859 at Wisconsin. They also raised John Conna. August enlisted at Menasha on Mar. 8, 1865. He was

LINK, August (cont.)
assigned as above and was promoted to Corporal in that company. He, along with most of that company, was transferred to Co. K, 51st Regt., Wis. Vol. Inf. under orders dated June 10, 1865. The transfer was completed on June 30, 1865 at Ft. Leavenworth, Kansas and the regiment returned to Madison, Wisconsin on Aug. 1, 1865. The men were mustered out by companies with the last being mustered out on Aug. 30, 1865. August was mustered out on Aug. 21, 1865. By 1889 he owned 120 acres in the town of Nekimi and another 160 acres of farmland in the state of Nebraska. He was listed in the veteran section of the 1885, 1895 and 1905 Wisconsin State census at P.O. Oshkosh. August was listed in the 1890 federal census as residing in the town of Nekimi at P.O. Oshkosh. He was listed in 1905 as retired and residing at 151 Eleventh Street in the city of Oshkosh.
{US 1860, 1890; WC-V 1885, 1895, 1905; ROV; Randall p.27; B-1905}

LINT, Henry - Pvt., Co. C, 53rd Regt., Wis. Vol. Inf.
Henry resided at Oshkosh and enlisted there on Mar. 8, 1865. He was assigned as above. Henry and most of the men from that company were transferred to Co. K, 51st Regt. Wis. Vol. Inf. under orders dated June 10, 1865. The transfer was completed on June 30, 1865 at Ft. Leavenworth, Kansas and the regiment then returned to Madison, Wisconsin Aug. 1, 1865. The men were mustered out by companies with the last being mustered out on Aug. 30, 1865.
{ROV}

LINZ, Joseph - Pvt., Co. C, 10th Regt., New York Cav.
Joseph was listed in 1883 at P.O. Menasha, where he had been receiving a pension of $4 per month since July 1881 for chronic rheumatism. He was listed as above in the veteran section of the 1885 Wisconsin State census at P.O. Menasha.
{WC-V 1885; LOP-1883}

LISK, Benjamin F. - Capt., Co. I, 52nd Regt., U.S. Colored Troops.
Benjamin resided at Neenah and enlisted there on Sept. 17, 1861. He was assigned as Private, Co. K, 11th Regt., Wis. Vol. Inf. Benjamin was promoted to Sergeant and then 1st Sergeant in that company and he was wounded at Vicksburg, Mississippi. He was commissioned as Captain of Co. I, 52nd Regt., U.S. Colored Troops on Oct. 12, 1863 and was then discharged on July 10, 1864.
{ROV}

LISK, Ezra R. - 1st Lt., Co. C, 1st Regt., Wis. Hvy. Art.
Ezra was born circa 1836 at New York. He was listed in the 1860 federal census as a painter residing with George Wilcox in the village of Neenah. Also residing there was Francis Lisk, brother of Ezra. This may be the Benjamin F. of a previous sketch. Ezra was married in Winnebago County on Mar. 13, 1861 to Elizabeth M. Jenkins. They were residing at Neenah when he enlisted in the above company. He was commissioned as 1st Lieutenant in that company on Oct. 9, 1863 and he then resigned his commission on Sept. 14, 1864. Ezra was listed in the veteran section of the 1885 Wisconsin State census at P.O. Oshkosh.
{US 1860; WC-V 1885; WCMR v.1, p.212, #1142; ROV}

LITNER, Leopold - Pvt., Co. B, 21st Regt., Wis. Vol. Inf.
Leopold resided at Oshkosh and enlisted there on Aug. 14, 1862. He was assigned as above and was mustered out on June 8, 1865.
{ROV}

LITTLE, James H. - Pvt., Co. D, 32nd Regt., Wis. Vol. Inf.
James resided at Rushford and enlisted there on Nov. 23, 1863. He was assigned as above and was then transferred to the Veteran Reserve Corps on Aug. 3, 1864.
{ROV}

LITTLE, Sylvester K. - Sgt., Co. C, 38th Regt., Wis. Vol. Inf.
Sylvester was born in 1830. Luella A., his wife, was born in 1833. Sylvester resided at Aurora, Waushara County and he enlisted there on Mar. 29, 1864. He was assigned as above and was promoted to Corporal and then Sergeant in that company. Sylvester was mustered out on July 26, 1865. Lucella died in 1869 and Sylvester died in 1870. He has a simple military marker. They are buried together in the town of Rushford at Waukau Cemetery.
{ROV; Cem. records}

LITTLEFIELD, Alvin S. - Pvt., Co. G, 3rd Regt., Wis. Vol. Inf.
Alvin was born circa 1841 at New Hampshire, a son of Japhet and Mary Littlefield and a brother of Lucien from a following sketch. Japhet was born circa 1801 at Maine and Mary was born circa 1801 at New Hampshire. They were listed in the 1860 federal census as residing in the village of Neenah. Listed with them were the following children: Annette, born circa 1831; Lucien; and Alvin. Alvin resided at Neenah and enlisted there on Apr. 20, 1861. He was assigned as above and was then discharged on Jan. 20, 1862 due to a disability.
{US 1860; ROV}

LITTLEFIELD, Lathrop - Pvt., Co. E, 6th Regt., Wis. Vol. Inf.
Lathrop was born on May 10, 1828 at Antwerp, New York. He was married Mar. 1, 1854 at Rome, Oneida County, New York to Almyra More. She was born on Apr. 7, 1831 at Canandaigua, New York and was of Holland Dutch descent. Her grandfather was an officer in the army during the American Revolution. Lathrop and Almyra removed to Wisconsin in December 1856. They settled for a time at Sheboygan, Sheboygan County and then removed to Oshkosh in 1864. Lathrop resided at Scott, Sheboygan County when he was drafted on Oct. 21, 1864. He was assigned as above and was then mustered out on July 12, 1865. Lathrop was listed in 1868 as a teamster residing at 28 Seventh Street in the city of Oshkosh. He was listed in the veteran section of the 1885 and 1895 Wisconsin State census at P.O. Oshkosh. He was listed in 1888 as a member of GAR Post #241 at Oshkosh. Lathrop was listed in the 1890 federal census as residing in Oshkosh and suffering from diatic rheumatism. He was not found in that section of the 1905 state census. On Mar. 1, 1904, Mr. & Mrs. Littlefield, then residing on Seventh Street in Oshkosh, had celebrated their 50th wedding anniversary. Lathrop was then a rural mail carrier. He and Almyra had four children, only one lived to see their golden anniversary. Anson Littlefield then resided on Tenth Street in Oshkosh.
{US 1890; WC-V 1885, 1895, 1905; ROV; T-1868; ODN 12 Mar 1904}

LITTLEFIELD, Lucien D. - Sgt., Co. I, 21st Regt., Wis. Vol. Inf.
Lucien was born circa 1837 at New Hampshire, a son of Japhet and Mary Littlefield and a brother of Alvin from a previous sketch. Lucien was listed in the 1860 federal census as a carpenter residing with his parents and their family in the village of Neenah. He enlisted at Neenah on Aug. 11, 1862. He was assigned as above and was promoted to Sergeant in that company. Lucien contracted a disease and he died on Nov. 21, 1862 at Mitchellsville, Tennessee.
{US 1860; ROV}

LITTON, John - Pvt., 8th Batt., Wis. Lt. Art.
John resided at Menasha and enlisted there on Feb. 27, 1864. He was assigned as above and was mustered out on Aug. 10, 1865. Mahala Litton, his mother, was listed in 1883 at P.O. Neenah. She was receiving a mother's pension of $8 per month.
{ROV; LOP-1883}

LLOYD, B.F. - Civil War Veteran?
B.F. was born in 1836 and died in 1912. Frances, his wife, was born in 1848 and died in 1902. Ura a son, was born in 1885 and died in 1941. All three are buried in the town of Clayton at Royer Cemetery. B.F. has a GAR marker at his grave. He may be the Frank Lloyd of a following sketch.
{Cem. records}

LLOYD, Charles Wesley - Pvt., 8th Batt., Wis. Lt. Art.
Charles was born on Feb. 8, 1842 at Farmington, Ohio. He came west with his parents about 1847 and settled on a farm in the town of Clayton. Charles ran away from home and enlisted at Green Bay, Brown County on Oct. 31, 1864. He was assigned as above and was then mustered out on Aug. 10, 1865. After his military service, Charles returned to Menasha and made that place his permanent home. He held several elected and political positions in that city. He was listed in the veteran section of the 1885, 1895 and 1905 Wisconsin State census at P.O. Menasha. He was listed in the 1890 federal census as residing in the city of Menasha. Charles was listed in 1905 as a stockman residing at 325 First Street in Menasha. Annie, John, Joseph, Minnie and Flora Lloyd were then residing with him. Charles was the last Civil War veteran in Menasha when he died there on May 1, 1933. He was survived by his wife, sons Joseph and John of Menasha, and daughters Anna and Flora of Menasha and Mrs. Anton Loerke, then of Kaukauna.
{US 1890; WC-V 1885, 1895, 1905; ROV; B-1905; ODN 02 May 1933}

LLOYD, Edward - Sgt., Co. B, 3rd Regt., Wis. Cav.
Edward resided at Oshkosh and he enlisted there on Dec. 12, 1861. He was assigned as above and was promoted to Commissary Sergeant of that company. He was mustered out on Feb. 14, 1865 at the end of his term of enlistment.
{ROV}

LLOYD, Elias W. - Pvt., Co. K, 11th Regt., Wis. Vol. Inf.
Elias resided at Neenah and enlisted there on Sept. 17, 1861. He was assigned as above. Elias contracted a disease and died on July 3, 1863 at Vicksburg, Mississippi.
{ROV}

LLOYD, Frank - Pvt., Co. C, 10th Regt., Wis. Vol. Inf.
Frank was born circa 1836 at New York. He was listed in the 1860 federal census as a carpenter residing in the town of Clayton at P.O. Neenah. Residing with him were a brother, Wesley, who was born circa 1842 at Ohio, and his mother, Mary, who was born circa 1802 at England. Frank listed his residence as Menasha when he enlisted there on Sept. 27, 1861. He was assigned as above and was transferred to the Marine Brigade on Mar. 11, 1863. Frank Lloyd was married in Winnebago County on Dec. 20, 1865 to Frances Nutter. He was listed (Co. E, 57th Regt., U.S. Colored Troops) in the veteran section of the 1885 Wisconsin State census at P.O. Winchester. He was listed in that section of the 1895 state census at P.O. Winchester and in that part of the 1905 state census at P.O. Larsen. Frank was listed in the 1910 federal census as a widower residing at the Wisconsin Veterans' Home at King.
{US 1860, 1890, 1910; WC-V 1885, 1895, 1905; WCMR v.1, p.295, #1801; ROV}

LLOYD, Henry - Pvt., Co. K, 11th Regt., Wis. Vol. Inf.
Henry was born circa 1840 at Ohio. He was listed in the 1860 federal census as a farm laborer for Rans. Sperry in the town of Clayton at P.O. Neenah. Henry enlisted at Clayton on Feb. 25, 1864. He was assigned as above and was mustered out on Sept. 4, 1865.
{US 1860; ROV}

LLOYD, Robert D. - Pvt., Co. B, 3rd Regt., Wis. Cav.
Robert resided at Oshkosh and enlisted there on Nov. 18, 1861. He was assigned as above and was then transferred to Co. I of the same regiment on Apr. 1, 1862. Robert was mustered out on Nov. 8, 1865. He was listed in the 1890 federal census as residing at 23 New York Avenue in the city of Oshkosh. He provided information that he was Quartermaster Sergeant of Co. M, 3rd Regt., Wis. Cav. when he was mustered out.
{US 1890; ROV}

LLOYD, William - Pvt., Co. I, 21st Regt., Wis. Vol. Inf.
William resided at Vinland and enlisted there on Aug. 15, 1862. He was assigned as above and was mustered out on June 8, 1865. William was listed in the 1890 federal census as residing in the city of Menasha. He was not found in the 1905 county directory.
{US 1890; ROV; B-1905}

LLOYD, William H. - Pvt., Co. A, 1st (3 yr.) Regt., Wis. Vol. Inf.
William was born on Mar. 13, 1830. Cornelia, his wife, was born on Sept. 18, 1837. William resided at Omro and enlisted there on Oct. 21, 1861. He was assigned as above and was taken prisoner at Chickamauga, Georgia. William was listed as absent prisoner when that regiment was mustered out on Oct. 13, 1864. Cornelia died on Aug. 9, 1884 and William died on Aug. 24, 1912. Both are buried, with others of their family, in the town of Rushford at Eureka Cemetery.
{ROV; Cem. records}

LOCKE, William H. - Pvt., Co. I, 1st Regt., Wis. Hvy. Art.
William resided at Benton, Lafayette County and enlisted there on Oct. 5, 1864. He was assigned as above and was discharged on June 29, 1865 due to a disability. A Benjamin Z. Locke was a member of that same company. William was not found in the veteran

LOCKE, William H. (cont.)
section of the 1885 Wisconsin State census. He was listed in the 1890 federal census as residing at 48 Hannah Street in the city of Oshkosh. William was listed in the veteran section of the 1895 and 1905 state census at P.O. Oshkosh.
{US 1890; WC-V 1885, 1895, 1905; ROV}

LOCKERBY, Matthew L. - Cpl., Co. B, 37th Regt., Wis. Vol. Inf.
Matthew was born circa 1825 at New York. Desire, his wife, was born circa 1824 at Maine. They removed to Winnebago County circa 1847 and they were listed in the 1860 federal census as residing on a farm in the town of Clayton at P.O. Neenah. Listed with them were the following children: William, born circa 1853; Charles, born circa 1854; Leaton, born circa 1855; Mary, born circa 1857; and John, born circa 1859. Matthew enlisted at Clayton on Mar. 30, 1864. He was assigned as above and was then listed as a veteran volunteer. Matthew was promoted to Corporal in that company and he was wounded on June 18, 1864 at Petersburg, Virginia. He was transferred to the Veteran Reserve Corps on Apr. 24, 1865.
{US 1860; ROV; OWN 07 Apr 1864}

LOCKHART, Benjamin F. - Pvt., Co. A, 36th Regt., Illinois Vol. Inf.
Benjamin was born in 1846 at Hendricks County, Indiana. He was a son of Emanuel and Patience (Blakemore) Lockhart and a brother of Jasper N. and Thomas A. Lockhart from following sketches. Emanuel was born on Apr. 27, 1806 at Virginia and was a son of Daniel and Mary (Ward) Lockhart. Daniel was of Scotch-Irish descent and Mary was of Irish descent. Emanuel was raised in Virginia. He was married on Jan. 1, 1829 to Mrs. Elizabeth (Belshey) Curl, a daughter of Joseph and Margaret (Ward) Belshey. She was born about 1801 and died in 1836. Shortly after their marriage, Emanuel and Elizabeth removed to Ohio, where they had two daughters: Mary, born on Mar. 1, 1830; and Julia E., born in Oct. 1832. After Elizabeth died, Emanuel returned to Virginia for a year. He was then married to Patience Blakemore, who was born in 1807 at Virginia. They removed to Indiana and remained there for about ten years. Emanuel and Patience had five children: Jasper N.; Jane C., born circa 1840; Martha A., born circa 1842; Thomas A.; and Benjamin F. Lockhart. Emanuel then came to Wisconsin with his family and settled in the town of Utica. They were listed in the 1860 federal census as residing on a farm in the town of Utica at P.O. Fisk's Corners. Patience died there in 1881. Emanuel remained there on a farm of 160 acres until 1885 and then removed to a farm of 40 acres in the town of Omro. He was married in Dec. 1881 to Mrs. Hannah Haley. Benjamin, the subject of this sketch, enlisted at Illinois and was assigned as a Private, Co. A. 36th Regt., Ill. Vol. Inf. Benjamin was married in 1872 to Ann Webster. She was a daughter of David Webster. They had four children: Jasper William; Olive May; Louis Roy; and Arthur. He was listed as above in the veteran section of the 1885 Wisconsin State census at P.O. Oshkosh. Benjamin was listed in the 1890 federal census as residing in the town of Utica at P.O. Elo. He listed his service dates as from Apr. 1864 to Nov. 1864. He was then suffering from piles, chronic diarrhea and a lung disease. He was listed in the veteran section of the 1895 state census at P.O. Elo and in that part of the 1905 state census at P.O. Pickett.
{US 1860, 1890; WC-V 1885, 1895, 1905; Research of Andrew Lockhart}
{Randall p.30, 52}

LOCKHART, Jasper N. - Sgt., Co. A, 38th Regt., Wis. Vol. Inf.
Jasper was born circa 1839 at Indiana, a son of Emanuel and Patience (Blakemore) Lockhart. He was a brother of Benjamin of a previous sketch and of Thomas of a following sketch. Jasper was listed in the 1860 federal census as residing with his parents and their family on a farm in the town of Utica at P.O. Fisk's Corners. He listed his residence as Waukau when he enlisted on Oct. 1, 1861. He was assigned as a Private to Co. G, 1st Regt., Wis. Cav. Jasper was promoted to Sergeant and then 1st Sergeant in that company. He was discharged due to a disability on Oct. 26, 1862. Jasper then listed his residence as Oshkosh when he re-enlisted on Mar. 24, 1864. He was assigned as above. He was then listed as a veteran. Jasper was promoted to Quartermaster Sergeant of that company on Apr. 15, 1864. He was commissioned as Quartermaster of the 38th Regt. on Mar. 23, 1865 but was not mustered at that rank. He was mustered out on July 26, 1865.
{US 1860; ROV; Randall p.30; Research of Andrew Lockhart}

LOCKHART, Thomas Andrew - Sgt., Co. B, 37th Regt., Wis. Vol. Inf.
Thomas was born on Mar. 10, 1844 at Hendricks County, Indiana. He was a son of Emanuel and Patience (Blakemore) Lockhart and a brother of Benjamin and Jasper from previous sketches. Thomas received a good common school education and he attended two terms at Lawrence University at Appleton, Outagamie County. He was listed in the 1860 federal census as residing with his parents and their family in the town of Utica at P.O. Fisk's Corners. Thomas enlisted at Utica on Sept. 7, 1861 and was assigned as a Private, Co. C, 1st Regt., Wis. Cav. He served in that company until being discharged on Oct. 22, 1862. Thomas re-enlisted at Utica on Mar. 31, 1864 and was assigned as a Private to Co. B, 37th Regt., Wis. Vol. Inf. He was promoted to Sergeant in that company. Thomas was then wounded on June 17, 1864 at Petersburg, Virginia when he took a musket shot in the face which took out his upper teeth. He was mustered out on July 27, 1865. Thomas was married in Winnebago County on Jan. 6, 1870 to Amanda Mary Wright. She was born in 1848, a daughter of John Heaton and Amanda Malissa (Brown) Wright. Amanda was born Nov. 9, 1821 at Addison, Addison County, Vermont. She was a daughter of Daniel Rockwell and Phoebe Jackson (Lewis) Brown. John H. and Amanda were married on Nov. 9, 1846 at Canton, St. Lawrence County, New York. Thomas and Amanda had the following children: Frances Jane "Jennie", born in 1871; Carl Wright, born in 1875, married Gladys Gale; Mary Florence, born in 1878, married George Foster; Georgia Wright; Frances Grace; and Patience Blossom. In 1889 they were living on his father's farm of 160 acres in the town of Utica. Thomas was listed in the 1890 federal census as residing in the town of Utica at P.O. Elo. He was suffering the effects of the gunshot wound and a lung disease. Thomas was listed in the veteran section of the 1905 state census at P.O. Oshkosh.
{US 1860, 1890; WC-V 1905; Family Research files of Andrew Lockhart}
{Randall p.30, 52; ROV; Family Research files of the author}

LOCKWOOD, Chauncey A. - Pvt., Co. H, 14th Regt., Wis. Vol. Inf.
Chauncey resided at Springvale when he enlisted on Mar. 31, 1862. He was assigned as above and was mustered out on Apr. 4, 1865 at the end of his term of enlistment. Augusta J., his widow, was listed in the 1890 federal census as residing at 583 Main Street in the city of Oshkosh.
{US 1890; ROV}

LOEHR, Thomas S. - Pvt., Co. C, 10th Regt., Wis. Vol. Inf.
Thomas resided at Menasha and enlisted as above on Sept. 3, 1861. He was killed on Oct. 8, 1862 at Perryville, Kentucky.
{ROV}

LOFFT, William H. - Pvt., Co. C, 91st Regt., Pennsylvania Vol. Inf.
William was born circa 1838 at England. His parents were natives of that country. William emigrated to the United States in 1848. He was listed as above in the veteran section of the 1905 Wisconsin State census at P.O. Oshkosh. He was also listed that same year as a resident at the Wisconsin Veterans' Home at King. Merinsee, his wife, was residing there with him. William had been received from Milwaukee and was credited for service with the above regiment for 15 months. He was listed in the 1910 federal census as residing at King. Marinsse was born circa 1843 at Indiana. Her parents were natives of Germany. That was the third marriage for William and the second for Marinsse.
{US 1910; WC-V 1905; GAR 40th}

LOGAN, Richard R. - Pvt., Co. B, 3rd Regt., Wis. Vol. Inf.
Richard was born circa 1822 at Maine. Mary, his wife, was born circa 1823 at Nova Scotia, Canada. Richard was listed in the 1860 federal census as a lumberman residing in the third ward of the city of Oshkosh. Residing with him were his wife and a son, Wilbert, who was born circa 1858 at Wisconsin. Richard resided at Oshkosh and enlisted there on June 10, 1861. He was assigned as above and was wounded in both arms at Antietam, Maryland on Sept. 17, 1862. Richard was discharged due to those wounds on Nov. 25, 1862.
{US 1860; ROV; OWN 02 Oct 1862}

LONGLEY, Prescott E. - Cpl., Co. F, 3rd (reorg.) Regt., Wis. Cav.
Prescott resided at Baraboo, Sauk County and enlisted there on Dec. 15, 1863. He was assigned to Co. F, 3rd Regt., Wis. Cav and was then transferred to Co. F., 3rd (reorg.) Regt., Wis. Cav. Prescott was promoted to Corporal in that company and was mustered out on June 29, 1865. He was not found in the veteran section of the 1885 Wisconsin State census. Prescott was listed in that section of the 1895 state census at P.O. Oshkosh and was not found in that part of the 1905 state census.
{WC-V 1885, 1895, 1905; ROV}

LONGSTAFF, Oren G.J. - Pvt., Co. G, 3rd Regt., Wis. Vol. Inf.
Oren resided at Menasha and enlisted there on Apr. 20, 1862. He was assigned as above and was wounded on May 3, 1863. Oren was mustered out on June 14, 1864 at the end of his term of enlistment.
{ROV}

LOOP, David W. - Cpl., Co. C, 29th Regt., Wis. Vol. Inf.
David resided at Hubbard, Dodge County and enlisted there on Aug. 21, 1862. He was assigned as above and was promoted to Corporal in that company. David was absent sick when the regiment was mustered out June 22, 1865. He was listed (Look) in the veteran section of the 1885 Wisconsin State census at P.O. Omro. He was listed in the 1890 federal census as residing in the town of Omro at P.O. Waukau. He was suffering from chronic diarrhea, piles and rheumatism. David died on Mar. 28, 1891 at age 66

LOOP, David W. (cont.)
years, 10 months and 7 days. Sally C., his wife, was born on Feb. 28, 1828 and died on Mar. 11, 1894. Both are buried at Omro Cemetery, Olin's Addition, Section B, plot 24. A daughter, Welthie J. (Loop) Philpott is also buried on that plot.
{US 1890; WC-V 1885; ROV; Cem. records}

LOPER - see also Soper

LOPER, George Penny - Pvt., Co. F, 18th Regt., Wis. Vol. Inf.
George was born on Sept. 8, 1843 at Sullivan County, New York. He was a son of Samuel Eldridge and Nancy (Carpenter) Loper and a brother of Lyman Amos Loper from a following sketch. Samuel was born on Dec. 13, 1807 at Long Island, New York and Nancy was born circa 1815 at New York. They were married on Aug. 12, 1830. Samuel and Nancy were listed in the 1860 federal census as residing on a farm in the town of Rushford at P.O. Delhi. Listed with them were the following children: Amos; Anna, born circa 1842; George; Martha, born circa 1845; Charles, born circa 1849; Joseph, born circa 1850; Edgar, born circa 1854; Ezra, born circa 1856; and Susan, born circa 1858. The three youngest children were born in Wisconsin and the others were all born in New York. Samuel died on Jan. 24, 1881 and Nancy died on Apr. 9, 1893 at DePere, Brown County, Wisconsin. George resided at Rushford and he enlisted there on Feb. 5, 1864. He was assigned as above and was taken prisoner at Allatoona, Georgia. George was mustered out on May 24, 1865. He was married by Oscar E. Loper on Mar. 29, 1868 at Rushford to Frances Utter. She was born in 1850 at Wisconsin and was a daughter of William Willis and Elizabeth (Crego) Utter. William was a son of James and Lola Utter and Elizabeth was a daughter of John and Elizabeth Crego. The parents of both William and Elizabeth were among the early settlers of Walworth County. George and Frances had at least one son, Arthur. George resided at Rushford and removed to the city of Oshkosh in the early 1870s. He was not found in the veteran section of the 1885 Wisconsin State census. He was listed (Soper) in 1888 as a member of GAR Post #241 at Oshkosh. He was listed in the 1890 federal census as residing at 21 Jefferson Avenue in the city of Oshkosh. George was suffering from a hernia and listed that he had been held prisoner at Andersonville, Libby and Florence Prisons. He was listed in the veteran section of the 1895 and 1905 state census at P.O. Oshkosh. George was listed in 1905 as a partner in Loper & Loper, a livery business. He then resided at 61 Waugoo Street in Oshkosh. George was elected as commander of GAR Post #241 at Oshkosh on Dec. 26, 1905. He died of pneumonia on Jan. 6, 1906.
{US 1860, 1890; WC-V 1885, 1895, 1905; ROV; WCMR v.1, p.373, #2279; B-1905}
{OWN 13 Jan 1906; Family Research files of the author}

LOPER, Lorenzo C. - Pvt., Co. F, 18th Regt., Wis. Vol. Inf.
Lorenzo was born circa 1845 at New York. He was a son of Oscar E. and Catherine Loper. Oscar was born circa 1818 at New York. He died on Apr. 22, 1909 at Rushford. He was a son of Amos Loper, an early settler at Ceresco, Fond du Lac County. Catherine was born on June 17, 1819 at Schoharie County, New York and she died on Dec. 15, 1903 at Rushford. Oscar was one of the five founders of the Republican Party at Ripon, Fond du Lac County. He was listed in the 1860 federal census as residing on a farm in the town of Rushford at P.O. Eureka. Listed with him were his wife and the following children: Lovina, born circa 1843; Lorena, born circa 1844; Lorenzo; Loren, born circa 1847; Ella, born circa 1850; Almeda, born circa 1852; Mary, born circa 1854;

LOPER, Lorenzo C. (cont.)
Edwin, born circa 1856; and Ida, born circa 1859. The three eldest children were born in New York and the others were all born in Wisconsin. Lorenzo resided at Rushford and enlisted there on Feb. 27, 1864. He was assigned as above and was taken prisoner at Allatoona, Georgia. Lorenzo died on Apr. 6, 1865 at St. Louis, Missouri at age 20 years, 1 month and 18 days. He is buried with his parents in the town of Rushford at Rushford Cemetery.
{US 1860; ROV; Cem. records; Family Research files of the author}

LOPER, Lyman Amos - Pvt., Co. B, 4th Regt., Wis. Cav.
Lyman was born on Mar. 25, 1840 at Forestburg, New York, a son of Samuel Eldridge and Nancy (Carpenter) Loper and a brother of George from a previous sketch. Amos was listed in the 1860 federal census as residing with his parents and their family in the town of Rushford at P.O. Delhi. Lyman resided at Delhi and enlisted on May 13, 1861. He was assigned as above and was listed as having deserted on July 27, 1861. Lyman died on Feb. 9, 1865.
{US 1860; ROV; Family Research files of the author}

LORD, Hiram M. - Pvt., Co. I, 1st Regt., Wis. Hvy. Art.
Hiram resided at Benton, Lafayette County and enlisted there on Oct. 15, 1864. He was assigned as above and was mustered out on June 26, 1865. Hiram was listed in the veteran section of the 1885 and 1895 Wisconsin State census at P.O. Oshkosh. He was listed in the 1890 federal census as residing in the city of Oshkosh. Hiram was listed in the veteran section of the 1905 state census at P.O. Antigo, Langlade County.
{US 1890; WC-V 1885, 1895, 1905; ROV}

LORD, Presbury W. - Sgt., Co. G, 5th Regt., Wis. Vol. Inf.
Presbury was a son of William and Mary (Jones) Lord. William was a native of England and was a British soldier in his youth. While serving in Ireland, he was married to Mary Jones. They soon emigrated to America, where William worked as a carpenter in New York. He went to Vermont for a year and then returned to New York, where he engaged in farming. William migrated to Ohio in 1839 and then removed to Winnebago County in 1849. He settled with his family in the town of Clayton, where William died in 1859. William and Mary had six sons and one daughter. Presbury resided at Rushford and enlisted there on May 1, 1861. He was assigned as above and re-enlisted at the end of his 3 month term. Presbury was promoted to Corporal and then Sergeant in that company. He was wounded at Spottsylvania and was then transferred to Co. B, Ind. Bn. on July 13, 1864. Presbury was killed in action on Apr. 2, 1865 at Petersburg, Virginia.
{ROV; Randall p.53}

LOUD, William - Pvt., Co. L, 3rd (reorg.) Regt., Wis. Cav.
William resided at Oshkosh and enlisted there on Dec. 23, 1863. He was assigned as above and was mustered out on Oct. 23, 1865.
{ROV}

LOUNECLIFFE, William - Pvt., Co. L, 1st Regt., Ohio Cav.
William was listed as above in the veteran section of the 1905 Wisconsin State census at

LOUNECLIFFE, William (cont.)
P.O. Menasha.
{WC-V 1905}

LOVELESS, Joseph R. - Pvt., Co. E, 1st Regt., Wis. Cav.
Joseph resided at Winneconne and enlisted there on Sept. 28, 1864. He was assigned as above and was mustered out on July 29, 1865.
{ROV}

LOWE, John - Cpl., Co. K, 5th (reorg.) Regt., Wis. Vol. Inf.
John resided at Utica and enlisted there on Sept. 2, 1864. He was assigned as above and was promoted to Corporal in that company. John was mustered out on June 20, 1865. He was listed in the veteran section of the 1885 Wisconsin State census at P.O. Waukau. John was listed in the 1890 federal census as residing in the town of Utica at P.O. Elo. He was listed in the veteran section of the 1895 Wisconsin State census at P.O. Elo. John was listed in that part of the 1905 state census at P.O. Fisk. He was listed in 1905, with his wife Matilda and son Harry, as residing on 35 acres of section 11 in the town of Utica.
{US 1890; WC-V 1885, 1895, 1905; ROV; B-1905}

LOWE, Robert - Pvt., Co. F, 18th Regt., Wis. Vol. Inf.
Robert resided at Rushford and he enlisted there on Feb. 8, 1864. He was assigned as above and was taken prisoner at Allatoona, Georgia. Robert was then mustered out on July 18, 1865.
{ROV}

LOWE, William - Pvt., Co. B, 21st Regt., Wis. Vol. Inf.
William was born in 1844. He resided at Rushford and enlisted there on Aug. 15, 1862. He was assigned as above and was discharged on Dec. 12, 1862 due to a disability. William then listed his residence as Utica and enlisted there on Sept. 2, 1864. He was assigned as a Private to Co. K, 5th (reorg.) Regt., Wis. Vol. Inf. and was promoted to Sergeant in that company. William was mustered out on June 13, 1865. Ann E., his wife, was born in 1845. They had at least one son, Robert, who was born in 1885. William died in 1911 and Ann died in 1924. They are buried with son Robert and his wife in the town of Plainfield, Waushara County at Plainfield Cemetery.
{ROV; Cem. records}

LOWERY, Samuel - Pvt., Co. H, 25th Regt., Wis. Vol. Inf.
Samuel resided at Potosi, Grant County and he enlisted there on Aug. 11, 1862. He was assigned as above. Samuel contracted a disease and died on Sept. 10, 1863 at Memphis, Tennessee. Eliza, his widow, was listed in 1883 at P.O. Oshkosh and receiving a pension of $8 per month. She was listed in the 1890 federal census as residing in the city of Oshkosh. She provided his unit designation as above. Eliza was listed in 1905 as residing at 217 Ninth Street in Oshkosh. Daughter Eleanor was residing with her.
{US 1890; ROV; LOP-1883; B-1905}

LUCE, William H. - Pvt., 3rd Batt., Wis. Lt. Art.
William enlisted on Sept. 13, 1861 and was assigned as above. He was mustered out on Oct. 10, 1864 at the end of his term of enlistment. There was a James R. Luce in that

LUCE, William H. (cont.)
same company. William was listed in 1868 as a saw filer residing at 15 Pearl Street in the city of Oshkosh. He was married to Emeline Damuth. They had a daughter, not yet named when her birth was registered, who was born in Oshkosh on Mar. 24, 1880. William was not found in the veteran section of the 1885 Wisconsin State census. He was listed in that section of the 1895 state census at P.O. Oshkosh and was not found in that part of the 1905 state census. William was listed in 1905 as a saw filer residing at 569 Algoma Street in Oshkosh. Benjamin F. and Henry H. Luce were then residing at that same address.
{WC-V 1885, 1895, 1905; ROV; T-1868; B-1905; WCBR v.2, p.190, #535}

LUCK, Christopher - Pvt., Co. B, 47th Regt., Wis. Vol. Inf.
Christopher resided at Princeton, Green Lake County and enlisted there on Feb. 4, 1865. He was assigned as above and was mustered out on Aug. 29, 1865. He was listed in the veteran section of the 1885 Wisconsin State census at P.O. Rush Lake. The name was alternately spelled Lueck.
{WC-V 1885; ROV}

LUCK, David - Pvt., Co. H, 21st Regt., Wis. Vol. Inf.
David resided at Vinland and enlisted there on Aug. 14, 1862. He was assigned as above and was transferred to the Veteran Reserve Corps on Apr. 22, 1864. David was then mustered out on June 30, 1865.
{ROV}

LUCK, Frederick - Pvt., Co. C, 21st Regt., Wis. Vol. Inf.
Frederick was born on Nov. 17, 1841 at Posen, Prussia. He was a son of John and Wilhelmina (Jausch) Luck. John was a teacher in Prussia before emigrating to America in 1858. Wilhelmina died on the ship and was buried at sea. The family remained in New York for two years and came to Wisconsin in the latter part of 1860. They settled at Winnebago County in the town of Winchester. Fred had been taught the trade of a carpenter and was thus engaged at Oshkosh for two years. He enlisted at Oshkosh on Aug. 12, 1862 and was was assigned as above. Frederick was wounded less than five minutes into his first battle, at Chaplin Hills, Kentucky on Oct. 8, 1862. He was struck in the right leg by a bullet and another passed through his body, grazing his left lung and breaking two ribs in the process. He was injured at about four in the afternoon and remained injured on the battlefield until late morning of the next day. He was then taken to a field hospital and remained there without surgical help for a week. Frederick was taken to a private house at Perryville and remained there for two months. He was then taken to Hospital #7 at Perryville. Frederick was discharged due to his wounds on Feb. 10, 1863. While travelling back to Wisconsin, Fred was required to stop along the way at hospitals in Covington and Louisville, Kentucky. He also was treated at Toledo, Ohio. He then arrived at Madison, Wisconsin on Dec. 1, 1863 and there his left leg was amputated on Jan. 3, 1864. He remained in the hospital until May 12, 1864 when he was sent to Chicago to be fitted for a cork leg. Frederick returned to Winnebago County, where he was married on Dec. 13, 1868 to Henrietta (Wendtland) Krantz. She was born in Germany and emigrated to America in 1868. Fred and Henrietta had two children, Emeline and Ottila. She died at Winneconne on May 21, 1883. On Oct. 9, 1883 Fred was married to Matilda Marten, a daughter of Frederick and Carolina Marten. Her father died in Germany and her mother was still residing there in 1888.

LUCK, Frederick (cont.)
Fred and Matilda had two children, Frederick W. and Amanda. Fred was unable to do much work since his return from military service. He removed to Winneconne in 1882. He was listed in 1883 at P.O. Winneconne and receiving a pension of $24 per month for the loss of his left leg. He was listed (Lueck) in the veteran section of the 1885 Wisconsin State census at P.O. Winneconne. Fred was listed in the 1890 federal census (Leck) as residing in the town of Winneconne at P.O. Winneconne. He was also listed in the veteran section of the 1895 and 1905 state census at P.O. Winneconne. Fred was listed in 1905 as residing on E. Water Street in the village of Winneconne. Fred Jr. and Amanda were then residing with him.
{US 1890; WC-V 1885, 1895, 1905; ROV; LOP-1883; SCA 1:720-1; B-1905}
{WCMR v.1, p.403, #2520; OWN 16 Oct 1862; OWN 07 May 1863}

LUCY, Patrick - Pvt., Co. C, 6th Regt., Wis. Vol. Inf.
Patrick resided at Utica and was drafted there on Sept. 30, 1864. He was assigned as above and was mustered out on June 6, 1865.
{ROV}

LUCY, Peter - Pvt., Co. E, 6th Regt., Wis. Vol. Inf.
Peter resided at Utica and was drafted there on Sept. 30, 1864. He was assigned as above and was wounded at Hatcher's Run. Peter was listed as absent wounded when that regiment was mustered out.
{ROV}

LUDER, Samuel - Pvt., Co. B, 3rd Regt., Wis. Cav.
Samuel resided at Oshkosh and enlisted there on Dec. 10, 1861. He was assigned as above and was listed as having deserted on June 8, 1862.
{ROV}

LUECK - see Luck

LUHM, Fred - Pvt., Co. B, 37th Regt., Wis. Vol. Inf.
Fred resided at Oshkosh and enlisted there on Mar. 31, 1864. He was assigned as above and was wounded on June 17, 1864 at Petersburg, Virginia. Fred contracted a disease and died on Nov. 18, 1864 at Washington, D.C.
{ROV}

LUKER, Stephen - Pvt., Co. D, 47th Regt., Wis. Vol. Inf.
Stephen was born on Mar. 4, 1822 at Woolshire, England. Mary, his wife, was born on Nov. 5, 1828 at England. She was a daughter of John and Dianna Nash. Stephen and Mary were listed in the 1860 federal census as residing on a farm in the town of Nepeuskun at P.O. Waukau. Stephen was listed in the military records as Looker although local records present the name as Luker. Stephen resided at Omro and enlisted there on Jan. 30, 1865. He was assigned as above and was mustered out on May 25, 1865. Stephen and Mary had at least eight children: George, born circa 1845 at England; John, born on Mar. 8, 1847 at England, died on July 3, 1927; Diana, born circa 1852 at England; Mary, born circa 1854 at Wisconsin; Edward, born circa 1857 at Wisconsin; Maria, born circa 1859 at Wisconsin; Charlie E., died on July 25, 1870 at age 3 months and 21 days; and Bessie E., died on Feb. 4, 1881 at age 9 years and 18

LUKER, Stephen (cont.)
days. Mary died on Feb. 13, 1887. Stephen was listed in the 1890 federal census as residing in the town of Nepeuskun at P.O. Rush Lake and suffering from the effects of diarrhea. He died on Feb. 22, 1891. Both are buried in the town of Nepeuskun at Koro Cemetery. Several members of their family are buried on that same plot.
{US 1860, 1890; ROV; Cem. records}

LULL, Edgar M. - Sgt., Co. H, 20th Regt., Wis. Vol. Inf.
Edgar was born circa 1830 at Vermont. He was a son of Levy and Fanny Lull. Both parents were natives of Vermont, the father born there circa 1788 and the mother born circa 1799. They were listed in the 1860 federal census as residing on a farm in the fifth ward of the city of Oshkosh. Listed with them were the following children: Edgar; Sophia, born circa 1843; and Laura, born circa 1845. The children were all born in Vermont. Edgar enlisted at Oshkosh on Aug. 14, 1862. He was assigned as above and was promoted to Corporal and then Sergeant in that company. Edgar was wounded at Prairie Grove and was discharged on Apr. 29, 1863 due to a disability. He was married in Winnebago County on June 10, 1863 to Emily Hayter. He was listed in 1868 as a partner in the firm of Lull & McNair, grocers, and residing at 8 N. Punhoqua Street in Oshkosh. Edgar was listed in 1883 at P.O. Oshkosh and receiving a pension of $4 per month for a wound to his right thigh. Fanny, his mother, was also listed in 1883 at P.O. Oshkosh and receiving a mother's pension of $8 per month since May 1881. Edgar was listed in 1888 as a member of GAR Post #241 at Oshkosh. He was listed in the veteran section of the 1885, 1895 and 1905 Wisconsin State census P.O. Oshkosh. Edgar was listed in the 1890 federal census as residing in Oshkosh. He was listed in 1905 as a carpenter residing at 359 Sixth Street in Oshkosh.
{US 1860, 1890; WC-V 1885, 1895, 1905; ROV; LOP-1883; B-1905}

LULL, Julius E. - Pvt., Co. E, 2nd Regt., Wis. Vol. Inf.
Julius resided at Oshkosh and enlisted there on May 18, 1861. He was assigned as above and was wounded slightly in the leg at Gainesville, Virginia on Aug. 28, 1862. He was discharged on Dec. 19, 1862 due to those wounds. Julius re-enlisted on Aug. 23, 1864 and was assigned as Private, Co. B, 3rd Regt., Wis. Cav. He was then transferred to Co. B, 3rd (reorg.) Regt., Wis. Cav. and was promoted to Corporal in that company. Julius died on June 16, 1865 at Jefferson Barracks, Missouri.
{ROV; OWN 11 Sep 1862}

LULL, Marcus S. - Cpl., Co. H, 36th Regt., Wis. Vol. Inf.
Marcus resided at Utica and enlisted on Feb. 29, 1864. He was assigned as above and was promoted to Corporal in that company. He was taken prisoner at Ream's Station. Marcus contracted a disease and died on Jan. 20, 1865 at Salisbury, North Carolina.
{ROV}

LUMISH, Wilber F. - Pvt., 84th Regt., Pennsylvania Vol. Inf.
Wilber was listed as above in the 1890 federal census as residing in the city of Oshkosh. He provided no other information on his military service.
{US 1890}

LUSCOMBE, Charles W. - Pvt., Co. I, 27th Regt., Wis. Vol. Inf.
Charles was born in 1846. He resided at Richfield, Washington County and enlisted

LUSCOMBE, Charles W. (cont.)
there on Dec. 25, 1863. He was assigned as above and was mustered out on Sept. 13, 1865. Charles was listed in the veteran section of the 1885, 1895 and 1905 Wisconsin State census at P.O. Omro. He was listed in the 1890 federal census as residing in the village of Omro. Charles was listed in 1905 as a painter residing at 310 Water Street in Omro. Also listed at that residence were Bonnie and Hazel Luscombe. Charles died in 1931. Elizabeth, his wife, was born in 1865 and died in 1943. Both are buried at Omro Cemetery, Original Section, plot 218.
{US 1890; WC-V 1885, 1895, 1905; ROV; B-1905; Cem. records}

LUSCOMBE, Francis E. - Pvt., Co. E, 17th Regt., Wis. Vol. Inf.
Francis was born in 1842. He resided at West Bend, Washington County and gave his name as Frank when he enlisted there on Jan. 8, 1862. He was assigned as above and was wounded on May 19, 1863. Frank was discharged on Sept. 17, 1863 due to a disability. He was married to Annie Pokorny. They had a son, Edward, who was born in Omro on May 15, 1877. Francis was listed in 1883 at P.O. Omro and receiving a pension of $24 per month for the loss of his left leg. Frank was listed in the veteran section of the 1885, 1895 and 1905 Wisconsin State census at P.O. Omro. He was listed in the 1890 federal census as residing in the village of Omro. He was listed in 1905 as residing at 315 Third Street in Omro. Francis died in 1921. He and Anna, his wife, are buried at Omro Cemetery, Pelton's Addition, Section D, plot 14. Edward C. Luscombe, their son, is also buried on that plot. He was a veteran of the Spanish-American War.
{US 1890; WC-V 1885, 1895, 1905; B-1905; Cem. records; WCBR v.2, p.39, #75}
{ROV; LOP-1883}

LUSCOMBE, Henry - Pvt., Co. E, 17th Regt., Wis. Vol. Inf.
Henry resided at West Bend, Washington County and enlisted there on Jan. 8, 1862. He was assigned as above and was mustered out on Jan. 24, 1865 at the end of his term of enlistment. He was listed in 1888 as a member of GAR Post #10 at Oshkosh. Henry was listed in the veteran section of the 1885 and 1895 Wisconsin State census at P.O. Oshkosh. He was listed in the 1890 federal census as residing in the city of Oshkosh. Henry was not found in the veteran section of the 1905 state census.
{US 1890; WC-V 1885, 1895, 1905; ROV}

LUSHA, Elisha W. - Sgt., Co. G, 3rd (reorg.) Regt., Wis. Cav.
Elisha resided at Oshkosh and he enlisted there on Dec. 4, 1863. He was assigned as above and was promoted to Sergeant in that company. Elisha was then mustered out on Oct. 27, 1865.
{ROV}

LUTHER, Seymour - Pvt., Co. A, 48th Regt., Wis. Vol. Inf.
Seymour resided at Rushford and enlisted there on Jan. 26, 1865. He was assigned as above and was mustered out on Dec. 30, 1865.
{ROV}

LUTTMAN, Charles G. - Sgt., Co. F, 12th Regt., Illinois Vol. Inf.
Charles was listed in the 1890 federal census as residing in the city of Neenah. He provided his unit designation as above and his service dates as having been July 12, 1861 to July 21, 1862. He also provided that he had then enlisted as a Private in Co. F, 96th

LUTTMAN, Charles G. (cont.)
Regt., Ill. Vol. Inf. on Aug. 13, 1862 and served with that regiment until June 10, 1865. Charles was listed as above in the veteran section of the 1885 and 1895 Wisconsin State census at P.O. Neenah.
{US 1890; WC-V 1885, 1895}

LYNCH, Joseph - Pvt., Co. C, 10th Regt., Wis. Vol. Inf.
Joseph resided at Menasha and he enlisted there on Sept. 3, 1861. He was assigned as above and was discharged on Oct. 20, 1862 due to a disability. Joseph was listed as having died prior to 1908.
{ROV; Lawson p.812}

LYNG, Eugene W. - Cpl., Co. F, 18th Regt., Wis. Vol. Inf.
Eugene resided at Oshkosh and enlisted there on Dec. 21, 1861. He was assigned as above and was promoted to Corporal in that company. Eugene contracted a disease and died on May 25, 1862 at Shiloh, Tennessee.
{ROV}

LYONS, Timothy - Pvt., Co. G, 1st Regt., Wis. Cav.
Timothy resided at Fisk and enlisted there on Oct. 8, 1861. He was assigned as above and was listed as having deserted on Mar. 20, 1864.
{ROV}

MACE, Frederick W. - Pvt., Co. D, 32nd Regt., Wis. Vol. Inf.
Frederick resided at Oshkosh and enlisted there on Nov. 24, 1863. He was assigned as above and was transferred to Co. D, 16th (reorg.) Regt., Wis. Vol. Inf. on June 4, 1865. The records of that company indicate that he had been mustered out on May 19, 1865. Frederick was married to Caroline E. Minert. They had a son, Albert Julius, who was born in Winneconne on Nov. 10, 1877. Frederick was listed in 1888 as a member of GAR Post #10 at Oshkosh. He was listed in the 1890 federal census as residing in the city of Oshkosh. Frederick was listed in the veteran section of the 1895 Wisconsin State census at P.O. Oshkosh.
{US 1890; WC-V 1895; ROV; WCBR v.2, p.82, #203}

MADDEN, Timothy - Pvt., Co. K, 32nd Regt., Wis. Vol. Inf.
Timothy resided at Oshkosh and enlisted there on Dec. 21, 1863. He was assigned as above and was transferred to Co. I, 16th Regt., Wis. Vol. Inf. on June 4, 1865. He was then mustered out on July 12, 1865. Timothy listed his residence as Lowville, Columbia County at the time of his transfer.
{ROV}

MADER, George - Pvt., Co. E, 5th (reorg.) Regt., Wis. Vol. Inf.
George was born circa 1845 at Pennsylvania. He was listed in the 1860 federal census as a farm laborer for Augustus Spies in the town of Winneconne. George listed his residence as Vinland when he enlisted on Aug. 11, 1864. He was assigned as above and was mustered out on June 20, 1865. George was listed in the 1890 federal census as residing in the town of Caledonia, Waupaca County. He was listed in the veteran section of the 1895 and 1905 Wisconsin State census at P.O. Winneconne. He was listed in 1905 as residing on Lake Avenue in the village of Winneconne. He was still listed in 1920 as

MADER, George (cont.)
residing at Winneconne.
{US 1860, 1890; WC-V 1895, 1905; ROV; B-1905; 21-33rd}

MAGLOWSKI, Frederick - Pvt., Co. B, 3rd Regt., Wis. Vol. Inf.
Frederick was born circa 1840 at Prussia. He was a son of Johann and Wilhelmine Magalowski. Johann was born circa 1810 and Wilhelmina was born circa 1812, both at Prussia. Johann was listed in the 1860 federal census as a wagon maker residing in the third ward of the city of Oshkosh. Then residing with him were his wife and the following children: Friedrich; Auguste, born circa 1844 at Prussia; Henriette, born circa 1846 at Prussia; and Anna, born circa 1855 at Wisconsin. Frederick resided at Oshkosh and enlisted there on May 22, 1861. He was assigned as above. Frederick was killed in action on Sept. 17, 1862 at Antietam, Maryland. His mother, Wilhelmina, was listed in 1883 at P.O. Oshkosh and receiving a mother's pension of $8 per month.
{US 1860; ROV; LOP-1883}

MAIER, Herman C. - Pvt., Co. A, 50th Regt., Wis. Vol. Inf.
Herman resided at Columbus, Columbia County and he enlisted there on Feb. 11, 1865. He was assigned as above and was mustered out on June 12, 1866 at the end of his term of enlistment. Herman was listed (Mayer) in 1888 as a member of GAR Post #241 at Oshkosh. He was listed in the 1890 federal census as residing in the city of Oshkosh. Herman was listed in the veteran section of the 1895 and 1905 Wisconsin State census at P.O. Oshkosh. He was listed (Meyer) in 1905 as a trimmer for T. Neville and residing at 31 Boyd Street in Oshkosh. Minnie H. and Fred C. Meyer were residing with him.
{US 1890; WC-V 1895, 1905; ROV; B-1905}

MAIN, Gilbert S. - Sgt., Co. E, 5th (reorg.) Regt., Wis. Vol. Inf.
Gilbert resided at Oshkosh and enlisted there on Aug. 27, 1864. He was assigned as above and was promoted to Corporal and then Sergeant in that company. Gilbert was mustered out on June 20, 1865.
{ROV}

MALLORY, Zadock K. - Pvt., Co. H, 18th Regt., Wis. Vol. Inf.
Zadock was born circa 1838 at New York. He was a son of Joseph and Lydia Mallory. Both parents were natives of New York, Joseph born there circa 1802 and Lydia born circa 1808. They were listed in the 1860 federal census as residing on a farm in the town of Rushford at P.O. Waukau. Listed with them were the following children: Luke, born circa 1828 at New York, with his family; Ebenezer, born circa 1830 at New York, with his family; Zadock; Henrietta, born circa 1851 at New York; and Samuel, born circa 1852 at Wisconsin. Zadock resided at Waukau and enlisted there on Dec. 27, 1861. He was assigned as above and was discharged on July 1, 1862 due to a disability. Zadock was married in Winnebago County on July 4, 1864 to Mary Hicks.
{US 1860; ROV; WCMR v.1, p.256, #1493*}

MALOY, James - Sgt., Co. H, 19th Regt., Wis. Vol. Inf.
James was born circa 1818 at New Brunswick, Canada. Margaret, his wife, was born circa 1821 near that same place. James was listed in the 1860 federal census as a lumberman residing in the third ward of the city of Oshkosh. Residing with him were his wife and a son, Alfred J., who was born circa 1847 at New Brunswick. James

MALOY, James (cont.)
resided at Oshkosh and enlisted on Jan. 27, 1862. He was assigned as above and he re-enlisted at the end of his term. James was promoted to Sergeant in that company and was transferred to Co. E of the same regiment on May 1, 1865. He was then mustered out on Aug. 9, 1865. James was listed in 1868 as a carpenter residing at 293 Main Street in Oshkosh.
{US 1860; ROV; T-1868}

MALOY, John - Pvt., Co. C, 12th Regt., Michigan Vol. Inf.
John was listed as above in the veteran section of the 1885 Wisconsin State census at P.O. Oshkosh.
{WC-V 1885}

MANDEVILLE, Byron - Pvt., Co. A, 16th Regt., Wis. Vol. Inf.
Byron was born circa 1841 at New York, a son of Thurston and Esther Mandeville. Both parents were natives of New York and both were born circa 1812. They were listed (Manderville) in the 1860 federal census as residing on a farm in the town of Nepeuskun at P.O. Berlin. Listed with them were the following children: Wellington, born circa 1835; Florentina, born circa 1832; Byron; Emma, born circa 1843; Harriet, born circa 1846; Celestine, born circa 1848; Mortimer, born circa 1850; and Mary, born circa 1854. The three eldest children were born in New York and the others were all listed as having been born in Wisconsin. Byron resided at Nepeuskun and enlisted there on Oct. 19, 1861. He was assigned as above and he re-enlisted at the end of his term. Byron was mustered out on July 12, 1865.
{US 1860; ROV}

MANLEY, Charles Oscar - Pvt., Co. D, 41st Regt., Wis. Vol. Inf.
Oscar was a son of Henry H. and Eliza (Elkins) Manley. Eliza was a daughter of Joseph and Elizabeth Elkins. She was married to Henry on July 4, 1845. Her grandfather was a veteran of the American Revolution and a brother served in the Union army during the Civil War. Henry was born on Mar. 8, 1825 at New York. He was a son of Luke and Charlotte (Streeter) Manley. Henry removed in 1845 and settled Licking County, Ohio. He remained there until 1857, when he settled in Wisconsin at the town of Ellington, Outagamie County. Henry and Eliza had the following children: Charles Oscar; Orson P., married Emeline Reimer of Ellington; John, married Harriet Scarboro, resided at Dakota; Martha Jane, married Dr. B.F. Strong, resided at Seymour; Emma, married Walton Cole, resided in the town of Vinland; Velma, married Frank Glass of Kaukauna; William, married Mary Bower, resided at Dakota; Maryett, married C. Pew of Dakota; and Leonard, at home in 1888. Oscar listed his residence as Menasha when he enlisted on May 16, 1864. He was assigned as above and was then mustered out on Sept. 23, 1864 at the end of his term of enlistment. Oscar was married to Loretta Cole. They had at least four children: Lida; Mertie; Stillman; and Bessie. Oscar was listed in the veteran section of the 1885, 1895 and 1905 Wisconsin State census at P.O. Neenah. He was listed in the 1890 federal census as residing in the city of Neenah and suffering the effects of chronic diarrhea. He was listed in 1905 as Oscar C. Manley, cheesemaker, residing at 415 W. Winneconne Avenue in Neenah. Bessie E. and Charles S. Manley were then residing at the same address.
{US 1890; WC-V 1885, 1895, 1905; ROV; SCA 1:595; B-1905}

MANN, Arnold - Pvt., Co. A, 3rd Regt., Wis. Vol. Inf.
Arnold enlisted on Apr. 18, 1861 and was assigned as above. He was wounded at Cedar Mountain and again at Antietam, Maryland. He was listed as absent on detached service when that company was mustered out on June 18, 1865. Arnold is buried with a simple military marker at Omro Cemetery, Original Section, plot 61. George, a son, died on Aug. 19, 1860 at age 14 years. Georgia Anna, a daughter, died on Apr. 21, 1863 at age 1 year and 8 months. Both are buried on the plot with their father.
{ROV; Cem. records}

MANN, Edward - Pvt., Co. C, 21st Regt., Wis. Vol. Inf.
Edward resided at Oshkosh and enlisted there on Aug. 14, 1862. He was assigned as above. He was listed as suffering from rheumatism and a patient at the General Hospital in Louisville, Kentucky in Nov. 1862. George was wounded at Chickamauga, Georgia and he died there from his wounds on Sept. 19, 1863.
{ROV; OWN 13 Nov 1862}

MANNING, S. Rodman - Pvt., Co. K, 14th Regt., Wis. Vol. Inf.
He was listed in the index to Roster of Wisconsin Volunteers as having been assigned as above. Rodman was listed in 1883 at P.O. Omro and he was then receiving a pension of $18 per month for a wound to his right wrist.
{ROV; LOP-1883}

MANNING, Thomas - Pvt., Co. F, 18th Regt., Wis. Vol. Inf.
Thomas resided at Oshkosh and enlisted on Jan. 2, 1862. He was assigned as above and was transferred to the Veteran Reserve Corps on Sept. 15, 1863. Thomas was mustered out on Feb. 7, 1865 at the end of his term of enlistment.
{ROV}

MANSFIELD, Solomon - Pvt., Co. H, 18th Regt., Wis. Vol. Inf.
Solomon was born circa 1835 at New York. He was listed in the 1860 federal census as a farmer residing with the family of L.M. Parsons in the town of Rushford at P.O. Waukau. Solomon resided at Waukau and he enlisted there on Jan. 6, 1862. He was assigned as above. Solomon was killed in action on Apr. 6, 1862 at Shiloh, Tennessee.
{US 1860; ROV}

MANTHEY, John - Cpl., Co. C, 53rd Regt., Wis. Vol. Inf.
John was born on Oct. 6, 1829 at Prussia. Lauretta, his wife, was born on Nov. 22, 1837, also at Prussia. They were listed in the 1860 federal census as residing on a farm in the town of Nekimi. Listed with them were two of their children. Amelia was born circa 1857 at Prussia and Albert was born circa 1859 at Wisconsin. John resided at Utica and enlisted there on Mar. 8, 1865. He was assigned as above and was promoted to Corporal in that company. The company was transferred to Co. K, 51st Regt., Wis. Vol. Inf. by orders dated June 10, 1865. The transfer was completed on June 30, 1865 at Ft. Leavenworth, Kansas. The regiment returned to Madison, Wisconsin on Aug. 1, 1865 and was then mustered out by companies. The last company was mustered out on Aug. 30, 1865. John was listed in the 1890 federal census as residing in the city of Oshkosh. He then provided information that he had been mustered out on Aug. 21, 1865 and that he had been a patient in the military hospital at Warrensburg, Missouri for rheumatism. John and Lauretta had a son, John, who was born on May 27, 1872

MANTHEY, John (cont.)
and died on Dec. 23, 1891. They had a daughter Linda who was married to Rev. L. Kaspar. She was born in 1874 and died in 1912. John died on Feb. 2, 1900 and Lauretta died on Nov. 6, 1902. Both are buried in the town of Algoma at Peace Lutheran Cemetery.
{US 1860, 1890; ROV; Cem. records}

MANTOR, Morris T. - Pvt., Co. F, 18th Regt., Wis. Vol. Inf.
Morris was born Mar. 1, 1831 at Otsego County, New York. He was a son of Thomas and Parmelia (Yagor) Mantor, both natives of New York. Along with Morris, they had a daughter Susan. The family removed to Pennsylvania in the early 1830s and Thomas died there. Parmelia and Morris came west in 1851 and located in Winnebago County. Parmelia later removed to Hortonville, Outagamie County and died there. Morris was married on Oct. 31, 1853 to Mariette "Margett" Cornell. She was born on Apr. 13, 1833/4 at Steuben County, New York and was a daughter of Zopher and Annie (Dawley) Cornell. Zopher was a native of Long Island, New York and Annie was a native of Steuben County in that state. They also had a son, David L. Cornell. Morris was listed in the 1860 federal census as a farmer residing in the town of Winneconne. Listed with him were his wife and the following children: Melvin, born in 1855, died in 1925; Martin, born in 1856, died in 1947; and Myron, born circa 1858. All three were born in Wisconsin. Morris enlisted at Winneconne on Feb. 25, 1864. He was assigned as above. He was wounded by an explosion at Columbia, S.C. and was sent to the hospital at Louisville, Kentucky. Morris was listed as absent sick when that regiment was mustered out on July 18, 1865. He was mustered out of the service from the hospital in 1865. He was listed in the veteran section of the 1885 Wisconsin State census at P.O. Winneconne. Morris was listed in the 1890 federal census as residing in the town of Winneconne at P.O. Winneconne. He was listed in the veteran section of the 1895 state census at P.O. Allenville and in that section of the 1905 state census at P.O. Winneconne. Morris and Mariette had several additional children: Ellen E., born on Mar. 18, 1859, date of birth questioned as she does not appear in the 1860 census, died on Aug. 5, 1900; and Etta E., born on June 20, 1868, died on Apr. 29, 1903. Morris and Marietta were listed in 1905, with son Martin H., as residing on 80 acres of section 2 in the town of Winneconne. Morris died on Nov. 9, 1913 and Mariette died on Aug. 22, 1925. Both are buried with their children in the town of Winneconne at Bell Cemetery.
{US 1860, 1890; WC-V 1885, 1895, 1905; ROV; Randall p.55; Cem. records; B-1905} {WCMR v.1, p.145, #600}

MANTZ, Amos E. - Pvt., Co. F, 29th Regt., Wis. Vol. Inf.
Amos was born circa 1844 at Ohio. His father was a native of Pennsylvania and his mother was born in Ohio. Amos resided at Berlin, Green Lake County and he enlisted there on Aug. 31, 1864. He was assigned as above and was mustered out on June 22, 1865. Amos was listed in the veteran section of the 1895 Wisconsin State census at P.O. Oshkosh and in that section of the 1905 state census as residing at the Wisconsin Veterans' Home at King. He was listed in 1905 as Amos C. Mantz. Amos was received at the veterans' home from Waupaca. He was listed in the 1910 federal census at King. Lenora, his wife of 2 years, was then residing there with him. She was born circa 1864 at Michigan. Her mother was a native of that state and her father was born in French Canada. That was the second marriage for both Amos and Lenora. Jesse E. Mantz, a

MANTZ, Amos E. (cont.)
brother of Amos, was residing with them. He was born circa 1857 at Ohio.
{US 1910; WC-V 1895, 1905; ROV; GAR 40th}

MANUEL, Mathias - Pvt., Co. B, 3rd Regt., Wis. Vol. Inf.
Mathias resided at Oshkosh and enlisted there on Apr. 19, 1861. He was assigned as above and was discharged by orders dated Oct. 25, 1862.
{ROV}

MANVILLE, Peter - Pvt., Co. C, 14th Regt., Wis. Vol. Inf.
Peter was born circa 1837 at Ohio. He was listed in the 1860 federal census as a saloon keeper residing in the first ward of the city of Oshkosh. Peter resided at Oshkosh and enlisted there on Sept. 25, 1861. He was assigned as above and he re-enlisted in that same company at the end of his term. Peter was mustered out on Oct. 9, 1865.
{US 1860; ROV}

MARBLE, William H. - Chaplain, 20th Regt., Wis. Vol. Inf.
William was born circa 1822 at New Hampshire. Jeanette, his wife, was born in that same state circa 1828. William was listed in the 1860 federal census as a Congregational minister residing in the fifth ward of the city of Oshkosh. Then residing with him were his wife and the following children: Mathilda, born circa 1853 at Ohio; William, born circa 1854 at Ohio; and Flora, born circa 1856 at Wisconsin. William resided at Oshkosh and was commissioned as the Chaplain of the above regiment on Aug. 27, 1862. He resigned on Mar. 2, 1863.
{US 1860; ROV}

MARDEN, Edward - Pvt., Co. E, 2nd Regt., Wis. Cav.
Edward was born circa 1844 at New York. He was a son of Edward and Mary Marden. The parents were both natives of England, the father born there circa 1822 and the mother born circa 1823. They were listed in the 1860 federal census as residing on a farm in the town of Algoma. Listed with them were the following children: Edward; Mary, born circa 1847 at Michigan; Adelaide, born circa 1848 at Michigan; Frances, born circa 1850; Emily, born circa 1854; Louis, born circa 1856; and Seymour, born circa 1857. The four youngest children were born in Wisconsin. Edward listed his residence as Oshkosh when he enlisted on Aug. 30, 1864. He was assigned as above and was mustered out on July 4, 1865. Edward was listed in the veteran section of the 1885 Wisconsin State census at P.O. Oshkosh. This listing credited him with having served in Co. B, 18th Regt., Wis. Vol. Inf. He does not appear in the records of that company. Edward was listed in 1888 as a member of GAR Post #241 at Oshkosh. He was listed in 1905 as a resident at the Wisconsin Veterans' Home at King. Rachel, his wife, was residing there with him. Both had been received from Oshkosh.
{US 1860; WC-V 1885; ROV; GAR 40th}

MARHEINE, Anton - Pvt., Co. C, 53rd Regt., Wis. Vol. Inf.
Anton was born circa 1833 at Hanover, Germany, a son of Anton Sr. and Friederike Marheine. The father was born circa 1801 and the mother circa 1803, both at Hanover. The father was listed in the 1860 federal census as a laborer residing in the second ward of the city of Oshkosh. Ricke, wife of Anton Jr., was born circa 1838 at Hanover. Both were listed in 1860 as residing with his parents. Theodore, their son, was born circa

MARHEINE, Anton (cont.)
1859 at Wisconsin. Anton resided at Oshkosh and enlisted there on Mar. 8, 1865. He was assigned as above. This company was transferred to Co. K, 51st Regt., Wis. Vol. Inf. under orders dated June 10, 1865. The transfer was completed on June 30, 1865 at Ft. Leavenworth, Kansas. The regiment returned to Madison, Wisconsin on Aug. 1, 1865 and was then mustered out by companies. The last company was mustered out on Aug. 30, 1865. Anton was listed in 1868 as a laborer residing at 121 Ceape Street in Oshkosh. He was listed in the 1890 federal census as residing in Oshkosh. Anton then provided that he had been discharged on a Surgeon's Certificate on Aug. 21, 1865. He was suffering from rheumatism. Anton was listed in 1905 as residing at 395 Waugoo Street in Oshkosh. Elizabeth Marheine was residing at that same address.
{US 1860; 1890; ROV; T-1868; B-1905}

MARHEINE, Frederick - Pvt., Co. C, 53rd Regt., Wis. Vol. Inf.
Frederick resided at Oshkosh and enlisted there on Mar. 8, 1865. He was assigned as above and was discharged on May 24, 1865 due to a disability. Frederick was listed in 1868 as a laborer residing at 34 Pearl Street in the city of Oshkosh. He was listed in the veteran section of the 1895 Wisconsin State census at P.O. Spirit, Pierce County. He was not found in that section of the 1905 state census.
{WC-V 1895, 1905; ROV; T-1868}

MARIHUGH, John - Cpl., Co. E, 42nd Regt., Wis. Vol. Inf.
John resided at Oshkosh and enlisted there on Aug. 17, 1864. He was assigned as above and was promoted to Corporal in that company. John was mustered out June 20, 1865.
{ROV}

MARK, James P. - Cpl., Co. K, 11th Regt., Wis. Vol. Inf.
James resided at Clayton and enlisted there on Sept. 28, 1861. He was assigned as above and he re-enlisted in that same company at the end of his term. James was promoted to Corporal in that company and was then mustered out on Sept. 4, 1865.
{ROV}

MARKHAM, Andrew J. - Capt., Co. B, 36th Regt., Wis. Vol. Inf.
Andrew resided at Oshkosh and he enlisted there on Feb. 22, 1864. He was assigned as above and was promoted to Corporal and then Sergeant in that company. He was then commissioned as Sergeant Major of that regiment on Nov. 1, 1864 and was promoted to Brevet Captain on Apr. 2, 1865. He was mustered out on July 12, 1865. Andrew was listed in the veteran section of the 1885, 1895 and 1905 Wisconsin State census at P.O. Winneconne. He was listed in the 1890 federal census as residing in the village of Winneconne. Andrew was listed in 1905 as residing on Lake Avenue in Winneconne.
{US 1890; WC-V 1885, 1895, 1905; ROV; B-1905}

MARKHAM, Ira - Sgt., Co. D, 32nd Regt., Wis. Vol. Inf.
Ira resided at Oshkosh and enlisted there on Aug. 18, 1862. He was assigned as above and was promoted to Corporal and then Sergeant in that company. Ira was mustered out on June 12, 1865.
{ROV}

MARKS, Seneca - Civil War Veteran?
Seneca was listed in 1883 at P.O. Elo. He had been receiving a pension of $6 per month since Dec. 1882 for chronic diarrhea as a result of his military service. Seneca was not found in the index to Roster of Wisconsin Volunteers.
{ROV; LOP-1883}

MARQUARDT, Michael - Pvt., Co. B, 37th Regt., Wis. Vol. Inf.
Michael was born circa 1829 at Poland. Julianna, his wife, was born circa 1834, also at Poland. They were listed in the 1860 federal census as residing on a farm in the town of Orihula at P.O. Fremont. Then listed with them were William, born circa 1855 at Wisconsin, and Auguste, born circa 1857 at Wisconsin. Michael resided at Wolf River and was drafted there on Nov. 5, 1864. He was assigned as above and was mustered out on July 27, 1865. Michael was listed in the 1890 federal census as residing at P.O. Symco, Waupaca County. He suffered from rheumatism as a result of his military service.
{US 1860, 1890; ROV}

MARSH, Leonard F. - Pvt., Co. K, 1st Regt., Wis. Hvy. Art.
Leonard was born circa 1827 at Vermont. He was listed in the 1860 federal census as a sawyer residing in the second ward of the village of Menasha. Melvina, his wife, was born circa 1828 at New York. Residing with them was Eliza, mother of Leonard. She was born circa 1798 at New Hampshire. Leonard enlisted at Menasha on Sept. 8, 1864. He was assigned as above and was mustered out on June 26, 1865.
{US 1860; ROV}

MARSHALL, Andrew - Pvt., Co. K, 11th Regt., Wis. Vol. Inf.
Andrew resided at Neenah and enlisted there on Sept. 17, 1861. He was assigned as above and was discharged on Aug. 17, 1862 due to a disability. Andrew was listed in the 1890 federal census as residing in the city of Waupaca, Waupaca County.
{US 1890; ROV}

MARSHALL, Edmund D. - Pvt., Co. B, 2nd Regt., New Hampshire Vol. Inf.
Edmund was born on Apr. 19, 1832 at New York. He was a son of Caleb and Eureta (Howe) Marshall. A biography shows that Edmund resided at New York until age 23 and then removed to Omro. He was married to Betsy O. Stearns on Sept. 22, 1861. Their marriage was recorded in Winnebago County. She was born on July 6, 1837 and was a daughter of George and Asenath (Webster) Stearns. Edmund worked at both the carpenter and carriage maker trades. He and Betsy had seven children: Effie J., born on June 3, 1863; Artie C., born on Oct. 3, 1864; Jessie A., born on Mar. 20, 1870; Julia E., born on Feb. 15, 1873; Hiram Wheat, born at Omro on Dec. 28, 1876; Frank Leo, born in the town of Omro on Dec. 2, 1879; and Narcissa Bella, born in the town of Omro on May 14, 1882. The biography listed that Edmund removed from the village of Omro about fourteen years after his arrival and then settled on a farm in section 9 of the town of Omro. It further listed that in 1871 he had purchased another farm, this being shown elsewhere as 80 acres of section 20 in the town of Omro. Edmund was listed as above in the veteran section of the 1885 Wisconsin State census at P.O. Omro. He was listed (22nd Regt., N.H. Vol. Inf.) in that same section of the 1895 state census at P.O. Oshkosh. Edmund was listed in 1905 as retired and residing on Division Street in the village of Omro. Julia and Leo Marshall were residing at that same address.

MARSHALL, Edmund D. (cont.)
Betsy died on May 6, 1909 and Edmund died on July 4, 1911. He had suffered for some time from facial cancer. Both are buried in the town of Omro at Omro Junction Cemetery.
{WC-V 1885, 1895; Randall p.30; WCBR v.3, p.61, #366; OmJ 13 Jul 1911; B-1905} {WCMR v.1, p.218, #1192; Harney p.30; WCBR v.2, p.31, #49; Cem. records} {WCBR v.2, p.189, #533}

MARSHALL, Edward - Pvt., Co. H, 1st Regt., Wis. Vol. Inf.
Edward listed his residence as Sheboygan, Sheboygan County and he enlisted there on Oct. 13, 1861. He was assigned as above and was mustered out on Oct. 14, 1864. Edward is buried with a simple military marker in the town of Omro at Omro Union Cemetery.
{ROV; Cem. records}

MARSHALL, John J. - Cpl., Co. K, 1st Regt., Vermont Cav.
John was born on June 6, 1844 at Addison County, Vermont. He was a son of John and Emily Marshall. John Jr. was thirteen when his father died. John enlisted on Oct. 28, 1861 and was assigned as above. He was soon promoted to Corporal and he was taken prisoner in 1862. He was confined at Libby Prison and was paroled after a few weeks. John was shot three times in a short period of time in the battle of Wilderness, Virginia. The first two shots caused minor damage but the third struck his right leg between the knee and instep. He was taken prisoner again at that time. He was taken first to Salisbury Prison and was transferred to Andersonville Prison, where he remained for some nine or ten months. He was then held at Charleston and Florence, S.C. John was paroled in Mar. 1865 and was immediately mustered out. He returned to his home at Vermont and, in the fall of that year, he removed to Wisconsin and located at Menasha. He engaged in the grocery business on Main Street at that place. John was married to Abbie Canfield/Kenfield in Winnebago County on Apr. 30, 1868. She was born Oct. 6, 1834 at New York. John was listed in 1883 at P.O. Menasha. He had been receiving a pension of $4 per month since May 1882 for a wound to his right leg. John was listed as above in the veteran section of the 1885 and 1895 Wisconsin State census at P.O. Menasha. He was listed in the 1890 federal census as residing in the city of Menasha. John died on May 18, 1898. Abbie, his widow, was listed in 1905 as residing at 163 Main Street in Menasha. She died on Aug. 22, 1911. Both are buried in the town of Algoma at Ellenwood Cemetery, Section F. Recollections from John appeared in the Oshkosh Northwestern.
{US 1890; WC-V 1885, 1895; LOP-1883; Randall p.20; Cem. records; B-1905} {WCMR v.1, p.387, #2396; OWN 11 Jun 1898}

MARSTEN, Stephen - Pvt., Co. C, 14th Regt., Wis. Vol. Inf.
Stephen was born circa 1824 at New York. Louisa, his wife, was born circa 1833, also at New York. They were listed in the 1860 federal census as residing on a farm in the town of Omro. Then listed with them were the following children: Georgiana, born circa 1847; Lucretia, born circa 1850; Mary, born circa 1857; and Sarah, born circa 1859. The younger two daughters were born in Wisconsin and the other two were born in New York. Stephen resided at Omro and he enlisted there on Sept. 21, 1861. He was assigned as above. Stephen contracted a disease and died on May 15, 1862 at Jefferson

MARSTEN, Stephen (cont.)
Barracks, Missouri.
{US 1860; ROV}

MARTELL, Prosper - Pvt., Co. H, 20th Regt., Wis. Vol. Inf.
Prosper resided at Oshkosh and enlisted there on Aug. 4, 1862. He was assigned as above and was mustered out on July 14, 1865.
{ROV}

MARTIN, Abner P.H. - Pvt., Co. E, 2nd Regt., Wis. Vol. Inf.
Abner resided at Oshkosh and enlisted there on Apr. 21, 1861. He was assigned as above and was discharged on Dec. 24, 1861 due to a disability.
{ROV}

MARTIN, Alexander - Pvt., Co. G, 17th Regt., Wis. Vol. Inf.
Alexander resided at Nepeuskun and enlisted there on Mar. 5, 1864. He was assigned as above and was listed as having deserted on June 7, 1864.
{ROV}

MARTIN, Edward - Pvt., Co. E, 3rd Regt., Wis. Cav.
Edward resided at Plymouth, Sheboygan County and enlisted there on Aug. 20, 1864. He was transferred to Co. C, 3rd (reorg.) Regt., Wis, Cav. on Feb. 1, 1865 and was mustered out on June 19, 1865. Edward was listed in the 1890 federal census as residing in the city of Oshkosh.
{US 1890; ROV}

MARTIN, Edwin - Cpl., Co. E, 1st Regt., Wis. Cav.
Edwin was born circa 1835 at Ohio. He was a son of John and Rachel Martin. They were listed in the 1860 federal census as residing on a farm in the town of Winneconne at P.O. Butte des Morts. John was a native of New Hampshire and Rachel was listed as born in Massachusetts. John died on Nov. 25, 1871 at age 77 years and 6 days. Rachel died on May 3, 1871 at age 71 years. Daniel, a brother of Edwin, was born on Apr. 13, 1829 and died on Nov. 6, 1890. Edwin was married in Winnebago County on July 4, 1859 to Almira W. Ball. She was born circa 1838 at Canada and was listed with Edwin and his parents in the 1860 census. Also listed then was William Ball, brother of Almira. He was born circa 1840 at Canada. The marriage of Edwin and Almira was recorded in June 1865. Edwin resided at Winneconne and enlisted on Sept. 23, 1864. He was assigned as above and was promoted to Corporal in that company. Edwin then contracted a disease and died at Mound City, Illinois on May 17, 1865. His marker lists his date of death as having been Mar. 24, 1865. Almira W., formerly the widow of Edwin, was listed in the 1890 federal census as residing in the village of Omro. Edwin is buried with his parents and brother in the town of Winneconne at Bell Cemetery.
{US 1860, 1890; ROV; Cem. records; WCMR v.1, p.277, #1658}

MARTIN, Henry - Pvt., Co. D, 8th Regt., Wis. Vol. Inf.
Henry resided at Oshkosh and enlisted there on Feb. 24, 1864. He was assigned as above and was mustered out on Sept. 5, 1865.
{ROV}

473

MARTIN, Henry - Pvt., Co. I, 47th Regt., Wis. Vol. Inf.
Henry was born in 1846 at England. Mary, his wife, was born in 1846 at New York. Henry resided at Ripon, Fond du Lac County and enlisted there on Jan. 20, 1865. He was assigned as above and was mustered out on Sept. 4, 1865. Henry and his wife, Mary Townsend, had a daughter, unnamed at registration, who was born at Eureka on July 21, 1881. Henry was listed in the veteran section of the 1885, 1895 and 1905 Wisconsin State census at P.O. Eureka. He was listed in the 1890 federal census as residing in the town of Rushford at P.O. Eureka. Henry was then suffering from catarrah and a kidney disease. He was listed in 1905 as working the government dredge at Eureka and residing in that village. Henry died in 1928 and Mary died in 1934. A son, Frank Burton, was born on June 10, 1886. He was married to Virginia Saltonstall and died on Oct. 17, 1960. All four are buried in the town of Rushford at Eureka Cemetery.
{US 1890; WC-V 1885, 1895, 1905; ROV; WCBR v.3, p.37, #219; Cem. records} {B-1905}

MARTIN, Henry E. - Pvt., 8th Batt., Wis. Lt. Art.
Henry resided at Neenah and enlisted there on Feb. 7, 1862. He was assigned as above and was discharged on Nov. 13, 1863 due to a disability. Henry re-enlisted on Jan. 4, 1864 and was assigned as Private, Co. G, 3rd Regt., Wis. Vol. Inf. He was wounded on May 25, 1864. Henry died from the effects of those wounds at Chattanooga, Tennessee on July 1, 1864.
{ROV}

MARTIN, Henry F. - Pvt., Co. E, 52nd Regt., Wis. Vol. Inf.
Henry resided at Neenah and enlisted there on Mar. 14, 1865. He was assigned as above and was mustered out on July 28, 1865.
{ROV}

MARTIN, James H. - Sgt., Co. A, 48th Regt., Wis. Vol. Inf.
James was born circa 1827 at New Hampshire. Ann, his wife, was born circa 1828 at New York. They were listed in the 1860 federal census as residing on a farm in the town of Rushford at P.O. Omro. Listed with them were the following children: Eugene, born circa 1850; Morris, born circa 1852; Adalaide, born circa 1854; Estella, born circa 1856; Isabel, born in 1859; and Isadora, a twin of Isabel, also born in 1859. All of the children were born in Wisconsin. James listed his residence as Somers, Kenosha County when he enlisted on Feb. 11, 1865. He was assigned as a wagoner in the above company and was promoted to Quartermaster Sergeant on Nov. 1, 1865. James was listed in 1905 as residing in the village of Eureka. He was then the treasurer for the town of Rushford. Residing with him at that time was Hilda, his wife.
{US 1860; ROV; B-1905}

MARTIN, Joseph - Pvt., Co. H, 50th Regt., Wis. Vol. Inf.
Joseph resided at Waldwick, Iowa County and enlisted there on Mar. 9, 1865. He was assigned as above and was listed as having deserted on Aug. 30, 1865. Joseph was not found in the veteran section of the 1885 Wisconsin State census. He was listed in that section of the 1895 state census at P.O. Clayton and was not found in that part of the 1905 state census.
{WC-V 1885, 1895, 1905; ROV}

MARTIN, Robert - Pvt., Co. G, 3rd Regt., Wis. Cav.
Robert resided at Oshkosh and enlisted there on Feb. 7, 1864. He was assigned as above and was discharged on Nov. 2, 1864 due to a disability.
{ROV}

MARTIN, Robert - Pvt., Co. L, 3rd (reorg.) Regt., Wis. Cav.
Robert resided at Oshkosh and enlisted there on Feb. 7, 1864. He was assigned as a bugler with the above company and was then mustered out on Oct. 23, 1865.
{ROV}

MARTIN, Samuel - Pvt., Co. D, 32nd Regt., Wis. Vol. Inf.
Samuel was born circa 1840 at England. He was listed in the 1860 federal census as a farm laborer for Gerrit Roberts in the town of Utica at P.O. Bothelli. Samuel listed his residence as Oshkosh when he enlisted on Aug. 21, 1862. He was assigned as above and was listed as having deserted on Oct. 7, 1862.
{US 1860; ROV}

MARTIN, Thomas - Pvt., unassigned, U.S. Colored Troops.
Thomas resided at Black Wolf and enlisted there on Apr. 2, 1864. Nothing further was found of him in the Wisconsin records.
{ROV}

MARTIN, Thomas - Pvt., Co. B, 3rd Regt., Wis. Cav.
Thomas resided at Oshkosh and enlisted there on Jan. 13, 1862. He was assigned as above. Thomas contracted a disease and died on Dec. 17, 1862 at Ft. Leavenworth, Kansas.
{ROV}

MARTIN, William M. - 1st Sgt., Co. A, 50th Regt., Wis. Vol. Inf.
William resided at Hebron, Jefferson County and enlisted there on Feb. 6, 1865. He was assigned as above and was then promoted to 1st Sergeant of that company. William was mustered out on June 6, 1865. He was listed in the veteran section of the 1885 Wisconsin State census at P.O. Eureka. He was not found in that section of the 1895 state census and was listed in that part of the 1905 state census at P.O. Oshkosh. William was listed in 1905 as residing at 420 Algoma Street in the city of Oshkosh.
{WC-V 1885, 1895, 1905; ROV; B-1905}

MASON, Bryan - Pvt., Co. K, 21st Regt., Wis. Vol. Inf.
Bryan resided at Manitowoc Rapids, Manitowoc County and enlisted there on Aug. 15, 1862. He was assigned as above and was discharged on Dec. 2, 1862 due to a disability. A Wesley Mason was in that same company. Bryan was not found in the veteran section of the 1885 Wisconsin State census. He was found (Byron) in that section of the 1895 state census at P.O. Neenah and was not found in that section of the 1905 state census. Abbie S., widow of Bryan, was listed in 1905 as residing at 206 E. Columbian Avenue in the city of Neenah. Edith I. and Miles H. Mason were residing at that same address.
{WC-V 1885, 1895, 1905; ROV; B-1905}

MASON, Joseph - Pvt., Co. C, 46th Regt., Wis. Vol. Inf.
Joseph resided at Winneconne and enlisted there on Feb. 6, 1865. He was assigned as

MASON, Joseph (cont.)
above and was mustered out on Sept. 27, 1865.
{ROV}

MATHEWS, Charles F. - Pvt., Co. F, 18th Regt., Wis. Vol. Inf.
Charles was born circa 1835 at New York. He was listed in the 1860 federal census as a laborer residing in the town of Rushford at P.O. Eureka. Jane, his wife, was born circa 1837 at Ireland. James, their son, was born circa 1859 at Wisconsin. Charles resided at Eureka and enlisted there on Nov. 26, 1861. He was assigned as above. Charles contracted a disease and died on May 11, 1862 at Hamburg, Tennessee.
{US 1860; ROV}

MATHEWS, James J. - Pvt., Co. H, 30th Regt., Wis. Vol. Inf.
James resided at Leon, Monroe County and enlisted there on Aug. 21, 1862. He was assigned as above and was mustered out on Sept. 20, 1865. He was listed in 1883 at P.O. Winneconne. He had been receiving a pension of $4 per month since Aug. 1882 for neuralgia in his left thigh. James was listed in the veteran section of the 1885 Wisconsin State census at P.O. Winneconne. He was listed in the 1890 federal census as residing in the village of Winneconne.
{US 1890; WC-V 1885; ROV; LOP-1883}

MATHEWS, Joseph - 1st Lt., Co. H, 30th Regt., Wis. Vol. Inf.
Joseph was born in 1832. Mary, his mother, was born in 1784 and died in 1873. Joseph was married in Waushara County on Dec. 17, 1854 to Martha Ann Cates. She was born in 1832. Joseph resided at Auroraville, Waushara County and enlisted on Aug. 18, 1862. He was assigned to the above company and was commissioned as 2nd Lieutenant of that company on Sept. 11, 1862. Joseph was promoted to 1st Lieutenant of that company on Mar. 7, 1863 and was mustered out on Sept. 20, 1865. Mary, his wife, died in 1867. Joseph was listed in the veteran section of the 1885 Wisconsin State census at Pine River and in that section of the 1895 state census at P.O. Auroraville, both in Waushara County. He was listed in the 1890 federal census as residing at P.O. Auroraville. Joseph was listed in the veteran section of the 1905 state census at P.O. Omro. He was listed in 1905 as retired and residing at 551 Waukau Road in the village of Omro. Joseph was married a second time and had at least two children. Theodore F. was born in 1872 and died in 1873. Mary Jessie was born in 1877 and died in 1880. Joseph is buried with his first wife, his mother, and the two listed children in the town of Aurora, Waushara County at Pine Grove Cemetery.
{US 1890; WC-V 1885, 1895, 1905; ROV; B-1905; Waushara Co. Marriage Records} {Cem. records}

MATHEWS, Lorenzo J. - Civil War Veteran?
Jenette, widow of Lorenzo, was listed in the 1890 federal census as residing in the city of Neenah. She provided no details for his military service. Lorenzo was not found in the index to the Roster of Wisconsin Volunteers. Jeanette was listed in 1905 as residing at 210 Elm Street in Neenah.
{US 1890; ROV; B-1905}

MATHEWS, Nathan H. - Pvt., Co. H, 30th Regt., Wis. Vol. Inf.
Nathan was listed in 1905 as a resident at the Wisconsin Veterans' Home at King.

MATHEWS, Nathan H. (cont.)
Catherine, his wife, was residing there with him. Nathan was credited with 37 months of service and was received at the veterans' home from Omro.
{GAR 40th}

MATHEWS, William J. - Pvt., Co. G, 2nd Regt., Wis. Cav.
William resided at Oshkosh and enlisted there on Dec. 3, 1861. He was assigned as a wagoner with the above company. William died on Oct. 10, 1862 at Springfield, Missouri.
{ROV}

MATHISON, Mathis - Pvt., Co. G, 13th Regt., Wis. Vol. Inf.
Mathis was listed as above in the veteran section of the 1885 Wisconsin State census at P.O. Winchester. He was listed in the Wisconsin Roster of Volunteers index as a member of Co. C, 15th Regt., Wis. Vol. Inf.
{WC-V 1885; ROV}

MATOXIN, Isaac - Pvt., Co. H, 18th Regt., Wis. Vol. Inf.
Isaac resided at Oshkosh and enlisted there on Nov. 4, 1862. He was assigned as above and was wounded and taken prisoner on May 14, 1863 at Jackson, Mississippi. Isaac was discharged due to a disability on Mar. 30, 1865.
{ROV}

MATTESON, Charles D. - Pvt., Co. D, 32nd Regt., Wis. Vol. Inf.
Charles resided at Oshkosh and enlisted there on Nov. 18, 1863. He was assigned as above and was transferred to Co. D, 16th (reorg.) Regt., Wis. Vol. Inf. on June 4, 1865. Charles was then mustered out on July 12, 1865.
{ROV}

MATTESON, Leroy W. - Sgt., Co. F, 10th Regt., New York Cav.
Leroy was listed as above in the veteran section of the 1885 Wisconsin State census at P.O. Omro. He was listed in the 1890 federal census as residing in the village of Omro. Leroy provided his service dates as having been from Sept. 8, 1864 to June 18, 1865. He was then suffering from rheumatism and heart trouble.
{US 1890; WC-V 1885}

MAXSON, Daniel - Pvt., Co. B, 21st Regt., Wis. Vol. Inf.
Daniel was married in Winnebago County on July 2, 1855 to Amelia Cole. He resided at Poygan and enlisted there on Aug. 14, 1862. He was assigned as above and was then transferred to the Veteran Reserve Corps. Daniel was mustered out on Aug. 16, 1865. He died on Feb. 16, 1869 at age 42 years, 1 month and 18 days. Charles H., a son, died on Oct. 8, 1863 at age 4 years, 10 months and 2 days. George F., another of his sons, died on Oct. 24, 1863 at age 7 years and 10 days. All three are buried in the town of Poygan at Oak Hill Cemetery.
{ROV; WCMR v.1, p.77, #336; Cem. records}

MAXSON, David S. - Sgt., Co. C, 14th Regt., Wis. Vol. Inf.
David was born on Aug. 15, 1825 at New York. He was a son of Jonathan and Nancy Maxson and a brother of George from a following sketch. David was married in

MAXSON, David S. (cont.)
Winnebago County on Nov. 11, 1856 to Amanda Maria Bunting. Amanda was born on Mar. 16, 1832 at Massachusetts. They were listed in the 1860 federal census as residing on a farm in the town of Poygan. David was then listed as born circa 1828 and Amanda as born circa 1830. Listed with them were the following children: Watson, born circa 1852 at Michigan; Ann, born circa 1855 at Michigan; George, born circa 1857 at Wisconsin; and Jonathan, born in 1860 at Wisconsin. His parents were then listed as residing on a nearby farm. Jonathan was born circa 1799 at Ohio and Nancy was born circa 1799 at New York. Then residing with the parents were daughter Emma, born circa 1833 at New York, and son George, born circa 1842 at Ohio. David resided at Poygan and enlisted there on Sept. 8, 1861. He was assigned as above and was promoted to Corporal and then Sergeant in that company. He was mustered out on Oct. 9, 1865. David was involved in an altercation at the saloon of Peter Deyoe at Waukau. One of David's sons was known to frequent the establishment and, becoming unruly on one occasion, Mr. Deyoe attempted to put him out. A scuffle ensued during which Mr. Deyoe was injured. He had David's son arrested and fined for assault and battery. David then had Mr. Deyoe charged with allowing a minor to loiter in his saloon. Deyoe was found guilty of the charge. David was listed in 1883 at P.O. Waukau. He had been receiving a pension of $6 per month since June 1881 for a disease of the lungs and a wound to his leg and ankle. David was listed in the 1890 federal census as residing in the town of Rushford at P.O. Waukau. He was suffering from piles and the effects of a gunshot wound. David was listed in the veterans section of the 1895 and 1905 Wisconsin State census at P.O. Waukau. His wife died on Sept. 14, 1902. Thaddeus, their son, died on Apr. 26, 1886 at age 11 years and 23 days. David was listed in 1905 as owning a barber shop in the village of Waukau. He died at Antigo, Langlade County on Mar. 24, 1917. All three are buried in the town of Rushford at Waukau Cemetery.
{US 1860, 1890; WC-V 1895, 1905; LOP-1883; WCMR v.1, p.99, #409*; B-1905}
{ROV; Cem. records; OmJ 14 Jan 1877}

MAXSON, George S. - Pvt., Co. C, 14th Regt., Wis. Vol. Inf.
George was born on May 30, 1841 at Ohio, a son of Jonathan and Nancy Maxson and a brother of David from a previous sketch. George was listed in the 1860 federal census as residing with his parents on a farm in the town of Poygan. He was married in Winnebago County on July 25, 1863 to Celestia B. Wilkinson. George enlisted at Omro on Nov. 26, 1863 and was assigned as above. He was mustered out on Oct. 9, 1865. George was married second in Winnebago County on Feb. 10, 1873 to Elva Hammond. He was listed in the veteran section of the 1885 Wisconsin State census at P.O. Waupun, Fond du Lac County and was not found in that section of the 1895 state census. George was listed in that section of the 1905 state census at P.O. Waukau. He was listed in 1905 as residing in the village of Waukau. Residing with him was a Beulah B. Maxson. George died on May 1, 1906. He was buried with a simple military marker in the town of Rushford at Waukau Cemetery.
{US 1860; WC-V 1885, 1895, 1905; B-1905; ROV; WCMR v.1, p.244, #1399}
{Cem. records}

MAXWELL, George T. - Pvt., Co. B, 3rd Regt., Wis. Vol. Inf.
George resided at Oshkosh and enlisted there on June 4, 1861. He was assigned as above. George was killed in action when shot in the head on Aug. 9, 1862 at Cedar

MAXWELL, George T. (cont.)
Mountain, Virginia.
{ROV; OWN 21 Aug 1862}

MAXWELL, John D. - Pvt., Co. B, 52nd Regt., Pennsylvania Vol. Inf.
John was born in 1840 and died in 1918. He is buried with members of his family in the town of Utica at Liberty Prairie Cemetery. His unit designation is included on his marker.
{Cem. records}

MAY, John - Confederate Civil War Veteran.
John had resided at Menasha prior to the Civil War. He moved south and fought with the confederate forces until captured by Menasha soldiers serving with Co. C, 10th Regt., Wis. Vol. Inf. at Huntsville, Alabama. John was recognized by several of the men. He was then reported to be a hard-core confederate.
{Lawson p.816}

MAYER, Gottlieb W. - Pvt., Co. F, 18th Regt., Wis. Vol. Inf.?
Gottlieb was listed as above in the veteran section of the 1905 Wisconsin State census at P.O. Winneconne. He was not found in the records of that company. George and Charlotte, his wife, were listed in 1905 as residing on 159 acres of section 11 in the town of Poygan. Hattie, Arthur, Richard and Silvia Mayer were residing with them.
{WC-V 1905; ROV; B-1905}

MAYNARD, Caleb Jr. - Pvt., Co. K, 12th Regt., Wis. Vol. Inf.
Caleb resided at Utica and enlisted there on Oct. 2, 1861. He was assigned as above and he re-enlisted in that same company at the end of his term. Caleb was then wounded on Aug. 12, 1864 at Atlanta, Georgia. He was transferred to the Veteran Reserve Corps on Apr. 24, 1865.
{ROV}

McALLISTER, Daniel - Pvt., Co. K, 11th Regt., Wis. Vol. Inf.
Daniel was born on May 1, 1819 at Vermont. Susan, his wife, was born in 1821, also at Vermont. They were listed in the 1860 federal census as residing on a farm in the town of Vinland. Mary McAllister, mother of Daniel, was residing with them. She was born circa 1789 at New Hampshire. Also listed were the following children: David, born circa 1842 at New Hampshire; Francis, born circa 1851 at Wisconsin; and Albert, born circa 1856 at Wisconsin. Daniel enlisted at Vinland on Sept. 17, 1861. He was assigned as above and was discharged on June 2, 1863 due to a disability. Daniel was listed in 1883 at P.O. Neenah. He had been receiving a pension of $6 per month since Mar. 1878 for asthma. Daniel was listed in the veteran section of the 1885 and 1895 Wisconsin State census at P.O. Neenah. He was listed in the 1890 federal census as residing in the town of Vinland at P.O. Neenah. Daniel died there on June 13, 1895 and Susan died in 1907. Both are buried with members of their family in the town of Menasha section of Oak Hill Cemetery.
{US 1860, 1890; WC-V 1885, 1895; LOP-1883; ROV; Cem. records}

McALLISTER, Matthew B. - Pvt., Co. C, 21st Regt., Wis. Vol. Inf.
Matthew was born circa 1843 at Maine. He was a son of Silas McAllister. Silas was

McALLISTER, Matthew B. (cont.)
born circa 1804 at Maine. The father was listed in the 1860 federal census as a lumberman residing in the fourth ward of the city of Oshkosh. Residing with him then were the following children: Olive, born circa 1832; Hannah, born circa 1839; Charlotte, born circa 1841; Matthew; Stephen, born circa 1853; and Frank, born circa 1859. The youngest was born in Wisconsin and the others were born in Maine. Matthew resided at Oshkosh and enlisted there on Aug. 12, 1862. He was assigned as above and was mustered out on June 8, 1865.
{US 1860; ROV}

McCABE, John - 1st Lt., Co. E, 5th (reorg.) Regt., Wis. Vol. Inf.
John was born on Nov. 1, 1823 at County Cavan, Ireland. He was a son of John and Catherine (Fitzpatrick) McCabe. John was a second cousin of Gen. Phil Sheridan. He received his education in his native land and then emigrated to America in May 1840. His parents had been to America in 1812 but returned to Ireland in 1815. John located with his parents at Ulster County, New York and was engaged there in the trade of a stone cutter. He was married there on May 16, 1845 to Ellen Coughlan. She was born circa 1822 in County Kings, Ireland and came to America with her sister. Her father, Michael Couglan, had died in Ireland in 1860. Her mother came to this country in 1861 and resided with John and Ellen until her death in 1866. John and Ellen removed to Wisconsin in 1848, landing at Milwaukee in September and then removing to Oshkosh on Oct. 9 of the same year. There he purchased a farm in the town of Vinland along with his brothers Cornelius and Francis. John and Ellen were listed in the 1860 federal census as residing on the farm in the town of Vinland. Listed with them were the following children: Catherine, born circa 1847; James, born circa 1849; Cornelius, born circa 1852; Eva, born circa 1855; and John, born circa 1857. Catherine was born in New York and the other children were born in Wisconsin. John was engaged as an enlisting officer during 1861-2. In 1863 he resigned from his position as Town Chairman and enlisted to help fill the quota for that town. He was commissioned as 1st Lieutenant of the above company on Sept. 12, 1864 and was mustered out on June 20, 1865 at Hall's Hill, Washington, D.C. He suffered from exposure during his military service which resulted in rheumatism. On returning home, John purchased a large farm in the town of Winneconne. Being unable to do hard labor, John leased out that farm and moved into the village of Winneconne, where he was engaged as a butcher for six years. He was there elected as Justice of the Peace, which lead to his studying of the law. At the age of 60 he was admitted to the bar at Oshkosh. All through his residency in Winnebago County, John held many various elected and appointed positions. He was commander of the GAR post at Winneconne in 1867. When that post was disbanded in 1873, John joined Post #241 at Oshkosh. He was listed in the veteran section of the 1885 Wisconsin State census at P.O. Winneconne. John and Ellen had eight children: Katie, married Edward Lee of Minnesota; James, married Anna Lyons, resided in Oregon; Cornelius, employed on a railroad in Minnesota; Eva, married John Manning, resided with her father as a widow in 1888; Mamie, married Frank Hildebrand of Rhinelander; Nellie, a teacher; Wendell Phillips, died in 1884 at age 14 years; and one who died in infancy. John was residing in Winneconne in 1888. He was listed in the 1890 federal census as residing in the city of Oshkosh. John died on Aug. 12, 1894 at Austin, Minnesota. He was returned to Oshkosh for burial in Riverside Cemetery. He had been stricken with paralysis while attending the funeral of an old Army comrade that he had not seen in years. Another article places the reason for his trip to Minnesota as being at the bedside

McCABE, John (cont.)
of a sister who was dying from typhoid-pneumonia. When word reached Oshkosh on Aug. 11 that John had been stricken, Frank McCabe, a nephew, and Mrs. John (Eva) Manning, his daughter, departed for Minnesota.
{US 1860, 1890; WC-V 1885; Randall p.55; SCA 1:405-6; OWN 18 Aug 1894; ROV} {OWN 01 Nov 1888}

McCABE, Terrence - Pvt., Co. B, 6th Regt., Wis. Vol. Inf.
Terrence resided at Oshkosh and enlisted there on May 22, 1861. He was assigned as Private, Co. B, 3rd Regt., Wis. Vol. Inf. and he was discharged by orders on Oct. 25, 1862. Terrence was then drafted at Clayton on Sept. 30, 1864. He was assigned as above and was wounded at Gravelly Run, Virginia. Terrence was then mustered out on June 21, 1865.
{ROV}

McCALLUM, Murray - Pvt., Co. I, 21st Regt., Wis. Vol. Inf.
Murray was born circa 1845 at New York, a son of William and Ann McCallum. The father was born circa 1814 at New York and Ann was born in that same state circa 1826. They were listed in the 1860 federal census as residing on a farm in the town of Clayton at P.O. Neenah. Listed with them were the following children: Murray; Margaret, born circa 1847; Peter, born circa 1850; and William, born circa 1854. The youngest was born in Wisconsin and the other children were born in New York. Murray listed his residence as Vinland when he enlisted there on Aug. 13, 1862. He was assigned as above and was transferred to the Veteran Reserve Corps on Feb. 6, 1864. Murray was married in Winnebago County on Aug. 20, 1868 to Sarah E. Ball. He was listed in the veteran section of the 1885, 1895 and 1905 Wisconsin State census at P.O. Neenah. Murray was listed in 1888 as a member of GAR Post #129 at Neenah. He was listed in the 1890 federal census as residing in the city of Neenah. Murray was listed in 1905 as a shipping clerk at the Kimberly-Clark Co. and residing at 324 W. Forest Avenue in Neenah. Etha E. and Theodosia McCallum were residing at that same address. Murray was listed as a resident of Neenah in 1920 and was still there in 1927.
{US 1860, 1890; WC-V 1885, 1895, 1905; ROV; WCMR v.1, p.391, #2428; B-1905} {21-33rd; 21-40th}

McCANDLESS, John M. - Pvt., Co. C, 10th Regt., Wis. Vol. Inf.
John was born circa 1833 at Scotland. He was listed in the 1860 federal census as a carpenter and joiner residing with others of his family in the second ward of the village of Menasha. John enlisted at Menasha on Sept. 27, 1861. He was assigned as above. John was reported as killed on Oct. 8, 1862 at Perryville, Kentucky. His name was still found in the veteran section of the 1885, 1895 and 1905 Wisconsin State census at P.O. Menasha. He was also listed in the 1890 federal census as residing in the city of Menasha. John was listed in 1905 as residing at 160 River Street in Menasha. Harriet McCandless was also residing at that address. John was still residing there in 1908.
{US 1860, 1890; WC-V 1885, 1895, 1905; ROV; B-1905; Lawson p.812}

McCARN, John - Pvt., Co. G, 22nd Regt., Wis. Vol. Inf.
John resided at Winchester and enlisted there on Mar. 3, 1865. He was assigned as above and was transferred as unassigned to the 3rd Regt., Wis. Vol. Inf. on June 10,

McCARN, John (cont.)
1865. John was then mustered out on June 24, 1865.
{ROV}

McCARN, John S. - Lt., 6th Regt., Miss. Colored Troops.
John resided at Omro and enlisted there on Sept. 8, 1861. He was assigned as a Private, Co. C, 14th Regt., Wis. Vol. Inf. John was discharged on Sept. 25, 1863 to accept his commission as 1st Lieutenant of the 6th Regt., Miss. Colored Troops.
{ROV}

McCARTY, Charles - Pvt., Co. B, 44th Regt., Wis. Vol. Inf.
Charles resided at Menasha and enlisted there on Sept. 27, 1864. He was assigned as above and was mustered out on June 26, 1865.
{ROV}

McCARTY, William - Sgt., Co. E, 5th (reorg.) Regt., Wis. Vol. Inf.
William was born circa 1825 at Ohio. He was listed in the 1860 federal census as a miller residing in the first ward of the city of Oshkosh. William resided at Oshkosh and enlisted there on Apr. 22, 1861. He was assigned as above and was taken prisoner at Winchester, Virginia. William was discharged on Oct. 25, 1862. He re-enlisted at Vinland on Aug. 18, 1864 and was assigned as Private, Co. E, 5th (reorg.) Regt., Wis. Vol. Inf. on Aug. 18, 1864. William was promoted to Sergeant in that company and was mustered out on June 20, 1865. William had a son, unnamed at registration, who was born in Oshkosh on May 1, 1882.
{US 1860; ROV; WCBR v.3, p.76, #454}

McCLUSKEY, Owen - Pvt., Co. A, 50th Regt., Wis. Vol. Inf.
Owen resided at Algoma and enlisted there on Feb. 27, 1865. He was assigned as above and was mustered out on June 12, 1866 at the end of his term of enlistment.
{ROV}

McCORD, James - Civil War Veteran?
James was born on Jan. 12, 1847 at New York. He was a son of William McCord and a brother of Thomas from a following sketch. William was born circa 1815 at Ireland. He removed with his family to the Omro area in 1849. He was listed (McCore) in the 1860 federal census as residing on a farm in the town of Omro. Listed with him were the following children: Thomas; Jane, born circa 1843 at New York; James; and Clarissa, born circa 1849 at New York. James was listed in the 1890 federal census as residing in the town of Omro at P.O. Omro. He provided information that he had been a mechanic in Gen. Brune's Department from Jan. 1, 1863 to July 1, 1863. Alma, his widow, was listed in 1905 as residing on Genesee Street in the village of Omro. James died on July 1, 1899 in Omro at the home of Dr. Petty, his brother-in-law. He had been ill with appendicitis for three weeks. James was survived by a brother in California and two sisters, one at Ripon and the other at Densmore, Kansas.
{US 1860, 1890; B-1905; OWN 08 Jul 1899}

McCORD, Thomas - Pvt., Co. C, 21st Regt., Wis. Vol. Inf.
Thomas was born circa 1839 at New York. He was a son of William McCord and a brother of James from a previous sketch. He was listed in the 1860 federal census as

McCORD, Thomas (cont.)
residing with his father on a farm in the town of Omro. Thomas resided at Omro and he enlisted there on Aug. 14, 1862. He was assigned as above and he was wounded on Oct. 8, 1862 at Chaplin Hills, Kentucky. Thomas died from those wounds on Oct. 15, 1862 at Sulphur Springs, Kentucky.
{US 1860; ROV; OWN 07 May 1863}

McCORMICK, John - Pvt., Co. E, 5th (reorg.) Regt., Wis. Vol. Inf.
John was born circa 1834 at Ireland. He was listed in the 1860 federal census as a farmer residing in the town of Oshkosh. Margaret, his mother, was residing with him. She was born circa 1800 at Ireland. Also listed were his brother Andrew, listed as born in Norway circa 1844, and sister Margaret, born circa 1846 at Ireland. John enlisted at Oshkosh on Aug. 14, 1862. He was assigned as Private, Co. F, 21st Regt., Wis. Vol. Inf. He was discharged on Feb. 22, 1863 due to a disability. John re-enlisted at Algoma on Aug. 27, 1864. He was assigned as above and was mustered out on June 20, 1865. John was listed in the veteran section of the 1885 Wisconsin State census at P.O. Winnebago. He was listed in the 1890 federal census as residing in the town of Oshkosh at P.O. Winnebago. He was then listed as being sick.
{US 1860, 1890; WC-V 1885; ROV}

McCORMICK, Samuel - Pvt., Co. D, 41st Regt., Wis. Vol. Inf.
Samuel resided at Menasha and enlisted there on May 9, 1864. He was assigned as above and was mustered out on Sept. 23, 1864 at the end of his term of enlistment.
{ROV}

McCORRISON, Orrin - Pvt., Co. A, 1st (3 yr.) Regt., Wis. Vol. Inf.
Orrin resided at New London, Waupaca County and enlisted on Sept. 24, 1861. He was assigned as above and was discharged on Nov. 25, 1862 due to a disability. Orrin was married to Louise M. Myers. They had a son, Arthur Edwin, who was born in Oshkosh on May 24, 1883. Orrin was listed in 1883 at P.O. Oshkosh. He had been receiving a pension of $4 per month since May 1881 for chronic diarrhea. He was listed in 1888 as a member of GAR Post #10 at Oshkosh. Orrin was listed in the veteran section of the 1885, 1895 and 1905 Wisconsin State census at P.O. Oshkosh. He was listed in the 1890 federal census as residing at 405 Main Street in the city of Oshkosh. Orrin provided information that during his military service he had been confined to a hospital for four months. He was suffering from chronic diarrhea and erysipelas. Orrin was commander of GAR Post #10 at Oshkosh in 1906.
{US 1890; WC-V 1885, 1895, 1905; GAR 40th; ROV; WCBR v.3, p.124, #742}
{LOP-1883}

McCOY, Charles - Pvt., Co. D, 5th Regt., Wis. Vol. Inf.
Charles was born in 1837 at Linden, Vermont. He listed his residence as Beaver Dam, Dodge County when he enlisted there on Apr. 22, 1861. He was assigned as above and was discharged in Sept. 1862 due to a disability. Charles was listed in the veteran section of the 1885 Wisconsin State census at P.O. Oshkosh. He was listed in 1888 as a member of GAR Post #10 at Oshkosh and Charles died in Oshkosh on Oct. 7, 1889. Kittie E., his widow, was listed in the 1890 federal census as residing in the city of Oshkosh. She provided that Charles had died of a heart disease.
{US 1890; WC-V 1885; ROV; OWN 10 Oct 1899}

McCOY, John - Pvt., 8th Batt., Wis. Lt. Art.
John resided at Neenah and enlisted there on Mar. 25, 1862. He was assigned as above and was mustered out on Apr. 1, 1865 at the end of his term of enlistment.
{ROV}

McCRELLIS, Joseph R. - Pvt., 17th Regt., Wis. Vol. Inf.
Joseph resided at Utica and was drafted there on Sept. 30, 1864. He was listed as unassigned within the above regiment and was mustered out on June 5, 1865.
{ROV}

McCRUMMY, Michael - Pvt., Co. B, 3rd Regt., Wis. Cav.
Michael was born circa 1830 at Ireland. Ann, his wife, was born circa 1832 at New Brunswick, Canada. Michael was listed in the 1860 federal census as a blacksmith residing in the second ward of the city of Oshkosh. Residing with him and his wife were the following children: Mary Ann, born circa 1852; Elizabeth, born circa 1844; Catherine, born circa 1856; and John, born circa 1858. All of the children were born in Wisconsin. Michael resided at Oshkosh and enlisted there on Dec. 5, 1861. He was assigned as a Farrier with the above company and was discharged on Nov. 27, 1862 due to a disability.
{US 1860; ROV}

McCULLICK, Jonas - Cpl., Co. A, 43rd Regt., Wis. Vol. Inf.
Jonas resided at Utica and enlisted on Aug. 17, 1864. He was assigned as above and was promoted to Corporal in that company. Jonas was mustered out on June 24, 1865.
{ROV}

McCURDY, Chandler - Pvt., Co. A, 1st (3 yr.) Regt., Wis. Vol. Inf.
Chandler was born in 1838 at Maine, a son of Chandler Sr. and Rachel (Simpson) McCurdy. The father is the subject of a following sketch. Deborah S., wife of Chandler, was born in 1838, also at Maine. Chandler was listed in the 1860 federal census as a laborer residing in the third ward of the city of Oshkosh. A son, Eddy J., was born at Oshkosh on Mar. 24, 1861 and died three days later. Chandler resided at Oshkosh and enlisted there on Sept. 16, 1861. He was assigned as above and was then discharged on Oct. 25, 1862 due to a disability. Chandler was listed in 1868 as a farmer residing near the end of Ohio Street in Oshkosh. Chandler Sr. was listed at that time as residing at 60 Kansas Street in Oshkosh. Chandler and Deborah had a daughter, Nettie E., who died on Nov. 14, 1873 at age 10 years and 7 months. Chandler was listed in 1883 at P.O. Oshkosh. He had been receiving a pension of $2 per month for an injury to his left arm. After residing at Oshkosh for most of his life, Chandler removed to Bayfield, Bayfield County where he managed sawmills in both Bayfield and Ashland. He died at Bayfield on Oct. 19, 1891 from the onset of a heart disease. Chandler was survived by six children, two of them being married. Deborah died in 1898. Both are buried, along with the son and daughter named above, in the town of Algoma at Ellenwood Cemetery, Section A.
{US 1860; ROV; LOP-1883; T-1868; Cem. records; OWN 29 Oct 1891}

McCURDY, Chandler Sr. - Pvt., Co. B, 37th Regt., Wis. Vol. Inf.
Chandler was born circa 1812 at Maine. He was engaged there and at New Brunswick, Canada in the lumber trade until he removed west with his family. They reached

McCURDY, Chandler Sr. (cont.)
Oshkosh on Oct. 10, 1850. Before coming west, Chandler was married in Maine to Rachel Simpson. They had a family of seven children: George and James, resided in western Wisconsin; Chandler, subject of a previous sketch; Daniel, resided in Nebraska; Robert and Benjamin of Oshkosh; and Louisa, married a Little, resided several miles outside of Oshkosh. Robert was at one time the Assistant State Treasurer. Chandler enlisted on Mar. 31, 1864 and was assigned as Private, Co. B, 37th Regt., Wis. Vol. Inf. He was discharged on July 11, 1865 due to a disability. Chandler was engaged at lumbering and farming near Oshkosh for 35 years. As his health was poor, Chandler moved to the Soldiers' Home at Milwaukee in 1883. He died there in April 1885 after a brief illness. Chandler was an uncle of John Buckstaff Jr. of Oshkosh. He was also related to Mrs. Benjamin Doughty.
{ROV; ODT 23 Apr 1885}

McCURDY, Henry W. - Civil War Veteran?
Henry was listed in the 1890 federal census as residing in the town of Winneconne at P.O. Winneconne. No military information was provided. Henry was not found in the index to Roster of Wisconsin Volunteers.
{US 1890; ROV}

McCURDY, James H. - Pvt., Co. F, 11th Regt., Wis. Vol. Inf.
James was born circa 1835 at New Brunswick, Canada. He was a son of James and Louisa McCurdy. Louisa was born circa 1814 at New Brunswick and James Sr. was born circa 1808 at Maine. James Sr. was a brother of Chandler McCurdy Sr. from a previous sketch. He was listed in the 1860 federal census as a boarding house keeper residing in the third ward of the city of Oshkosh. Residing with him were his wife and the following children: James; Lucy, born circa 1840; Victoria, born circa 1842; and Sarah, born circa 1850. Sarah was born in Wisconsin and the others were born in New Brunswick. James resided at Oshkosh and enlisted there on Sept. 27, 1861. He was assigned as above and he re-enlisted in that same company at the end of his term. He was mustered out on Sept. 4, 1865. James was listed in 1868 as a river man boarding at 13 Sixth Street in Oshkosh. This was the home of James McCurdy, his father. James was not listed in the veteran section of the 1885 Wisconsin State census. He was listed in the 1890 federal census as residing at 366 Algoma Street in Oshkosh. James was listed in the veteran section of the 1895 state census at P.O. Oshkosh and was not found in that section of the 1905 state census. He was not listed in the 1905 county directory.
{US 1860, 1890; WC-V 1885, 1895, 1905; ROV; T-1868; B-1905}

McCUSKER, Cornelius - Pvt., Co. B, 96th Regt., Illinois Vol. Inf.
Cornelius was listed as above in the veteran section of the 1885, 1895 and 1905 Wisconsin State census at P.O. Oshkosh. He was listed in the 1890 federal census as residing in the city of Oshkosh. Cornelius provided his unit designation as above and his service dates as being from sometime in 1862 to June 10, 1865. He was listed in 1888 as a member of GAR Post #241 at Oshkosh. Cornelius was listed in 1905 as a patrolman residing at 36 Wright Street in Oshkosh. Gertrude A., John F., Kathleen A. and Marguerite McCusker were residing at that same address.
{US 1890; WC-V 1885, 1895, 1905; B-1905}

McDANIELS, Harvey - Pvt., Co. E, 2nd Regt., Wis. Vol. Inf.
Harvey resided at Oshkosh and enlisted there on May 18, 1861. He was assigned as above and was wounded in the first battle of Bull Run, Virginia. Harvey was wounded slightly in the hand at Beverly Ford on Aug. 21, 1862 and was then taken prisoner at Gettysburg, Pennsylvania. He was mustered out on June 28, 1864 at the end of his term of enlistment. He was listed in 1888 as a member of GAR Post #241 at Oshkosh. Col. Harshaw reported that Harvey was residing at Michigan in 1899.
{ROV; OWN 11 Sep 1862; ODN 07 May 1899}

McDERMOTT, Patrick A. - Pvt., Co. E, 2nd Regt., Wis. Vol. Inf.
Patrick resided at Oshkosh and he enlisted there on May 25, 1861. He was assigned as above and was discharged due to a disability on June 20, 1862. He was listed in the 1890 federal census as residing in the town of Oshkosh at P.O. Oshkosh. Patrick was listed in the veteran section of the 1895 Wisconsin State census at P.O. Oshkosh. He was listed in that section of the 1905 state census as residing at the Wisconsin Veterans' Home at King. Christine, his wife, was residing there with him. Christina was listed in the 1910 federal census as a widow residing at King. She was born circa 1856 at French Canada. Her parents were both natives of that place. She came to the United States in 1867. She had been married to Patrick for 19 years and had 5 children, four then living.
{US 1890, 1910; WC-V 1895, 1905; ROV; GAR 40th}

McDONNELL, James - Pvt., 3rd Regt., Wis. Cav.
James resided at Oshkosh and enlisted there on Dec. 29, 1863. He was assigned to the above regiment but his name does not appear in the records for any company within that regiment.
{ROV}

McFADDEN, William - Cpl., Co. D, 32nd Regt., Wis. Vol. Inf.
William was born circa 1839 at New York. He was listed in the 1860 federal census as a farm laborer for C.W. Thrall in the town of Utica at P.O. Welaunee. William resided at Utica and enlisted there on Aug. 21, 1862. He was assigned as above and was then promoted to Corporal in that company. William was mustered out on June 12, 1865.
{US 1860; ROV}

McFALL, Daniel - Pvt., Co. H, 49th Regt., Wis. Vol. Inf.
Daniel was born circa 1839 at New York. He was a son of Sylvester and Sabrina McFall. Sylvester was born circa 1794 at New York and Sabrina was born circa 1800 at Rhode Island. They were listed in the 1860 federal census as residing on a farm in the town of Winneconne. Listed with them was a daughter, Alzina, who was born circa 1844 at New York. Daniel and his wife were also residing with his parents. Daniel had been married in Winnebago County on Nov. 10, 1859 to Harriet Fairbanks. She was born circa 1840 at New York. Daniel listed his residence as Winneconne when he enlisted there on Feb. 7, 1865 and was assigned as above. He was then mustered out on Nov. 8, 1865. Daniel is buried with a simple military marker at Omro Cemetery, Pelton's Addition, Section F, plot 4. Adaline, his wife, was born in 1840 and died in 1915. She is buried at his side.
{US 1860; ROV; WCMR v.1, p.195, #1002; Cem. records}

McFARLAND, Alexander B. - Cpl., Co. I, 47th Regt., Wis. Vol. Inf.
Alexander resided at Utica and he enlisted there on Jan. 28, 1865. He was assigned as above and was promoted to Corporal in that company. Alexander was mustered out on Sept. 4, 1865.
{ROV}

McFARLAND, Edwin P. - Cpl., Co. B, 3rd Regt., Wis. Vol. Inf.
Edwin resided at Oshkosh and enlisted there on Jan. 4, 1864. He was assigned as above and was promoted to Corporal in that company. Edwin was wounded at Dallas, Georgia and was mustered out on July 18, 1865.
{ROV}

McFETRICH, John - Pvt., Co. A, 2nd Regt., Wis. Cav.
John resided at Oshkosh and enlisted on Dec. 1, 1861. He was assigned as above and was listed as having deserted on May 16, 1862. Daniel McFetrich was a member of that same company. He enlisted on the same date and was discharged on Jan. 28, 1865. Daniel was listed in the 1890 federal census as residing at New London, Waupaca County.
{US 1890; ROV}

McGILLIS, Angus - Cpl., Co. H, 21st Regt., Wis. Vol. Inf.
Angus resided at Oshkosh and he enlisted there on Aug. 12, 1862. He was assigned as above and was promoted to Corporal in that company. Angus was then mustered out on May 18, 1865.
{ROV}

McGOWAN, Abram - Pvt., Co. B, 3rd Regt., Wis. Vol. Inf.
Abram resided at Oshkosh and enlisted there on June 14, 1861. He was assigned as above and was mustered out on June 29, 1864 at the end of his term of enlistment.
{ROV}

McGREGOR, Alexander - Pvt., Co. D, 1st Regt., Wis. Cav.
Alexander was born circa 1830 at Scotland. He was a son of Duncan and Margaret McGregor and a brother of Andrew from a following sketch. Both parents were natives of Scotland, Duncan born there circa 1800 and Margaret born circa 1806. They were listed in the 1860 federal census as residing on a farm in the town of Nepeuskun at P.O. Ripon. Listed with them were the following children: Alexander; Neil, born circa 1836; John, born circa 1838; Isabella, born circa 1841; Jennette, born circa 1843; and Andrew. All of the children were born in Scotland. Alexander enlisted on Sept. 1, 1864 and was assigned as above. He was mustered out on July 19, 1865. Alexander was listed in the veteran section of the 1885 and 1895 Wisconsin State census at P.O. Rush Lake. He was listed in the 1890 federal census as residing in the town of Aurora, Waushara County at P.O. Berlin. Alexander then listed that he was a re-enlisted veteran. He was listed in that same census as residing in the town of Nepeuskun at P.O. Rush Lake. He was listed in the veteran section of the 1905 state census at P.O. Eureka and has having been a member of the 10th Regt., N.Y. Vol. Inf. He was listed in 1905 with Maggie, his wife, as residing in the village of Eureka.
{US 1860, 1890; WC-V 1885, 1895, 1905; ROV; B-1905}

McGREGOR, Andrew - Pvt., Co. K, 20th Regt., Wis. Vol. Inf.
Andrew was born circa 1845 at Scotland. He was a son of Duncan and Margaret McGregor and a brother of Alexander from a previous sketch. Andrew was listed in the 1860 federal census as residing with his parents on a farm in the town of Nepeuskun at P.O. Ripon. He resided at Nepeuskun and enlisted there on Aug. 15, 1862. He was assigned as above and was mustered out on July 14, 1865.
{US 1860; ROV}

McGREGOR, James - Pvt., Co. B, 3rd Regt., Wis. Vol. Inf.
James resided at Oshkosh and enlisted there on Apr. 22, 1861. He was assigned as above and was mustered out on June 29, 1864 at the end of his term of enlistment.
{ROV}

McGUIRE, Patrick - Cpl., Co. D, 12th Regt., Maine Vol. Inf.
Patrick was born on Oct. 19, 1837 at St. Patrick, New Brunswick, Canada. When a young boy he removed to Calais, Maine with his parents. He enlisted there on Nov. 11, 1861 and was assigned to the 12th Regt., Maine Vol. Inf. He was wounded twice and was promoted to Corporal in that company. Patrick was discharged on Apr. 18, 1866. He removed to Oshkosh shortly after his discharge. Patrick was listed in 1868 as a lumberman boarding at the Peters House in the city of Oshkosh. He was married in 1871 to Flavia Thibodeaux. They had a son, James W., who was born in Oshkosh on July 20, 1879. A daughter, unnamed at registration, was born in Oshkosh on May 23, 1881. Patrick was also listed as the father of an unnamed daughter who was born in Oshkosh on Dec. 31, 1881. He was listed in 1883 at P.O. Oshkosh. He had then been receiving a pension of $2 per month since Mar. 1881 for a wound to his right hand. Patrick (McWire) was listed in the veteran section of the 1885 Wisconsin State census at P.O. Oshkosh as a veteran of the 12th Mass. Vol. Inf. He was listed in the 1890 federal census as residing in Oshkosh. Patrick was listed again in the veteran section of the 1905 state census at P.O. Oshkosh and as having been assigned to Co. K, 12th Regt., Maine Vol. Inf. He was listed in that year as a laborer residing at 249 Bowen Street in Oshkosh. Albert P. and Cora A. McGuire were residing at the same address. Patrick died in Oshkosh on Nov. 15, 1924. He was buried there in Calvary Cemetery. Patrick was survived by his widow and five children: Charles and Albert McGuire of Oshkosh; James McGuire of Sheboygan; and Mrs. Cora Middlestead and Mrs. F.W. Cowen, both of Oshkosh.
{US 1890; WC-V 1885, 1905; LOP-1883; B-1905; WCBR v.2, p.151, #411; T-1868}
{WCBR v.3, p.25, #146; WCBR v.3, p.85, #509; ODN 15 Nov 1924}

McINTOSH, Lochlin L. - Pvt., Co. E, 2nd Regt., Wis. Vol. Inf.
Lochlin was born circa 1833 at Canada. Mary, his wife, was born circa 1839 at Rhode Island. Lochlin was listed in the 1860 federal census as a laborer residing in the fourth ward of the city of Oshkosh. Residing with him were his wife and the following children: Mary, born circa 1852; James, born circa 1855; and Laughlin, born circa 1859. Lochlin resided at Oshkosh and he enlisted there on Apr. 21, 1861. He was assigned as above. Lochlin was killed in action on Sept. 17, 1862 at Antietam, Maryland.
{US 1860; ROV; OWN 11 Sep 1862}

McINTOSH, Thomas - Pvt., Co. G, 3rd Regt., Wis. Vol. Inf.
Thomas resided at Manitowoc, Manitowoc County when he was drafted on Sept. 30,

McINTOSH, Thomas (cont.)
1864. He was assigned as above and was then mustered out on June 9, 1865. Thomas was listed in the 1890 federal census as residing in the city of Oshkosh. He died in a fire at his apartment in Oshkosh on May 29, 1894. He had resided there for five weeks. Thomas had no relatives in Oshkosh. His family lived in the east. He was said to have owned considerable property in Manitowoc County.
{US 1890; ROV; OWN 02 Jun 1894}

McKENNA, Thomas - Pvt., Co. B, 3rd Regt., Wis. Cav.
Thomas resided at Oshkosh and enlisted there on Dec. 27, 1861. He was assigned as above. Thomas was discharged on Jan. 23, 1863 under sentence of a General Court Martial.
{ROV}

McKILLIP, Charles F. - Pvt., Co. H, 18th Regt., Wis. Vol. Inf.
Charles resided at Waukau and enlisted there on Jan. 8, 1862. He was assigned as above and was mustered out on Mar. 14, 1865 at the end of his term of enlistment.
{ROV}

McKILLIP, John - Pvt., Co. C, 10th Regt., Wis. Vol. Inf.
John was married in Winnebago County on Oct. 1, 1861 to Sarah Stanley. He resided at Menasha and enlisted there on Sept. 3, 1861. He was assigned as above. John was killed on Oct. 8, 1862 at Perryville, Kentucky. His marriage was registered again in June 1865.
{ROV; WCMR v.1, p.122, #502*; WCMR v.1, p.275, #1646}

McKINLEY, William - Cpl., Co. A, 47th Regt., Wis. Vol. Inf.
William was born on Oct. 24, 1834 at Ohio. Milly, his wife, was born circa 1837, also at Ohio. They were listed in the 1860 federal census as residing on a farm in the town of Clayton at P.O. Neenah. William enlisted at Winchester on Feb. 11, 1865. He was assigned as above and was promoted to Corporal in that company. William was then mustered out on Sept. 4, 1865. He was listed in the veteran section of the 1885 and 1895 Wisconsin State census at P.O. Winchester. William was listed in the 1890 federal census as residing in the town of Clayton at P.O. Winchester. He was listed in the veteran section of the 1905 state census at P.O. Oshkosh. He was listed that year with Lucinda, his wife, as residing on 40 acres of section 18 in the town of Clayton. William died on Apr. 13, 1918. Amelia, his wife, died on Feb. 23, 1892 at age 55 years and 23 days. Elizabeth S., a daughter, died on Oct. 27, 1857 at age 3 months and 18 days. All three are buried in the town of Clayton at Royer Cemetery. Other members of their family are buried in that same cemetery.
{US 1860, 1890; WC-V 1885, 1895, 1905; ROV; B-1905; Cem. records}

McKINNEY, Daniel E. - Sgt., Co. B, 1st Regt., Maine Lt. Art.
Daniel was born circa 1835. He was listed (McKenney) as above in the veteran section of the 1885 Wisconsin State census at P.O. Oshkosh. He was listed (McKenny) in 1888 as a member of GAR Post #241 at Oshkosh. He was listed again (McKinney) in the veteran section of the 1895 census at P.O. Oshkosh. Daniel was listed in the 1890 federal census as residing in the city of Oshkosh. He then provided his unit designation as above and his service dates as having been from Mar. 20, 1865 to Apr. 5, 1866. Daniel died

McKINNEY, Daniel E. (cont.)
at Oshkosh on Nov. 26, 1897 after a sickness of about two months. He had been engaged in lumbering on the Wolf River since the Civil War and, shortly before his death, he was employed by the Conlee Lumber Company. He was survived by his wife and one son.
{US 1890; WC-V 1885, 1895; ODN 26 Nov 1897}

McLAUGHLIN, William Judson - Pvt., Co. B, 41st Regt., Wis. Vol. Inf.
William was born on Nov. 8, 1842 at Indiana. He was a son of George and Sarah (Miller) McLaughlin. George was born on Nov. 5, 1809 at North Carolina and Sarah was born on May 3, 1820 at Virginia. They came to Wisconsin with their family in 1848 and settled in the town of Nepeuskun. They were listed in the 1860 federal census as residing on a farm in the town of Nepeuskun. Listed with them were the following children: Mary, born circa 1840; William; Silas, born circa 1845; Harriet, born circa 1848; Ann, born circa 1850; and Melvina, born circa 1856. The three youngest children were born in Wisconsin and the others were born in Indiana. George died at Nepeuskun on June 1, 1874 and Sarah died there on Jan. 22, 1879. William remained on the farm of his parents for fifteen years and then worked as a blacksmith at Berlin, Green Lake County for eight months. In 1864 he travelled to Indianapolis, Indiana and worked as a carpenter for three months. He then returned to Winnebago County and settled at Eureka. William enlisted at Nepeuskun on May 13, 1864. He was assigned as above and was mustered out on Sept. 23, 1864 at the end of his term of enlistment. William was married on Feb. 14, 1866 to Louisa A. Kolb. She was born on Feb. 22, 1846 and was a daughter of George and Harriet (Schneider) Kolb. William and Louisa had three children: Blanche, born on Oct. 25, 1874; Alvin J., born Aug. 11, 1879, died Sept. 7, 1880; and a stillborn son born in Eureka on Feb. 26, 1882. William was listed in the veteran section of the 1885 and 1895 Wisconsin State census at P.O. Eureka. He was listed in the 1890 federal census as residing in the town of Rushford at P.O. Eureka. William listed that he was suffering from chronic diarrhea. He was not found in the veteran section of the 1905 state census. His parents are buried in the town of Nepeuskun at Koro Cemetery. Others of their family are buried on the same plot.
{US 1860, 1890; WC-V 1885, 1895, 1905; Randall p.51-2; ROV; Cem. records}
{WCBR v.3, p.66, #392}

McLEOD, Norman - Pvt., Co. E, 1st (3 yr) Regt., Wis. Vol. Inf.
Norman resided at Rushford and enlisted there on May 12, 1864. He was assigned as above and was then transferred to Co. G, 21st Regt., Wis. Vol. Inf. on Sept. 19, 1864. He was transferred again to the 3rd (reorg.) Regt., Wis. Vol. Inf. on June 8, 1865 and was mustered out on July 18, 1865.
{ROV}

McMAHON, John - Pvt., Co. C, 14th Regt., Wis. Vol. Inf.
John was born on Apr. 13, 1829 at Ireland. He was a son of Edmund and Mary (McSweeney) McMahon and a brother to Patrick from a following sketch. They came to America in 1849 and located at Waterville, Maine. John worked there as a laborer. He was married at Lewiston Falls, Maine on June 11, 1851 to Hannah Cunningham. She was born circa 1834 at Ireland and she had come to this country in Sept. 1850 with her cousins James and Bridget (McGrath) Cunningham. John and Hannah removed to Wisconsin in 1856 and settled in Racine County. Soon thereafter they removed to

McMAHON, John (cont.)
Winnebago County and settled near Omro. They were listed in the 1860 federal census as residing on a farm in the town of Winneconne. Listed with them were the following children: Edmund, born circa 1853 at Maine; Maria, born circa 1854 at Maine; James, born circa 1856 at Wisconsin; and John, born circa 1858 at Wisconsin. John enlisted at Poygan on Sept. 25, 1861 and was assigned as above. He was wounded slightly in the battle at Corinth, Mississippi and was wounded again three times, once in a knee, once in a hip and the other in a shoulder on May 22, 1863 at Vicksburg, Mississippi. His wounds occurred at about noon on the second day of the battle and he lay wounded on the battlefield until sundown on the third day. He was then placed on a hospital boat and removed to Young's Point. John was transferred to Union Hospital at Memphis, Tennessee and then on to the Marine Hospital at St. Louis, Missouri. He was finally taken to the Harvey Hospital at Madison, Wisconsin where he was then mustered out on Dec. 7, 1864 at the end of his term of enlistment. He returned home and carried with him for the rest of his life the rifle ball in his shoulder. John and Hannah had the following children: Maria, married Arthur Richardson; James C., resided at Minnesota; John A., resided at Minnesota; William H., resided at Fifield, Price County; Edmund Shiloh, named after that battle as he was born on the day after his father fought on that battlefield; Maggie A., married Charles Welcher; Lenora; and George Washington McMahon. John was listed in 1883 at P.O. Winneconne. He had then been receiving a pension of $8 per month since Jan. 1878 for wounds to his right leg and hip. John was not found in the veteran section of the 1885 Wisconsin State census. He was listed in the 1890 federal census as residing in the village of Omro. He was listed in that section of the 1895 and 1905 state census at P.O. Omro. John and Hannah were both listed in 1905 as residing at the Wisconsin Veterans' Home at King. John is buried with a simple military marker in the town of Omro at Oak Grove Cemetery.
{US 1860, 1890; WC-V 1885, 1895, 1905; GRI; SCA p.622-3; LOP-1883; ROV}
{GAR 40th}

McMAHON, Patrick - Pvt., Co. G, 32nd Regt., Wis. Vol. Inf.
Patrick was born in 1836 at Ireland. He was a son of Edmund and Mary (McSweeney) McMahon and a brother of John from a previous sketch. Mary Moonan, his wife, was born in 1836. Patrick resided at Omro when he enlisted on Nov. 20, 1863. He was assigned as above and was wounded on Feb. 3, 1865 at River's Bridge, S.C. Patrick was wounded on Mar. 21, 1865 at Bentonville, N.C. His wounds resulted in the amputation of a leg. Patrick was then transferred to Co. H, 16th (reorg.) Regt., Wis. Vol. Inf. on June 4, 1865 and he was mustered out on June 19, 1865. Patrick was listed in the veteran section of the 1885 Wisconsin State census at P.O. Mauston, Juneau County. He died in 1894 and Mary died in 1895. Both are buried in the town of Omro at Oak Grove Cemetery.
{WC-V 1885; SCA p.623; GRI; ROV; Cem. records}

McMANUS, William - Pvt., Co. H, 36th Regt., Wis. Vol. Inf.
William resided at Utica and enlisted there on Feb. 29, 1864. He was assigned as above and was mustered out on July 12, 1865.
{ROV}

McMILLAN, David H. - Pvt., Co. D, 5th (reorg.) Regt., Wis. Vol. Inf.
David resided at Wausau, Marathon County and enlisted there on Aug. 29, 1864. He

McMILLAN, David H. (cont.)
was assigned as above and was mustered out on June 20, 1865. David was not found in the veteran section of the 1885 Wisconsin State census. He was listed in 1888 as a member of GAR Post #10 at Oshkosh. David was listed in the 1890 federal census as residing in the town of Oshkosh at P.O. Oshkosh. He was listed in the veteran section of the 1895 state census at P.O. Oshkosh. David was listed in that section of the 1905 state census as residing at the Wisconsin Veterans' Home at King.
{US 1890; WC-V 1885, 1895, 1905; ROV; GAR 40th}

McMILLEN, Michael S. - Pvt., Co. D, 6th Regt., Wis. Vol. Inf.
Michael resided at Clayton and was drafted there on Mar. 20, 1865. He was assigned as above and he was listed as absent without leave when that regiment was mustered out on July 14, 1865.
{ROV}

McMULLEN, John E. - Pvt., Co. B, 3rd Regt., Wis. Vol. Inf.
John resided at Oshkosh and he enlisted on Apr. 21, 1861. He was assigned as above. John was wounded at Antietam, Maryland and again at Gettysburg, Pennsylvania. He was mustered out on June 29, 1864 at the end of his term of enlistment. John was married in Winnebago County on July 4, 1866 to Mary A. Cochran. He was listed in 1868 as a mill man residing at 13 Sixth Street in the city of Oshkosh. John was listed in 1888 as a member of GAR Post #205 at Chilton, Calumet County.
{ROV; T-1868; WCMR v.1, p.301, #1856*}

McMULLEN, Thomas - Cpl., Co. A, 1st (3 yr) Regt., Wis. Vol. Inf.
Thomas was born circa 1845 at New Brunswick, Canada. He was listed in the 1860 federal census as a servant for John Buckstaff Jr. in the third ward of the city of Oshkosh. Thomas resided at Oshkosh when he enlisted on Sept. 17, 1861 and was assigned as above. He was wounded at Chickamauga, Georgia. Thomas was mustered out on Oct. 13, 1864 at the end of his term of enlistment. He was listed in 1868 as boarding at the Peters House in the city of Oshkosh. He was listed in 1883 at P.O. Oshkosh. Thomas had then been receiving a pension of $4 per month since Dec. 1882 for the loss of the second toe and metatarsal bone of his left foot. He was a member of the old volunteer fire department at Oshkosh and was one of the first members of the paid department. Thomas died in April 1888.
{US 1860; ROV; T-1868; LOP-1883; OWN 19 Apr 1888}

McNAIR, John - Sgt., Co. G, 142nd Regt., New York Vol. Inf.
John was listed in 1868 as a partner in the firm of Lull & McNair in Oshkosh. He was then boarding at 8 North Punhoqua Street in the city of Oshkosh. John was listed as above in the veteran section of the 1885 Wisconsin State census at P.O. Oshkosh. He was listed in 1888 as a member of GAR Post #241 at Oshkosh. John was listed in the 1890 federal census as residing in Oshkosh.
{US 1890; WC-V 1885; T-1868}

McNAMEE, Patrick H. - Pvt., Co. C, 89th Regt., Illinois Vol. Inf.
Patrick was listed as above in the veteran section of the 1885 Wisconsin State census at P.O. Rosendale, Fond du Lac County. He was listed in that same section of the 1905 state census at P.O. Oshkosh. Patrick was then listed as a blacksmith for J.L. Clark and

McNAMEE, Patrick H. (cont.)
residing at 308 High Street in the city of Oshkosh.
{WC-V 1885, 1905; B-1905}

McNUTT, Erasmus - Pvt., Permanent Guard, Wis. Vol. Inf.
Erasmus resided at Green Bay, Brown County and was drafted there on Sept. 30, 1864. He was assigned as above and was discharged on Jan. 29, 1865 as he had then furnished a substitute. He was listed as E. McNutt in the veteran section of the 1885 Wisconsin State census at P.O. Winneconne.
{WC-V 1885; ROV}

McWILLIAMS, John - Pvt., Co. G, 1st (3 yr) Regt., Wis. Vol. Inf.
John resided at Oshkosh and enlisted there on Sept. 13, 1861. He was assigned as above and was mustered out on Oct. 14, 1864 at the end of his term of enlistment.
{ROV}

McWILLIAMS, Robert N. - Pvt., Co. F, 18th Regt., Wis. Vol. Inf.
Robert was born circa 1843 at Pennsylvania, a son of Job and Amanda McWilliams. Job was born in 1819 at Pennsylvania. Amanda died on Oct. 7, 1856 at age 36 years, 5 months and 4 days. Job was married second to Maria, who was born circa 1834 at New York. He was listed in the 1860 federal census as residing on a farm in the town of Nekimi at P.O. Oshkosh. Listed with him were the following children: Nelson; Amelia, born circa 1845; Euthelia, born circa 1849; Eugene, born circa 1852; and Amanda, born circa 1857. Job died in 1905. Robert resided at Oshkosh and enlisted there on Mar. 10, 1862. He was assigned as above. Robert was killed in action on Apr. 6, 1862 at Shiloh, Tennessee at age 19 years and 6 months. He is buried with his parents in the town of Algoma at Ellenwood Cemetery, Section A.
{US 1860; ROV; Cem. records}

MEDBURY, Alvin Bartlett - Pvt., Co. E, 52nd Regt., Wis. Vol. Inf.?
Alvin was born on Mar. 17, 1843 at Porter's Corners near Saratoga, New York. He came west with his parents circa 1853 and settled at Eagle, Waukesha County. He served in the Civil War during 1863 and 1864. Alvin removed to Oshkosh circa 1866 and was employed there by William B. Folds at McCay Bros. & Folds. He was a clerk there for five years. Alvin was married in Winnebago County on July 3, 1867 to Sarah Cordelia Knapp. She was born on July 16, 1849 at Sherburne, Chenango County, New York and was a daughter of George Young and Phila (Cushman) Knapp. She was also descended from Robert Cushman of the "Mayflower" and she came to Wisconsin with her parents in 1852. Alvin was listed in 1868 as a clerk boarding at 60 Warren Street in the city of Oshkosh. That was the residence of Charles L. Medberry. Alvin then went to Illinois and was involved in a merchandise business with John H. Stanhilber. After several other engagements, Alvin returned to Oshkosh and engaged in a paper business with E.E. Bemis. Alvin was listed (A.B.) as above in the veteran section of the 1885 Wisconsin State census at P.O. Oshkosh. He was not found in the records of that regiment and he was not found in the Roster of Wisconsin Volunteers. A.B. was listed in 1905 as the president of Medberry-Findeisen Co. of Oshkosh. They dealt in wholesale paper, notions and woodenware. He was residing at 67 W. Irving Street in Oshkosh. Alma C. and Fannie K. Medberry were also residing at that address. Sarah Medberry died in Oshkosh on Jan. 26, 1935. She was survived by three daughters: Mrs. Henry

MEDBURY, Alvin Bartlett (cont.)
(Ethel Mae) Barber; Mrs. Harry S. (Alma M.) Mallery; and Fannie Knapp Medberry. She was also survived by a sister, Mrs. Newton Holmes of Antigo, Langlade County. Sarah was taken to Milwaukee for cremation.
{WC-V 1885; ROV; T-1868; WCMR v.1, p.347, #2074; ODT 27 Aug 1899; B-1905} {ODN 26 Jan 1935}

MEIER - see Maier, Mayer, Meyer

MEKENTIER, Thain - Pvt., Co. G, 3rd Regt., Wis. Vol. Inf.?
He was listed as above in the veteran section of the 1885 Wisconsin State census at P.O. Oshkosh but was not found in the records of that regiment.
{WC-V 1885; ROV}

MELLOR, Edmond - Cpl., Co. E, 5th (reorg.) Regt., Wis. Vol. Inf.
Edmond resided at Oshkosh and enlisted there on Aug. 17, 1864. He was assigned as above and was wounded at Sailor's Creek. Edmond was mustered out on June 9, 1865.
{ROV}

MELTON, Frank - Pvt., Co. D, 8th Regt., Wis. Vol. Inf.
Frank resided at Oshkosh and enlisted there on Feb. 27, 1864. He was assigned as above and was listed as having deserted in Apr. 1864.
{ROV}

MENSIOR, William - Cpl., Co. F, 19th Regt., Wis. Vol. Inf.
William resided at Oshkosh and enlisted there on Jan. 31, 1862. He was assigned as above and was promoted to Corporal in that company. William was mustered out on Apr. 29, 1865 at the end of his term of enlistment.
{ROV}

MENTCH, Jacob N.B. - Pvt., 9th Batt., Wis. Lt. Art.
Jacob was born circa 1812 at Pennsylvania. Sarah, his wife, was born circa 1831 at New York. They were listed in the 1860 federal census as residing in the town of Omro. Listed with them were the following children: Maroni, subject of a following sketch; Abram, born circa 1853; Isaac, born circa 1856; Hiram, born circa 1858; and Jacob, born in 1860. The two eldest sons were born in Illinois and the other children were born in Wisconsin. Jacob listed his residence as Oshkosh when he enlisted on Feb. 10, 1862. He was assigned as above and was discharged due to a disability on Dec. 16, 1862. Jacob died in the town of Algoma on Sept. 18, 1863 aged circa 50 years. He is buried with a simple military marker in the town of Omro at Omro Union Cemetery.
{US 1860; OWN 24 Sep 1863; Cem. records; ROV}

MENTCH, Meronia - Pvt., Co. E, 5th (reorg.) Regt., Wis. Vol. Inf.
Meronia (Maroni) was born circa 1850 at Illinois. He was a son of Jacob Mentch from a previous sketch. Maroni was listed in the 1860 federal census as residing with his parents in the town of Omro. He listed his residence as Oshkosh when he enlisted on Sept. 3, 1864. He was assigned as above and was mustered out on June 20, 1865.
{US 1860; ROV}

MENTZEL, Robert - Sgt., Co. B, 178th Regt., New York Vol. Inf.
Minnie, widow of Robert, was listed in the 1890 federal census as residing in the city of Oshkosh. She provided his unit designation as above and his service dates as having been from May 18, 1863 to Apr. 20, 1866. She added that Robert had been shot in the leg. Minnie was listed in 1905 as residing at 307 Waugoo Street in Oshkosh. Julius R. Mentzel, a son, was also listed at that address.
{US 1890; B-1905}

MERBACH, John - Pvt., Co. F, 6th Regt., Wis. Vol. Inf.
John resided in the town of Harrison, Waupaca County and he was drafted there on Mar. 9, 1865. He was assigned as above and was then mustered out on July 14, 1865. John was listed in the veteran section of the 1885 Wisconsin State census at P.O. Menasha.
{WC-V; ROV}

MERGES, Peter - Pvt., Co. B, 3rd Regt., Wis. Cav.
Peter was born circa 1844 at Prussia. He was a son of Mary Merges. Mary was born circa 1822 at Prussia. She was listed in the 1860 federal census as residing in the fourth ward of the city of Oshkosh. Residing with her were the following children: Peter; Nicholas, born circa 1847; and Mary, born circa 1856. All of the children were born in Prussia. Peter enlisted at Oshkosh on Nov. 27, 1861. He was assigned as above and was mustered out on Jan. 27, 1865 at the end of his term of enlistment. Peter was listed in 1868 as a marble engraver boarding at 64 Merritt Street in Oshkosh. That was the home of Mary M. Merges, his mother.
{US 1860; ROV; T-1868}

MERKLEY, Hyronimous - Pvt., Co. C, 1st Regt., Wis. Hvy. Art.
Hyronimus was born circa 1837 at Wurtemburg, a son of John and Helina Merkley. Both parents were born circa 1810, also at Wurtemburg. They were listed in the 1850 and 1860 federal census as residing on a farm in the town of Vinland. With them were the following children: Heronimus; James (Simon), born circa 1841 at Germany; Margaret, born circa 1843 at Germany; Martha (Matheus), born circa 1849 at Wisconsin; Maria, born circa 1851 at Wisconsin; Elizabeth, born circa 1856 at Wisconsin; and John, born circa 1857 at Wisconsin. Helina Merkley died in the town of Vinland of general debility in Dec. 1894. Hyronimous listed his residence as Neenah when he enlisted on Sept. 28, 1863. He was assigned as above and was mustered out on Sept. 21, 1865. Hieronimous was married on Dec. 23, 1868 in Winnebago County to Margareth Schwarz. He was listed in 1883 at P.O. Neenah. He had then been receiving a pension of $8 per month since Feb. 1880 for an injury to his abdomen. Hyronimous was listed in the veteran section of the 1885, 1895 and 1905 Wisconsin State census at P.O. Neenah. He was listed in the 1890 federal census as residing in the town of Vinland at P.O. Neenah and suffering the effects of a rupture and piles as a result of his military service. Hyronimous and Margaret, his wife, were listed in 1905 as residing on 40 acres of section E-17 in the town of Vinland. John, William and Lewis Merkley were also listed as residing there.
{US 1860, 1890; WC-V 1885, 1895, 1905; ROV; WCMR v.1, p.399, #2492; B-1905}
{LOP-1883; OWN 15 Dec 1894}

MERRILL, James H. - Cpl., Co. B, 47th Regt., Wis. Vol. Inf.
James was born on Feb. 9, 1846 at Batavia, New York. He was a son of James B. Merrill. The family removed to Wisconsin in 1849 and settled at Milwaukee. James H. remained there for a time and then moved to East Troy, Walworth County. He enlisted in the Navy on June 15, 1863 and was assigned on the Mississippi River and the Gulf Squadron. He was assigned as a Landsman to the "Eastport," which was torpedoed. James was seriously injured in the explosion and was given up for dead. He was discharged on June 23, 1864 and returned home. After recovering from his wounds, James enlisted at East Troy on Jan. 23, 1865. He was then listed as a Veteran Volunteer and was assigned as above. James was promoted to Corporal in that company and was mustered out on Sept. 4, 1865. He then returned to New York and studied law in the office of his uncle, William Merrill. He returned to East Troy in 1867 and resumed law studies in the office of his father. James was admitted to the Bar of Wisconsin at Elkhorn and then removed to Winneconne to open his practice. He remained there until 1875, when he removed to Oshkosh. He was listed in the veteran section of the 1885 and 1895 Wisconsin State census at P.O. Oshkosh. James was listed in the 1890 federal census as residing at 123 E. Irving Street in the city of Oshkosh. During his military service, James had suffered the crushing of his left foot and the crippling of the great toe on that foot. He was also suffering from a hearing impairment. James was the Mayor of Oshkosh when, in June 1900, he left for a trip to New York City to visit a sister, Mrs. James (Jane) Kimberley. While there, he died suddenly on June 28, 1900. Frances, his wife, was then visiting a brother in Pierce City, Missouri and James was expected to meet her there shortly. He was survived by his wife, a sister-in-law Mrs. Sara Willis of Oshkosh, his sister in New York, one niece and one nephew. Frances, his widow, was listed in 1905 as residing at 197 Grand Avenue in Oshkosh. James was the namesake for Merrill Elementary and Junior High Schools in Oshkosh.
{US 1890; WC-V 1885, 1895, 1905; ROV; B-1905; ODN 28 June 1900}

MERRILL, Wilber F. - Pvt., Co. C, 46th Regt., Wis. Vol. Inf.
Wilber was born at Wilmington, Essex County, New York. He was a son of John Merrill and a brother of William W. from a following sketch. They were descendants of the original Merrill settlers in this country. The family was located in New Hampshire and Vermont. John was married to Hannah, daughter of Abner and Lois Hickok. He was also a soldier in the War of 1812. Wilber came to Wisconsin in 1862. John died at Omro in 1876. Son Wilber was listed as his executor. Wilber listed his residence as Omro when he enlisted on Feb. 3, 1865 and was assigned as above. He was promoted to Corporal when that company was mustered in on Mar. 2, 1865. Three days later the regiment left for Louisville, Kentucky where they were assigned to guard the Nashville & Decatur Railroad. About May 1 of that year, while in the midst of an attack of chronic diarrhea, Wilber suffered a sunstroke. He was relieved of duty and sent to Decatur, Alabama for four weeks. Wilber received orders on May 15, 1865 to report immediately for duty as a clerk for the Acting Assistant Adjutant General and remained in that position until he was mustered out at Nashville, Tennessee on Sept. 27, 1865. On Oct. 2, 1865 he arrived at Madison, Wisconsin. There he was paid and formally discharged. Wilber was married at Appleton, Outagamie County on Aug. 20, 1873 to Elma W., daughter of Rev. Merritt and Cyrene (Wood) Preston. Wilber and Elma had three children: Willard Jay; Leroy; and John. Elma died on Oct. 9, 1884. Wilber was listed in the veteran section of the 1885 Wisconsin State census at P.O. Appleton and in

MERRILL, Wilber F. (cont.)
that same section of the 1905 state census as a resident at the Wisconsin Veterans' Home at King.
{WC-V 1885, 1905; SCA p.642-3; ROV; GAR 40th; OmJ 21 Sep 1876}

MERRILL, William W. - Pvt., Co. C, 46th Regt., Wis. Vol. Inf.
William was a son of John and Hannah (Hickok) Merrill and a brother of Wilber from a previous sketch. He resided at Omro and enlisted there on Jan. 28, 1865. William was assigned as above and was promoted to Sergeant in that company. He was mustered out on Sept. 27, 1865.
{SCA p.642; ROV}

MERRITT, John James - Pvt., Co. K, 60th Regt., New York Vol. Inf.
John was married to Mary Louisa Boyd. They had a daughter, unnamed at registration, who was born in the town of Black Wolf on May 13, 1879. John was listed as above in the veteran section of the 1885 Wisconsin State census at P.O. Omro. Mary, widow of John, was listed in 1905 as residing at 139 Church Street in the city of Oshkosh. Daughter Mildred E. was residing at that same address. Mary died at her home in Oshkosh on Feb. 16, 1925 after an illness of about three months. Daughter Mildred E. was her only survivor.
{WC-V 1885; B-1905; WCBR v.2, p.152, #412; ODN 17 Feb 1925}

MERRY, Edward N. - Pvt., Co. B, 32nd Regt., Wis. Vol. Inf.
Edward resided at Springvale, Fond du Lac County and enlisted there on Aug. 21, 1862. He was assigned as above and was mustered out on June 12, 1865. Edward was listed in the veteran section of the 1885 Wisconsin State census at P.O. Rosendale, Fond du Lac County. He was listed in that section of the 1895 and 1905 state census at P.O. Neenah. Edward was listed in 1905 as a laborer residing at 202 E. Columbian Avenue in the city of Neenah. E.W. and Lillian E. Merry were also residing at that address.
{WC-V 1885, 1895, 1905; ROV; B-1905}

MESSINGER, Francis C. - Pvt., Co. C, 46th Regt., Wis. Vol. Inf.
Francis was born circa 1812 at Massachusetts. Mildred Agnes, his wife, was born circa 1820 at Virginia. Francis was listed in the 1860 federal census as a printer residing in the first ward of the city of Oshkosh. Listed with him were his wife and a son, Charles, who was born circa 1836 at Virginia. Francis resided at Oshkosh and enlisted there on Jan. 30, 1865. He was assigned as above and was mustered out on Sept. 27, 1865.
{US 1860; ROV}

METTAM, Thomas - Pvt., Co. F, 37th Regt., Wis. Vol. Inf.
Thomas was born on Nov. 1, 1820 at Lincolnshire, England. He mas married there on July 15, 1848 to Sarah Walker. She was born on Aug. 15, 1824 at Nottinghamshire, England and was a daughter of John and Sarah (Wells) Walker. Thomas and Sarah emigrated to America in 1849 and settled in Winnebago County on a farm in the town of Poygan, where they were listed in the 1860 federal census. They then had the following children: Edward, born circa 1850 at Wisconsin; Sarah Ann, died on Feb. 2, 1862 at age 9 years, 10 months and 10 days; Eliza Jane, died on Feb. 13, 1862 at age 8 years; Mary M., born circa 1858 at Wisconsin; and George H. Mettam, born after 1860. Thomas was drafted at Poygan on Nov. 5, 1864. He was assigned as above and was

METTAN, Thomas (cont.)
mustered out on July 27, 1865. He returned to Poygan and engaged there in farming. Thomas died at Poygan on Feb. 27, 1877. Sarah was listed in the 1890 federal census as residing in the town of Poygan at P.O. Omro. She was listed in 1905 as residing on 130 acres of section 35 in the town of Poygan. She died there on Feb. 20, 1906. Thomas and Sarah are buried with daughters Eliza and Sarah in the town of Poygan at Oak Hill Cemetery.
{US 1860, 1890; Randall p.50; Cem. records; ROV; B-1905}

METZIG, Benjamin - Pvt., Co. D, 50th Regt., Wis. Vol. Inf.
Benjamin was born on Aug. 29, 1823 at Saxony. Johanna R., his wife, was born there on Oct. 26, 1827. They were listed in the 1860 federal census as residing on a farm in the town of Winchester. Listed with them were the following children: Charles, born circa 1851 at Saxony; William, born circa 1853 at Saxony; Julia, born circa 1857 at Wisconsin; and Henrietta, born circa 1859 at Wisconsin. His brother Godhelf, subject of a following sketch, lived nearby. Benjamin listed his residence as Oakland, Jefferson County when he enlisted on Feb. 11, 1865. He was assigned as above and was mustered out on June 12, 1866 at the end of his term of enlistment. His brother Gothelf and an August Metzig were also assigned to that company. Benjamin was not found in the veteran section of the 1885 Wisconsin State census. He was listed in the 1890 federal census as residing in the town of Wolf River at P.O. Zittau. At that time Benjamin was listed as receiving a pension. He was listed in the veteran section of the 1895 state census at P.O. Zittau. Benjamin died on Dec. 15, 1898. Johanna then resided with Mrs. H. Moser in the town of Wolf River until she died on Feb. 18, 1905. Both are buried in the town of Wolf River at Immanuel Lutheran Cemetery. Others of the Metzig family are buried in that same cemetery.
{US 1860, 1890; WC-V 1885, 1895, 1905; ROV; B-1905; Cem. records}

METZIG, Gothelf - Sgt., Co. D, 50th Regt., Wis. Vol. Inf.
Gothelf was born circa 1823 at Saxony. He was a brother of Benjamin from a previous sketch. Gothelf was listed as Gottlieb when he was married in Winnebago County on Dec. 4, 1859 to Ernestina Lueck. She was born circa 1835 at Prussia. They were listed in the 1860 federal census as residing on a farm in the town of Winchester. Gothelf listed his residence as Otsego, Columbia County when he enlisted there on Feb. 11, 1865. He was assigned as above and was promoted to Corporal and then Sergeant in that company. He was mustered out on June 12, 1866 at the end of his term of enlistment. Gothelf was listed in the veteran section of the 1885 Wisconsin State census at P.O. Zittau. Ernestine, his widow, was listed in the 1890 federal census as residing in the town of Wolf River at P.O. Zittau. She provided that her husband had died of cancer on Jan. 19, 1877. Ernestina was listed in 1905 as residing with Fred W. and Albertina Metzig in section 13 of the town of Wolf River.
{US 1860, 1890; WC-V 1885; ROV; B-1905; WCMR v.1, p.196, #1008}

MEYER - see also: Maier, Mayer, Meier

MEYER, Carl - Cpl., Co. D, 13th Regt., Ohio Cav.
Carl was listed in the Wisconsin records as having enlisted at Oshkosh on June 4, 1861. He was assigned as a Private to the 3rd Regt., Wis. Cav. and was listed as having deserted on Sept. 10, 1862. Charles was married in Winnebago County on June 5, 1867

MEYER, Carl (cont.)
to Ernestine Louise Steinke. Carl was listed in the veteran section of the 1885 Wisconsin State census as a veteran of the 3rd Regt., Wis. Vol. Inf. and residing at Oshkosh. He does not appear in the records of that regiment. While on a reunion excursion with members of GAR Post #10 from Oshkosh, Carl fell overboard and was drowned in Lake Winnebago on Sept. 1, 1886. He was 50 years old at the time of his death and he left a wife and a large family in Oshkosh. Louise, widow of Carl, was listed in the 1890 federal census as residing in the city of Oshkosh. She provided his unit designation as above and his enlistment date as having been May 5, 1864. Carl was still listed in the veteran section of the 1895 Wisconsin State census as a veteran of the 2nd Regt., Wis. Cav. at P.O. Oshkosh. Louisa was listed in 1905 as residing at 170 Thirteenth Street in Oshkosh. Son Bernhard was then residing with her. Louisa was born on Apr. 16, 1850 and died on July 4, 1929. Carl is buried with a simple military marker. A son, Eduard, was born on Feb. 16, 1872 and died on Nov. 3, 1882. All three are buried in the town of Algoma at Peace Lutheran Cemetery.
{US 1890; WC-V 1885, 1895; ODN 01 Sep 1886; WCMR v.1, p.325, #2048; B-1905} {Cem. records; ROV; OWN 09 Sep 1886}

MEYER, Frederick - Pvt., Co. B, 3rd Regt., Wis. Vol. Inf.
Fred enlisted at Oshkosh on June 4, 1861 and was assigned as above. He was wounded in the hip at Antietam, Maryland on Sept. 17, 1862 and was mustered out on June 29, 1864 at the end of his term of enlistment. Fred was listed in 1883 at P.O. Oshkosh. He was then receiving a pension of $2 per month for a wound to his right hip joint. He was listed in 1888 as a member of GAR Post #10 at Oshkosh. Fred was listed in the veteran section of the 1885, 1895 and 1905 Wisconsin State census at P.O. Oshkosh. His name was spelled variously as Meier, Myer and Meyer.
{US 1890; WC-V 1885, 1895, 1905; ROV; OWN 02 Oct 1862; LOP-1883}

MEYER, Simon - Pvt., Co. I, 11th Regt., Wis. Vol. Inf.
Simon resided at Madison, Dane County and enlisted there on Feb. 8, 1865. He was assigned as above and was mustered out on Sept. 4, 1865. Simon was listed in the 1890 federal census as residing in the city of Oshkosh.
{US 1890; ROV}

MICHELSON, Andrew - 1st Sgt., Co. K, 11th Regt., Wis. Vol. Inf.
Andrew resided at Clayton and enlisted there on Sept. 28, 1861. He was assigned as above and he re-enlisted in that same company at the end of his term. Andrew was promoted to Corporal, Sergeant and 1st Sergeant in that company. He was mustered out on Sept. 4, 1865. Andrew was listed in the veteran section of the 1885 Wisconsin State census at P.O. Neenah. Mary, his widow, was listed in 1905 as residing with her daughter Anna at 301 S. Commercial Street in the city of Neenah.
{WC-V 1885; ROV; B-1905}

MILES, Clark G. - Pvt., Co. A, 3rd Regt., Wis. Cav.
Clark resided at Algoma and enlisted there on Dec. 6, 1863. He was assigned as above and was then transferred to Co. K, 3rd (reorg.) Regt., Wis. Cav. on Mar. 23, 1865. He was mustered out on July 19, 1865. Elizabeth, wife of Clark, died on Apr. 7, 1869 at age 28 years, 6 months and 28 days. Clifford C., a son, died on Dec. 13, 1869 at age

MILES, Clark G. (cont.)
8 months and 23 days. Elizabeth and Clifford are buried in the town of Algoma at Ellenwood Cemetery, Section B.
{ROV; Cem. records}

MILES, John F. - Pvt., Co. E, 2nd Regt., Wis. Vol. Inf.
John was born circa 1843 at Ohio. Esther, his mother, was born circa 1811 at Pennsylvania. She was listed in the 1860 federal census as residing with Morrell Bailey in the town of Algoma. Listed with her were the following children: John; Jane, born circa 1846 at Ohio; Esther, born circa 1851 at Wisconsin; and Alice, born circa 1853 at Wisconsin. John resided at Algoma and enlisted there on Apr. 21, 1861. He was assigned as above and was discharged on Sept. 25, 1861 due to a disability. John re-enlisted on Nov. 11, 1861 and was assigned as Private, Co. F, 18th Regt., Wis. Vol. Inf. He was discharged again on July 12, 1862. John was married in Winnebago County on Aug. 9, 1868 to Elisabeth Holmes. He was listed that same year as a filer residing at 6 Wisconsin Street in the city of Oshkosh. John was reported to be living at Hurley, Iron County in a 1899 article by Col. Harshaw
{US 1860; ROV; T-1868; ODN 07 May 1899; WCMR v.1, p.387, #2395}

MILES, Martin M. - Pvt., Co. C, 53rd Regt., Wis. Vol. Inf.
Martin was born circa 1825 at New York. According to her marker, his wife Betsey died on Aug. 11, 1856 at age 24 years. She is buried in the town of Nepeuskun at Koro Cemetery. Martin was married second to Elizabeth Ostrander in Winnebago County on June 5, 1858. She was born circa 1836 at New York. They were listed in the 1860 federal census as residing on a farm in the town of Utica at P.O. Oshkosh. George, their son, was born circa 1859 at Wisconsin. Also residing with them was a Mary Ostrander who was born circa 1830 at New York and her daughter, E.A. Ostrander, who was born circa 1854 at Wisconsin. Martin resided at Utica and enlisted there on Mar. 8, 1865. He was assigned as above. That company was transferred to Co. K, 51st Regt., Wis. Vol. Inf. by orders dated June 10, 1865. The transfer was completed on June 30, 1865 at Ft. Leavenworth, Kansas. The regiment then returned to Madison, Wisconsin on Aug. 1, 1865 and was mustered out by companies. The last company was mustered out on Aug. 30, 1865.
{US 1860; ROV; WCMR v.1, p.185, #925; Cem. records}

MILLARD, Napoleon B. - Pvt., Co. B, 3rd Regt., Wis. Cav.
Napoleon was born circa 1820 at New York. He was in Winnebago County in 1849 when he claimed ownership of the lands of Frederick Preston. He was married in Winnebago County in 1855 to Mariam Neff. Napoleon was listed in the 1860 federal census as a lumberman residing in the fourth ward of the city of Oshkosh. Residing with him were: Mary, his wife, born circa 1838 at New York; Edna, born circa 1857 at Wisconsin; and Bonaparte, born circa 1858 at Wisconsin. Napoleon enlisted at Oshkosh on Nov. 23, 1861. He was assigned as above and was listed as having deserted on Jan. 21, 1863. Napoleon returned to that company on Apr. 25, 1865 and was mustered out on May 15, 1865. He was listed in 1868 as a lumberman then residing at 150 Nebraska Street in Oshkosh. He was listed in the veteran section of the 1885 Wisconsin State census at P.O. Oshkosh.
{US 1860; WC-V 1885; ROV; T-1868; OTD 11 May 1849; OWC 12 Sep 1855}

MILLARD, Wellington H. - Cpl., Co. C, 21st Regt., Wis. Vol. Inf.
Wellington was born circa 1830 at New York. He was listed in the 1860 federal census as a lumberman residing with the family of William R. Garrick in the third ward of the city of Oshkosh. Wellington resided at Oshkosh and enlisted there on Aug. 14, 1862. He was assigned as above and was promoted to Corporal in that company. Wellington was killed on Oct. 8, 1862 at Chaplin Hills, Kentucky.
{US 1860; ROV; OWN 07 May 1863}

MILLER - see also: Mueller, Muller

MILLER, A.L. - Civil War Veteran?
His wife was listed in the 1920 reunion booklet of the 21st Regt., Wis. Vol. Inf. as then residing at Winneconne. Associate members of that unit were veterans of the Civil War from other regiments or wives of Civil War veterans.
{21-33rd}

MILLER, Adam - Sgt., Co. H, 105th Regt., Pennsylvania Vol. Inf.
Adam was born in May 1844 at Pennsylvania. His parents were both natives of that state. Adam was listed in the 1900 federal census as residing at the Wisconsin Veterans' Home at King. He had been married then for two years and his wife was not residing there with him. Adam was listed as above in the veteran section of the 1905 Wisconsin State census at P.O. Oshkosh.
{US 1900; WC-V 1885}

MILLER, Alonzo E. - Lt., 6th Regt., Mississippi Colored Troops.
Alonzo was born circa 1840 at New Brunswick, Canada. He was a son of George and Mary Miller and a brother of Charles from a following sketch. George and Mary were both natives of New Brunswick, he born circa 1817 and she born circa 1819. They were listed in the 1860 federal census as residing on a farm in the town of Utica at P.O. Welaunee. Listed with them were the following children: Ira, born circa 1839; Alonzo; Charles; Ezra, born circa 1846; Helen, born circa 1847; George, born circa 1849; Eugene, born circa 1851; Albert, born circa 1853; Orlena, born circa 1855; Orin, born circa 1856; and Franklin, born circa 1858. The first four children were born in New Brunswick and the others were all born in Wisconsin. Colin, brother of George and subject of a following sketch, was also residing with them. Alonzo resided at Utica and enlisted on Sept. 16, 1861. He was assigned as Private, Co. C, 14th Regt., Wis. Vol. Inf. and was promoted to Corporal and then Sergeant in that company. He was wounded at Shiloh, Tennessee. Alonzo was discharged on June 10, 1863 to accept his commisison as a Lieutenant, 6th Regt., Mississippi Colored Troops.
{US 1860; ROV}

MILLER, Charles - Pvt., Co. G, 26th Regt., Illinois Vol. Inf.
Charles was listed as above in the veteran section of the 1885 Wisconsin State census at P.O. Menasha.
{WC-V 1885}

MILLER, Charles H. - Cpl., Co. B, 21st Regt., Wis. Vol. Inf.
Charles was born circa 1844 at New Brunswick, Canada. He was a son of George and Mary Miller and a brother of Alonzo from a previous sketch. Charles was listed in the

MILLER, Charles H. (cont.)
1860 federal census as residing with his parents and their family in the town of Utica at P.O. Welaunee. He enlisted at Utica on Aug. 12, 1862. He was assigned as above and was promoted to Corporal in that company. Charles was wounded at Dallas, Georgia and was mustered out on June 8, 1865. He was listed in the veteran section of the 1885 and 1895 Wisconsin State census at P.O. Waukau. Charles was listed in the 1890 federal census as residing in the town of Rushford at P.O. Waukau. He listed that he had suffered a wound to his right arm. Charles was listed in the veteran section of the 1905 state census at P.O. Oshkosh. He was listed in 1905 as residing at 321 Wisconsin Avenue in the city of Oshkosh. Letta M. Miller was residing with him. Charles was listed in 1920 as residing at Tacoma, Washington.
{US 1860, 1890; WC-V 1885, 1895, 1905; ROV; 21-33rd; B-1905}

MILLER, Colin - 1st Lt., Co. C, 14th Regt., Wis. Vol. Inf.
Colin was born circa 1820 at New Brunswick, Canada. He was listed in the 1860 federal census as a speculator residing with the family of George Miller, his brother, in the town of Utica at P.O. Welaunee. Colin was an uncle of Alonzo and Charles Miller of previous sketches. He resided at Utica and enlisted there on Sept. 8, 1861. He was assigned as a Private in the above company and was then commissioned as 1st Lieutenant of that company on Oct. 1, 1861. He was placed temporarily in command of Co. F of the same regiment and was wounded on May 22, 1863 at Vicksburg, Mississippi. Colin died of those wounds on May 23, 1863.
{US 1860; ROV}

MILLER, John F. - Pvt., Co. B, 17th Regt., Wis. Vol. Inf.
John was drafted on Sept. 22, 1864. He was assigned as above and was mustered out on June 2, 1865. He was listed in the veteran section of the 1885 Wisconsin State census at P.O. Neenah. John was listed in the 1890 federal census as residing in the town of Clayton at P.O. Neenah. He was listed in 1905 as retired and residing at 416 Washington Street in the city of Neenah. Edward C., Helen A., Hulda E. and Lena Miller were then residing at that same address.
{US 1890; WC-V 1885; ROV; B-1905}

MILLER, John Leverett - Pvt., Co. E, 2nd Regt., Wis. Vol. Inf.
John was born in 1839. He listed his residence as Oshkosh when he enlisted there on May 18, 1861. He was assigned as above and was mustered out on June 28, 1864 at the end of his term of enlistment. John was married in Winnebago County on Oct. 17, 1867 to Marietta Bunten. They had at least the following children: Ida J., born in 1872, died in 1958; Charles L., born in 1874, died in 1950; twin sons, both unnamed at registration, who were born in Oshkosh on Feb. 9, 1879; and Charlotte C., born in 1882, died in 1957. John was listed in the veteran section of the 1885 and 1905 Wisconsin State census at P.O. Oshkosh. He was listed in the 1890 federal census as residing in the city of Oshkosh. John listed that he had suffered a foot wound during his military service. He was listed in 1905 as a laborer residing at 327 Tenth Street in Oshkosh. John died in 1910. Marietta was born in 1842 and died in 1925. They are buried with several of their children in the town of Algoma at Ellenwood Cemetery, Section F.
{US 1890; WC-V 1885, 1905; WCMR v.1, p.361, #2185; Cem. records; B-1905; ROV}
{WCBR v.2, p.136, #364}

MILLER, John W. - Pvt., Co. I, 21st Regt., Wis. Vol. Inf.
John resided at Vinland and enlisted there on Aug. 13, 1862. He was assigned as above and was taken prisoner at Chickamauga, Georgia on Sept. 20, 1863. John was mustered out on June 8, 1865. He was listed in 1883 at P.O. Neenah, where he had then been receiving a pension of $4 per month since Mar. 1882 for chronic diarrhea and a kidney disease.
{ROV; LOP-1883; Lawson p.833}

MILLER, Leonard J. - Sgt., Co. B, 21st Regt., Wis. Vol. Inf.
Leonard was born in 1834 at York County, New Brunswick, Canada. He was a son of Isaac and Harriet Miller. They came to Winnebago County in 1850. Leonard received a common school education and was engaged in farming. He was also engaged in the lumbering business in northern Wisconsin. Leonard listed his residence as Winneconne when he enlisted on Aug. 13, 1862. He was assigned as above and was promoted to Corporal and then Sergeant in that company. Leonard was wounded at Resaca, Georgia and recovered enough to rejoin the regiment at Goldsboro. He was mustered out on June 8, 1865. Leonard was married in 1865 to Mary A. Benedict. The records of marriage for Winnebago County list her as Mary A. Cross and provide a marriage date of Nov. 17, 1868. After their marriage, Leonard and Mary moved to a farm at Utica. They had three children: Winifred; Warren A.; and Della M. Miller. He was listed in 1883 at P.O. Elo. Leonard was then receiving a pension of $4 per month for wounds to his face and side. He was listed in the 1890 federal census as residing in the town of Utica at P.O. Elo. Leonard reported that he had suffered a gunshot wound to his face, neck and side. He died at his home in Utica on Nov. 3, 1900. Leonard was survived by his wife, a daughter, Mrs. T.R. Lewellyn of Utica, a son, Warren A. Miller, principal of Park School at Kaukauna, and a brother, John A. Miller of Washington state. Mary A., his widow, was listed in 1905 as residing on 80 acres of section 16 in the town of Utica.
{US 1890; ROV; LOP-1883; Randall p.52; WCMR v.1, p.388, #2400*; B-1905}
{ODN 04 Nov 1900}

MILLER, Miles P. - Pvt., 9th Batt., Wis. Lt. Art.
Miles was born circa 1838 at Pennsylvania. He was a son of Abram and Ann Miller and a brother to Solomon of a following sketch. Ann was born circa 1810 at Pennsylvania and Abram was born circa 1800 at Switzerland. He was listed in the 1860 federal census as a mason residing in the third ward of the city of Oshkosh. Residing with him were his wife and the following children: Eleanor, born circa 1834; Richard, born circa 1836; Miles; Solomon; John, born circa 1845; Daniel, born circa 1847; and George, born circa 1850. All of the children were born in Pennsylvania. Miles resided at Oshkosh when he enlisted on Oct. 19, 1861. He was assigned as above and he re-enlisted in that same company at the end of his term. Miles was mustered out on Sept. 30, 1865. He was married in Winnebago County on July 14, 1866 to Mary Jacobs. He was listed in the veteran section of the 1905 state census at P.O. Oshkosh. He was listed in 1905 as retired and rooming at 202 Tenth Street in the city of Oshkosh. Miles died on June 7, 1923. He is buried in Oshkosh at Riverside Cemetery, GAR Plot, east row, #24 from the south.
{US 1860; WC-V 1905; Cem. records; B-1905; WCMR v.1, p.302, #1863; ROV}

MILLER, Nelson - Pvt., Co. B, 21st Regt., Wis. Vol. Inf.
Nelson resided at Winneconne and enlisted there on Aug. 14, 1862. He was assigned as above. Nelson contracted a disease and died on Nov. 24, 1862 at Mitchellville, Tennessee.
{ROV}

MILLER, Solomon - Pvt., 9th Batt., Wis. Lt. Art.
Solomon was born circa 1842/4 at Pennsylvania. He was a son of Abram and Ann Miller and a brother of Miles of a previous sketch. Solomon was listed in the 1860 federal census as a farm hand for Fred. Chittenden in the town of Black Wolf. He listed his residence as Oshkosh when he enlisted on Oct. 19, 1861. He was assigned as above and re-enlisted in that same company at the end of his term. He was then mustered out on Sept. 30, 1865. Solomon was listed (Saul) in the veteran section of the 1885 Wisconsin State census at P.O. Waupaca, Waupaca County. He was listed in 1888 as a member of GAR Post #21 at Waupaca and he was listed in the 1890 federal census as residing in the city of Waupaca.
{US 1860, 1890; WC-V 1885; ROV; SCA}

MILLER, Tannes E. - Pvt., Co. C, 1st Regt., Wis. Hvy. Art.
Tannes was born circa 1841 at Norway. He was a son of Andrew and Sophie Miller. The parents were also natives of Norway and were both born circa 1814. They were listed in the 1860 federal census as residing on a farm in the town of Winneconne. Listed with them were the following children: Tonnes; Frederick, born circa 1845; Andrew, born circa 1848; Sophia, born circa 1851; and Barent, born circa 1853. The children were all born in Norway. Tannes listed his residence as Winneconne when he enlisted on Sept. 23, 1863. He was assigned as a Musician with the above company and he was mustered out on Sept. 21, 1865.
{US 1860; ROV}

MILLER, Theron F. - Pvt., Co. B, 161st Regt., New York Vol. Inf.
Theron was listed in the 1890 federal census as residing in the town of Rushford at P.O. Eureka. He then provided his unit designation as above and his service dates as having been from June 14, 1864 to Nov. 12, 1865. Theron also provided that he had suffered a wound to the knee. He was listed in the veteran section of the 1895 Wisconsin State census at P.O. Eureka.
{US 1890; WC-V 1895}

MILLER, Tobias C. - Pvt., Co. C, 14th Regt., Wis. Vol. Inf.
Tobias was born on Oct. 8, 1841 at Norway. He was a son of Tobias and Christina Miller and a brother of Tonnes from a following sketch. The parents were also natives of Norway, the father born there circa 1809 and the mother born circa 1816. They were listed in the 1860 federal census as residing on a farm in the town of Winneconne. Listed with them were the following children: Tonnes; Tobias; Amelia, born circa 1845; Conrad, born circa 1848; Henry, born circa 1854; and Ludwig, born circa 1858. The two youngest children were born in Wisconsin and the others were born in Norway. Tobias enlisted at Omro on Feb. 2, 1864 and was assigned as above. He was mustered out on Oct. 9, 1865. Tobias was married in Winnebago County on Apr. 7, 1866 to Ann Halverson. He was married second in Winnebago County on June 29, 1871 to Florence E. Henry. Tobias and his second wife had a daughter, Inez Luella, who was born in

MILLER, Tobias C. (cont.)
Winneconne on Nov. 26, 1877. Tobias was listed as a member of GAR Post #241 at Oshkosh in 1888. He was listed in the veteran section of the 1885, 1895 and 1905 Wisconsin State census at P.O. Winneconne. He was listed in the 1890 federal census as residing in the town of Winneconne at P.O. Winneconne. Tobias was listed in 1905 as residing on 169 acres of section 15 in the town of Winneconne. A Subert Miller was then residing with him. Tobias was still residing on that land in 1909. He died Dec. 27, 1923 and is buried at Winneconne Cemetery, Block 4, lot 14.
{US 1860, 1890; WC-V 1885, 1895, 1905; WCP-1909; WCMR v.1, p.295, #1808*}
{GRI; ROV; WCMR v.1, p.502, #3313; WCBR v.2, p.83, #205}

MILLER, Tonnes O. - Pvt.,Co. C, 1st Regt., Wis. Hvy. Art.
Tonnes was born circa 1839 at Norway. He was a son of Tobias and Christina Miller and a brother of Tobias from a previous sketch. Tonnes enlisted on Sept. 1, 1864. He was assigned as above and was mustered out on June 16, 1865. Tonnes was married in Winnebago County on Apr. 7, 1866 to Ann Halverson.
{US 1860; ROV; WCMR v.1, p.295, #1808*}

MILLHISER, Frank - Pvt., Co. B, 13th Regt., Wis. Vol. Inf.
Frank listed his residence as Waukegan, Illinois when he enlisted on Sept. 10, 1861. He was assigned as above and he re-enlisted in that same company at the end of his term. Frank was mustered out on Nov. 24, 1865. He was listed in the veteran section of the 1885 Wisconsin State census at P.O. Oshkosh.
{WC-V 1885; ROV}

MILLIKEN, L.B. - Pvt., Co. F, 12th Regt., Maine Vol. Inf.
He was listed as above in the veteran section of the 1905 Wisconsin State census at P.O. Oshkosh. He was listed then as residing at 223 Elm Street in the city of Oshkosh. Alice Milliken was residing at that same address.
{WC-V 1905; B-1905}

MILLS, Eugene W. - Pvt., Co. A, 48th Regt., Wis. Vol. Inf.
Eugene was born on Aug. 8, 1847 at Wisconsin. He was a son of William E. and Emily C. (Hatch) Mills. William was born on Dec. 20, 1821 at Ohio. He was a son of Isaac and Polly (Adams) Mills. William was reared on a farm in Portage County, Ohio. He was married on Oct. 16, 1845 to Emily. She was born July 10, 1825 at Ohio and was a daughter of Moses and Cornelia (French) Hatch. William and Emily had the following children: Eugene W.; Alma, born on Aug. 13, 1850; Ellery Duane, born on Mar. 3, 1853; Harry V., born on Dec. 17, 1857; Frank L., born on Apr. 23, 1860; and Hattie M., born on Apr. 16, 1862. William removed to a farm of 70 acres in the town of Omro. Eugene listed his residence as Algoma when he enlisted on Feb. 11, 1865. He was assigned as a musician in the above company and was mustered out on Dec. 30, 1865. Eugene died on July 5, 1870.
{US 1860; ROV; Randall p.30}

MILLS, George - Pvt., Co. E, 5th (reorg.) Regt., Wis. Vol. Inf.
George was born circa 1820 at New York. Abigail, his wife, was also born circa 1820 at New York. They were listed in the 1860 federal census as residing on a farm in the town of Vinland. Listed with them were a daughter, Jane, who was born circa 1845 at

MILLS, George (cont.)
New York, and a son, Eugene, who was born circa 1848 at New York. George listed his residence as Winneconne when he enlisted on Sept. 3, 1864. He was assigned as above. George was killed in action on Apr. 6, 1865 at Sailor's Creek, Virginia. Abigail, his wife, was listed in 1883 at P.O. Butte des Morts. She was then receiving a widow's pension of $8 per month. Abigail was listed in the 1890 federal census as residing in the village of Winneconne. She was listed in 1905 as residing in the village of Butte des Morts.
{US 1860, 1890; ROV; LOP-1883; B-1905}

MINCKLER, Levi - Pvt., Co. F, 18th Regt., Wis. Vol. Inf.
Levi listed his residence as Oshkosh when he enlisted there on Oct. 21, 1861. He was assigned as above and was taken prisoner at Shiloh, Tennessee. Levi contracted a disease and died on June 16, 1862 at Montgomery, Alabama. Mary A., wife of Levi, died on May 7, 1864 at age 42 years, 10 months and 1 day. She is buried in the town of Omro at Minckler Cemetery.
{ROV; Cem. records}

MIRACLE, John - Pvt., Co. C, 1st Regt., Wis. Hvy. Art.
John resided at Oshkosh and enlisted there on Sept. 12, 1863. He was assigned as above and was mustered out on Sept. 21, 1865.
{ROV}

MIRACLE, Lawrence - Pvt., Co. E, 15th Regt., Michigan Vol. Inf.
Lawrence was listed as above in the veteran section of the 1885, 1895 and 1905 Wisconsin State census at P.O. Menasha. He was listed in the 1890 federal census as residing in the city of Menasha. He then provided that he had lost his right leg during his military service. Lawrence was listed in 1905 as retired and residing at 631 Tayco Street in Menasha. Dottie Miracle was residing at that same address.
{US 1890; WC-V 1885, 1895, 1905; B-1905}

MITCHELL, James A. - Cpl., Co. D, 41st Regt., Wis. Vol. Inf.
James was born circa 1845 at New Brunswick, Canada. He was a son of Thomas and Mary Mitchell and a brother of Thomas H. from a following sketch. Thomas was born circa 1815 at Ireland. He was listed in the 1860 federal census as a dry goods and grocery dealer residing in the second ward of the village of Menasha. Mary, his wife, was born circa 1817, also at Ireland. Listed with them were the following children: Sarah, born circa 1842; Eliza, born circa 1843; James; Thomas, born circa 1847; David, born circa 1849; Mary, born circa 1852; John, born circa 1855; Anna, born circa 1857; and Margaret, born circa 1860. The last four children were born in Wisconsin and the others were born in New Brunswick. James enlisted at Menasha on May 2, 1864. He was assigned as above and was promoted to Corporal in that company. James was then mustered out on Sept. 23, 1864 at the end of his term of enlistment. He drowned at St. Paul, Minnesota circa 1876.
{US 1860; ROV; Lawson p.840}

MITCHELL, James Harley - Pvt., Co. B, 37th Regt., Wis. Vol. Inf.
James was born on Apr. 24, 1846. Anna, his wife, was born on Mar. 21, 1852. James resided at Utica and enlisted there on Mar. 31, 1864. He was assigned as above and was

MITCHELL, James Harley (cont.)
mustered out on July 27, 1865. James was married in Winnebago County on Aug. 13, 1866 to Amy Perkins. He was listed in the veteran section of the 1885 Wisconsin State census at P.O. Auroraville and in that section of the 1895 census at P.O. Fargoville, both in Waupaca County. James was listed in that section of the 1905 state census at P.O. Omro. He was listed in 1905 as residing on 60 acres of section 5 in the town of Rushford. Then residing with him were his wife and Ella, William, Nellie, Ray and Lucy Mitchell. James died on Feb. 9, 1921 and Anna died on Sept. 23, 1930. Both are buried in the town of Rushford at Eureka Cemetery.
{WC-V 1885, 1895, 1905; B-1905; WCP-1909; ROV; WCMR v.1, p.305, #1883}
{Cem. records}

MITCHELL, Samuel B. - Pvt., Co. C, 6th Regt., Wis. Vol. Inf.
Samuel was born circa 1816 at Maine. Caroline, his wife, was born circa 1825 at New York. They were listed in the 1860 federal census as residing on a farm in the town of Neenah. Listed with them were the following children: Mary, born circa 1851; Alice, born circa 1853; and Nellie, born circa 1859. All three children were born in Wisconsin. Samuel was drafted at Clayton on Mar. 20, 1865. He was assigned as above and was mustered out on July 14, 1865. Caroline, his widow, was listed in 1905 as residing on 80 acres of section 34 in the town of Neenah.
{US 1860, ROV; B-1905}

MITCHELL, Thomas - Pvt., Permanent Guard, Wis. Vol. Inf.
Thomas resided at Nekimi and enlisted there on Mar. 4, 1865. He was assigned as above and was transferred to Co. K, 22nd Regt., Wis. Vol. Inf. on May 11, 1865. Thomas was again transferred as unassigned to the 3rd Regt., Wis. Vol. Inf. on June 10, 1865 and he was mustered out on June 24, 1865.
{ROV}

MITCHELL, Thomas H. - Pvt., Co. D, 41st Regt., Wis. Vol. Inf.
Thomas was born circa 1847 at New Brunswick, Canada. He was a son of Thomas and Mary Mitchell and a brother of James A. from a previous sketch. Thomas resided at Menasha and enlisted there on May 2, 1864. He was assigned as above and was then mustered out on Sept. 23, 1864 at the end of his term of enlistment.
{US 1860; ROV}

MOFFSHER, Jacob J. - Pvt., Co. M, 9th Regt., Pennsylvania Cav.
Jacob was listed as above in the veteran section of the 1895 Wisconsin State census at P.O. Oshkosh.
{WC-V 1895}

MOHR, Hans - Pvt., Co. F, 19th Regt., Wis. Vol. Inf.
Hans resided at Oshkosh and enlisted there on Sept. 5, 1864. He was assigned as above and was then transferred to Co. C of that same regiment on May 1, 1865. Hans was mustered out on June 26, 1865.
{ROV}

MOLL, Henry - Pvt., Co. G, 9th Regt., Wis. Vol. Inf.
Henry resided at Oshkosh and enlisted there on Sept. 19, 1861. He was assigned as

MOLL, Henry (cont.)
above and was taken prisoner at Newtonia. Henry was mustered out on Dec. 3, 1864 at the end of his term of enlistment. He was listed in 1905 as a laborer residing at the corner of Ninteenth and Alaska Streets in the city of Oshkosh.
{ROV; B-1905}

MOLL, Joseph - Pvt., Co. D, 51st Regt., Wis. Vol. Inf.
Joseph resided at Menasha and enlisted there on Mar. 10, 1865. He was assigned as above and was mustered out on Aug. 29, 1865.
{ROV}

MOLLET, Jacob S. - Pvt., Co. F, 32nd Regt., Wis. Vol. Inf.
Jacob resided at Oshkosh and enlisted there on Jan. 1, 1864. He was assigned as above and was then transferred to Co. G, 16th Regt., Wis. Vol. Inf. on June 4, 1865. He listed his address at that time as being Ellington, Outagamie County. Jacob was mustered out on July 12, 1865.
{ROV}

MONEAUX, A. - Civil War Veteran?
He was listed in the veteran section of the 1895 Wisconsin State census at P.O. Clayton as a veteran from the state of Michigan.
{WC-V 1895}

MONREAU, Michael - Pvt., Co. B, 46th Regt., Wis. Vol. Inf.
Michael resided at Berlin, Green Lake County and enlisted there on Jan. 30, 1865. He was assigned as above and was mustered out on Sept. 27, 1865. Michael was listed in the 1890 federal census as residing in the town of Nepeuskun at P.O. Rush Lake. He then provided information that he was suffering from the effects of asthma and a heart disease.
{US 1890; ROV}

MONROE, Sylvanus - Sgt., Co. C, 128th Regt., Indiana Vol. Inf.
Sylvanus was listed as a member of the 29th Regt., Indiana Vol. Inf. in the veteran section of the 1905 Wisconsin State census at P.O. Oshkosh. He was listed that year as a dealer in stationery and books residing at 56 S. Main Street in the city of Oshkosh. Sylvanus is buried in Oshkosh at Riverside Cemetery, GAR plot, west row, #4 from the south. His marker provides his unit designation as above.
{WC-V 1905; B-1905; Cem. records}

MONTGOMERY, Frank L. - Pvt., Co. C, 46th Regt., Wis. Vol. Inf.
Frank was born circa 1847 at New Hampshire, a son of W.S. and Mary Montgomery. The father was born circa 1821 at New Hampshire and Mary was born circa 1828 at England. They were listed in the 1860 federal census as residing on a farm in the town of Omro. Listed with them were the following children: Frank; George, born circa 1851 at Wisconsin; and Mary, born circa 1859 at Wisconsin. Frank listed his residence as Oshkosh when he enlisted on Jan. 18, 1865. He was assigned as above and was mustered out on Oct. 28, 1865.
{US 1860; ROV}

MOODY, Manley - Cpl., Co. A, 50th Regt., Wis. Vol. Inf.
Manley was born in 1833. Desiah, his wife, was born in 1838. Manley resided at Rushford and enlisted there on Feb. 6, 1865. He was assigned as above and was then promoted to Corporal in that company. He was mustered out on June 6, 1865. Manley was listed in the veteran section of the 1885 Wisconsin State census at P.O. Omro, in the 1890 federal census as residing at Clintonville, Waupaca County, and in the veteran section of the 1895 state census at P.O. Clintonville. In that section of the 1905 state census he was back at P.O. Omro. He was listed in 1905 as retired and residing on Poygan Road in the village of Omro. Manley died on Nov. 18, 1921 and Desiah died in 1918. She is buried at Omro Cemetery, Olin's Addition, Section B, plot 77. That plot was owned by A.B. Neal. Manley is buried at Omro Cemetery, Olin's Addition, Section C, plot 11. Several members of his family are buried on that same plot.
{US 1890; WC-V 1885, 1895, 1905; ROV; B-1905; Cem. records}

MOODY, Russell R. - Pvt., Co. G, 118th Regt., New York Vol. Inf.
Russell was born circa 1840 at New York. His father was a native of that state and his mother was born in Vermont. Russell was listed as above in the veteran section of the 1885 and 1895 Wisconsin State census at P.O. Omro. He was listed in the 1890 federal census as residing in the town of Omro. Russell provided his service dates as having been from Dec. 8, 1863 to Nov. 26, 1864. He suffered from chronic diarrhea as a result of his military service. He was listed in the veteran section of the 1905 state census as residing at the Wisconsin Veteran's Home at King. Frances, his wife, was then residing with him. Russell was listed in the 1910 federal census at King. Frances, his wife of 6 years, was residing there with him. Each had been married once before. Frances was born circa 1846 at New York.
{US 1890, 1910; WC-V 1885, 1895, 1905; GAR 40th}

MOODY, William Manley - Pvt., Co. A, 50th Regt., Wis. Vol. Inf.
William was born in 1832. Nancy, his wife, was born in 1840. William resided at Rushford and enlisted there on Feb. 6, 1865. He was assigned as above and was then mustered out on June 6, 1865. William was listed in the veteran section of the 1885, 1895 and 1905 Wisconsin State census at P.O. Omro. He was listed in the 1890 federal census as residing in the village of Omro. William was then suffering from deafness and chronic diarrhea. He was listed in 1905 as residing on High Street in Omro. William died in 1907 and Nancy died in 1924. Both are buried at Omro Cemetery, Pelton's Addition, Section C, plot 20. Other members of their family are also buried on that plot.
{US 1890; WC-V 1885, 1895, 1905; ROV; B-1905; Cem. records}

MOON, Francis H. - Pvt., Co. B, 21st Regt., Wis. Vol. Inf.
Francis resided at Vinland and enlisted there on Aug. 14, 1862. He was assigned as above and was wounded at Chaplin Hills, Kentucky. Francis was then listed as absent wounded when the regiment was mustered out on June 8, 1865.
{ROV}

MOON, James R. - Pvt., Co. B, 32nd Regt., Wis. Vol. Inf.
James resided at Chester, Dodge County and enlisted there on Jan. 4, 1864. He was assigned as above and was transferred to Co. H, 16th (reorg.) Regt., Wis. Vol. Inf. on June 4, 1865. He was mustered out on July 12, 1865. Henry C. Moon was also assigned

MOON, James R. (cont.)
to Co. B, 32nd Regt., Wis. Vol. Inf. James was listed in the veteran section of the 1885 Wisconsin State census at P.O. Oshkosh. He was then shown as having been a member of Co. B, 3rd Regt., Wis. Vol. Inf. He was listed in 1888 as a member of GAR Post #10 at Oshkosh. James was listed in the 1890 federal census as residing in the town of Oshkosh at P.O. Oshkosh.
{US 1890; WC-V 1885; ROV}

MOON, Jeremiah - Pvt., Co. K, 2nd Regt., New York Vol. Inf.
Jeremiah was born on Oct. 31, 1847. He was listed in 1905 as a foreman at the Paine Lumber Co. and residing at 346 Main Street in the city of Oshkosh. Inez Moon also resided at that address. Jerry was listed as above in the veteran section of the 1905 Wisconsin State census at P.O. Oshkosh. He died at Oshkosh on Apr. 11, 1919. His marker shows him as a member of Co. B, 3rd Regt., Wis. Vol. Inf. Cemetery records provide his service dates as having been from Nov. 27, 1863 to July 18, 1865. Jeremiah is buried at Riverside Cemetery, GAR plot, west row, #17 from the south.
{WC-V 1905; B-1905; Cem. records}

MOONEY, Thomas - Pvt., Co. C, 1st Regt., Wis. Hvy. Art.
Thomas resided at Neenah and enlisted there on Sept. 10, 1863. He was assigned as above and was mustered out on Sept. 21, 1865.
{ROV}

MOORE, Duane R. - Pvt., Co. B, 32nd Regt., Wis. Vol. Inf.
Duane resided at Springvale, Fond du Lac County and enlisted there on Aug. 15, 1862. He was assigned as above and was wounded on July 27, 1864 at Courtland, Alabama. Duane was mustered out on May 26, 1865. He was listed in the veteran section of the 1885 Wisconsin State census at P.O. Pickett. He was listed as a mail carrier in 1905. With Caroline, his wife, he was residing on 2 acres of section 31 in the town of Utica at the village of Pickett.
{WC-V 1885; ROV; B-1905}

MOORE, Elisha - Unassigned, Wis. Vol. Inf.
Elisha resided at Utica and was drafted there on Sept. 30, 1864. He was not found in the records as having been assigned to any regiment and was mustered out on June 30, 1865.
{ROV}

MOORE, William H. - Sgt., Co. C, 1st Regt., Colorado Vol. Inf.
William was listed as above in the 1890 federal census as residing in the city of Neenah. He provided his service dates as having been from Sept. 17, 1861 to Sept. 20, 1866. He was then suffering the effects of bronchial consumption. William was listed as such in the veteran section of the 1895 Wisconsin State census at P.O. Neenah.
{US 1890; WC-V 1895}

MORAN, Edward V. - Lt., Co. G, 3rd Regt., Wis. Vol. Inf.
Edward resided at Butte des Morts and enlisted there on Apr. 20, 1861. He was assigned as above and was promoted to Corporal, Sergeant and then 1st Sergeant in that company. Edward was commissioned as 2nd Lieutenant of that company on Apr. 20,

MORAN, Edward V. (cont.)
1865. He was mustered out on July 18, 1865. He was listed in 1905 as the proprietor of a sample room and residing on Lake Avenue in the village of Winneconne. Nellie Moran was residing at the same address and Ed. Jr. resided nearby. Edward is buried with a simple military marker in the town of Winneconne at Bell Cemetery. June, a daughter of E. & E.R. Moran, is buried on that same plot.
{ROV; B-1905; Cem. records}

MOREY, John H. - Pvt., Co. C, 1st (3 yr.) Regt., Wis. Vol. Inf.
John resided at Winneconne and enlisted there on Sept. 8, 1861. He was assigned as above and was discharged due to a disability on Nov. 28, 1862. John was then drafted on Nov. 25, 1863 and was assigned as a Private to Co. C, 14th Regt., Wis. Vol. Inf. He was transferred as a Private to Co. I, 21st Regt., Wis. Vol. Inf. on Sept. 19, 1864 and was transferred to Co. I, 3rd Regt., Wis. Vol. Inf. on June 8, 1865. John was mustered out on July 18, 1865. He had a daughter, unnamed, who died on the day she was born, Sept. 27, 1879.
{ROV; WCBR v.2, p.158, #430}

MOREY, Loraine C. - Sgt., Co. C, 1st Regt., Wis. Hvy. Art.
Loraine resided at Neenah and enlisted there on Sept. 1, 1863. He was assigned as above and was promoted to Corporal and then Sergeant in that company. He was mustered out on Sept. 21, 1865.
{ROV}

MORGAN, Andrew H. - Pvt., Co. E, 13th Regt., Vermont Vol. Inf.
Andrew was listed as above in the 1890 federal census and he was then residing in the city of Oshkosh. He provided his service dates as having been from Sept. 8, 1862 through July 21, 1863. He also provided that he had served as a Private in Co. E, 1st Regt., Vermont Cav. from Aug. 15, 1864 to June 21, 1865.
{US 1890}

MORGAN, Benjamin F. - Lt., Co. K, 1st (3 yr.) Regt., Wis. Vol. Inf.
Benjamin resided at Black Wolf and enlisted there on Sept. 21, 1861. He was assigned as a private to the above company and was then promoted to Sergeant in that company. Benjamin was commissioned as 1st Lieutenant of that company on July 1, 1864 and was mustered out on Oct. 14, 1864.
{ROV}

MORGAN, Charles H. - Capt., Co. H, 21st Regt., Wis. Vol. Inf.
Charles was born on Dec. 10, 1813 at Rushford, Allegheny County, New York. He was a son of Samuel Huntington and Lucy (Culver) Morgan. Samuel was born on Nov. 2, 1786 in Connecticut and was of Welsh ancestry. Lucy Culver was born on Apr. 14, 1784 at Wethersfield, Vermont. Samuel died on Mar. 3, 1843 at New York and Lucy died in Apr. 1861. Charles was married on Mar. 10, 1836 to Mary P. Medbury. She was born on Feb. 20, 1815 at New York and was a daughter of William F. and Betsy (Wilber) Medbury. William was born Mar. 16, 1783 at Scituate, Rhode Island. Betsy was born June 17, 1789 at New York. William died on May 29, 1836 and Betsy died in June 1871. Charles was engaged in lumbering on the Allegheny River in winter and in farming in the summer, along with his father and brothers, until the death of the father. Charles

MORGAN, Charles H. (cont.)
then continued on his own in the lumbering business for three years. In 1845 he entered into dairy farming. Then, on Mar. 10, 1857 he sold all of his personal effects and removed to Wisconsin with his family. After lumbering here for two years he traded his mill for the farm in the town of Black Wolf, known as the Lone Elm, upon which he spent the rest of his life. Charles and Mary were listed in the 1860 federal census as residing with most of their family on a farm in the town of Black Wolf. They then had the following children: America T., born on Feb. 6, 1837; Orissa Mary, born Jan. 28, 1839 at New York; William Montrose, the subject of a following sketch; Harriet M., born on Sept. 5, 1848 at New York; and Ella E., born on Sept. 30, 1853 at New York. Charles engaged in the lumbering business for two years with a brother. He was elected Chairman of the town of Black Wolf in 1859. He enlisted at Black Wolf on Apr. 20, 1861 and was assigned as a Private, Co. I, 1st (3 mo.) Regt., Wis. Vol. Inf. He was mustered out on Aug. 21, 1861 at the end of his term. Charles re-enlisted on Sept. 3, 1861 and was assigned as a Private to Co. K, 1st (3 yr.) Regt., Wis. Vol. Inf. He was promoted to Sergeant in that company. He was commissioned as Sergeant Major of the regiment on Mar. 1, 1862. Charles was then taken prisoner at Perryville, Kentucky on Oct. 8, 1862 and was paroled on the field that same day. He was awaiting exchange at Camp Lew Wallace near Columbus, Ohio on Oct. 29, 1862. He was promoted to 2nd Lieutenant and assigned to Co. F, 21st Regt., Wis. Vol. Inf. on Aug. 12, 1862. He was taken prisoner at Chaplin Hills, Kentucky on Sept. 20, 1863 and was then promoted to Captain, Co. H of that same regiment on Apr. 11, 1865. Charles was mustered out on June 8, 1865. He died at Black Wolf on Oct. 16, 1891. He was survived by the following children: Mrs. J. Gordon of Oshkosh; Mrs. Orissa M. Harney of Black Wolf; W.M. Morgan of Black Wolf, subject of a following sketch; and Mrs. C.W. Knapp of Black Wolf. Mrs. W.J. Fleming, a daughter was deceased.
{US 1860; Randall p.17; CBR-FRV p.1193-5; ODT 17 Oct 1891; OWN 13 Nov 1862} {ROV}

MORGAN, John W. - Pvt., Co. C, 21st Regt., Wis. Vol. Inf.
John resided at Oshkosh and enlisted there on Aug. 12, 1862. He was assigned as above and was wounded at Chaplin Hills, Kentucky on Oct. 8, 1862. John was a patient in the hospital at Louisville, Kentucky on Apr. 16, 1863 and he was transferred to the Department of the Navy on May 14, 1863. He was listed in 1920 as residing at Lake Nebagamon, Douglas County. John was listed in 1927 as residing at Glendale, Oregon.
{ROV; 21-33rd; 21-40th; OWN 07 May 1863}

MORGAN, William Montrose - Cpl., Co. K, 1st (3 yr.) Regt., Wis. Vol. Inf.
William Montrose Morgan was born on Jan. 14, 1842 at Cuba, Allegheny County, New York. He was a son of Charles H. Morgan from a previous sketch. William received a good education at Oshkosh and was engaged in farming with his father. He was listed in the 1860 federal census as residing with his father in the town of Black Wolf. William enlisted at Black Wolf on Oct. 4, 1861. He was assigned as above and was promoted to Corporal in that company. William received a slight wound to the hand at Chaplin Hills, Kentucky. Twenty-two men were shot down beside him. William was one of the 6,000 Union soldiers taken prisoner at Chickamauga, Georgia. He was confined at Belle Isle for several weeks and was then transferred to Richmond, Virginia. They were housed in warehouses and factories as Libby Prison was filled with officers. He was moved to Danville, then to Andersonville. In Sept. 1864 he was moved to Charleston,

MORGAN, William Montrose (cont.)
S.C. and after several weeks was taken to Florence. William made his escape Feb. 28, 1865 while on parole to do work outside of the prison. He reached the Union lines at Georgetown, S.C.. After several stops along the way he arrived at Washington, D.C., where he received his discharge and transportation home. William returned to his 70 acres in the town of Black Wolf and continued farming. He was married in Winnebago County on Nov. 16, 1867 to Isabella Harney. She was a daughter of John Harney, a pioneer of Winnebago County. William and Isabella had nine children: Flora M.; Grace I.; Libbie H.; Charles F.; Gertrude H.; Harriet O.; Mollie L.; Neeley Emma; and Carter Montrose Morgan. He was listed in the veteran section of the 1885, 1895 and 1905 Wisconsin State census at P.O. Oshkosh. William was listed in 1888 as a member of GAR Post #241 at Oshkosh. He was listed in the 1890 federal census as residing in the city of Oshkosh. William was elected in 1892 to the position of Winnebago County Register of Probate. After his term of office William returned to Black Wolf. He and Belle were listed in 1905 as residing on 63 acres of section 7 in the town of Black Wolf.
{US 1860, 1890; WC-V 1885, 1895, 1905; Randall p.17; CBR-FRV p.1193-5; ROV}
{B-1905; WCMR v.1, p.360, #2180}

MORIARITY, Jeremiah - Pvt., 3rd Regt., Wis. Cav.
Jeremiah resided at Rushford and enlisted there on Feb. 29, 1864. He was assigned as above and was placed on detached service. His last report within that regiment was being on detached service at Ft. Riley, Kansas in Feb. 1865. Jeremiah was listed in the veteran section of the 1895 Wisconsin State census at P.O. Omro. He died in 1902 and is buried at Oakwood Cemetery in Berlin, Green Lake County.
{WC-V 1895; ROV; GRI}

MORLEY, Aden - Cpl., Co. C, 46th Regt., Wis. Vol. Inf.
Aden was born circa 1822 at New York. He was a son of Warren and Laura Morley. Warren was born circa 1796 at Massachusetts. Laura was born circa 1802 at New York. Warren was listed in the 1860 federal census as a blacksmith residing in the town of Black Wolf. Listed with him were two sons, Francis M. and Albert, both subjects of following sketches. Aden resided on an adjoining farm. Mary, his wife, was born circa 1815 at New York. Nancy, their daughter, was born circa 1855 at Wisconsin. Aden enlisted at Oshkosh on Feb. 13, 1865. He was assigned as above and was promoted to Corporal in that company. Aden was mustered out on Sept. 27, 1865. He was listed in 1868 as a steamboat captain residing at 12 Bay Street in the city of Oshkosh. He was listed in the veteran section of the 1885 Wisconsin State census at P.O. Oshkosh. Aden was listed in the 1890 federal census as residing in Oshkosh. Angeline, his widow, was listed in 1905 as residing at 157 E. Irving Street in Oshkosh.
{US 1860, 1890; WC-V 1885; ROV; T-1868; B-1905}

MORLEY, Albert - Pvt., Co. K, 1st (3 yr.) Regt., Wis. Vol. Inf.
Albert was born circa 1843 at New York. He was a son of Warren and Laura Morley and a brother of Aden, Asahel and Francis M. of other sketches. Albert was listed in the 1860 federal census as residing with his parents in the town of Black Wolf. Albert enlisted on Sept. 21, 1861. He was assigned as above and was discharged due to a disability on Dec. 31, 1862. Albert died of consumption at the home of his parents in Black Wolf on May 3, 1871. He was survived by his parents and a brother, Hiram, of

MORLEY, Albert (cont.)
Oshkosh. Albert was still listed in the veteran section of the 1885 Wisconsin State census at P.O. Oshkosh.
{US 1860; WC-V 1885; ROV; OWN 11 May 1871}

MORLEY, Arnel - Pvt., Co. K, 1st (3 yr.) Regt., Wis. Vol. Inf.
Arnel resided at Black Wolf and enlisted there on Sept. 17, 1861. He was assigned as above and was discharged on June 16, 1862 due to a disability. He was listed as having re-enlisted as a Private in Co. I, 3rd (reorg.) Regt., Wis. Cav.
{ROV}

MORLEY, Asahel W. - Cpl., Co. B, 3rd Regt., Wis. Vol. Inf.
Asahel was born circa 1835 at New York. He was a son of Warren and Laura Morley and a brother of Aden, Albert and Francis M. Morley of other sketches. Asahel was married in Winnebago County on June 4, 1856 to Rachel Ella Groat. She was born circa 1837 at New York. Asahel was listed in the 1860 federal census as residing on a farm near his father in the town of Black Wolf. Listed with him were his wife and the following children: Mary M., born circa 1857 at Wisconsin; and Ella S., born in 1859 at Wisconsin. Asahel resided at Black Wolf and enlisted on June 17, 1861. He was assigned as above and was promoted to Corporal in that company. Asahel was wounded and taken prisoner at Winchester, Virginia. He was discharged on July 29, 1862 due to a disability. Asahel was listed in 1868 as a carpenter residing at 15 Sixth Street in the city of Oshkosh.
{US 1860; ROV; WCMR v.1, p.165, #760; T-1868}

MORLEY, Francis M. - Pvt., Co. D, 41st Regt., Wis. Vol. Inf.
Francis was born circa 1841 at New York. He was a son of Warren and Laura Morley and a brother of Aden, Albert and Asahel Morley from previous sketches. Francis was listed in the 1860 federal census as residing with his father in the town of Black Wolf. He listed his residence as Menasha when he enlisted on May 30, 1864. He was assigned as above and was mustered out on Sept. 23, 1864 at the end of his term of enlistment. Francis died prior to 1908.
{US 1860; ROV; Lawson p.840}

MORLEY, Harmon O.R. - Pvt., Co. K, 1st (3 yr.) Regt., Wis. Vol. Inf.
Harmon resided at Black Wolf and enlisted on Sept. 21, 1861. He was assigned as above. Harmon contracted a disease and died on Sept. 27, 1862 at Nashville, Tennessee.
{ROV}

MORLEY, Richard - Pvt., Co. K, 1st (3 yr.) Regt., Wis. Vol. Inf.
Richard resided at Black Wolf and enlisted there on Sept. 21, 1861. No further mention of him was found in the records of that company.
{ROV}

MORLEY, Thomas G.W. - Pvt., Co. L, 4th Batt., New York Lt. Art.
Thomas was listed as above in the veteran section of the 1885 Wisconsin State census at P.O. Menasha.
{WC-V 1885}

MORRIS, Archibald - Pvt., Co. B, 3rd Regt., Wis. Cav.
Archibald resided at Vinland and enlisted there on Dec. 10, 1861. He was assigned as above and was mustered out on Feb. 14, 1865.
{ROV}

MORRIS, Benjamin J. - Pvt., Co. C, 21st Regt., Wis. Vol. Inf.
Benjamin resided at Oshkosh and enlisted there on Aug. 12, 1862. He was assigned as above. Benjamin contracted a disease and died on Mar. 16, 1863 at Murfreesboro, Tennessee.
{ROV}

MORRIS, Luther - Pvt., Co. B, 3rd Regt., Wis. Cav.
Luther was listed in the 1860 federal census as a farm laborer for Henry Gardner in the town of Vinland. He was then listed as born circa 1840 at New York. He was listed in that same census as a farm laborer for Rufus Lambert in the town of Oshkosh. Luther was then shown as born circa 1835 at New York. He listed his residence as Vinland when he enlisted on Dec. 11, 1861. He was assigned as above and was listed as having deserted on Feb. 27, 1862.
{US 1860; ROV}

MORRIS, Monroe J. - Cpl., Co. C, 46th Regt., Wis. Vol. Inf.
Monroe was born in 1836 at Ohio. He was married on Aug. 22, 1858 to Lomirah M. Hewitt in Winnebago County. She was born in 1838, also at Ohio. They were listed in the 1860 federal census as residing on a farm in the town of Omro at P.O. Oshkosh. Monroe enlisted at Algoma on Feb. 4, 1865 and was assigned as above. He was then promoted to Corporal in that company and was mustered out on Sept. 27, 1865. Monroe was listed in the veteran section of the 1885 Wisconsin State census at P.O. Omro. He was listed in the 1890 federal census as residing in the town of Omro at P.O. Omro and suffering from the effects of malarial fever. He was listed in the veteran section of the 1895 and 1905 state census at P.O. Oshkosh. He was listed in 1905, along with his wife and daughter Mira R., as residing on 40 acres of section 24 in the town of Omro. Monroe died in 1905 yet the farm remained in his name in 1909. Lomirah died in 1927. Daughter Mira was born in 1870 and died in 1945. All three are buried in the town of Omro at Omro Junction Cemetery.
{US 1860, 1890; WC-V 1885, 1895, 1905; ROV; WCP-1909; Cem. records; B-1905}
{WCMR v.1, p.191, #968}

MORRIS, Thomas - Pvt., Co. H, 36th Regt., Wis. Vol. Inf.
Thomas resided at Utica and enlisted there on Feb. 29, 1864. He was assigned as above. Thomas was killed in action on May 26, 1864 at North Anna, Virginia.
{ROV}

MORRIS, Thomas W. - Pvt., Co. F, 1st Regt., Wis. Hvy. Art.
Thomas resided at Utica and enlisted there on Sept. 5, 1864. He was assigned as above and was mustered out on June 26, 1865.
{ROV}

MORSER, Jacob - Civil War veteran?
Jacob was born circa 1817. He moved to Wisconsin from New York circa 1869. Jacob

MORSER, Jacob (cont.)
died at Oshkosh in July 1892. He had moved there from Clintonville, Waupaca County in April 1891. Jacob was a prominent member of the G.A.R. He was returned to his former home at Clintonville for burial. Jacob was survived by seven children: Mrs. O.M. Doty of Chicago; Mrs. A.V. DerMotte of Clintonville; both J.H. Morser and C.H. Morser of Antigo, Langlade County; W.C. Morser of Fresno, California; and E.L. Morser and W.S. Morser of Oshkosh.
{OWN 16 Jul 1892}

MORTON, Charles Calvin - Sgt. Maj., 48th Regt., Wis. Vol. Inf.
Charles was born circa 1838 at New York. He was a son of Levi and Jane P. (Barrett) Morton and a brother of George O. from a following sketch. Levi was born on Jan. 7, 1805 at Massachusetts. Jane was born on Apr. 28, 1809 at Vermont and died on Nov. 19, 1907. Levi and Jane were listed in the 1860 federal census as residing on a farm in the town of Winneconne. Listed with them were sons Charles and George. Charles enlisted there on Sept. 9, 1861 and was assigned as a Private to Co. E, 1st Regt., Wis. Cav. He was discharged on Dec. 30, 1862. Charles then re-enlisted at Winneconne on Feb. 6, 1865 and was assigned as a Private to Co. A, 48th Regt., Wis. Vol. Inf. He was promoted to 1st Sergeant in that company and was then commissioned as Sergeant Major of the 48th Regiment on Dec. 1, 1865. Charles was mustered out on Dec. 30, 1865. Levi, his father, died at the residence of Ansel Jones in Oshkosh on Apr. 23, 1885. Charles was listed in the veteran section of the 1885, 1895 and 1905 Wisconsin State census at P.O. Omro. He was listed in the 1890 federal census as residing in the village of Omro. He was listed in 1905 as being in partnership with J.B. Treleven, J.T. Orchard and S.D. Gilman in the operation of a planing mill on Pearl Street in Omro. He was then residing on Park Street at the corner of Second Street in Omro. Jane P., his mother, was listed as residing with him. Lois Samantha, wife of Charles, was born on Jan. 2, 1843 and died on Nov. 10, 1927. Charles is buried with a simple military marker at Omro Cemetery, Olin's Addition, Section C, plot 36. His wife and parents are buried on that same plot.
{US 1860, 1890; WC-V 1885, 1895, 1905; Cem. records; ODN 24 Apr 1885; ROV}
{B-1905}

MORTON, George O. - Pvt., Co. B, 21st Regt., Wis. Vol. Inf.
George was born on June 17, 1840 at Canton, St. Lawrence County, New York. He was a son of Levi and Jane P. (Barrett) Morton and a brother of Charles from a previous sketch. Levi Morton was of "Mayflower" ancestry. Jane's family was from Cornwall, Litchfield County, Connecticut. George came to Winnebago County with his parents in 1855 and was listed with them in the 1860 federal census as residing on a farm in the town of Winneconne. He enlisted there on Aug. 11, 1862 and was assigned as above. He was discharged on Mar. 6, 1863 due to a disability. George re-enlisted on Sept. 1, 1864 and was assigned as a Private to Co. C, 1st Regt., Wis. Hvy. Art. He was then mustered out on June 16, 1865. George was married in Winnebago County on Oct. 10, 1865 to Jane E. Arnold. She was born in 1842. George was a mechanic by trade until 1866, when he changed to the pursuit of an agricultural career. George and Jane had two sons: William Everett, born on Oct. 18, 1877; and Lewis A. Morton. George was listed in the veteran section of the 1885 and 1895 Wisconsin State census at P.O. Omro. He was listed in the 1890 federal census as residing in the town of Omro at P.O. Omro. He was not found in the veteran section of the 1905 state census but he was listed in that

MORTON, George O. (cont.)
year as residing on 160 acres of section 8 in the town of Omro. Residing with him at that time were his wife and son Lewis with his wife Minnie. Jane died in 1911 and George died in 1917. Both are buried at Omro Cemetery, Pelton's Addition, Section B, plot 28.
{US 1860, 1890; WC-V 1885, 1895, 1905; ROV; Randall p.29; W-HP p.603; B-1905} {Cem. records}

MOSCRIP, Daniel H. - Cpl., Co. B, 21st Regt., Wis. Vol. Inf.
Daniel was born circa 1833 at New York. Mary E., his wife, was born circa 1834, also at New York. Daniel was listed in the 1860 federal census as a farmer residing in the first ward of the city of Oshkosh. He and Mary had a daughter, Alvi Izora, who was born circa 1859 at Wisconsin. Also residing with them were Esther Crandell, born circa 1787 at Rhode Island, and Edward, brother of Daniel and subject of a following sketch. Daniel resided at Winneconne and enlisted there on Aug. 14, 1862. He was assigned as above and was promoted to Corporal in that company. Daniel was wounded at Buzzard's Roost, Georgia and was then transferred to the Veteran Reserve Corps on Dec. 20, 1864. He was mustered out on Aug. 12, 1865.
{US 1860; ROV}

MOSCRIP, Edward - Pvt., Co. E, 2nd Regt., Wis. Vol. Inf.
Edward was born circa 1837 at New York. He was a brother of Daniel from a previous sketch. Edward was listed in the 1860 federal census as a wagon maker residing with brother Daniel in the first ward of the city of Oshkosh. Edward listed his residence as Winneconne when he enlisted on Apr. 21, 1861. He was assigned as above and was wounded in the battle at Wilderness, Virginia. Edward was listed as being in the hospital when that regiment was mustered out.
{US 1860; ROV}

MOSCRIP, William S. - Sgt., Co. K, 19th Regt., Wis. Vol. Inf.
William was born circa 1830 at New York. Clarissa A., his wife, was born circa 1838 at Pennsylvania. William was listed in the 1860 federal census as a wagon maker residing in the fourth ward of the city of Oshkosh. He and Clarissa had one daughter, Carrie A., who was born circa 1858 at Wisconsin. Also residing with them was William W. Arnett, subject of a previous sketch. William was shown as having enlisted at Winneconne on Apr. 21, 1861. He was assigned as a Private to Co. B, 3rd Regt., Wis. Vol. Inf. and two days later he was commissioned as 1st Lieutenant of that company. William then resigned his commission on Jan. 16, 1862. He re-enlisted on Mar. 1, 1862 and was assigned as a Private to Co. K, 19th Regt., Wis. Vol. Inf. He was promoted to Corporal and then Sergeant in that company. William was commissioned as Sergeant Major of that regiment on Mar. 14, 1863 but he rejected the commission and was returned to Co. K. William was wounded and he died of those wounds on Sept. 14, 1864 at Ft. Monroe, Virginia.
{US 1860; ROV}

MOSES, John - Pvt., Co. C, 21st Regt., Wis. Vol. Inf.
John resided at Nekimi and enlisted there on Aug. 14, 1862. He was assigned as above and was discharged due to a disability on Mar. 9, 1863.
{ROV; OWN 07 May 1863}

MOSES, Richard - Pvt., Co. C, 21st Regt., Wis. Vol. Inf.
Richard resided at Nekimi and enlisted there on Aug. 14, 1862. He was assigned as above and was mustered out on June 8, 1865. Richard was listed in 1920 as residing at Winifred Lake, South Dakota.
{ROV; 21-33rd}

MOSHER, Augustus - Pvt., Co. F, 1st Regt., Wis. Hvy. Art.
Augustus was born on June 9, 1835. Philetta, his wife, was born on Mar. 13, 1837. Augustus resided at Utica and enlisted there on Sept. 5, 1864. He was assigned as above and was mustered out on June 26, 1865. Augustus and Philetta had at least two sons. Charles J. died on Jan. 30, 1887 at age 16 years, 9 months and 13 days. Ovett died on Jan. 11, 1878 at age 5 years, 4 months and 6 days. Augustus was listed in the 1890 federal census as residing in the town of Aurora, Waushara County at P.O. Berlin. He provided that he had contracted diarrhea while in the military. Augustus died Jan. 3, 1913 and Philetta died on Oct. 11, 1922. Both are buried with the above sons in the town of Aurora at Shead Island Cemetery.
{US 1890; ROV; Cem. records}

MOSHER, Simon F. - Cpl., Co. F, 18th Regt., Wis. Vol. Inf.
Simon resided at Eureka and enlisted there on Nov. 26, 1861. He was assigned as above and was promoted to Corporal in that company. Simon was taken prisoner at Allatoona, Georgia and was mustered out on July 18, 1865.
{ROV}

MOSHIER, Franklin H. - Cpl., Co. G, 18th Regt., Wis. Vol. Inf.
Franklin resided at Centralia, Wood County and enlisted there on Dec. 16, 1861. He was assigned as above and was then promoted to Corporal in that company. He was mustered out on July 18, 1865. Franklin was listed in the 1890 federal census as residing in the city of Oshkosh.
{US 1890; ROV}

MOSLEY, Charles R. - Pvt., Co. A, 16th Regt., Wis. Vol. Inf.
Charles was born on Aug. 21, 1841 and Almyra, his wife, was born on June 6, 1845. Charles enlisted at Otsego, Columbia County on Sept. 6, 1861 and was assigned as above. He was mustered out on Dec. 21, 1864 at the end of his term of enlistment. A John Mosley had been a member of that same company. Charles was listed in the veteran section of the 1885 Wisconsin State census at P.O. Eureka. He was listed in the 1890 federal census as residing in the town of Rushford at P.O. Eureka. He was listed in the veteran section of the 1895 and 1905 state census at P.O. Omro. Charles was listed in 1905 as retired and residing on Pleasant Street in the village of Omro. He still owned 100 acres of section 24 in the town of Poygan. That land was then being rented by Harley and Ethel Mosley. Charles died on Apr. 7, 1913 and Almyra died on Dec. 5, 1928. A son, Maurice, was born on Apr. 2, 1871 and died on Feb. 19, 1930. All three are buried at Omro Cemetery, Olin's Addition, Section C, plot 80.
{US 1890; WC-V 1885, 1895, 1905; ROV; B-1905; Cem. records}

MOSS, Edgar - Pvt., Co. K, 16th Regt., New York Vol. Inf.
Edgar was listed as above in the veteran section of the 1895 and 1905 Wisconsin State census at P.O. Oshkosh. He was not found in that section of the 1885 state census.

MOSS, Edgar (cont.)
Edgar was listed in 1905 as a rural mail carrier residing at 373 Ceape Street in the city of Oshkosh. Fay V., Irving and Vida Moss were also listed at that address.
{WC-V 1885, 1895, 1905; B-1905}

MOSSMAN, William W. - Pvt., Co. F, 22nd Regt., Wis. Vol. Inf.
William was born in 1841. He enlisted at Waterford, Racine County on Aug. 15, 1862 and was assigned as above. William was discharged due to a disability on Apr. 9, 1864. He was listed in the veteran section of the 1885 Wisconsin State census at P.O. Oshkosh and he was listed in the 1890 federal census as residing in the city of Oshkosh. William was listed in 1905 as an engineer on the Wisconsin Central Railroad and residing at 366 Thirteenth Street in Oshkosh. Mabel R. and Mildred Mossman were listed at that same address. William W. died in 1924. Annie M., his wife, was born in 1858 and died in 1937. Both are buried in the town of Algoma at Ellenwood Cemetery.
{US 1890; WC-V 1885; ROV; Cem. records; B-1905}

MOSSOP, John C. - Pvt., Co. D, 41st Regt., Wis. Vol. Inf.
John was born circa 1846 at England. He was listed in the 1860 federal census as residing with the family of Thomas Palmer in the town of Clayton at P.O. Neenah. John enlisted at Neenah on May 16, 1864. He was assigned as above and was mustered out on Sept. 23, 1864 at the end of his term of enlistment. John was listed (Massok) in the veteran section of the 1885 Wisconsin State census at P.O. Neenah. He was listed in that section of the 1895 census at P.O. Menasha and in that section of the 1905 state census at P.O. Eau Claire, Eau Claire County.
{US 1860; WC-V 1885, 1895, 1905; ROV}

MOTT, Wesley - Pvt., Co. D, 49th Regt., Wis. Vol. Inf.
Wesley was born circa 1835 at New York, a son of Mayhew and Mary Mott. Both of his parents were born in New York, the father circa 1795 and the mother circa 1794. Wesley was listed in the 1860 federal census as residing with his parents on a farm in the town of Winchester. Mayhew died at Winchester on Sept. 24, 1869. Wesley enlisted there on Feb. 14, 1865. He was assigned as above and was discharged on Oct. 20, 1865 due to a disability. Wesley was married to Harriet Lavinia Porter. They had at least three children: Florence Beatrice, born in Winchester on Aug. 10, 1872; Wesley Mayhew, born in Winchester on May 3, 1874; and Harriet Elizabeth, born in Winchester on Jan. 16, 1879. Wesley was listed in the veteran section of the 1885 Wisconsin State census at P.O. Winchester. He was listed in the 1890 federal census as residing in the city of Neenah. Wesley was listed in the veteran section of the 1895 and 1905 state census at P.O. Neenah. He was listed in 1905 as a member of Mott & Mott, attorneys. Wesley was then residing at 205 Third Street in Neenah. Elizabeth, Florence B. and Mayhew Mott were also residing at that address.
{US 1860, 1890; WC-V 1885, 1895, 1905; B-1905; WCBR v.2, p.170, #478; ROV}
{WCBR v.2, p.170, #479; WCBR v.2, p.170, #477; OsJ 02 Oct 1869}

MOULTON, Truman T. - Lt., Co. D, 41st Regt., Wis. Vol. Inf.
Truman was born circa 1831 at Vermont. He was listed in the 1860 federal census as a mason residing in the village of Neenah. Olive, his wife, was born circa 1833 at New York. They had a daughter, Ella, who was born circa 1853 at Wisconsin. Truman enlisted at Menasha and was assigned to the above company. He was commissioned as

MOULTON, Truman T. (cont.)
2nd Lieutenant of that company on June 9, 1864 and was mustered out on Sept. 23, 1864 at the end of his term of enlistment. In Aug. 1872 Truman constructed a lime kiln at Neenah. He was listed in the 1890 federal census as residing in the city of Neenah. Truman was listed in the veteran section of the 1895 Wisconsin State census at P.O. Neenah and in that section of the 1905 state census at P.O. Oshkosh. He was listed in 1905 as residing at 574 High Street in the city of Oshkosh. Louis Moulton was also residing at that address. Truman was listed in the 1910 federal census as a widower residing at the Wisconsin Veterans' Home at King. He had been married for 11 years.
{US 1860, 1890, 1910; WC-V 1895, 1905; B-1905; ROV; HN 1878 p.98}

MOUNTAIN, Robert G. - Sgt., Co. K, 21st Regt., Wis. Vol. Inf.
Robert resided at Manitowoc, Manitowoc County and enlisted there on Aug. 14, 1862. He was assigned as above and was promoted to Corporal and then Sergeant in that company. Robert was taken prisoner at Chaplin Hills, Kentucky and he was mustered out on June 8, 1865. He was listed in the veteran section of the 1885 Wisconsin State census at P.O. Marion, Waupaca County. Robert was not found in that section of the 1895 state census and was listed in that part of the 1905 state census at P.O. Oshkosh.
{WC-V 1885, 1895, 1905; ROV}

MOWERS, Henry - Pvt., Co. D, 52nd Regt., Wis. Vol. Inf.
Henry resided at Oshkosh and enlisted there on Mar. 4, 1865. He was assigned as above and was mustered out on July 28, 1865.
{ROV}

MUELLER - see also: Miller, Muller

MUELLER, Jost - Pvt., Co. E, 27th Regt., Wis. Vol. Inf.
Jost resided at Alto, Fond du Lac County and he enlisted there on Feb. 1, 1865. He was assigned as above and was mustered out on Aug. 29, 1865. Jost was listed in the veteran section of the 1885 Wisconsin State census at P.O. Winchester and in that part of the 1895 census at P.O. Oshkosh. He was listed (Co. E, 31st Regt., Wis. Vol. Inf.) in the 1890 federal census as residing in the town of Clayton at P.O. Neenah. He was not found in the veteran section of the 1905 state census. Jost was listed in 1905 as retired and residing at 310 Bond Street in the city of Neenah.
{US 1890; WC-V 1885, 1895, 1905; ROV; B-1905}

MUELLER, Moritz - Pvt., Co. A, 32nd Regt., Wis. Vol. Inf.
Moritz resided at Oshkosh and enlisted there on Aug. 21, 1862. He was assigned as above and was mustered out on June 12, 1865.
{ROV}

MULANEY, Thomas - Pvt., Co. C, 21st Regt., Wis. Vol. Inf.
Thomas resided at Omro and enlisted there on Aug. 14, 1862. He was assigned as above and was wounded on May 14, 1864. Thomas died of those wounds on May 23, 1864 at Resaca, Georgia.
{ROV}

MULASKEY, Charles - Pvt., Co. B, 21st Regt., Wis. Vol. Inf.
Charles resided at Oshkosh and enlisted there on Aug. 11, 1862. He was assigned as above and was taken prisoner on Sept. 20, 1863. Charles contracted a disease and died on Nov. 8, 1864 while in the rebel prison at Andersonville, Georgia. He was buried there in grave #11,936.
{ROV}

MULLER - see also: Miller, Mueller

MULLER, Heronimus - Pvt., Co. F, 19th Regt., Wis. Vol. Inf.
Heronimus resided at Vinland and enlisted there on Feb. 27, 1864. He was assigned as above and was transferred to Co. C of that same regiment on May 1, 1865. Heronimus was then listed as absent sick when the regiment was mustered out on Aug. 9, 1865.
{ROV}

MULLER, William C. - Pvt., Co. F, 48th Regt., Wis. Vol. Inf.
William resided at Oshkosh and enlisted there on Feb. 25, 1865. He was assigned as above and was mustered out on May 23, 1865. William was married on June 28, 1866 in Winnebago County to Clara Tix.
{ROV; WCMR v.1, p.301, #1855}

MULLIKEN, David R. - Pvt., Co. H, 36th Regt., Wis. Vol. Inf.
David resided at Utica and enlisted there on Feb. 19, 1864. He was assigned as above and was mustered out on July 12, 1865.
{ROV}

MULVEY, John - Sgt., Co. C, 12th Regt., Maine Vol. Inf.
John was listed as above in the 1890 federal census as residing in the town of Oshkosh at P.O. Oshkosh. He provided his discharge date as having been Jan. 3, 1865.
{US 1890}

MUNSIL, Ai F. - Pvt., Co. C, 46th Regt., Wis. Vol. Inf.
A.I. was born circa 1845 at New York. He was a son of Rufus and Emily Munsil. Rufus was born circa 1816 at New York and Emily was born circa 1817 at Vermont. They removed to Winnebago County circa 1850 and they were listed in the 1860 federal census as residing on a farm in the town of Utica at P.O. Welaunee. Listed with them were the following children: A.I.; William, born circa 1847; Abby, born circa 1849; John, born circa 1852; and Emma, born circa 1856. The elder two children were born in New York and the younger ones were born in Wisconsin. Also residing with them was a Benjamin Munsil and his family. Rufus died at Utica on Aug. 24, 1891. Ai resided at Utica and enlisted there on Feb. 9, 1865. He was assigned as above and was mustered out on Sept. 27, 1865.
{US 1860; ROV; OWN 27 Aug 1891}

MUNSON, Torger - Pvt., Co. B, 15th Regt., Wis. Vol. Inf.
Torger resided at Clayton and he enlisted there on Feb. 25, 1864. He was assigned as above and was then transferred to Co. H of that regiment on Dec. 1, 1864. Torger was mustered out on Nov. 24, 1865. He was also listed in the index to Roster of Wisconsin

MUNSON, Torger (cont.)
Volunteers as having been assigned to Co. I, 13th Regt., Wis. Vol. Inf.
{ROV}

MURPHY, Henry M. - Pvt., Co. D, 8th Regt., Wis. Vol. Inf.
Henry was born in 1840. He enlisted at Omro on Nov. 26, 1863 and was assigned as above. He was mustered out on June 5, 1865. Henry was married on July 4, 1865 in Winnebago County to Julia M. Paddleford. She was born in 1843. They had a stillborn daughter in Omro on Feb. 28, 1877. He was listed in the veteran section of the 1885, 1895 and 1905 Wisconsin State census at P.O. Omro. He was listed in the 1890 federal census as residing in the town of Omro at P.O. Omro. Henry and Julia were listed in 1905 as residing on 120 acres of section 11 in the town of Omro. A John H. Murphy was residing with them. Henry died in 1922 and Julia died in 1930. Lillian, a daughter, died on Mar. 17, 1877 at age 2 years, 8 months and 6 days. John, a son, was born in 1883 and died in 1953. All are buried in the town of Omro at Omro Union Cemetery.
{US 1890; WC-V 1885, 1895, 1905; ROV; WCMR v.10, p.11, #516; Cem. records}
{B-1905; WCBR v.2, p.21, #20}

MURPHY, James E. - Pvt., Co. K, 5th (reorg.) Regt., Wis. Vol. Inf.
James was born circa 1844 at New York. He was listed in the 1860 federal census as residing with the family of John J. Rowen in the town of Rushford at P.O. Eureka. James resided at Rushford and enlisted there on Aug. 30, 1864. He was assigned as above and was mustered out on June 20, 1865. James was married on Apr. 3, 1866 in Winnebago County to Eliza Ann White.
{US 1860; ROV; WCMR v.1, p.296, #1809}

MURPHY, Michael - Sgt., Co. B, 3rd Regt., Wis. Vol. Inf.
Michael resided at Oshkosh and enlisted there on Apr. 21, 1861. He was promoted to Sergeant in that company and was discharged due to a disability on Feb. 20, 1863. Michael re-enlisted on Jan. 4, 1864 and was assigned as a Private to Co. B, 3rd Regt., Wis. Cav. He was then transferred to Co. B, 3rd (reorg.) Regt., Wis. Cav. on Feb. 1, 1865 and was promoted to Corporal in that company. Michael was mustered out on Sept. 8, 1865.
{ROV}

MURPHY, Patrick - Pvt., Co. D, 31st Regt., Wis. Vol. Inf.
Patrick was born circa 1843 at Massachusetts. He was a son of Margaret Murphy and a brother of William from a following sketch. Margaret was born circa 1820 at Ireland. She was listed in the 1860 federal census as residing on a farm in the town of Black Wolf. Listed with her were the following children: William; Maurice, born circa 1841; Patrick; Ellen, born circa 1846; and John, born circa 1851. John was born in Wisconsin and the others were listed as born in Massachusetts. Patrick listed his residence as Utica when he enlisted on Aug. 15, 1862. He was assigned as above and was mustered out on July 29, 1865.
{US 1860; ROV}

MURPHY, William - Cpl., Co. C, 21st Regt., Wis. Vol. Inf.
William was born circa 1838 at Rhode Island. He was a son of Margaret Murphy and a brother of Patrick from a previous sketch. William was listed in the 1860 federal

MURPHY, William (cont.)
census as residing with his mother on a farm in the town of Black Wolf. He enlisted at Black Wolf on Aug. 21, 1862. He was assigned as above and was promoted to Corporal in that company. William was mustered out on June 8, 1865.
{US 1860; ROV}

MURTY, Patrick - Pvt., Co. E, 2nd Regt., Wis. Vol. Inf.
Patrick was born circa 1844 at Ireland. He was a son of Patrick and Ellen Murty. Both parents were natives of Ireland, the father born there circa 1805 and the mother born circa 1815. They were listed in the 1860 federal census as residing on a farm in the town of Nekimi. Listed with them were son Patrick and a daughter, Ann, who was born circa 1843 at Ireland. Patrick listed his residence as Oshkosh when he enlisted on May 25, 1861. He was assigned as above and he was taken prisoner at Gettysburg, Pennsylvania. Patrick was then mustered out on June 28, 1864 at the end of his term of enlistment. He was listed as having died prior to the 1899 article by Col. Harshaw.
{US 1860; ROV; ODN 07 May 1899}

MUTTART, Jarvis - Sgt., Co. K, 11th Regt., Wis. Vol. Inf.
Jarvis was born on June 1, 1845 at Canada West, a son of John and Ellen (Pardon) Muttart. John was born circa 1813 at Prince Edward Island, Canada. Ellen was born circa 1825 at Canada West. They settled in Wisconsin in 1853. John and Ellen were listed in the 1860 federal census as residing on a farm in the town of Neenah. Listed with them were the following children: Jarvis; William L., born May 21, 1852, resided at Oshkosh; George, born June 14, 1855, resided at Oshkosh; Edmund, born Mar. 3, 1857; and Sarah, born in 1859. The two oldest sons were born in Canada West and the other children were born in Wisconsin. They had another daughter, Mary, who was born on May 28, 1864. John died in Winnebago County in 1891. Jarvis resided at Neenah and enlisted there on Oct. 8, 1861. He was assigned as above and he re-enlisted in that same company at the end of his term. Jarvis was promoted to Corporal and then Sergeant in that company. He was mustered out on Sept. 4, 1865. Jarvis was married on Apr. 1, 1866 to Fannie Cowling. She was a daughter of George and Jane Cowling of Winnebago County. In June of that same year they removed to Osborn, Outagamie County. He bought 80 acres of timber land at $4 per acre. He cleared his land by hand and expanded until, by 1895, he owned 156 acres of good farm land there. Jarvis and Fannie had a family of 10 children: Mary Ann; Agnes and Alice B., twins; William L.; Sarah; Martha; Fannie; Jarvis; Isabella; and George. Jarvis held elected positions in his town and county. He was still residing at Osborn in 1895.
{US 1860; ROV; CBR-FRV p.686-7}

MUZZY, Artemus H. - Pvt., Co. E, 192nd Regt., New York Vol. Inf.
Artemus was married in Winnebago County on June 2, 1873 to Sarah Jane Hallam. He was listed in the veteran section of the 1895 Wisconsin State census at P.O. Brillion, Calumet County and as having been assigned as above. Artemus was listed in the same section of the 1905 state census at P.O. Oshkosh. He was born in 1847 and died in 1913. Sarah, his wife, was born in 1855 and died in 1941. Both are buried at Omro Cemetery, Olin's Addition, Section A, plot 20.
{WC-V 1895, 1905; B-1905; Cem. records; WCMR v.1, p.581, #3948}

MYATT, Joseph - Sgt., Co. I, 21st Regt., Wis. Vol. Inf.
Joseph was born circa 1818 at New York. He was listed in the 1860 federal census as a laborer residing in the town of Neenah. Mary, his wife, was born circa 1836 at New York. Listed with them were the following children: Louisa, born circa 1854; Ellen, born circa 1856; and Anna, born in 1859. All three children were born in Wisconsin. Joseph resided at Neenah and enlisted there on Aug. 19, 1862. He was assigned as above and was promoted to Corporal and then Sergeant in that company. He was mustered out on June 8, 1865.
{US 1860; ROV}

MYER - see also: Maier, Mayer, Meier, Meyer

MYER, Joseph - Pvt., 8th Batt., Wis. Lt. Art.
Joseph resided at Menasha and enlisted there on Jan. 28, 1864. No further mention of him was found in the Wisconsin military records.
{ROV}

MYRE, Ole Olsen - Pvt., Co. G, 3rd Regt., Wis. Vol. Inf.
Ole resided at Neenah and enlisted there on Apr. 23, 1861. He was assigned as above and was mustered out on June 29, 1864 at the end of his term of enlistment. Ole was listed in the veteran section of the 1885 and 1895 Wisconsin State census at P.O. Neenah.
{WC-V 1885, 1895; ROV}

NACHTRAB, Johann W. - Pvt., Co. C, 53rd Regt., Wis. Vol. Inf.
Johann was born on Dec. 23, 1829 and Anna M., his wife, was born on Feb. 2, 1826. Johann resided at Aztalan, Jefferson County and enlisted there on Mar. 9, 1865. He was assigned as above and was mustered out on June 29, 1865. Johann was listed in the veteran section of the 1885 Wisconsin State census at P.O. Nekimi. He was listed in the 1890 federal census as residing at 50 Kansas Street in the city of Oshkosh. He provided then that he had suffered from and inflamation of the bowels since his military service. Johann was listed in the veteran section of the 1895 and 1905 state census at P.O. Oshkosh. He and Anna were listed in 1905 as residing in section 26 of the town of Nekimi. John died there on Aug. 1, 1908 and Anna died on Aug. 25, 1908. Both are buried in the town of Nekimi at Scheller Cemetery.
{US 1890; WC-V 1885, 1895, 1905; ROV; B-1905; Cem. records}

NAGEL, John J. - Pvt., Co. B, 8th Regt., New York Hvy. Art.
John was listed in 1883 at P.O. Neenah. He was then receiving a pension of $8 per month for a wound to his right hip. John was listed as above in the veteran section of the 1885 Wisconsin State census at P.O. Neenah. He was listed in the 1890 federal census as residing in the town of Clayton at P.O. Neenah. John then provided his dates of service as having been from Aug. 1, 1862 to Dec. 10, 1864. He was listed in the veteran section of the 1905 state census at P.O. Neenah. John was then listed as a farmer residing at 231 Third Street in the city of Neenah.
{US 1890; WC-V 1885, 1905; LOP-1883; B-1905}

NAHRING, Herman - Pvt., Co. F, 19th Regt., Wis. Vol. Inf.
Herman resided at Winchester and enlisted there on Mar. 31, 1862. He was assigned as above and was wounded on Oct. 27, 1864 at Fair Oaks, Virginia. Herman was then

NAHRING, Herman (cont.)
transferred to Co. C of that regiment on May 1, 1865 and was mustered out on Aug. 18, 1865. He was listed in the veteran section of the 1885 Wisconsin State census at P.O. Winchester. Herman was listed in the 1890 federal census as residing in the town of Winchester at P.O. Readfield, Waupaca County. He listed that he then suffered the effects of chronic rheumatism. Amelia, widow of Herman, was listed in 1905 as residing on 113 acres of section 5 in the town of Winchester. Richard, August and Alex Nahring were also residing there.
{US 1890; WC-V 1885; ROV; B-1905}

NAILER, Jerome B. - Pvt., Co. I, 3rd (reorg.) Regt., Wis. Cav.
Jerome resided at Nepeuskun and enlisted there on Nov. 27, 1863. He was assigned as above and was mustered out on July 14, 1865. Jerome was listed (Naylor) in the 1890 federal census as residing in the city of Waupaca, Waupaca County.
{US 1890; ROV}

NARRACONG, Israel W. - Pvt., Co. G, 3rd Regt., Wis. Vol. Inf.
Israel was born circa 1809 at New Jersey. Phoebe, his wife, was born circa 1812 at England. Israel was listed in the 1850 federal census as a carpenter residing in the town of Neenah. With him were his wife and daughter Maria. She was born circa 1849 at Wisconsin. Also residing with the family was Franklin Powers, who was born circa 1838 at Maine. Israel was listed in the 1860 federal census as a ship carpenter residing in the second ward of the village of Menasha. He was listed as born circa 1815 at Ohio. Phoebe was then listed as born circa 1823 at Ireland. Maria was listed as Anna. Israel and Phoebe then had two additional children. Mary was born circa 1852 at Wisconsin and Lewis was born circa 1855 at Wisconsin. Israel resided at Menasha and enlisted there on July 5, 1861. He was assigned as above. Israel contracted a disease and died on Dec. 15, 1861 at Frederick, Maryland. Phebe, his wife, was listed in 1883 at P.O. Menasha and receiving a widow's penion of $8 per month.
{US 1850, 1860; ROV; LOP-1883}

NATHAN, John - Pvt., Co. F, 18th Regt., Wis. Vol. Inf.
John resided at Rushford and enlisted there on Feb. 25, 1864. He was assigned as above and was taken prisoner at Allatoona, Georgia. John contracted a disease and was sent home to Waukau, where he died on Mar. 16, 1865.
{ROV}

NAUMER, Nicholas - Pvt., Co. C, 27th Regt., Wis. Vol. Inf.
Nicholas resided at Manitowoc, Manitowoc County and enlisted there on Sept. 20, 1864. He was assigned as above and was mustered out on July 14, 1865. Nicholas was listed in the 1890 federal census as residing in the town of Oshkosh at P.O. Oshkosh. He was listed as being sick at that time. Nicholas was listed in the veteran section of the 1895 Wisconsin State census at P.O. Oshkosh. He was not found in that section of the 1885 or 1905 state census.
{US 1890; WC-V 1885, 1895, 1905; ROV}

NEAL, Alanson - Pvt., Co. A, 50th Regt., Wis. Vol. Inf.
Alanson was born on Oct. 22, 1849. He was a son of Alanson B. and Eleanor Neal. The father is the subject of a following sketch. Alanson resided at Algoma and enlisted

NEAL, Alanson (cont.)
there on Feb. 6, 1865. He was assigned as above. Alanson contracted a disease and died on Mar. 24, 1865 at Madison, Wisconsin. He is buried on the plot of his parents at Omro Cemetery, Olin's Addition, Section B, plot 77.
{ROV; GRI; Cem. records}

NEAL, Alanson B. - Pvt., Co. C, 188th Regt., New York Vol. Inf.
Alanson was born on Oct. 14, 1806. Eleanor, his wife, was born July 25, 1808. They were the parents of Alanson from a previous sketch. Eleanor was listed in 1883 at P.O. Omro. She was then receiving a mother's pension of $8 per month. Alanson B. died on Jan. 26, 1890 and Eleanor died on Feb. 14, 1897. Both are buried at Omro Cemetery, Olin's Addition, Section B, plot 77.
{LOP-1883; GRI; Cem. records}

NEAL, Isaac M. - Pvt., Co. I, 21st Regt., Wis. Vol. Inf.
Isaac resided at Clayton and enlisted there on Aug. 11, 1862. He was assigned as above and was discharged due to a disability on Nov. 17, 1862.
{ROV}

NEAL, Ralsey M. - Pvt., Co. C, 118th Regt., New York Vol. Inf.
Ralsey was listed in the 1890 federal census as residing in the town of Rushford at P.O. Eureka. He provided his unit designation as above and his service dates as having been from Aug. 11, 1862 to July 8, 1865. Ralsey was listed as above in the veteran section of the 1895 and 1905 Wisconsin State census at P.O. Omro. He was listed in 1905 as residing at 410 Mary Street in the village of Omro. Ralsey is buried with a simple military marker at Omro Cemetery, Olin's Addition, Section B, plot 77. That plot was owned by Alanson B. Neal, the subject of a previous sketch.
{US 1890; WC-V 1895, 1905; B-1905; GRI; Cem. records}

NEFF, Johann C. - Pvt., Co. D, 41st Regt., Wis. Vol. Inf.
Johann resided at Menasha and enlisted there on May 12, 1864. He was assigned as above and was mustered out on Sept. 23, 1864 at the end of his term of enlistment. John died circa 1898 at Appleton.
{ROV; Lawson p.840}

NEILSON, Christian J. - Pvt., Co. G, 3rd Regt., Wis. Vol. Inf.
Christian resided at Neenah and enlisted there on Jan. 5, 1864. He was assigned as above and was wounded on June 30, 1864. He was then listed as absent sick when the regiment was mustered out on July 18, 1865. Christian was listed in the veteran section of the 1895 and 1905 Wisconsin State census at P.O. Neenah. He was not found in that section of the 1885 state census.
{WC-V 1885, 1895, 1905; ROV}

NEIS, Mathias - Pvt., Co. H, 1st (3 mo.) Regt., Wis. Vol. Inf.
Mathias was born circa 1835 at Prussia. He was a son of Johan B. and Elizabetha Neiss. Elizabeth and Johan were both born circa 1806 at Prussia. John was listed in the 1860 federal census as a laborer residing in the first ward of the city of Oshkosh. Residing with him and his wife were the following children: Mathias; Catherine, born circa 1838; Josephine, born circa 1842; and Johan, born circa 1847. All of the children were born

NEIS, Mathias (cont.)
in Prussia. Mathias was listed again in that same census as a butcher residing with the family of Conrad Ernst in the third ward of Oshkosh. Mathias resided at Oshkosh and enlisted there on Apr. 16, 1861. He was assigned as above and was then mustered out on Aug. 21, 1861. Mathias was listed in 1868 as a butcher residing at 154 Main Street in Oshkosh.
{US 1860; ROV; T-1868}

NEITZEL, Charles - Pvt., Co. C, 53rd Regt., Wis. Vol. Inf.
Carl was born circa 1820 at Prussia. He came to America during the Mexican War and served in the final ten months of that contest. He then came to Wisconsin in 1849 and settled on a farm in the town of Black Wolf. Carolina, his wife, was born circa 1827 at Prussia. They were listed in the 1860 federal census as residing on a farm in the town of Black Wolf. Listed with them were the following children: Rosa, born circa 1851; Charles, born circa 1853; Caroline, born circa 1855; Louis, born circa 1858; and Robert, born in 1860. All of the children were born in Wisconsin. Charles enlisted at Black Wolf on Mar. 1, 1865. He was assigned as above and was mustered out June 27, 1865 after having been confined in the hospital at St. Louis, Missouri. Charles removed to Minnesota in 1878 and returned to Wisconsin in 1882, settling then in the city of Oshkosh. He was listed in the veteran section of the 1885 Wisconsin State census at P.O. Oshkosh. Charles was listed in the 1890 federal census as residing in Oshkosh. He then listed that he had served during the Mexican War as a Private with Co. F, 1st Regt., Mich. Vol. Inf. from Nov. 15, 1847 to Aug. 15, 1848.
{US 1860, 1890; WC-V 1885; Randall p.17; ROV}

NELLIS, Marvin - Pvt., Co. H, 1st Regt., Wis. Vol. Inf.
Marvin was a son of William Nellis. The father was a soldier in the Seminole War in Florida and lost an eye while in service. Marvin resided at Meeme, Manitowoc County and enlisted there on Nov. 27, 1863. He was assigned as above and was wounded at Kenesaw Mountain and again at Pumpkin Vine Creek. Marvin was then transferred to Co. D, 21st Regt., Wis. Vol. Inf. on Sept. 20, 1864. He was again transferred as unassigned to the 3rd Regt., Wis. Vol. Inf. on June 8, 1865 and was mustered out on July 18, 1865. Marvin provided his residence as Neenah when he was transferred to the 3rd Regt. Seward, a brother of Marvin, was also a veteran of the Civil War and was wounded in service. Amanda C. Nellis, a sister, was married in June 1871 to William Boaz Johns, who was also a Civil War veteran and later resided at Antigo, Langlade County.
{ROV; SCA 1:483-4}

NELSON, Christian C. - Sgt., Co. K, 11th Regt., Wis. Vol. Inf.
Christian resided at Clayton and enlisted there on Sept. 28, 1861. He was assigned as above and was promoted to Corporal and then Sergeant in that company. Christian was wounded at Vicksburg, Mississippi. He contracted a disease and died on Oct. 10, 1864 at New Orleans, Louisiana.
{ROV}

NELSON, John - Pvt., Co. H, 20th Regt., Wis. Vol. Inf.
John resided at Ripon, Fond du Lac County and he enlisted there on Feb. 20, 1864. He was assigned as above and was then transferred to Co. E, 35th Regt., Wis. Vol. Inf. on

NELSON, John (cont.)
July 12, 1865. John was mustered out on Mar. 15, 1866. He was not found in the veteran section of the 1885 Wisconsin State census. He was listed in that section of the 1895 state census at P.O. Oshkosh and was not found in that part of the 1905 state census. John was listed in 1888 as a member of GAR Post #10 at Oshkosh. He had been elected as a member of that post on Apr. 2, 1885.
{WC-V 1885, 1895, 1905; ROV}

NELSON, Nels - Pvt., Co. D, 32nd Regt., Wis. Vol. Inf.
Nels resided at Utica and enlisted there on Aug. 21, 1862. He was assigned as above and was mustered out on June 12, 1865.
{ROV}

NELSON, Nels - Pvt., Co. A, 47th Regt., Wis. Vol. Inf.
Nels resided at Winchester and enlisted there on Feb. 11, 1865. He was assigned as above. Nels contracted a disease and died on Mar. 29, 1865 at Tullahoma, Tennessee.
{ROV}

NELSON, Peter - Pvt., Co. A, 11th Regt., Wis. Vol. Inf.?
Peter was listed as above in the veteran section of the 1905 Wisconsin State census at P.O. Oshkosh. He was not found in the records of that regiment. Peter and Christiana, his wife, were listed in that year as residing on 50 acres of section 18 in the town of Algoma. Clarence and Clara Nelson were then residing with him.
{WC-V 1905; B-1905}

NELSON, Simeon B. - Capt., Co. I, 21st Regt., Wis. Vol. Inf.
Simeon was born on Mar. 7, 1828 at Roxbury, Cheshire County, New Hampshire, a son of William and Lucy (Batchelder) Nelson. William was a native of England and Lucy was born in Massachusetts. Simeon was educated in the common schools and attended two terms at an academy. He learned the trade of manufacturing woodenware at age 18 years in Westport, New Hampshire. Simeon was married on May 4, 1852 to Louisa M. Bailey of Swanzey, New Hampshire. She was born circa 1824. They had three children: Eugene F., born circa 1854, died prior to 1888, also listed as Imogene; Emma S.; and Lulie L. In 1853 he began the manufacturing of sash, doors and blinds with two partners. Simeon removed to Wisconsin on Sept. 8, 1857 and settled at Menasha. He was then engaged as a foreman at the Menasha Wooden Ware Co. Simeon was named as the Recruiting Officer at Menasha for the 21st Regt., Wis. Vol. Inf. and held that position from July 28, 1862 until Sept. 5, 1862. He was then commissioned as Captain of the above company on Aug. 26, 1862. Simeon was listed as missing and actually was taken prisoner at Jefferson, Kentucky on Dec. 30, 1862. He was paroled after 36 hours. He was sent to Nashville and then to Camp Chase. In April 1863 he was sent to Benton Barracks at St. Louis to await his exchange. Simeon resigned his commission Apr. 25, 1863 due to a disease brought on by exposure. He then returned to Menasha and concentrated on returning to good health. Louisa had died on Feb. 10, 1863. Simeon returned to his former position but found that he was too ill to continue. He purchased a farm and operated it for two years. Simeon was married a second time on May 4, 1864 to Lestina E. Holt. They had three children: Elwin F.; Flora May; and Roy B. Nelson. Simeon was engaged in taking charge of a manufacturing concern at Peshtigo, Oconto County. He operated that establishment until the great fire which occurred nine

NELSON, Simeon B. (cont.)
years to the day from his involvement in the disaster at Perryville, Kentucky. He returned to Menasha and his former work at the woodenware company. Simeon then removed to Oshkosh in April 1878 and formed a business with George Kennan, a former asoociate from the 21st Regt. They formed the Wisconsin Manufacturing Company and continued under different partnership arrangements. In 1883 they purchased an interest in the Tustin Mill property. Simeon was listed in the veteran section of the 1885 and 1895 Wisconsin State census at P.O. Oshkosh. He was listed in 1888 as a member of GAR Post #10 at Oshkosh. He was listed in the 1890 federal census residing at 44 Mt. Vernon Street in Oshkosh. Simeon was then suffering from bronchitis and a chronic inflammation of the kidney and bladder. He was not found in the veteran section of the 1905 state census.
{US 1860, 1890; WC-V 1885, 1895, 1905; ROV; SCA 1:730-1; OWN 22 Jan 1863}

NESS, John - Pvt., Co. H, 1st Regt., Wis. Hvy. Art.
John resided at Clayton and enlisted there on Aug. 30, 1864. He was assigned as above and was mustered out on June 26, 1865.
{ROV}

NESS, Lans K. - Pvt., Co. H, 1st Regt., Wis. Hvy. Art.
Lans resided at Clayton and enlisted there on Aug. 30, 1864. He was assigned as above and was mustered out on June 26, 1865.
{ROV}

NEUDECK, Emil - Pvt., Co. F, 19th Regt., Wis. Vol. Inf.
Emil resided at Oshkosh and enlisted there on Sept. 3, 1864. He was assigned as above and was transferred to Co. C of that same regiment on May 1, 1865. Emil was mustered out on June 26, 1865. He was listed in 1883 at P.O. Neenah. Emil had then been receiving a pension of $4 per month since Dec. 1882 for an injury to his abdomen. He was listed in the veteran section of the 1885, 1895 and 1905 Wisconsin State census at P.O. Neenah. Emil was listed in the 1890 federal census as residing in the city of Neenah. He was listed in 1905 as residing at 111 E. Wisconsin Avenue in Neenah. A.H., Clara, Lottie, G.J. and W.H. Neudeck were also residing at that address.
{US 1890; WC-V 1885, 1895, 1905; ROV; LOP-1883; B-1905}

NEUMAN, Friedrich - Pvt., Co. F, 19th Regt., Wis. Vol. Inf.
Friedrich was born on Sept. 9, 1836 at Prussia. He was listed in the 1860 federal census as a tailor residing with the family of Johann Matzeck in the third ward of the city of Oshkosh. Emilie C., his wife, was born on Apr. 15, 1841. Friedrich enlisted at Winneconne on Jan. 24, 1862. He was assigned as above and was wounded on May 16, 1864. Friedrich was mustered out on Apr. 29, 1865 at the end of his term of enlistment. He was listed in 1883 at P.O. Winchester, where he was receiving a pension of $6 per month for a wound to his left leg. He was listed in the veteran section of the 1885 Wisconsin State census at P.O. Winchester and in that section of the 1895 state census at P.O. Zittau. Emilie died on Nov. 20, 1890. Frederick was listed in the 1890 federal census as residing in the town of Winchester at P.O. Winchester. He died on July 13, 1904. Friedrich is buried with his wife in the town of Winchester at St. Peter's Evangelical Lutheran Cemetery.
{US 1860, 1890; WC-V 1885, 1895, 1905; ROV; LOP-1883; Cem. records}

NEUMAN, George William - Sgt., Co. F, 19th Regt., Wis. Vol. Inf.
George was born on Sept. 2, 1836 at Rueckerhausen, Nassau, Prussia. He was a son of Peter and Henrietta (Crass) Neumann. The family emigrated to America in 1847. They came directly to Wisconsin and settled on a farm in Washington County. Both parents died there and are buried at Fillmore, Washington County. George removed to Oshkosh in 1854. He was occupied there as a shoemaker. He was married on Oct. 25, 1859 to Catherine Scherff of Winneconne. He was listed as William in the 1860 federal census and was then residing in the third ward of the city of Oshkosh. Kate, his wife, was born circa 1838 at Bavaria. George enlisted at Oshkosh on Jan. 28, 1862. He was assigned as above and was promoted to Sergeant and then 1st Sergeant of that company. George was wounded on July 17, 1864 and was taken prisoner on Oct. 27, 1864 at Fair Oaks, Virginia. He was sent to Richmond, where he remained in Libby Prison for ten days. He was then sent to the stockade prison at Salisbury, N.C. He was commissioned as 2nd Lieutenant of the company on Nov. 28, 1864 but was not mustered at that rank as he was still being held at Salisbury. George was released from prison on Mar. 1, 1865 and was then mustered out at Madison, Wisconsin on Apr. 29, 1865 at the end of his term of enlistment. He returned to Oshkosh. George and Catherine had six children: Helen, married August Moak; Martin J., born on Oct. 31, 1863, died at Oshkosh on Nov. 3, 1925; William J., resided later at Nogales, Arizona; George F.; Katherine "Katie," married to H.H. Nettekoven; and Annie Neumann, married to L.H. Boehm, resided at Chicago. George was listed in the veteran section of the 1885, 1895 and 1905 Wisconsin State census at P.O. Oshkosh. He was listed in 1888 as a member of GAR Post #241 at Oshkosh. He was listed in the 1890 federal census as residing in the town of Oshkosh at P.O. Oshkosh. George was listed in 1905 as residing at 165 Waugoo Street in the city of Oshkosh. George F., Katherine and Anna were residing at that same address. Kate, his wife, died at Oshkosh on Jan. 18, 1900. George was stricken with an illness while attending a GAR convention at Madison, Wisconsin in June 1914. He was returned to his residence at 165 Waugoo Street in Oshkosh. George died in Oshkosh on Apr. 6, 1915.
{US 1860, 1890; WC-V 1885, 1895, 1905; ROV; Randall p.43; SCA 1:580-2; B-1905}
{ODN 16 Jun 1914; ODN 3 Nov 1925; ODN 07 Apr 1915}

NEVITT, Charles R. - Capt., Co. E, 5th (reorg.) Regt., Wis. Vol. Inf.
Charles was born circa 1825 at New York. Elizabeth, his wife, was born circa 1832, also at New York. Charles was listed in the 1860 federal census as a printer residing in the fourth ward of the city of Oshkosh. Listed with him and his wife were the following children: Robert, born circa 1853; Charles, born circa 1855; and William J., born in Oshkosh on Dec. 21, 1857, died at Oshkosh on May 16, 1924. All three sons were born in Wisconsin. Charles resided at Oshkosh when he was commissioned as Captain of the above company on Sept. 12, 1864. He was mustered out on June 20, 1865. Charles was listed in 1868 as a dealer in insurance and real estate. He was then residing at 22 Mt. Vernon Street in Oshkosh. He was listed in 1888 as a member of GAR Post #241 at Oshkosh. Charles was listed in the veteran section of the 1895 and 1905 Wisconsin State census at P.O. Oshkosh. He was not found in that section of the 1885 state census. He was listed in 1905 as a dealer in real estate, insurance and loans. Charles was then residing at 111 High Street in Oshkosh.
{US 1860; WC-V 1885, 1895, 1905; ROV; T-1868; B-1905; ODN 17 May 1924}

NEWCOMB, Joseph A. - Pvt., Co. H, 18th Regt., Wis. Vol. Inf.
Joseph resided at Nepeuskun and enlisted there on Jan. 25, 1864. He was assigned as above and was mustered out on Aug. 3, 1865.
{ROV}

NEWGARD, Amon L. - Cpl., Co. K, 11th Regt., Wis. Vol. Inf.
Amond was born circa 1839 at Norway, a son of Lars and Mary Newgard. Both parents were natives of Norway, the father born there circa 1812 and the mother born circa 1805. They were listed in the 1860 federal census as residing on a farm in the town of Clayton at P.O. Neenah. Also listed with them was Martha, a daughter, who was born circa 1844 at Norway. Amon resided at Clayton and enlisted there on Sept. 17, 1861. He was assigned as above and was promoted to Corporal in that company. Amon was discharged due to a disability on Apr. 7, 1863.
{US 1860; ROV}

NEWGARD, Armud L. - Pvt., Co. G, 3rd Regt., Wis. Vol. Inf.
Armud resided at Clayton and enlisted there on Apr. 28, 1861. He was assigned as above and was discharged on July 15, 1861 due to a disability. Armud re-enlisted in that same company on Jan. 23, 1864 and was wounded on May 25, 1864. He was mustered out on July 18, 1865.
{ROV}

NEWTON, Calvin W. - Pvt., Co. D, 41st Regt., Wis. Vol. Inf.
Calvin resided at Menasha and enlisted there on May 13, 1864. He was assigned as above and was mustered out on Sept. 23, 1864 at the end of his term of enlistment.
{ROV}

NICHOLS, Homer K. - Pvt., Co. F, 18th Regt., Wis. Vol. Inf.
Homer resided at Oshkosh and enlisted there on Nov. 8, 1861. He was assigned as above and was wounded and taken prisoner at Shiloh, Tennessee. Homer was taken prisoner again at Allatoona, Georgia. He was listed as absent on detached service when the regiment was mustered out on July 18, 1865. Homer was listed in the veteran section of the 1885, 1895 and 1905 Wisconsin State census at P.O. Oshkosh. He was listed in 1905 as a painter residing at 393 Main Street in the city of Oshkosh. Edwin Nichols was also residing at that address. Homer was born in 1838 and died in 1924. Catie, his wife, was born in 1845 and died in 1913. Both are buried in the town of Algoma at Peace Lutheran Cemetery.
{WC-V 1885, 1895, 1905; ROV; B-1905; Cem. records}

NICHOLS, Horace - Pvt., Co. C, 29th Regt., Wis. Vol. Inf.
Horace resided at Hubbard, Dodge County and he enlisted there on Aug. 21, 1862. He was shown in the records as having been discharged due to a disability on Sept. 8, 1863. Nancy E. Robinson, his widow, was listed in the 1890 federal census as residing in the city of Oshkosh. She provided his unit designation as above. She also listed that Horace had died in the service in Oct. 1863.
{US 1890; ROV}

NICHOLS, Isaac - Pvt., Co. D, 32nd Regt., Wis. Vol. Inf.
Isaac was born circa 1823 at New York. Elisabeth, his wife, was born circa 1828, also

NICHOLS, Isaac (cont.)
at New York. They were listed in the 1860 federal census as residing on a farm in the town of Nekimi at P.O. Oshkosh. Listed with them then were the following children: Addison, born circa 1853; Eugene, born circa 1855; and Emma, born circa 1859. All of the children were born in Wisconsin. Thomas and Caleb, brothers of Isaac, resided on a nearby farm. Isaac enlisted at Nekimi on Aug. 21, 1862. He was assigned as above and was mustered out on June 12, 1865.
{US 1860; ROV}

NICHOLS, John H. - Pvt., 11th Regt., Wis. Vol. Inf.
John resided at Madison, Dane County and enlisted on Oct. 1, 1861. He was assigned as a musician in the regimental band and was mustered out on July 29, 1862. John was listed in the veteran section of the 1885 Wisconsin State census at P.O. Madison. He was listed in that section of the 1905 state census at P.O. Oshkosh. John was listed then as a bookkeeper at the Commercial National Bank and residing at 51 Franklin Avenue in the city of Oshkosh. Mary Nichols, his wife, was also listed then as the senior vice-president of the Womans' Relief Corps and residing at that same address.
{WC-V 1885, 1905; ROV; B-1905}

NICHOLS, John N. - Cpl., Co. H, 20th Regt., Wis. Vol. Inf.
John resided at Oshkosh and enlisted there on Aug. 14, 1862. He was assigned as above and was promoted to Corporal in that company. John was killed in action at Prairie Grove, Arkansas on Dec. 7, 1862.
{ROV}

NICHOLS, Thomas C. - Cpl., Co. L, 3rd (reorg.) Regt., Wis. Cav.
Thomas resided at Oshkosh and enlisted there on Nov. 25, 1863. He was assigned as above and was promoted to Corporal in that company. Thomas was then mustered out on Oct. 23, 1865.
{ROV}

NICHOLSON, Andrew - Sgt., Co. K, 11th Regt., Wis. Vol. Inf.
Andrew resided at Clayton and was drafted there on Sept. 28, 1861. He was assigned as above and was mustered out on Sept. 30, 1865. Andrew was listed in the 1890 federal census as residing in the city of Neenah. He provided his unit designation as above and his service dates as having been from Aug. 15, 1861 to Sept. 4, 1865. Andrew added that he was then suffering from protruding piles.
{US 1890; ROV}

NICHOLSON, Frederick - Pvt., Co. C, 43rd Regt., Wis. Vol. Inf.
Frederick resided at Utica and enlisted there on Aug. 16, 1864. He was assigned as above and was mustered out on June 24, 1865. Frederick was listed in the veteran section of the 1885 Wisconsin State census at P.O. Soldiers' Grove, Crawford County. He was listed in that section of the 1895 state census at P.O. Clayton and he was not found in that section of the 1905 state census.
{WC-V 1885, 1895, 1905; ROV}

NICHOLSON, Henry William - Cpl., Co. B, 49th Regt., Wis. Vol. Inf.
Henry was born on July 8, 1821 at Randolph, Vermont. He was a son of Richard H.

NICHOLSON, Henry William (cont.)
and Almira (Elmen) Nicholson. Almira was born circa 1796 at Vermont. Henry remained in Vermont until fourteen years of age and then removed to New Hampshire for two years. He was married on Sept. 25, 1843 to Sarah Howe. They removed to Wisconsin in 1846 and settled in Fond du Lac County at the Fourrerite Settlement now known as Ripon. In 1848 he removed to Winnebago County and settled on a farm near Eureka in the town of Rushford. Henry and Sarah had three children: Almira, born in 1846 at New Hampshire; Henry Hudson, subject of a following sketch; and Parker, born in 1854 at Wisconsin. Sarah died in Jan. 1857. Henry was then married in Feb. 1858 to Jane E. Mosley. She was born circa 1837 at New York. They were listed in the 1860 federal census as residing on a farm in the town of Rushford at P.O. Eureka. Almira, mother of Henry, was also residing with them. Henry enlisted at Eureka on Feb. 4, 1865. He was assigned as above and was promoted to Corporal in that company. He was discharged due to a disability on Sept. 20, 1865. Henry and Jane had four children: Dexter, born in 1860; Charlotte B., born in 1862; Charles, born in 1863; and Jessie, born in 1864. Henry was listed in the veteran section of the 1885 Wisconsin State census at P.O. Eureka and in that section of the 1895 state census at P.O. Omro. He owned 185 acres in the town of Rushford in 1889. He was listed in the 1890 federal census as residing in the town of Rushford at P.O. Eureka. Henry moved into the village of Omro in 1893. He was not found in the veteran section of the 1905 state census, but Henry was listed in 1905 as retired and residing at 207 Exchange Street in Omro. Jessie F. Nicholson was then also residing at that address. Henry died on Apr. 3, 1911. He is listed as having been buried in the town of Rushford at Eureka Cemetery but no marker has been found for him. Henry was survived by his wife, five children and one sister.
{US 1860, 1890; WC-V 1885, 1895, 1905; ROV; B-1905; GRI; Randall p.52}
{OmJ 06 Apr 1911}

NICHOLSON, Henry Hudson - Pvt., Co. B, 49th Regt., Wis. Vol. Inf.
Hudson was born circa 1851 at Wisconsin. He was a son of Henry W. Nicholson from a previous sketch. Hudson was listed in the 1860 federal census as residing with his father on a farm in the town of Rushford at P.O. Eureka. He enlisted at Rushford on Feb. 4, 1865. He was assigned as above and was discharged on Sept. 20, 1865 due to a disability.
{US 1860; ROV}

NICHOLSON, Samuel - Pvt., Co. C, 43rd Regt., Wis. Vol. Inf.
Samuel resided at Utica and enlisted there on Aug. 16, 1864. He was assigned as above and was mustered out on May 18, 1865. Samuel was listed in the veteran section of the 1885 Wisconsin State census at P.O. Soldiers' Grove, Crawford County. He was listed in that same section of the 1895 state census at P.O. Clayton and in that section of the 1905 state census at P.O. Richland Center, Richland County.
{WC-V 1885, 1895, 1905; ROV}

NICHOLSON, William - Pvt., Co. C, 43rd Regt., Wis. Vol. Inf.
William resided at Utica and enlisted there on Aug. 16, 1864. He was assigned as above and was mustered out on June 24, 1865. William was listed in the veteran section of the 1885 Wisconsin State census at P.O. Soldiers' Grove, Crawford County. He was listed in that section of the 1895 state census at P.O. Clayton and in the same section of the

NICHOLSON, William (cont.)
1905 state census at P.O. Viola, Richland County.
{WC-V 1885, 1895, 1905; ROV}

NICKEL, John R. - Pvt., Co. L, 3rd (reorg.) Regt., Wis. Cav.
John was born on Nov. 1, 1823. Mary J., his wife, was born on May 25, 1832. John resided at Algoma and enlisted there on Feb. 22, 1864. He was assigned as above and was mustered out on Oct. 23, 1865. John was listed in 1888 as a member of GAR Post #46 at New London, Waupaca County. He was listed in the 1890 federal census as residing in the town of New London. John was listed in the veteran section of the 1895 Wisconsin State census at P.O. New London. He was listed in that section of the 1905 state census at P.O. Omro. John was a brother-in-law of James C. Turney from a following sketch. Mary J. died on Oct. 28, 1898 and John died on Aug. 7, 1908. Both are buried in the town of Mukwa, Waupaca County at Floral Hill Cemetery.
{US 1890; WC-V 1895, 1905; ROV; Cem. records; SCA}

NIEDERGALL, J. - Seaman, "Cricket," U.S. Navy.
He was listed as above in the veteran section of the 1885 Wisconsin State census at P.O. Oshkosh.
{WC-V 1885}

NIEGENFIND, Herman - Pvt., Co. F, 19th Regt., Wis. Vol. Inf.
Herman was born circa 1829 at Prussia. Caroline, his wife, was born circa 1840 at Prussia. They were listed in the 1860 federal census as residing on a farm in the town of Winchester at P.O. Rat River. Listed with them was their son, William, who was born in 1860 at Wisconsin. Robert, a brother of Herman, resided nearby with his family. Herman enlisted at Winchester on Feb. 3, 1862. He was assigned as above. Herman contracted a disease and died on Oct. 15, 1864 at Point of Rocks, Virginia.
{US 1860; ROV}

NIELSEN, Hendrick - Pvt., Co. D, 52nd Regt., Wis. Vol. Inf.
Hendrick resided at Oshkosh and enlisted there on Mar. 4, 1865. He was assigned as above and was mustered out on July 28, 1865.
{ROV}

NILSON, Lars - Pvt., Co. H, 15th Regt., Wis. Vol. Inf.
Lars resided at Neenah and enlisted there on Dec. 22, 1861. He was assigned as above. Lars contracted a disease and died on Feb. 25, 1863 at Nashville, Tennessee.
{ROV}

NITSCHKE, Gottfried - Pvt., Co. C, 9th Regt., Wis. Vol. Inf.
Gottfried resided at Oshkosh and enlisted there on Sept. 16, 1861. He was assigned as above and was then transferred to Co. G of the same regiment. Gottfried was last reported as being absent sick from Ft. Leavenworth, Kansas on Oct. 31, 1864.
{ROV}

NOBLE, Richard P. - Pvt., 3rd Regt., Wis. Vol. Inf.
Richard was born June 19, 1825 at Elizabeth, New York. He was married in Winnebago County on May 6, 1849 to Genervia M. Porter. She was born circa 1833 at New York.

NOBLE, Richard P. (cont.)
They were listed in the 1860 federal census as residing on a farm in the town of Rushford at P.O. Eureka. Listed with them were the following children: Eleanor, born circa 1854; Frederick, born circa 1856; and Philo, born in 1860. All three children were born in Wisconsin. Residing nearby were Mosea and Fanny Noble, probably parents of Richard. Richard listed his residence as Oshkosh when he was shown as enrolled in the 3rd Regt., Wis. Vol. Inf. He was then shown as residing at Gratiot, Lafayette County when he enlisted on Aug. 21, 1862 and was assigned as a Private in Co. H, 33rd Regt., Wis. Vol. Inf. He was mustered out from that unit on Aug. 9, 1865. Richard was married second in Winnebago County on Apr. 6, 1865 to Louise Fellows. He was listed as a member of GAR Post #42 at Tomah, Monroe County. The register of that post shows that Richard had been discharged at Washington, D.C. due to a disability. It also shows that he died on Aug. 12, 1908 and was buried at Olympia, Washington.
{US 1860; WCMR v.1, p.9, #33; WCMR v.1, p.303, #1870; Post #42 Register; ROV}

NOE, Charles - Cpl., Co. F, 19th Regt., Wis. Vol. Inf.
Charles resided at Oshkosh and enlisted there on Feb. 1, 1862. He was assigned as above and was promoted to Corporal in that company. Charles was then mustered out on Apr. 29, 1865 at the end of his term of enlistment. He was listed in 1868 as a carpenter residing at 6 Seventh Street in the city of Oshkosh. Charles was married to Augusta Siefeld. They had a son, unnamed at registration, who was born in Oshkosh on May 25, 1882. Charles was listed in the veteran section of the 1885 and 1895 Wisconsin State census at P.O. Oshkosh. He was listed in 1888 as a member of GAR Post #241 at Oshkosh. Carl was listed in the 1890 federal census as residing at 30 Rosalia Street in Oshkosh.
{US 1890; WC-V 1885, 1895; ROV; T-1868; WCBR v.3, p.57, #338}

NOE, John - Pvt., Co. F, 19th Regt., Wis. Vol. Inf.
John resided at Oshkosh and enlisted there on Nov. 28, 1863. He was assigned as above and he was transferred to Co. C of that same regiment on May 1, 1865. John was then mustered out on Aug. 9, 1865. He was listed in 1868 as an edger boarding at the home of Sebastian Noe at 26 Cemetery Street in the city of Oshkosh.
{ROV; T-1868}

NOGGLE, Lyman H. - Pvt., Co. H, 16th (reorg.) Regt., Wis. Vol. Inf.
Lyman resided at Utica and enlisted there on Feb. 20, 1865. He was assigned as above and was mustered out on July 12, 1865. Lyman was listed in the veteran section of the 1885 Wisconsin State census at P.O. Lynxville, Crawford County.
{WC-V 1885; ROV}

NOLTE, Frederick - Pvt., Co. C, 32nd Regt., Wis. Vol. Inf.
Frederick was born in 1842 at Hanover, a son of Friedrich and Louise Nolte. The parents were also natives of Hanover, the father born there circa 1804 and the mother born circa 1814. They were listed in the 1860 federal census as residing on a farm in the town of Oshkosh. Listed with them were Frederick and another son, Gustav, who was born circa 1847 at Hanover. Frederick enlisted at Oshkosh on Dec. 7, 1863. He was assigned as above and was transferred to Co. G, 16th Regt., Wis. Vol. Inf. on June 4, 1865. Frederick was mustered out on July 12, 1865. He was married in Winnebago County on Oct. 14, 1867 to Mary Jane Sanderson. Frederick died in 1882. Margaret,

NOLTE, Frederick (cont.)
his widow, was born in 1851. She was listed in 1905 as residing at 117 S. Main Street in the city of Oshkosh. She died in 1920. A son, George A., was born in 1874 and died in 1939. All three are buried in the town of Algoma at Ellenwood Cemetery, Section F. His wife was listed in the 1890 federal census as Fredericka. She was then residing in the town of Nekimi at P.O. Oshkosh.
{US 1860, 1890; ROV; B-1905; Cem. records; WCMR v.1, p.351, #2108}

NORSTRANDT, Isaac H. - Pvt., Co. C, 53rd Regt., Wis. Vol. Inf.
Isaac was married in Winnebago County on July 2, 1862 to Mrs. Eleanor C. Sherman. He resided at Oshkosh and enlisted there on Mar. 6, 1865. He was assigned as above. That company was transferred to Co. K, 51st Regt., Wis. Vol. Inf. under orders dated June 10, 1865. The transfer was completed on June 30, 1865 at Ft. Leavenworth, Kansas. The regiment returned to Madison, Wisconsin on Aug. 1, 1865 and was then mustered out by companies. The last company was mustered out on Aug. 30, 1865. Isaac died on Sept. 8, 1866 at age 28 years, 6 months and 16 days. He is buried in the town of Nekimi at Salem Baptist Cemetery. This name may also be found as Nostrant.
{ROV; WCMR v.1, p.228, #1269; Cem. records}

NORTHAM, Eli R. - Pvt., Co. F, 18th Regt., Wis. Vol. Inf.
Eli resided at Oshkosh and enlisted there on Jan. 17, 1862. He was assigned as above. Eli contracted a disease and died on June 30, 1862 at Hamburg, Tennessee.
{ROV}

NORTHAM, Jay V. - Pvt., Co. D, 41st Regt., Wis. Vol. Inf.
Jay resided at Menasha and enlisted there on May 12, 1864. He was assigned as above and was mustered out on Sept. 23, 1864 at the end of his term of enlistment. Jay died circa 1904 at Chicago.
{ROV; Lawson p.840}

NORTHAM, Norman W. - Cpl., Co. C, 21st Regt., Wis. Vol. Inf.
Norman resided at Oshkosh and enlisted on Aug. 13, 1862. He was assigned as above and was promoted to Corporal in that company. He was mustered out on June 8, 1865. Norman was listed in 1868 as a clerk boarding at 7 Sixth Street in the city of Oshkosh.
{ROV; T-1868}

NORTHAM, Simon R. - Sgt., Co. C, 10th Regt., Wis. Vol. Inf.
Simon was born circa 1836 at New York. He was a son of Eli and Barthena Northum and a brother of Wesley from a following sketch. Eli was born circa 1812 at New York and his wife was born circa 1813 in that same state. They were listed in the 1860 federal census as residing in the second ward of the village of Menasha. Listed with them were the following children: Simon; Wesley; Wilson, born circa 1843; and Vincent, born circa 1848. All of the children were born in New York. Simon was then listed as a boatman. He resided at Menasha and enlisted there on Sept. 16, 1861. He was assigned as above and was promoted to Corporal and then Sergeant in that company. He was wounded at Perryville and was taken prisoner at Chickamauga, Georgia. Simon contracted a disease and died in the rebel prison at Andersonville, Georgia on Aug. 7, 1864. He was buried there in grave #4,980.
{US 1860; ROV}

NORTHAM, Wesley - Pvt., Co. G, 3rd Regt., Wis. Vol. Inf.
Wesley was born circa 1841 at New York. He was a son of Eli and Barthena Northam and a brother of Simon from a previous sketch. Wesley was listed in the 1860 federal census as residing with his parents in the second ward of the village of Menasha. He resided there when he enlisted on Apr. 20, 1861 and was assigned as above. Wesley was discharged due to a disability on Oct. 13, 1862.
{US 1860; ROV}

NORTON, Charles - Pvt., Co. D, 32nd Regt., Wis. Vol. Inf.
Charles was born on Oct. 3, 1815. He removed to Winnebago County and settled in the town of Algoma in 1849. Charles enlisted in Algoma on Aug. 18, 1862. He was assigned as above and was transferred to the Veteran Reserve Corps on July 17, 1865. Charles was listed in 1883 at P.O. Oshkosh. He had then been receiving a pension since August 1878 for rheumatism. Charles was listed in the veteran section of the 1885, 1895 and 1905 Wisconsin State census at P.O. Oshkosh. He was listed in the 1890 federal census as residing at 236 Knapp Street in Oshkosh. Charles celebrated his 75th birthday at the home of his daughter, Mrs. F.E. Morehouse, on Eleventh Street in Oshkosh. He was listed in 1905 as residing at 33 Georgia Street in Oshkosh.
{US 1890; WC-V 1885, 1895, 1905; LOP-1883; B-1905; OWN 09 Oct 1890; ROV}

NORTON, Joseph - Pvt., Co. A, 52nd Regt., Wis. Vol. Inf.
Joseph was born on Jan. 20, 1824 at County Wicklow, Ireland. He was the eldest son of James and Catherine (Kelly) Norton. They had fourteen children. Joseph attended the common schools of his home until age 15, when he commenced farming with his father. He left home on Mar. 17, 1850 with the assistance of his father and proceeded to Liverpool, England. He then took passage on the "Kossuth" bound for America. He commenced work as a farm hand in Onondaga County, New York for Caleb Brown. Joseph remained there for five years. In Oct. 1855 he removed and settled in Wisconsin at DePere, Brown County. He purchased 80 acres in the town of Rockland and added another 80 acres in the following year. For his first five years in Wisconsin, Joseph was engaged in sawmills near DePere. He was married on July 24, 1858 to Bridget Forestal. She was a native of County Kilkenny, Ireland. Her father, Thomas Forestal, died before she was born. She came to America with her mother and brothers Thomas and Edward. Joseph and Bridget had the following children: Katie C., resided at home; Mary A., married William Powers of Nahma, Michigan; Sarah, married John Shaughnessy of Ft. Howard; James; Timothy; and Anna. Joseph listed his residence as Menasha when he enlisted on Mar. 1, 1865. He was assigned as above but saw no actual service as he contracted small pox at St. Louis, Missouri and was then discharged on June 3, 1865. Joseph owned 600 acres in Wrightstown and Rockland in 1895.
{ROV; CBR-FRV 358-9}

NORTON, Samuel G. - Pvt., Co. E, 5th (reorg.) Regt., Wis. Vol. Inf.
Samuel resided at Oshkosh and enlisted there on Sept. 3, 1864. He was assigned as above and was mustered out on June 20, 1865. Samuel was married to Hannah J., a daughter of Reuben M. Parkinson. Reuben was born on May 10, 1808 at Schoharie County, New York and was a son of Reuben and Nannie (McCurdy) Parkinson. He was married in 1833 to Sarah A. Woodard. She died in 1838, leaving two children, Hannah and Joseph Parkinson. Reuben came to Oshkosh with his second wife and his family in 1850. When Reuben died in Oshkosh on Apr. 25, 1893, Samuel and Hannah were listed

NORTON, Samuel G. (cont.)
as residing in Jasper County, Missouri.
{ROV; OWM 29 Apr 1893}

NORTON, William S. - Pvt., Co. F, 17th Regt., Massachusetts Vol. Inf.
William was listed as above in the veteran section of the 1885 Wisconsin State census at P.O. Neenah. He was listed in that section of the 1905 state census at P.O. Oshkosh. William was listed in 1905 as a laborer residing at 79 Merritt Street in the city of Oshkosh.
{WC-V 1885, 1905; B-1905}

NOSTRANT, James Monroe - Pvt., Co. C, 21st Regt., Wis. Vol. Inf.
James was born circa 1843. He resided at Nekimi and enlisted there on Aug. 12, 1862. He was assigned as above and was mustered out on June 8, 1865. James died at the home of a daughter in Oshkosh on Dec. 25, 1905. He was survived by four children: Mrs. Fred W. Lambert of Oshkosh; Mrs. M. Halversen and James Nostrant, both of Anamoose, North Dakota; and Mrs. S.M. Cook of Chicago. He was also survived by two sisters, Mrs. O.A. Tooker of Green Bay and Mrs. Daniel Quincy of Stevens Point, and a brother, William Nostrant, also of Stevens Point.
{ROV; ODN 26 Dec 1905}

NOYES, George B. - Cpl., Co. C, 146th Regt., Illinois Vol. Inf.
George was born in May 1846 at Canada. His father was born in Massachusetts and his mother was a native of Vermont. George was listed as above in the veteran section of the 1885 Wisconsin State census at P.O. Winneconne. He was listed in the 1890 federal census as residing in the village of Winneconne. George then provided his unit designation as above and his service dates as having been from Aug. 30, 1864 to July 1865. He was listed in the 1900 federal census as residing at the Wisconsin Veterans' Home at King. Amelia A., his wife of 25 years, was residing there with him. She was born in Dec. 1856 in Wisconsin. Her father was a native of Wales and her mother was born in New York. George and Amelia had 6 children, three still living in 1900, including Sarah, who was born in Apr. 1886 and Julia, who was born in Apr. 1890. Both named daughters were also residing at King in 1900.
{US 1890, 1900; WC-V 1885}

NOYES, Joshua Copp - Surg., 32nd Regt., Wis. Vol. Inf.
Joshua resided at Fairwater, Fond du Lac County. He was commissioned as 2nd Assistant Surgeon of the above regiment on Dec. 9, 1863 and was promoted to 1st Assistant Surgeon on Oct. 19, 1864. Joshua was promoted to Surgeon on Feb. 1, 1865 and was mustered out on June 12, 1865. He was listed in 1868 as a physician boarding at 13 Washington Street in the city of Oshkosh. Joshua was listed in the veteran section of the 1885 and 1895 Wisconsin State census at P.O. Oshkosh. He was listed in 1888 as a member of GAR Post #10 at Oshkosh. Joshua was listed in the 1890 federal census as residing at 65 Washington Street in Oshkosh. Catherine, his widow, was listed in 1905 as residing at 65 Washington Street in Oshkosh. Helen and Miriam Noyes were also residing at that address. Dr. George B. Noyes also had his office at that address.
{US 1890; WC-V 1885, 1895; ROV; T-1868; B-1905}

NUGENT, Alfred A. - Pvt., Co. I, 21st Regt., Wis. Vol. Inf.
Alfred was a son of Henry B. and Jane Nugent and a brother of John B. of a following sketch. Alfred resided at Menasha and enlisted there on Jan. 4, 1864. He was assigned as above and was wounded at Bentonsville. Alfred was discharged due to those wounds on May 16, 1865. When Henry died in 1898, Alfred was listed as an attorney residing at Kaukauna, Outagamie County.
{ROV; ODN 11 Feb 1898}

NUGENT, John B. Sr. - Pvt., Co. G, 3rd Regt., Wis. Vol. Inf.
John was born on Oct. 13, 1834 at Marysburg, Prince Edward, Canada. He was a son of Henry B. and Jane Nugent, both natives of Canada. He was also a brother of Alfred A. and William H. Nugent from other sketches. Henry was born circa 1811. In about 1839 he removed with his family to Upper Canada and remained there until John was sixteen years of age. Jane died during that time while on a trip back to Marysburg. In 1850, John removed with his father and step-mother to Michigan. Four years later they removed to Wisconsin and settled in Calumet County. John was engaged there as a lumberman and farmer. Henry remained in Calumet County until about 1889 and he then moved to Menasha and resided with son John. He died at Menasha on Feb. 10, 1898. Henry was survived by eight children: John B. Nugent of Menasha; Alfred A. Nugent of Kaukauna; Fred and Daniel Nugent of Florida; Mrs. T. Moore of Menasha; Mrs. Nancy Blake and Flora Nugent of Marinette; and Mrs. Jessie Hart of Canada. John enlisted at Clifton, Monroe County on Apr. 30, 1861. He was assigned as above and was discharged on May 28, 1862 due to a disability. John was married on Jan. 1, 1864 to Josephine V. Collins. She was born Nov. 27, 1843 at Washington, Sullivan County, New Hampshire and was a daughter of Tristram and Emilia Collins. John and Josephine had nine children: James C.; John B.; Kittie M.; Alice M.; Emilla J.; Charles H.; William H.; Mary J.; and Belle M. Nugent. John was listed in the veteran section of the 1885 Wisconsin State census at P.O. Sherwood, Calumet County. He removed to Menasha in the spring of 1887. This move was for the education of his children and John retained his farm in Calumet County. He remained in Menasha and was listed there in the 1890 federal census. He was listed in the veteran section of the 1895 state census at P.O. Menasha and was not found in that part of the 1905 state census. He was listed in 1905 as residing in the village of Winnebago. Belle, Mollie, Milicent, John and Harry Nugent were listed as residing with him.
{US 1890; WC-V 1885, 1895, 1905; ROV; Randall p.20; ODN 11 Feb 1898; B-1905}

NUGENT, William H. - Sgt., Co. C, 10th Regt., Wis. Vol. Inf.
William was a son of Henry B. and Jane Nugent. He was a brother of Alfred A. and John B. Nugent from previous sketches. William resided at Menasha and enlisted there on Sept. 3, 1861. He was assigned as above and was promoted to Sergeant in that company. William contracted a disease and he died on Mar. 28, 1862 at Nashville, Tennessee.
{ROV}

NUTT, Silas J. - Pvt., Co. C, 21st Regt., Wis. Vol. Inf.
Silas resided at Oshkosh and enlisted there on Aug. 20, 1862. He was assigned as a musician in the above company and was mustered out on June 8, 1865.
{ROV}

NUTTER, George - Pvt., Co. E, 2nd Regt., Wis. Vol. Inf.
George resided at Oshkosh and enlisted there on May 25, 1861. He was assigned as above. George was killed in action on Sept. 14, 1862 at South Mountain, Maryland.
{ROV; OWN 02 Oct 1862}

NUTTING, Isaac W. - Pvt., Co. A, 1st Batt., Maine Lt. Art.
Isaac was born in 1843. Frances Berray, his wife, was born in 1850. Isaac was listed as above in the veteran section of the 1885 and 1895 Wisconsin State census at P.O. Eureka. He was listed as above in the 1890 federal census as residing in the town of Rushford at P.O. Eureka. Isaac then provided his service dates as having been from Feb. 1864 to July 16, 1865. He was suffering from chronic diarrhea and a lung disease. Isaac was listed in the veteran section of the 1905 state census at P.O. Omro. Isaac was listed in 1905 as a carpenter residing on Poygan Avenue in the village of Omro. He died in 1924 and Frances died in 1935. Both are buried in the town of Poygan at Oak Hill Cemetery.
{US 1890; WC-V 1885, 1895, 1905; ROV; B-1905; Cem. records}

NUTTING, Warren - Pvt., Co. K, 5th (reorg.) Regt., Wis. Vol. Inf.
Warren resided at Rushford and enlisted there on Aug. 30, 1864. He was assigned as above and was then mustered out on June 20, 1865. Sarah C., his wife, was born on June 2, 1842 and died on Jan. 15, 1873. Charles E. a son, died on Feb. 15, 1882 at age 12 years, 7 months and 13 days. Sarah and Charles are buried in the town of Aurora, Waushara County at Shead Island Cemetery.
{ROV; Cem. records}

NYE, Frederick W. - Sgt., Co. C, 48th Regt., Wis. Vol. Inf.
Fred was married in Winnebago County on Jan. 25, 1865 to Minnie Rumsey. He resided at Omro and enlisted there on Jan. 30, 1865. He was assigned as above and was then promoted to 1st Sergeant in that company. Frederick was discharged on July 14, 1865 due to a disability. Almeda, former widow of Fred, was listed in the 1890 federal census as residing in the village of Omro.
{US 1890; ROV; WCMR v.1, p.268, #1592*}

OAKLEY, James H. - Civil War Veteran.
James was born circa 1831. He was a son of Peter and Betsey E. Oakley. Peter was born circa 1808 and died on July 27, 1853. Betsey was born on June 30, 1810 and died on June 25, 1900. James died in the battle at Pittsburg Landing, Tennessee on Aug. 6, 1862 at age 31 years. His estate was entered into probate in the records of Winnebago County on Apr. 16, 1870. James is buried with his parents in the town of Nepeuskun at Koro Cemetery.
{Cem. records; WCPR v.14, p.285-292}

OATMAN, Albert - Civil War Veteran?
Albert was born circa 1841 at New York. He was a son of Reuben Bates and Sarah (Safford) Oatman and a brother of Charles, Isaac and Safford Oatman of other sketches. Albert was listed in the 1860 federal census as residing with his parents in the town of Neenah. He enlisted in an unknown Wisconsin unit. He was sent to an invalid hospital and then returned home, where he died three weeks later.
{US 1860; SCA 1:221-2}

OATMAN, Charles A. - Pvt., Co. I, 32nd Regt., Wis. Vol. Inf.
Charles was born circa 1843 at New York. He was a son of Reuben Bates and Sarah (Safford) Oatman and a brother of Albert, Isaac and Safford Oatman of other sketches. Charles was listed in the 1860 federal census as residing with his parents in the town of Neenah. He enlisted at Neenah on Oct. 28, 1863. He was assigned as above and was then transferred to Co. C, 16th Regt., Wis. Vol. Inf. on June 4, 1865. Charles was mustered out on July 12, 1865.
{US 1860; ROV; SCA 1:221-2}

OATMAN, Isaac - Pvt., Co. E, 2nd Regt., Wis. Vol. Inf.
Isaac was a son of Reuben Bates and Sarah (Safford) Oatman and a brother of Albert, Charles and Safford Oatman from other sketches. Isaac listed his residence as Oshkosh when he enlisted on May 25, 1861. He was assigned as above and received an ankle wound while in service. He was mustered out on June 28, 1864 at the end of his term of enlistment. Isaac listed his residence as Menasha when he re-enlisted on Feb. 22, 1865. He was assigned as a Private to Co. F, 50th Regt., Wis. Vol. Inf. and was promoted to Corporal in that company. Isaac was mustered out on Feb. 23, 1866 at the end of his term of enlistment. He was listed by Col. Harshaw as residing in Northern Wisconsin in 1899.
{ROV; SCA 1:221-2; ODN 07 May 1899}

OATMAN, Safford - Pvt., Co. G, 3rd Regt., Wis. Vol. Inf.
Safford was born on Dec. 7, 1835 at Brattleboro, Vermont. He was a son of Reuben Bates and Sarah (Safford) Oatman and a brother to Albert, Charles and Isaac Oatman of other sketches. Reuben was born circa 1807 in Bennington, Vermont. Sarah was born circa 1812 at Salem, Washington County, New York. She was a daughter of Aden Safford, a veteran of the War of 1812. Safford Oatman removed with his parents to Pineville, Oswego County, New York. They were residents there for 16 years and Safford received his education there in the district schools. The family removed to Wisconsin in 1853 and settled in the town of Neenah. Reuben and Sarah also had at least one daughter, Mary, who was born circa 1844 at New York. Safford was married at Neenah on May 12, 1856 (Sept. 6, 1855) to Charlotte (Emma) Hoha. She was born circa 1836 at New York and was a daughter of Charles and Charlotte Hoha. Both of her parents were natives of Prussia, the father born there circa 1803 and the mother born circa 1804. They were listed in the 1860 federal census as residing on a farm near Safford and his family in the town of Clayton at P.O. Neenah. Safford and Charlotte had eleven children: Nettie, born circa 1856, married Charles Moss of Ingalls, Mich.; Emma, born circa 1857, married John Lynch of Ingalls, Mich.; Ellen, born circa 1858, married William Smith of Menomonee, widowed prior to 1888; Byron, born in late 1859, married Ettie Williams, resided north of Menomonee; Mattie; General; Jin; Jessie; Helen, died in infancy; Elmer, died in infancy; and Willie, died in infancy. Safford listed his residence as Clayton when he enlisted on May 30, 1861. He was assigned as above and was discharged on Aug. 31, 1862 due to a disability. At enlistment, Safford had suffered from floating cartilage. He suffered from exposure which caused one of his limbs to swell to three times its normal size. He returned to Neenah and worked at his trade as a carpenter until 1866. He then removed to Menomonee, Michigan. Safford was engaged there as a contractor and builder. He was still residing at Menomonee in 1888. He was listed in the 1910 federal census as a widower residing at the Wisconsin

OATMAN, Safford (cont.)
Veterans' Home at King. He had been married for 30 years.
{US 1860, 1910; SCA 1:221-2; WCMR v.1, p.85, #362; ROV}

OBORN, John Sanford - Cpl., Co. G, 36th Regt., Wis. Vol. Inf.
John resided at Menasha and enlisted there on Feb. 28, 1864. He was assigned as above and was promoted to Corporal in that company. He was mustered out on July 12, 1865. John was married in Winnebago County on Dec. 25, 1866 to Carrie A. Henry.
{ROV; WCMR v.1, p.315, #1961}

OBORN, William - Pvt., Co. D, 41st Regt., Wis. Vol. Inf.
William resided at Menasha and enlisted there on May 6, 1864. He was assigned as above and was mustered out on Sept. 23, 1864 at the end of his term of enlistment.
{ROV}

O'BRIEN, Edward - Pvt., Co. I, 21st Regt., Wis. Vol. Inf.
Edward resided at Menasha and enlisted there on Aug. 9, 1862. He was assigned as above. Edward contracted a disease and died on Dec. 6, 1863 at Nashville, Tennessee.
{ROV}

O'BRIEN, Patrick - Pvt., Co. F, 1st Regt., Wis. Cav.
Patrick resided at Ft. Atkinson, Jefferson County and enlisted there on Nov. 3, 1861. He was assigned as above and he was discharged due to a disability on Oct. 21, 1862. Patrick re-enlisted at Oshkosh on Feb. 25, 1865 and was assigned as Private, Co. E, 48th Regt., Wis. Vol. Inf. He was mustered out on Dec. 30, 1865. Patrick was listed in the veteran section of the 1885 and 1905 Wisconsin State census at P.O. Winneconne. He was listed in the 1890 federal census as residing in the village of Winneconne. Patrick was listed in 1905 as a sailor residing on George Street in Winneconne.
{US 1890; WC-V 1885, 1905; ROV; B-1905}

O'BRIEN, Richard - Pvt., 8th Batt., Wis. Lt. Art.
Richard resided at Menasha and enlisted there on Feb. 26, 1864. He was assigned as above and was mustered out on Aug. 10, 1865. Richard was listed in the 1890 federal census as residing in the city of Menasha. He was then suffering from deafness. Sarah, widow of Richard, was listed in 1905 as residing at 459 Tayco Street in Menasha. Edward J. and Flavia H. O'Brien were also residing at that address.
{US 1890; ROV; B-1905}

OCHNER, Fred - Pvt., Co. D, 51st Regt., Wis. Vol. Inf.
Fred resided at Oshkosh and enlisted there on Mar. 4, 1865. He was assigned as above and was mustered out on Aug. 29, 1865.
{ROV}

O'CONNELL, James Jr. - Sgt., Co. E, 42nd Regt., Wis. Vol. Inf.
James was born circa 1845 at Massachusetts, a son of James and Mary (Murphy) O'Connell and a brother of Michael of a following sketch. The father was a native of Ireland, born there circa 1810. Mary was born circa 1820 at Ireland. Elizabeth Murphy, her mother, was born circa 1790 at Ireland. James and Mary were listed in the 1860 federal census as residing on a farm in the town of Black Wolf. Listed with

O'CONNELL, James Jr. (cont.)
them were the following children: Daniel, born circa 1841; Michael; James; Mary, born circa 1846; Elisabeth, born circa 1848; Margaret, born circa 1850; Morris, born circa 1853; and William, born circa 1856. The three youngest children were all born in Wisconsin and the others were born in Massachusetts. Elizabeth Murphy was also residing with them. James Jr. resided at Black Wolf and he enlisted there on Feb. 20, 1862. He was assigned as Private, Co. C, 17th Regt., Wis. Vol. Inf. and was then discharged on Mar. 27, 1863 due to a disability. James re-enlisted on Aug. 22, 1864 and was assigned as Private, Co. E, 42nd Regt., Wis. Vol. Inf. He was promoted to Corporal and then Sergeant in that company. James was mustered out June 20, 1865.
{US 1860; ROV}

O'CONNELL, Michael - Pvt., Co. E, 42nd Regt., Wis. Vol. Inf.
Michael was born circa 1843 at Massachusetts, a son of James and Mary O'Connell and a brother of James from a previous sketch. Michael resided at Black Wolf and enlisted there on Aug. 22, 1864. He was assigned as above and was mustered out June 20, 1865.
{US 1860; ROV}

O'CONNER, Patrick - Pvt., Co. B, 3rd Regt., Wis. Cav.
Patrick was married to Ellen McDonald in Winnebago County on Sept. 21, 1853. He resided at Oshkosh and enlisted there on Mar. 24, 1862. He was assigned as a wagoner in the above company. Patrick was then transferred to Co. B, 3rd (reorg.) Regt., Wis. Cav. on Feb. 1, 1865. He contracted a disease and died on Feb. 6, 1865 at Little Rock, Arkansas.
{ROV; WCMR v.1, p.149, #635}

ODELL, Charles H. - Pvt., Co. D, 32nd Regt., Wis. Vol. Inf.
Charles enlisted at Oshkosh on Dec. 7, 1863 and was assigned as above. He was then transferred to Co. D, 16th (reorg.) Regt., Wis. Vol. Inf. on June 4, 1865. At that time he provided his address as Omro. Charles was mustered out on July 12, 1865.
{ROV}

ODELL, Columbus P. - Pvt., Co. H, 21st Regt., Wis. Vol. Inf.
Columbus was born circa 1828 at New York. Ann, his wife, was born circa 1828 at Ireland. They were listed in the 1860 federal census as residing on a farm in the town of Black Wolf. Listed with them were the following children: James H., born circa 1850 at New York; Nathan, born circa 1852 at New York; Agnes, born circa 1858 at Wisconsin; and Lena, born in 1859 at Wisconsin. Columbus listed his residence as Oshkosh when he enlisted on Aug. 14, 1862. He was assigned as above and was then discharged on Apr. 22, 1863 due to a disability. Columbus re-enlisted on Feb. 13, 1865 and was assigned as a Private, Co. C, 46th Regt., Wis. Vol. Inf. He was mustered out on Aug. 21, 1865. Columbus was listed in 1868 as a drag sawyer residing at 38 Warren Street in the city of Oshkosh. He was listed in 1883 at P.O. Oshkosh and receiving a pension of $8 per month for chronic myelitis. Dr. H.W. Gubera, a brother-in-law residing at Keokuk, Iowa had visited with Columbus in April 1885. Columbus was listed as a member of GAR Post #241 at Oshkosh in 1888. He was listed in the 1890 federal census as residing in the town of Omro at P.O. Omro. Columbus was listed in the veteran section of the 1895 and 1905 Wisconsin State census at P.O. Oshkosh. He was not found in that part of the 1885 state census. Columbus was listed in 1905 as residing

ODELL, Columbus P. (cont.)
at 111 Vine Street in the city of Oshkosh. Charles A., Lillian A. and Valeria A. Odell were also residing at that address.
{US 1860, 1890; WC-V 1885, 1895, 1905; ROV; T-1868; LOP-1883; B-1905}
{ODT 23 Apr 1885}

ODELL, James Henry - Pvt., Co. E, 42nd Regt., Wis. Vol. Inf.
James resided at Menasha and enlisted there on Aug. 18, 1864. He was assigned as above and was mustered out on June 20, 1865. James was listed in the veteran section of the 1885 and 1905 Wisconsin State census at P.O. Menasha. He was not found in that section of the 1895 census. James was listed in the 1890 federal census as residing in the city of Menasha. He was listed in 1905 as a foreman for the Chicago, Milwaukee & St. Paul Railroad and residing at 537 First Street in Menasha. John Odell was also listed at that address.
{US 1890; WC-V 1885, 1895, 1905; ROV; B-1905}

OEHLER, Henry - Pvt., Co. E, 52nd Regt., Wis. Vol. Inf.
Henry was born on July 9, 1824. Fredrica, his wife, was born on Oct. 27, 1832. Henry resided at Winchester and enlisted there on Mar. 13, 1865. He was assigned as above and was mustered out on July 28, 1865. Fredrica died on July 22, 1878 and Henry died on June 1, 1906. Both are buried in the town of Nekimi at Salem Baptist Cemetery.
{ROV; Cem. records}

O'HARROW, Joel S. - Pvt., Co. C, 46th Regt., Wis. Vol. Inf.
Joel was born in 1843 at New York. Sarah, his mother, was born circa 1800 at New York. She was listed in the 1860 federal census as residing in the town of Nekimi at P.O. Oshkosh. Then listed with her were the following children: William H., subject of a following sketch; Joel; and Ellen, born circa 1836 at New York. Joel resided at Nekimi and enlisted there on Feb. 14, 1865. He was assigned as above and was mustered out on Sept. 27, 1865. Joel was listed in the veteran section of the 1885 Wisconsin State census at P.O. Nekimi. He was listed in the 1890 federal census as residing in the town of Nekimi at P.O. Oshkosh. He was listed in that section of the 1895 and 1905 state census at P.O. Oshkosh. Joel died in 1916. Frances I., his wife, was born in 1854 and died in 1936. They are buried with members of their family in the town of Nekimi at Salem Baptist Cemetery.
{US 1860, 1890; WC-V 1885, 1895, 1905; ROV; Cem. records}

O'HARROW, William H. - Pvt., Co. F, 18th Regt., Wis. Vol. Inf.
William was born circa 1841 at New York, a son of Henry and Sarah O'Harrow. Henry died on Sept. 20, 1857 at age 59 years. Sarah died on Dec. 1, 1886 at age 85 years. William listed his residence as Oshkosh when he enlisted on Nov. 24, 1861. He was assigned as above and was taken prisoner at Allatoona, Georgia. William was mustered out on May 25, 1865. He died on Sept. 29, 1867 at age 26 years, 10 months and 17 days. William is buried with his parents in the town of Nekimi at Salem Baptist Cemetery.
{US 1860; ROV; Cem. records}

OLANS, Nels - Pvt., Co. B, 15th Regt., Wis. Vol. Inf.
Nels resided at Winchester and enlisted there on Jan. 6, 1862. He was assigned as above

OLANS, Nels (cont.)
and was taken prisoner at Chickamauga, Georgia. Nels was mustered out on Jan. 18, 1865 at the end of his term of enlistment.
{ROV}

OLDS, Ebenezer - Pvt., Co. C, 38th Regt., Wis. Vol. Inf.
Ebenezer was married in Winnebago County on Oct. 7, 1861 to Lucretia Lowell. He resided at Oshkosh and enlisted there on Mar. 31, 1864. He was assigned as above and was mustered out on July 26, 1865.
{ROV; WCMR v.1, p.219, #1197}

OLESON, Andrew - Pvt., Co. H, 1st Regt., Wis. Hvy. Art.
Andrew resided at Winchester and enlisted there on Aug. 31, 1864. He was assigned as above and was mustered out on June 26, 1865.
{ROV}

OLESON, Johannes - Pvt., Co. H, 1st Regt., Wis. Hvy. Art.
Johannes resided at Winchester and enlisted on Aug. 30, 1864. He was assigned as above and was mustered out on June 26, 1865.
{ROV}

OLESON, John - Pvt., unassigned, 11th Regt., Wis. Vol. Inf.
John resided at Winchester and enlisted there on Feb. 22, 1864. He was not found on the rolls of any company within that regiment.
{ROV}

OLESON, Ole - Pvt., Co. E, 2nd Regt., Wis. Vol. Inf.
Ole was born on Dec. 30, 1839 at Upper Tillemarken, Norway. He was the oldest of ten children. He emigrated to the United States with his parents in 1843 and settled at Wisconsin in Racine County. They removed to Winnebago County in 1853 and settled in the town of Winchester. In 1859 Ole moved into Oshkosh as he did not care for life on the farm. He was then engaged on the river steamers. Ole listed his residence as Winchester when he enlisted on June 1, 1861. He was originally assigned as above. He was detached to the Naval Gunboat Service in Feb. 1862 at Cairo, Illinois and was assigned to the "Mound City." Ole was dropped from the rolls by order of the War Dept. on Nov. 13, 1863. He returned to Oshkosh and resumed working as a boatman. Ole was married in 1871 to Mary Ann Petford. She was a daughter of Thomas Petford of Butte des Morts. Ole served two four-year terms as the appointed Postmaster of Oshkosh. He was listed as a member of GAR Post #10 at Oshkosh in 1888. Ole was listed in the 1890 federal census as residing in the city of Oshkosh. He was listed in the veteran section of the 1895 Wisconsin State census at P.O. Oshkosh. Ole was seized with a stroke of apoplexy while seated on the "S.W. Hollister" on the evening of Aug. 13, 1905. He died early the following morning at his home. Ole was survived by his wife, an invalid for many years, and one daughter, Mrs. John Harmon of Oshkosh. He was also survived by a brother, Martin Oleson of Oshkosh and sisters Mrs. M. Halverson of Los Angeles, California (also given as Mrs. Ole Halverson of Winneconne) and Mrs. Anna Jackson (also given as from Oshkosh) of Omaha, Nebraska. Ole was buried in

OLESON, Ole (cont.)
Oshkosh at Riverside Cemetery.
{US 1890; WC-V 1895; ODN 14 Aug 1905; ODN 08 Feb 1898; OWN 04 Jun 1898}
{ROV; ODN 14 Aug 1905; ODN 09 Dec 1905}

OLESON, Ole Andrew - Pvt., 2nd Batt., Wis. Lt. Art.
Ole was born in 1840. He enlisted on Sept. 18, 1861 and was assigned as above. He was mustered out on Oct. 1, 1864 at the end of his term of enlistment. Ole was married in Winnebago County on Nov. 9, 1866 to Amelia Miller. She was born in 1844. Ole was listed in the veteran section of the 1885, 1895 and 1905 Wisconsin State census at P.O. Winneconne and he was listed in the 1890 federal census as then residing in the village of Winneconne. Ole was listed in 1905 as residing on 80 acres of section 10 in the town of Winneconne. Amelia died in 1929 and Andrew died in 1931. Both are buried with members of their family in the town of Winneconne at Bell Cemetery.
{US 1890; WC-V 1885, 1895, 1905; ROV; B-1905; WCMR v.1, p.310, #1922*}
{Cem. records}

OLESON, Ole B. - Pvt., Co. D, 32nd Regt., Wis. Vol. Inf.
Ole resided at Clayton and enlisted there on Aug. 21, 1862. He was assigned as above. Ole died on July 10, 1863 at Memphis, Tennessee.
{ROV}

OLESON, Ole Souby - Pvt., Co. D, 32nd Regt., Wis. Vol. Inf.
Ole listed his residence as Clayton when he enlisted on Aug. 20, 1862. He was assigned as above and was discharged due to a disability on Aug. 10, 1863. Ole listed his residence as Winchester when he re-enlisted on Aug. 31, 1864. He was assigned as a Private, Co. H, 1st Regt., Wis. Hvy. Art. Ole was then mustered out on June 26, 1865. He was married in Winnebago County on Mar. 4, 1866 to Anna Danielson.
{ROV; WCMR v.1, p.293, #1789*}

OLIN, Charles H. - Pvt., Co. G, 32nd Regt., Wis. Vol. Inf.
Charles listed his residence as Dartford, Green Lake County and he enlisted there on Aug. 14, 1862. He was assigned as above and he was mustered out on June 12, 1865. Charles was listed in the veteran section of the 1885 Wisconsin State census at P.O. Berlin, Green Lake County. He was listed in the 1890 federal census as residing in the city of Oshkosh. Eliza J., his widow, was listed in 1900 and again in 1905 as residing at 193 Ninth Street in Oshkosh.
{US 1890; ROV; WC-V 1885, 1905; B-1905}

OLIN, Edwin D. - Pvt., Co. B, 1st Regt., Wis. Cav.
Edwin was born circa 1841 at Wisconsin. He was a son of Nelson and Lucy L. (Jones) Olin and a brother of Uriel from a following sketch. Edwin was listed in the 1860 federal census as residing with the family of Milo Bushnell in the town of Omro. Residing with him was Lois Olin, who was born circa 1843 at Wisconsin. Nelson Olin, his father, resided on the adjoining farm. Edwin resided at Omro and enlisted there on Oct. 15, 1861. He was assigned as a bugler in the above company and was taken prisoner at L'Anguille Ferry, Arkansas. Edwin was paroled and he was then discharged on Dec. 23, 1862 while on parole. He was residing at Cincinnati, Ohio in 1888.
{US 1860; ROV; SCA p.665; Randall p.31}

OLIN, Luman D. - Capt., Co. C, 48th Regt., Wis. Vol. Inf.
Luman was born circa 1838 at New York. He was listed in the 1860 federal census as a laborer on the farm of James M. Olin, his brother, in the town of Omro. James was born circa 1821 at New York. Luman listed his residence as Oshkosh when he enlisted on Oct. 19, 1861. He was assigned as a Private to Co. F, 18th Regt., Wis. Vol. Inf. and was promoted to Sergeant in that company. Luman was then commissioned as 2nd Lieutenant of Co. C, 48th Regt., Wis. Vol. Inf. on Feb. 23, 1865 and was promoted to Captain of that company on Oct. 23, 1865. He was mustered out on Mar. 24, 1866. He provided his residence as Omro when he was commissioned.
{US 1860; ROV}

OLIN, Uriel P. - Sgt., Co. B, 2nd Regt., Wis. Vol. Inf.
Uriel was born on Feb. 3, 1837. He was a son of Nelson and Lucy L. (Jones) Olin and a brother of Edwin from a previous sketch. Nelson was born on May 22, 1809 at New York and died on Aug. 4, 1895. Lucy was born on Nov. 18, 1811 at New York and died of consumption in Omro on Feb. 17, 1853. Nelson's second wife was Orpha C. (Bushnell) Skinner. She was born at Vermont on Nov. 15, 1822 and died on Aug. 4, 1864. He was married third on Mar. 4, 1865 to Zilpha (Hill) Ferris, widow of Richard Ferris and mother of Elisha P. Ferris, both the subject of previous sketches. His fourth wife was Josephine L. (Lane) Steele. Prior to the war, Uriel was foreman in the office of the LaCrosse Republican. He enlisted at LaCrosse, LaCrosse County on Apr. 18, 1861. He was assigned as above and was promoted to Corporal and then Sergeant in that company. Uriel was wounded in action when shot through the bowels on Sept. 17, 1862 at Antietam, Maryland. He died from his wounds that same day and he was buried on the battlefield there. His parents are buried at Omro Cemetery, Original Section, plot 1 south.
{SCA p.665; OWN 16 Oct 1862; WCMR v.1, p.272, #1618; Randall p.30-1; ROV} {OWD 25 Feb 1853}

OLIVER, William - Pvt., Co. G, 5th (reorg.) Regt., Wis. Vol. Inf.
William was a son of Stephen and Emily Mahala (Wells) Moore Oliver. She was born in 1809 at Vermont. Emily was first married in 1826 to William Moore. They had six children and, after William died, she was married in 1845 to Stephen Oliver. Stephen and Emily removed to Wisconsin in 1857 and resided in Sheboygan County for eight years. They then removed to a farm in the town of Utica. William listed his residence as Omro when he enlisted on Aug. 29, 1864. He was assigned as above and he was mustered out on June 20, 1865. Records notwithstanding, his marker shows that he died at Camp Randall, Madison, Wisconsin on Dec. 26, 1864 at age 23 years, 7 months and 26 days. His marker also shows him as a member of Co. D, 12th Regt., Wis. Vol. Inf. although he does not appear in the records of that company. He was then listed in the 1890 federal census as residing in the town of Poygan at P.O. Poygan. Stephen Oliver died on Aug. 31, 1876 at age 73 years, 2 months and 23 days. Emily, his wife, died on May 19, 1894 at age 85 years and 24 days. William is buried with his parents in the town of Omro at Omro Union Cemetery.
{US 1890; ROV; Randall p.52; Cem. records}

OLMSTEAD, George W. - Pvt., Co. G, 3rd Regt., Wis. Cav.
George resided at Dunn, Dane County and he enlisted there on Nov. 28, 1863. He was assigned as above and was mustered out on Oct. 27, 1865. A James J. Olmstead was

OLMSTEAD, George W. (cont.)
also listed in the records of that company. George was married in Winnebago County on Nov. 27, 1865 to Eliza Osborn. He was listed in the 1890 federal census as residing in the village of Winneconne. He was listed in the veteran section of the 1895 Wisconsin State census at P.O. Winneconne. He was not found in that section of the 1885 or 1905 state census.
{US 1890; WC-V 1885, 1895, 1905; ROV; WCMR v.1, p.286, #1729}

OLMSTEAD, Lamar - Sgt., Co. K, 10th Regt., Wis. Vol. Inf.
Lamar was born on Feb. 20, 1842 at Chemung, New York, a son of Orrin L. and Mary Jane (Fuller) Olmstead. The father was a native of Connecticut. Orrin and Mary removed to Georgia about 1844 and remained between there and Alabama for seven years. They then removed with their family to Wisconsin and settled at Waupun, Fond du Lac County. Lamar was educated there in the common schools and then attended Ripon College. He listed his residence as Trenton, Dodge County when he enlisted at Waupun on Sept. 7, 1861 and was assigned as above. When the company was being organized Lamar was promoted to Corporal. He was later promoted to Sergeant in that company. Lamar was taken prisoner on Sept. 20, 1863 at Chickamauga, Georgia. He was held at Atlanta for several days and was then taken to Libby Prison, where he remained but one day. He was moved to Richmond on Sept. 18, 1863 and remained at the Pemberton Building there until Dec. 1, 1863. Lamar was transferred to Danville Prison and remained there until Apr. 20, 1864. He was taken back to Georgia and was held at Andersonville Prison until Sept. 10, 1864. He was then taken to Charleston, S.C. and remained there until being sent to Florence, S.C. on Nov. 1, 1864. He remained there until Feb. 15, 1865. He was finally released and returned to the Union lines. Of the 26 comrades from his company to be captured, only nine lived to see freedom. Lamar was taken to Annapolis, Maryland and then to St. Louis, Missouri. He was furloughed home and went to Milwaukee to receive his discharge as his term had by then expired. He returned to Waupun and remained there for a year while recruiting his health. He removed to Fond du Lac in 1866 and was engaged in the manufacturing of flour. He then removed Winnebago County and settled at Neenah. Lamar was working there in the flour mill of J.H. Kimberly when he received serious injuries while at work in Jan. 1872. He eventually settled at Appleton, Outagamie County in 1879. He was there engaged with the Appleton Machine Company. Lamar was married on Aug. 16, 1886 to Ellen Corbitt. They had three children: Mary C.; John A.; and one who died in infancy. Lamar was residing at Appleton in 1888 and was then a member of GAR Post #133. Mary, his mother, was listed in 1905 as residing at 115 W. Forest Avenue in the city of Neenah. J. Elizabeth and Lutie Olmstead were residing with her.
{ROV; SCA 1:578-9; B-1905; HN 1878 p.96}

OLOFF, Frank - Pvt., Co. D, 12th Regt., Wis. Vol. Inf.?
Frank was listed as above in the veteran section of the 1895 Wisconsin State census at P.O. Menasha. He was not found in the records of that company and was not found in the index to Roster of Wisconsin Volunteers.
{ROV; WC-V 1895}

OLSEN, Arne - Pvt., Co. K, 11th Regt., Wis. Vol. Inf.
Arne resided at Clayton and enlisted there on Sept. 19, 1861. He was assigned as above

OLSEN, Arne (cont.)
and was discharged due to a disability on Mar. 6, 1863.
{ROV}

OLSEN, Christian - Pvt., Co. A, 47th Regt., Wis. Vol. Inf.
Christian resided at Winchester and enlisted there on Feb. 10, 1865. He was assigned as above and was mustered out on Aug. 29, 1865.
{ROV}

OLSEN, Henry - Pvt., Co. C, 46th Regt., Wis. Vol. Inf.
Henry resided at Winchester and enlisted there on Jan. 30, 1865. He was assigned as above and was mustered out on Sept. 27, 1865. Henry was in poor health at the time of his discharge and he died in Winchester in October 1865. He was survived by his wife and three children. Irene, his widow, was listed in the 1890 federal census as residing in the town of Winchester at P.O. Winchester. She provided information that Henry was sick while in the army and that he died on Oct. 27, 1865.
{US 1890; ROV; OWN 02 Nov 1865}

OLSEN, Ingbrit - Pvt., Co. A, 47th Regt., Wis. Vol. Inf.
Ingbrit resided at Winchester and enlisted there on Feb. 10, 1865. He was assigned as above and was mustered out on Sept. 4, 1865. Ingbrit was listed in the 1890 federal census as residing in the town of Winchester at P.O. Winchester. He was listed in the veteran section of the 1895 Wisconsin State census at P.O. Winchester. Inga, his widow, was listed in 1905 as residing on 120 acres of section 22 in the town of Winchester. Albert, Clara and Florence Olson were then residing with her.
{US 1890; WC-V 1885, 1895, 1905; ROV; B-1905}

OLSEN, John - Pvt., Co. G, 3rd Regt., Wis. Vol. Inf.
John resided at Winneconne and enlisted there on July 1, 1861. He was assigned as above and was then transferred to the Veteran Reserve Corps on Nov. 15, 1863. John was mustered out on June 29, 1864 at the end of his term of enlistment.
{ROV}

OLSEN, Olans C. - Sgt., Co. G, 3rd Regt., Wis. Vol. Inf.
Olans resided at Clayton and enlisted there on Apr 20, 1861. He was assigned as above and was promoted to Corporal and then Sergeant in that company. Olans was wounded on May 25, 1864 and was mustered out on July 18, 1865.
{ROV}

OLSON, Christian - Pvt., Co. B, 15th Regt., Wis. Vol. Inf.
Christian resided at Winchester and enlisted there on Jan. 2, 1862. He was assigned as above and was then transferred to Co. H of that regiment on Jan. 14, 1865. Christian was attached to the 24th Regt., Wis. Vol. Inf. on Feb. 13, 1865 but he was listed there as having been mustered out on Feb. 8, 1865.
{ROV}

OLSON, Daniel - Pvt., Co. C, 1st Regt., Wis. Hvy. Art.
Daniel resided at Neenah and enlisted there on Sept. 11, 1863. He was assigned as

OLSON, Daniel (cont.)
above. Daniel died on June 30, 1865 at Davenport, Iowa.
{ROV}

OLSON, Nels - Pvt., Co. B, 6th Regt., Wis. Vol. Inf.
Nels resided at Utica and was drafted there on Oct. 29, 1864. He was assigned as above and was wounded at Gravelly Run, Virginia. Nels was mustered out on May 15, 1865.
{ROV}

OLSON, Ole - Pvt., Co. I, 21st Regt., Wis. Vol. Inf.
Ole resided at Menasha and enlisted there on Aug. 6, 1862. He was assigned as above and was mustered out on June 8, 1865. Ole was listed in the 1890 federal census as residing in the city of Neenah. He was then listed as "quite deaf in both ears." Ole was listed in the veteran section of the 1895 Wisconsin State census at P.O. Neenah.
{US 1890; WC-V 1895; ROV}

OLSON, Thomas - Pvt., Co. K, 2nd Regt., 1st Army Corps Vet. Vol.
Thomas resided at Algoma and enlisted there on Feb. 23, 1865. He was assigned as above. Thomas must have had two years of previous honorable service prior to joining that organization. He was mustered out on Feb. 23, 1866 at the end of his term of enlistment.
{ROV}

ONDERDONK, George E. - Cpl., Co. B, 37th Regt., Wis. Vol. Inf.
George resided at Oshkosh and enlisted there on Mar. 26, 1864. He was assigned as above and was promoted to Corporal in that company. George was wounded June 17, 1864 at Petersburg, Virginia. He was mustered out on July 27, 1865.
{ROV}

ONDERDONK, Harley W. - Pvt., Co. F, 18th Regt., Wis. Vol. Inf.
Harley resided at Oshkosh and enlisted there on Jan. 10, 1862. He was assigned as above and was wounded at Shiloh, Tennessee. Harley soon died from those wounds on Apr. 9, 1862.
{ROV}

O'NEIL, Bartley - Pvt., Co. A, 17th Regt., Wis. Vol. Inf.
Bartley resided at Utica and was drafted there on Sept. 29, 1864. He was assigned as above and was mustered out on June 2, 1865.
{ROV}

O'NEIL, John - Pvt., Co. C, 1st Regt., Wis. Hvy. Art.
John resided at Winneconne and enlisted there on Sept. 2, 1864. He was assigned as above and was mustered out on June 16, 1865.
{ROV}

ONSEN, Samuel Christian - Pvt., Co. B, 21st Regt., Wis. Vol. Inf.
Samuel resided at Winneconne and enlisted there on Aug. 14, 1862. He was assigned as above and was taken prisoner on Jan. 2, 1863. Samuel was also wounded at Resaca,

ONSEN, Samuel Christian (cont.)
Georgia. He was mustered out on June 8, 1865. Samuel was married in Winnebago County on Oct. 15, 1867 to Regina Anderson.
{ROV; WCMR v.1, p.353, #2123}

OPP, George - Pvt., Co. C, 53rd Regt., Wis. Vol. Inf.
George resided at Utica and enlisted there on Mar. 10, 1865. He was assigned as above. That company was transferred to Co. K, 51st Regt., Wis. Vol. Inf. under orders dated June 10, 1865. The transfer was completed on June 30, 1865 at Ft. Leavenworth, Kansas. George was then mustered out on July 15, 1865, before the regiment returned to Wisconsin.
{ROV}

OPP, John - Cpl., Co. C, 53rd Regt., Wis. Vol. Inf.
John George Opp was married in Winnebago County on Dec, 29, 1864 to Lawine Opp. He resided at Utica and enlisted there on Mar. 10, 1865. He was assigned as above and was promoted to Corporal in that company. This company was transferred to Co. K, 51st Regt., Wis. Vol. Inf. under orders dated June 10, 1865. The transfer was completed on June 30, 1865 at Ft. Leavenworth, Kansas. The regiment returned to Madison, Wisconsin on Aug. 1, 1865 and was mustered out by companies. The last company was mustered out on Aug. 30, 1865.
{ROV; WCMR v.1, p.266, #1573}

O'RILEY, Alexander - Cpl., Co. D, 32nd Regt., Wis. Vol. Inf.
Alexander was born in 1832 at County Mayo, Ireland. He was a son of Dennis and Margaret (Hollerin) O'Reily and a brother of Thomas from a following sketch. Dennis and his wife were both born circa 1820 at Ireland. With their eight children, they emigrated to America in 1846. At that time they located in Jersey City, New Jersey. They removed to Wisconsin in 1855 and settled in the town of Poygan. They were listed in the 1860 federal census as residing in their farm in Poygan. Then residing with them were sons Thomas and John. Alexander listed his residence as Nepeuskun when he enlisted on Aug. 20, 1862. He was assigned as above and was promoted to Corporal in that company. Alexander was mustered out on June 12, 1865. He was married in that same year to Maria, daughter of John and Mary Flanigan. Alexander and Maria had the following children: Annie; Mary; Katy; Sarah; Agnes; Bridget; and Lizzie. One of the daughters was born in the town of Poygan on Feb. 22, 1878. Mary, his wife, died on Aug. 5, 1880 at age 31 years. Alice, his second wife, was born in 1853 and died in 1922. David, a son of Alexander and Alice, was born in 1888 and died in 1956. Alexander was listed in the veteran section of the 1885 Wisconsin State census at P.O. Poygan. He was listed in the 1890 federal census as residing in the town of Poygan at P.O. Winneconne. He listed then that he had been stabbed with a knife at Memphis, Tennessee. Alexander was listed (Alex. O. Riley) in the veteran section of the 1895 state census at P.O. Winneconne and in that part of the 1905 state census at P.O. Omro. He was listed in 1905, along with his wife Alice, as residing on 80 acres of section 24 in the town of Poygan. Alexander died in 1922. He is buried with both wives in the town of Poygan at St. Thomas Cemetery.
{US 1860, 1890; WC-V 1885, 1895, 1905; ROV; B-1905; WCBR v.2, p.93, #237}
{Randall p.50; Cem. records}

O'RILEY, Thomas - Pvt., Co. D, 3rd Regt., Wis. Vol. Inf.
Thomas was born circa 1844 at Ireland. He was a son of Dennis and Margaret O'Riley and a brother of Alexander from a previous sketch. Thomas was listed in the 1860 federal census as residing on the farm of his parents in the town of Poygan. He resided there when he enlisted on Apr. 22, 1861. He was assigned as above and was listed as having deserted on Dec. 4, 1861. Thomas then enlisted at Taycheedah, Fond du Lac County on Sept. 14, 1864 and was assigned as Private, Co. I, 2nd Regt., Wis. Cav. He was mustered out on June 12, 1865. Thomas was listed in the veteran section of the 1885 Wisconsin State census at P.O. Poygan. He was listed in the 1890 federal census as residing in the village of Winneconne.
{US 1860, 1890; WC-V 1885; ROV}

ORTON, David - Pvt., Co. G, 8th Regt., Illinois Vol. Inf.
David died on Sept. 4, 1876 at age 39 years, 3 months and 4 days. He is buried in the town of Nepeuskun at Koro Cemetery. His unit designation is included on his marker.
{Cem. records}

OSBORN, Charles D. - Pvt., Co. G, 5th Regt., Wis. Vol. Inf.
Charles was born circa 1841 at Ohio. He was a son of Lafayette and Moriah Osborn. Both parents were natives of New York, the father born there circa 1806 and the mother born circa 1815. They were listed in the 1860 federal census as residing on a farm in the town of Nepeuskun at P.O. Koro. Listed with them were the following children: Mary, born circa 1836 at New York; George, born circa 1838 at Ohio; Julia, born circa 1839 at Ohio; Charles; Amelia, born circa 1843 at Ohio; Almira, born circa 1847 at Wisconsin; and Jesse, born circa 1852 at Wisconsin. Lafayette died on Dec. 19, 1872 at age 62 years and 2 months. Moriah died May 17, 1885 at age 72 years, 2 months and 26 days. Charles enlisted on Apr. 17, 1861 and was assigned as above. He was promoted to Corporal in that company. Charles contracted a disease and died at Hagerstown, Maryland on Nov. 24, 1862 at age 22 years. He was buried there. A monument was erected for him on the plot of his parents in the town of Nepeuskun at Koro Cemetery.
{US 1860; ROV; Cem. records}

OSBORN, Horace - Pvt., Co. B, 47th Regt., Wis. Vol. Inf.
Horace was born circa 1821 at New York. He was listed in the 1860 federal census as residing on a farm in the town of Nepeuskun at P.O. Koro. Jerusha A., his wife, was born in 1824 at Pennsylvania. Then listed with them were the following children: Mary, born circa 1850; James, born circa 1852; Harriet, born circa 1854; and Laura, born circa 1856. All of the children were born in Wisconsin. Horace resided at Nepeuskun and enlisted there on Jan. 23, 1865. He was assigned as above and was mustered out on Sept. 4, 1865. Horace was listed in the 1890 federal census as residing in the town of Aurora, Waushara County at P.O. Berlin. He is buried with a simple military marker in the town of Aurora at Shead Island Cemetery. Jerusha died in 1901 and is buried at his side.
{US 1860, 1890; ROV; Cem. records}

OSBORNE, William J. - Sgt., Co. H, 1st Regt., Wis. Hvy. Art.
William resided at Algoma and enlisted there on Aug. 31, 1861. He was assigned as

OSBORNE, William J. (cont.)
above and was promoted to Sergeant in that company. William was mustered out on June 26, 1865.
{ROV}

OSCAR, Thomas - Pvt., Co. H, 36th Regt., Wis. Vol. Inf.
Thomas resided at Utica and enlisted on Feb. 29, 1864. He was assigned as above and was taken prisoner at Ream's Station. Thomas was mustered out on July 19, 1865.
{ROV}

OSGOOD, Augustus B. - Sgt., Co. F, 18th Regt., Wis. Vol. Inf.
Augustus resided at Rushford and enlisted there on Feb. 6, 1862. He was assigned as above and was promoted to Sergeant in that company. Augustus was taken prisoner at Allatoona, Georgia and was mustered out on May 31, 1865.
{ROV}

OSGOOD, Nathaniel A. - Pvt., Co. F, 18th Regt., Wis. Vol. Inf.
Nathaniel resided at Rushford and enlisted there on Feb. 6, 1862. He was assigned as above and was taken prisoner at Shiloh, Tennessee. Nathaniel was then discharged on Jan. 10, 1863 due to a disability.
{ROV}

OSTERTAG, John - Pvt., Co. E, 26th Regt., Wis. Vol. Inf.
John was born circa 1844 at Wurtemburg. He was a son of Valentine and Mary A. (Ruedinger) Ostertag and a brother of Sebastian of a following sketch. John was listed in the 1860 federal census as residing with his parents and their family in the town of Nekimi at P.O. Oshkosh. He listed his residence as Fond du Lac, Fond du Lac County when he enlisted on Aug. 21, 1862. He was assigned as above. John contracted a disease and died at Chattanooga, Tennessee on May 2, 1864.
{US 1860; ROV; SCA 1:152-3}

OSTERTAG, Sebastian - Pvt., Co. E, 2nd Regt., Wis. Vol. Inf.
Sebastian was born on Apr. 21, 1839 at Wurtemburg, Germany, a son of Valentine and Mary A. (Ruedinger) Ostertag, both natives of Wurtemburg, Germany. Sebastian was also a brother of John of a previous sketch. Valentine was born circa 1810 and Mary was born circa 1814. At the age eight years, Sebastian emigrated to America with his parents. They settled in the town of Nekimi. Valentine and Mary were listed in the 1860 federal census as residing on a farm in the town of Nekimi at P.O. Oshkosh. Listed with them were the following children: Sebastian; Catharine, born circa 1842; John; Mary, born circa 1847; Valentine, born circa 1850; and Ellen, born circa 1856. The three youngest children were born in Wisconsin and the others had been born in Wurtemburg. Sebastian resided with his parents and worked on the family farm until he enlisted at Oshkosh on Apr. 21, 1861. He was assigned as above and was wounded on July 21, 1861 during the first battle at Bull Run, Virginia when a shot hit him in the right thigh. Sebastian was wounded again on Aug. 28, 1862 at Gainesville, Virginia when his right hip was injured. He was taken prisoner then and was sent to St. Joseph's Hospital at Philadelphia, Pennsylvania . He remained there until just before Christmas of 1862. He was sent to Camp Distribution to recover his health and came home on furlough. While home, Sebastian was married on Jan. 20, 1863 to Sophia Kuebler. She was born in 1844

OSTERTAG, Sebastian (cont.)
at Bavaria, Germany. Sebastian rejoined his regiment at the front just three weeks later. He was again wounded at Gettysburg, Pennsylvania on July 1, 1863 when a bullet passed through his left cheek under the eye. The shell passed through his face behind his nose and was lodged behind the right eye near the temple. The ball was removed on July 11, 1863 in the hospital at West Philadelphia. Sebastian was transferred to the Veteran Reserve Corps at Washington, D.C. on Mar. 15, 1864 and was then mustered out there on June 16, 1864 at the end of his term of enlistment. On returning to Wisconsin, Sebastian was employed with the Chicago & Northwestern Railroad. In Nov. 1865 he engaged in the grocery business. He removed to Appleton for two years and then returned to his grocery business at Oshkosh. He started in the hardware business in 1884 and continued for three years. Sebastian owned 83 acres in the town of Algoma about two miles from the city of Oshkosh. He and Sophia had six children: John Albert; Edward Sebastian, born on Mar. 15, 1865, married Mary Ellen Murphy; Ida Mary; Catherine, died on Mar. 26, 1868 at age 16 months; Theodore Louis; and Lydia Helena Sophia, an adopted daughter, died on Oct. 15, 1879 at age 9 years and 6 months. Sebastian was listed in 1883 at P.O. Oshkosh. He was receiving a pension of $8 per month for a wound to his face. He was listed as a member of GAR Post #241 at Oshkosh in 1888. Sebastian was listed in the veteran section of the 1885, 1895 and 1905 Wisconsin State census at P.O. Oshkosh. He was listed in the 1890 federal census as residing in the town of Algoma at P.O. Oshkosh. Sebastian was listed in 1905 as retired and residing at 17 Pleasant Avenue in the city of Oshkosh. Daughter Lydia F. was then residing with him. Mary, a sister of Sebastian, was married on May 18, 1867 to August Ernest Nitschke of Appleton.
{US 1860, 1890; WC-V 1885, 1895, 1905; LOP-1883; Randall p.16, 27; B-1905}
{ROV; CBR-FRV p.1181-2; CBR-FRV p.305-7; SCA 1:152-3}

OSTRANDER, Charles - Pvt., Co. D, 32nd Regt., Wis. Vol. Inf.
Charles resided at Utica and enlisted there on Aug. 21, 1862. He was assigned as above and was listed as having deserted on Oct. 7, 1862.
{ROV}

OTIS, Andrew A. - Pvt., Co. D, 16th (reorg.) Regt., Wis. Vol. Inf.
Andrew resided at Winchester and enlisted there on Sept. 8, 1864. He was assigned as above and was mustered out on May 25, 1865.
{ROV}

OTIS, Anson M. - Pvt., Co. D, 16th (reorg.) Regt., Wis. Vol. Inf.
Anson resided at Winchester and enlisted there on Sept. 8, 1864. He was assigned as above. Anson contracted a disease and died on Feb. 1, 1865 at Beauford, S.C.
{ROV}

OTIS, Charles F. - Civil War Veteran?
Charles was born in 1829 at Vermont. M. Maria, his wife, was born in 1834 at Canada. They were listed in the 1860 federal census as residing on a farm in the town of Utica at P.O. Fisk's Corners. Listed with them were the following children: E.J., born circa 1852 at New York; Agnes, born circa 1854 at New York; John, born circa 1856 at New York; and Frances, born circa 1858 at Wisconsin. Charles died in 1900 and Maria died in 1908. Both are buried with members of their family in the town of Algoma at

OTIS, Charles F. (cont.)
Ellenwood Cemetery. A GAR marker has been placed at the grave of Charles. He was not found in the index to the Roster of Wisconsin Volunteers.
{US 1860; ROV; Cem. records}

OTTO, August - Pvt., Co. B, 37th Regt., Wis. Vol. Inf.
August was born circa 1820 at Prussia. He was married to Louise Ludke on Sept. 29, 1856 in Winnebago County. She was born circa 1836, also at Prussia. They were listed in the 1860 federal census as residing on a farm in the town of Orihula at P.O. Fremont. Listed with them were Rudolph, subject of a following sketch, and Louisa, born circa 1859 at Wisconsin. August resided at Wolf River and was drafted there on Nov. 5, 1864. He was assigned as above and was mustered out on July 27, 1865.
{US 1860; ROV; WCMR v.1, p.105, #436}

OTTO, Rudolph - Pvt., Co. B, 21st Regt., Wis. Vol. Inf.
Rudolph was born circa 1844 at Prussia. He was listed in the 1860 federal census as residing in the town of Orihula at P.O. Fremont with August Otto, subject of a previous sketch. He may have been a son of August by a first marriage. Rudolph listed his residence as Oshkosh when he enlisted on Aug. 13, 1862. He was assigned as above and was mustered out on June 8, 1865.
{US 1860; ROV}

OVIATT, Lunson S. - Pvt., Co. A, 3rd Regt., Wis. Cav.
Lunson was born Feb. 20, 1831 at Hadley, Saratoga County, New York. He was a son of Samuel and Apollonia (Brooks) Oviatt. Samuel had a family of ten children: Lucinda; Anson; Louisa; David; Lunson; Chloe; Normal; Ravina; and Laura. Lunson began to fend for himself at age 8 years. He worked for his board and clothes with Henry Blackwood for 5 years and then for the next 8 years he worked for Ebenezer Johnson. From 1852 to 1854 he remained at Saratoga County, learning the trade of a carpenter. Lunson then removed to Wisconsin and settled at Oshkosh. After three years he removed to Shiocton, Outagamie County and purchased 40 acres there. Lunson was married at Oshkosh to Susan Griffith. She was a daughter of James and Betsey Griffith. Lunson listed his residence as Oshkosh when he enlisted on Dec. 7, 1863. He was assigned as above and was then transferred to Co. K, 3rd (reorg.) Regt., Wis. Cav. on Mar. 23, 1865. Lunson was mustered out on Sept. 29, 1865. The following year he added 40 acres to his original farm. He and Susan had eight children: Laverna; Mary; Ida; Temmie; Bertha; Matilda; James; and Norman Oviatt. Lunson was residing in the town of Bovina, Outagamie County in 1895.
{ROV; CBR-FRV p.850-1}

OWEN, Albert H. - Pvt., Co. I, 21st Regt., Wis. Vol. Inf.
Albert was born circa 1834 at New York. He was a son of Albert and Julia Owen and a brother of George from a following sketch. The parents were natives of New York, the father born there circa 1799 and the mother born circa 1811. They were listed in the 1860 federal census as residing on a farm in the second ward of the village of Menasha. Listed with them were the following children: Albert, a sailor; George; Harriet, born circa 1842; and Mary, born circa 1846. The children were all born in New York. Albert resided at Menasha and enlisted there on Aug. 19, 1862. He was assigned as a drummer in the above company and was mustered out on June 8, 1865. Albert was

OWEN, Albert H. (cont.)
married in Winnebago County on Nov. 5, 1866 to Mary Jane Morey.
{US 1860; ROV; Lawson p.831; WCMR v.1, p.310, #1923}

OWEN, George W. - Pvt., Co. D, 41st Regt., Wis. Vol. Inf.
George was born circa 1837 at New York. He was a son of Albert and Julia Owens and a brother of Albert H. from a previos sketch. George was listed in the 1860 federal census as a sailor residing with his parents in the second ward of the village of Menasha. He enlisted at Menasha on May 2, 1864. He was assigned as above and was mustered out on Sept. 23, 1864 at the end of his term of enlistment.
{US 1860; ROV}

OWEN, Rufus C. - Sgt., Co. C, 46th Regt., Wis. Vol. Inf.
Rufus was born circa 1842 at Ohio. He was listed in the 1860 federal census as residing on a farm in the town of Winneconne. That farm was owned by Abner and Jemima Owen. Both were born in Vermont, Abner born circa 1788 and Jemima born circa 1798. They were probably parents of Rufus but could be his grandparents. Rufus was married in Winnebago County on Feb. 6, 1865 to Frances Thrall. He resided at Winneconne and enlisted there on Feb. 8, 1865. He was assigned as above and was promoted to Sergeant in that company. He was mustered out on Sept. 27, 1865. Rufus was listed in the veteran section of the 1885 Wisconsin State census at P.O. Winneconne.
{US 1860; WC-V 1885; WCMR v.1, p.281, #1695; ROV}

OWEN, William S. - Pvt., Co. C, 21st Regt., Wis. Vol. Inf.
William resided at Oshkosh and he enlisted there on Aug. 13, 1862. He was assigned as above. William was killed on Oct. 8, 1862 at Chaplin Hills, Kentucky.
{ROV; OWN 07 May 1863}

OWENS, Albert - Pvt., Co. G, 3rd Regt., Wis. Vol. Inf.
Albert resided at Menasha and enlisted there on Apr. 20, 1861. He was assigned as above and was discharged due to a disability on Jan. 18, 1862.
{ROV}

OWENS, David J. - Seaman, "Juliet," Gunboat Service, U.S. Navy
David was born circa 1828 at Wales. He was listed in the 1860 federal census as a turner residing in the village of Neenah. Elizabeth, his wife, was born circa 1830 at Wales. Listed with them were the following children: John, born circa 1854; David, born circa 1858; and Maria, born circa 1859. The children were born in Wisconsin. David enlisted on Aug. 17, 1864 for duty with the Naval Gunboat Service. After training he was assigned to the gunboat "Juliet." David was listed as a carpenter with the above assignment in the veteran section of the 1885 and 1905 Wisconsin State census at P.O Neenah. He was listed in 1905 as residing at 314 Elm Street in the city of Neenah.
{US 1860; WC-V 1885, 1905; Lawson p.831; B-1905}

OWENS, Edward C. - Pvt., Co. C, 1st Regt., Wis. Hvy. Art.
Edward was born on Mar. 18, 1846 at Montgomeryshire, North Wales. He was a son of Evan and Sarah (Morris) Owens. Evan was born on Apr. 15, 1817 at Tilaulligan, Wales and Sarah was born on Jan. 29, 1819 at Montgomeryshire, North Wales. They were married in Mynavon parish, Wales on Jan. 11, 1843. They emigrated to America

OWENS, Edward C. (cont.)
in 1849 with their three children, John, Evan and Edward. They remained in Philadelphia, Pennsylvania for a year. They then removed to Wisconsin and settled at Neenah. Six years later they removed to a farm in the town of Oshkosh, where they were listed in the 1860 federal census. Listed with them were some of their children: John, born circa 1844, resided later at Tower, Minnesota; Edward; Evan, born circa 1849, resided at Oshkosh; William D., born circa 1850, resided in Algoma; Richard F., born circa 1852, resided in Algoma; Margaret, born circa 1855, married C. Whiting, resided in Algoma; Robert Thomas, born circa 1856, resided later at Two Harbors, Minnesota; Samuel, born circa 1858, later postmaster at Tower, Minnesota; Sarah, born circa 1859, married Emerson Lake, resided in Algoma. Another daughter married W.H. McMillen and resided in Algoma. They also included as a son a Frank Spurbeck. The three oldest children were born in Wales and the others were born in Wisconsin. In 1860 they moved to a farm in the town of Algoma. At that same home on Jan. 11, 1893 the family, Evan and Sarah with all eleven children, their spouses and all but four of the grandchildren, three of them being dead, gathered to celebrate their golden wedding anniversary. A collection was taken among the family to allow the parents to return to Wales for a visit. Less then three months later, in early April, Sarah died. She was buried in Oshkosh at Riverside Cemetery. Edward was reared on the family farm at Neenah and was educated in the common schools. He enlisted at Neenah on Sept. 17, 1863. He was assigned as above and was mustered out on Nov. 30, 1865 at Madison, Wisconsin. Edward had contracted small pox while at St. Louis, Missouri. After the war he took a course at a commercial college and then taught school for two years. In 1869 he was engaged as a bookkeeper for an Oshkosh firm and remained in that position for five years. Edward then removed to Stevens Point, Portage County. There he was engaged in the milling business for four years. In spring of 1876 Edward was married to Clara W., daughter of D.L. Johnson. She died in spring of 1884 at age 28 years. They had one child which died in spring of 1878 at age eight months. Edward then spent a year in the Black Hills area of South Dakota before returning to Oshkosh. He was employed by R.C. McMillen & Co., where he was stationed at Mitchell, South Dakota and was placed in charge of the company lumber yard at that place. He again returned to Oshkosh in the fall of 1880 and was given charge of the yards for that company in this area. Edward was listed in 1883 at P.O. Oshkosh. He had been receiving a pension of $6 per month since June 1881 for vericose veins in his left leg. He was listed as a member of GAR Post #10 at Oshkosh in 1888. Edward was listed in the veteran section of the 1895 Wisconsin State census at P.O. Oshkosh. Emma B., his widow, was listed in 1905 as residing at 296 Elm Street in the city of Oshkosh.

{US 1860; WC-V 1895; ROV; Randall p.16, 43; LOP-1883; SCA 1:467-8; B-1905}
{OWN 21 Jan 1893; OWN 08 Apr 1893}

PAAPE, Herman - Pvt., Co. K, 24th Regt., Wis. Vol. Inf.?
Herman was married to Maria Demmad in Winnebago County on Sept. 17, 1859. He was listed as above in the veteran section of the 1885 Wisconsin State census at P.O. Neenah. He was not found in the records of that company.
{WC-V 1885; ROV; WCMR v.1, p.196, #1013}

PACE, John W. - Pvt., Co. C, 10th Regt., Wis. Vol. Inf.
John resided at Menasha and enlisted there on Sept. 3, 1861. He was assigned as above and he was dropped from the rolls as a deserter on Aug. 7, 1862. John was listed in

PACE, John W. (cont.)
1888 as a member of GAR Post #46 at New London, Waupaca County. He was listed in the 1890 federal census as a veteran of Co. H, 16th Regt., Wis. Vol. Inf. and residing at New London.
{US 1890; ROV; SCA}

PACKARD, Allen - Sgt., Co. K, 5th (reorg.) Regt., Wis. Vol. Inf.
Allen was born circa 1844 at Ohio. He was a son of Emaline Packard. She was born circa 1812 at New York. Emeline was listed in the 1860 federal census as residing on a farm in the town of Utica at P.O. Waukau. Listed with her were the following children: James, born circa 1838; Asa, born circa 1839; Sarah, born circa 1842; Allen; Josephine, born circa 1845; Walter, born circa 1847; Emma, born circa 1850; Oscar, born circa 1852; and Frank, born circa 1854. The three eldest children were born in New York and the others were all born in Ohio. Allen enlisted at Utica on Aug. 15, 1862. He was assigned as a Private to Co. B, 21st Regt., Wis. Vol. Inf. He was discharged due to a disability on Mar. 10, 1863. Allen re-enlisted at Nepeuskun on Aug. 30, 1864. He was assigned as above and was promoted to Sergeant in that company. Allen was mustered out on June 20, 1865. Katie, his wife, was born on Aug. 20, 1849 and died on Feb. 28, 1932. Daughter Helen L. was born in 1879 and died in 1880. Daughter Alice A. was born in 1885 and died in 1916. Allen is buried with a simple military marker in the town of Rushford at Waukau Cemetery. His wife and daughters are buried on that same plot.
{US 1860; ROV; Cem. records}

PAGE, Charles - Pvt., Co. H, 30th Regt., Wis. Vol. Inf.
Charles was born in 1832. He enlisted on Aug. 21, 1862 and was assigned as above. Charles was home on furlough at the end of the war and never received a formal discharge. He was listed in the 1890 federal census as residing in the town of Aurora, Waushara County at P.O. Auroraville. Charles died in 1920. Nancy, his wife, was born in 1860 and died in 1933. Both are buried in the town of Rushford at Rushford Cemetery.
{US 1890; Cem. records}

PAINE, Charles N. - Capt., Co. B, 21st Regt., Wis. Vol. Inf.
Charles was born on Sept. 3, 1831 at Orwell, Pennsylvania. He was a son of Edward L. and Eleanor (Ross) Paine. Edward was born May 29, 1801 at Pomfret, Connecticut. He was married on Aug. 5, 1824 at Brooklyn, Susquehanna County, Pennsylvania to Eleanor Ross. She was born circa 1807 in Pennsylvania and she was a daughter of Jesse Ross. Edward removed to Orwell, Pennsylvania and then to Elmyra and Canisteo, New York. He came to Wisconsin in 1854 and located at Milwaukee. The following year he came to Oshkosh with son Charles. They erected a sawmill which was the foundation of the Paine Lumber Company. Edward was listed in the 1860 federal census as a lumberman residing in the fifth ward of the city of Oshkosh. Residing with him were his wife, his mother, and the following children: Charles; George, born circa 1834; and Nathan, subject of a following sketch. All of the sons were born in Pennsylvania. Charles was listed as a lumberman and George was a dentist. Charles resided at Oshkosh when the Civil War began. After enlisting there he was commissioned as Captain of the above company on Aug. 26, 1862. Charles resigned his commission on Dec. 2, 1863 due to a disability, he having suffered from poor health. He returned to

PAINE, Charles N. (cont.)
Oshkosh and to his position as president of Paine Lumber Company. He was listed in 1868 at 14 South Algoma Street in Oshkosh. Charles died in Milwaukee at the residence of his sister Mrs. R.P. Elmore on May 3, 1885.
{US 1860; ROV; T-1868; Randall p.43-4}

PAINE, Hosea Ballou - Pvt., Co. C, 21st Regt., Wis. Vol. Inf.
Hosea was married in Winnebago County on Sept. 1, 1853 to Lydia Murphy Buckstaff. He resided at Oshkosh and enlisted there on Aug. 21, 1862. He was assigned as a musician with the above company and was listed as absent sick when that regiment was mustered out on June 8, 1865. Hosea died at Wilmington, N.C. on Apr. 1, 1865 at age 40 years. Lydia, his wife, died on July 9, 1860 at age 31 years, 4 months and 12 days. Charlie, a son, died on July 1, 1856 at age 5 months. Hosea and Lydia, along with Charlie and an infant daughter, Georgia, are buried in the town of Algoma at Ellenwood Cemetery, Section A. Their marriage was re-filed in Winnebago County in June 1866.
{ROV; WCMR v.1, p.146, #610; Cem. records; WCMR v.1, p.301, #1850*}

PAINE, Nathan - Maj., 1st Regt., Wis. Cav.
Nathan was born on Sept. 20, 1835 at Orwell, Pennsylvania. He was the youngest son of Maj. Edward L. and Eleanor (Ross) Paine and a brother of Charles N. Paine from a previous sketch. He was listed in the 1860 federal census as a student residing with his father's family in the fifth ward of the city of Oshkosh. Nathan graduated with high honors from Lawrence University at Appleton, Outagamie County in 1860. He then completed the law course of Albany Law School at New York in 1861. Nathan returned to Oshkosh and was married there to Olive, daughter of Rev. David Copeland. Nathan enlisted on Aug. 6, 1861 and was assigned to Co. G, 1st Regt., Wis. Cav. He was elected to the position of 2nd Lieutenant at the organization of that company. He was then promoted to 1st Lieutenant on Oct. 31, 1861. Nathan was promoted to Captain of that company on Nov. 16, 1861. On Sept. 28, 1863, he was commissioned as Major of the regiment for gallant and meritorious conduct on the field of battle. Nathan was killed in action on July 28, 1864 while leading his regiment in a charge near Campbelltown, Georgia. He was buried there on the battlefield. Nathan's remains were returned to Oshkosh after the war and, on Apr. 21, 1867, he was laid to rest at Riverside Cemetery with military honors. He was survived by his wife and a daughter who died at age 18 years. The daughter was born while Nathan was in the service and he never saw her. Olive was residing at Los Angeles, California in 1888.
{US 1860; ROV; OWN 18 Aug 1864; ODN 20 Oct 1934; WCPR v.X, p.398-405}
{Randall p.44}

PALM, Wilhelm - Pvt., Co. F, 19th Regt., Wis. Vol. Inf.
Wilhelm resided at Oshkosh and enlisted there on Jan. 24, 1862. He was assigned as above and was mustered out on Apr. 29, 1865 at the end of his term of enlistment. He was listed in 1868 as a tailor residing at 164 Main Street in the city of Oshkosh. William had been an early settler at Oshkosh and he removed to Appleton, Outagamie County about 1881. His wife died there in May 1891 and was returned to Oshkosh for burial in Riverside Cemetery. Wilhelm was listed in the veteran section of the 1895 Wisconsin State census at P.O. Oshkosh.
{WC-V 1895; ROV; T-1868; OWN 21 May 1891}

PALMER, Charles P. - Sgt., Co. I, 3rd Regt., Wis. Cav.
Charles was born on Aug. 16, 1822. He enlisted in the above regiment on Jan. 1, 1862 and served until Jan. 7, 1865. He was listed in 1888 as a member of GAR Post #133 at Appleton, Outagamie County. Charles was listed in 1905 as engaged in real estate and residing at 29 Pleasant Avenue in the city of Oshkosh. He died at Oshkosh on Nov. 21, 1911. He was survived by his widow. Charles is buried in Oshkosh at Riverside Cemetery, GAR plot, west row, #7 from the south.
{B-1905; Cem. records; SCA}

PALMER, Richard - Pvt., Co. D, 24th Regt., Michigan Vol. Inf.
Richard was listed as above in the 1890 federal census as residing in the city of Oshkosh. He provided his unit designation as above and his service dates as having been Aug. 13, 1862 to Apr. 11, 1864. Richard was listed in the veteran section of the 1895 and 1905 Wisconsin State census at P.O. Oshkosh. He was listed in 1905 as a laborer at the Foster-Lothman Mills and residing at 155 Sixth Street in Oshkosh. Frank and William Palmer were also listed at that address.
{US 1890; WC-V 1895, 1905; T-1868; B-1905}

PALMER, Samuel - Pvt., Co. E, 5th (reorg.) Regt., Wis. Vol. Inf.
Samuel resided at Algoma and enlisted there on Aug. 30, 1864. He was assigned as above and was mustered out on June 20, 1865.
{ROV}

PALMER, William H. - Pvt., Co. K, 11th Regt., Wis. Vol. Inf.
William was born circa 1844 at Maine, a son of John and Cordelia Palmer. Cordelia was born circa 1823 at Maine and John was born circa 1820 in that same state. He was listed in the 1850 federal census as a farmer residing in the town of Clayton. Listed with them were the following children: William H.; Susan T., born circa 1845 at Maine; John N., born circa 1846 at Maine; and Lloyd M., born in 1849 at Wisconsin. John and Cordelia were listed in the 1860 federal census as residing on a farm in the town of Clayton at P.O. Neenah. They then had the following additional children: Frederick, born circa 1852; George, born circa 1854; Augusta, born circa 1857; Alfred, born circa 1858; Alferretta, born circa 1858; and May, born in 1860. These children were all born in Wisconsin. William resided at Clayton and enlisted there on Oct. 5, 1861. He was assigned as above and was discharged on Jan. 3, 1863 due to a disability.
{US 1850, 1860; ROV}

PANSIE, Herman - Pvt., Co. H, 18th Regt., Wis. Vol. Inf.
Herman was born on Jan. 30, 1845. He resided at Nepeuskun and he enlisted there on Jan. 20, 1864. He was assigned as above and was mustered out on July 18, 1865. Herman was listed in the veteran section of the 1905 Wisconsin State census at P.O. Fisk. He was listed in that year with Ettie, his wife, as residing on 167 acres of section 12 in the town of Utica. Son Edward was also residing with them. Herman died on June 30, 1928. Etta, his wife, was born on Jan. 27, 1856 and died on Jan. 5, 1939. Both are buried in the town of Algoma at Ellenwood Cemetery, Section H.
{WC-V 1905; ROV; B-1905; Cem. records}

PAQUE, Alphonse - Cpl., Co. G, 17th Regt., Wis. Vol. Inf.
Alphonse resided at Nepeuskun and enlisted there on Mar. 5, 1864. He was assigned as

PAQUE, Alphonse (cont.)
above and was promoted to Corporal in that company. Alphonse was mustered out on July 14, 1865.
{ROV}

PARCELL, Melvin H. - Pvt., Co. K, 5th (reorg.) Regt., Wis. Vol. Inf.
Melvin resided at Rushford and enlisted there on Aug. 30, 1864. He was assigned as above and he was wounded at Sailor's Creek. Melvin died of his wounds on Apr. 19, 1865 at Annapolis, Maryland. His marker shows that he died on Apr. 19, 1864 at age 34 years, 5 months and 5 days. Anna E., daughter of M.H. and N.M. Parcell, died on Dec. 1, 1873 at age 14 years, 5 months and 1 day. She is buried with her father in the town of Rushford at Rushford Cemetery
{ROV; Cem. records}

PARK, John H. - Cpl., Co. E, 5th (reorg.) Regt., Wis. Vol. Inf.
John resided at Oshkosh and enlisted on Sept. 2, 1864. He was assigned as above and was promoted to Corporal in that company. John was mustered out on June 20, 1865.
{ROV}

PARKER, DeWitt C. - Pvt., Co. D, 41st Regt., Wis. Vol. Inf.
DeWitt was born circa 1845 at New York. He was listed in the 1860 federal census as a laborer on the farm of James Ladd in the town of Menasha. DeWitt enlisted at Menasha on May 11, 1864. He was assigned as above and was then mustered out on Sept. 23, 1864 at the end of his term of enlistment.
{US 1860; ROV}

PARKER, Edwin M. - Pvt., Co. C, 32nd Regt., Wis. Vol. Inf.
Edwin resided at Omro and enlisted there on Nov. 28, 1863. He was assigned as above and was then transferred to Co. G, 16th Regt., Wis. Vol. Inf. on June 4, 1865. He was mustered out on July 21, 1865.
{ROV}

PARKER, George E. - Pvt., Co. F, 4th Regt., Wis. Cav.
George was born circa 1842 at New York. He was listed in the 1860 federal census as a teamster residing with the family of Alonzo Granger in the second ward of the village of Menasha. George listed his residence as Oshkosh when he enlisted on June 1, 1861. He was assigned as above and he re-enlisted in that same company at the end of his term. George was wounded on June 14, 1863 at Port Hudson, Louisiana. He was then transferred to Co. D of the same regiment on Aug. 22, 1865 and was mustered out on Apr. 13, 1866. George was listed in the veteran section of the 1885, 1895 and 1905 Wisconsin State census at P.O. Menasha. He was listed in the 1890 federal census as residing in the city of Menasha. George provided that he had suffered a gunshot wound during his military service. He was listed in 1905 as retired and residing at 248 Kaukauna Street in Menasha. Son George J. Parker was also listed at that address.
{US 1860, 1890; WC-V 1885, 1895, 1905; ROV; B-1905}

PARKER, Harry - Pvt., Co. G, 3rd Regt., Wis. Vol. Inf.
Harry resided at Menasha and enlisted there on Apr. 30, 1861. He was assigned as

PARKER, Harry (cont.)
above and was taken prisoner on May 24, 1862. Harry was then discharged due to a disability.
{ROV}

PARKER, Henry J. - Cpl., Co. G, 36th Regt., Wis. Vol. Inf.
Henry resided at Neenah and enlisted there on Feb. 23, 1864. He was listed as a veteran volunteer and was assigned as above. Henry was then promoted to Corporal in that company. He was mustered out on June 7, 1865.
{ROV}

PARKER, Richard R. - Pvt., Co. H, 36th Regt., Wis. Vol. Inf.
Richard resided at Utica and enlisted there on Feb. 29, 1864. He was assigned as above and was taken prisoner at Ream's Station. Richard contracted a disease and died on Jan. 16, 1865 at Salisbury, N.C.
{ROV}

PARKER, Thomas - Civil War Veteran?
Thomas was born circa 1843 at England. He was listed in the 1860 federal census as residing with George Blake in the town of Winneconne. George is the subject of a previous sketch. Jane Parker, sister of Thomas, was born circa 1848 at Indiana. She was also residing with George Blake in 1860. Thomas was listed in the 1890 federal census as residing in the town of Winneconne at P.O. Winneconne. He listed that he was a teamster in the army from Oct. 5, 1864 to May 2, 1865. Thomas was formerly known as Thomas Blake.
{US 1860, 1890}

PARKER, William J. - Sgt., 9th Regt., Connecticut Cav.
William was married in Winnebago County on July 22, 1856 to Julia A. Harding. Julia, widow of William, was listed in the 1890 federal census as residing in the town of Nepeuskun at P.O. Rush Lake. She provided William's unit designation as above and his service dates as having been from Apr. 13, 1861 to Sept. 15, 1865.
{US 1890; WCMR v.1, p.106, #439}

PARKER, William N. - Pvt., Co. K, 17th Regt., New York Vol. Inf.
William was listed as above in the veteran section of the 1885 and 1895 Wisconsin State census at P.O. Menasha. He was listed in the 1890 federal census as residing in the town of Menasha at P.O. Menasha. William provided his service dates as having been from July 24, 1861 to June 24, 1865. He was listed in 1905 as a resident at the Wisconsin Veterans' Home at King. Martha A., his wife, was also residing there. William had been received from Menasha and Martha from LaCrosse.
{US 1890; WC-V 1885, 1895; GAR 40th}

PARKS, John E. - Pvt., Co. C, 1st Regt., Wis. Hvy. Art.
John was born circa 1842 at New York. He was a son of Morris and Julianne Parks. The parents were both natives of New York, the father born there circa 1813 and the mother born circa 1818. They were listed in the 1860 federal census as residing on a farm in the town of Vinland. Listed with them were the following children: John; Mary, born circa 1848 at New York; Jane, born circa 1853 at Wisconsin; and James, born circa

PARKS, John E. (cont.)
1856 at Wisconsin. John resided at Winnebago and enlisted there on Sept. 28, 1863. He was assigned as above and was mustered out on May 29, 1865. John was listed in the veteran section of the 1885 Wisconsin State census as a veteran of Co. C, 19th Regt., Wis. Vol. Inf. He was not found in the records of that company. John was listed in 1890 as above and residing in the town of Neenah at P.O. Neenah. He was suffering from rheumatism of the heart. John was listed in the veteran section of the 1895 and 1905 Wisconsin State census at P.O. Neenah. He was listed in 1905 as residing at 610 Isabella Street in the city of Neenah. Bertha Parks was also residing at that address.
{US 1860, 1890; WC-V 1885; 1895, 1905; ROV; B-1905}

PARMELEE, Franklin H. - Pvt., Co. E, 1st Regt., Wis. Cav.
Franklin was born circa 1847 at New York. He was listed in the 1860 federal census as residing with Timothy and Huldah Parmalee in the town of Omro at P.O. Waukau. It is not known if they were his parents or grandparents. Franklin enlisted at Omro on Nov. 16, 1863. He was assigned as above and was mustered out July 29, 1865. Franklin was listed in the veteran section of the 1885 Wisconsin State census at P.O. Markesan, Green Lake County. He was listed in that section of the 1895 and 1905 state census at P.O. Ripon, Fond du Lac County. He was also listed as residing there in 1920.
{US 1860; WC-V 1885; 1895, 1905; 21-33rd; ROV}

PARMENTER, Eugene - Pvt., Co. I, 47th Regt., Wis. Vol. Inf.
Eugene resided at Utica and enlisted there on Jan. 30, 1865. He was assigned as above and was mustered out on Sept. 4, 1865.
{ROV}

PARMENTER, Frederick - Pvt., Co. I, 47th Regt., Wis. Vol. Inf.
Frederick resided at Utica and enlisted there on Jan. 30, 1865. He was assigned as above and was mustered out on Aug. 31, 1865.
{ROV}

PARSONS, Albertus A. - Pvt., Co. H, 18th Regt., Wis. Vol. Inf.
Albertus was born circa 1849 at Massachusetts. He was a son of Samuel F. and Matilda Parsons. Samuel was born circa 1811 at Connecticut and Matilda was born circa 1819 at Massachusetts. They were listed in the 1860 federal census as residing on a farm in the town of Rushford at P.O. Eureka. Listed with them were the following children: Frances, born circa 1844; Sarah, born circa 1845; Albertus; and Charles, born in 1860. Charles was born in Wisconsin and the other children were born in Massachusetts. Albertus listed his residence as Holland, Brown County when he enlisted on Mar. 14, 1864. He was assigned as above and was mustered out on July 18, 1865. Lewis A., son of A.A. and J.A. Parsons, was born in 1878 and died in 1879. He is buried in the town of Rushford at Rushford Cemetery. Albertus was listed in the veteran section of the 1885 and 1895 Wisconsin State census at P.O. Eureka. He was listed in the 1890 federal census as residing in the town of Rushford at P.O. Eureka. Albertus was suffering from chronic gastritis. He was listed in that section of the 1905 state census at P.O. Omro. Albertus was listed in 1905 as a gardener residing on Quarter Street in the village of Omro. William and Burt Parsons were also residing at that address. Albertus died in 1929. He is buried with a simple military marker. Julia A., his wife, died on May 30, 1882 at age 40 years, 2 months and 8 days. Both are buried in the town of Rushford at

PARSONS, Albertus A. (cont.)
Rushford Cemetery. Albertus had been married second to Tillie Kresal. She was born on Nov. 5, 1876 at Germany and was a daughter of Paul Kresal. Their family removed to America and resided at Berlin, Green Lake County and then Eureka and Omro. Tillie also resided at the Wisconsin Veterans' Home for a while. She went to live with her daughter in 1964. Tillie was listed in 1972 as the final surviving widow of a Civil War veteran still residing in Wisconsin.
{US 1860, 1890; WC-V 1885, 1895, 1905; ROV; B-1905; ODN 03 Nov 1972}
{Cem. records}

PARSONS, Alonzo O. - Pvt., Co. I, 3rd (reorg.) Regt., Wis. Cav.
Alonzo was born circa 1824 at New York. Margaret, his wife, was born circa 1838 at Canada. Alonzo was listed in the 1860 federal census as a harness maker residing in the first ward of the city of Oshkosh. Then residing with him were his wife and the following children: Orson Alonzo, born circa 1855; Edgar Case P., born circa 1856; and Willie, born circa 1858. All three sons were born in Wisconsin. Alonzo enlisted at Oshkosh on Aug. 12, 1862. He was assigned as a Private in Co. C, 21st Regt., Wis. Vol. Inf. He was discharged on Feb. 28, 1863 due to a disability. Alonzo re-enlisted at Oshkosh on Jan. 5, 1864. He was assigned as above and was mustered out on July 14, 1865. Alonzo was married second in Winnebago County on Dec. 15, 1866 to Eliza/Elizabeth Hurley. He was listed in 1868 as a harness maker residing at 75 Jackson Street in Oshkosh.
{US 1860; ROV; T-1868; WCMR v.1, p.317, #1984; OWN 07 May 1863}

PARTRIDGE, Edwin D. - Capt., Co. G, 11th Regt., Wis. Vol. Inf.
Edwin resided at Clayton and enlisted on Aug. 26, 1861. He was assigned as above and was commissioned as 1st Lieutenant on Oct. 10, 1861. Edwin was promoted to Captain of that company on May 14, 1862. He resigned his commission on Mar. 18, 1863.
{ROV}

PATRICK, Francis - Pvt., Co. C, 10th Regt., Wis. Vol. Inf.
Francis resided at Menasha and enlisted there on Sept. 3, 1861. He was assigned as above and was taken prisoner at Chickamauga, Georgia. Francis died in the rebel prison at Danville, Virginia on Apr. 6, 1864.
{ROV}

PATTERSON, Robert - Pvt., Co. B, 3rd Regt., Wis. Cav.
Robert was born circa 1842 at Canada. He was listed in the 1860 federal census as residing with the family of Alonzo O. Parsons in the first ward of the city of Oshkosh. Robert enlisted at Oshkosh on Dec. 11, 1861. He was assigned as above and was then mustered out on Feb. 14, 1865 at the end of his term of enlistment.
{US 1860; ROV}

PATTON, Worthington H. - Sgt., Co. E, 6th Regt., Wis. Vol. Inf.
Worthie resided at Appleton, Outagamie County and enlisted there on June 28, 1861. He was assigned as above and was promoted to Sergeant and then 1st Sergeant in that company. Worthie was wounded in the battle at Wilderness, Virginia. He was mustered out on July 15, 1864 at the end of his term of enlistment. Worthington was married in Winnebago County on Oct. 10, 1867 to Susan Maria Heath. He was listed in 1868 as a

PATTON, Worthington H. (cont.)
bookkeeper at the Oshkosh Post Office. He was then boarding at 26 Waugoo Street in Oshkosh. He was listed in 1888 as a member of GAR Post #10 at Oshkosh. Worthie was listed in the 1890 federal census as residing in the city of Oshkosh. He provided that he had served 12 months and 5 days as a prisoner, among other places at Andersonville and Florence Prisons. Worthie was listed in the veteran section of the 1895 Wisconsin State census at P.O. Oshkosh.
{US 1890; WC-V 1895; ROV; T-1868; WCMR v.1, p.353, #2122}

PAUS, Samuel - Pvt., Co. F, 19th Regt., Wis. Vol. Inf.
Samuel resided at Black Wolf and enlisted there on Sept. 1, 1864. He was assigned as above and was then transferred to Co. C of the same regiment on May 1, 1865. Samuel was mustered out on June 26, 1865.
{ROV}

PAYNE, John - Lt., Co. E, 36th Regt., Wis. Vol. Inf.
John resided at Cascade, Sheboygan County and enlisted there on Feb. 18, 1864. He was assigned as above and was promoted to Corporal, Sergeant and then 1st Sergeant in that company. John was commissioned as 2nd Lieutenant of the company on Oct. 19, 1864 and was mustered out on July 12, 1865. He was listed in the 1890 federal census as residing in the city of Menasha. John was suffering from neuralgia and rheumatism. He was listed in the veteran section of the 1895 Wisconsin State census at P.O. Menasha.
{US 1890; WC-V 1895; ROV}

PAYNE, Thomas - Pvt., Co. B, 3rd Regt., Wis. Cav.
Thomas resided at Oshkosh and enlisted there on Dec. 3, 1861. He was assigned as above and was listed as having deserted on Mar. 27, 1862.
{ROV}

PAYNE, William H. - Pvt., Co. A, 43rd Regt., Wis. Vol. Inf.
William resided at Utica and enlisted there on Aug. 29, 1864. He was assigned as above and was mustered out on May 14, 1865.
{ROV}

PAYTON, John R. - Pvt., Co. F, 1st Regt., Wis. Cav.
John was listed as above in the veteran section of the 1895 Wisconsin State census at P.O. Omro. He was not found in the records of that company. Effie Payton was listed in 1905 as residing at 519 Pearl Street in the village of Omro.
{WC-V 1895; ROV; B-1905}

PAYTON, James W. - Pvt., Co. K, 40th Regt., Wis. Vol. Inf.
James resided at Madison, Dane County and enlisted there on June 2, 1864. He was assigned as above and was mustered out on Sept. 16, 1864 at the end of his term of enlistment. The GRI lists his name as Joseph and provides Jan. 2, 1855 as his date of birth. That would have made James 9 years of age at the time of his enlistment. That file also shows his date of death as being Sept. 22, 1876. James is buried at Omro Cemetery, Olin's Addition, Section A, plot 70. Samuel Payton, the subject of a following sketch, is buried on that same plot.
{ROV; GRI; Cem. records}

PAYTON, Samuel - Pvt., Co. A, 3rd Regt., Wis. Vol. Inf.
Samuel was born on Jan. 21, 1831. He resided at New London, Waupaca County and enlisted there on Sept. 24, 1861. Samuel was assigned as above and was discharged due to a disability on Sept. 12, 1862. He died on Feb. 17, 1881. Samuel is buried at Omro Cemetery, Olin's Addition, Section A, plot 70. James Payton, the subject of a previous sketch, is buried on that same plot.
{ROV; GRI; Cem. records}

PEARSON, Frank - Cpl., Co. I, 21st Regt., Wis. Vol. Inf.
Frank resided at Menasha and enlisted there on Aug. 15, 1862. He was assigned as above and was then promoted to Corporal in that company. Frank was wounded at Chickamauga, Georgia on Sept. 20, 1863 and was transferred to the Veteran Reserve Corps on Sept. 13, 1864. He was mustered out on Aug. 19, 1865. He was listed as Frank Pearse in one history.
{ROV; Lawson p.834}

PEARSON, John - Pvt., Co. F, 18th Regt., Wis. Vol. Inf.
John resided at Oshkosh and enlisted there on Oct. 26, 1861. He was assigned as above and was taken prisoner at Shiloh, Tennessee. John contracted a disease and died on Sept. 28, 1862 at Macon, Georgia.
{ROV}

PEASLEE, Jonathan B. - Cpl., Co. B, 21st Regt., Wis. Vol. Inf.
Jonathan resided at Winneconne and enlisted there on Aug. 14, 1862. He was assigned as above and was promoted to Corporal in that company. Jonathan was discharged due to a disability on Sept. 7, 1863.
{ROV}

PECK, Calvin - Pvt., Co. D, 6th Regt., Wis. Vol. Inf.
Calvin resided at Utica and was drafted there on Mar. 20, 1865. He was assigned as above and was mustered out on July 14, 1865.
{ROV}

PECK, Cyrus W. - Cpl., Co. H, 36th Regt., Wis. Vol. Inf.
Cyrus resided at Utica and enlisted there on Feb. 1, 1862. He was assigned as a Private to Co. A, 6th Regt., Wis. Vol. Inf. Cyrus was then discharged on Mar. 4, 1863 due to a disability. He re-enlisted at Utica on Feb. 26, 1864. He was assigned as above and was promoted to Corporal in that company. He was wounded June 18, 1864 at Petersburg, Virginia. He was then transferred to the Veteran Reserve Corps on Apr. 17, 1865.
{ROV}

PECK, Matthew C. - Pvt., Co. C, 10th Regt., Wis. Vol. Inf.
Mathew was born circa 1821 at New Hampshire. His wife was also a native of that state. They were listed in the 1860 federal census as residing in the first ward of the village of Menasha. Listed with them were the following children: Truman, subject of a following sketch; Amanda, born circa 1849; Adelaide, born circa 1850; Ellridge, born circa 1853; Mariner, born circa 1855; and Harriet, born circa 1858. The three younger children were born in Wisconsin and the others were born in New Hampshire. Matthew resided

PECK, Matthew C. (cont.)
at Menasha he and enlisted there on Sept. 3, 1861. He was assigned as above and was mustered out on Nov. 3, 1864.
{US 1860; ROV}

PECK, Oliver P. - Cpl., Co. H, 36th Regt., Wis. Vol. Inf.
Oliver resided at Utica and enlisted there on Feb. 26, 1864. He was assigned as above and was promoted to Corporal in that company. Oliver was wounded on June 18, 1864 at Petersburg, Virginia. He was then transferred to a company of the Veteran Reserve Corps on Apr. 17, 1865.
{ROV}

PECK, Reuben - Pvt., Co. A, 48th Regt., Wis. Vol. Inf.
Reuben resided at Algoma and enlisted there on Feb. 6, 1865. He was assigned as above and was listed as having deserted on Sept. 15, 1865.
{ROV}

PECK, Truman - Pvt., Co. G, 36th Regt., Wis. Vol. Inf.
Truman was born circa 1846 at New Hampshire, a son of Mathew Peck from a previous sketch. Truman was listed in the 1860 federal census as residing with his father in the first ward of the village of Menasha. He listed his residence as Neenah when he enlisted on Feb. 29, 1864. He was assigned as above. Truman contracted a disease and died on Apr. 12, 1864 at Madison, Wisconsin.
{US 1860; ROV}

PECK, Watrous - Pvt., Co. G, 24th Regt., Iowa Vol. Inf.
Watrous was listed as above in the veteran section of the 1885 Wisconsin State census at P.O. Menasha. He was listed in the 1890 federal census as residing in the city of Menasha. Watrous then provided his service dates as having been from Aug. 11, 1862 to July 11, 1865. He added that he was transferred to the Veteran Reserve Corps on June 18, 1864. Watrous was suffering from rheumatism in 1890.
{US 1890; WC-V 1885}

PECKHAM, Joshua - Pvt., Co. F, 3rd Regt., Wis. Vol. Inf.
Joshua resided at Clayton and was drafted there on Sept. 30, 1864. He was assigned as above and was mustered out on June 9, 1865.
{ROV}

PEDOLSKY, Theodore - Pvt., 101st Regt., Pennsylvania Vol. Inf.
Theodore was listed as above in the 1890 federal census. He was residing in the town of Oshkosh at P.O. Oshkosh. Theodore provided his service dates as having been from Feb. 2, 1865 to Aug. 28, 1865.
{US 1890}

PEEBLES, Dennis R. - Pvt., Co. K, 1st Regt., U.S. Colored Cav.
Dennis was listed as above in the veteran section of the 1885 Wisconsin State census at P.O. Menasha. He was listed in the 1890 federal census as residing in the city of Menasha. Dennis then provided his service dates as having been from Sept. 19, 1864 to

PEEBLES, Dennis R. (cont.)
Nov. 21, 1865.
{US 1890; WC-V 1885}

PEEBLES, Morris - Pvt., Co. G, 3rd (reorg.) Regt., Wis. Cav.
Morris resided at Cross Plains, Dane County and enlisted there on Nov. 27, 1863. He was assigned as above and was mustered out on Oct. 27, 1865. Morris was listed in the veteran section of the 1895 Wisconsin State census at P.O. Oshkosh.
{WC-V 1895; ROV}

PEETZKE, Wilhelm - Pvt., Co. B, 37th Regt., Wis. Vol. Inf.
Wilhelm resided at Oshkosh and enlisted there on Mar. 31, 1864. He was assigned as above and was mustered out on July 27, 1865.
{ROV}

PEISKEE, Louis - Pvt., Co. C, 1st Regt., Ohio Sharpshooters.
Louis was listed as above in the veteran section of the 1905 Wisconsin State census at P.O. Oshkosh. The name could possibly be Paske.
{WC-V 1905}

PELTON, Charles - Pvt., Co. C, 47th Regt., Wis. Vol. Inf.
Charles was born in 1844 at New York. He was a son of Alfred and Eliza A. Pelton. Margaret, his wife, was born in 1847, also at New York. Charles resided at Green Bay, Brown County and enlisted there on Feb. 1, 1865. He was assigned as above and was mustered out on Sept. 2, 1865. Alfred Pelton, father of Charles, died on Mar. 28, 1875 at age 73 years. Charles was listed in the 1880 federal census as a dry goods merchant residing in the town of Omro. Also residing with him at that time were Eliza Pelton, his mother, who was born circa 1810 at Connecticut and John Mead, his brother-in-law. Eliza died on Mar. 28, 1884 at age 75 years. Charles was listed in the veteran section of the 1885, 1895 and 1905 Wisconsin State census at P.O. Omro. He was listed in the 1890 federal census as residing in the village of Omro. Charles listed then that he had a finger shot off during his military service. He was listed in 1905 as being in business with H.B. Winslow. They were dealers in general merchandise under the name of Charles Pelton & Co. Charles was then residing on Prospect Street in Omro. He died on Mar. 18, 1924 and Margaret died on Sept. 10, 1937. Both are buried, with his parents, in Omro Cemetery, Olin's Addition, Section B, plot 1.
{US 1880, 1890; WC-V 1885, 1895, 1905; ROV; B-1905; Cem. records}

PENDLETON, Jerome - Pvt., Co. I, 21st Regt., Wis. Vol. Inf.
Jerome was born circa 1842 at Wisconsin. He was a son of Peter and Sarah Pendleton. The name is also found as Pembleton. Peter was born circa 1797/1812 at New York. Sarah was born circa 1812 in that same state. Peter was listed in the 1850 census as a farmer residing in the town of Neenah. With him were his wife and the following children: William, born circa 1831; Robert, born circa 1834; John, born circa 1836; Frances, born circa 1840; Elisa, born circa 1842; Jerome; Maria, born circa 1845; Silas, born circa 1847; and Louis, born circa 1848. William was listed as born in New York and the rest of the children were born in Wisconsin. All members of the family were listed as mulatto. They were still listed at that farm in the 1860 federal census. Peter and Sarah then had the additional children: Russell, born circa 1852; Theodore, born

PENDLETON, Jerome (cont.)
circa 1854; Catherine, born circa 1855; Elmira, born circa 1856; Elvira, born circa 1856; and Julia, born circa 1858. Jerome resided at Menasha and enlisted there on Aug. 12, 1862. He was assigned as above and was wounded at Chaplin Hills, Kentucky. Jerome died of those wounds on Jan. 29, 1863 at New Albany, Indiana.
{US 1850, 1860; ROV}

PENES, Lewis - Pvt., Co. G, 32nd Regt., Wis. Vol. Inf.
Lewis resided at Oshkosh and enlisted there on Nov. 20, 1863. He was assigned as above and was then transferred to Co. D, 16th (reorg.) Regt., Wis. Vol. Inf. on June 4, 1865. Lewis was mustered out on July 12, 1865.
{ROV}

PERKINS, Albert H. - Sgt., Co. B, 3rd Regt., Wis. Cav.
Albert was born circa 1835 at Vermont. Cordelia, his wife, was born circa 1838 at New York. Albert was listed in the 1860 federal census as a carpenter residing in the third ward of the city of Oshkosh. Also listed were his wife and Cora, a daughter, who was born circa 1859 at Wisconsin. Albert enlisted at Oshkosh on Nov. 6, 1861. He was assigned as above and was promoted to Sergeant and Quartermaster Sergeant in that company. Albert was transferred to Co. B, 3rd (reorg.) Regt., Wis. Cav. on Feb. 1, 1865. He was commissioned as 2nd Lieutenant of that company on Sept. 15, 1865 but was not mustered at that rank. Albert was mustered out on Sept. 20, 1865.
{US 1860; ROV}

PERKINS, Frederick B. - Pvt., Co. K, 8th Regt., Wis. Vol. Inf.
Frederick was born in 1825. Sarah, his wife, was born in 1835. Frederick resided at Mt. Pleasant and enlisted there on Jan. 25, 1864. He was assigned as above and was mustered out on Sept. 5, 1865. Frederick was listed in the veteran section of the 1885 and 1895 Wisconsin State census at P.O. Waukau. He was listed in that section of the 1905 state census at P.O. Omro. He was listed as Frank B. in the 1890 federal census and residing in the town of Rushford at P.O. Waukau. Fred and Sarah were listed in 1905 as residing in the village of Waukau. Frederick died in 1918 and Sarah died in 1917. A son, F.O. Perkins, was born in 1861 and died in 1923. All three are buried in the town of Rushford at Waukau Cemetery.
{US 1890; WC-V 1885, 1895, 1905; ROV; B-1905; Cem. records}

PERKINS, Goveneur M. - Pvt., Co. C, 14th Regt., Wis. Vol. Inf.
Goveneur resided at Omro and enlisted there on Sept. 8, 1861. He was assigned as above and was wounded at Corinth, Mississippi. He was discharged due to a disability on Dec. 19, 1862.
{ROV}

PERKINS, Marcus - Pvt., Co. F, 18th Regt., Wis. Vol. Inf.
Marcus resided at Oshkosh and enlisted there on Dec. 20, 1861. He was assigned as a musician in the above company and was then discharged on June 3, 1862. This may be the same person as the following sketch.
{ROV}

PERKINS, Marcus A. - Pvt., Co. F, 18th Regt., Wis. Vol. Inf.
Marcus was born circa 1833 at New York. Frances E., his wife, was born circa 1839, also at New York. Marcus was listed in the 1860 federal census as a blacksmith residing in the first ward of the city of Oshkosh. Residing with him were his wife and two children. Martha was born circa 1858 and Fred Eugene was born circa 1859. Both children were born in Wisconsin. Marcus enlisted at Oshkosh on Dec. 26, 1861. He was assigned as a musician in the above company and was discharged on Aug. 17, 1862.
{US 1860; ROV}

PERRY, Alanson F. - Pvt., Co. C, 38th Regt., Wis. Vol. Inf.
Alanson was born circa 1843 at Indiana. He was a son of Willard and Lucinda Perry and a brother of Jefferson Perry from a following sketch. Willard was born circa 1808 at Vermont and Lucinda was born circa 1808 at New York. They were listed in the 1860 federal census as residing on a farm in the town of Nepeuskun at P.O. Koro. Listed with them were the following children: Martin, born circa 1839; Marion, born circa 1841; Alanson; Sylvania, born circa 1845; Jefferson; Abigail, born circa 1847; Cassius, born circa 1849; Marcus and Marshall, both born circa 1850; and Lucinda, born circa 1851. The eldest son was born in Michigan, the four youngest children were born in Wisconsin and the others were born in Indiana. Alanson resided at Koro and enlisted there on Mar. 21, 1864. He was assigned as above and was wounded at Petersburg, Virginia on June 16, 1864. Alanson was mustered out on July 26, 1865. He was married in Winnebago County on May 19, 1867 to Sarah Parsons. He was listed in the veteran section of the 1885, 1895 and 1905 Wisconsin State census at P.O. Neenah. He was listed as Alonzo F. in the 1890 federal census and as residing in the town of Neenah at P.O. Neenah. He was then suffering from a disease of the lungs. Alanson was listed in 1905 as residing at 415 South Commercial Street in the city of Neenah. Olla M. Perry was also listed at that address.
{US 1860, 1890; WC-V 1885, 1895, 1905; ROV; WCMR v.1, p.324, #2039; B-1905}

PERRY, Benjamin F. - Cpl., Co. D, 41st Regt., Wis. Vol. Inf.
Benjamin resided at Menasha and enlisted there on May 2, 1864. He was assigned as above and was then promoted to Corporal in that company. Benjamin was mustered out on Sept. 23, 1864 at the end of his term of enlistment.
{ROV}

PERRY, Clark A. - Pvt., Co. B, 47th Regt., Wis. Vol. Inf.
Clark resided at Nepeuskun and enlisted there on Jan. 24, 1865. He was assigned as above and was mustered out on Sept. 4, 1865.
{ROV}

PERRY, Evan - Pvt., Co. C, 21st Regt., Wis. Vol. Inf.
Evan resided at Neenah and enlisted there on Aug. 14, 1862. He was assigned as above and was taken prisoner at Chickamauga, Georgia on Sept. 20, 1863.
{ROV}

PERRY, Franklin W. - Capt., Co. C, 10th Regt., Wis. Vol. Inf.
Franklin was born circa 1827 at Massachusetts. He was listed in the 1860 federal census as a lawyer residing in the village of Neenah. Sophronia, his wife, was born circa 1828, also at Massachusetts. Frank enlisted at Neenah on Sept. 2, 1861. He was assigned as

PERRY, Franklin W. (cont.)
above and was then commissioned as 1st Lieutenant of that company on Sept. 30, 1861.
Frank was promoted to Captain of Co. I in that regiment on Mar. 24, 1863. He was
taken prisoner during the fight at Chickamauga, Georgia. Frank was held in the rebel
prisons at Andersonville, Georgia and Charleston, S.C. He was then mustered out on
Mar. 11, 1865. Frank listed his residence as Menasha at the time of his promotion to
Captain.
{US 1860; ROV; Lawson p.810}

PERRY, George E. - Pvt., Co. B, 41st Regt., Wis. Vol. Inf.
George resided at Nepeuskun and enlisted there on May 13, 1864. He was assigned as
above and was mustered out on Sept. 23, 1864 at the end of his term of enlistment.
{ROV}

PERRY, George W. - Pvt., Co. K, 194th Regt., New York Vol. Inf.
George was listed as above in the 1890 federal census as residing at 408 Jackson Street
in the city of Oshkosh. He provided his service dates as having been from Mar. 24, 1865
to May 10, 1865. George was listed in the veteran section of the 1905 Wisconsin State
census at P.O. Oshkosh.
{US 1890; WC-V 1905}

PERRY, Gilford C. - Pvt., Co. F, 18th Regt., Wis. Vol. Inf.
Gilford resided at Oshkosh and enlisted there on Dec. 21, 1861. He was assigned as
above and was discharged on July 12, 1862. Gilford died on Aug. 12, 1862 at age 19
years, 7 months and 24 days. He is buried with two of his sisters in the town of Algoma
at Ellenwood Cemetery, Section B.
{ROV; Cem. records}

PERRY, Jefferson - Pvt., Co. B, 47th Regt., Wis. Vol. Inf.
Jefferson was born circa 1846 at Indiana. He was a son of Willard and Lucinda Perry
and a brother to Alanson of a previous sketch. Jefferson was listed in the 1860 federal
census as residing with his parents and their family in the town of Nepeuskun at P.O.
Koro. He enlisted at Nepeuskun on Jan. 26, 1865. He was assigned as above and was
then mustered out on Sept. 4, 1865. Jefferson was married in Winnebago County on
Sept. 27, 1868 to Maggie Dwire.
{US 1860; ROV; WCMR v.1, p.394, #2447}

PERRY, John - Pvt., Co. D, 32nd Regt., Wis. Vol. Inf.
John resided at Oshkosh and enlisted on Dec. 4, 1863. He was assigned as above and
was transferred to Co. D, 16th (reorg.) Regt., Wis. Vol. Inf. on June 4, 1865. He listed
his residence at that time as Waushara. John was mustered out on July 12, 1865.
{ROV}

PERRY, John - Pvt., Co. C, 10th Regt., Wis. Vol. Inf.
John resided at Menasha and enlisted there on Sept. 3, 1861. He was assigned as above
and was discharged due to an illness on Nov. 18, 1862.
{ROV; Lawson p.831}

PERRY, John C. - Cpl., Co. K, 11th Regt., Wis. Vol. Inf.
John was born circa 1832 at Wisconsin. Susan, his wife, was born circa 1838 at New York. They were listed in the 1860 federal census as residing with the family of George Lindsley in the village of Neenah. Listed with them were two children. Daughter Carrie was born circa 1856 at Wisconsin and son Frederick was born circa 1858 at Wisconsin. John enlisted at Neenah on Nov. 5, 1861. He was assigned as above and was promoted to Corporal in that company. John was mustered out on Mar. 7, 1865.
{US 1860; ROV}

PERRY, John J. - Pvt., Co. D, 1st Regt., Wis. Hvy. Art.
John resided at Nepeuskun and enlisted there on Sept. 2, 1864. He was assigned as above and was mustered out on June 30, 1865.
{ROV}

PERRY, Leander - Seaman, "Pensacola," U.S. Navy.
Leander was listed as above in the veteran section of the 1885 Wisconsin State census at P.O. Neenah.
{WC-V 1885}

PERRY, Sumner M. - Pvt., Co. E, 12th Regt., Michigan Vol. Inf.
Sumner was listed (S.H.) as above in the veteran section of the 1885 Wisconsin State census at P.O. Eureka. He is buried with a simple military marker in the town of Aurora, Waushara County at Shead Island Cemetery. Others of his family are buried on the same plot.
{WC-V 1885; Cem. records}

PERRY, William M. - Pvt., Co. F, 7th Regt., Ohio Vol. Inf.
William was listed in 1888 as a member of GAR Post #241 at Oshkosh. He was listed as above in the veteran section of the 1895 and 1905 Wisconsin State census at P.O. Oshkosh. William was listed in 1905 as a mason contractor residing at 283 High Street in the city of Oshkosh.
{WC-V 1895, 1905; B-1905}

PETERS, Cobus - Pvt., Co. G, 3rd (reorg.) Regt., Wis. Cav.
Cobus resided at Oshkosh and enlisted there on Feb. 12, 1864. He was assigned as above and was mustered out on Oct. 27, 1865.
{ROV}

PETERSON, Alexander - Lt., Co. B, 21st Regt., Wis. Vol. Inf.
Alexander resided at Oshkosh and enlisted there on Aug. 14, 1862. While the regiment was being organized, Alex was married on Aug. 24, 1862 to Harriet Hotchkiss. He was assigned as above and was promoted to Corporal and then 1st Sergeant of that company. Alexander was commissioned as 2nd Lieutenant of that company on Apr. 11, 1865 and was he mustered out on June 8, 1865. He was listed in 1920 as residing at Belle Plaine, Shawano County. He was listed in 1927 as residing at Embarrass, Waupaca County.
{21-33rd; 21-40th; WCMR v.1, p.229, #1276; ROV}

PETERSON, Charles A. - Pvt., Co. B, 21st Regt., Wis. Vol. Inf.
Charles was born in 1844. He resided at Shawano, Shawano County and enlisted there

PETERSON, Charles A. (cont.)
on Aug. 11, 1862. He was assigned as above. He was taken prisoner at Chickamauga, Georgia on June 7, 1864 and was held in confinement with Henry Courtney Scott, the subject of another sketch. He was mustered out on June 8, 1865. Charles was married in Winnebago County on June 21, 1866 to Esther J. Scott, sister of Henry. She was born in 1847. Charles was listed in the 1890 federal census as residing in the village of Omro. He reported that he had suffered a bayonette wound in the back during his military service. Charles was listed in the veteran section of the 1895 and 1905 Wisconsin State census at P.O. Omro. He was employed by Henry Scott in 1895 and was listed in 1905 as an engineer residing at the corner of Elizabeth Street and Third Street in the village of Omro. A daughter Helen was residing with him. Esther died in 1922 and Charles died on Nov. 11, 1926. Both are buried at Omro Cemetery, Original Section, plot 82.
{US 1890; WC-V 1895, 1905; ROV; Cem. records; WCMR v.1, p.302, #1860*; B-1905}

PETERSON, Christian - Pvt., Co. D, 32nd Regt., Wis. Vol. Inf.
Christian resided at Clayton and enlisted there on Aug. 21, 1862. He was assigned as above and was discharged on May 13, 1863 due to a disability.
{ROV}

PETERSON, Henry - Pvt., Co. K, 11th Regt., Wis. Vol. Inf.
Henry resided at Winchester and enlisted there on Feb. 22, 1864. He was assigned as above and was mustered out on Sept. 4, 1865.
{ROV}

PETERSON, Jens Peter - Pvt., Co. B, 38th Regt., Wis. Vol. Inf.
Jens resided at Oshkosh and enlisted there on Sept. 14, 1864. He was assigned as above and was mustered out on June 2, 1865.
{ROV}

PETERSON, John - Pvt., unassigned, 3rd Regt., Wis. Cav.
John resided at Oshkosh and enlisted there on Feb. 2, 1863. He was not found on the rolls of any company within that regiment.
{ROV}

PETERSON, John - Pvt., Co. B, 17th Regt., Wis. Vol. Inf.
John resided at Oshkosh and enlisted there on Feb. 27, 1862. He was assigned as above and was wounded on July 22, 1864. John was then discharged on June 26, 1865 due to his wounds.
{ROV}

PETERSON, Samuel - Pvt., Co. C, 46th Regt., Wis. Vol. Inf.?
Samuel was listed as above in the veteran section of the 1885 Wisconsin State census at P.O. Winneconne. He was not found in the records of that company.
{WC-V 1885; ROV}

PETERSON, William D. - Pvt., Co. E, 5th (reorg.) Regt., Wis. Vol. Inf.
William resided at Winneconne and enlisted there on Aug. 26, 1864. He was assigned

PETERSON, William D. (cont.)
as above and was discharged due to a disability on May 17, 1865.
{ROV}

PETRIE, Sandusky - Pvt., Co. C, 10th Regt., Wis. Vol. Inf.
Sandusky resided at Menasha and enlisted there on Sept. 12, 1861. He was assigned as above and was mustered out on Nov. 3, 1864.
{ROV}

PETTINGILL, Eugene N. - Pvt., Co. K, 65th Regt., Illinois Vol. Inf.
Eugene was listed as above in the veteran section of the 1885 and 1895 Wisconsin State census at P.O. Oshkosh. He was listed as Eugene E. in the 1890 federal census as residing in the town of Algoma at P.O. Oshkosh. Eugene then provided his service dates as having been from May 15, 1862 to May 15, 1865. He is buried with a simple military marker in the town of Algoma at Ellenwood Cemetery, Section C. Priscilla Waterman Jones Pettingill, his wife, is buried at his side. There are no dates on her marker.
{US 1890; WC-V 1885, 1895; Cem. records}

PETTINGILL, George S. - Pvt., Co. D, 15th Regt., Illinois Vol. Inf.
George was listed in the veteran section of the 1885 Wisconsin State census at P.O. Oshkosh. He was then listed as a veteran of Co. E, 95th Regt., Wis. Vol. Inf. but there was no such unit. George was listed as a veteran of the 15th Regt., Ill. Vol. Inf. in the 1890 federal census. He was then residing at 205 Central Avenue in the city of Oshkosh and he provided his service dates as having been from May 24, 1861 to June 14, 1864. George was listed in the veteran section of the 1895 and 1905 state census at P.O. Oshkosh and having been assigned as above. He was listed in 1905 as an employee of the R. McMillen Co. and residing at 20 W. Irving Street in Oshkosh. Bella A. Pettingill was also residing at that address.
{US 1890; WC-V 1885, 1895, 1905; B-1905}

PETTINGILL, Lemuel R. - Lt., Co. B, 58th Regt., U.S. Colored Troops.
Lemuel R. was listed in the veteran section of the 1885 Wisconsin State census at P.O. Oshkosh as having been assigned as a Private to Co. B, 6th Regt., Miss. Vol. Inf. He was listed in 1888 as a member of GAR Post #10 at Oshkosh. He was listed in the 1890 federal census as having been a Private in Co. B, 95th Regt., Ill. Vol. Inf. He was listed in the veteran section of the 1895 state census at P.O. Oshkosh and as having been assigned as 2nd Lieutenant, Co. B, 58th Regt., U.S. Colored Troops. Lemuel was listed as S.R. Pettingill in the 1905 state census as residing at P.O. Oshkosh. He was listed in that year as an employee of the Paine Lumber Co. and residing at 676 High Street in the city of Oshkosh. Claude H. Pettingill was also listed at that address.
{US 1890; WC-V 1885, 1895; 1905; B-1905}

PETTIT, Reuben - Pvt., Co. C, 32nd Regt., Wis. Vol. Inf.
Reuben resided at Oshkosh and enlisted there on Dec. 28, 1863. He was assigned as above and was mustered out on Aug. 12, 1865.
{ROV}

PETTY, John - Pvt., Co. C, 21st Regt., Wis. Vol. Inf.?
John was listed as above in the veteran section of the 1885 Wisconsin State census at

PETTY, John (cont.)
P.O. Oshkosh. He was not found in the records of that company. John was listed in 1888 as a member of GAR Post #10 at Oshkosh. He was not found in the index to the Roster of Wisconsin Volunteers.
{WC-V 1885; ROV}

PFAUNSCHMIDT, Andreas J. - Pvt., Co. H, 45th Regt., Wis. Vol. Inf.
Andreas resided at Milwaukee, Milwaukee County and enlisted there on Nov. 21, 1864. He was assigned as above and was mustered out on July 17, 1865. Andreas was listed in the veteran section of the 1885, 1895 and 1905 Wisconsin State census at P.O. Oshkosh. He was listed in the 1890 federal census as residing as 18 Peck Court in the city of Oshkosh. He then provided that he suffered a bayonette wound to his left wrist, piles, bronchitis and an inflammation of the bowels during his military service.
{US 1890; WC-V 1885, 1895, 1905; ROV}

PHELPS, Allen J. - Pvt., Co. C, 10th Regt., Wis. Vol. Inf.
Allen resided at Menasha and enlisted there on Nov. 1, 1861. He was assigned as a drummer in the above company and was mustered out on Nov. 3, 1864.
{ROV}

PHELPS, Frank M. - Pvt., Co. C, 10th Regt., Wis. Vol. Inf.
Frank resided at Menasha and enlisted there on Sept. 28, 1861. He was assigned as above and was discharged by order dated Mar. 18, 1864.
{ROV}

PHELPS, Pliny J. - Pvt., Co. D, 32nd Regt., Wis. Vol. Inf.
Pliny resided at Utica and enlisted there on Nov. 20, 1863. He was assigned as above. Pliny contracted a disease and died on Aug. 27, 1864 at Decatur, Alabama.
{ROV}

PHELPS, William M. - Pvt., Co. D, 32nd Regt., Wis. Vol. Inf.
William was born circa 1838 at New York. He was a son of M.W. and Louisa Phelps. The father was born circa 1804 at Connecticut and the mother was born circa 1801 at Massachusetts. M.W. was listed in the 1860 federal census as a shoemaker residing in the town of Utica at P.O. Fisk's Corners. Listed with them were sons George, William and Leonard, all born at New York. William enlisted at Utica on Nov. 20, 1863. He was assigned as above and was transferred to Co. D, 16th (reorg.) Regt., Wis. Vol. Inf. on June 4, 1865. William was then mustered out on July 12, 1865.
{US 1860; ROV}

PHETTEPLACE, Luther A. - Pvt., Co. G, 3rd Regt., Wis. Vol. Inf.
Luther was born circa 1842 at New York. He was listed in the 1860 federal census as employed in a pail factory and residing with the family of Owen Jones in the first ward of the village of Menasha. Luther enlisted at Menasha on Apr. 30, 1861. He was assigned as above and he re-enlisted in that company at the end of his term. Luther was wounded on Sept. 17, 1862 and he was wounded again on May 25, 1864. While home on a veteran furlough, Luther was married in Winnebago County on Jan. 6, 1864 to Jane Theresa Eldridge. He was mustered out on June 5, 1865. He was listed in 1883 at P.O. Menasha. He was then receiving a pension of $4 per month for an injury to his

PHETTEPLACE, Luther A. (cont.)
abdomen. Luther was listed in the veteran section of the 1885 Wisconsin State census at P.O. Menasha. He was listed (Louis A.) in the 1890 federal census as residing in the town of Menasha at P.O. Menasha. Luther was listed in the veteran section of the 1895 and 1905 state census at P.O. Neenah.
{US 1860, 1890; WC-V 1885, 1895, 1905; ROV; WCMR v.1, p.255, #1485; LOP-1883}

PHILLIPS, Eugene - Pvt., Co. E, 24th Regt., Wis. Vol. Inf.
Eugene was born on Sept. 20, 1840. He resided at Brookfield, Waukesha County and enlisted there on Aug. 14, 1862. He was assigned as above and was mustered out on June 10, 1865. Eugene was listed in the veteran section of the 1895 Wisconsin State census at P.O. Omro. He was listed in 1905 as a farmer residing on Waukau Road in the village of Omro. A Hattie Phillips was also listed with him. Magdalena, his wife, was born in 1854 and died in 1896. Eugene died on Mar. 29, 1913. Both are buried at Omro Cemetery, Pelton's Addition, Section B, plot 25. A son, Ed. Phillips, was listed in the cemetery records as residing at Berkshire, New York.
{WC-V 1895; ROV; GRI; B-1905; Cem. records}

PHILLIPS, George - Pvt., Co. E, 42nd Regt., Wis. Vol. Inf.
George resided at Menasha and enlisted there on Sept. 2, 1864. He was assigned as above and was transferred to Co. G of that regiment on Sept. 14, 1864. George was discharged due to a disability on May 6, 1865. He was listed in the 1890 federal census as residing in the town of Bear Creek, Waupaca County. George was suffering from protapous ani as a result of chronic diarrhea. He then stated "I am used up totally."
{US 1890; ROV}

PHILLIPS, Tyler D. - Sgt., Co. G, 36th Regt., Wis. Vol. Inf.
Tyler was born on Oct. 14, 1841. Fannie, his wife, was born on July 29, 1842. Tyler resided at Menasha and enlisted there on Feb. 28, 1864. He was assigned as above and was promoted to Corporal and then Sergeant in that company. Tyler was wounded on June 18, 1864 near Petersburg, Virginia. He was mustered out on July 12, 1865. Tyler was listed in the veteran section of the 1885, 1895 and 1905 Wisconsin State census at P.O. Menasha. He was listed in the 1890 federal census as residing in the town of Menasha at P.O. Menasha. Fannie died on Aug. 6, 1918 and Tyler died Nov. 4, 1921. Everett, a son, was born in 1875 and died in 1951. All three are buried in the town of Menasha section of Oak Hill Cemetery.
{US 1890; WC-V 1885, 1895, 1905; ROV; Cem. records}

PICKLE, Henry M. - Cpl., Co. C, 46th Regt., Wis. Vol. Inf.
Henry was born circa 1838 at New York. He was listed in the 1860 federal census as a laborer residing with the family of Jacob Lonas in the town of Winneconne at P.O. Butte des Morts. Henry enlisted at Winneconne on Feb. 6, 1865. He was assigned as above and was then promoted to Corporal in that company. Henry was mustered out on Sept. 27, 1865.
{US 1860; ROV}

PICKLE, Lancelotte H. - Pvt., Co. B, 21st Regt., Wis. Vol. Inf.
Lancelotte resided at Winneconne and enlisted there on Aug. 9, 1862. He was assigned

PICKLE, Lancelotte H. (cont.)
as above and was mustered out on June 8, 1865.
{ROV}

PICKLE, Mansuette - Pvt., Co. B, 21st Regt., Wis. Vol. Inf.
Mansuette resided at Winneconne and enlisted there on Dec. 10, 1863. He was assigned as above and was taken prisoner on Mar. 24, 1865. Mansuette was then transferred as unassigned to the 3rd Regt., Wis. Vol. Inf. on June 8, 1865. The records of that company show him as having been mustered out on May 12, 1865.
{ROV}

PIERCE, A.E. - Pvt., Co. G, 11th Regt., Vermont Vol. Inf.
He was listed as above in the veteran section of the 1885 Wisconsin State census at P.O. Eureka.
{WC-V 1885}

PIERCE, Albert C. - Pvt., Co. H, 49th Regt., Wis. Vol. Inf.
Albert was born on Sept. 3, 1847 at Vermont. He was a son of Jeremiah C. Pierce and a brother of Gustavus from following sketches. Albert was listed in the 1860 federal census as residing with his parents and their family in the town of Omro. He enlisted at Omro on Feb. 7, 1865 and was assigned as above. He contracted a disease and died on Aug. 14, 1865 at St. Louis, Missouri. Albert is buried with his parents at Omro Cemetery, Original Section, plot 152.
{US 1860; ROV; Cem. records}

PIERCE, Alvin - Pvt., Co. B, 3rd Regt., Wis. Cav.
Alvin was born circa 1838 at Maine. He was listed in the 1860 federal census as a farmer residing in the town of Oshkosh. Betsey, his wife, was born circa 1842 at Vermont. Alvin enlisted at Oshkosh on Nov. 27, 1861. He was assigned as above and was discharged due to a disability on Nov. 27, 1862. Alvin was listed in 1868 as a farmer residing at 14 Pearl Street in the city of Oshkosh.
{US 1860; ROV; T-1868}

PIERCE, Amos - Pvt., Co. D, 32nd Regt., Wis. Vol. Inf.
Amos was born circa 1821 at New York. Phoebe, his wife, was born circa 1820, also at New York. They were listed in the 1860 federal census as residing on a farm in the town of Rushford at P.O. Eureka. Listed with them were the following children: Lillis, born circa 1843; Elisabeth, born circa 1848; and Amos, born circa 1853. All three children were born in New York. Amos enlisted at Rushford on Aug. 21, 1862. He was assigned as above and was then listed as having deserted on Dec. 29, 1862.
{US 1860; ROV}

PIERCE, Gustavus A. - Pvt., Co. H, 49th Regt., Wis. Vol. Inf.
Gustavus was born circa 1851 at Vermont. He was a son of Jeremiah C. Pierce from a following sketch. Gustavus was listed in the 1860 federal census as residing with his parents and their family on a farm in the town of Omro. He resided at Omro and enlisted on Feb. 7, 1865. He was assigned as above and was mustered out on Nov. 8, 1865. Gustavus was listed in 1874 as an eligible voter in the town of Omro.
{US 1860; ROV}

PIERCE, Halvah H. - Pvt., Co. C, 46th Regt., Wis. Vol. Inf.
Halvah was born on July 19, 1843 at Vermont, a son of Simeon and Hannah Pierce and a brother of William from a following sketch. Simeon was born circa 1810 at New Hampshire and Hannah was born circa 1808 at Massachusetts. They were listed in the 1860 federal census as residing on a farm in the town of Algoma. Listed with them were the following children: Lizzie, born circa 1838 at Massachusetts; William; Halvah; and Nelson, born circa 1849 at Massachusetts. Halvah enlisted at Oshkosh on Jan. 28, 1865. He was assigned as above and was mustered out on May 27, 1865. Halvah was married in Winnebago County on Mar. 26, 1873 to Ellen A. Atherton. He was listed in the veteran section of the 1885, 1895 and 1905 Wisconsin State census at P.O. Oshkosh. Halvah was listed in the 1890 federal census as residing in the town of Algoma at P.O. Oshkosh. He resided on a farm in the town of Algoma, on Omro Road just west of Oakwood Road. Halvah and Ellen were listed in 1905 as residing on 10 acres of section 17 in the town of Algoma. Also residing with them were Arthur L. and Clara A. Pierce. Clara died in 1952. Halvah on died Sept. 1, 1913 and Ellen died in 1916. Both are buried with members of their family in the town of Omro at Omro Junction Cemetery.
{US 1860, 1890; WC-V 1885, 1895, 1905; ROV; WCMR v.1, p.568, #3842; B-1905} {Cem. records}

PIERCE, James G. - Pvt., Co. I, 21st Regt., Wis. Vol. Inf.
James was born circa 1838 at New York. He was a son of Charles and Sarah S. Pierce and a brother to Myron of a following sketch. Charles was born circa 1805 at Vermont and Sarah was born in that same state circa 1818. They were listed in the 1860 federal census as residing on a farm in the town of Poygan. Listed with them then were the following children: James; Myron; Charles, born circa 1841; Harvey, born circa 1844; and Franklin, born circa 1852. All of the children were born in New York. James enlisted at Menasha on Aug. 5, 1862 and was assigned as above. He was mustered out on May 29, 1865. He was listed in the 1890 federal census as residing in the town of Poygan at P.O. Omro. James was then listed as suffering from rheumatism resulting from a disease of the heart. He was again listed in the veteran section of the 1895 and 1905 Wisconsin State census at P.O. Omro. James is buried with a simple military marker in the town of Poygan at Oak Hill Cemetery. His parents and others of their family are buried on that same plot.
{US 1860, 1890; WC-V 1895, 1905; ROV; Cem. records}

PIERCE, Jeremiah C. - Pvt., Co. C, 14th Regt., Wis. Vol. Inf.
Jeremiah was born on July 14, 1813 at Vermont. Edna R., his wife, was born Nov. 22, 1823, also at Vermont. They were listed in the 1860 federal census as residing on a farm in the town of Omro. Listed with them were the following children: Emeretta, born circa 1846; Albert, subject of a previous sketch; Gustavus, subject of a previous sketch; Frank, born circa 1853; Viola, born circa 1855; and Laurinda, born circa 1859. The three youngest children were born in Wisconsin and the others were born in Vermont. Jeremiah enlisted at Omro on Sept. 8, 1861. He was assigned as above and was then discharged due to a disability on June 10, 1862. Jeremiah was listed in 1874 as an eligible voter in the town of Omro. He was listed in the veteran section of the 1885 Wisconsin State census at P.O. Wild Rose, Waushara County. Jeremiah died June 26, 1886. Edna died on Oct. 9, 1909. Both are buried with members of their family at Omro Cemetery, Original Section, plot 152.
{US 1860; WC-V 1885; ROV; Cem. records}

PIERCE, Merritt R. - Pvt., Co. C, 1st Regt., Wis. Hvy. Art.
Merritt was born circa 1826 at New York. He was a son of Rufus and Elizabeth Pierce. Rufus was born circa 1795 at Vermont and Elizabeth was born circa 1899 at New York. Both were listed in the 1850 federal census as residing in the town of Vinland. Merritt was married in Winnebago County on Mar. 7, 1849 to Elizabeth Doughty. He was listed as residing next to his father in the 1850 census. Merritt and Elizabeth then had a son, Ira, who had been born in 1850. Merritt listed his residence as Winneconne when he enlisted on Sept. 8, 1863. He was assigned as above and was mustered out on Sept. 21, 1865. The above needs to be confirmed as there may have been a second Merritt Pierce in Vinland in 1860.
{US 1850, 1860; ROV; WCMR v.1, p.15, #58}

PIERCE, Myron L. - Pvt., Co. I, 21st Regt., Wis. Vol. Inf.
Myron was born on Nov. 24, 1838 at Essex, Essex County, New York. He was a son of Charles and Sarah S. Pierce and a brother of James from a previous sketch. Myron removed to the town of Poygan at age 20 years and he was listed in the 1860 federal census as a farm laborer for Washington Blinn in the town of Omro. He listed his residence as Poygan when he enlisted on Aug. 15, 1862. He was transferred to the Veteran Reserve Corps on Aug. 19, 1863 and was mustered out July 5, 1865 at Detroit, Michigan. Myron was married to Mary J. White in Winnebago County on Mar. 15, 1873. They had a daughter, Sarah Myrtle Pierce, who was born in the town of Poygan on Dec. 3, 1879. Myron was listed in the veteran section of the 1885, 1895 and 1905 Wisconsin State census at P.O. Omro. He was listed in the 1890 federal census as residing in the village of Omro. He was suffering from kidney disease as a result of exposure during his military service. Myron was listed in 1905 as a canvasser residing at the corner of East Street and Poygan Road in Omro. Also listed at that address were Lillie Pierce, a school teacher, and Myron W. Pierce, a student. Myron died in Omro on Oct. 4, 1915. Mary Jane, his wife, was born on Aug. 7, 1852 and died on Mar. 8, 1932. Alice May, a daughter, died on Sept. 1, 1878 at age 7 months and 12 days. Myron, Mary Jane and Alice are buried in the town of Poygan at Oak Hill Cemetery.
{US 1860, 1890; WC-V 1885, 1895, 1905; ROV; WCMR v.1, p.573, #3879; B-1905}
{Cem. records; WCBR v.2, p.189, #532; 21-29th}

PIERCE, William Franklin - Pvt., Co. A, 3rd Regt., Wis. Cav.
William was born on Aug. 28, 1840 at Vermont. He was a son of Simeon and Hannah Pierce and a brother of Halvah from a previous sketch. Simeon was born circa 1810 at New Hampshire and Hannah was born circa 1808 at Massachusetts. William was listed in the 1860 federal census as residing with his parents in the town of Algoma. He listed his residence as Oshkosh when he enlisted on Jan. 4, 1864. He was assigned as above and was transferred to Co. K, 3rd (reorg.) Regt., Wis. Cav. on Mar. 23, 1865. He was mustered out on Sept. 29, 1865. William was listed in 1874 as an eligible voter in the town of Omro. He was listed in the veteran section of the 1885, 1895 and 1905 Wisconsin State census at P.O. Oshkosh. He was listed in the 1890 federal census as residing in the town of Algoma at P.O. Oshkosh. William had suffered a wound to the head and was reported in poor health. He was listed in 1905 as residing on 25 acres of section 18 in the town of Algoma. This was just west of Leonard Road and about a mile west of brother Halvah's farm. Residing with him at that time were Anna E., his wife, and Erna and Vernon Pierce. William was a member of GAR Post #10 at Oshkosh in 1888. He died on Feb. 10, 1908. Anna was born in 1857 and died in 1935. Both are

PIERCE, William Franklin (cont.)
buried in the town of Omro at Omro Union Cemetery.
{US 1860, 1890; WC-V 1885, 1895, 1905; ROV; B-1905; Cem. records}

PIERCE, William H. - Pvt., Co. D, 32nd Regt., Wis. Vol. Inf.
William resided at Utica and enlisted there on Nov. 28, 1863. He was assigned as above and was then transferred to Co. D, 16th (reorg.) Regt., Wis. Vol. Inf. on June 4, 1865. William was mustered out on July 12, 1865.
{ROV}

PIERCOTT, Joseph - Pvt., Co. C, 9th Regt., Wis. Vol. Inf.
Joseph was born circa 1833 at Prussia. He was listed in the 1860 federal census as a farm laborer for George Lathrop in the town of Algoma. Joseph listed his residence as Oshkosh when he enlisted on Sept. 24, 1861. He was assigned as above and he then re-enlisted in that same company at the end of his term. Joseph was transferred to Co. A, 9th (reorg.) Regt., Wis. Vol. Inf. and he was mustered out on Jan. 30, 1866.
{US 1860; ROV}

PILLAR, James - Pvt., Co. B, 21st Regt., Wis. Vol. Inf.
James was born circa 1844 at England, a son of James and Charlotte Pillar. Both parents were natives of England, the father born there circa 1812 and the mother born circa 1802. James Jr. was listed in the 1860 federal census as residing with his parents on a farm in the town of Vinland. Also listed was a sister, Elizabeth, who was born circa 1850 at England. James enlisted at Vinland on Aug. 14, 1862. He was assigned as above. James was killed in action on Sept. 20, 1863 at Chickamauga, Georgia. His father died prior to 1894. He had then been a widower for some time and there was a dispute over the settlement of his will. Elizabeth, listed above, had married a Bowron and was trying to gain an interest in the estate.
{US 1860; ROV; OWN 17 Feb 1894}

PINE, James H. - Pvt., unassigned, 3rd Regt., Wis. Cav.
James resided at Oshkosh and enlisted there on Feb. 22, 1864. He was listed in the records of that regiment as serving on detached service until he was mustered out on May 27, 1865.
{ROV}

PINGEL, Fritz - Pvt., Co. D, 51st Regt., Wis. Vol. Inf.
Fritz resided at Appleton, Outagamie County and enlisted there on Feb. 28, 1865. He was assigned as above and was mustered out on Aug. 29, 1865. Fritz was listed in the veteran section of the 1895 Wisconsin State census at P.O. Neenah. He and his wife were listed in 1905 as residing on 80 acres of section 15 in the town of Clayton.
{WC-V 1895; ROV; B-1905}

PINGRY, Fred - Pvt., Co. I, 51st Regt., Wis. Vol. Inf.?
Fred was listed as above in the veteran section of the 1885 Wisconsin State census at P.O. Neenah. The only Pingry in that company was Winfield Pingray. He enlisted at Sylvester, Green County on Mar. 17, 1865. This company was then mustered out at Milwaukee, Wisconsin on May 6, 1865 before joining the regiment.
{WC-V 1885; ROV}

PINGRY, Gilman E. - Pvt., Co. F, 18th Regt., Wis. Vol. Inf.
Gilman was born circa 1846 at New Hampshire, a son of Walker and Mary Pingry. Both parents were natives of New Hampshire and both were born circa 1820. They were listed (Pingrey) in the 1860 federal census as residing on a farm in the town of Rushford at P.O. Eureka. Listed with them were the following children: Gilman; Mary, born circa 1848 at New Hampshire; and Adaline, born circa 1857 at Wisconsin. Gilman enlisted at Rushford on Feb. 17, 1862. He was assigned as above. Gilman contracted a disease and died at Monterey on June 11, 1862.
{US 1860; ROV}

PINKHAM, Comfort - Sgt., Co. I, 7th Regt., Wis. Vol. Inf.
Comfort resided at Clayton and enlisted there on Sept. 20, 1861. He was assigned as above and was promoted to Sergeant in that company. Comfort was listed as having deserted on June 21, 1865.
{ROV}

PIPER, Asa - Pvt., Co. K, 15th Regt., Maine Vol. Inf.
Asa was listed as above in the veteran section of the 1885 Wisconsin State census at P.O. Neenah. He was listed in the 1890 federal census as residing in the town of Neenah at P.O. Neenah and as having been a musician with Co. K, 15th Regt., Mich. Vol. Inf. Asa then provided his service dates as having been from Feb. 1, 1862 to Mar. 6, 1863. He was suffering from diarrhea and blindness. Orinda, widow of Asa, was listed in 1905 as residing on 60 acres of section 20 in the town of Neenah. Ora Piper was then residing with her. Orenda had been listed in 1883 as residing at P.O. Neenah and receiving a mother's pension of $8 per month.
{US 1890; WC-V 1885; B-1905; LOP-1883}

PIPER, Fred M. - Pvt., Co. A, 3rd Regt., Wis. Vol. Inf.
Fred enlisted on Sept. 2, 1864 and was assigned as above. He was then mustered out on June 9, 1865. Fred was listed in 1888 as a member of GAR Post #10 at Oshkosh. He was listed that same year as a member of GAR Post #241, also at Oshkosh. Fred was listed as above in the veteran section of the 1885 Wisconsin State census at P.O. Oshkosh. He was married to Henrietta Ripple. They had a son, unnamed when his birth was resigtered, who was born in the town of Black Wolf on Dec. 8, 1878.
{WC-V 1885; ROV; WCBR v.2, p.127, #339}

PIRKEY, Joseph - Pvt., Co. D, 41st Regt., Wis. Vol. Inf.
Joseph resided at Menasha and enlisted there on May 6, 1864. He was assigned as above and was mustered out on Sept. 23, 1864 at the end of his term of enlistment.
{ROV}

PITCHER, Sylvester D. - Pvt., Co. E, 2nd Regt., Wis. Vol. Inf.
Sylvester was born circa 1838 at New York. He was listed in the 1860 federal census as a laborer residing with the family of Joel L. Mead in the first ward of the city of Oshkosh. Sylvester listed his residence as Fond du Lac, Fond du Lac County when he enlisted on Apr. 21, 1861. He was assigned as above. Sylvester was wounded and taken prisoner in the first battle at Bull Run, Virginia. He was mustered out on June 28, 1864 at the end of his term of enlistment. Sylvester was listed in 1883 at P.O. Oshkosh. He had then been receiving a pension of $8 per month since Jan. 1882 for the partial loss

PITCHER, Sylvester D. (cont.)
of his left index and second fingers, a wound to his right leg and vericose veins. Sylvester was listed in the veteran section of the 1885, 1895 and 1905 Wisconsin State census at P.O. Oshkosh. He was also listed in 1888 as a member of GAR Post #10 at Oshkosh. He was listed in the 1890 federal census as residing in the city of Oshkosh. He was listed in a 1898 article as preparing to leave for the Klondike with a party from Waupaca County. Sylvester was listed in 1905 as a commercial traveler residing at 130 Waugoo Street in Oshkosh. Herbert, Jennie, Lulu and Edith Pitcher were also residing at that address.
{US 1860, 1890; WC-V 1885, 1895, 1905; B-1905; OWN 19 Feb 1898; LOP-1883} {ROV}

PITT, Frederick - Pvt., Co. F, 19th Regt., Wis. Vol. Inf.
Frederick was born circa 1820 at Prussia. Wilhelmina, his wife, was born circa 1826, also at Prussia. They were listed in the 1860 federal census as residing on a farm in the town of Winchester. Listed with them were the following children: Ernestine, born circa 1847; Augusta, born circa 1852; Henrietta, born circa 1857; and Amelia, born circa 1859. The two older daughters were born in Prussia and the others were all born in Wisconsin. Frederick enlisted at Winchester on Jan. 30, 1862. He was assigned as above and was discharged on July 23, 1862 due to a disability. Frederick was listed in 1868 as the proprietor of a boarding house at 43 Ceape Street in Oshkosh. Wilhelmina suffered from asthma. She died at their home at the corner of Ceape and Broad Streets in Oshkosh in April 1891. She was survived by her husband, two sons and four daughters. All were residents of Oshkosh except a son who resided at Idaho. Fred was listed in the veteran section of the 1895 Wisconsin State census at P.O. Oshkosh. Minnie Pitt was listed in 1905 as residing at 131 Ceape Street in Oshkosh. William Pitt was residing with her.
{US 1860; WC-V 1895; ROV; T-1868; B-1905; OWN 23 Apr 1891}

PITT, Horace Coker - Pvt., Co. B, 37th Regt., Wis. Vol. Inf.
Horace was born circa 1846 at New York, a son of Charles and Patience Pitt. Both parents were natives of Vermont, the father born there circa 1822 and the mother born circa 1827. They were listed in the 1860 federal census as residing on a farm in the town of Orihula at P.O. Fremont, Waupaca County. Listed with them were the following children: Mary, born circa 1845; Horace; William, born circa 1848; Betsey, born circa 1854; Henry, born circa 1856; George, born circa 1858; and Harriet, born in 1860. The last three children were born in Wisconsin and the others were born in New York. Horace enlisted at Fremont on Mar. 17, 1864. He was assigned as above and he was wounded on June 18, 1864 at Petersburg, Virginia. Horace was then mustered out on July 27, 1865. He was married to Anna Mae Bell and they had a son, Charles William Pitt, who was born in the town of Wolf River on June 15, 1879. Horace was listed in the 1890 federal census as residing in the town of Wolf River at P.O. Fremont. He listed that he had suffered a gunshot wound and that he was receiving a pension.
{US 1860, 1890; ROV; WCBR v.2, p.149, #403}

PIXLEY, Willis C. - Pvt., Co. A, 38th Regt., Wis. Vol. Inf.
Willis resided at Vinland and enlisted there on Aug. 31, 1864. He was assigned as above and was mustered out on July 26, 1865.
{ROV}

PLANK, N.G. - Pvt., Co. F, 186th Regt., New York Vol. Inf.
He was listed as above in the veteran section of the 1885 Wisconsin State census at P.O. Menasha.
{WC-V 1885}

PLUMMER, Harrison H. - Sgt., Co. C, 10th Regt., Wis. Vol. Inf.
Harrison resided at Menasha and enlisted there on Aug. 12, 1861. He was assigned as above and was promoted to Corporal and then Sergeant in that company. Harrison was wounded at Chickamauga, Georgia and was then mustered out on Nov. 3, 1864. He was listed in the veteran section of the 1895 Wisconsin State census at P.O. Neenah. Harrison was listed in 1905 as a dealer in plumbing supplies and a cement contractor. He was residing at 420 S. Commercial Street in the city of Neenah. Olive and Zilpha Plummer were also residing at that address.
{WC-V 1895; ROV; B-1905}

PLUMMER, Jefferson L. - Sgt., Co. C, 10th Regt., Wis. Vol. Inf.
Jefferson resided at Menasha and enlisted there on Aug. 22, 1861. He was assigned as above and was promoted to Corporal and then Sergeant in that company. He was taken prisoner at Chickamauga, Georgia. Jefferson died on Jan. 22, 1865 at Annapolis, Maryland.
{ROV}

POHLMAN, George - Pvt., Co. C, 46th Regt., Wis. Vol. Inf.
George was born circa 1830 at New York, a son of William and Margaret Pohlman and a brother of Hiram from a following sketch. Both parents were natives of New York, the father born there circa 1806 and the mother born circa 1805. They were listed in the 1860 federal census as residing on a farm in the town of Clayton at P.O. Neenah. Listed with them were the following children: George; William, born circa 1836 at New York; and Hiram. George enlisted at Neenah on Feb. 4, 1865. He was assigned as above and was mustered out on Sept. 27, 1865.
{US 1860; ROV}

POHLMAN, Hiram A. - Cpl., Co. K, 11th Regt., Wis. Vol. Inf.
Hiram was born circa 1840 at New York, a son of William and Margaret Pohlman and a brother of George from a previous sketch. Hiram was listed in the 1860 federal census as residing with his parents on a farm in the town of Clayton at P.O. Neenah. He enlisted at Clayton on Sept. 28, 1861. He was assigned as above and was promoted to Corporal in that company. Hiram contracted a disease and died on July 15, 1864 at Brashear City, Louisiana.
{US 1860; ROV}

POLAI, John - Pvt., Co. E, 5th (reorg.) Regt., Wis. Vol. Inf.
John resided at Oshkosh and enlisted there on Aug. 17, 1864. He was assigned as above and was wounded at Sailor's Creek. John was mustered out on June 20, 1865.
{ROV}

POLLACK, Frederich J. - Pvt., Co. B, 3rd Regt., Wis. Cav.
Frederich resided at Black Wolf and enlisted there on Dec. 23, 1861. He was assigned

POLLACK, Frederich J. (cont.)
as above. Frederich contracted a disease and died on Apr. 10, 1862 at St. Louis, Missouri.
{ROV}

POND, William H. - Lt., Co. G, 16th Regt., Wis. Vol. Inf.
William resided at Eau Claire, Eau Claire County and enlisted there on Nov. 1, 1861. He was assigned as above and was commissioned as 1st Lieutenant of that company on Jan. 4, 1862. William resigned his commission on Sept. 3, 1862. Elizabeth, his widow, was listed in the 1890 federal census as residing at 51 New York Avenue in the city of Oshkosh.
{US 1890; ROV}

POOL, Elijah C. - Pvt., Co. B, 49th Regt., Wis. Vol. Inf.
Elijah resided at Utica and enlisted there on Feb. 10, 1865. He was assigned as above and was mustered out on Nov. 1, 1865.
{ROV}

POOLER, Reuben F. - Pvt., Co. L, 3rd (reorg.) Regt., Wis. Cav.
Reuben resided at Jefferson and enlisted there on Mar. 10, 1864. He was assigned as above and was mustered out Oct. 23, 1865. Reuben had a son, unnamed at registration, who was born in Oshkosh on May 21, 1882. Reuben was listed in the veteran section of the 1885 and 1905 Wisconsin State census at P.O. Oshkosh. He was listed in 1888 as a member of GAR Post #10 at Oshkosh. He was listed in the 1890 federal census as residing in the city of Oshkosh. Reuben was listed in 1905 as a grinder at the Oshkosh Logging Tool Co. and residing at 75 School Street in Oshkosh. Earl A. and Roy F. Pooler were also residing at that address.
{US 1890; WC-V 1885, 1905; ROV; B-1905; WCBR v.3, p.81, #483}

POPE, Charlemagne - Pvt., Co. D, 41st Regt., Wis. Vol. Inf.
Charlemagne was born circa 1845 at New York. He was listed in the 1860 federal census as a drug clerk for and residing with Augustus E. Bates in the first ward of the village of Menasha. Charlemagne enlisted at Menasha on May 2, 1864. He was assigned as above and was mustered out on Sept. 23, 1864 at the end of his term of enlistment. He was killed in a sawmill accident at Menasha.
{US 1860; ROV; Lawson p.840}

POPE, George M. - Pvt., Co. C, 10th Regt., Wis. Vol. Inf.
George was born circa 1817 at New York. He was listed in the 1860 federal census as a sawyer residing in the second ward of the village of Menasha. Elmira, his wife, was born circa 1826 at New York. Sophronia, their daughter, was born circa 1848, also at New York. George enlisted at Menasha on Sept. 3, 1861. He was assigned as a fifer in the above company and was discharged on Apr. 9, 1863 due to a disability. George died in 1901 at Nebraska.
{US 1860; ROV; Lawson p.811}

POPE, William A. - Lt., Co. F, 18th Regt., Wis. Vol. Inf.
William was born circa 1826 at New York. Harriet, his wife, was born circa 1830 at Pennsylvania. William was listed in the 1860 federal census as a painter residing in the

POPE, William A. (cont.)
third ward of the city of Oshkosh. Listed with him were his wife and the following children: Ophelia, born circa 1849 at New Jersey; Henry, born circa 1852 at Wisconsin; Edwin, born circa 1857 at Wisconsin; and Benjamin, born circa 1859 at Wisconsin. William enlisted at Oshkosh on Nov. 19, 1861. He was assigned as above and was promoted to Corporal and then Sergeant in that company. He was taken prisoner at Allatoona, Georgia. He was commissioned as 1st Lieutenant of that company Apr. 19, 1864 and was mustered out on May 15, 1865. William was listed in 1868 as a machinist residing at 124 Ohio Street in Oshkosh. He was listed in the veteran section of the 1885 Wisconsin State census at P.O. Oshkosh. William was listed in the 1890 federal census as residing at 490 Ohio Street in Oshkosh and suffering from a disease of the lungs. He died on Jan. 28, 1892 at age 66 years. Harriet, his wife, was born on Mar. 7, 1831 and died on July 22, 1898. Both are buried with members of their family in the town of Algoma at Ellenwood Cemetery, Section F.
{US 1860, 1890; WC-V 1885; ROV; T-1868; Cem. records; OWN 4 Feb 1892}

PORLIER, Charles L. - Pvt., Co. B, 21st Regt., Wis. Vol. Inf.
Charles was born in 1841/9 at Wisconsin, a son of Louis B. and Sophia (Grignon) Porlier. Louis was born circa 1818 at Wisconsin. His obituary states that he was born on Jan. 1, 1814 at Green Bay. Charles and his father were listed in the 1860 federal census as residing in the town of Oshkosh. They were residing with Augustine Grignon, father of Sophia. She was not listed there at that time. Louis died at the Grignon homestead near Butte des Morts in May 1896. Charles enlisted at Oshkosh on Aug. 9, 1862. He was assigned as above and was then transferred to the Veteran Reserve Corps on Apr. 10, 1864. Charles re-joined his company on July 5, 1864 and was mustered out on June 8, 1865. He was married in Winnebago County on Nov. 19, 1866 to Josephine DuChien. Charles was listed in 1883 at P.O. Butte des Morts. He had been receiving a pension of $4 per month since Oct. 1879 for an injury to his abdomen. Charles was listed in the veteran section of the 1885 and 1895 Wisconsin State census at P.O. Omro. He was listed in the 1890 federal census as residing in the village of Omro and suffering from breech and kidney troubles. He was listed in the veteran section of the 1905 state census at P.O. Oshkosh. Charles was listed in 1905 as an employee of the Paine Lumber Co. and residing at 17 Vinland Road in the city of Oshkosh. Also at that address were Charles P., Jesse G., Joseph L., Louis D., and Rossie E. Porlier. Charles died in 1918.
{US 1860, 1890; WC-V 1885, 1895, 1905; ROV; WCMR v.1, p.313, #1946; B-1905}
{LOP-1883; OWN 18 May 1896}

PORTER, Joel W. - Pvt., Co. H, 16th Regt., Wis. Vol. Inf.?
Joel was born on Nov. 24, 1824 in the town of Naples, New York. He removed west circa 1846 and spent a year at Richmond, Illinois. Joel then moved to Winnebago County in November 1847 and settled at the then village of Oshkosh. Several years later, circa 1856, he was married to Julia Hammond from Ripon. Joel was a contractor and builder. He constructed many of the lumber mills along the Fox River at Oshkosh. He also constructed the first permanent bridge over the river. Joel and Julia had a large home at the corner of High and New York in Oshkosh. He was listed as above in the veteran section of the 1885 Wisconsin State census at P.O. Oshkosh. He was not found in the records of that company and was not found in the Index to Roster of Wisconsin Volunteers. Joel was listed in the 1890 federal census as residing in the city of Oshkosh. He listed his unit assignment as above and included that he had also served with Co. G,

PORTER, Joel W. (cont.)
158th Regt., Ill. Vol. Inf. Joel was listed in the veteran section of the 1895 state census as a veteran of Co. G, 158th Regt., Ill. Vol. Inf. He was listed in 1905 as residing at 730 High Street in Oshkosh. Joel and Julia celebrated their golden wedding anniversary circa 1906 and she died about two years later. Joel then moved to the home of his daughter, Mrs. Nellie E. Dale, where he died on Mar. 13, 1913. He was buried in Oshkosh at Riverside Cemetery. Joel was survived by a sister, Mrs. Abigail Pritchard, of Cleveland, Ohio. His brother died much earlier at Buffalo, New York. Joel was also survived by his only daughter and her three sons, she the widow of Dr. Harvey B. Dale.
{US 1890; WC-V 1885, 1895; ROV; B-1905; OWN 14 Mar 1913}

PORTER, William R. - Pvt., Co. B, 3rd Regt., Wis. Cav.?
William was listed in 1868 as a builder residing at 170 Algoma Street in the city of Oshkosh. He was listed as above in the veteran section of the 1885 Wisconsin State census at P.O. Oshkosh. He was not found in the records of that company and was not found in the index to Roster of Wisconsin Volunteers.
{WC-V 1885; T-1868; ROV}

POSSELT, Carl Ernest - Pvt., Co. D, 50th Regt., Wis. Vol. Inf.
Carl was born on Apr. 16, 1833. He was married in Winnebago County on Oct. 30, 1861 to Ernestine Apollonia Engel. She was born in 1837. Carl listed his residence as Elba, Dodge County when he enlisted on Feb. 11, 1865. He was assigned as above and was mustered out on June 12, 1866 at the end of his term of enlistment. Carl was listed in the 1890 federal census as residing in the town of Wolf River at P.O. Zittau. He was listed in the veteran section of the 1895 Wisconsin State census at P.O. Zittau. Carl died on Mar. 14, 1903. Appolonia was listed in 1905 as residing with the family of Fred W. Posselt in section 12 of the town of Wolf River. She died in 1925. Both are buried in the town of Wolf River at Immanuel Lutheran Cemetery.
{US 1890; WC-V 1895; Cem. records; WCMR v.1, p.220, #1203; B-1905; ROV}

POST, Albert M. - Cpl., Co. G, 3rd Regt., Wis. Vol. Inf.
Albert was born on Aug. 27, 1837 at Camillus, New York. He was a son of Eliaz and Experience (Rice) Post. Experience died at New York in 1838 and Eliaz died there about 10 years later. Eliaz was a veteran of the War of 1812. Albert was a brother of Mrs. Harvey Sackett, a resident of Appleton, Outagamie County. A sister-in-law, Mrs. G.W. Post resided at Milton Junction, Rock County. Albert came to Wisconsin in 1859 and was engaged at farming until the start of the war. He listed his residence as Appleton, Outagamie County when he enlisted at Fond du Lac, Fond du Lac County on June 28, 1861 and was assigned as above. Albert was taken prisoner on May 25, 1862 during the second battle at Winchester, Virginia. He was taken to Lynchburg and later to Belle Isle, where he was paroled on Sept. 13. He went to Annapolis, Maryland and rejoined his regiment in December 1862. Albert was then discharged on Dec. 20, 1863 and he immediately re-enlisted in that same company. While home on furlough, Albert was married on Jan. 9, 1864 to Margaret M. Hartshiem. She was born in Germany. Albert was soon promoted to Corporal in that company for bravery, the officers of the company considering him brave for having gotten married in the midst of army life. Albert was home on furlough when his regiment returned to the state. He was discharged July 18, 1865. Albert resided at Appleton and Neenah after returning. He eventually took a soldier's homestead in Shawano County, removing there in March 1884. Albert and

POST, Albert M. (cont.)
Margaret had seven children: Elford; Oscar W.; Elsie E.; Grace P.; Anna S., died young; Arthur M., died young; and Everett E., died young. Albert was a member of GAR Post #81 at Shawano in 1888.
{ROV; SCA 1:652-3}

POTTER, Albert - Pvt., Co. D, 32nd Regt., Wis. Vol. Inf.
Albert was born circa 1830 at Vermont. He was married on Feb. 17, 1852 to Lucretia Doughty in Winnebago County. Albert was listed in the 1860 federal census as residing on a farm in the town of Rushford at P.O. Eureka. Charlotte, his wife, was born circa 1839 at New York. Listed with them were a son, Hobart, who was born circa 1856 at Wisconsin, and a daughter, Charlotte, who was born in 1860. Albert enlisted at Eureka on Nov. 20, 1863. He was assigned as above and was transferred to Co. D, 16th (reorg.) Regt., Wis. Vol. Inf. on June 4, 1865. Albert was mustered out on July 12, 1865. He was listed in the veteran section of the 1885 and 1895 Wisconsin State census at P.O. Eureka. Albert was listed in the 1890 federal census as residing in the town of Rushford at P.O. Eureka. He is buried with a simple military marker in the town of Rushford at Eureka Cemetery. C.M., his widow, was listed in 1905 as residing on a lot in section 21 of the town of Rushford.
{US 1860, 1890; WC-V 1885, 1895; B-1905; WCMR v.1, p.72, #314; Cem. records}
{ROV}

POTTER, Erwin W. - Lt., 15th Regt., U.S. Inf.
Erwin was born circa 1831 at Pennsylvania. He was listed in the 1860 federal census as a clerk residing in the first ward of the city of Oshkosh. Erwin enlisted at Oshkosh on Apr. 21, 1861. He was assigned as a Private to Co. E, 2nd Regt., Wis. Vol. Inf. and was promoted to Corporal in that company. While stationed at Chain Bridge, the regiment was visited by General McClellan, Secretary Cameron, and Gov. and Mrs. Curtin of Pennsylvania. Erwin was acquainted with Mrs. Curtin and, as her carriage stopped, he made his way through the crowd and approached her. He requested her assistance in receiving a commission in the Regular Army. As a favor to her, Gen. McClellan made arrangements and, on Sept. 16, 1861, Erwin was commissioned as a 1st Lieutenant in the 15th Regt., U.S. Army. According to an article in 1899 by Col. Harshaw, Erwin died at Texas while in the service.
{US 1860; OWN 27 Dec 1861; ODN 07 May 1899; ROV}

POTTER, Horace H. - Pvt., Co. K, 5th (reorg.) Regt., Wis. Vol. Inf.
Horace was born circa 1845 at Wisconsin. He was a son of Wilber Potter. Wilber was born circa 1818 at New York. He was listed in the 1860 federal census as residing on a farm in the town of Rushford at P.O. Waukau. Maria, his wife, was born circa 1832 at Ireland. Listed with them were the following children: Horace; Matilda, born circa 1847; David, born circa 1852; Harriet, born circa 1853; Alice, born circa 1855; Charles, born circa 1858; and Adelbert, born in 1859. All of the children were born in Wisconsin. Horace resided at Nepeuskun and enlisted there on Aug. 30, 1864. He was assigned as above and was mustered out on June 20, 1865.
{US 1860; ROV}

POTTER, Jacob L. - Surg., 29th Regt., Wis. Vol. Inf.
Jacob was commissioned as 2nd Assistant Surgeon of the above regiment on Feb. 20,

POTTER, Jacob L. (cont.)
1864. He was promoted to 1st Asst. Surg. on Aug. 31, 1863 and was then promoted to Surgeon on Aug. 23, 1864. Jacob was mustered out on June 22, 1865.
{ROV}

POTTER, James B. - Pvt., Co. K, 1st Regt., Indiana Cav.
James was listed in 1888 as a member of GAR Post #10 at Oshkosh. He was listed as above in the veteran section of the 1895 Wisconsin State census at P.O. Oshkosh. He was listed in the 1890 federal census as residing in the city of Oshkosh. James then provided that he had been a member of Co. B of the above regiment from June 1861 until Nov. 19, 1864.
{US 1890; WC-V 1895}

POTTER, John Jr. - Sgt., Co. D, 41st Regt., Wis. Vol. Inf.
John was born circa 1821 at Pennsylvania. He was married in Winnebago County on Nov. 27, 1853 to Susanna Lull. She was born circa 1823 at Vermont. John was listed in the 1860 federal census as a lawyer residing in the first ward of the village of Menasha. Listed with him was his wife and Martha Lull, her mother. Martha was born circa 1797 at New York. John enlisted at Menasha on May 11, 1864. He was assigned as above and was promoted to Commissary Sergeant in that company on June 8, 1864. John was mustered out on Sept. 24, 1864 at the end of his term of enlistment. He re-enlisted on Feb. 7, 1865 and was assigned as a Private to Co. C, 29th Regt., Wis. Vol. Inf. John was transferred to Co. G, 14th Regt., Wis. Vol. Inf. on June 22, 1865. He was then listed as absent sick when that regiment was mustered out on Oct. 9, 1865. John died circa 1877.
{US 1860; ROV; WCMR v.1, p.145, #601; Lawson p.841}

POTTS, Oscar F. - Pvt., Co. C, 1st Regt., Wis. Vol. Inf.
Oscar enlisted on Nov. 13, 1861 and was assigned as above. He was taken prisoner and was discharged on Oct. 29, 1862. Oscar was listed in 1868 as a teamster residing at 184 Main Street in the city of Oshkosh. He was listed in the veteran section of the 1885 Wisconsin State census at P.O. Oshkosh. Joanna, his widow, was listed in the 1890 federal census as residing in Oshkosh. She provided that Oscar had died in May 1890.
{US 1890; WC-V 1885; ROV; T-1868}

POWER, John - Pvt., Co. B, 3rd Regt., Wis. Cav.
John resided at Oshkosh and enlisted there on Dec. 25, 1861. He was assigned as above and was listed as having deserted on June 9, 1862.
{ROV}

POWERS, Alvin - Pvt., Co. C, 21st Regt., Wis. Vol. Inf.
Alvin was born circa 1839 at Vermont. He was a son of Nelson Powers, the subject of a following sketch. Alvin was listed in the 1860 federal census as residing with his father in the fifth ward of the city of Oshkosh. He enlisted there on Aug. 14, 1862. He was assigned as above and was mustered out on June 8, 1865. Alvin was listed in 1868 as partners with Nelson Powers, his father. They were ice dealers and both resided at 39 Sixth Street in Oshkosh. Alvin was married in Winnebago County on Aug. 18, 1868 to Etta Eliza Drew.
{US 1860; T-1868; WCMR v.1, p.398, #2477; ROV}

POWERS, George A. - Civil War Veteran?
George was listed as a veteran in the 1890 federal census as residing in the city of Oshkosh. No additional information was provided. He was listed in 1905 as a carpenter residing at 30 Rosalia Street in Oshkosh. Mrs. Martha (Lewis) Powers, widow of George, died at the home of her sister in Rochester, New York on Oct. 28, 1926. She had only recently removed east, George having died late in the summer of 1925. Martha was returned to Oshkosh for burial.
{US 1890; B-1905; ODN 29 Oct 1926}

POWERS, John A. - Pvt., Co. C, 40th Regt., Wis. Vol. Inf.
John was born on Oct. 8, 1844 at Ontario, Canada near Niagara Falls. He was a son of Philo Powers and was one of six children, there having been five boys and one girl. George A. Powers from a preceding sketch was a brother. John was brought to Wisconsin as a young boy and his family settled in Fond du Lac County. He resided at Milton, Rock County and enlisted there on May 16, 1864. He was assigned as above and was mustered out on Sept. 16, 1864 at the end of his term of enlistment. John was married in Fond du Lac (a published obit says Rock County) on Mar. 14, 1866 to Nancy Ann Camp. They did reside near Milton at the time they were married. They had four children: a son who died in infancy; Jennie L., died prior to 1917; Aura E.; and Harry W. Powers. John and Nancy removed to Oshkosh in 1886. John was listed in the veteran section of the 1895 and 1905 Wisconsin State census at P.O. Oshkosh. He was listed in 1905 as president of the Home Purchasers Association, dealing in real estate and insurance. John was then residing at 18 Evans Street in the city of Oshkosh. Aura E. and Harry W. Powers were also listed at that address. Nancy died at her home in Oshkosh on Thanksgiving Day, Nov. 25, 1915. She was survived by her husband, two children and two sisters, Mrs. J.C. Stedman and Mrs. William Drinkwater, both of Monticello, Ohio. John died in Oshkosh on Aug. 3, 1917. Both are buried in Oshkosh at Riverside Cemetery.
{WC-V 1895, 1905; ROV; B-1905; ODN 04 Aug 1917; ODN 26 Nov 1915}

POWERS, Nelson - Pvt., Co. C, 21st Regt., Wis. Vol. Inf.
Nelson was born circa 1817 at Vermont. He was listed in the 1860 federal census as a farmer residing in the fifth ward of the city of Oshkosh. Elizabeth, his wife, was born circa 1822 at New Hampshire. Listed with them were the following children: Alvin, subject of a previous sketch; Charles, born circa 1842; Ellen, born circa 1844; Christina, born circa 1851; and Frank, born circa 1855. Christina was born in New Hampshire and the other children were born in Vermont. Nelson enlisted at Oshkosh on Jan. 29, 1864. He was assigned as above and was transferred as unassigned to the 3rd Regt., Wis. Vol. Inf. on June 8, 1865. He was listed within that regiment as having been mustered out on May 8, 1865. Nelson was listed in 1868 as a partner with son Alvin. They were ice dealers and both resided at 39 Sixth Street in Oshkosh.
{US 1860; ROV; T-1868}

POWERS, Silas H. - Pvt., Co. C, 2nd Regt., Wis. Vol. Inf.
Silas resided at Clayton and enlisted there on Jan. 23, 1864. He was assigned as above and was transferred to the Independent Battalion on June 10, 1864.
{ROV}

POWERS, William B. - Pvt., Co. F, 18th Regt., Wis. Vol. Inf.
William resided at Rushford and enlisted there on Jan. 2, 1864. He was assigned as above and was taken prisoner at Allatoona, Georgia. William was then mustered out on July 18, 1865. He was listed in 1888 as a member of GAR Post #10 at Oshkosh.
{ROV; SCA}

PRATT, David A. - Pvt., Co. K, 1st Regt., Wis. Hvy. Art.
David resided at Menasha and enlisted there on Sept. 8, 1864. He was assigned as above and was mustered out on June 26, 1865.
{ROV}

PRATT, Edward - Pvt., 8th Batt., Wis. Lt. Art.
Edward resided at Menasha and enlisted there on Feb. 13, 1864. He was assigned as above and was mustered out on Aug. 10, 1865.
{ROV}

PRATT, Erastus H. - Cpl., Co. C, 10th Regt., Wis. Vol. Inf.
Erastus resided at Menasha and enlisted there on Sept. 3, 1861. He was assigned as above and was discharged due to a disability on Apr. 3, 1863. Erastus died in 1888 at Calumet County.
{ROV; Lawson p.812}

PRENTICE, Worthy A. - Pvt., Co. D, 2nd Regt., Wis. Cav.
Worthy resided at Osceola, Fond du Lac County and enlisted there on Mar. 16, 1865. He was assigned as above and was mustered out on Nov. 15, 1865. Worthy was listed in the veteran section of the 1895 Wisconsin State census at P.O. Clayton. He was listed in that section of the 1905 state census at P.O. Algoma.
{WC-V 1895, 1905; ROV}

PRENTISS, George S. - Pvt., Co. K, 4th Regt., Wis. Cav.
George resided at Forest, Fond du Lac County and enlisted there on Oct. 1, 1864. He was assigned as above and was mustered out on June 20, 1865. George was listed in the veteran section of the 1895 Wisconsin State census at P.O. Oshkosh.
{WC-V 1895; ROV}

PRICE, John - Pvt., Co. E, 35th Regt., Iowa Vol. Inf.
John was listed as above in the veteran section of the 1905 Wisconsin State census at P.O. Oshkosh. He was listed that same year as retired and residing at 760 Main Street in the city of Oshkosh. Cleora M. and W.M. Price were also residing at that address.
{WC-V 1905; B-1905}

PRICKETT, William H. - Pvt., Co. C, 21st Regt., Wis. Vol. Inf.
William resided at Oshkosh and enlisted there on Aug. 15, 1862. He was assigned as above and was discharged on Mar. 27, 1863 due to a disability.
{ROV}

PRIEBE, Adolph - Pvt., Co. I, 9th Regt., Wis. Vol. Inf.
Adolph was born on Apr. 8, 1844 at Baernbruch, Germany. He was a son of Frederick and Christina (Kloetz) Priebe. The father and Emil Priebe, a brother, are subjects of

PRIEBE, Adolph (cont.)
following sketches. When Adolph was age 7 years the family came to this country and they settled at Wisconsin in the town of New Berlin, Green Lake County. Adolph enlisted at Berlin on Feb. 8, 1862 and was assigned as a Private to Co. D of the above regiment. He was listed on the muster rolls of that company as absent on sick leave to Wisconsin in Sept. 1864. A later pension application shows that Adolph was wounded in the right shoulder by a musket ball on Apr. 30, 1864 at Jenkin's Ferry, Arkansas. Adolph was later transferred to Co. I of that same regiment and was mustered out on Feb. 10, 1865 at the end of his term of enlistment. He was listed in 1868 as a saloon keeper residing at 88 Main Street in the city of Oshkosh. He provided information on his pension application that he had resided in Michigan from about 1876 to 1878. He stated that he was married on June 3, 1877 at Newport, R.P. (?) to Augusta Hanson. They had ten children: Alida, born in Mar. 1878; Mary, born on Mar. 1, 1880, married a Barsch; Sarah, born Jan. 16, 1882, married a McEachron; Max Paul, born Oct. 14, 1883, died prior to his father; Titus M., born on Jan. 1, 1885, a veteran of the Spanish American War and WW-1, resided at Santa Rosa, Calif.; Evelyn, born on Jan. 12, 1887; Adolph E., born on Sept. 5, 1888, resided at Oshkosh; Clara, born on Nov. 28, 1890; Walter A., born July 12, 1893, resided at Waukesha, Wis.; and Harry Earl, born on Apr. 28, 1895, resided at Oshkosh. Adolph was listed in 1888 as a member of GAR Post #241 at Oshkosh, having been mustered in to that post on Feb. 12, 1885. He was listed in the 1890 federal census as residing at 58 Fremont Street in Oshkosh. He was listed in 1905 as a paper hanger residing at 58 Ashland Avenue in Oshkosh. Adolph died at Oshkosh on Dec. 25, 1943 of organic heart disease due to arteriosclersis. His wife preceeded him in death. He is buried at Riverside Cemetery in Oshkosh.
{US 1890; WC-V 1895; ROV; ODN 26 Dec 1943; T-1868; USDI-BP; B-1905}

PRIEBE, Emil G. - Pvt., Co. D, 32nd Regt., Wis. Vol. Inf.
Emil was born on May 24/6, 1842 in the province of Posen, Prussia. He was a son of Frederick Priebe from a following sketch and a brother of Adolph Priebe from a previous sketch. Emil emigrated to this country when 17 years of age and he resided for many years at Berlin, Green Lake County. He enlisted at Berlin on Aug. 20, 1862. He was assigned as above and was wounded on Mar. 2, 1865 in a battle near Cheraw, S.C. He received a bullet thru his left leg below the knee. According to Roster of Wisconsin Volunteers, Emil contracted a disease and died on Apr. 28, 1865 at Beaufort, S.C. Pension records show that Emil was honorably discharged from the U.S. Hospital at Newark, New Jersey on June 13, 1865. He was married on May 13, 1883 to Anna Kiel of West Bend in the Lutheran church at Wrightstown, Brown County. She was born in 1856. Emil was listed in the 1890 federal census as residing in the town of Poy Sippi, Waushara County. He was listed in 1905 as retired and residing at 36 Knapp Street in the city of Oshkosh. Ernest, Flora, Fred W., Lottie, Paul and William Priebe were also listed at that address. In a pension declaration dated 1918, Emil reported that he had resided at Oshkosh, Berlin, the National Home in Milwaukee, Wittenberg, Wrightstown, Portage and Fisk. He was then residing at Fisk. Anna died in 1925. Emil died of arteriosclerosis on Nov. 30, 1936 at the home of his daughter, Mrs. August Folska, in Fisk. He was survived by seven children: Fred Priebe of Spring Lake; Mrs. Folska of Fisk; Mrs. Florence Klank of Chicago; William, Ernest and Paul Priebe of Oshkosh; and Bertha Priebe of Oshkosh. Emil and Anna are buried in the town of Algoma at Peace Lutheran Cemetery, Section F. Bertha, a daughter, was born in 1895 and died in 1980.

PRIEBE, Emil G. (cont.)
She is buried with her parents.
{US 1890; ROV; Cem. records; USDI-BP; B-1905; ODN 01 Dec 1936}

PRIEBE, Frederick - Pvt., Co. G, 9th Regt., Wis. Vol. Inf.
Frederick was married on Sept. 2, 1838 at Schubin, Prussia to Christine Celeps (Clapps), who was born circa 1810. A witness to their marriage was Wilhelm Hildebrand, who later became a resident of Oshkosh. Frederick enlisted at Berlin, Green Lake County on Oct. 12, 1861. He was assigned as above and was discharged on May 24, 1862 at Milwaukee due to a disability, it being a disease of the eyes. Frederick was listed as enrolling in Co. C, 9th Regt., Wis. Vol. Inf. on July 1, 1864 and he was transferred to Co. H, 8th Regt., Veteran Reserve Corps by general orders dated Dec. 30, 1864. Frederick was then discharged on Nov. 16, 1865 at Cairo, Illinois. His records include a furlough from the National Asylum for Disabled Volunteer Soldiers at Milwaukee to enable him to travel to Oshkosh in Aug. 1875. A letter from that institution to the Pension Office in 1879 listed Frederick as being totally blind. He was trying to get a pension for both himself and his wife, who was listed as being without support for over 14 years. Frederick died in Oshkosh on Oct. 19, 1884. Christina, his wife, resided with son Adolph at Oshkosh in 1890 when she filed for a widow's pension. She was awarded pension #285,881 of $8 per month until her death on Jan. 3, 1898.
{US 1890; ROV; USDI-BP}

PRINK, Oscar H. - Sgt., Co. E, 1st Regt., Wis. Cav.
Oscar enlisted on Sept. 15, 1861 and was assigned as above. He was promoted to Sergeant in that company and was then taken prisoner at L'Anguille Ferry, Arkansas. He was mustered out on Oct. 31, 1864 at the end of his term of enlistment. Eugene A. Prink had been a member of that same company. Oscar was married to Mary Aurilla Dowd. She was a sister of George W. Dowd from a previous sketch. They had a son, unnamed at registration, who was born on July 10, 1880 in Oshkosh. They also had a daughter, Olive May, who was born in Oshkosh on Mar. 26, 1882. Oscar was listed in 1883 at P.O. Oshkosh. He had then been receiving a pension of $4 per month since Jan. 1881 for an injury to his right side and a wound to his left thigh.
{ROV; LOP-1883; WCBR v.3, p.22, #130; WCBR v.3, p.77, #460}

PROCKNOW, August - Pvt., Co. F, 6th Regt., Wis. Vol. Inf.
August resided at Montpelier, Kewaunee County and was drafted there on Mar. 22, 1865. He was assigned as above and was mustered out on July 14, 1865. August was not found in the veteran section of the 1885 or 1895 Wisconsin State census. He was listed in that section of the 1905 state census at P.O. Oshkosh. August was listed then as retired and residing at 272 Bowen Street in the city of Oshkosh. His name was given as Brocknow in military records.
{WC-V 1885, 1895, 1905; ROV; B-1905}

PROUTY, Ira Jr. - Pvt., Co. G, 3rd Regt., Wis. Vol. Inf.
Ira was born circa 1840 at Ohio, a son of Ira and Mardula Prouty and a brother of Warren from a following sketch. The parents were both natives of New York, the father born there circa 1797 and the mother born circa 1805. They were listed in the 1860 federal census as residing with members of their family on a farm in the town of Menasha. Ira enlisted at Menasha on Apr. 20, 1861. He was assigned as above and was

PROUTY, Ira Jr. (cont.)
wounded on Sept. 17, 1862. Ira was mustered out on June 29, 1864 at the end of his term of enlistment. He was married in Winnebago County on Nov. 3, 1864 to Laura Minnie Lisk.
{US 1860; ROV; WCMR v.1, p.262, #1538*}

PROUTY, Warren C. - Pvt., Co. I, 21st Regt., Wis. Vol. Inf.
Warren was born circa 1838 at Ohio. He was a son of Ira and Mardula Prouty and a brother of Ira Jr. from a previous sketch. Warren was married in Winnebago County on Mar. 14, 1859 to Matilda Willard. She was born circa 1839 at New York. They were listed in the 1860 federal census as residing with his parents and others of their family on a farm in the town of Menasha. Warren enlisted there on Aug. 21, 1862. He was assigned as above. Warren contracted a disease and died on Feb. 14, 1863 at Nashville, Tennessee.
{US 1860; ROV; WCMR v.1, p.179, #873}

PRUYN, William F. - Pvt., Co. B, 21st Regt., Wis. Vol. Inf.
William resided at Winneconne and enlisted there on Feb. 6, 1864. He was assigned as above and was then transferred to Co. B, 3rd Regt., Wis. Vol. Inf. on June 8, 1865. William was mustered out on July 18, 1865.
{ROV}

PRYOR, Henry D. - Sgt., Co. B, 14th Regt., Wis. Vol. Inf.
Henry resided at Waupaca, Waupaca County and enlisted there on Oct. 1, 1861. He was assigned as above and was promoted to Corporal, Sergeant and then 1st Sergeant in that company. Henry was taken prisoner and was then mustered out on Oct. 9, 1865. He was listed in the veteran section of the 1885 Wisconsin State census at P.O. Omro. Henry was listed in the 1890 federal census as residing in the village of Omro. He then provided that he had been wounded at Vicksburg, Mississippi.
{US 1890; WC-V 1885; ROV}

PUFFER, Frank A. - Pvt., Co. C, 10th Regt., Wis. Vol. Inf.
Francis was born circa 1841 at New York. He was a son of Lucy Puffer. She was born circa 1799 at New York. She was listed in the 1850 federal census as residing in the town of Neenah. With her were the following children: Isaac, born circa 1823; Courtney, born circa 1824; Charles, born circa 1826; Jane, born circa 1832; Dolly, born circa 1834; Wilson, born circa 1838; and Francis. All of the children were listed as having been born at New York. Frank listed his residence as Menasha when he enlisted there on Sept. 3, 1861. He was assigned as above and was transferred to the Marine Brigade on Mar. 11, 1863.
{US 1850; ROV}

PUGH, George W. - Sgt., Co. G, 35th Regt., Wis. Vol. Inf.
George resided at Clayton and enlisted there on Nov. 23, 1863. He was assigned as a Private to Co. C of the above regiment and was transferred to Co. G of that regiment on Apr. 1, 1864. George was promoted to Sergeant and then 1st Sergeant in Co. G and was mustered out on Mar. 15, 1866.
{ROV}

PULASKI, John - Pvt., Co. D, 8th Regt., Wis. Vol. Inf.
John was listed in the 1860 federal census as a laborer on the farm of John Hammer in the town of Algoma. He was listed as born circa 1844 at Prussia. John enlisted at Omro on Oct. 1, 1861 and was assigned as above. He was wounded at Spanish Fort, Alabama and was mustered out on Sept. 5, 1865.
{US 1860; ROV}

PURATH, August John - Pvt., Co. B, 3rd Regt., Wis. Vol. Inf.
August was born circa 1836 at Prussia. He was a son of Frederick and Mena Purath and a brother of Ernest from a following sketch. Both parents were natives of Prussia, the father born there circa 1804 and the mother born circa 1814. They were listed in the 1860 federal census as residing on a farm in the town of Winchester. Listed with them were the following children: August, a boatman; Ernest, a boatman; Yetta, born circa 1846; Willie, born circa 1850; Ernestina, born circa 1854; Julius, born circa 1857; and John, born in 1860. The three youngest children were born in Wisconsin and the others were born in Prussia. August listed his residence as Winneconne when he enlisted on Apr. 21, 1861. He was assigned as above and was wounded at Antietam, Maryland. August was discharged by orders dated Oct. 25, 1862. He was married in Winnebago County on Oct. 9, 1867 to Wilhelmine Witt. August was listed in 1888 as a member of GAR Post #241 at Oshkosh. He died at his home at 265 Merritt Street in Oshkosh in July 1891 at age 57 years. August was survived by his wife and one son.
{US 1860; ROV; WCMR v.1, p.352, #2110; OWN 23 Jul 1891}

PURATH, Ernest - Pvt., Co. B, 3rd Regt., Wis. Vol. Inf.
Ernest was born circa 1839 at Prussia. He was a son of Frederick and Mena Purath and a brother of August from a previous sketch. Ernest was listed in the 1860 federal census as a boatman residing with his parents in the town of Winchester. He listed his residence as Oshkosh when he enlisted on May 22, 1861. He was assigned as above and he was wounded in the side at Antietam, Maryland on Sept. 17, 1862. Ernest was mustered out on June 29, 1864 at the end of his term of enlistment.
{US 1860; ROV; OWN 02 Oct 1862}

PUTNAM, David - Pvt., Co. D, 32nd Regt., Wis. Vol. Inf.
David was born circa 1827 at New York. He was a brother of Ransom from a following sketch. Both alternated spelling of the name between Putnam and Putman. David was listed in the 1860 federal census as residing on a farm in the town of Poygan. Elvira, his wife, was born circa 1826 at New York. Listed with them were the following children: Frederick, born circa 1854 at New York; Alice, born circa 1856 at Wisconsin; and Clinton, born circa 1859 at Wisconsin. David enlisted at Poygan on Aug. 21, 1862. He was assigned as above and was mustered out on June 12, 1865. David was listed in the 1890 federal census as residing in the town of Omro at P.O. Omro. He was listed in 1905 as residing on E. Division Street in the village of Omro.
{US 1860; 1890; ROV; B-1905}

PUTNAM, Ransom - Cpl., Co. C, 14th Regt., Wis. Vol. Inf.
Ransom was born circa 1824 at New York. He was a brother of David from a previous sketch. Both alternated the spelling of their name between Putnam and Putman. Ransom was listed in the 1860 federal census as residing on a farm in the town of Poygan. Eliza, his wife, was born circa 1826 at New York. They had a son, Justus, who

PUTNAM, Ransom (cont.)
was born circa 1851 at New York. Ransom enlisted at Poygan on Sept. 8, 1861. He was assigned as above and was promoted to Corporal in that company. Ransom was killed in action on Oct. 3, 1862 at Corinth, Mississippi.
{US 1860; ROV}

QUACKENBUSH, H. - Pvt., Co. K, 26th Regt., Michigan Vol. Inf.
He was listed as above in the veteran section of the 1885 Wisconsin State census at P.O. Oshkosh. He was also listed in 1888 as a member of GAR Post #10 at Oshkosh.
{WC-V 1885}

QUIMBY, John F. - Pvt., Co. B, 36th Regt., Wis. Vol. Inf.
John was born on Apr. 21, 1855? Elizabeth C., his wife, was born on Nov. 28, 1833. John listed his residence as Poygan when he enlisted on Feb. 25, 1864. He was assigned as above and was wounded on June 18, 1864 at Petersburg, Virginia. John was then transferred to the Veteran Reserve Corps on Mar. 7, 1865 and was mustered out on Sept. 1, 1865. Willard J., a son of John and Elizabeth, was born on Apr. 21, 1855 and died on Dec. 12, 1871. John was listed in the 1890 federal census as residing in the town of Weyauwega, Waupaca County. He died there on Sept. 20, 1910. There is no death date on Elizabeth's marker. They are buried in the town of Weyauwega at Evanswood Cemetery. Moses C., a brother of John, was also a veteran of the Civil War, having served as a Private in Co. B, 14th Regt., Wis. Vol. Inf. He is buried with his family in that same cemetery.
{US 1890; ROV; Cem. records}

QUINN, George P. - Cpl., Co. C, 10th Regt., Wis. Vol. Inf.
George resided at Menasha and enlisted there on July 20, 1862. He was assigned as above and was promoted to Corporal in that company. George was mustered out on Nov. 3, 1864.
{ROV}

RACE, William W. - Pvt., Co. C, 41st Regt., Wis. Vol. Inf.
William was born on May 4, 1839. He was married to E.B. Thom. William resided at Omro and enlisted there on May 7, 1864. He was assigned as above and was mustered out on Sept. 23, 1864 at the end of his term of enlistment. William was listed in the veteran section of the 1885 and 1895 Wisconsin State census at P.O. Omro. He was listed in the 1890 federal census as residing in the village of Omro. Eva E., a daughter, was born on May 30, 1883 and died on Mar. 11, 1896. William died on July 11, 1897. He is buried with his daughter in Omro Cemetery, Olin's Addition, Section A, plot 43.
{US 1890; WC-V 1885, 1895; ROV; Cem. records}

RADDATZ, William - Pvt., Co. C, 53rd Regt., Wis. Vol. Inf.
William was married in Winnebago County on Jan. 12, 1864 to Maria Schwelge. He resided at Oshkosh and enlisted there on Mar. 9, 1865. He was assigned as above and that company was transferred to Co. K, 51st Regt., Wis. Vol. Inf. under orders dated June 10, 1865. The transfer was completed June 30, 1865 at Ft. Leavenworth, Kansas. The regiment returned to Madison, Wisconsin on Aug. 1, 1865 and was mustered out by companies. The last company was mustered out on Aug. 30, 1865. William was listed in the veteran section of the 1885 Wisconsin State census at P.O. Nekimi. He was listed

RADDATZ, William (cont.)
in the 1890 federal census as residing in the town of Nekimi at P.O. Oshkosh. William was listed in the veteran section of the 1895 and 1905 state census at P.O. Oshkosh. He was listed in 1905 as residing on 100 acres of section 27 in the town of Nekimi. John C. Raddatz was also residing there.
{US 1890; WC-V 1885, 1895, 1905; ROV; WCMR v.1, p.248, #1425; B-1905}

RADFORD, James - Pvt., Co. G, 1st Regt., Wis. Cav.
James resided at Ripon, Fond du Lac County and he enlisted there on Nov. 17, 1863. He was assigned as above and was mustered out on July 19, 1865. James was listed in the 1890 federal census as a resident at the Northern Hospital for the Insane. He was listed in the veteran section of the 1895 Wisconsin State census at P.O. Oshkosh.
{US 1890; WC-V 1895; ROV}

RAHR, Charles - Sgt., Co. H, 9th Regt., Wis. Vol. Inf.
Charles was born on Nov. 27, 1836 at Wessel, Province of Rhine, Prussia. He was a son of Frederick and Johanna (Huffstadt) Rahr. Charles emigrated alone to America about 1857 and settled in Wisconsin at Maitowoc, Manitowoc County. He was engaged there as a gunsmith for a year and one half and then removed to Davenport, Iowa. He returned to Wisconsin and settled at his trade in Green Bay, Brown County. Charles resided there when he enlisted on Oct. 21, 1861. He was assigned as above and was promoted to Corporal in that company. Charles was promoted to Commissary Sergeant of that company on Jan. 1, 1863. He was mustered out on Dec. 3, 1864 at the end of his term of enlistment. After the war Charles returned to Green Bay for two months, during which he was married on Jan. 1, 1865 to Caroline Hochgrave, before removing to Oshkosh. Charles was listed in 1868 as a brewer residing on Lake Street in the city of Oshkosh. He was listed in 1883 at P.O. Oshkosh, where he had been receiving a pension of $4 per month since Dec. 1882 for an incised wound to the right side of his back. Charles was listed in the veteran section of the 1885 and 1905 Wisconsin State census at P.O. Oshkosh. He was listed in 1888 as a member of GAR Post #241 at Oshkosh. He was listed in the 1890 federal census as residing on Rosalia Street in Oshkosh. Charles and Caroline had six children: Charles, born in Oshkosh in 1865, died in Oshkosh on Nov. 4, 1925; Caroline; Clara; Annie; Ella Mary; and Olga Rahr. He was listed in 1905 as the proprietor of Rahr's Brewery and residing at 81 Rahr Avenue in Oshkosh. Daughters Ella and Marie were residing at the same address and son Charles Jr. resided nearby.
{US 1890; WC-V 1885, 1905; T-1868; LOP-1883; SCA 1:614-5; ODN 04 Nov 1925}
{ROV; B-1905}

RAMORE, Daniel - Cpl., Co. D, 1st Regt., Wis. Hvy. Art.
Daniel resided at Menasha and enlisted there on Nov. 3, 1863. He was assigned as above and was promoted to Corporal in that company. Daniel was mustered out on Aug. 18, 1865.
{ROV}

RAND, Philo - Civil War Veteran.
Philo died about Jan. 4, 1898. His obituary listed him as a veteran of the Civil War and a member of the GAR.
{ODN 07 Jan 1898}

RANDALL, A.G. - Civil War Veteran?
A.G. Randall was born circa 1814. He died in Oshkosh early in 1898, preceeded in death by his wife and all five of their daughters, including Annie, Edith, and Mrs. Jessie Anderson. A.G. had been a member of the legislature from the state of Maine and had served in the Civil War as a Captain.
{OWN 05 Mar 1898}

RANDALL, Henry - Pvt., Co. E, 43rd Regt., Wis. Vol. Inf.
Henry was born circa 1822 at Rhode Island. Sarah, his wife, was born circa 1826 at New York. They were listed in the 1860 federal census as residing on a farm in the town of Winchester. Henry enlisted at Winchester on Sept. 5, 1864. He was assigned as above and was mustered out on June 24, 1865.
{US 1860; ROV}

RANDALL, John G. - Pvt., Co. D, 7th Regt., Wis. Vol. Inf.
John listed his residence as Chilton, Calumet County. He was drafted there on Dec. 28, 1864. He was assigned as above and was mustered out on July 28, 1865. John was married to Rosella Johnson. They had at least one son, James J. Randall, who was born on Nov. 10, 1880 at Oshkosh. John was listed in the veteran section of the 1885 Wisconsin State census at P.O. Oshkosh. He was listed in the 1890 federal census as residing in the town of Rushford at P.O. Omro. John was then suffering the effects of a hernia and lung disease. He was listed in the veteran section of the 1895 state census at P.O. Omro. John was born in 1824 and died in 1899. Mrs. Rosella Randall, widow of John G., was listed in 1905 as residing with Frank Appley and his wife on 79 acres of section 23 in the town of Rushford. John is buried in Omro Cemetery, Pelton's Addition, Section A, plot 8.
{US 1890; WC-V 1885, 1895; B-1905; WCBR v.3, p.8, #44; Cem. records; ROV}

RANDALL, Murray N. - Pvt., Co. I, 32nd Regt., Wis. Vol. Inf.
Murray resided at Oshkosh and enlisted there on Nov. 23, 1863. He was assigned as above and was transferred to Co. C, 16th Regt., Wis. Vol. Inf. on June 4, 1865. He was mustered out on July 12, 1865.
{ROV}

RANDALL, Philester - Pvt., Co. D, 1st Regt., Wis. Cav.
Philester was born circa 1820 at Vermont. R.F., his wife, was born circa 1820 at Ohio. They were listed in the 1860 federal census as residing on a farm in the town of Nepeuskun. Lemuel, their son, was born circa 1849 at New York. Philester enlisted at Nepeuskun on Sept. 22, 1864. He was assigned as above and was then mustered out on July 19, 1865.
{US 1860; ROV}

RANNEY, Homer C. - Pvt., Co. I, 21st Regt., Wis. Vol. Inf.
Homer was born circa 1842 at Vermont, a son of Bradford and Elizabeth Ranney. Both parents were natives of Vermont, the father born there circa 1809 and the mother born circa 1814. They were listed in the 1860 federal census as residing in the village of Neenah. Homer was then residing with them, as was a daughter, Jane, who was born circa 1845 at Vermont. Homer enlisted at Neenah on Aug. 21, 1862. He was assigned

RANNEY, Homer C. (cont.)
as above. Homer contracted a disease and died on Nov. 12, 1862 at Lebanon, Kentucky.
{US 1860; ROV}

RANSOM, Leonard - Pvt., Co. G, 3rd Regt., Wis. Vol. Inf.
Leonard was born circa 1840 at New York, a son of William and Margareth Ransom. William was born circa 1808 at New York and Margareth was born circa 1820 in that same state. William was listed in the 1850 federal census as a carpenter residing in the town of Winnebago. With him were his wife and the following children: Leonard; Frances A., born circa 1842 at New York; Mary J., born circa 1846 at Wisconsin; and Robert B., born circa 1848 at Wisconsin. They were then residing with the family of Solomon Blodgett. Leonard was listed in the 1860 federal census as a laborer residing with the family of Edwin Barns in the town of Vinland. He enlisted at Vinland May 6, 1861. He was assigned as above and he re-enlisted in that same company at the end of his term. Leonard was wounded on Sept. 17, 1862 and was taken prisoner at Atlanta, Georgia. He was mustered out on July 18, 1865. Leonard was not found in the veteran section of the 1885, 1895 or 1905 Wisconsin State census.
{US 1850, 1860; WC-V 1885, 1895, 1905; ROV}

RANSOM, Luther H. - Pvt., Co. C, 51st Regt., Wis. Vol. Inf.
Luther was born on Aug. 20, 1825 at New York, a son of George Ransom. George was born on Oct. 23, 1782 at Colchester, Connecticut. He was a son of Bliss and Sarah (Mumford) Ransom. George was married on May 26, 1808 to Lydia Bebee. They had ten children: Addison, born on Apr. 2, 1809, married Ruby Hendy on Nov. 16, 1841, died at Perrysburg, New York on Apr. 3, 1862; Orrin, born on Dec. 8, 1810 in New York, married Nancy Chase on Feb. 9, 1836, married second to Betsy Gregory in 1847, died on Feb. 21, 1853 in New York; Louisa L., born Mar. 9, 1816, died in Wisconsin on Feb. 16, 1900; Julius B., born on Oct. 15, 1818, married Minerva St. John on July 21, 1843 in Wisconsin, died in 1864 in Texas; Justin B., born Sept. 17, 1822 in New York, married Barbara Ingersol on Mar. 27, 1850 in Ohio; Luther H.; Edwin M., born on Mar. 2, 1828 in New York, married to Sarah Brown on Jan. 25, 1858 in Wisconsin; Edward B., born on Mar. 2, 1828 in New York, married on July 3, 1864 at Carey, Wyandotte County, Ohio to Wealthy J. Turner, died on Aug. 7, 1919 in Winnebago County; Jehiel; and Lucius. Luther was married on Nov. 19, 1863 in Wisconsin to Mary Elizabeth Brown, a daughter of Nathaniel and Rebecca Redd. She was born in 1844 and she did list her maiden name as Brown in a later birth record. Nathaniel was born in 1810 and died in 1907. Rebecca was born in 1816 and died in 1901. Luther was listed in the 1860 federal census as residing on a farm in the town of Utica at P.O. Fisk's Corners. His wife's parents and their family were also listed there. Luther listed his residence as Jackson, Washington County when he enlisted on Mar. 2, 1865. He was assigned as above and was mustered out at Madison, Dane County on Aug. 19, 1865. Luther and Elizabeth had a daughter, Maude Rebecca, who was born in Utica on June 17, 1880. Luther was listed in the 1890 federal census as residing in the town of Utica at P.O. Fisk. He died in 1914 and Mary died on Jan. 6, 1919. Both are buried with her parents in the town of Utica at Liberty Prairie Cemetery.
{US 1860, 1890; ROV; Cem. records; WCBR v.3, p.22, #128; WCPR v.27, p.107}
{Research of Don E. Ransom Jr. of Colorado}

RANSOM, Seth M. - Pvt., Co. B, 3rd Regt., Wis. Vol. Inf.
Seth resided at Utica and enlisted there on Apr. 22, 1861. He was assigned as above and was shot through the chest at Antietam, Maryland on Sept. 17, 1862. Seth was mustered out on June 29, 1864 at the end of his term of enlistment.
{ROV; OWN 02 Oct 1862}

RASMUSSEN, Anthony C. - Pvt., Co. B, 44th Regt., Wis. Vol. Inf.
Anthony was born circa 1838 at Denmark. He emigrated to the United States about 1853 and settled in the east. His obituary listed that he came to Wisconsin after the war but he resided at Sheboygan, Sheboygan County and enlisted there on Sept. 29, 1864. He was assigned as above and was mustered out on July 2, 1865. After the war, Anthony came to Winnebago County and settled on a farm in the town of Algoma. He was listed in the veteran section of the 1885 Wisconsin State census at P.O. Oshkosh. He was listed in 1888 as a member of GAR Post #241 at Oshkosh. He was listed in the 1890 federal census as residing in the town of Algoma at P.O. Oshkosh. Six months prior to his death Anthony removed into the city of Oshkosh, where he died on Apr. 19, 1893. He was survived by his wife.
{US 1890; WC-V 1885; ROV; OWN 22 Apr 1893; OWN 29 Apr 1893}

RASMUSSEN, Christian - Pvt., 2nd Regt., Wis. Vol. Inf.
Christian was born circa 1825 at Norway. Caren, his wife, was born circa 1821, also at Norway. Christian was listed in the 1860 federal census as a music teacher residing in the first ward of the village of Menasha. Listed with him were his wife and the following children: John, born circa 1847; Frederick, born circa 1851; Mary, born circa 1853; Robert, born circa 1857; and Catherine, born in 1860. The three youngest children were born in Wisconsin and the others were born in Norway. Christian enlisted at Menasha on June 6, 1861. He was assigned as a musician to the above regiment and was mustered out on Aug. 24, 1862.
{US 1860; ROV}

RATTAY, Joseph - Pvt., Co. F, 19th Regt., Wis. Vol. Inf.
Joseph resided at Oshkosh and enlisted there on Feb. 20, 1862. He was assigned as above and was transferred to the Veteran Reserve Corps on Sept. 4, 1863. Joseph was mustered out on Apr. 5, 1865 at the end of his term of enlistment. He was listed in 1868 as a laborer residing at 35 Eleventh Street in the city of Oshkosh.
{ROV; T-1868}

RAUN, Louis - Pvt., Co. D, 52nd Regt., Wis. Vol. Inf.
Louis resided at Oshkosh and enlisted there on Mar. 4, 1865. He was assigned as above and was mustered out on June 7, 1865.
{ROV}

RAY, Walter H. - Pvt., Co. C, 81st Regt., New York Vol. Inf.
Walter was listed as above in the veteran section of the 1885 Wisconsin State census at P.O. Neenah.
{WC-V 1885}

RAYMOND, Albert M. - Pvt., Co. A, 48th Regt., Wis. Vol. Inf.
Albert was born in 1836 at Vermont. He was a son of Joseph H. and Edna J. Raymond

RAYMOND, Albert M. (cont.)
and a brother of Sidney from a following sketch. Joseph died on Apr. 2, 1873 at age 65 years. Edna was born on July 17, 1801 and died on Apr. 18, 1878. Albert enlisted at Somers, Kenosha County on Feb. 1, 1865 and was assigned as above. He contracted a disease and died on Feb. 28, 1865 at Milwaukee, Wisconsin. Albert is buried with his parents in the town of Omro at Omro Union Cemetery. He must have been married as "father" is engraved on his marker.
{ROV; Cem. records}

RAYMOND, Elam - Pvt., Co. G, 3rd Regt., Wis. Vol. Inf.
Elam was born circa 1840 at Vermont. He was listed in the 1860 federal census as a farm laborer for Frederick Wheeler in the town of Clayton at P.O. Neenah. Elam enlisted on May 6, 1861 and was assigned as above. He was discharged on Feb. 7, 1863 due to a disability.
{US 1860; ROV}

RAYMOND, Israel - Pvt., Co. G, 3rd Regt., Wis. Vol. Inf.
Israel was born circa 1844 at West Canada. He was a son of Edward and Basahise? Raymond. Both parents were natives of West Canada, the father born there circa 1804 and the mother born circa 1807. They were listed in the 1860 federal census as residing in the second ward of the village of Menasha. Listed with them were the following children: Agnes, born circa 1840 at Michigan, listed as insane; Israel; and Daniel, born circa 1846 at West Canada. Israel listed his residence as Clayton and he enlisted there on Feb. 3, 1864. He was then assigned as above. Israel contracted a disease and died on Oct. 11, 1864 at Nashville, Tennessee.
{US 1860; ROV}

RAYMOND, Sidney - Pvt., Co. B, 21st Regt., Wis. Vol. Inf.
Sidney was born circa 1838 at Vermont, a son of Joseph H. and Edna J. Raymond and a brother of Albert from a previous sketch. Joseph was listed in the 1860 federal census as residing in the town of Dakota, Waushara County. Sidney listed his residence as Omro when he enlisted there on Aug. 13, 1862 and was assigned as above. He was wounded in the right elbow at Chaplin Hills, Kentucky in Oct. 1862. Sidney died of those wounds on Nov. 18, 1862 at Perryville, Kentucky.
{US 1860; ROV; OWN 16 Oct 1862; OWN 23 Oct 1862}

REA, James A. - Lt., Co. F, 46th Regt., Wis. Vol. Inf.
James was born circa 1827 in Cumberland County, Pennsylvania. In 1840 he removed to Wisconsin and settled in Fond du Lac County. He moved to Winnebago County in 1848 and settled in the city of Oshkosh. Lucinda, his wife, was born circa 1831 at Ohio. James was listed in the 1860 federal census as a hotel keeper residing in the third ward of Oshkosh. Listed with him were his wife and the following children: Ida, born circa 1853; Alfred, born circa 1855; Lulilia, born circa 1857; and Merch, born circa 1859. All of the children were born in Wisconsin. James enlisted at Oshkosh and he was commissioned as 1st Lieutenant of the above company on Feb. 22, 1865. He was mustered out on Sept. 27, 1865. James was listed in 1868 as the proprietor of the Empire House at 107 Main Street in Oshkosh, which burned in 1878. James purchased a flour mill at Sparta, Monroe County in 1872 and he removed to that place. He removed to Minnesota in 1878. Lucinda, his wife, died of cancer on Aug. 28, 1883 at

REA, James A. (cont.)
Minneapolis, Minnesota. James took her back to Oshkosh for burial in Riverside Cemetery as other relatives were already buried there. James removed to Michigan in 1888. He died at Alaska, Michigan on Mar. 31, 1894. James had been married twice. He was survived by his wife, six sons, and one daughter, Mrs. C.W. Graves of Viroqua, Bad Axe County, Wisconsin.
{US 1860; ROV; OWN 30 Aug 1883; ODN 23 Aug 1883; ODN 06 Apr 1894; T-1868}

READ - see Reed

READER, John H. - Pvt., Co. D, 16th Regt., Wis. Vol. Inf.
John resided at Winchester and enlisted there on Sept. 8, 1864. He was assigned as above and was mustered out on June 2, 1865. John was listed in 1888 as a member of GAR Post #78 at Antigo, Langlade County.
{ROV; SCA}

REARDAN, Jeremiah H. - Pvt., Co. F, 13th Regt., Wis. Vol. Inf.
Jerry resided at Janesville, Rock County and enlisted there on Oct. 17, 1861. He was assigned as above and was discharged due to a disability on Jan. 26, 1862. Jeremiah was listed in 1868 as a painter residing at 111 Waugoo Street in the city of Oshkosh. He was listed (Riordan) in 1888 as a member of GAR Post #241 at Oshkosh. Jeremiah was listed in the 1890 federal census as residing in Oshkosh. He had then been suffering from lung disease and a running sore on his left leg since his discharge. Jerry was listed in the veteran section of the 1905 Wisconsin State census at P.O. Oshkosh. He was not found in that section of the 1885 state census. Jeremiah was listed in 1905 as a piano mover residing at 15 Winnebago Street in Oshkosh. George H. and Katherine M. Reardon were also residing at that address. Jeremiah died on Oct. 11, 1915 at his home in Manitowoc, Manitowoc County at the age of 72 years, 4 months and 8 days. He was survived by Mary, his wife, and by 2 daughters and three grandchildren.
{US 1890; WC-V 1885, 1905; ROV; T-1868; B-1905; 21-29th}

REARDON, John - Pvt., Co. H, 21st Regt., Wis. Vol. Inf.
John resided at Oshkosh and enlisted there on Aug. 15, 1862. He was assigned as above and was listed as having deserted on Oct. 8, 1862.
{ROV}

REBENSTORFF, Frederich - Pvt., Co. B, 3rd Regt., Wis. Cav.
Friedrich was born circa 1841 at Hanover, Germany. He was a son of Friedrich and Caroline Rebensdorf. Both parents were born circa 1810, the father at Mecklenburg and the mother at Hanover. Friedrich Sr. was listed in the 1860 federal census as a carpenter residing in the second ward of the city of Oshkosh. Listed with him were his wife and the following family members: Sophia, born circa 1843; Wilhelm, born circa 1826; Friedrich; and Carl, born circa 1846. All were born in Hanover. Frederich enlisted at Oshkosh and enlisted on Dec. 10, 1861. He was assigned as above and was transferred to Co. B, 3rd (reorg.) Regt., Wis. Cav. on Feb. 1, 1865. Frederich was mustered out on July 29, 1865. He was listed in 1868 as a carpenter residing at 141 Ceape Street in Oshkosh. Fred died on Dec. 15, 1876. He had been engaged to work in the pineries. He froze to death on the road near Shawano, Shawano County after "a little more warm whiskey than he could carry." Fred is buried at Oshkosh in Riverside

REBENSTORFF, Frederich (cont.)
Cemetery, GAR Plot, east row, #4 from the south. He was survived by his wife and five children, with another on the way. Anna, his widow, was listed in 1905 as residing at 213 Ceape Street in Oshkosh. Son Louis was also residing at that address.
{US 1860; ROV; T-1868; B-1905; Cem. records; OWN 21 Dec 1876}

REDFORD, Robert - Pvt., Co. C, 22nd Regt., Wis. Vol. Inf.
Robert resided at Geneva, Walworth County and enlisted there on Aug. 14, 1862. He was assigned as above. Robert was taken prisoner at Brentwood and was wounded at Lost Mountain. He was mustered out on June 12, 1865. He was listed in 1888 as a member of GAR Post #10 at Oshkosh. Robert was listed in the 1890 federal census as residing in the city of Oshkosh. He was listed in the veteran section of the 1895 and 1905 Wisconsin State census at P.O. Oshkosh. Robert was listed in 1905 as a mail carrier residing at 112 Central Avenue in Oshkosh. Also listed at that address were Addie B., Alice M., E.B. and Morris Redford.
{US 1890; WC-V 1895, 1905; ROV; B-1905}

REED, A.D. - Pvt., 1st Regt., Wis. Cav.?
He was listed as above in the GAR Post #7 cemetery roster. He was listed as buried at Omro Cemetery. His grave was not found there and he does not appear in the Index to Roster of Wisconsin Volunteers.
{ROV}

REED, Edward H. - Cpl., Co. I, 21st Regt., Wis. Vol. Inf.
Edward resided at Menasha and he enlisted there on Aug. 8, 1862. He was assigned as above and was promoted to Corporal in that company. Edward was then discharged on Mar. 10, 1863.
{ROV}

REED, George - Pvt., Co. H, 3rd (reorg.) Regt., Wis. Cav.
George resided at Winneconne and enlisted there on Feb. 12, 1864. He was assigned as above and was mustered out on Sept. 29, 1865.
{ROV}

REED, Henry W. - Cpl., Co. B, 21st Regt., Wis. Vol. Inf.
Henry was born circa 1841 at Vermont. He was listed in the 1860 federal census as residing at the boarding house of Maria Parsons in the town of Rushford at P.O. Waukau. Henry enlisted at Rushford on Aug. 15, 1862. He was assigned as above and was promoted to Corporal in that company. Henry was taken prisoner at Nolansville, Tennessee. He was mustered out on June 8, 1865. Henry suffered for some time from dyspepsia and an article on Aug. 24, 1882 stated that it was thought he could not survive. He is buried with a simple military marker in the town of Rushford at Waukau Cemetery.
{US 1860; OmJ 24 Aug 1882; Cem. records; ROV}

REED, Ichabod - Pvt., Co. G, 30th Regt., Wis. Vol. Inf.
Ichabod was listed in the 1860 federal census as residing in the town of Dakota, Waushara County. He was born circa 1825 at England. Joanna, his wife, was born circa 1837, also at England. Ichabod enlisted at Dakota on Aug. 21, 1862 and was

REED, Ichabod (cont.)
assigned as above. He was discharged on Sept. 10, 1865 due to a disability. He was listed in 1883 at P.O. Omro and he was then receiving a pension of $12 per month for a wound to his left hand. Ichabod was listed in the veteran section of the 1885 Wisconsin State census at P.O. Omro. He was listed in the 1890 federal census as residing in the village of Omro. Ichabod provided that he had lost a hand in a railroad accident. He is buried with a simple military marker at Omro Cemetery, Pelton's Addition, Section B, plot 27. The plot was owned by a J. Reed, probably his wife.
{US 1860, 1890; WC-V 1885; ROV; LOP-1883; Cem. records}

REED, James - Pvt., Co. B, 52nd Regt., Wis. Vol. Inf.
James resided at Oshkosh and enlisted there on Mar. 8, 1865. He was assigned as above and was mustered out on July 28, 1865.
{ROV}

REED, John L. - Pvt., Co. C, 14th Regt., Wis. Vol. Inf.
John was married in Winnebago County on July 29, 1856 to Jane Hills. He enlisted at Omro on Oct. 1, 1861 and was assigned as above. He was discharged on Dec. 28, 1862 due to a disability. John listed his residence as Algoma when he re-enlisted on Feb. 29, 1864. He was assigned as a Private to Co. B, 3rd Regt., Wis. Cav. John was then transferred to Co. B, 3rd (reorg.) Regt., Wis. Cav. on Feb. 1, 1865 and was mustered out on Sept. 8, 1865. He was married second in Winnebago County on Aug. 28, 1867 to Orcetta Franklin. John is buried with a simple military marker in the town of Rushford at Rushford Cemetery.
{ROV; WCMR v.1, p.96, #397; WCMR v.1, p.389, #2407; Cem. records}

REED, John W. - Pvt., Co. L, 3rd (reorg.) Regt., Wis. Cav.
John resided at Oshkosh and enlisted there on Feb. 19, 1864. He was assigned as above. John was listed as being on detached service at Lawrence, Kansas when that company was mustered out on Oct. 23, 1865.
{ROV}

REED, Lorenzo B. - Capt., Co. B, 3rd (reorg.) Regt., Wis. Cav.
Lorenzo was born in June 1819 at Lowville, Lewis County, New York. He was married in Jan. 1847 to Marian Moran of Lewis County. She was born circa 1824 at New York. Lorenzo came to Oshkosh in 1849 with his mother and family. They joined his brother, O.B., who had arrived in 1847 and had taken up farming in the town of Vinland. Lorenzo was listed in the 1850 federal census as residing in the town of Winnebago. With him then were his wife and a son, Orlando B. Reed, who was born circa 1848 at New York. The brothers, with a Mr. Wyman, erected a steam sawmill, the second in the city. O.B. Reed died in the fall of 1858 and Lorenzo continued in the business. He was listed in the 1860 federal census as a lumber merchant residing in the third ward of the city of Oshkosh. With him were his wife, son Orlando and two daughters. Jennie E. was born circa 1852 and Clara E. was born circa 1854. Also residing with them was Barnard Moran, father of Marian. He was born circa 1788 at Ireland. Lorenzo enlisted at Oshkosh on Nov. 13, 1861. He was assigned as a Private to Co. B, 3rd Regt., Wis. Cav. and was then commissioned as 2nd Lieutenant of that company on Dec. 13, 1861. Lorenzo was promoted to 1st Lieutenant of that company on June 14, 1862. He was commissioned as Captain and was assigned to Co. B, 3rd (reorg.) Regt., Wis. Cav. on

REED, Lorenzo B. (cont.)
Mar. 9, 1865. Lorenzo was commissioned as Major of that regiment on Sept. 15, 1865 but was not mustered at that rank as he had been mustered out on Sept. 8, 1865. He was listed in 1868 as a shingle manufacturer residing at 42 Sixth Street in the city of Oshkosh. Lorenzo sold his interest in the sawmill in 1875 to pursue his interest in boating. He became the owner and manager of the side-wheel steamer "O.B. Reed." Lorenzo was listed in 1888 as a member of GAR Post #241 at Oshkosh. He was listed in the 1890 federal census as residing in the town of Oshkosh at P.O. Oshkosh. He and Marian had four children, including: Orlando B., residing at California in 1889, at Marinette in 1894; and Thaxter, chief engineer of the "O.B. Reed." Lorenzo died at his home in Oshkosh on Feb. 11, 1894. He was survived by his wife and both sons. He was also survived by two sisters, Mrs. George F. Stroud and Mrs. Elizabeth M. Spencer, both of Oshkosh. Marian, widow of Lorenzo, was listed in 1905 as residing at 403 Algoma Street in Oshkosh. Son Thaxter was then residing with her.
{US 1850, 1860; 1890; ROV; T-1868; B-1905; Randall p.44; ODN 12 Feb 1894}
{OWN 17 Feb 1894}

REED, Philander - Sgt., Co. A, 48th Regt., Wis. Vol. Inf.
Philander was born on Feb. 24, 1830 at St. Lawrence County, New York. He was the third son and one of seven children of Richard Reed Sr. Philander came to Wisconsin in 1848 and settled at Omro. He resided there for the rest of his life. Philander was married in Winnebago County on Nov. 19, 1853 to Catharine Sloan. Kate was born circa 1838 at New York. She was a daughter of William and Betsey Sloan and a sister of Douglas Sloan from a following sketch. Philander and Catharine were listed in the 1860 federal census as residing on a farm in the town of Omro. Listed with them was Alice, their daughter, who was born circa 1855 at Wisconsin. Philander enlisted at Omro on Feb. 6, 1865. He was assigned as above and was promoted to Corporal and then Sergeant in that company. He was mustered out on Dec. 30, 1865. He was listed in 1874 as an eligible voter in the town of Omro. Philander and Kate were listed in the 1880 federal census as residing in the village of Omro. He was engaged as a lumberman. Residing with them was a school teacher, Hosea Rood, the subject of a following sketch. Philander died on June 17, 1883. He is buried at Omro Cemetery, Olin's Addition. Section B, plot 70. He was survived by his father, aged 86 years. A brother had died a few weeks earlier.
{US 1860, 1880; Cem. records; WCMR v.1, p.145, #604; ODN 19 Jun 1883; ROV}

REED, Richard - Capt., Co. A, 43rd Regt., New York Vol. Inf.
Richard was listed as above in the veteran section of the 1885 and 1895 Wisconsin State census at P.O. Oshkosh. He was a bartender for C.E. Follett in 1893 when he was awarded a bronze medal given by the State of New York to survivors of the battle at Gettysburg.
{WC-V 1885, 1895; OWN 07 Oct 1893}

REED, Richard - Pvt., Co. C, 14th Regt., Wis. Vol. Inf.
Richard resided at Omro and enlisted there on Feb. 18, 1864. He was assigned as above and was mustered out on Oct. 9, 1865. Richard was listed in the veteran section of the 1885 Wisconsin State census at P.O. Omro. He was listed as a member of GAR Post #241 at Oshkosh in 1888. Richard was listed in the veteran section of the 1895 and 1905 state census at P.O. Rhinelander, Oneida County. He was still residing at Rhinelander

REED, Richard (cont.)
in 1920 when he was elected president of the 14th Regt. Association.
{WC-V 1885, 1895, 1905; ROV; ODN 21 Jun 1920}

REED, Richard - Pvt., Co. A, 2nd Regt., Wis. Cav.
Richard resided at Rosendale, Fond du Lac County and enlisted there on Nov. 18, 1863. He was assigned as above and was mustered out on Sept. 2, 1865. Richard was listed in the veteran section of the 1885 and 1895 Wisconsin State census at P.O. Oshkosh. He was listed in the 1890 federal census as residing in the city of Oshkosh. Richard died on Oct. 4, 1895 at age 59 years. Hannah Morgan Reed, his wife, was born on Dec. 24, 1837. She was listed in 1905 as owning a restaurant and residing at 45 S. Main Street in Oshkosh. Daughter Ada, born at Oshkosh on Aug. 13, 1876, was then residing with her. Hannah died on Dec. 23, 1909. She is buried with Richard in the town of Algoma at Ellenwood Cemetery, Section F.
{US 1890; WC-V 1885, 1895; B-1905; WCBR v.2, p.71, #169; Cem. records; ROV}

REED, Robert - Pvt., Co. C, 21st Regt., Wis. Vol. Inf.
Robert enlisted at Oshkosh on Aug. 13, 1862. He was assigned as above and was wounded at Jefferson, Tennessee. Robert was mustered out on June 8, 1865.
{ROV}

REED, Royal W. - Cpl., Co. C, 14th Regt., Wis. Vol. Inf.
Royal was born circa 1828 at New York. He was a son of Richard and Cynthia Reed and a brother of Philander from a previous sketch. The father was born circa 1798 at Vermont and the mother was born in that same state circa 1803. They were listed in the 1860 federal census as residing on a farm in the town of Omro. Listed with them were Royal and his family. Mary Jane Hammond, his wife, was born circa 1835 at Maine. Both of her parents were natives of that state. Royal and Mary then had sons Clarence, born circa 1855 at Wisconsin, and Marshall, born circa 1857 at Wisconsin. Royal enlisted at Omro on Feb. 18, 1864. He was assigned as above and was promoted to Corporal in that company. Royal was mustered out on Oct. 9, 1865. He was listed in the 1880 federal census as residing in the town of Omro. Royal and Mary had at least the following children: Marshall, born circa 1858; Royal W., born circa 1865; Ulysses S., born circa 1868; and Mabel E., born circa 1875. Also residing with the family in 1880 was Olive Hammond, aged 82 years, the mother of Mary Jane. Royal was listed in the veteran section of the 1885 and 1895 Wisconsin State census at P.O. Omro. He was listed in the 1890 federal census as residing in the village of Omro. Royal was still suffering the effects of dropsy due to exposure during his military service.
{US 1860, 1880, 1890; WC-V 1885, 1895; ROV}

REED, Theophilus L. - Cpl., Co. G, 3rd Regt., Wis. Vol. Inf.
Theophilus was born circa 1837 at New York. He was listed in the 1860 federal census as a carpenter residing with the family of William Bailey in the town of Clayton at P.O. Neenah. Theophilus enlisted at Neenah on Apr. 20, 1861. He was assigned as above and was promoted to Corporal in that company. Theophilus was wounded on May 23, 1862 and was then discharged on Jan. 8, 1863 due to a disability.
{US 1860; ROV}

REED, William - Pvt., Co. A, 50th Regt., Wis. Vol. Inf.
William resided at Rushford and enlisted there on Feb. 4, 1865. He was assigned as above and was mustered out on June 12, 1866 at the end of his term of enlistment.
{ROV}

REED, William H. - Pvt., Co. A, 48th Regt., Wis. Vol. Inf.
William was born on June 12, 1845 at Potsdam, New York. He later provided that his father was a native of New Hampshire and his mother was born in New York, although he was a son of Richard Reed Sr. and a brother of Philander and Royal W. Reed from previous sketches. William came west in 1849 and settled with his parents at Waukesha. He removed to Winnebago County and settled at Omro. William enlisted at Omro on Feb. 4, 1865. He was assigned as above and was mustered out on Dec. 30, 1865. William was listed in the 1880 federal census as a grocery clerk residing in the village of Omro. Also listed was Julia Sloan, his wife. She was born circa 1846 and was a daughter of William Sloan. Her brother Douglas is the subject of a following sketch. William and Julia had a daughter, Lizzie, born circa 1868, and a son, Douglas, born in the village of Omro on Nov. 18, 1877. All four were residing with her father in 1880. William was listed in the 1890 federal census as residing at 56 Jefferson Avenue in the city of Oshkosh. He died on Apr. 30(obit)/June 12(marker), 1898 and Julia died in 1904. Both are buried at Omro Cemetery, Olin's Addition, Section B, plot 70. Philander Reed, the subject of a previous sketch, is buried on that same plot. William was survived by his wife, one daughter, Mrs. G.W. Ulrich, one son, Douglas Reed, one sister, Mrs. Orrie Perkins of Omro, and two brothers, Royal and Richard, both subjects of previous sketches.
{US 1880, 1890; ROV; Cem. records; WCBR v.2, p.86, #214; ODN 02 May 1898}
{OWN 07 May 1898}

REES, John G. - Pvt., Co. C, 53rd Regt., Wis. Vol. Inf.
John resided at Black Wolf and enlisted there on Feb. 27, 1865. He was assigned as above. That company was transferred to Co. K, 51st Regt., Wis. Vol. Inf. under orders dated June 10, 1865. The transfer was completed on June 30, 1865 at Ft. Leavenworth, Kansas. The regiment returned to Madison, Wisconsin on Aug. 1, 1865 and was then mustered out by companies. The last company was mustered out on Aug. 30, 1865. Elizabeth, wife of John, died in the town of Utica on Apr. 27, 1893. She had suffered for a year from dropsy of the heart. Elizabeth was 76 years old. She was survived by her husband and the following children: David of Utica; Henry of Sioux Rapids, Iowa; John G. of Washington; G.L. of Oshkosh; Maggie of Utica; Lettisha of Utica; Mrs. John Pritchard of Utica; Mrs. T.C. Lloyd of Utica; Mrs. John Owens of Utica; and Mrs. Hugh E. Jones of Sioux Rapids, Iowa. Elizabeth had been a resident of Utica since about 1848.
{ROV; OWN 29 Apr 1893}

REES, Thomas - Pvt., Co. D, 32nd Regt., Wis. Vol. Inf.
Thomas resided at Nekimi and enlisted there on Aug. 21, 1862. He was assigned as above. Thomas was taken prisoner on Mar. 1, 1865 near Cheraw, S.C. He was then mustered out on May 15, 1865. Thomas was listed in the veteran section of the 1885, 1895 and 1905 Wisconsin State census at P.O. Oshkosh. He was listed in 1888 as a member of GAR Post #10 at Oshkosh. He was listed in the 1890 federal census as residing at 302 Jefferson Avenue in the city of Oshkosh. Thomas then provided that he

REES, Thomas (cont.)
had been held at Libby Prison for about three months. He was suffering from the effects of a hernia, chronic diarrhea and a general debility. Thomas was residing at that same address in 1905.
{US 1890; WC-V 1885, 1895, 1905; ROV; B-1905}

REES, Thomas Jr. - Seaman, "Undine," Gunboat Service, U.S. Navy.
Thomas enlisted in the Naval Gunboat Service and was then assigned to the gunboat "Undine." He was injured while in service.
{Lawson p.841}

REES, Thomas L. - Cpl., Co. K, 51st Regt., Wis. Vol. Inf.
Thomas resided at Utica and enlisted there on Mar. 23, 1865. He was assigned as a private to Co. C, 53rd Regt., Wis. Vol. Inf. That company was then transferred with Co. K, 51st Regt., Wis. Vol. Inf. by orders dated June 10, 1865. The transfer was completed on June 30, 1865 at Ft. Leavenworth, Kansas. The regiment returned to Madison, Wisconsin on Aug. 1, 1865 and the men were mustered out by companies. The last company was mustered out on Aug. 30, 1865.
{ROV}

REIL, John - Pvt., Co. D, 1st Regt., Wis. Hvy. Art.
John resided at Menasha and enlisted there on Oct. 31, 1863. He was assigned as above and was listed as having deserted on Jan. 31, 1864.
{ROV}

REINERT, Friedrich - Pvt., Co. F, 19th Regt., Wis. Vol. Inf.
Friedrich was born on Jan. 12, 1816 at Prussia. Catharine, his wife, was born circa 1824, also at Prussia. They were listed (Reinhard) in the 1860 federal census as residing on a farm in the town of Winchester. Listed with them were the following children: Gotfried, subject of a following sketch; Frederick, born circa 1844 at Prussia; and Elisa, born circa 1856 at Wisconsin. Frederick enlisted at Winchester on Feb. 23, 1862. He was assigned as above and was discharged due to a disability on Apr. 6, 1863. Frederick was listed in 1868 as operating a grocery and saloon at 10 Main Street in the city of Oshkosh. He was listed in 1883 at P.O. Winchester and receiving a pension of $8 per month for an injury to his abdomen. He was listed in the 1890 federal census as residing in the town of Winchester at P.O. Winchester. Friedrich was listed in the veteran section of the 1905 Wisconsin State census at P.O. Larsen. He was listed in 1905 as residing with the family of Rudolph Reinert in section 18 of the town of Winchester. His children Fred Jr., Elmeda and Albert were residing with him. He died on Mar. 25, 1912. Friedrich is buried in the town of Winchester at St. Johannes Cemetery.
{US 1860, 1890; WC-V 1905; LOP-1883; T-1868; B-1905; Cem. records; ROV}

REINERT, Gottfried - Pvt., Co. C, 1st Regt., Wis. Cav.
Gotfried was born circa 1842 at Prussia. He was a son of Frederick Reinert from a previous sketch. Gotfried was listed in the 1860 federal census as residing with his parents on a farm in the town of Winchester. He was married in Winnebago County on Mar. 7, 1862 to Harriet Engel. Gottfried resided at Winchester and was drafted there on Nov. 24, 1863. He was assigned as above and was mustered out on July 19, 1865. He was listed (Godfrey) in 1868 as boarding at 11 Fifth Street in the second ward of the

REINERT, Gottfried (cont.)
city of Oshkosh. Gottfried was listed in the veteran section of the 1885 and 1895 Wisconsin State census at P.O. Winchester. He was listed in the 1890 federal census as residing in the town of Winchester at P.O. Winchester.
{US 1860, 1890; WC-V 1885, 1895; T-1868; ROV; WCMR v.1, p.225, #1246}

REINHARDT, Frank L. - Pvt., Co. C, 53rd Regt., Wis. Vol. Inf.
Frank was listed in the 1860 federal census as residing on a farm in the town of Algoma. Listed with him then were Louise, his wife, and the following children: Gustav, born circa 1852; Oscar, born circa 1855; and Emilie, born circa 1858. The children were all born in Wisconsin. Frank enlisted at Oshkosh on Mar. 9, 1865. He was assigned as above. That company was transferred to Co. K, 51st Regt., Wis. Vol. Inf. under orders dated June 10, 1865. The transfer was completed on June 30, 1865 at Ft. Leavenworth, Kansas. The regiment returned to Madison, Wisconsin on Aug. 1, 1865 and the men were mustered out by companies. He was mustered out on Aug. 21, 1865. Frank was listed in 1868 as residing at 34 Ninth Street in the city of Oshkosh. He was listed in the veteran section of the 1885 Wisconsin State census at P.O. Nekimi. Frank was listed in the 1890 federal census as residing in the town of Nekimi at P.O. Oshkosh. He was listed in the veteran section of the 1895 and 1905 state census at P.O. Oshkosh. Frank was listed in 1905 as residing at 224 Michigan Street in Oshkosh. That Frank L. Reinhardt was born Mar. 7, 1830 at Prussia and died on June 12, 1909. Louise M., his wife, was born on Oct. 3, 1831 at Prussia and died in Oshkosh on Sept. 22, 1878. Both are buried in the town of Algoma at Peace Lutheran Cemetery. There is also a Frank L. Reinhardt buried with a simple military marker in the town of Omro at Omro Union Cemetery. His unit designation as shown on the marker is the same as above.
{US 1860, 1890; WC-V 1885, 1895, 1905; T-1868; B-1905; Cem. records; ROV}

REINKE, Christlieb - Pvt., Co. E, 7th Regt., Wis. Vol. Inf.
Christlieb resided at Nekimi and enlisted there on Feb. 24, 1865. He was assigned as above and was mustered out on July 3, 1865.
{ROV}

REMINGTON, Charles Franklin - Pvt., Co. A, 48th Regt., Wis. Vol. Inf.
Charles was born in 1848 at Wisconsin, a son of William H. and Esther Remington. The father was born circa 1813 at New York and the mother was born circa 1824 at Massachusetts. They were listed in the 1860 federal census as residing on a farm in the town of Omro. Listed with them were the following children: Charles F.; Frederick, born circa 1852; Clara, born circa 1854; Alice, born circa 1856; and Theodore, born in 1860. All of the children were born in Wisconsin. Also listed with them was Priscilla Pillsbury, who was born circa 1789 at New Hamsphire. Charles enlisted on Feb. 10, 1865 and was assigned as above. He was mustered out on Dec. 10, 1865. Charles was married in Winnebago County on Nov. 12, 1870 to Eunice Achsah Childs. She was born in 1850. They had twins, one stillborn and the other unnamed at registration, who were born in Omro on June 5, 1878. Charles died in 1926 and Eunice died in 1928. Both are buried at Omro Cemetery, Original Section, plot 35.
{US 1860; ROV; WCMR v.1, p.470, #3053; WCBR v.2, p.108, #280; Cem. records}

REMINGTON, Marshall D. - Pvt., Co. H, 18th Regt., Wis. Vol. Inf.
Marshall resided at Omro and enlisted there on Jan. 8, 1862. He was assigned as above.

REMINGTON, Marshall D. (cont.)
Marshall contracted a disease and died on July 16, 1862 at Keokuk, Iowa.
{ROV}

REPE, Charles - Pvt., "Orion," Gunboat Service, U.S. Navy.
Charles was born on July 22, 1849 at Prussia. He was a son of Fred and Caroline Repe. His parents emigrated to America with their family in 1855. They came directly from New York to Wisconsin and settled at Milwaukee. Charles remained there until spring of 1865. He then went to Chicago, Illinois and enlisted on Mar. 20, 1865 as a landsman in the marine service. Charles became ill at Vicksburg, Mississippi and was sent on the "Red Rover" to Mound City, Illinois. He was discharged due to a disability in Sept. 1865. His name was entered on the military rolls as Charles Ripp. Charles returned to Milwaukee and continued learning the trade of a paper maker. He took ill in 1872 and was forced to leave that position. He then learned the trade of a stone cutter and removed to Oshkosh in that same year. Charles was married on June 25, 1873 to Francelia Thew. He worked for Alfred Chapple for 14 years. At the death of Mr. Chapple, Charles purchased the company. He was listed in the veteran section of the 1885 Wisconsin State census at P.O. Oshkosh. No unit designation or other information was provided. He was listed as above in the 1890 federal census as residing at 216 Mt. Vernon Street in Oshkosh. Charles then provided his service dates as having been from Mar. 20, 1865 to Aug. 22, 1865. He added that he had suffered a gunshot wound to his right leg. Charles and Francelia had two sons, Willie Elmer and Robert Buron Repe. He was listed in 1905 as owning a stoneyard and being a stone cutter. He was then residing at the same address and son Robert B. was also residing there.
{US 1890; WC-V 1885; SCA 1:571-2; B-1905}

RESCH, Michael - Pvt., Co. C, 9th Regt., Wis. Vol. Inf.
Michael resided at Fond du Lac, Fond du Lac County. He enlisted there on Sept. 10, 1861. He was assigned as above and was transferred to Co. G of the same regiment on June 5, 1864. Michael was then mustered out on Dec. 3, 1864 at the end of his term of enlistment. He was listed in the veteran section of the 1885, 1895 and 1905 Wisconsin State census at P.O. Menasha. Michael was listed in the 1890 federal census as residing in the town of Menasha at P.O. Menasha. He was listed in 1905 as residing at 224 Second Street in the city of Menasha. Son Albert was listed at that same address. Kate, widow of Louis Resch, resided next door with her family.
{US 1890; WC-V 1885, 1895, 1905; ROV; B-1905}

RETZACK, Gustav - Cpl., Co. C, 9th Regt., Wis. Vol. Inf.
Gustav was born circa 1836 at Prussia. Ernestine, his wife, was born circa 1842, also at Prussia. Gustav was listed in the 1860 federal census as residing with the family of Anton Okrug in the third ward of the city of Oshkosh. Listed with him were his wife and a daughter, Emma May, who was born circa 1856 at Wisconsin. Also listed were his brother August, born circa 1850 at Prussia, and sister Julianna, born circa 1848 at Prussia. Gustav enlisted at Oshkosh on Oct. 9, 1861. He was assigned as above and was promoted to Corporal in that company. Gustav was then mustered out on Dec. 3, 1864 at the end of his term of enlistment. He was listed in 1868 as a mill man residing at 15 Thirteenth Street in Oshkosh. He was listed in the veteran section of the 1885, 1895 and 1905 Wisconsin State census at P.O. Oshkosh. Gustav was listed in the 1890 federal census as residing in the city of Oshkosh. He then provided that he suffered from

RETZACK, Gustav (cont.)
rheumatism and that he had been in the hospital at Ft. Scott. Gustav was listed in 1905 as a hardware merchant residing at 215 Thirteenth Street in Oshkosh. Son George was residing on Fifteenth Street. He had been born in Oshkosh on July 19, 1873 and died there on Mar. 21, 1913. His father had died about two and one-half years earlier and his mother followed in about six months of her husband.
{US 1860, 1890; WC-V 1885, 1895, 1905; ROV; T-1868; ODN 22 Mar 1913; B-1905}

RETZER, Mathias - Pvt., Co. B, 3rd Regt., Wis. Cav.
Mathias was born circa 1844 at Germany. His parents were natives of that country. Mathias came to the United States in 1860. He was residing at New London, Waupaca County when he enlisted on Dec. 3, 1861. He was assigned as above and was transferred to Co. B, 3rd (reorg.) Regt., Wis. Cav. on Feb. 1, 1865. Mathias was then mustered out on Sept. 8, 1865. He was listed in the 1890 federal census as residing in the city of Oshkosh. Mathias was listed in the veteran section of the 1895 and 1905 Wisconsin State census at P.O. Oshkosh. He was listed in the 1910 federal census as residing at the Wisconsin Veterans' Home at King. He had been married once for 42 years. He was not listed as a widower but his wife was not residing with him.
{US 1890, 1910; WC-V 1895, 1905; ROV}

REYNOLDS, Charles - Civil War Veteran?
Charles was listed in 1888 as a member of GAR Post #241 at Oshkosh.
{SCA}

REYNOLDS, James H. - Pvt., Co. D, 8th Regt., Wis. Vol. Inf.
James resided at Oshkosh and enlisted there on Nov. 26, 1863. He was assigned as above and was listed as having deserted on July 23, 1864.
{ROV}

REYNOLDS, James M. - Pvt., Co. B, 123rd Regt., New York Vol. Inf.
James was listed in 1888 as a member of GAR Post #10 at Oshkosh. He was listed as above in the 1890 federal census as residing in the town of Oshkosh at P.O. Oshkosh. He then provided his service dates as having been Sept. 23, 1862 to Apr. 28, 1865. James was listed as above in the veteran section of the 1895 Wisconsin State census at P.O. Oshkosh.
{US 1890; WC-V 1895}

RHEINER, Jacob - Pvt., Co. D, 21st Regt., Wis. Vol. Inf.
Jacob was born in Jan. 1831 at Switzerland. His parents were natives of that country. He emigrated to the United States in 1852. Jacob resided at Menasha and enlisted there on Jan. 4, 1864. He was assigned as above and was transferred as unassigned to the 3rd Regt., Wis. Vol. Inf. on June 8, 1865. He was mustered out on July 18, 1865. Jacob was listed in the veteran section of the 1885 Wisconsin State census at P.O. Menasha. He was listed in the 1890 federal census as residing in the town of Menasha at P.O. Menasha. Jacob was listed in the 1900 federal census as residing at the Wisconsin Veterans' Home at King. Martha, his wife of 21 years, was residing there with him. She was born in Feb. 1831 at Germany and she came to this country in 1850. Jacob was listed (Rhyner) in 1905 as residing King. He was listed (Rhyner) in the 1910 federal

RHEINER, Jacob (cont.)
census at King as having been a widower for 8 years.
{US 1890, 1900, 1910; WC-V 1885; ROV; GAR 40th}

RHOADES, Solomon - Sgt., Co. I, 32nd Regt., Wis. Vol. Inf.
Solomon resided at Medina, Outagamie County and he enlisted there on Aug. 19, 1862. He was assigned as above and was promoted to Corporal and then Sergeant in that company. Solomon was wounded Feb. 3, 1865 at River's Bridge, S.C. He was mustered out on June 12, 1865. A Hiram Rhoades was assigned to that same company. Solomon was listed in the veteran section of the 1895 and 1905 Wisconsin State census at P.O. Oshkosh. He was listed in 1905 as residing at 238 Merritt Street in the city of Oshkosh. John F. Rhoades was listed at that same address.
{WC-V 1895, 1905; ROV; B-1905}

RHYNER, John - Pvt., Co. C, 46th Regt., Wis. Vol. Inf.
John was born in 1847. He resided at Black Wolf and enlisted there on Feb. 2, 1865. He was assigned as above and was mustered out on Sept. 27, 1865. John was listed in the veteran section of the 1885, 1895 and 1905 Wisconsin State census at P.O. Oshkosh. He was listed in the 1890 federal census as residing in the town of Black Wolf at P.O. Oshkosh. John was accepted as a member of the GAR on Sept. 23, 1886. He was listed in 1888 as a member of GAR Post #241 at Oshkosh. John was listed in 1905 with Judith, his wife, as residing on 80 acres of section 29 in the town of Black Wolf. Son Benjamin S. Rhyner was also residing there. John died in 1921. His wife, E. Rhyner, was born in 1845 and died in 1928. A son, John H., was born in 1869 and died in 1887. All three are buried in the town of Algoma at Peace Lutheran Cemetery.
{US 1890; WC-V 1885, 1895, 1905; ROV; B-1905; Cem. records}

RICE, Ai - Pvt., Co. K, 11th Regt., Wis. Vol. Inf.
Ai was born in March 1841 in New York. His father was a native of Ireland and his mother was born in Scotland. Ai resided at Oshkosh and enlisted there on Sept. 17, 1861. He was assigned as above and was mustered out on Sept. 4, 1865. Ai was listed in the veteran section of the 1895 Wisconsin State census at P.O. Oshkosh. He was listed in the 1900 federal census as residing at the Wisconsin Veterans' Home at King. Ellen, his wife of 2 years, was residing there with him. She was born in July 1845 at England. Ai is buried in the town of Poygan at Oak Hill Cemetery. His marker reads Co. K, 11th Regt., Mo. Inf.
{US 1900; WC-V 1895; ROV; Cem. records}

RICE, Arthur D. - Pvt., Co. B, 38th Regt., Wis. Vol. Inf.
Arthur was born on Sept. 26, 1847 at Boston, Massachusetts. He was a son of Micajah Henry and Olive (Lilley) Rice. Henry was a native of Massachusetts and Olive was born in New York. They came to Wisconsin in Oct. 1852 and settled on a farm in Waupaca County. Arthur grew up on the farm and was educated in the common schools prior to his enlistment. His father enlisted in the same company. Arthur resided at Dayton, Waupaca County and enlisted there on Mar. 17, 1864. He was assigned as above and was wounded on June 17, 1864 at Petersburg, Virginia. He was accidentally wounded on Apr. 4, 1865 and, as a result, his left leg was amputated. He was discharged due to his wounds on Aug. 12, 1865. Arthur returned to his father's farm. In Jan. 1868 he went to Milwaukee and attended Spencer's Business College and learned the trade of a

RICE, Arthur D. (cont.)
cigar maker. He returned to Waupaca, purchased a team and set out for Iowa. He drove stage there and worked with horses until fall of 1869, when he entered work as a clerk in a merchandise store. After about a year, Arthur opened a cigar shop at Mason City, Iowa. He conducted that business for three years. He was married on Apr. 26, 1873 to Mary Bailey. She was a daughter of John D. and Martha (Noyes) Bailey. John was born in New York and Martha was a native of Vermont. Arthur then returned to Waupaca and engaged in farming. He sold his farm after a year and moved into the city of Waupaca, where he was engaged as a cooper. He removed to Antigo, Langlade County in Nov. 1882. There he was employed with a hardware firm. Arthur was listed in 1888 as a member of GAR Post #78 at Antigo. He also held elected positions there. Arthur and Mary had five children: Irwin L.; Claude H.; Gertrude; Fred; and Hazel. An uncle of Arthur, Dexter Munger, was killed in the battle at Perryville, Kentucky. Arthur was listed in the veteran section of the 1905 Wisconsin State census at P.O. Oshkosh. He was listed in 1905 as residing at 65 Prospect Avenue in the city of Oshkosh. Fred M. and Hazel V. Rice were also residing at that address. Arthur's portrait appears on page 336 of Soldiers' and Citizens' Album, vol. 1. Micajah was listed in the 1890 federal census as residing in the town of Dayton, Waupaca County at P.O. Rural.
{US 1890; WC-V 1905; ROV; SCA 1:343-4; B-1905}

RICE, Hiram M. - Pvt., Co. A, 48th Regt., Wis. Vol. Inf.
Hiram was born circa 1837 at New York. He was married in Winnebago County on Feb. 10, 1859 to Lavina VanDoren. She was born circa 1831 at New York. They were listed in the 1860 federal census as residing on a farm in the town of Omro at P.O. Waukau. Listed with them were Sarah, Jane and Mary VanDoren, sisters of Lavina. Hiram enlisted at Somers, Kenosha County on Feb. 6, 1865 and was assigned as above. He was listed as absent sick when that regiment was mustered out on Feb. 19, 1866. Cora Bell, a daughter of Hiram and Lavina, died on Oct. 11, 1867 at age 10 months and 20 days. She is buried on the VanDoren plot at Minckler Cemetery in the town of Omro. Hiram was listed (McRice) in the veteran section of the 1885 Wisconsin State census at P.O. Omro. He was listed in the 1890 federal census as residing in the town of St. Lawrence at P.O. Ogdensburg, Waupaca County. Hiram then provided that he suffered an injury to his stomach. He was listed in that section of the 1895 state census at P.O. Waupaca and in that part of the 1905 state census at P.O. Ogdensburg, both in Waupaca County. Hiram was a brother of William H. Rice from a following sketch.
{US 1860, 1890; WC-V 1885, 1895, 1905; WCMR v.1, p.176, #854; Cem. records} {ROV; SCA 1:618-9}

RICE, Horace F. - Pvt., Co. B, 3rd Regt., Wis. Vol. Inf.
Horace resided at Oshkosh and enlisted there on June 10, 1861. He was assigned as above and was discharged on Feb. 21, 1863 due to a disability.
{ROV}

RICE, James M. - Pvt., Co. C, 4th Regt., Minnesota Vol. Inf.
James was married in Winnebago County on July 29, 1850 to Mary Foley (Fraleigh). He was listed as above in the veteran section of the 1885 Wisconsin State census at P.O. Whitcomb, Shawano County. James was then listed in that section of the 1895 state

RICE, James M. (cont.)
census at P.O. Omro.
{WC-V 1885, 1895; WCMR v.1, p.31, #133}

RICE, John Walter - Sgt., Co. B, 3rd (reorg.) Regt., Wis. Cav.
John was born on Aug. 27, 1832 at New York. He was a son of Benjamin Rice. The father was born in 1807 and died in 1874. He was listed in the 1860 federal census as residing in the town of Omro. Nancy, his wife, was born circa 1817 at Vermont. Benjamin's will was probated in Winnebago County on Dec. 17, 1874. John resided at Algoma and enlisted there on Nov. 28, 1861. He was assigned as a Private to Co. B, 3rd Regt., Wis. Cav. John was transferred to reorg. Co. B on Feb. 1, 1865 and was then promoted to Quartermaster Sergeant of that regiment on Feb. 20, 1865. His residence was then listed as Oshkosh. He was mustered out on Sept. 8, 1865. John was listed in the 1880 federal census as a grocer residing in the village of Omro. Amanda H., his wife, was born in 1837 at Vermont. A daughter, Lucinda Della, was born in the village of Omro on Nov. 7, 1878. John was listed in the veteran section of the 1885, 1895 and 1905 Wisconsin State census at P.O. Omro. He was listed in the 1890 federal census as residing in the village of Omro. He was listed in 1905 as residing on Exchange Street in Omro. Lucinda, their daughter, was listed as a school teacher and residing at that same address. Amanda died in 1910 and John died on Oct. 31, 1916. Both are buried with his father at Omro Cemetery, Original Section, plot 92.
{US 1880, 1890; WC-V 1885, 1895, 1905; Cem. records; WCBR v.2, p.124, #329}
{WCPR v.20, p.497-9; B-1905; ROV}

RICE, Martin VanBuren - Pvt., Co. D, 32nd Regt., Wis. Vol. Inf.
VanBuren was born circa 1841 at New York. He was listed in the 1860 federal census as a laborer on the farm of Gilman Lowd in the town of Omro at P.O. Waukau. Martin listed his residence as Oshkosh when he enlisted on Nov. 20, 1863. He was assigned as above and was wounded on Feb. 3, 1865 at River's Bridge, S.C. Martin was transferred to Co. D, 16th (reorg.) Regt., Wis. Vol. Inf. on June 4, 1865 and was mustered out on June 6, 1865. He was listed in the veteran section of the 1905 Wisconsin State census at P.O. Oshkosh. Martin was listed in that year as residing at 336 W. Algoma Street in the city of Oshkosh.
{US 1860; WC-V 1905; ROV; B-1905}

RICE, Nelson - Pvt., Co. B, 21st Regt., Wis. Vol. Inf.
Nelson was born on Apr. 6, 1845 at Watertown, Jefferson County, Wisconsin. He was a brother of Ai and James M. Rice from other sketches. Nelson listed his residence as Oshkosh when he enlisted on Aug. 13, 1862 and was assigned as above. He received a flesh wound in the leg on Oct. 8, 1862 at Chaplin Hills, Kentucky. He was hospitalized for about six months before returning to his regiment. Nelson was then mustered out on June 8, 1865 at Milwaukee, Wisconsin. He was married at Menasha on Feb. 6, 1867/8 to Mrs. Margaret (Redhead) Worden. She was the widow of George C. Worden, the subject of a following sketch. Nelson and Margaret had seven children: Cora E.; Franklin N.; Walter L.; Orpha M.; Maggie J.; Leah J.; and Alfie M. Rice. John Rice, oldest brother of Nelson, was a soldier in the Mexican War. He died there from the effects of exposure. Nelson was listed in 1920 as residing at St. Louis Park, Minnesota.
{ROV; SCA 1:307; OWN 16 Oct 1862; WCMR v.1, p.365, #2216; OWN 23 Oct 1862}
{21-33rd}

RICE, Roscoe Clayton - Pvt., Co. B, 49th Regt., Wis. Vol. Inf.
Roscoe resided at Berlin, Green Lake County and enlisted there on Feb. 15, 1865. He was assigned as above and was mustered out on Nov. 1, 1865. Roscoe was married to Mary Elmyra Everett. They had a son, Percy Roy Rice, who was born in Oshkosh on Oct. 22, 1880. Another son, Roscoe Leslie, was born in Oshkosh on Oct. 3, 1882. Roscoe was listed in the veteran section of the 1895 and 1905 Wisconsin State census at P.O. Oshkosh. He was listed in 1905 as an engineer residing at 306 Merritt Street in the city of Oshkosh. Lester, Maud and Percey R. Rice were also listed at that address.
{WC-V 1895, 1905; WCBR v.3, p.62, #371; WCBR v.3, p.14, #79; ROV; B-1905}

RICE, William H. - Pvt., Co. H, 16th Regt., Wis. Vol. Inf.
William was born on Sept. 11, 1844 at Russell, St. Lawrence County, New York. He was a son of William S. and Jennett (Stembing) Rice. His parents removed to Wisconsin in 1855 and settled at Waupaca County. William enlisted at Wautoma in Nov. 1861 and was assigned as above. He was mustered into service in Jan. 1862 with his residence listed as Little Wolf and he was then assigned to Co. I of the same regiment. William was wounded in the arm during the battle at Pittsburg Landing. He was sent to a hospital at Newberg, Indiana. The hospital was raided by rebels on Oct. 31, 1862 and all of the patients were captured. They were paroled and were sent to the Salt Mills hospital at Evansville, Indiana. William then rejoined his regiment at Grand Junction, Tennessee. He was sent as a parolee to St. Louis to await exchange. He grew tired of waiting there and joined a group that went aboard a boat and was taken downriver to Lake Providence, Louisiana, where William met up with his regiment. He had been detained at St. Louis due to his wounds while others had been exchanged and furloughed to home. William had not been informed that he had been exchanged and, as such, his commanding officers would not issue him a gun. Being captured with one while on parole was cause for being shot. William was eventually reinstated and, in the action at Peach Tree Creek in Georgia, he was hit by a shell that had killed four others before striking him and another afterwards. He was injured in the hips and was permanently disabled. William was then hospitalized for 14 months. He was discharged due to a disability on Apr. 25, 1865 and returned to the home of his parents near Waupaca. William was married on Mar. 31, 1866 to Mary E. Kennedy. He was a resident of various locations near his parents until 1888. He was listed in that year as a member of GAR Post #197 at Plainfield. William was listed in the 1890 federal census as residing at Plainfield. He was engaged in keeping a hotel at Plainfield, Waushara County. William and Mary had two sons, Ira A. and Ruel A. Rice. Three of his brothers served in Wisconsin regiments, Martin in the 8th, Miner in the 42nd, and Hiram, subject of a previous sketch, served in the 48th. William died in 1937. He is buried with members of his family in the town of Plainfield, Waushara County, at Plainfield Cemetery.
{US 1890; ROV; SCA 1:618-9; Cem. records}

RICH, Zephus C. - Pvt., Co. C, 118th Regt., New York Vol. Inf.
Zephus was born on July 15, 1841. He was married to Caroline (Neal) Wagner. She was the widow of Henry Wagner. Henry died in the army in July 1865. Zephus and Caroline had a son, Loyal Alton Rich, who was born in the village of Omro on July 22, 1879. Zephus was listed as above in the veteran section of the 1885, 1895 and 1905 Wisconsin State census at P.O. Omro. He was listed in 1905 as a mason residing at 523 Pleasant Street in the village of Omro. Lyndon Rich was also residing at that address. Zephus died on Apr. 17, 1906. Caroline, his wife, was born in 1846 and died in 1926.

RICH, Zephus C. (cont.)
Both are buried at Omro Cemetery, Pelton's Addition, Section D, plot 35. Other members of their family are buried on that same plot.
{WC-V 1885, 1895, 1905; Cem. records; WCBR v.2, p.150, #408; B-1905}

RICHARDS, Bradley - Pvt., Co. B, 29th Regt., Wis. Vol. Inf.
Bradley resided at Watertown, Jefferson County and enlisted there on Aug. 14, 1862. He was assigned as above. Bradley contracted a disease and died on May 1, 1863 at Milliken's Bend, Louisiana. Cornelia H. Forbes, his widow, was listed in the 1890 federal census as residing at 36 Hannah Street in the city of Oshkosh. She had then been married to J.B. Forbes. She was listed as his widow in 1905 and was residing at 14 Park Street in Oshkosh.
{US 1890; ROV; B-1905}

RICHARDS, J. - Seaman, "Juliet," Gunboat Service, U.S. Navy.
He enlisted on Aug. 17, 1864 and was assigned to the Naval Gunboat Service. He was trained on the Great Lakes at Chicago and was then assigned to the gunboat "Juliet."
{Lawson p.840-1}

RICHARDSON, Andrew J. - Capt., Co. C, 10th Regt., Wis. Vol. Inf.
Andrew was born circa 1829 at Massachusetts. He was listed in the 1860 federal census as a teacher residing in the first ward of the village of Menasha. Lucy E., his wife, was born circa 1829 at Rhode Island. Andrew enlisted at Menasha and he was commissioned as Captain of the above company on Sept. 30, 1861. He then resigned his commission on Apr. 12, 1862. Andrew was appointed as 1st Lieutenant of Co. G, 10th Regt., Wis. Vol. Inf. on Oct. 1, 1862. He resigned that commission on June 2, 1863. Andrew died in 1881 at Kansas.
{US 1860; ROV; Lawson p.810}

RICHARDSON, Edwin O. - Pvt., Co. C, 1st Regt., New York Sharpshooters.
Edwin was listed (E.A.) as above in the veteran section of the 1885 and 1895 Wisconsin State census at P.O. Menasha. He was listed in the 1890 federal census as residing in the city of Menasha. He then provided his service dates as having been from Aug. 1862 to June 28, 1865. Edwin added that he had been held prisoner at Belle Isle and was suffering from deafness.
{US 1890; WC-V 1885, 1895}

RICHARDSON, H. Stone - Pvt., 76th Regt., New York Vol. Inf.
Rev. H. Stone Richardson was listed as above in the veteran section of the 1885 and 1895 Wisconsin State census at P.O. Oshkosh. He died in Feb. 1899 at Oshkosh. Charlotte, his widow, was listed in 1905 as residing at 53 Forest Avenue in Oshkosh. Glenn and William C. Richardson were also listed at that address. H. Stone Richardson is buried in Oshkosh at Riverside Cemetery.
{WC-V 1885, 1895; B-1905; OWN 18 Feb 1899}

RICHARDSON, James - Civil War Veteran?
James died on Feb. 13, 1862 at age 38 years and 6 months. He is buried in the town of Vinland at Allenville Cemetery. A GAR marker has been placed at his grave. A brother

RICHARDSON, James (cont.)
George is buried on that same plot.
{Cem. records}

RICHMOND, Abial - Pvt., Co. I, 32nd Regt., Wis. Vol. Inf.
Abial resided at Oshkosh and enlisted there on Dec. 25, 1863. He was assigned as above and was then transferred to Co. C, 16th Regt., Wis. Vol. Inf. on June 4, 1865. Abial was mustered out on July 12, 1865. He was listed in 1888 as a member of GAR Post #81 at Shawano, Shawano County.
{ROV; SCA}

RICHMOND, Tabor C. - Pvt., Co. B, 3rd Regt., Wis. Vol. Inf.
Tabor was born circa 1844 at Vermont. He was a son of Gilbert and Sarah Richmond. The father was born circa 1808 at Vermont and the mother was born circa 1818 at New York. They were listed in the 1860 federal census as residing on a farm in the town of Utica at P.O. Welaunee. Listed with them were the following children: Tabor; Jacob, born circa 1846 at Vermont; and Otis, born circa 1857 at Wisconsin. Tabor enlisted at Utica on Apr. 21, 1861. He was assigned as above and was wounded in the ankle at Antietam, Maryland on Sept. 17, 1862. Tabor was discharged on Feb. 23, 1863 due to his wound.
{US 1860; ROV; OWN 02 Oct 1862}

RICKARD, Edgar J. - Cpl., Co. K, 1st Regt., Michigan Vol. Inf.
Edgar was listed (E.D.) as above in the veteran section of the 1885 Wisconsin State census at P.O. Oshkosh. He was listed in 1888 as a member of GAR Post #10 at Oshkosh. He was listed in the 1890 federal census as residing in the city of Oshkosh. Edgar added that he had served as a Private in Co. I of the same regiment. He had enlisted on Sept. 17, 1861 and was mustered out on June 30, 1866. Edgar died in Oshkosh in Feb. 1891. Clara, his widow, was listed in 1905 as residing at 195 Jefferson Avenue in Oshkosh. Alice Rickard was also listed at that address.
{US 1890; WC-V 1885; B-1905; OWN 12 Feb 1891}

RICKER, Andrew - Pvt., Co. H, 14th Regt., Wis. Vol. Inf.
Andrew resided at Barton, Washington County and was drafted there on Dec. 1, 1864. He was assigned as above and was mustered out on Oct. 9, 1865. Andrew was listed in the veteran section of the 1885 Wisconsin State census at P.O. Menasha. He was listed in 1905 as a resident at the Wisconsin Veterans' Home at King. Andrew had been received there from Appleton, Outagamie County.
{WC-V 1885; ROV; GAR 40th}

RIDEOUT, William K. - Pvt., Co. F, 43rd Regt., Wis. Vol. Inf.
He was listed variously as William K. and Wanton K., but usually as W.K. Rideout. William was born on July 15, 1840 at Richmond, Maine. He was a son of W.S. and Eleanor (Perry) Rideout. Both parents were natives of Maine, the mother being a descendant of Commodore Perry. W.S. died on Jan. 2, 1847 and Eleanor then came to Wisconsin with her son. She died in Oshkosh on Sept. 14, 1893 at the age of 82 years. Eleanor was buried in Hortonville, Outagamie County. William arrived in Oshkosh in spring of 1857 but remained only one week. He then removed to Hortonville, where he was married on June 22, 1861 to Eliza J. Hagen. Her parents were natives of Scotland

RIDEOUT, William K. (cont.)
and she was born on Nov. 3, 1839 at New York. Eliza removed to Branford, Canada with her parents when she was a child. In 1858 the family came to Hortonville. William learned the carpenter and joiner trades and worked in that field until 1860. He then began a small-scale business of manufacturing wagons and houses. William continued as such until he enlisted on Aug. 27, 1864. He was assigned as above and was mustered out on June 24, 1865. William then returned to Hortonville and was engaged in the manufacturing of doors and sash, which he continued until 1886. He also began in the lumber business in 1870 by purchasing pine timber and then cutting and marketing the logs at Oshkosh and Fond du Lac. During this same time he operated a sawmill at Hortonville. William operated that mill until Jan. 1889 when it was removed north. In 1880 he went to Eland Junction, Shawano County and erected a sawmill, then becoming extensively engaged in lumbering. He located permanently at Oshkosh in Aug. 1885. William was listed in the 1890 federal census as residing in the city of Oshkosh. He and Eliza had three children, including Permelia E. "Ella,", died in childhood; M.C., married Judge Porter of Lincoln County, died circa 1902; and William A. Rideout. William was listed in 1905 as involved in several business enterprises and residing at 350 Algoma Street in Oshkosh. Eliza died at Oshkosh on June 25, 1909 after an illness of many years. She was buried at Hortonville. William died in June 1936 and his second wife died in June 1950.
{US 1890; Randall p.44-5; B-1905; ODN 16 Sep 1893; OWN 23 Sep 1893; ROV}
{ODN 16 Jul 1927; ODN 26 Jun 1936; ODN 12 Jun 1950}

RIFENBURGH, Ebenezer - Pvt., Co. K, 11th Regt., Wis. Vol. Inf.
Ebenezer resided at Neenah and enlisted there on Oct. 9, 1861. Before his regiment was organized and sent from the state, Ebenezer was married on Nov. 1, 1861 in Winnebago County to Julia Morrow. He was assigned as above and was discharged on July 30, 1862 due to a disability.
{ROV; WCMR v.1, p.221, #1210}

RILEY - see also: O'Riley

RILEY, Barnard - Pvt., Co. K, 11th Regt., Wis. Vol. Inf.
Barnard resided at Neenah and enlisted there on Oct. 5, 1861. He was assigned as above and was listed as having deserted on Nov. 15, 1861.
{ROV}

RILEY, James E. - Pvt., Co. K, 5th (reorg.) Regt., Wis. Vol. Inf.
James resided at Rushford and enlisted there on Aug. 25, 1864. He was assigned as above and was mustered out on June 20, 1865. James was listed in the 1890 federal census as residing in the town of Rushford at P.O. Eureka.
{US 1890; ROV}

RILLY, James - Sgt., Co. F, 46th Regt., Wis. Vol. Inf.
James resided at Oshkosh and enlisted on Feb. 7, 1865. He was assigned as above and was promoted to Sergeant in that company. He was mustered out on Sept. 27, 1865.
{ROV}

RILLING, John Frederick - Pvt., Co. A, 16th Regt., Wis. Vol. Inf.
Fred was born on Sept. 18, 1823 at Gomaringen, Germany. He was a son of Johann Friedrich and Catharina B. (Hermann) Rilling. Fred was married on Feb. 15, 1847 at West Turin, Lewis County, New York to Anna Maria Ingle, daughter of John Jacob and Rosina Hayse. Anna was born Sept. 22, 1831 at West Turin. Fred resided at Concord, Jefferson County and he was drafted there on Sept. 20, 1864. He was assigned to the 44th Regt., Wis. Vol. Inf. and was transferred to Co. A, 16th Regt., Wis. Vol. Inf. Fred was mustered out on June 2, 1865. He and Anna had the following children: John Frederick, born on Feb. 20, 1848 at West Turin; Charles Joseph, born June 18, 1850 at West Turin, married Amelia Butler; James Henry, born on May 13, 1852 at Concord, married Orlena Morrison; Anna Maria, born Nov. 16, 1853 at Concord; David Elliott, born July 26, 1855 at Concord, married Evangeline Sage; Sarah Rosina, born Dec. 7, 1858 at Concord, married David M. Aspinwall; Wilson Edward, born on Oct. 21, 1861 at Concord, married Anna Brownell; Albert A., born on Jan. 8, 1867 at Floyd, Iowa, married Anna B. Coates; and Joseph Miles, born on Sept. 26, 1869 at Farmington, Jefferson County, married Minnie Adeline Walter. John died on Sept. 17, 1900 at Omro. He is buried there with a simple military marker at Omro Union Cemetery. Anna died on Feb. 29, 1904 and is buried in the town of Rushford at Rushford Cemetery.
{ROV; Cem. records; Family Research files of the author}

RINGLING, Frederick - Pvt., Co. K, 5th (reorg.) Regt., Wis. Vol. Inf.
Frederick resided at Nepeuskun and enlisted there on Sept. 2, 1864. He was assigned as above and was mustered out on June 20, 1865. Frederick is buried with a simple military marker at Borth Cemetery in the town of Poysippi, Waushara County.
{ROV; Cem. records}

RIPLEY, Daniel O. - Pvt., Co. E, 5th Regt., Wis. Vol. Inf.
Daniel resided at Janesville, Rock County and enlisted there on May 10, 1861. He was assigned as above and was wounded at Gaines' Mill. Daniel was discharged on Dec. 29, 1862 due to a disability. He was listed in the veteran section of the 1885 Wisconsin State census at P.O. Menasha. Daniel was listed in the 1890 federal census as a resident at the Northern Hospital for the Insane. After having been in that hospital for about 7 years, Daniel died there on Sept. 20, 1891. He was survived by his wife. She had taken work at the hospital to be near him. Daniel was a brother of Mrs. Curtis Reed of Menasha. He left considerable property in Menasha.
{US 1890; WC-V 1885; ROV; OWN 24 Sep 1891}

RIPLEY, Smith - Pvt., Co. B, 21st Regt., Wis. Vol. Inf.
Smith was born circa 1835 at New York. Lydia, his mother, was born circa 1808 at New York. They were listed in the 1860 federal census as residing in the town of Utica at P.O. Welaunee. Also listed was Julia Ripley. She was born circa 1850 at Wisconsin. Smith was married in Winnebago County on Aug. 11, 1861 to Harriet Aldrich. He enlisted at Utica on Aug. 15, 1862. He was assigned as above. Smith contracted a disease and died on Mar. 5, 1863 at Nashville, Tennessee.
{US 1860; ROV; WCMR v.1, p.217, #1183}

RIPPLE, Andrew C. - Pvt., Co. F, 11th Regt., Wis. Vol. Inf.
Andrew resided at Oshkosh and enlisted there on Sept. 27, 1861. He was assigned as

RIPPLE, Andrew C. (cont.)
above and was wounded at Port Gibson. Andrew was then transferred to the Veteran Reserve Corps on July 7, 1864 and he was transferred to Co. K, 3rd Regt., Wis. Vol. Inf. on Feb. 7, 1865. He was mustered out on July 18, 1865. Andrew was married in Winnebago County on Mar. 28, 1866 to Martha Jane Potter. They had a son, unnamed at registration, who was born in the town of Algoma on July 7, 1877. Andrew was listed in 1883 at P.O. Oshkosh. He had been receiving a pension of $2 per month since May 1881 for a wound to his right foot. Andrew was listed in 1888 as a member of GAR Post #10 at Oshkosh. He was listed in the 1890 federal census as residing in the city of Oshkosh. Andrew was listed in the veteran section of the 1895 and 1905 Wisconsin State census at P.O. Oshkosh. He was listed in 1905 as a watchman residing at 114 Jefferson Avenue in Oshkosh. Jennie and Walter Ripple were also listed at that address.
{US 1890; WC-V 1895, 1905; LOP-1883; B-1905; WCBR v.2, p.61, #141; ROV}
{WCMR v.1, p.295, #1806}

RIPPLE, Henry - Cpl., Co. B, 3rd Regt., Wis. Vol. Inf.
Henry resided at Black Wolf and enlisted there on Apr. 19, 1861. He was assigned as above and was promoted to Corporal in that company. He was then taken prisoner on Aug. 9, 1862 and was mustered out on June 29, 1864 at the end of his term of enlistment. Henry was married in Winnebago County on May 12, 1866 to Isabella O'Brien. He was listed in 1868 as a lumberman residing at 63 Seventh Street in the city of Oshkosh. He was listed in the veteran section of the 1885 Wisconsin State census at P.O. Nekimi. Carrie, his widow, was listed in 1905 as residing on 50 acres of section 23 in the town of Nekimi. Son Ernst was residing with her.
{WC-V 1885; ROV; T-1868; B-1905; WCMR v.1, p.298, #1828*}

RIST, Charles A. - Pvt., Co. A, 3rd Regt., Wis. Cav.
Charles resided at Oshkosh and enlisted there on Dec. 18, 1863. He was assigned as above and was then transferred as a blacksmith to Co. K, 3rd (reorg.) Regt., Wis. Cav. Mar. 23, 1865. Charles was mustered out on Sept. 29, 1865.
{ROV}

RITCH, William G. - Adj., 46th Regt., Wis. Vol. Inf.
William was born circa 1830 at New York. Olive M., his wife, was born circa 1834 at Vermont. William was listed in the 1860 federal census as an architect residing in the third ward of the city of Oshkosh. He and Olive had a son William who was born circa 1859 at Wisconsin. Also residing with them was a Dilly McIntyre, born circa 1825 at Vermont. This may be a sister of Olive. William was commissioned as Adjutant of the above regiment on Jan. 2, 1865. He was mustered out on Sept. 27, 1865. William was listed in 1868 as a solicitor of patents residing at 21 Ninth Street in Oshkosh.
{US 1860; ROV; T-1868}

ROACH - see also: Roche

ROACH, Andrew - Pvt., Co. F, 21st Regt., Wis. Vol. Inf.
Andrew resided at Winneconne and enlisted there on Aug. 15, 1862. He was assigned as above and was taken prisoner at Chickamauga, Georgia. Andrew contracted diarrhea and died in the rebel prison at Andersonville, Georgia on June 16, 1864. He was buried

ROACH, Andrew (cont.)
there in grave #2,028.
{ROV}

ROACH, Daniel - Pvt., Co. B, 21st Regt., Wis. Vol. Inf.
Daniel resided at Winneconne and enlisted there on Aug. 14, 1862. He was assigned as above and was transferred as an artificer to the U.S. Veteran Volunteer Engineers on July 29, 1864. Daniel was mustered out on June 30, 1865.
{ROV}

ROACH, Thomas - Pvt., Co. D, 32nd Regt., Wis. Vol. Inf.
Thomas was born circa 1833 at England. He was listed in the 1860 federal census as a tailor residing in the town of Winneconne. Listed with him was a Laura Roach, his wife. She was born circa 1843 at Ohio. Thomas enlisted at Winneconne on Aug. 21, 1862. He was assigned as above and was mustered out on June 12, 1865. Laura, his widow, was listed in the 1890 federal census as residing in the town of Leon, Waushara County at P.O. Auroraville. She provided that Thomas had suffered from consumption while in service.
{US 1860, 1890; ROV}

ROBBINS, America C. - Cpl., Co. B, 3rd Regt., Wis. Vol. Inf.
America resided at Omro and enlisted there on Apr. 21, 1861. He was assigned as above and was promoted to Corporal in that company. He was wounded on May 3, 1863 and again on May 25, 1864. America was mustered out on June 29, 1864 at the end of his term of enlistment. He was listed in 1868 and 1876 as a laborer residing at 13 Wren Street in the city of Oshkosh. Isabella, his widow, was listed in 1905 as residing at 188 W. Lincoln Avenue in Oshkosh.
{ROV; T-1868; 1876; B-1905}

ROBBINS, Andrew J. - Sgt., Co. F, 18th Regt., Wis. Vol. Inf.
Andrew was born on Feb. 15, 1844 at Maine, a son of Charles and Mary Robbins and a brother of Rufus from a following sketch. Both parents were natives of Maine, the father born there circa 1805 and the mother born circa 1815. They were listed in the 1860 federal census as residing on a farm in the town of Algoma. Listed with them were the following children: William, born circa 1832, listed with his wife and a daughter; Samuel, born circa 1839; Andrew; Rufus; and Frances, born circa 1852. The children were all born in Maine. Charles died in Algoma on Oct. 5, 1885. He had been a resident of Winnebago County for 32 years and was survived by his wife and six children, being three sons and three daughters. Andrew listed his residence as Omro when he enlisted there on Dec. 1, 1861. He was assigned as above and was promoted to Corporal and then Sergeant in that company. Andrew was taken prisoner at Allatoona, Georgia and was mustered out on July 18, 1865. He was married to Almeda Wilmarth. They had a son, unnamed at registration, who was born in Omro on Aug. 13, 1880. Andrew was listed in the 1890 federal census as residing at 255 Central Avenue in Oshkosh. He was listed in the veteran section of the 1895 and 1905 Wisconsin State census at P.O. Oshkosh. Andrew was listed in 1905 as a gardener residing at 430 West Algoma in Oshkosh. Also at that address was a Ray J. Robbins. Andrew died Aug. 1, 1917. Almeda W., his wife, was born in 1846 and died in 1938. Both are buried in the

ROBBINS, Andrew J. (cont.)
town of Omro at Omro Union Cemetery.
{US 1860, 1890; WC-V 1895, 1905; B-1905; WCBR v.3, p.5, #26; Cem. records}
{ROV; OWN 10 Dec 1885}

ROBBINS, David R. - Pvt., Co. D, 41st Regt., Wis. Vol. Inf.
David resided at Neenah and enlisted there on May 16, 1864. He was assigned as a drummer in the above company and was mustered out on Sept. 23, 1864 at the end of his term of enlistment.
{ROV; Lawson p.840}

ROBBINS, Erwin - Pvt., Co. G, 3rd Regt., Wis. Vol. Inf.
Erwin was born circa 1841 at Illinois, a son of Oliver and Mary Robbins. Oliver was born circa 1810 and Mary was born circa 1815, both at New York. Oliver was listed in the 1860 federal census as a farmer residing in the fifth ward of the city of Oshkosh. Listed with him were his wife and the following children: Erwin, a lumberman; Herbert, born circa 1850 at Wisconsin; and Melvin, born circa 1859 at Wisconsin. Erwin enlisted at Oshkosh on Apr. 25, 1861. He was assigned as above and was wounded at Antietam, Maryland. Ervin was discharged by order Oct. 26, 1862 to enlist in the regular army.
{US 1860; ROV; Lawson p.808}

ROBBINS, Henry A. - Pvt., Co. B, 16th (reorg.) Regt., Wis. Vol. Inf.
Henry was born in 1833 at Prince Edward Island, Canada. He was a son of Thomas and Ann Robbins and a brother of James, Stephen and William Robbins from following sketches. Thomas was born circa 1790 at England and Ann was born circa 1800 at Prince Edward Island. They were listed in the 1860 federal census as residing on a farm in the town of Black Wolf. Listed with them were the following children: James; George, born circa 1830; Henry; Stephen; Jane, born circa 1843; and William. The children were all born at Prince Edward Island. Mary Craw, wife of Henry, was born in 1843, also at Prince Edward Island. Henry resided at Nekimi and enlisted there on Mar. 5, 1864. He was assigned as above and was mustered out on June 30, 1865. Henry was listed in the veteran section of the 1905 Wisconsin State census at P.O. Oshkosh. He was listed then as residing at 23 Huron Street in the city of Oshkosh. Henry died in 1920 and Mary died in 1931. Both are buried at Omro Cemetery, Olin's Addition, Section B, plot 84.
{US 1860; WC-V 1905; B-1905; Cem. records; ROV}

ROBBINS, James - Pvt., Co. B, 16th (reorg.) Regt., Wis. Vol. Inf.
James was born circa 1826 at Prince Edward Island, Canada. He was a son of Thomas and Ann Robbins and a brother of Henry; Stephen and William Robbins from other sketches. James was listed in the 1860 federal census as residing on a farm adjoining his parents land in the town of Black Wolf. Mary Ann, his wife, was born circa 1835 at Scotland. Listed with them were two sons who were born in Wisconsin. Thomas was born circa 1856 and George was born circa 1859. James resided at Nekimi and enlisted there on Mar. 5, 1861. He was assigned as above. James was killed in action July 22, 1864 at Atlanta, Georgia. Mary A. King, formerly his widow, was listed in the 1890 federal census as residing in the town of Oshkosh at P.O. Oshkosh.
{US 1860, 1890; ROV}

ROBBINS, Leonard H. - Civil War Veteran?
Leonard was born circa 1833 at Maine. Ann, his wife, was born circa 1839 at New York. They were listed in the 1860 federal census as residing in the town of Omro. Katie, their daughter, was born in 1859 at Wisconsin. Leonard enlisted at Omro on Apr. 21, 1861. He was assigned as above and was wounded in the hand at Antietam, Maryland on Sept. 17, 1862. Leonard was mustered out on June 29, 1864 at the end of his term of enlistment.
{US 1860; ROV; OWN 02 Oct 1862}

ROBBINS, Rufus - Pvt., Co. F, 18th Regt., Wis. Vol. Inf.
Rufus was born in 1844 at Maine. He was a son of Charles and Mary Robbins and a brother of Andrew from a previous sketch. Rufus was listed in the 1860 federal census as residing with brother William and his family in the town of Algoma. He enlisted at Omro on Dec. 2, 1861 and was assigned as above. He was discharged from that company. Rufus re-enlisted at Algoma on Feb. 9, 1865 and was assigned as a Private in Co. C, 46th Regt., Wis. Vol. Inf. He was mustered out on Sept. 27, 1865.
{US 1860; ROV}

ROBBINS, Stephen - Pvt., Co. B, 16th (reorg.) Regt., Wis. Vol. Inf.
Stephen was born circa 1839 at Prince Edward Island, Canada. He was a son of Thomas and Ann Robbins and a brother of Henry, James and William Robbins from other sketches. Stephen was listed in the 1860 federal census as residing with his parents and their family in the town of Black Wolf. He was married in Winnebago County on Jan. 8, 1863 to Hannah Foster. Stephen listed his residence as Nekimi when he enlisted on Mar. 5, 1864. He was assigned as above and was discharged on Dec. 6, 1864 due to a disability. Stephen was listed in 1868 as a farmer residing at 118 High Street in the city of Oshkosh. He was listed at P.O. Oshkosh in 1883. Stephen had then been receiving a pension of $8 per month since Aug. 1880 for a disease of the lungs. He was listed in the 1890 federal census as residing in Oshkosh. Stephen was listed in the veteran section of the 1885, 1895 and 1905 Wisconsin State census at P.O. Oshkosh. He was listed in 1905 as residing at 76 Cedar Street in Oshkosh.
{US 1860, 1890; WC-V 1885, 1895, 1905; ROV; T-1868; WCMR v.1, p.303, #1867*}
{LOP-1883; B-1905}

ROBBINS, William - Pvt., Co. C, 46th Regt., Wis. Vol. Inf.
William was born circa 1845 at Prince Edward Island, Canada. He was a son of Thomas and Ann Robbins and a brother of Henry, James and Stephen Robbins from other sketches. William was listed in the 1860 federal census as residing with his parents in the town of Black Wolf. He enlisted at Black Wolf on Feb. 14, 1865. He was assigned as above and was mustered out on Sept. 27, 1865. William was married in Winnebago County on June 17, 1866 to Roseana Howard.
{US 1860; ROV; WCMR v.1, p.300, #1845*}

ROBERTS, Aaron - Pvt., Co. I, 29th Regt., U.S. Colored Troops.
Aaron was listed as above in the veteran section of the 1895 Wisconsin State census at P.O. Oshkosh. He was listed in 1905 as a carpenter residing at 55 Custer Street in the city of Oshkosh.
{ROV; B-1905}

ROBERTS, Edgar G. - Pvt., Co. C, 21st Regt., Wis. Vol. Inf.
Edgar was born circa 1846 at New York. He was a son of Stephen and Cynthia Roberts. Stephen was born circa 1812 and Cynthia was born circa 1811, both at New York. Stephen was listed in the 1860 federal census as a liveryman residing in the second ward of the city of Oshkosh. Listed with him were his wife and the following children: Edgar; Clara, born circa 1853 at New York; Ida, born circa 1856 at Illinois; and Willie, born circa 1858 at Wisconsin. Edgar enlisted at Oshkosh on Aug. 13, 1862. He was assigned as above. Edgar contracted a disease and died on Dec. 1, 1862 at Bowling Green, Kentucky.
{US 1860; ROV; OWN 25 Dec 1862; OWN 07 May 1863}

ROBERTS, James B. - Pvt., Co. C, 21st Regt., Wis. Vol. Inf.
James resided at Oshkosh and enlisted there on Aug. 12, 1862. He was assigned as above and was listed as missing since the action at Chaplin Hills, Kentucky on Oct. 8, 1862. James was listed on Apr. 16, 1863 as having deserted.
{ROV; OWN 07 May 1863}

ROBERTS, Joseph W. - Capt., Co. F, 18th Regt., Wis. Vol. Inf.
Joseph was born circa 1838 at England. He was a son of James and Ann Roberts. Both were born circa 1800 at Wales. James was listed in the 1860 federal census as a carpenter residing in the first ward of the city of Oshkosh. Listed with him were his wife, son Joseph and a daughter, Catherine Ann, who was born circa 1844 at England. Joseph enlisted at Oshkosh on Apr. 21, 1861. He was assigned as above and was then promoted to Sergeant in that company. Joseph was wounded in the first battle of Bull Run, Virginia. He was commissioned as Captain of Co. F, 18th Regt., Wis. Vol. Inf on Dec. 20, 1861. Joseph was commissioned as Major of that regiment on July 1, 1865 but was not mustered at that rank. He was mustered out on July 18, 1865. Joseph was married to L.A. Noble. Their marriage was registered on Aug. 3, 1866 in Winnebago County. Joseph was listed in 1868 as a builder residing at 34 Pearl Street in Oshkosh.
{US 1860; T-1868; WCMR v.1, p.304, #1875*; ROV}

ROBERTS, Robert - Pvt., Co. A, 2nd Regt., Wis. Cav.
Robert resided at Nekimi and enlisted there on Oct. 21, 1861. He was assigned as above and he was listed as having deserted on Mar. 24, 1862. Robert then enlisted at Nekimi on Aug. 14, 1862 and was assigned as a Private to Co. C, 21st Regt., Wis. Vol. Inf. He was reported to have fallen out of ranks on Dec. 31, 1862 while the regiment was marching to the front lines at Murfreesboro, Tennessee. He went with the wagons that were ordered to Nashville the next day and was taken prisoner. Robert was reported as a deserter.
{ROV; OWN 07 May 1863}

ROBERTS, Solomon D. - Pvt., Co. I, 21st Regt., Wis. Vol. Inf.
Solomon was born circa 1845 at Wisconsin. He was listed in the 1860 federal census as a farm laborer for Apollus Austin in the town of Clayton at P.O. Neenah. Solomon enlisted at Clayton on Aug. 14, 1862. He was assigned as above and was wounded in the fight at Chickamauga, Georgia on Sept. 19, 1863. Solomon was then mustered out on June 8, 1865.
{US 1860; ROV; Lawson p.833}

ROBIE, Benjamin F. - Cpl., Co. G, 3rd Regt., Wis. Vol. Inf.
Benjamin was born circa 1839 at Maine. He was listed in the 1860 federal census as a farm laborer for Artemus Wheeler in the town of Clayton at P.O. Neenah. Benjamin resided at Vinland and enlisted there on May 6, 1861. He was assigned as above and was then promoted to Corporal in that company. He was wounded on May 25, 1864 and was transferred to the Veteran Reserve Corps on Mar. 12, 1865. Benjamin was married in Winnebago County on Sept. 8, 1867 to Viola F. Wheeler. Her sister was married to William Wheeler of a following sketch. Benjamin was listed in 1888 as residing at Webster City, Iowa.
{US 1860; ROV; SCA 1:477-8; WCMR v.1, p.393, #2444}

ROBIE, Charles F. - Pvt., Co. B, 3rd Regt., Wis. Vol. Inf.
Charles was born circa 1837 at Maine. He was listed in the 1860 federal census as a farm laborer for David Brown in the town of Omro at P.O. Oshkosh. Charles resided at Vinland and enlisted there on Apr. 20, 1861. He was assigned as above and was shot in the jaw at Cedar Mountain. Charles was discharged on Oct. 26, 1862.
{US 1860; ROV; OWN 21 Aug 1862}

ROBINSON, Andrew - Cpl., Co. C, 10th Regt., Wis. Vol. Inf.
Andrew was born circa 1838 at Wisconsin, a son of Samuel and Elizabeth Robinson and a brother of John S. from a following sketch. Samuel was born circa 1812 at Ireland and Elizabeth was born circa 1812/5 at New York. He was listed in the 1850 federal census as a carpenter residing in the town of Neenah. With him were his wife and the following children: Andrew; Jane E., born circa 1840; John S.; Sarah, born circa 1845; Martha, born circa 1847; and William Frank, born circa 1850. All of the children were listed as born in Wisconsin. Elizabeth was listed in the 1860 federal census as residing in the first ward of the village of Menasha. Also listed at that time was a daughter, Minnie, who had been born circa 1855 at Wisconsin. Andrew enlisted at Menasha on Aug. 22, 1861. He was assigned as above and was promoted to Corporal in that company. Andrew was then taken prisoner at Chickamauga, Georgia. He died in the rebel prison at Andersonville, Georgia on Aug. 18, 1864.
{US 1850, 1860; ROV}

ROBINSON, Charles A. - Pvt., Co. D, 41st Regt., Wis. Vol. Inf.
Charles was born circa 1843 at Vermont. He was a son of Amos and Lois Robinson and a brother of William from a following sketch. The parents were both natives of Vermont, the father born there circa 1799 and the mother born circa 1800. They were listed in the 1860 federal census as residing in the second ward of the village of Menasha. Charles was married in Winnebago County on July 3, 1862 to Olive L. Parker. He resided at Menasha and enlisted there on May 19, 1864. He was assigned as above and was mustered out on Sept. 23, 1864 at the end of his term of enlistment. Charles was listed in the veteran section of the 1885, 1895 and 1905 Wisconsin State census at P.O. Menasha. He was listed in the 1890 federal census as residing in the town of Menasha at P.O. Menasha. Charles was listed in 1905 as a partner in the firm of Robinson & Hennig. They ran the Menasha Ice & Fuel Co. Charles was then residing at 132 Main Street in the city of Menasha.
{US 1860, 1890; WC-V 1885, 1895, 1905; ROV; B-1905}

ROBINSON, Cyrus D. - Cpl., Co. I, 21st Regt., Wis. Vol. Inf.
Cyrus resided at Menasha and enlisted there on Aug. 14, 1862. He was assigned as above and was promoted to Corporal in that company. Cyrus contracted a disease and died on Feb. 17, 1863 at Nashville, Tennessee.
{ROV}

ROBINSON, George H. - Cpl., Co. D, 44th Regt., Wis. Vol. Inf.
George resided at Eldorado, Fond du Lac County and enlisted there on Oct. 5, 1864. He was assigned as above and was then promoted to Corporal in that company. He was mustered out on Aug. 28, 1865. George was listed in the veteran section of the 1885, 1895 and 1905 Wisconsin State census at P.O. Oshkosh. He was listed in 1888 as a member of GAR Post #241 at Oshkosh. He was listed in the 1890 federal census as residing in the city of Oshkosh. George was listed in 1905 as a fireman at the Brooklyn Fire House and residing at 274 Eighth Street in Oshkosh. Sons George W. and Harley G. Robinson were also listed at that address.
{US 1890; WC-V 1885, 1895, 1905; ROV; B-1905}

ROBINSON, Henry - Seaman, "Chilicothe," Gunboat Service, U.S. Navy.
Henry enlisted in the Naval Gunboat Service and he was assigned to the gunboat "Chilicothe."
{Lawson p.841}

ROBINSON, Henry Orpheus - Pvt., Co. C, 14th Regt., Wis. Vol. Inf.
Henry was born on Oct. 19, 1847 at DePeyster, St. Lawrence County, New York. He was a son of Henry and Margaret Elizabeth (Curtis) Robinson. Henry was born circa 1824 at Vermont and Margaret was born circa 1826 at New York. She was a daughter of Leavens and Mary Curtis. Levens was born circa 1801 at New York and his wife was born circa 1804 in that same state. The subject of this sketch came to Wisconsin with his parents in 1856 and settled in the town of Omro. Henry and Margaret were listed in the 1860 federal census as residing on that farm. Listed with them were the following children: Henry O.; Levens, born circa 1851 at New York; and Charles, born circa 1855 at New York. Also listed with them were Levens and Mary Curtis. Henry O. enlisted at Omro on Nov. 7, 1861 and was assigned as above. He was mustered out on Jan. 30, 1865 at the end of his term of enlistment. After returning to Omro, Henry was engaged in lumbering on the Fox River for twelve years. In 1866 he had begun studying steam engines and their many applications. His expertise in that area eventually led to his position as Chief Engineer at the water works in Oshkosh after having removed there in 1882. Henry was married to Mary Jane Fraleigh in Winnebago County on Nov. 19, 1867. She was born in 1849 and was a daughter of Orval and M. Fraleigh. Orval was born in 1828 and died in 1881. The mother was born in 1828 and died in 1899. Both are buried in the town of Poygan at Oak Hill Cemetery. Florence, a daughter of Henry and Mary, died on Sept. 14, 1872 at age 1 month and 26 days. Mary Jane died in 1914. She and her daughter are buried with her parents.
{US 1860; ROV; SCA p.686; Cem. records; WCMR v.1, p.367, #2235}

ROBINSON, Hugh - Cpl., Co. B, 3rd (reorg.) Regt., Wis. Cav.
Hugh resided at Oshkosh and enlisted there on Nov. 23, 1861. He was assigned as a Private to Co. B, 3rd Regt., Wis. Cav. Hugh was then transferred to Co. B, 3rd (reorg.) Regt., Wis. Cav. on Feb. 1, 1865 and was promoted to Corporal in that

ROBINSON, Hugh (cont.)
company. He was mustered out on Sept. 8, 1865.
{ROV}

ROBINSON, James T. - Pvt., Co. E, 42nd Regt., Wis. Vol. Inf.
James resided at Menominie, Brown County and enlisted there on Sept. 2, 1864. He was assigned as above and was mustered out on June 20, 1865. James was listed in the veteran section of the 1885 Wisconsin State census at P.O. Oshkosh. He was listed in the 1890 federal census as residing in the city of Oshkosh. James then provided that he had been a Corporal assigned to Co. D, 3rd Regt., Kentucky Cav. He provided his service dates as having been from Oct. 1, 1861 to Oct. 6, 1862. James added that he had been discharged at Athens, Alabama due to chronic diarrhea. James was also listed as a member of the Kentucky Cav. in the veteran section of the 1895 Wisconsin State census at P.O. Oshkosh.
{US 1890; WC-V 1885, 1895; ROV}

ROBINSON, John - Pvt., Co. I, 21st Regt., Wis. Vol. Inf.
John resided at Neenah and enlisted there on Aug. 14, 1862. He was assigned as above and was wounded at Chickamauga, Georgia. John was killed in action on May 31, 1864 at Dallas, Georgia.
{ROV}

ROBINSON, John S. - Cpl., Co. D, 41st Regt., Wis. Vol. Inf.
John was born circa 1842 at Wisconsin. He was a son of Samuel and Elizabeth Robinson and a brother of Andrew from a previous sketch. Samuel died on Mar. 20, 1859 and Elizabeth died on Sept. 29, 1886. John listed his residence as Menasha when he enlisted there on May 2, 1864. He was assigned as above and was promoted to Corporal in that company. John was then mustered out on Sept. 23, 1864 at the end of his term of enlistment. He died circa 1872 and is buried with a simple military marker next to his parents in the town of Menasha section of Oak Hill Cemetery.
{US 1850, 1860; Lawson p.840; ROV; Cem. records}

ROBINSON, Nathaniel S. - Surg., 1st Regt., Wis. Cav.
Nathaniel was born circa 1827 at Maine. Sarah, his wife, was born circa 1829 at Maine. He was listed in the 1860 federal census as a physician residing in the village of Neenah. Listed with him were his wife and two children. Charles was born circa 1855 at Wisconsin and Mary was born circa 1858 at Wisconsin. Nathaniel enlisted at Neenah and he was commissioned as Assistant Surgeon of the above regiment on Jan. 13, 1865. He was promoted to Surgeon on July 11, 1865 and was mustered out on July 19, 1865. Nathaniel was elected to the State Assembly on November 1874. He removed with his family to Portland, Maine soon thereafter. Nathaniel returned to Neenah in January 1876 and remained there. He was listed in the veteran section of the 1885 and 1895 Wisconsin State census at P.O. Neenah. He was listed in the 1890 federal census as residing in the city of Neenah. Nathaniel was listed in 1905 as a physician residing at 204 E. Forest Avenue in Neenah.
{US 1860, 1890; WC-V 1885, 1895; B-1905; HN 1878 p.104 & 107; ROV}

ROBINSON, William J. - Pvt., Co. B, 3rd Regt., Wis. Vol. Inf.
William was born circa 1843 at England. His parents were natives of that country.

ROBINSON, William J. (cont.)
William was brought to this country in 1847. He resided at Oshkosh and enlisted there on Apr. 20, 1861. He was assigned as above and was wounded in the arm at Antietam, Maryland on Sept. 17, 1862. William was mustered out on June 29, 1864 at the end of his term of enlistment. He was listed in 1868 as a laborer boarding at 52 Hancock Street in the city of Oshkosh. William was listed in the 1890 federal census as residing in Oshkosh. He then provided that he had been shot in the left arm. He was listed in the veteran section of the 1895 Wisconsin State census at P.O. Oshkosh. William and Elizabeth E., his wife, were listed in 1905 as residing at the Wisconsin Veterans' Home at King. Both were listed in the 1910 federal census at King. They had been married for 41 years and had two children, both then living. Elizabeth was born circa 1845 at Pennsylvania. Her parents were both natives of New York.
{US 1890, 1910; WC-V 1895; ROV; T-1868; GAR 40th; OWN 02 Oct 1862}

ROBINSON, William M. - Cpl., Co. C, 10th Regt., Wis. Vol. Inf.
William was born circa 1839 at Vermont. He was a son of Amos and Lois Robinson and a brother of Charles from a previous sketch. William was listed in the 1860 federal census as a painter residing with his parents in the second ward of the village of Menasha. He enlisted at Menasha on Aug. 22, 1861. William was assigned as above and was promoted to Corporal in that company. He was taken prisoner at Chickamauga, Georgia. William contracted a diease and died in the rebel prison at Andersonville, Georgia on Aug. 18, 1864. He was buried there in grave #6,088.
{US 1860; ROV}

ROBLEE, William B. - Sgt., Co. K, 11th Regt., Wis. Vol. Inf.
William was born circa 1822 at New York. He was listed in the 1850 federal census as a farmer residing in the town of Clayton. He was residing with a brother, Julius Roblee, and his family. Several of the children were born in Illinois prior to 1840 and the younger children were born after 1840 at Wisconsin. William enlisted at Clayton on Sept. 25, 1861. He was assigned as above and was promoted to Corporal and then Sergeant in that company. William was wounded at Vicksburg, Mississippi. He died from those wounds on May 28, 1863 at Vicksburg.
{US 1850; ROV}

ROCHE - see also: Roach

ROCHE, Thomas - Seaman, "Syren," Gunboat Service, U.S. Navy.
Thomas was born on May 17, 1842 at St. George, Quebec, Canada, a son of William and Mary Roche. Both were natives of County Kerry, Ireland, the father born circa 1813 and the mother born circa 1814. They came to Oshkosh with their family in the 1850s. William was listed in the 1860 federal census as a laborer residing in the third ward of the city of Oshkosh. Residing with him were his wife and the following children: Thomas; Mary, born circa 1844; Margaret, born circa 1846; Sarah, born circa 1850; Ellen, born circa 1853; and Agnes, born circa 1859. Agnes was born in Wisconsin and the other children were born in Canada. Thomas learned the trade of a mechanical engineer and was for several years the engineer on steamers of the Oshkosh area. He enlisted as a seaman on Aug. 17, 1864 at Chicago, Illinois. He was assigned to the "Syren" and was mustered out as a second class fireman at Mound City, Illinois in June 1865. Thomas was listed in 1868 as an engineer then boarding at 64 Knapp Street in

ROCHE, Thomas (cont.)
Oshkosh. That was the residence of William Roche, his father. Thomas joined the city fire department in 1873. He was promoted to second assistant chief during the term of Chief Weisbrod. In 1884 he was named first assistant chief. He was listed in 1888 as a member of GAR Post #241 at Oshkosh. Thomas was listed in the 1890 federal census as residing in Oshkosh. He was listed in the veteran section of the 1885, 1895 and 1905 Wisconsin State census at P.O. Oshkosh. Thomas was listed in 1905 as the city electrician and residing at 54 Doty Street in Oshkosh. Daughter Nellie D. was also listed at that address. He died at Oshkosh on Dec. 1, 1915. He had been injured in 1906 when a fire truck he was on overturned. He had sustained shock and injuries which followed him until death. Thomas was survived by two sisters, Mrs. Mary Delaney of St. Paul, Minnesota, and Mrs. Edward Allen of Oshkosh. He was also survived by his wife and four children: William Roche of Los Angeles, California; Mrs. John Martineau of Oshkosh; Mrs. J.M. Conley of Oshkosh; and Dorothy Ellen Roche of Milwaukee.
{US 1860, 1890; WC-V 1885, 1895, 1905; T-1868; SCA 1:235-6; ODN 02 Dec 1915}
{B-1905}

ROCKEFELLER, Simeon - Seaman, "Gem of the Sea," U.S. Navy.
Simeon was born July 1, 1846 at Gallatin, Columbia County, New York. He was listed in 1868 as an upholsterer boarding at 7 Sixth Street in the city of Oshkosh. He was listed as above in the veteran section of the 1885 and 1895 Wisconsin State census at P.O. Oshkosh. Simeon was married on Feb. 25, 1897 to Emma Fox. He was listed in 1905 as an engineer engaged at the Foster-Lothman Mills and residing at 161 Main Street in Oshkosh. Simeon died at his home in Oshkosh on Dec. 15, 1928. He was survived by his wife and several nephews in the east.
{WC-V 1885, 1895; T-1868; B-1905; ODN 15 Dec 1928}

ROE, John Peter - Chaplain, 97th Regt., New York Vol. Inf.
John was born in 1834 at New York, a son of Peter and Susan E. Roe of Moodna, near Cornwall-on-the-Hudson, New York. John Peter graduated from Williams College at Williamstown, Massachusetts and the Auburn, New York Theological Seminery. He then entered the ministry of the Presbyterian Church. He served two years as the Chaplain for the 97th Regt., N.Y. Vol. Inf. John was married in 1864 to Mary Bliss of Troy, New York. She was born in 1844/6. He soon came west to Wisconsin, where he was listed in 1868 as the pastor of the Congregational Church in the city of Oshkosh. He continued in that position for three years. His health failing, John gave up on his ministerial work and purchased the Lake Rest Fruit Farm in the town of Algoma, where he became a successful fruit grower. John and Mary had seven children, including: Julia N.; James W.; Mary E.; Carrie F.; and Charles A. Roe. John was listed in 1888 as a member of GAR Post #10 at Oshkosh. He was listed in the 1890 federal census as residing in the town of Algoma at P.O. Oshkosh. He then provided his unit designation as above and his dates of service as having been from Mar. 29, 1865 to June 30, 1865. John died in 1909 and Mary died in 1920. Both are buried in the town of Algoma at Peace Lutheran Cemetery.
{US 1890; T-1868; Randall p.16-7; Cem. records; OWN 09 Jan 1909}

ROGERS, Andrew J. - Pvt., Co. D, 32nd Regt., Wis. Vol. Inf.
Andrew was born circa 1833 at New York. He was a son of Asahel and Mary Rogers. Both parents were natives of New York and both were born circa 1805. Andrew was

ROGERS, Andrew J. (cont.)
married in Winnebago County on Sept. 20, 1854 to Julia Drace. She was born circa 1836 at New York. Andrew and Julia were listed in the 1860 federal census as residing on a farm in the town of Omro at P.O. Waukau. Listed with them were two daughters who were born in Wisconsin. Frances was born circa 1854 and Ida was born circa 1858. Listed on an adjoining farm were Asahel and Mary Rogers. Andrew enlisted at Omro on Nov. 20, 1863. He was assigned as above and was transferred to the 16th Regt., Wis. Vol. Inf. on June 4, 1865. He was then transferred to the Veteran Reserve Corps and was mustered out on July 24, 1865. Andrew was listed on an 1874 list of eligible voters from the town of Omro. He was listed in the veteran section of the 1885 and 1895 Wisconsin State census at P.O. Symco, Waupaca County. Andrew was listed in the 1890 federal census as residing in the town of Union, Waupaca County at P.O. Symco. He then reported that he suffered from a hernia.
{US 1860, 1890; WC-V 1885, 1895; ROV; WCMR v.1, p.153, #667}

ROGERS, Benjamin F. - Chaplain, 15th Regt., Illinois Vol. Inf.
Benjamin was born on July 23, 1831 at Piermont, Grafton County, New Hampshire. He was a son of Captain Charles and Permelia (Ramsey) Rodgers. Benjamin was educated in the common schools of his home and at the Bradford Academy in Vermont. He taught several terms in schools and academies in the east before removing to Illinois in the fall of 1855. He managed academies at Crystal Lake and Wauconda for two years. In May of 1857 Benjamin settled at Fox Lake, Dodge County, Wisconsin as the pastor of the Universalist Society. He was ordained there on Aug. 26, 1858. Benjamin was married on Oct. 11, 1860 to Elizabeth Caroline Vedder. Benjamin was then listed as Barton Tyler Rogers. Elizabeth was born in Saratoga County, New York and came to Wisconsin with her parents in childhood. Benjamin entered the service at Wauconda, Ill. and was commissioned as Chaplain of the above regiment on Dec. 17, 1862. He was mustered out at Springfield, Ill. on Sept. 30, 1865. Benjamin then officiated at Wisconsin in the churches of Jefferson, Ft. Atkinson, Whitewater and Oshkosh. In Iowa he was pastor at Cedar Rapids and Marshalltown. For three years Benjamin was the superintendent of the Universalist churches at Iowa. During his administrations, the first Universalist churches were built at Ft. Atkinson, Oshkosh, Whitewater, Wausau and Lodi, Wisconsin. He became the pastor at Wausau in 1886 and then removed to Illinois in 1888, where he was the pastor at Earlville. Benjamin and Elizabeth had the following children: Anna A.; Ellis E.; William W.; Mary M., and Grace G. Rogers. Benjamin had five brothers who also served in the Union army: George C., Col. of the 15th Regt., Ill. Vol. Inf.; William H., Private in that same regiment; Charles, served 2 years with the 2nd Regt., Wis. Cav. and afterwards with a Vermont Regt.; James, served in the Kansas Home Guards; and Thomas, served with the 2nd Kansas Mounted Infantry and died in Arkansas. A photo of Benjamin can be found in the Soldiers' and Citizens' Album on p. 432.
{SCA 1:435-6; WCMR v.1, p.242, #1381*}

ROGERS, Chester T. - Pvt., Co. B, 21st Regt., Wis. Vol. Inf.
Chester was born circa 1837 at New York. Emaline, his wife, was born circa 1841 at New York. They were listed in the 1860 federal census as residing on a farm in the town of Utica at P.O. Fisk's Corners. Arthur, their son, was born in 1860 at Wisconsin. Chester enlisted at Utica on Aug. 15, 1862. He was assigned as above and was discharged on Jan. 8, 1863. Chester was listed in the 1890 federal census as residing at

ROGERS, Chester T. (cont.)
P.O. Clintonville, Waupaca County. He then listed that he suffered from a lung disease and had been discharged on a Surgeon's Certificate.
{US 1860, 1890; ROV}

ROGERS, Daniel R. - Pvt., Co. B, 3rd Regt., Wis. Cav.
Daniel resided at Oshkosh and enlisted there on Jan. 5, 1862. He was assigned as above. Daniel contracted a disease and died on Oct. 3, 1864 at Little Rock, Arkansas.
{ROV}

ROGERS, Francis M. - Pvt., Co. C, 21st Regt., Wis. Vol. Inf.
Francis resided at Omro and enlisted there on Aug. 13, 1862. He was assigned as above. Francis contracted a disease and died on Dec. 30, 1862 at Nolansville, Tennessee.
{ROV}

ROGERS, Francis Marion - Pvt., Co. E, 1st Regt., Wis. Cav.
Francis was born on May 17, 1842 at Lee, Oneida County, New York. He was a son of Charles L. and Anna (Tubbs) Rogers. Charles was born circa 1821 at Michigan and Anna was born circa 1819 at New York. Francis was four years old when his parents removed with their family to Wisconsin and settled at Summit, Waukesha County. Four years later they moved to Winnebago County and settled at Omro. They were listed in the 1860 federal census as residing on a farm in the town of Omro. Listed with them were the following children: Francis; Merion, born circa 1844, possibly the subject of the preceeding sketch; Alfred, born circa 1846; Harriet, born circa 1848; Warren, born circa 1851; Edward, born circa 1853; and Ida, born circa 1855. The three eldest children were born in New York and the others were all born in Wisconsin. Francis was educated in the town schools and then attended school in Ripon, Fond du Lac County for three years. He learned the trade of a carpenter and worked at that occupation at intervals prior to enlisting. Francis was married on July 4, 1862 to Lucinda C. Buck. He listed his residence as Hebron, Jefferson County when he enlisted on Aug. 17, 1864. He was assigned as above and was then mustered out on July 19, 1865 at Edgefield, Tennessee. After the war Francis returned to Wisconsin, settling at Whitewater, Walworth County. He was a builder and contractor there for two years. He then worked in that same trade at Jefferson for three years and removed to Oshkosh in 1876. Francis applied for membership in GAR Post #10 at Oshkosh on Mar. 26, 1885 but his application was rejected the following week. He and Lucinda had nine children: Elmer A., died prior to 1888; Emma A.; Ina A.; Birdena M.; Katie L., died prior to 1888; Dora M.; Frank M.; Earl, died prior to 1888; and Charles Rogers. Francis was married second on May 18, 1879 to Ruth Hopkins. She soon died, leaving one child, Edna A. Rogers. He was married again to Alice Rogers, who was still living in 1888. Francis was listed in the 1890 federal census as residing at 42 Ackerman Street in the city of Oshkosh. He was then suffering from the effects of chronic diarrhea and rheumatism. Francis was listed in the veteran section of the 1895 Wisconsin State census at P.O. Oshkosh.
{US 1860, 1890; WC-V 1895; ROV; SCA 1:682-3}

ROGERS, Hosea M. - Pvt., Co. C, 1st Regt., Wis. Hvy. Art.
Hosea listed his residence as Neenah when he enlisted on Aug. 29, 1863. He was assigned as above and was mustered out on Sept. 21, 1865. Hosea was listed in the

ROGERS, Hosea M. (cont.)
veteran section of the 1885 Wisconsin State census at P.O. Winchester. He was listed in the 1890 federal census as residing in the town of Vinland at P.O. Allenville. Hosea is buried with a simple military marker in the town of Winchester at Winchester Cemetery. He is on the plot of Samuel Rogers, father of Samuel N. of a following sketch.
{US 1890; WC-V 1885; ROV; Cem. records}

ROGERS, John F. - Pvt., Co. D, 32nd Regt., Wis. Vol. Inf.
John resided at Omro and enlisted there on Oct. 24, 1863. He was assigned as above and was transferred to Co. D, 16th (reorg.) Regt., Wis. Vol. Inf. on June 4, 1865. John was mustered out on July 12, 1865. He was listed in 1874 as an eligible voter in the town of Omro. He was listed in the veteran section of the 1885 Wisconsin State census at P.O. Symco, Waupaca County. John was listed in the 1890 federal census as residing in the town of Union, Waupaca County at P.O. Symco. He then listed that he suffered from rheumatism.
{US 1890; WC-V 1885; ROV}

ROGERS, Samuel N. - Pvt., Co. D, 49th Regt., Wis. Vol. Inf.
Samuel was born on Apr. 26, 1843 at Paris, Oneida County, New York. He was a son of Samuel and Mary M. (Enos) Rogers. Samuel was a son of Samuel and Marinda Rogers. The eldest Samuel was born on June 3, 1760 at Connecticut and he died on Sept. 10, 1852 at Winchester. He is the only known veteran of the American Revolution buried in Winnebago County. Marinda was born on July 3, 1777 and died on Aug. 28, 1851. Their son Samuel was born on Dec. 25, 1805 and died on Nov. 18, 1885. Mary (Enos) Rogers was born on June 26, 1810 and died on Jan. 22, 1887. All four are buried in the town of Winchester at Winchester Cemetery. They removed to Wisconsin with their families in 1847 and settled at Spring Prairie, Walworth County. After a year, they moved to Winnebago County and settled on a farm in the town of Winchester. Samuel was engaged there as a farmer when he enlisted at Menasha on Feb. 14, 1865. He was married the next day to Anna Christine Davison. Samuel was assigned as above and was mustered out on Nov. 1, 1865 at Benton Barracks, St. Louis, Missouri. He then returned to Winchester. Anna died on Feb. 9, 1867 at age 19 years and 27 days. She is buried with his parents. Samuel was then married on June 28, 1868 to Mary Jane Cliff. They had a daughter, Harriet, who was born in 1870. Samuel remained at Winchester until 1885. He then purchased a farm in the town of Mukwa, Waupaca County. He was still residing there in 1888. Samuel was listed in the 1890 federal census as residing in the town of Mukwa at P.O. New London. He provided that he had suffered an injury to his back. Hosea M. Rogers, subject of a previous sketch, is also buried on the plot of Samuel Rogers at Winchester Cemetery.
{US 1890; ROV; SCA 1:264; Cem. records; WCMR v.1, p.268, #1587*}

ROGERS, William H. - Pvt., Co. A, 8th Regt., Wis. Vol. Inf.
William resided at Winchester and enlisted there on Aug. 31, 1861. He was assigned as above and was taken prisoner on Mar. 1, 1864 in Mississippi. William was mustered out on Dec. 10, 1864. He was listed in 1883 at P.O. Winneconne and receiving a pension of $12 per month for a wound to his left shoulder and hand. William was listed in 1888 as a member of GAR Post #10 at Oshkosh. He was listed in the veteran section of the 1885 and 1905 Wisconsin State census at P.O. Winneconne. He was listed in the 1890

ROGERS, William H. (cont.)
federal census as residing in the village of Winneconne. William was listed in 1905 as a furrier residing on Lake Avenue in Winneconne. Carl W. and Daisy E. Rogers were also residing there.
{US 1890; WC-V 1885, 1905; ROV; LOP-1883; B-1905; OWN 07 Apr 1864}

ROHAN, Thomas J. - Cpl., Co. B, 21st Regt., Wis. Vol. Inf.
Thomas was born circa 1843 at Germany. He was a son of John and Julia Rohan. Both parents were natives of Germany and both were born circa 1813. They were listed in the 1860 federal census as residing on a farm in the town of Rushford at P.O. Waukau. Listed with them were the following children: Leopold, born circa 1835; Thomas; Eva, born circa 1847; and Anna, born circa 1852. All of the children were born in Germany. Thomas enlisted at Rushford on Aug. 15, 1862. He was assigned as above and was then promoted to Corporal in that company. He was wounded at Peach Tree Creek, Georgia and was mustered out on June 8, 1865. Thomas was listed in 1905 as residing at the Wisconsin Veterans' Home at King. He was received there from Superior. Thomas was listed in 1920 as residing at Washburn, Bayfield County.
{ROV; 21-33rd; GAR 40th}

ROLLAN, Louis S. - Pvt., Co. D, 41st Regt., Wis. Vol. Inf.
Louis resided at Menasha and enlisted there on May 15, 1864. He was assigned as above and was mustered out on Sept. 23, 1864 at the end of his term of enlistment.
{ROV}

ROLOFF, Heinrich - Pvt., Co. K, 11th Regt., Wis. Vol. Inf.
Heinrich resided at Nekimi and enlisted there on Mar. 10, 1865. He was assigned as above and was mustered out on Sept. 4, 1865.
{ROV}

ROLPH, Columbus T. - Pvt., Co. G, 1st Regt., Wis. Cav.
Columbus was born on Sept. 10, 1830 at New York, a son of John and Sarah Rolph. John was born circa 1793 at Massachusetts and Sarah was born circa 1797 at Vermont. Columbus was married in Winnebago County on Nov. 23, 1858 to Alice E. Atherton. She was born circa 1845 at Prince Edward Island, Canada and she was a daughter of Elisabeth Atherton. Elisabeth was born circa 1805 at England. Columbus was listed in the 1860 federal census as born circa 1834 and residing on a farm in the town of Utica at P.O. Oshkosh. Also residing there were his parents and Alice's mother. Columbus listed his residence as Waukau when he enlisted on Oct. 8, 1861. He was assigned as above. Columbus contracted a disease and died at St. Louis, Missouri on Feb. 13, 1863 at age 31 years. He is buried in the town of Omro at Tice Cemetery. Members of his family are buried on the same plot.
{US 1860; ROV; WCMR v.1, p.175, #840; Cem. records}

ROLPH, George W. - Pvt., Co. C, 21st Regt., Wis. Vol. Inf.
George was born on Oct. 1, 1833 at New York. He was married in Winnebago County on Aug. 28, 1855 to Clarissa Rogers. She was born on July 28, 1835 at New York and was a daughter of Jude F. and Adaline (Warner) Rogers. Jude was born circa 1811 at New York. George and Clarissa were listed in the 1860 federal census as residing with her father and members of his family on a farm in the town of Omro at P.O. Waukau.

ROLPH, George W. (cont.)
George listed his residence as Utica when he enlisted on Aug. 13, 1862. He was assigned as above and was killed at Chaplin Hills, Kentucky on Oct. 8, 1862. George and Clarissa had a son, Eugene A., who was born on Nov. 27, 1857. George W., another son, was born circa 1858 and was listed with his parents in the 1860 census. George is buried in the town of Omro at Minckler Cemetery. Clarissa was married again in Winnebago County on Sept. 25, 1865 to John S. Baker, he being the subject of a previous sketch.
{US 1860; WCMR v.1, p.159, #713; Randall p.29; WCMR v.1, p.159, #713; ROV}
{Cem records; OWN 07 May 1863; WCMR v.1, p.282, #1759}

ROOD, Frank Hiram - Pvt., Co. F, 18th Regt., Wis. Vol. Inf.
Frank resided at Oshkosh and enlisted there on Jan. 9, 1862. He was assigned as a musician in the above company and was then promoted to Principle Musician of that regiment on Aug. 5, 1863. Frank was mustered out on Mar. 14, 1865.
{ROV}

ROOD, Hosea Whitford - Cpl., Co. E, 12th Regt., Wis. Vol. Inf.
Hosea was born on May 30, 1845 at Persia, Cattaraugus County, New York. He was a son of Charles P. and Marianne (Thorngate) Rood. Charles was born on May 13, 1823 at Highgate, Franklin County, Vermont and was a son of Burrell and Mary Rood. He was married in July 1844 at Clarence, Jefferson County, New York to Marianne, daughter of George and Matilda Thorngate. Charles and Marianne, along with her parents and their family, removed to Wisconsin in Sept. 1845. They landed in the village of Milwaukee and then removed to a farm in the town of Lake, Milwaukee County. After two years, Charles and Marianne moved to Johnstown, Rock County. In 1850 they removed to Waushara County. The Thorngate family settled there in the town of Dakota. The Rood family settled west of there in the town of Richford, where Charles and Marianne settled in a log home on May 13, 1850. The subject of this sketch, received permission from his father to go "on the prairie" in 1861 and hire out for the summer season. He walked the 70 miles to Dane County and found work with Dwight Brown in the town of Vienna. At the outbreak of the war, Hosea enlisted at Vienna on Oct. 6, 1861 and was assigned as above. In Jan. 1863, while the regiment was at Natchez, Mississippi Hosea and most of the regiment re-enlisted. On Mar. 13, 1863 the regiment began a "veteran furlough" and then joined the 17th Army Corps, travelling to join Gen. Sherman at Kenesaw Mountain, Georgia. Hosea was slightly wounded on July 21, 1863 at Bald Hill, Georgia. After remaining with his company for a week, he was sent to a hospital due to pain and fatigue. He re-joined his company in time for the "march to the sea." The regiment was then mustered out on July 16, 1865 at Louisville, Kentucky. Hosea returned home at the same time that his father and a brother were returning from their military service. Of this entire family, the father and three sons served in the Union Army. Four brothers of Hosea's mother also served in the military. Charles Rood died on Mar. 18, 1877 at North Loup, Nebraska. His wife and her father survived him at that place. Hosea was married in Waushara County on Oct. 13, 1866 to Ann E. Munroe. They had four children: Louis P. Harvey, born in 1867; Minnie May, died in infancy in 1869; Ida Lillian, born in 1870; and Lola Grace, born in 1885. Hosea began to teach in the common schools of Waushara County immediately after the war ended. He was principal at the following high schools: Sun Prairie, 1 year; Pewaukee, 1 year; Cadott, 1 year; Omro, 6 years; and Palmyra, at least four years.

ROOD, Hosea Whitford (cont.)
Hosea was listed in the veteran section of the 1885 Wisconsin State census at P.O. Omro. He was listed in that section of the 1905 state census at P.O. Madison, Dane County.
{WC-V 1885, 1905; ROV; SCA p.604-8}

ROOD, J.B. - Chaplain, 49th Regt., New York Vol. Inf.
He was listed as above in the veteran section of the 1895 Wisconsin State census at P.O. Oshkosh.
{WC-V 1895}

ROOD, Jeremiah - Pvt., Unassigned, 3rd Regt., Wis. Vol. Inf.
Jeremiah resided at Oshkosh and enlisted there on Sept. 1, 1862. He was listed as unassigned in the 3rd Regt. and was not found in the records of any company within that regiment.
{ROV}

ROOT, Charles - Pvt., Co. M, 3rd Regt., Wis. Cav.
Charles was born in March 1845 at New York. His parents were both natives of Pennsylvania. Charles resided at Fulton, Rock County and enlisted on Nov. 2, 1863. He was assigned as above and was transferred to Co. F, 3rd (reorg.) Regt., Wis. Cav. on Mar. 23, 1865. He was mustered out on Sept. 29, 1865. Charles was listed in the 1890 federal census as residing in the city of Oshkosh. He was listed in the veteran section of the 1895 Wisconsin State census at P.O. Oshkosh. Charles was listed in the 1900 federal census as residing at the Wisconsin Veterans' home at King. Olive B., his wife of 27 years, was residing there with him. She was born in Aug. 1853 at New York and her parents were both natives of that state. Charles and Olive had no children. Charles and Olive were listed in 1905 as residing at King. Both were again listed there in the 1910 federal census.
{US 1890, 1900, 1910; WC-V 1895; ROV; GAR 40th}

ROOT, Josiah M. - Pvt., Co. K, 43rd Regt., Wis. Vol. Inf.
Josiah was born on Sept. 26, 1833 at Litchfield County, Connecticut. He was a son of Ira and Sallie Ann (Morse) Root. Ira died in Connecticut in 1842 and Sallie died there circa 1856. Josiah was educated mainly at Norwalk, Ohio where he spent about five years in school and clerking. He then learned the baker's trade and followed such for a number of years in many places, mostly in Ohio and Indiana. Josiah then established his own shop at Norwalk, Ohio. In the course of his travels, he met Elizabeth E. Ripley of Logansport, Indiana. They were married on Nov. 21, 1854. She was born in Ohio on Oct. 28, 1830 and was a daughter of David and Christina Ripley. Both parents were natives of Pennsylvania. Josiah sold his business at Norwalk in 1856 and removed to Wisconsin, where he settled on a farm of over 200 acres in the town of Brooklyn, Green County. Josiah and Elizabeth had three children: Jennie, born on Feb. 8, 1857; Florett "Ettie," born on Nov. 13, 1858, died in Sept. 1885; and John, born on Nov. 13, 1860, married Fannie E., died in 1931. Josiah was residing at Brooklyn, Green County when he enlisted on Aug. 29, 1864. He was assigned as above and was then mustered out on June 24, 1865. William L. and Mortimer Root were assigned to that same company. Josiah was listed in the 1890 federal census as residing in the town of Nepeuskun at P.O. Berlin, Green Lake County. He was listed in 1905, with Elizabeth, as residing on 162 acres of section 7 in the town of Nepeuskun. Josiah died on Mar. 21, 1908 and Elizabeth

ROOT, Josiah M. (cont.)
died on Mar. 5, 1922. Both are buried with members of their family in the town of Nepeuskun at Koro Cemetery.
{US 1890; ROV; Randall p.28-9; Cem. records; B-1905}

ROOT, Russell L. - Pvt., Co. D, 32nd Regt., Wis. Vol. Inf.
Russell resided at Oshkosh and enlisted there on Dec. 8, 1863. He was assigned as above and was transferred to Co. D, 16th (reorg.) Regt., Wis. Vol. Inf. on July 4, 1865. Russell was mustered out on July 12, 1865.
{ROV}

RORABACK, John W. - Cpl., Co. H, 74th Regt., New York National Guard.
John was listed as above in the 1890 federal census as residing at 45 Mt. Vernon Street in the city of Oshkosh. No service dates or other information were provided.
{US 1890}

ROSE, James - Pvt., 9th Batt., Wis. Lt. Art.
James resided at Oshkosh and enlisted there on Oct. 19, 1861. He was assigned as above and was mustered out on Sept. 30, 1865.
{ROV}

ROSE, Phillip - Pvt., Co. D, 21st Regt., Wis. Vol. Inf.
Phillip was born on Apr. 11, 1836 at Ballston Spa, New York. He removed to Wisconsin in 1857. He was married at Greenville, Outagamie County on Feb. 3, 1861 to Mrs. Sarah A. Brien. She was born on July 27, 1842 at LeRoy, Jefferson County, New York and was a daughter of George W. and Phoebe A. Boone. Sarah came west with her parents in 1851 and settled at Greenville. Phillip resided at Ellington, Outagamie County and enlisted there on Aug. 14, 1862. He was assigned as above and was discharged on Aug. 28, 1863 due to wounds received in the battle at Perryville. Phillip then removed to Oshkosh, where he was listed in 1868 as a filer residing at 25 South Algoma in the city. He was listed in the veteran section of the 1885, 1895 and 1905 Wisconsin State census at P.O. Oshkosh. Phillip was listed in the 1890 federal census as residing in Oshkosh. He was listed in 1905 as an employee of the R. McMillen Co. and residing at 38 Congress Street in Oshkosh. Sarah died on Feb. 9, 1920 at Oshkosh and Phillip died three days later, on Feb. 12, 1920. They shared a common funeral and were buried in the same grave. They were survived by daughters Mrs. Dora M. Welton and Mrs. G.W. Hutchinson and son George E. Rose. Phillip was a member of GAR Post #10 at the time of his death.
{US 1890; WC-V 1885, 1895, 1905; ROV; T-1868; 21-33rd; B-1905}

ROSE, William - Pvt., Co. D, 7th Regt., Wis. Vol. Inf.
William resided at Liberty and was drafted there on Dec. 28, 1864. He was assigned as above and was mustered out on July 3, 1865. William was listed in the veteran section of the 1885 Wisconsin State census at P.O. Poygan.
{WC-V 1885; ROV}

ROSENOW, Charles Bernard - Pvt., Co. I, 21st Regt., Wis. Vol. Inf.
Charles was born circa 1839 at Prussia. He was listed in the 1860 federal census as a turner residing with the family of Noel Coates in the first ward of the village of

ROSENOW, Charles Bernard (cont.)
Menasha. Charles enlisted first as a Private in Co. G, 10th Regt., Wis. Vol. Inf. He was promoted to Corporal in that company and was discharged on July 15, 1862 due to a disability. Charles still resided at Menasha when he re-enlisted on Dec. 19, 1863. He was assigned as above and was then transferred to Co. G, 3rd Regt., Wis. Vol. Inf. on June 8, 1865. Charles was mustered out on July 18, 1865. He was listed in 1868 as a clerk boarding at the Adams House in the city of Oshkosh. Charles was married in Winnebago County on Aug. 12, 1868 to Emeline Clarissa Wilkins.
{US 1860; ROV; T-1868; Lawson p.807; WCMR v.1, p.392, #2430}

ROSENTHAL, Rudolph W. - Pvt., Co. C, 9th Regt., Wis. Vol. Inf.
Rudolph was born in 1832 and Charlotte F., his wife, was born in 1840. Rudolph resided at Oshkosh and enlisted there on Sept. 10, 1861. He was assigned as above and was transferred to Co. G of that same regiment on June 5, 1864. Rudolph was again transferred to Co. B, 9th (reorg.) Regt., Wis. Vol. Inf. and he was then mustered out on Jan. 30, 1866. He was listed (Rosenther) in 1868 as a mill man boarding at the Winnebago Hotel in the city of Oshkosh. Rudolph was listed in 1905, with Lottie, as residing on 80 acres of section 11 in the town of Vinland. Richard and Mattie Rosenthal were also residing there. Rudolph died in 1911 and Charlotte died in 1922. Both are buried in the town of Vinland at Brooks Cemetery.
{ROV; T-1868; B-1905; Cem. records}

ROSENWATER, Ole - Pvt., Co. B, 6th Regt., Wis. Vol. Inf.
Ole resided at Utica and was drafted there on Sept. 30, 1864. He was assigned as above and was mustered out on June 8, 1865.
{ROV}

ROSS, John - Sgt., Co. G, 44th Regt., Wis. Vol. Inf.
John was born on May 5, 1830. He resided at Springdale, Dane County and enlisted on Jan. 8, 1865. He was assigned as above and was promoted to Sergeant in that company. He was mustered out on Aug. 28, 1865. John was listed in the veteran section of the 1885 and 1895 Wisconsin State census at P.O. Omro. He was listed in the 1890 federal census as residing in the town of Omro at P.O. Omro. John died on July 21, 1902. Anna, his wife, was born on Nov. 24, 1835 and died on Nov. 1, 1883. Both are buried at Omro Cemetery, Olin's Addition, Section B, plot 22. Several members of their family are buried on that same plot.
{US 1890; WC-V 1885, 1895; ROV; Cem. records}

ROUGHT, George M. - Pvt., Co. C, 1st Regt., Wis. Hvy. Art.
George was born circa 1845 at New York. He was a son of Jacob and Christina Rought. Both parents were natives of New York, the father born there circa 1822 and the mother born circa 1823. They were listed (Raught) in the 1860 federal census as residing on a farm in the town of Clayton at P.O. Neenah. Listed with them were George and a daughter, Margaretta, who was born circa 1848 at New York. Also listed with them was Jacob Raught, father of Jacob. He was born circa 1775 at Germany. George enlisted at Neenah on Aug. 29, 1863. He was assigned as above and then was mustered out on Sept. 21, 1865. George was married in Winnebago County on Nov. 28, 1865 to June Slover.
{US 1860; ROV; WCMR v.1, p.293, #1787}

ROUSE, Walter R. - Sgt., Co. E, 2nd Regt., Wis. Vol. Inf.
He was listed as Walker Rouse in the 1860 federal census and residing in the first ward of the city of Oshkosh. Walter was then shown as a painter. He was born circa 1840 at New York. Walter enlisted at Oshkosh on Apr. 21, 1861. He was assigned as above and was promoted to Corporal, Sergeant and then 1st Sergeant in that company. Walter was wounded in the first battle at Bull Run, Virginia and he was wounded and taken prisoner at Gainesville, Virginia on Aug. 28, 1862. He was wounded on July 1, 1863 at Gettysburg, Pennsylvania. Walter died of those wounds on July 11, 1863. He is buried at Gettysburg National Cemetery in the innermost arc of one semi-circle of graves.
{US 1860; ROV; ODN 11 Nov ___; OWN 11 Sep 1862}

ROWE, John - Cpl., Co. I, 7th Regt., Wis. Vol. Inf.
John resided at Wautoma, Waushara County and enlisted there on Aug. 2, 1861. He was assigned as above and was promoted to Corporal in that company. He was then mustered out on July 3, 1865. John was listed in the veteran section of the 1885 Wisconsin State census at P.O. Pine River, Waushara County. He was listed in 1888 as a member of GAR Post #10 at Oshkosh. John was listed in the 1890 federal census as residing in the town of Weyauwega, Waupaca County. He was listed in the veteran section of the 1895 and 1905 Wisconsin State census at P.O. Omro. He was listed in 1905 as a laborer residing on Pearl Street in the village of Omro.
{US 1890; WC-V 1885, 1895, 1905; ROV; B-1905}

ROWELL, Daniel E. - Pvt., Co. H, 37th Regt., New York Vol. Inf.
Mary J., widow of Daniel, was listed in the 1890 federal census as residing in the town of Omro at P.O. Omro. She then provided his unit designation as above. She also provided his dates of service as having been from May 10, 1861 to Sept. 15, 1861.
{US 1890}

ROWLEY, Stephen N. - Pvt., Co. G, 30th Regt., Michigan Vol. Inf.
Stephen was listed as above in the veteran section of the 1905 Wisconsin State census at P.O. Oshkosh. He was listed in that year as a commercial traveler residing at 164 W. Lincoln Avenue in the city of Oshkosh.
{WC-V 1905; B-1905}

ROYER, Albert H. - Pvt., Co. A, 47th Regt., Wis. Vol. Inf.
Albert was born circa 1830 at Ohio. He was a son of Ephraim and Catharine Royer and a brother of Henry and James from following sketches. Ephraim was born circa 1805 and Catharine was born circa 1807. They were listed in the 1860 federal census as residing on a farm in the town of Winchester. Listed with them were the following children: Albert; Henry; James; Annie, born circa 1843; Amelia, born circa 1845; and Catharine, born circa 1848. All of the children were born in Ohio. Albert enlisted at Winchester on Feb. 11, 1865. He was assigned as above and was then mustered out on Sept. 4, 1865.
{US 1860; ROV}

ROYER, Christian - Cpl., Co. A, 47th Regt., Wis. Vol. Inf.
Christian was born circa 1840 at Ohio. He was a son of Margaret Royer and a brother of George from a following sketch. Margaret was born circa 1821 at Ohio. She was listed in the 1860 federal census as residing on a farm in the town of Winchester at P.O.

ROYER, Christian (cont.)
Rat River. Listed with her were the following children: Christian; George; Miranda, born circa 1845 at Ohio; and Sarah, born circa 1848 at Ohio. Christian enlisted at Winchester on Feb. 10, 1865. He was assigned as above and was promoted to Corporal in that company. Christian was mustered out on Sept. 4, 1865.
{US 1860; ROV}

ROYER, George - Pvt., Co. A, 47th Regt., Wis. Vol. Inf.
George was born circa 1842 at Ohio. He was a son of Margaret Royer and a brother of Christian from a previous sketch. George was listed in the 1860 federal census as residing with his mother and her family on a farm in the town of Winchester at P.O. Rat River. He enlisted at Winchester on Feb. 10, 1865. He was assigned as above and was then mustered out on Sept. 4, 1865.
{US 1860; ROV}

ROYER, Henry W. - Cpl., Co. A, 47th Regt., Wis. Vol. Inf.
Henry was born circa 1832 at Ohio. He was a son of Ephraim P. and Catharine Royer and a brother of Albert and James from other sketches. Henry resided at Winchester and enlisted there on Feb. 10, 1865. He was assigned as above and was promoted to Corporal in that company. Henry was then mustered out on Sept. 4, 1865. He died on Dec. 19, 1868 at age 36 years, 10 months and 5 days. Henry is buried with members of his family in the town of Clayton at Royer Cemetery.
{US 1860; ROV; Cem. records}

ROYER, James D. - Pvt., Co. K, 11th Regt., Wis. Vol. Inf.
James was born circa 1834 at Ohio. He was a son of Ephraim and Catharine Royer and a brother of Albert and Henry from previous sketches. James was listed in the 1860 federal census as residing with his parents and their family on a farm in the town of Winchester. He enlisted at Winchester on Oct. 20, 1861. He was assigned as above. James contracted a disease and died on June 28, 1862 at Batesville, Arkansas.
{US 1860; ROV}

RUBACH, Theodore - Cpl., Co. C, 10th Regt., Wis. Vol. Inf.
Theodore resided at Menasha and enlisted there on Aug. 14, 1861. He was assigned as above and was promoted to Corporal in that company. He was wounded at Perryville, Kentucky and again at Chickamauga, Georgia. He was mustered out on Nov. 3, 1864.
{ROV}

RUBACH, William - Pvt., Co. I, 21st Regt., Wis. Vol. Inf.
William resided at Menasha and enlisted there on Aug. 9, 1862. He was assigned as above and was discharged on Jan. 8, 1863 due to a disability. William re-enlisted on June 4, 1864 and was assigned as a Private to Co. D of the same regiment. He was transferred to the 3rd Regt., Wis. Vol. Inf. on June 8, 1865 and was mustered out on July 18, 1865.
{ROV}

RUBY, James N. - Capt., Co. B, 34th Regt., Wis. Vol. Inf.
James was born on Dec. 17, 1835 at Mt. Vernon, Knox County, Ohio. He was a son of James and Marcia A. (Reynolds) Ruby. The father was born in 1811 at St. Johns, New

RUBY, James N. (cont.)
Brunswick, Canada and the mother was born in 1812 at New York. They were married on Jan. 1, 1832 at Malone, New York. The following spring they settled in Knox County, Ohio. In 1853 they removed to Wisconsin and settled at Baraboo, Sauk County. They removed to Berlin, Green Lake County in 1857 and to Oshkosh in 1859. The father was a carpenter by trade and he died in Oshkosh in 1866 as the result of falling from a building. Marcia died in 1875 at Westfield, Marquette County. James, the subject of this sketch, left home at age fourteen years. For several years he was variously employed in different states. In 1853 he located at Philadelphia, Pennsylvania and worked there as a painter for two years. James joined the Unites States Army in 1855 and served for five years. At the end of his term of enlistment he came to Oshkosh and joined his parents. James enlisted at Oshkosh on Apr. 21, 1861. He was assigned as a Private to Co. E, 2nd Regt., Wis. Vol. Inf. and was promoted to Sergeant in that company. James was promoted to Sergeant Major of that regiment. He was then commissioned as 2nd Lieutenant of that company on Aug. 8, 1861 and he resigned on Nov. 27, 1861. James re-enlisted at Oshkosh on Dec. 2, 1861 and was commissioned as Captain of Co. B, 34th Regt., Wis. Vol. Inf. He was mustered out on Sept. 8, 1863 at the end of his term of enlistment. James was married on Mar. 16, 1864 to Sarah J. Willoch. She was born on Jan. 9, 1844 at Lowell, Massachusetts and was a daughter of James and Margaret (Mason) Willoch. James and Sarah had three children: Margaret W., born on Mar. 26, 1866; Katie E., born on Feb. 5, 1868; and James M., born on Nov. 26, 1873. James was listed in 1868 as a carpenter residing at 83 High Street in the city of Oshkosh. He was listed in the 1890 federal census as residing at 401 Main Street in Oshkosh. James was listed in the veteran section of the 1885, 1895 and 1905 Wisconsin State census at P.O. Oshkosh. He was listed in 1905 as a rural mail carrier residing at 401 Main Street in of Oshkosh. Son James M. Ruby was also listed at that address.
{US 1890; WC-V 1885, 1895, 1905; ROV; T-1868; Randall p.45; B-1905}

RUEGE, William - Pvt., Co. C, 53rd Regt., Wis. Vol. Inf.
William was married in Winnebago County on Dec. 13, 1861 to Frederica Brandt. He resided at Menasha and enlisted there on Mar. 8, 1865. He was assigned as above. That company was then transferred to Co. K, 51st Regt., Wis. Vol. Inf. under orders dated June 10, 1865. The transfer was completed at Ft. Leavenworth, Kansas on June 30, 1865 and the regiment returned to Madison, Wisconsin on Aug. 1, 1865. The men were mustered out by companies with the last having been mustered out on Aug. 30, 1865.
{ROV; WCMR v.1, p.222, #1219}

RUMSEY, George W. - Pvt., Co. A, 38th Regt., Wis. Vol. Inf.
George was born on June 6, 1838 at New York. Iphelia, his mother, was born circa 1815 at New York. She was listed in the 1860 federal census as residing in the town of Omro. Listed with her were the following children: Richard, born circa 1839 at New York; George; and Almeda, born circa 1850 at Illinois. George listed his residence as Fond du Lac when he enlisted on Mar. 21, 1864. He was assigned as above and was discharged on Aug. 10, 1864 due to a disability. He was listed in the 1880 federal census as residing in the town of Omro. George was also listed in the veteran section of the 1885, 1895 and 1905 Wisconsin State census at P.O. Omro. He was listed in the 1890 federal census as residing in the village of Omro. George listed that he was suffering from rheumatism and a heart disease as a result of exposure. He was listed in 1905 as

RUMSEY, George W. (cont.)
retired and residing at 214 High Street in Omro. Sarah H. Pool, his wife, was born Mar. 29, 1842 at Wisconsin and she died on Aug. 8, 1908. Her parents were born in Scotland. The death date on George's marker is submerged. Both are buried at Omro Cemetery, Original Section, plot 18.
{US 1860, 1880, 1890; WC-V 1885, 1895, 1905; B-1905; Cem. records; ROV}

RUMSEY, George W. - Pvt., Co. K, 48th Regt., Wis. Vol. Inf.
George resided at Waupun, Fond du Lac County and he enlisted there on Mar. 13, 1865. He was assigned as above and was mustered out on July 18, 1865. George was listed in the veteran section of the 1905 Wisconsin State census at P.O. Oshkosh.
{WC-V 1905; ROV}

RUPPERT, Joseph - Pvt., Co. C, 9th Regt., Wis. Vol. Inf.
Joseph resided at Oshkosh and enlisted there on Sept. 8, 1861. He was assigned as above and was transferred to Co. A of that same regiment on Jan. 1, 1864. Joseph was mustered out on Dec. 3, 1864 at the end of his term of enlistment. He was listed in the 1890 federal census as residing at the Wisconsin Veterans' Home at King. Joseph then provided that he had also served with the 5th Regt., Veteran Reserve Corps.
{US 1890; ROV}

RUSH, Thomas - Pvt., Co. B, 37th Regt., Wis. Vol. Inf.
Thomas resided at Oshkosh and enlisted there on Mar. 26, 1864. He was assigned as above and was listed as having deserted on Apr. 28, 1864.
{ROV}

RUSHTON, Thomas - Pvt., Co. H, 18th Regt., Wis. Vol. Inf.
Thomas was born in Feb. 1828 at England. His parents were both natives of that country. Thomas emigrated to the United States in 1853. He was listed in the 1860 federal census as a farm laborer for Robert S. Mathe in the town of Nepeuskun at P.O. Waukau. Thomas enlisted at Waukau on Dec. 19, 1861. He was assigned as above and was mustered out on Mar. 14, 1865 at the end of his term of enlistment. Thomas was listed in the 1890 federal census as residing at the Wisconsin Veterans' Home at King. He was listed again in the 1900 federal census at King. Thomas had been married then for 50 years. He was not listed as a widower but his wife was not residing with him.
{US 1860, 1890, 1900; ROV}

RUSSELL, Charles - Pvt., Co. C, 46th Regt., Wis. Vol. Inf.
Charles resided at Algoma and enlisted there on Feb. 10, 1865. He was mustered out on Sept. 27, 1865.
{ROV}

RUSSELL, Charles H. - Pvt., Co. E, __ Regt., New York Vol. Inf.
Charles was listed as above in the veteran section of the 1885 Wisconsin State census at P.O. Omro. A Charles Russell was married in Winnebago County on Sept. 28, 1852 to Sarah Ann Bower. A Charles Russell is listed in "Wisconsin - History and People" on pages 64-5. That sketch makes it appear that he is the same person as the previous Charles Russell but it also provides conflicting information. The Charles who married

RUSSELL, Charles H. (cont.)
Sarah was listed in the 1860 federal census in Winnebago County on p. 160.
{US 1860; WC-V 1885}

RUSSELL, David W. - Pvt., Co. A, 13th Regt., Wis. Vol. Inf.
David resided at Janesville, Rock County and enlisted there on Sept. 5, 1861. He was assigned as above and was discharged due to a disability on May 27, 1862. David was listed in the veteran section of the 1895 Wisconsin State census at P.O. Eureka.
{WC-V 1895; ROV}

RUSSELL, Francis T. - Pvt., Co. B, 1st Regt., Wis. Cav.
Francis enlisted on Aug. 30, 1864 and was assigned as above. He was mustered out on July 19, 1865. Frank T. Russell was married in Winnebago County on Dec. 11, 1868 to Elletta Brown. Francis was listed as above in the veteran section of the 1885 and 1895 Wisconsin State census at P.O. Neenah. He was listed (Frank F.) in the 1890 federal census as residing in the city of Neenah. Frank was listed in 1905 as a manufacturer residing at 115 Harrison Street in Neenah. Gregg and John Russell were also residing at that address.
{US 1890; WC-V 1885, 1895; ROV; B-1905; WCMR v.1, p.405, #2534}

RUSSELL, Hiram - Lt., Co. B, 21st Regt., Wis. Vol. Inf.
Hiram was born on Dec. 4, 1828 at Salisbury, Connecticut. He came to Wisconsin in 1849 and settled at Oshkosh, where he was employed as a clerk in the store of H.C. Jewell in Algoma. After 4 years, he bought out his employer and continued the store alone for another two years. Hiram then sold out and removed to Fremont, Waupaca County where he formed a partnership with Flavious George in the lumber business. Hiram enlisted at Fremont. He was commissioned as 1st Lieutenant of the above company on Aug. 26, 1862. Hiram was wounded and taken prisoner at Chickamauga, Georgia on Sept. 20, 1863. He was soon exchanged and then returned home. He was then promoted to Captain of that company on Dec. 26, 1863 and, although commanding the company, he was not mustered at that rank. He then resigned his commission on Aug. 6, 1864 due to a disability. Hiram was listed in 1868 as an agent for the Wolf River Boom Co. and boarding at the Empire House in the city of Oshkosh. He entered into a business with J.H. Weed and removed with his family to Barnum, Adams County. The family resided there until 1878, when they returned to Oshkosh. Hiram left Oshkosh for the woods on Oct. 25, 1879 to commence winter operations. He arrived at Stevens Point and went into the woods the following day. Hiram contracted a cold and returned to Stevens Point. This turned into inflammatory rheumatism and, with his wife by his side, Hiram died there on Nov. 17, 1879. He was survived by his wife, three sons and two daughters. Hiram was returned to Oshkosh for burial. Marie M., his widow, was listed in 1883 at P.O. Winneconne. She had been receiving a widow's pension of $8 per month since April 1881. She was listed in the 1890 federal census as residing in the village of Winneconne.
{US 1890; ROV; T-1868; LOP-1883; OCT 22 Nov 1879}

RUSSELL, Jacob - Pvt., Co. A, 113th Regt., Illinois Vol. Inf.
Jacob was born circa 1825 at New York. Both of his parents were natives of that state. Jacob was listed as above in the 1890 federal census and residing in the town of Rushford at P.O. Waukau. He then provided his service dates as having been from Mar. 1861 to

RUSSELL, Jacob (cont.)
Aug. 1864. Jacob was listed in the 1910 federal census as residing at the Wisconsin Veterans' Home at King. He had been married twice, the last 35 years to Emmie. She was born circa 1844 at New York. It was her only marriage and they had no children.
{US 1890, 1910}

RUSSELL, John - Pvt., Co. E, 8th Regt., Illinois Vol. Inf.
John was listed as above in the veteran section of the 1885 Wisconsin State census at P.O. Neenah. He was listed in the 1890 federal census as residing in the city of Neenah. John provided no information on his military service at that time. He was listed there in the veteran section of the 1895 state census as having been a Sergeant Major in that regiment. John was listed at Neenah in that part of the 1905 state census as having been a Private in the 4th Regt., Ill. Vol. Inf. He was listed in 1905 as residing at 430 Second Street in Neenah.
{US 1890; WC-V 1885, 1895, 1905; B-1905}

RUSSELL, John - Sgt., Co. B, 4th Regt., Wis. Cav.
John resided at Ripon, Fond du Lac County and enlisted there on Nov. 9, 1861. He was assigned as above and was promoted to Corporal and then Sergeant in that company. He was mustered out on Nov. 4, 1865. John was listed in the veteran section of the 1905 Wisconsin State census at P.O. Oshkosh. He was listed that same year as residing at 23 Division Street in the city of Oshkosh.
{WC-V 1905; ROV; B-1905}

RUSSELL, Joseph H. - Pvt., Co. D, 40th Regt., New York Vol. Inf.
Joseph was listed as above in the 1890 federal census as residing in the town of Oshkosh at P.O. Oshkosh. He then provided his service dates as having been from Feb. 1864 to July 1865.
{US 1890}

RUSSELL, Lewis A. - Pvt., Co. E, 5th (reorg.) Regt., Wis. Vol. Inf.
Lewis resided at Nepeuskun and enlisted there on Sept. 3, 1864. He was assigned as above and was mustered out on June 20, 1865.
{ROV}

RUSSELL, Thomas P. Jr. - Asst. Surg., 2nd Regt., Wis. Vol. Inf.
Thomas was born Apr. 19, 1827 at Bethel, Vermont. He was a son of Thomas Pember and Martha Russell. The father was born on Aug. 31, 1792 at Windsor, Connecticut. When he was a young boy, his father moved the family to Windsor County, Vermont. Thomas Sr. was raised there. At a young age he was elected as Probate Judge for that district and he held the position for 16 years. Thomas removed to Wisconsin in 1854 and settled at Oshkosh. He was attracted there by his son, the subject of this sketch. Martha, wife of Hon. Thomas Russell, was born circa 1892 at Vermont. Thomas Sr. was listed in the 1860 federal census as residing in the second ward of the city of Oshkosh. Residing with him were his wife and a daughter, Martha, who was born circa 1825 at Vermont. The family of Solomon Blodgett was also residing with him. Thomas Jr. was listed in that same census as a physician residing in the first ward of the city of Oshkosh. Sophia, his wife, was born circa 1830 at New York. Thomas W., their son, was born circa 1858 at Wisconsin. He was the only one of their three children to reach

RUSSELL, Thomas P. Jr. (cont.)
majority age. Thomas Sr. died in Oshkosh on Dec. 22, 1876. Thomas Jr. graduated from the Vermont Medical College in 1852. He practiced for two years at Weston, Vermont and then removed to Oshkosh. His wife of several years, Myra F. Edgerton, died at Oshkosh about 1856. Thomas was then married in 1856 to Sophia M. Edgerton, a cousin of Benjamin Edgerton of Oshkosh. Sophia was apparently not related to his first wife. Thomas Jr. enlisted at Oshkosh and was commissioned as 1st Assistant Surgeon of the above regiment on May 10, 1861. He resigned his commission in July 1861. His obituary stated that he was later assigned to the 1st Regt., Wis. Cav. In 1868 he was listed as Thomas P. Russell Jr., a physician residing at 12 Algoma Street in Oshkosh. Thomas was listed in the veteran section of the 1885 Wisconsin State census at P.O. Oshkosh. He was listed in 1888 as a member of GAR Post #10 at Oshkosh. He was listed in the 1890 federal census as residing in Oshkosh. Sophia died in Oshkosh on Dec. 14, 1904. Thomas was listed in 1905 as a physician and surgeon residing at 26 Algoma Street in Oshkosh. Son Thomas was also residing there. After an illness of just one day, Thomas died at his home in Oshkosh on Oct. 5, 1917. He is buried there in Riverside Cemetery.
{US 1860, 1890; WC-V 1885; T-1868; ODN 23 Dec 1876; ODN 14 Dec 1904; B-1905}
{ODN 06 Oct 1917; ROV}

RUSSELL, Willard A. - Pvt., Co. B, 21st Regt., Wis. Vol. Inf.
Willard resided at Winneconne and enlisted there on Aug. 14, 1862. He was assigned as above. Willard contracted a disease and died on Feb. 17, 1863 at Murfreesboro, Tennessee.
{ROV}

RUSSELL, William H. - Pvt., 2nd Regt., Marine Brigade.
William was listed as above in the veteran section of the 1905 Wisconsin State census at P.O. Neenah.
{WC-V 1905}

RUTHERFORD, Joseph - Pvt., Co. C, 52nd Regt., Wis. Vol. Inf.
Joseph resided at Oakland, Jefferson County and enlisted there on Mar. 8, 1865. He was assigned as above and was mustered out on July 28, 1865. Joseph was listed in the veteran section of the 1885 Wisconsin State census at P.O. Menasha. He was listed in the 1890 federal census as residing on East Polk Street in the city of Oshkosh. He was listed in the veteran section of the 1895 and 1905 state census at P.O. Oshkosh. Joseph was listed in 1905 as a carpenter residing at 327 Mt. Vernon Street in Oshkosh. Lulu, May and Grace A. Rutherford were also listed at that address.
{US 1890; WC-V 1885, 1895, 1905; ROV; B-1905}

RYAN, David Johnston - Cpl., Co. D, 41st Regt., Wis. Vol. Inf.
David was born June 20, 1840 at Ft. Howard, Brown County, Wisconsin. He was a son of Col. Samuel and Martha (Johnston) Ryan and a brother of Sam Ryan of a following sketch. David enlisted at Menasha on Aug. 5, 1862. He was then assigned as a Private to Co. I, 21st Regt., Wis. Vol. Inf. David was shot in the battle at Perryville, Kentucky less than a month after the regiment left Wisconsin. He was left on the field as dead until discovered the following day by Rev. O.P. Clinton, Chaplain of that regiment. He was discharged due to those wounds on Mar. 21, 1863. David re-enlisted on May 15,

RYAN, David Johnston (cont.)
1864 and was assigned as a Private to Co. D, 41st Regt., Wis. Vol. Inf. He was promoted to Corporal in that company and was mustered out on Sept. 23, 1864 at the end of his term of enlistment. David returned to Menasha and resided with his parents until his father died in 1876. He then moved to Appleton with his mother and was still residing there and unmarried in 1888. He was then listed as a member of GAR Post #133 at Appleton. David was still listed at Appleton in 1908.
{ROV; SCA 1:470; SCA 1:385-8; Lawson p.840}

RYAN, Edward - Pvt., Co. C, 45th Regt., Wis. Vol. Inf.
Edward resided at Chilton, Calumet County and enlisted there on Feb. 24, 1865. He was assigned as above and was mustered out on July 17, 1865. He was listed in the 1890 federal census as residing in the city of Oshkosh. Edward was listed in the veteran section of the 1905 Wisconsin State census at P.O. Oshkosh. He was listed in that same year as residing at 181 Cherry Avenue in Oshkosh. D.H. and Sarah Ryan also resided at that address.
{US 1890; WC-V 1905; ROV; B-1905}

RYAN, John - Pvt., Co. B, 3rd Regt., Wis. Cav.
John resided at Oshkosh and enlisted there on Dec. 21, 1861. He was assigned as above and was listed as having deserted on Feb. 7, 1863.
{ROV}

RYAN, Patrick - Pvt., Co. B, 21st Regt., Wis. Vol. Inf.
John resided at Oshkosh and he enlisted on Aug. 14, 1862. He was killed accidentally by a Provost Guard on Aug. 6, 1863 at Nashville, Tennessee.
{ROV}

RYAN, Samuel - Sgt., 5th Regt., Wis. Cav.
Sam was born on Mar. 13, 1824 at Sackett's Harbor, Jefferson County, New York. He was a son of Col. Samuel and Martha (Johnston) Ryan. The father was born circa 1789 at Nenagh, County Tipperary, Ireland. He was an impressed seaman in the British Navy in 1800. He was on a vessel stationed off the American coast during the War of 1812 and he deserted with others of the crew. He was later connected with the United States Army for 20 years, during which he came to Ft. Howard, Brown County, Wisconsin. During that period he also served in the Mexican War. He retired from military service in 1832 and was then engaged by the War Department and the Indian Bureau. He was associated with Governors Cass and Dodge in completing various Indian treaties. Col. Ryan was engaged with the U.S. Land Office about 1843 and moved to Menasha in 1852 to serve as the receiver. His commission as Colonel was issued by Gov. Dodge. Col. Ryan died at Menasha on Apr. 19, 1876 at age 87 years. Martha, his wife, was born in Ireland. After the death of Col. Ryan she removed to Appleton with her son David. She died there in 1883 at age 83 years. Their son Samuel received a small amount of education in the post school at Ft. Howard and in the mission school among the Stockbridge Indians. He was a pupil in the first public school at Green Bay after organization of the Wisconsin Territory. In 1841 he entered employment with Henry O. Sholes at the Green Bay Republican. There he learned the trade of a printer, experiencing every position from roller boy to editor. Samuel was married at Green Bay on June 1, 1847 to Laura Elvira Knappen of Plattsburg, New York. He removed the

RYAN, Samuel (cont.)
business to Fond du Lac, Fond du Lac County in Jan. 1848, where it was then known as the Fond du Lac Republican. He was appointed Postmaster there in 1849. His business soon failed through no fault of his own. Shortly thereafter, on Nov. 2, 1850, Laura died. Samuel resigned his position and returned to Green Bay the following month. He removed to Appleton on Dec. 31, 1852. On Feb. 27, 1853 the first issue of his new Appleton Crescent appeared. Sam was married in 1853 to Calista M. Crane. She was a daughter of W.B. Crane, an early settler of Grand Chute, Outagamie County. Soon after the news of the attack in Charleston Harbor Samuel enlisted a company of which he was made Captain. They went to camp at Fond du Lac with 69 men and were assigned to the 14th Regt., Wis. Vol. Inf. The Adjutant General ordered the company disbanded as it was not filled to regulation size. Most of the men then enlisted in other companies. Sam went to Madison to plead his case but was not successful. About the first day of January in 1862 he enlisted in the 3rd Regt., Wis. Cav. By an oversight he was not formally mustered until Feb. 18, 1862. He was then appointed as the Battalion Quartermaster Sergeant at the head of the regimental Commissary Department. Samuel became ill while at Ft. Leavenworth, Kansas and he was discharged on Dec. 29, 1862 and received his papers in Feb. 1863. Sam returned to Appleton and worked to regain his health. He resumed his former position in May 1864. Sam held many elected and appointed positions within Outagamie County. Calista, his wife, died of consumption in 1869. Sam was then married on Sept. 26, 1870 to Martha S. Driggs. She was a daughter of John J. Driggs, an early settler at Green Bay and a former classmate of his. A photo of Sam can be found in the Soldiers' and Citizens' Album on p. 384. He was elected as a judge in Outagamie County in April 1865 and held that position for eight years. Samuel was appointed in 1895 as U.S. Consul to St. Johns, Newfoundland. Martha died in March 1907 at Appleton. On the way to the cemetery during her funeral Samuel contracted pneumonia. He died on Mar. 26, 1907. Samuel left no immediate family but he was survived by brothers James, Henry and David Ryan, all of Appleton.
{ROV; SCA 1:385-8; OWN 30 Mar 1907; OWN 20 Apr 1876}

SABIN, Levi P. - Cpl., Co. H, 1st Regt., Wis. Hvy. Art.
Levi resided at Menasha and enlisted there on Sept. 8, 1864. He was assigned as above and was promoted to Corporal in that company. Levi was discharged due to a disability on Apr. 27, 1865.
{ROV}

SAFFORD, Adelbert - Pvt., Co. E, 42nd Regt., Wis. Vol. Inf.
Adelbert resided at Omro and enlisted there on Aug. 6, 1864. He was assigned as above and was mustered out on June 7, 1865. Adelbert was married in Winnebago County on Aug. 18, 1872 to Ida E. Tritt. She was a daughter of William Tritt, he the subject of a following sketch. Adelbert was listed in the veteran section of the 1885 and 1895 Wisconsin State census at P.O. Manawa, Waupaca County. He was listed in the 1890 federal census as residing in the town of Little Wolf, Waupaca County at P.O. Manawa. Mrs. Ida E. Safford, widow of Adelbert, was listed in 1905 as residing with William Tritt Sr. on 567 acres in section 26 of the town of Poygan.
{US 1890; WC-V 1885, 1895; ROV; B-1905; WCMR v.1, p.539, #3612}

SAFFORD, Charles A. - Pvt., Co. K, 32nd Regt., Wis. Vol. Inf.
Charles resided at Buffalo, Marquette County and enlisted there on Dec. 25, 1863. He

SAFFORD, Charles A. (cont.)
was assigned as above and was wounded on Aug. 18, 1864 at Atlanta, Georgia. Charles was transferred to Co. I, 16th (reorg.) Regt., Wis. Vol. Inf. on June 4, 1865. He was mustered out on July 12, 1865. Charles was listed in the veteran section of the 1885 Wisconsin State census at P.O. Waupaca, Waupaca County. He was listed in that section of the 1895 state census at P.O. Vernon, Waukesha County and in that part of the 1905 state census at the Wisconsin Veterans' Home at King. Charles is buried with a simple military marker in the town of Omro at Omro Junction Cemetery.
{WC-V 1885, 1895, 1905; ROV; Cem. records}

SAFFORD, Charles O. - Cpl., Co. D, 32nd Regt., Wis. Vol. Inf.
Charles was born on May 18, 1843 at Canada. He was a son of David Safford and a brother of David Wellington Safford from a following sketch. The father was born circa 1816 at Massachusetts, a son of David Safford who was born in 1793 at Connecticut. The father and grandfather were both listed in the 1860 federal census as residing on a farm in the town of Poygan at P.O. Omro. Listed with them then were the following children: Julia, born circa 1840 at Ohio; Charles; Mary, born circa 1845 at Vermont; Wellington; Emerson, born circa 1849 at Vermont; Elzina, born circa 1854 at Wisconsin; and Adelbert, born circa 1859 at Wisconsin. Charles enlisted at Omro on Aug. 20, 1862. He was assigned as above and was promoted to Corporal in that company. He was then mustered out on June 12, 1865. Charles was married in Winnebago County on July 4, 1874 to Katie Stevens. He died June 2, 1882 and is buried at Omro Cemetery, Original Section, plot 101.
{US 1860; ROV; WCMR v.1, p.627, #4314; Cem. records}

SAFFORD, David Wellington - Pvt., Co. D, 32nd Regt., Wis. Vol. Inf.
David was born on Dec. 3, 1848 at Vermont. He was a son of David Safford and a brother of Charles O. from a previous sketch. Wellington was listed in the 1860 federal census as residing with his father on a farm in the town of Poygan at P.O. Omro. He enlisted at Poygan on Dec. 5, 1863. He was assigned as above and was transferred to Co. D, 16th (reorg.) Regt., Wis. Vol. Inf. on June 4, 1865. David was mustered out on July 12, 1865. He provided his residence as Waukau at the time of his transfer. David was married in Winnebago County on Feb. 11, 1871 to Jane M. "Jennie" Lowe. He was listed as William when recording the birth of their daughter Ernestine Stewartson Safford. She was born at Waukau on Nov. 4, ? He was listed in the veteran section of the 1895 Wisconsin State census at P.O. Blair, Trempeleau County and in that section of the 1905 state census at P.O. Omro. David and Jennie were listed in 1905 as residing on 80 acres of section 24 in the town of Rushford. Jennie died in 1894 and David died on Nov. 29, 1923. Both are buried in the town of Rushford at Waukau Cemetery. Emerson, a brother of David, was born in 1850 and died in 1932. He served after the Civil War as a Sergeant in Co. H, 4th Regt., U.S. Army. He was married to Elizabeth A. Thompson. She was born in 1860 and died in 1927. Both are also buried at Waukau Cemetery.
{US 1860; WC-V 1895, 1905; ROV; Cem. records; WCMR v.1, p.487, #3196; B-1905}
{WCBR v.3, p.17, #98}

SAGE, Philo D. - Pvt., Co. C, 14th Regt., Wis. Vol. Inf.
Philo was born in 1824 at New York. He was a son of Daniel T. and Phoebe (Rider) Sage. Daniel was a descendant of David Sage, a settler of Connecticut about 1650. Philo

SAGE, Philo D. (cont.)
was married to Martha Knapp, who was born in 1824 at Vermont. They were listed in the 1860 federal census as residing in the town of Rushford at P.O. Eureka. Philo was then listed as born circa 1830. They had the following children: Emaline, born in 1847; Henrietta, born in 1853; Romaetta, born in 1857, married a Shiner, died in 1880; Daniel G., born on Oct. 13, 1859, married Delia Ott, died on Feb. 12, 1955; and Nellie, born in 1861, married a Read, died in 1899. Philo enlisted at Rushford on Oct. 16, 1861. He was assigned as above and was discharged on Jan. 10, 1863 due to a disability. Philo died in 1873. Martha was listed in 1883 at P.O. Omro and receiving a widow's pension of $8 per month since April 1880. She died in 1888. Both are buried with his parents in the town of Rushford at Rushford Cemetery. Daughters Romaetta and Nellie are buried on the same plot.
{US 1860; ROV; Cem. records; Family Research files of the author; LOP-1883}

SAINDON, Alphonse - Civil War Veteran?
Alphonso was born circa 1837 at Canada. He was listed in the 1860 federal census as residing on a farm with the family of Paul Coates in the town of Rushford at P.O. Eureka. Alphonse died on Aug. 31, 1898 at age 65 years when burned in a fire which destroyed his house. He was described as an "old hermit" and was reputed to have been murdered by the husband of Mrs. Effie Campfield. Alphonse reportedly left a will which left his entire estate to Mrs. Campfield. The will was proven to have a forged signature but Mrs. Campfield appealed the decision. Alphonse is buried in the town of Rushford at Rushford Cemetery. A GAR marker has been placed at his grave. Within an article on the contested will is an etching of Alponse in what appears to be a military uniform.
{US 1860; Cem. records; OWN 06 May 1899}

SALADAY, H.G. - Pvt., 31st Regt., New Jersey Vol. Inf.
He was listed as above in the veteran section of the 1895 Wisconsin State census at P.O. Winneconne. He was also listed (31st Regt., N.Y. Vol. Inf.) in that section of the 1905 state census at P.O. Oshkosh.
{WC-V 1895, 1905}

SAMPHIER, James W. - Sgt., Co. F, 18th Regt., Wis. Vol. Inf.
James was born in 1845 at New York. Both of his parents were natives of Canada and he was a brother of Peter from a following sketch. James removed to Wisconsin in 1845 and settled in Omro. He was listed in the 1860 federal census as residing with brother Peter in the town of Omro. James enlisted at Omro on Oct. 19, 1861 and was assigned as above. He was promoted to Corporal and then Sergeant in that company and was taken prisoner at Allatoona, Georgia. James was mustered out on July 18, 1865. He was married at Macomb, New York on Nov. 29, 1877 to Senora Tullar. She was born on May 25, 1847 in New York and was a daughter of John Snyder. He was listed in the 1880 federal census as residing in the town of Omro. Listed with him was his wife Senora. Both of her parents were natives of New York. Also residing with him was a son Charles J., who was born in 1878 at New York. James was listed in 1883 at P.O. Omro. He was then receiving a pension of $8 per month for wounds to his face and right hand. James was listed in the 1890 federal census as residing in the town of Omro at P.O. Omro. He then reported that he had been shot in the jaw and right hand. James was listed in the veteran section of the 1885, 1895 and 1905 Wisconsin State

SAMPHIER, James W. (cont.)
census at P.O. Omro. He was listed in 1905 as a justice of the peace residing at 307 Lincoln Street in the village of Omro. James died on Mar. 11, 1908. He was survived by his wife and two sons, Charles of Catawba, Pierce County and Blaine of Omro. Blaine died on July 11, 1914. Charles died in 1963. James and Charles are buried at Omro Cemetery, Original Section, plot 47. Senora died at Omro on Sept. 17, 1940. She was survived by son Charles and a sister, Mrs. Serena Wilson of Ogdensburg, New York. She was returned to New York for burial in the plot of her family.
{US 1860, 1880, 1890; WC-V 1885, 1895, 1905; ROV; LOP-1883; Cem. records}
{B-1905; ODN 13 Mar 1908; ODN 17 Sep 1940}

SAMPHIER, Peter - Pvt., Co. C, 3rd Regt., Wis. Cav.
Peter was born in 1835 at New York. He was a brother of James of a previous sketch. Peter was listed in the 1860 federal census as a shoemaker residing in the town of Omro. Mary, his wife, was born circa 1838 at New York. Both of her parents were later shown as natives of England. Peter enlisted at Omro on Feb. 23, 1864 and was assigned as above. He was transferred to Co. H, 3rd (reorg.) Regt., Wis. Cav. on Mar. 23, 1865 and was mustered out on Sept. 29, 1865. Peter was listed in the 1880 federal census as engaged in the operation of a shoe store with his brother James. He was then residing in the village of Omro. Peter was listed in 1883 at P.O. Omro and receiving a pension of $4 per month for a disease of the eyes. He was listed in the veteran section of the 1885 Wisconsin State census at P.O. Omro. Peter died in 1900 and Mary died in 1909. Both are buried at Omro Cemetery, Original Section, plot 26.
{US 1860, 1880; WC-V 1885; ROV; LOP-1883; Cem. records}

SAMSCOTT, Richard - Pvt., Co. F, 19th Regt., Wis. Vol. Inf.
Richard resided at Oshkosh and enlisted there on Mar. 31, 1862. He was assigned as a wagoner in the above company and was transferred to Co. C of that same regiment on May 1, 1865. Richard was mustered out on Aug. 9, 1865. He is buried with a simple military marker in Oshkosh at Riverside Cemetery, GAR Plot, east row, #3 from the south.
{ROV; Cem. records}

SANBORN, Edmund B. - Pvt., Co. H, 2nd Regt., New Hampshire Vol. Inf.
Edmund was listed as above in the veteran section of the 1885 Wisconsin State census at P.O. Oshkosh. He was listed in 1888 as a member of GAR Post #10 at Oshkosh. He was listed as a veteran of Co. B of that same regiment in the veteran section of the 1895 state census, also at P.O. Oshkosh. Edmund was listed in the 1890 federal census as residing at 52 Ackerman Street in the city of Oshkosh. He then provided his unit designation as Co. H of the above regiment and provided his service dates as having been from Sept. 8, 1862 to Oct. 9, 1863. Edmund listed that he had suffered from a hernia while in the service. His widow was listed in 1905 as residing at 134 E. Irving Street in Oshkosh.
{US 1890; WC-V 1885, 1895; B-1905}

SANDERS, Elias - Pvt., Co. G, 3rd Regt., Wis. Cav.
Elias was born in 1836 at Camillus, New York. He was a son of Ichabod and Irena (Rhoades) Sanders. The parents were both natives of New York and both were born circa 1809. Ichabod was listed in the 1850 federal census as residing in the town of

SANDERS, Elias (cont.)
Vinland. Listed with him were his wife and the following children: Lauretta, born circa 1832 at New York; Elias; Phena, born circa 1836; and Mary Amanda, born circa 1837. The last two were born in Medina, Ohio. In 1854 Ichabod purchased a lot in the village of Butte des Morts and built the family home. He was a shoemaker and carpenter. Ichabod was still residing at Butte des Morts in 1860. Elias was married at Greenville, Outagamie County on Oct. 5, 1859 to Betsy Root. They removed to the town of Dale, Outagamie County, where son Charles Alfred was born. On Feb. 27, 1864 Elias enlisted at Dale and was assigned as above. He was discharged on June 19, 1865 at Ft. Riley Kansas due to a stomach disease. Elias returned to Dale, where his daughter Gertie Diette was born in 1867. Elias died in the town of Dale on Dec. 6, 1869. His burial place is unknown.
{US 1850, 1860; ROV; information from granddaughter Luida E. Sanders}

SANFORD, Luther H. - Pvt., Co. A, 14th Regt., Wis. Vol. Inf.
Luther was born circa 1847 at Wisconsin. He was a son of Burritt and Grace Sanford. The father was born circa 1840 at Connecticut and the mother was born circa 1826 at New York. Burritt was listed in the 1860 federal census as a carpenter residing in the first ward of the village of Menasha. Listed with him were his wife and the following children: Luther; Minot, born circa 1854; and Amy, born circa 1855. All three children were born in Wisconsin. Luther listed his residence as Greenfield when he enlisted on Feb. 6, 1864. He was listed as Arthur. He was assigned as above and was mustered out on Oct. 9, 1865. He was listed in the veteran section of the 1885 Wisconsin State census at P.O. Menasha. Luther was listed in that section of the 1895 state census at P.O. Neenah. He was listed in the 1890 federal census as residing in Neenah. Phebe, his widow, was listed in 1905 as residing at 407 Nicolet Avenue in Neenah.
{US 1860, 1890; WC-V 1885, 1895; B-1905; ROV}

SANFORD, Orange E. - Pvt., Co. C, 10th Regt., Wis. Vol. Inf.
Orange was born circa 1842 at Ohio. He was a son of Benjamin and Adelia Sanford. Both parents were natives of New York, the father born there circa 1818 and the mother born circa 1823. Benjamin was listed in the 1860 federal census as a cooper residing in the first ward of the village of Menasha. Listed with him were his wife and the following children: Orange; Alma, born circa 1844; Alice, born circa 1846; and George, born circa 1850. All four children were born in Ohio. Orange enlisted at Menasha on Sept. 3, 1861. He was assigned as above and was then transferred to the Veteran Reserve Corps on Apr. 22, 1864.
{US 1860; ROV}

SANVILLE, Eclaire - Cpl., Co. G, 17th Regt., Wis. Vol. Inf.
Eclaire resided at Nepeuskun and enlisted there on Mar. 5, 1864. He was assigned as above and was promoted to Corporal in that company. He was wounded on June 18, 1864 and was then mustered out on July 14, 1865.
{ROV}

SARGENT, Samuel C. - Pvt., Co. C, 21st Regt., Wis. Vol. Inf.
Samuel was married in Winnebago County on Oct. 10, 1855 to Amanda Peterson. He resided at Oshkosh and enlisted there on Aug. 12, 1862. He was assigned as above and

SARGENT, Samuel C. (cont.)
was mustered out on June 8, 1865.
{ROV; WCMR v.1, p.162, #737}

SATTERLY, Harrison H. - Pvt., Co. C, 41st Regt., Wis. Vol. Inf.
Harrison was born circa 1841 at New York. He was a son of Asa Satterlee. The father was born circa 1803 at New York. Both were listed in the 1860 federal census as residing on a farm with James McAllister in the town of Poygan. Harrison listed his residence as Omro when he enlisted on May 18, 1864. He was assigned as above and was mustered out on Sept. 23, 1864 at the end of his term of enlistment.
{US 1860; ROV}

SAUER, Ferdinand Sr. - Pvt., Co. K, 1st Regt., Wis. Cav.
Ferdinand enlisted on Feb. 1, 1862 and was assigned as above. He was mustered out on Nov. 1, 1864 at the end of his term of enlistment. A Frederick Sauer was assigned to that same company. Ferdinand was listed in the veteran section of the 1885 and 1895 Wisconsin State census at P.O. Neenah. He was listed in the 1890 federal census as residing in the town of Menasha at P.O. Neenah. Ferdinand provided information that he had been kicked in the head by a horse during his military service. Sophia, his widow, was listed in 1905 as residing at 321 Madison Street in the city of Menasha.
{US 1890; WC-V 1885, 1895; ROV; B-1905}

SAWYER, Chauncey - Civil War Veteran?
Chauncey was born circa 1822 at New York. Lucina, his wife, was also born circa 1822 at New York. Chauncey was listed in the 1860 federal census as a carpenter residing in the village of Neenah. Listed with him were his wife and the following children: Harriet, born circa 1843; Charles, born circa 1846; James, born circa 1848, possibly the subject of a following sketch; George, born circa 1850; Ira, born circa 1855; Wallace, born circa 1857; and Myron, born in 1860. The three oldest children were born in Michigan and the others were born in Wisconsin. Chauncey was listed in the veteran section of the 1885 Wisconsin State census at P.O. Neenah. No unit designation or other information was provided. He was not found in the index to Roster of Wisconsin Volunteers.
{US 1860; WC-V 1885; ROV}

SAWYER, James F. - Pvt., Co. K, 21st Regt., Wis. Vol. Inf.
James listed his residence as Gibralter, Door County when he enlisted on Mar. 28, 1864. He was assigned as above and was wounded at Savannah, Georgia. He was transferred as unassigned to the 3rd (reorg.) Regt., Wis. Vol. Inf. on June 8, 1865 and was mustered out on July 18, 1865. James was listed in the veteran section of the 1885 Wisconsin State census at P.O. Omro. He was a charter member of GAR Post #7 at Omro and was the namesake of that post. Nancy E., his widow, was listed in the 1890 federal census as residing in the town of Omro at P.O. Omro. She provided his unit designation as above and information that he had suffered a bullet wound to his neck during his military service. He is buried with a simple military marker. Nancy was born on Feb. 26, 1830 and died on June 5, 1905. She was listed in 1905 as his widow and was then residing at 201 Exchange Street in the village of Omro. Both are buried at Omro Cemetery, Olin's Addition, Section A, plot 8.
{US 1890; WC-V 1885; ROV; B-1905; Cem. records}

SAWYER, Wesley C. - Pvt., Co. A, 23rd Regt., Massachusetts Vol. Inf.
Wesley was listed in 1883 at P.O. Oshkosh. He was receiving a pension of $24 per month for the loss of his left leg and thigh. He was listed as above in the veteran section of the 1885 Wisconsin State census at P.O. Oshkosh.
{LOP-1883; WC-V 1885}

SAXTON, John - Pvt., Co. E, 2nd Regt., Wis. Vol. Inf.
John was born in Feb. 1821. He resided at Oshkosh and enlisted there on May 18, 1861. He was assigned as above and was wounded at Gettysburg, Pennsylvania. John was then mustered out on June 28, 1864 at the end of his term of enlistment. He is buried with a simple military marker in Oshkosh at Riverside Cemetery, GAR Plot, east row, #5 from the south. He was listed in an 1899 article by Col. Harshaw as having died at Oshkosh.
{ROV; Cem. records; ODN 07 May 1899}

SAYLES, Derius Jr. - Pvt., Co. K, 20th Regt., Wis. Vol. Inf.
Derius Jr. was born circa 1845 at Indiana. Derius, his father, was born circa 1786 at New York. Derius Sr. was listed in the 1860 federal census as residing on a farm in the town of Nepeuskun. Eliza, his wife, was born circa 1801 at Vermont. Derius Jr. was then residing with them. He enlisted at Nepeuskun on Aug. 14, 1862. He was listed as Dennis and was assigned as above. Derius contracted typhoid fever and he died from it on Dec. 17, 1862 at Springfield, Missouri.
{US 1860; ROV; OWN 08 Jan 1863}

SCANANDOAH, Daniel - Pvt., 3rd Regt., Wis. Cav.
Daniel resided at Oshkosh and enlisted there on Jan. 4, 1864. He was last reported as serving with a detachment at Ft. Riley, Kansas in Feb. 1865.
{ROV}

SCANANDOAH, John P. - Pvt., 3rd Regt., Wis. Cav.
John resided at Oshkosh and enlisted there on Feb. 6, 1864. He was last reported as serving with a detachment at Lawrence, Kansas.
{ROV}

SCHEDLER, Christian - Pvt., Co. F, 19th Regt., Wis. Vol. Inf.
Christian resided at Winchester and enlisted there on Feb. 25, 1862. He was assigned as above and was transferred to the Veteran Reserve Corps on Sept. 4, 1863. Christian was mustered out on Mar. 31, 1865 at the end of his term of enlistment. He was then married in Winnebago County on Nov. 3, 1866 to Augusta Bohlmann. Christian was listed in the 1890 federal census as residing in the town of Winchester at P.O. Zittau. He was listed in the veteran section of the 1895 Wisconsin State census at P.O. Zittau.
{US 1890; WC-V 1895; ROV; WCMR v.1, p.311, #1930*}

SCHEIN, Conrad - Pvt., Co. I, 28th Regt., Wis. Vol. Inf.
Conrad was born on Apr. 15, 1843. He listed his residence as Spring Prairie, Walworth County when he enlisted on Aug. 19, 1862. He was assigned as above and was mustered out on Aug. 23, 1865. Conrad died on Aug. 7, 1882. Elizabeth, his widow, was listed in the 1890 federal census as residing in the city of Oshkosh. She was listed in that same year as residing at 609 Ninth Street in Oshkosh. Elizabeth was born on Jan. 7, 1847 and

SCHEIN, Conrad (cont.)
died on Dec. 23, 1905. She is buried with Conrad in the town of Algoma at Ellenwood Cemetery, Section C.
{US 1890; ROV; B-1905; Cem. records}

SCHELLER, Henry - Pvt., Co. C, 53rd Regt., Wis. Vol. Inf.
J. Heinrich was born Apr. 7, 1831 at Switzerland. He was married on July 17, 1859 in Winnebago County to Mrs. Catharina Opp. She was born on Nov. 2, 1839 at Prussia. They were listed in the 1860 federal census as residing in the town of Nekimi. Listed with them was a son, Henry, who was born in 1860 at Wisconsin. Henry listed his residence as Aztalan, Jefferson County when he enlisted on Mar. 9, 1865. He was assigned as above. Most of that company was transferred to Co. K, 51st Regt., Wis. Vol. Inf. under orders dated June 10, 1865. The transfer was completed at Ft. Leavenworth, Kansas on June 30, 1865 and the regiment then returned to Madison, Wisconsin on Aug. 1, 1865. The men were mustered out by companies with the last being mustered out on Aug. 30, 1865. Henry was listed in the veteran section of the 1885 Wisconsin State census at P.O. Nekimi. He was listed in the 1890 federal census as residing in the town of Nekimi at P.O. Nekimi. Henry listed then that he suffered from rheumatism and a disease of the kidneys. He died in Nekimi on Apr. 11, 1892. Katherine was listed in 1905 as residing on 40 acres of section 26 in the town of Nekimi. She died on Mar. 5, 1916. Both are buried with members of their family in the town of Nekimi at Scheller Cemetery. Son Henry died when struck by a train on Jan. 18, 1899 while on his way home from Fond du Lac.
{US 1860, 1890; WC-V 1885; Cem. records; WCMR v.1, p.182, #896; ROV; B-1905}
{OWN 21 Jan 1899}

SCHELLHORN, Franz - Pvt., Co. I, 45th Regt., Wis. Vol. Inf.
Franz resided at Cedarburg, Ozaukee County and enlisted there on Oct. 10, 1864. He was assigned as above and was mustered out on July 17, 1865. He was listed in the 1890 federal census as residing in the city of Oshkosh. Franz was listed in the veteran section of the 1895 and 1905 Wisconsin State census at P.O. Oshkosh. Frank was listed in 1905 as a laborer residing at 288 Eighth Street in Oshkosh.
{US 1890; WC-V 1895, 1905; ROV; B-1905}

SCHENDEL, Martin - Pvt., Co. C, 53rd Regt., Wis. Vol. Inf.
Martin was born circa 1831 at Germany. He resided at Utica and he enlisted there on Mar. 8, 1865. He was assigned as above. Most of that company was then transferred to Co. K, 51st Regt., Wis. Vol. Inf. under orders dated June 10, 1865. The transfer was completed at Ft. Leavenworth, Kansas on June 20, 1865 and the regiment returned to Madison, Wisconsin on Aug. 1, 1865. The men were mustered out by companies with the last being mustered out on Aug. 30, 1865. Martin was listed in 1868 as a laborer residing at 18 Seventh Street in the city of Oshkosh. He was listed in the veteran section of the 1905 Wisconsin State census at P.O. Oshkosh. Martin was then residing at 266 Sixteenth Street in Oshkosh. He was listed in the 1910 federal census as a widower residing at the Wisconsin Veterans' Home at King. He had been married for 43 years.
{US 1910; WC-V 1905; ROV; T-1868; B-1905}

SCHERFF, John - Pvt., Co. C, 46th Regt., Wis. Vol. Inf.
John was born circa 1844 at Ohio. He was a son of Jacob and Margaretta Scherff and

SCHERFF, John (cont.)
a brother of Martin from a following sketch. Jacob was born circa 1802 at Bavaria and Margaretta was born circa 1809, also at Bavaria. They were listed in the 1850 federal census as residing in the town of Winnebago, where Jacob was a shoemaker. Listed with them were the following children: Martin; Catherine, born circa 1837 at Germany; Hellen, born circa 1841 at Germany; and John. Both parents were listed in the 1860 federal census as residing in the town of Winneconne. Son John was listed as residing with them. He was also listed in the 1860 federal census as a clerk residing in the first ward of the city of Oshkosh. John listed his residence as Winneconne when he enlisted on Feb. 14, 1865. He was assigned as above and was mustered out on Nov. 2, 1865. John was married in Winnebago County on Mar. 1, 1865 to Mary E. Ball. They had at least one daughter, Annie, who was born in the village of Winneconne on Apr. 4, 1878.
{US 1850, 1860; ROV; WCMR v.1, p.273, #1625; WCBR v.2, p.104, #269}

SCHERFF, Martin - Capt., Co. F, 19th Regt., Wis. Vol. Inf.
Martin was born circa 1834 at Bavaria. He was a son of Jacob and Margaretta Scherff and a brother of John from a previous sketch. Martin was listed in the 1860 federal census as residing with his parents in the town of Winneconne. He listed his residence as Oshkosh when he enlisted on Jan. 16, 1862. He was assigned as above and was then commissioned as Captain of that company on Mar. 27, 1862. Martin was taken prisoner on Oct. 27, 1864. He was mustered out on Mar. 30, 1865 at the end of his term of enlistment.
{US 1850, 1860; ROV}

SCHERMERHORN, Edward - Pvt., Co. E, 1st Regt., Wis. Cav.
Edward resided at Rushford and enlisted there on Nov. 20, 1863. He was assigned as above and was wounded in action. Edward was then transferred to the Veteran Reserve Corps in May 1865. He was discharged on Aug. 18, 1865. Edward was listed in the 1890 federal census as residing at P.O. Clintonville, Waupaca County. He provided then that his ring finger had been shot off.
{US 1890; ROV}

SCHEUER, Anton - Pvt., Co. H, 45th Regt., Wis. Vol. Inf.
Anton resided at Milwaukee, Milwaukee County and enlisted there on Nov. 2, 1864. He was assigned as above and was mustered out on July 17, 1865. Anton was married in Winnebago County on Oct. 4, 1868 to Margaretha Habig. He was listed (Schener) in the veteran section of the 1885 Wisconsin State census at P.O. Oshkosh. He was listed in that section of the 1895 state census, also at P.O. Oshkosh. He was listed in 1888 as a member of GAR Post #241 at Oshkosh. Anton was listed in the 1890 federal census as residing on Jefferson Avenue in the city of Oshkosh. He was listed in 1905 as a cigar manufacturer residing at 344 Jefferson Avenue in Oshkosh. Anton Jr., Josie, Frank and John Scheuer also resided at that address.
{US 1890; WC-V 1885, 1895; ROV; B-1905; WCMR v.1, p.396, #2465*}

SCHINTZ, Louis - Cpl., Co. E, 2nd Regt., Wis. Vol. Inf.
Louis was born on May 8, 1839 at Zurich, Switzerland. He was a son of Henry and Regula (Hofmeister) Schintz. Both parents were natives of Switzerland, the father born there circa 1793 and the mother born circa 1801. Three of his brothers came to this

SCHINTZ, Louis (cont.)
country prior to Louis. Herman was in the U.S. Artillery during the Seminole War in Florida. The oldest brother, Henry, was born circa 1822 at Switzerland. He located at Oshkosh. Theodore settled at Oshkosh and eventually removed to Chicago. Louis came to America in 1851 with his parents. They came to Wisconsin and settled on a farm in the town of Black Wolf. They were listed as residing there in the 1860 federal census. In 1859 Louis had moved into Oshkosh and worked in the office of brother Theodore, who was then a Magistrate and Notary Public. Theodore was married on Sept. 30, 1851 in Winnebago County to Barbara Zentner. Louis then worked almost two years in the office of Gabe Bouck. He was listed in the 1860 federal census as a law student residing with the family of brother Theodore in the second ward of the city of Oshkosh. He then removed to Appleton, Outagamie County about Jan. 1, 1861 and assumed management of the local interests of Perry H. Smith. Louis listed his residence as Oshkosh when he enlisted on Apr. 21, 1861. He was assigned as above and was promoted to Corporal in that company. Louis was slightly wounded in the first battle at Bull Run, Virginia. A bullet passed through his coat and was deflected by a suspender buckle, preventing more serious damage. Louis contracted lung fever at Arlington Heights, Virginia. The illness kept him hospitalized for three weeks. Louis was discharged on Feb. 8, 1863 at Belle Plain, Virginia so that he could accept a commission as 2nd Lt., 27th Regt., Wis. Vol. Inf. That regiment had a full staff of line officers so he did not muster at that rank. Louis returned to Oshkosh and was employed there for 6 months before again settling at Appleton. He was married on June 8, 1863 to Catherine Ostertag. She was a sister of Sebastian Ostertag, the subject of a previous sketch. Louis was associated with Anson Ballard until Mr. Ballard's death in Mar. 1873. Louis then operated as a real estate and loan agent. He and Catherine had the following children: George L.; Henry W.; Edgar W.; Hugo J.; Louis E.; and Alma, died at age 8 years and 9 months. Louis was still residing at Appleton in 1888. He was listed in the 1890 federal census as residing on Elm Street in Appleton. He was listed as having died recently in an 1899 article by Col. Harshaw.
{US 1860, 1890; SCA 1:654-5; ODN 07 May 1899; WCMR v.1, p.37, #155*; ROV}

SCHMIDT, Andreas - Pvt., Co. C, 9th Regt., Wis. Vol. Inf.
Andreas resided at Oshkosh and enlisted there on Sept. 6, 1861. He was assigned as above and was discharged on Oct. 1, 1862 due to a disability.
{ROV}

SCHMIDT, Casper - Pvt., Co. F, 19th Regt., Wis. Vol. Inf.
Casper was born on Dec. 10, 1842 in the village of Greisnagh, Germany. He emigrated to this country in 1856 and located at Oshkosh. Casper enlisted at Oshkosh on Feb. 4, 1862. He was assigned to the above company as a musician. Casper was a patient at the Chesapeake general hospital for three months and he received a flesh wound in the arm at Petersburg, Virginia. He was mustered out on Apr. 29, 1865 at the end of his term of enlistment. A few days after the final attack on Richmond, Virginia, Casper was among the troops who had served past their time and were sent to Washington, D.C. There he was privileged to see Abraham Lincoln just three days before the President was assassinated. Casper was listed (Smith) in the veteran section of the 1885 Wisconsin State census at P.O. Oshkosh. He was listed in 1888 as a member of GAR Post #241 at

SCHMIDT, Casper (cont.)
Oshkosh. Mary, his widow, was listed in the 1890 federal census as residing in the city of Oshkosh.
{US 1890; WC-V 1885; ROV; SCA 1:638-9}

SCHMIDT, Christian - Pvt., Co. C, 53rd Regt., Wis. Vol. Inf.
Christian resided at Black Wolf and enlisted there on Mar. 20, 1865. He was assigned as above. Most of that company was transferred to Co. K, 51st Regt., Wis. Vol. Inf. under orders dated June 10, 1865. The transfer was completed at Ft. Leavenworth, Kansas on June 30, 1865 and the regiment returned to Madison, Wisconsin on Aug. 1, 1865. The men were mustered out by companies with the last being mustered out on Aug. 30, 1865.
{ROV}

SCHMIDT, Emil - Pvt., Co. F, 19th Regt., Wis. Vol. Inf.
Emil resided at Oshkosh and enlisted there on Feb. 4, 1862. He was assigned as a musician in the above company and was mustered out on Apr. 29, 1865 at the end of his term of enlistment. Emil was listed in the veteran section of the 1885 Wisconsin State census at P.O. Oshkosh. He was listed in 1888 as a member of GAR Post #241 at Oshkosh. Henrietta, his widow, was listed in the 1890 federal census as residing in the city of Oshkosh. She was listed in 1905 as residing at 169 Tenth Street in Oshkosh.
{US 1890; WC-V 1885; ROV; B-1905}

SCHMIDT, Friedrich - Pvt., Co. F, 19th Regt., Wis. Vol. Inf.
Friedrich resided at Oshkosh and enlisted there on Jan. 16, 1862. He was assigned as above and was discharged on Nov. 13, 1862 due to a disability.
{ROV}

SCHMIDT, Henry - Pvt., Co. D, 1st Regt., New York Engineers.
Henry was listed in 1868 as boarding at 77 Otter Street in the city of Oshkosh. He was listed (H. Schmidt) as above in the veteran section of the 1885 Wisconsin State census at P.O. Oshkosh. Josephine, his widow, was listed in the 1890 federal census as residing at 99 Merritt Street in Oshkosh. She listed his unit designation as Pvt., Co. D, 1st Regt., U.S. Vet. Engineers. She also provided his service dates as having been from Oct. 7, 1864 to Sept. 26, 1865.
{US 1890; WC-V 1885; T-1868}

SCHMIDT, John - Pvt., Co. C, 32nd Regt., New York Vol. Inf.
John was listed as above in the veteran section of the 1885 Wisconsin State census at P.O. Winchester.
{WC-V 1885}

SCHMIDT, John - Pvt., Co. G, 2nd Regt., Wis. Cav.
He was listed as above in the 1905 Wisconsin State census at P.O. Larsen. He was not found in the records of that company. He was listed in 1905 with Wilhelmina, his wife, as residing in the town of Winchester. This is probably the same John as the subject of the previous sketch.
{WC-V 1905; B-1905}

SCHMIDT, Peter - Pvt., 10th Batt., Wis. Lt. Art.
Peter resided in Washington County and enlisted there on Dec. 31, 1862. He was assigned as above and was listed as a veteran recruit. He was mustered out on June 7, 1865. Peter was listed in the 1890 federal census as residing at 210 Jefferson Avenue in the city of Oshkosh. He then provided his unit designation as above and his service dates as having been from Apr. 27, 1861 to June 10, 1865. Peter listed that he had suffered a wound to his ankle and that his general health was impared. Katherine, his widow, was listed in 1905 as residing at 186 Jefferson Avenue in Oshkosh.
{US 1890; ROV; B-1905}

SCHMITZ, Lambert - Pvt., Co. F, 19th Regt., Wis. Vol. Inf.
Lambert resided at Oshkosh and enlisted there on Nov. 31, 1863. He was assigned as above and was transferred to Co. C of that same regiment on May 1, 1865. Lambert was mustered out on Aug. 9, 1865.
{ROV}

SCHNEIDER, Christian - Pvt., Co. G, 9th Regt., Wis. Vol. Inf.
Christian was born circa 1839 at Prussia. He was listed in the 1860 federal census as a farm larborer for James Gillespie in the town of Nekimi at P.O. Oshkosh. Christian enlisted at Oshkosh on Sept. 18, 1861. He was assigned as above and was then mustered out on Dec. 3, 1864 at the end of his term of enlistment. Christian was listed in 1868 as a laborer boarding at 91 Doty Street in the city of Oshkosh.
{US 1860; ROV; T-1868}

SCHNEIDER, Jacob - Pvt., Co. D, 21st Regt., Wis. Vol. Inf.
Jacob resided at Menasha and enlisted there on Jan. 4, 1864. He was assigned as above and was transferred to the 3rd Regt., Wis. Vol. Inf. on June 8,1865. Jacob was then mustered out on July 18, 1865.
{ROV}

SCHNEIDER, Jacob - Pvt., Co. F, 19th Regt., Wis. Vol. Inf.
Jacob resided at Winneconne and enlisted there on Feb. 3, 1862. He was transferred to the Veteran Reserve Corps on Feb. 4, 1865 and was mustered out on Mar. 20, 1865 at the end of his term of enlistment.
{ROV}

SCHNEIDER, John - Pvt., Co. C, 53rd Regt., Wis. Vol. Inf.
John was born circa 1837 at Prussia. Anna, his wife, was born circa 1838 at Austria. John was listed in the 1860 federal census as a cabinet maker residing in the first ward of the village of Menasha. Listed with him were his wife and a daughter, Mary, who was born in 1859 at Wisconsin. John enlisted at Menasha on Mar. 9, 1865. He was assigned as above. Most of that company was then transferred to Co. K, 51st Regt., Wis. Vol. Inf. under orders dated June 10, 1865. The transfer was completed June 30, 1865 at Ft. Leavenworth, Kansas and the regiment returned to Madison, Wisconsin on Aug. 1, 1865. The men were mustered out by companies with the last being mustered out on Aug. 30, 1865. John was listed in the veteran section of the 1885 and 1895 Wisconsin State census at P.O. Oshkosh.
{US 1860; WC-V 1885, 1895; ROV}

SCHNEIDER, John - Pvt., Co. I, 3rd (reorg.) Regt., Wis. Cav.
John resided at Oshkosh and enlisted there on Feb. 6, 1864. He was assigned as above and was mustered out on Sept. 29, 1865.
{ROV}

SCHNEIDER, Phillip - Civil War Veteran?
Phillip was listed in the 1890 federal census as residing in the city of Oshkosh. He listed that he was an ambulance driver while in the military during 1865.
{US 1890}

SCHNELLBECKER, Peter - Pvt., Co. G, 3rd Regt., Wis. Vol. Inf.
Peter resided at Neenah and enlisted there on Apr. 20, 1861. He was assigned as above and he re-enlisted in that same company at the end of his term. While home on a veterans' furlogh, Peter was married in Winnebago County on Jan. 13, 1864 to Amelia Hasse. He returned to his unit and was then mustered out on July 18, 1865.
{ROV; WCMR v.1, p.249, #1435}

SCHOBLASKI, John - Pvt., Co. F, 19th Regt., Wis. Vol. Inf.
John was born circa 1835 at Germany. He was married on Aug. 20, 1855 in Winnebago County to Christiana Dahl. She was born circa 1833 at Mecklenberg. They were listed (Shibalaski) in the 1860 federal census as residing on a farm in the town of Nekimi. Listed with them were son Frank, born circa 1858, and daughter Jane, born in 1860. John listed his residence as Oshkosh when he enlisted on Mar. 21, 1862. He was assigned as above and was discharged Feb. 15, 1863 due to a disability. John was listed in 1868 as a laborer working for Kusche & Hitz at Oshkosh. He was listed in the veteran section of the 1885 and 1895 Wisconsin State census at P.O. Oshkosh. John was listed in the 1890 federal census as residing at 322 Minnesota Street in the city of Oshkosh. He reported that he had suffered from the effects of rheumatism as a result of his military service. Dora, widow of John, was listed in 1905 as residing at 322 Minnesota Street in Oshkosh. Sons Edward and Emil were also residing at that address.
{US 1860, 1890; WC-V 1885, 1895; T-1868; WCMR v.1, p.78, #341; ROV; B-1905}

SCHOFIELD, Cyrus N. - Pvt., Co. B, 1st Regt., Rhode Island Cav.
Cyrus was listed in the 1890 federal census as residing in the city of Oshkosh. He then provided his unit designation as above and his service dates as having been Feb. 28, 1865 to Aug. 5, 1865. He was listed as above in the veteran section of the 1895 Wisconsin State census at P.O. Oshkosh.
{US 1890; WC-V 1895}

SCHOLLKOPF, John - Pvt., Co. D, 3rd Regt., Wis. Cav.
John resided at Oshkosh and enlisted there on Dec. 22, 1863. He was assigned as above and was transferred to Co. I, 3rd (reorg.) Regt., Wis. Cav. on Mar. 23, 1865. John was then mustered out on Sept. 29, 1865. He was listed in 1868 as operating a saloon and residing at 184 Main Street in the city of Oshkosh.
{ROV; T-1868}

SCHOONOVER, Daniel M. - Pvt., Co. D, 49th Regt., Wis. Vol. Inf.
Daniel was born circa 1832 at New York, a son of Eunice Schoonover and a brother of Richard from a following sketch. Eunice was born circa 1806 at New York. Maria, wife

SCHOONOVER, Daniel M. (cont.)
of Daniel, was born circa 1833 at New York. They were listed in the 1860 federal census as residing on a farm in the town of Nekimi. Listed with them was Job, their son. He was born circa 1854 at New York. Also listed was Jeannette Scott and Lucius, her son. Daniel listed his residence as Oshkosh when he enlisted on Feb. 9, 1865. He was assigned as above and was mustered out on Nov. 1, 1865. He was listed in 1868 as a blacksmith residing at 88 Jefferson Avenue in Oshkosh. Daniel died on May 16, 1881 at the age of 48 years and 10 months. He is buried in the town of Vinland at Brooks Cemetery.
{US 1860; ROV; T-1868; Cem. records}

SCHOONOVER, Richard Bailey - Pvt., Co. C, 21st Regt., Wis. Vol. Inf.
Richard was born circa 1838 at New York. He was a son of Eunice Schoonover and a brother of Daniel from a previous sketch. Richard was listed in the 1860 federal census as residing on the farm of brother Daniel in the town of Nekimi. He was married in Winnebago County on Oct. 24, 1860 to Mary L. Rose. Bailey listed his residence as Oshkosh when he enlisted on Aug. 13, 1862. He was assigned as above and was then transferred to the Veteran Reserve Corps on Sept. 13, 1863. Bailey was mustered out on June 22, 1865.
{US 1860; ROV; WCMR v.1, p.207, #1098}

SCHRAEDER, William - Pvt., Co. C, 1st Regt., Wis. Hvy. Art.
William resided at Neenah and enlisted there on Aug. 3, 1863. He was assigned as above and was mustered out on Sept. 21, 1865.
{ROV}

SCHROEDER, Charles Jr. - Sgt., Co. H, 37th Regt., Wis. Vol. Inf.
Charles resided at Winchester and was drafted there on Nov. 24, 1863. He was assigned as above and was promoted to Corporal and then Sergeant in that company. Charles was wounded on June 17, 1864 at Petersburg, Virginia and was mustered out on July 27, 1865. He was listed in the 1890 federal census as residing in the town of Dale, Outagamie County. Charles then provided that he had been wounded while he was in the service and that he had suffered from chronic diarrhea.
{US 1890; ROV}

SCHROTTKY, Hugo - Pvt., Co. F, 20th Regt., New York Vol. Inf.
Hugo was married on May 26, 1864 at Milwaukee to Louisa Lieber. She was born on Sept. 8, 1843 at Fort Plain, New York. They located at Ripon, Fond du Lac County until 1880 and then removed to Oshkosh. Hugo was listed in 1888 as a member of GAR Post #10 at Oshkosh. He was listed in the 1890 federal census as residing in the city of Oshkosh. He then provided his unit designation as Pvt., Co. F, 2nd Regt., N.Y. Vol. Inf. and he listed his service dates as having been from May 6, 1861 to June 28, 1865. Hugo was listed in the veteran section of the 1895 and 1905 Wisconsin State census at P.O. Oshkosh as a veteran of the 20th Regt., N.Y. Vol. Inf. He was listed in 1905 as a carpenter residing at 118 Central Avenue in Oshkosh. Son Charles was also residing at that address. Hugo and Louisa had three sons, Henry, Edward and Charles. They also had three daughters, Mrs. Anna Hemple and Mrs. Charles Otto of Milwaukee and Mrs. Bertha Allen of Oshkosh. Louisa died at Oshkosh on May 7, 1926, shorlty after the death of Hugo. She was survived by the above children. She was also survived by a

SCHROTTKY, Hugo (cont.)
brother, Obert Lieber and two sisters, Mrs. Bertha Deffer and Mrs. Strothman, all of Milwaukee.
{US 1890; WC-V 1895, 1905; B-1905; ODN 10 May 1926}

SCHRUPP, Phillip Henry - Pvt., Co. H, 34th Regt., Wis. Vol. Inf.
Phillip resided at Wayne, Washington County and enlisted there on Nov. 24, 1862. He was assigned as above and was transferred to Co. F of that same regiment on Dec. 27, 1862. He was mustered out on Sept. 8, 1863 at the end of his term of enlistment. Phillip was listed in the veteran section of the 1895 Wisconsin State census at P.O. Oshkosh.
{WC-V 1895; ROV}

SCHULER, Joseph - Pvt., Co. C, 45th Regt., Wis. Vol. Inf.
Joseph resided at Milwaukee, Milwaukee County and he enlisted there on Feb. 7, 1865. He was assigned as above and was mustered out on July 17, 1865. Joseph was listed in the veteran section of the 1885 Wisconsin State census at P.O. Menasha.
{WC-V 1885; ROV}

SCHULTZ, Christian - Pvt., Co. I, 21st Regt., Wis. Vol. Inf.
Christian resided at Neenah and enlisted there on Aug. 11, 1862. He was assigned as above. He contracted a disease and died on Nov. 29, 1862 at Louisville, Kentucky.
{ROV}

SCHULZE, Carl - Pvt., Co. F, 19th Regt., Wis. Vol. Inf.
Carl (Schulz) was born on Oct. 5, 1831. He resided at Oshkosh and enlisted there on Mar. 31, 1862. He was assigned as above and was transferred to Co. C of that regiment on May 1, 1865. Carl was then mustered out on Aug. 9, 1865. He died on Oct. 30, 1918. He is buried in the town of Black Wolf at Knack Cemetery.
{ROV; Cem. records}

SCHURI, Conrad - Sgt., Co. F, 19th Regt., Wis. Vol. Inf.
Conrad was born on Mar. 25, 1839 at Bavaria, Germany. He enlisted on Apr. 14, 1861 at Brooklyn, New York and was assigned as a Private to Co. F, 28th Regt., N.Y. Vol. Inf. That regiment was mustered out on July 28, 1861 at the end of its term. Conrad soon removed to Wisconsin and settled at Oshkosh in fall of 1861. He enlisted at Oshkosh on Feb. 13, 1862. He was assigned as above and was promoted to Corporal and then Sergeant in that company. He was mustered out at Madison on Apr. 29, 1865 at the end of his term of enlistment. Conrad was married on Oct. 11, 1865 in Winnebago County to Mary Catherine Elizabeth Kranz. He was listed in 1868 as then operating a saloon at 7 Main Street and residing at 77 Otter Street, both in the city of Oshkosh. He was listed in 1888 as a member of GAR Post #241 at Oshkosh. Conrad was listed in the veteran section of the 1885 and 1895 Wisconsin State census at P.O. Oshkosh. He was listed in the 1890 federal census as residing in Oshkosh. Mary, his widow, was listed in 1905 as residing at 165 Otter Street in Oshkosh.
{US 1890; WC-V 1885, 1895; T-1868; SCA 1:704-5; WCMR v.1, p.280, #1687; ROV} {B-1905}

SCHUVANDER, Berthold - Pvt., Co. I, 21st Regt., Wis. Vol. Inf.
Berthold resided at Menasha and enlisted there on Aug. 11, 1862. He was assigned as

SCHUVANDER, Berthold (cont.)
above and was wounded at Chaplin Hills, Kentucky. Berthold was discharged due to his wounds on Jan. 14, 1863.
{ROV}

SCHWARZMUELLER, Ch. - Pvt., 2nd Batt., Missouri Lt. Art.
He was listed as such in the veteran section of the 1885 Wisconsin State census at P.O. Oshkosh.
{WC-V 1885}

SCHWEGER, Herman - Pvt., Co. A, 2nd Regt., Wis. Cav.
Herman was born circa 1846 at Hungary, a son of Krago and Mary Schweger. Both parents were natives of Hungary, the father born there circa 1809 and the mother born circa 1806. They were listed (Schweker) in the 1860 federal census as residing in the first ward of the village of Menasha. Listed with them were the following children: Mary, born circa 1842; Theresa, born circa 1844; Herman; and Robert, born circa 1848. All of the children were born in Hungary. Herman enlisted at Menasha on Sept. 8, 1864. He was assigned as above and was mustered out on June 12, 1865.
{US 1860; ROV}

SCHWINZER, Frederick - Pvt., Co. F, 16th (reorg.) Regt., Wis. Vol. Inf.
Frederick resided at Oshkosh and enlisted there on Feb. 14, 1865. He was assigned as above and was mustered out on July 12, 1865.
{ROV}

SCOTT, Andrew J. - Cpl., Co. A, 14th Regt., Wis. Vol. Inf.
Andrew resided at Oshkosh and enlisted there on Oct. 27, 1861. He was assigned as above and was promoted to Corporal in that company. Andrew was then discharged on Oct. 15, 1862 due to a disability.
{ROV}

SCOTT, Ebenezer H. - Pvt., Co. E, 5th (reorg.) Regt., Wis. Vol. Inf.
Ebenezer was married in Winnebago County on Apr. 29, 1856 to Eunice Schoonover. He resided at Oshkosh and enlisted there on Sept. 3, 1864. He was assigned as above and was mustered out on July 13, 1865. Ebenezer was listed in the 1890 federal census as residing in the town of Rose, Waushara County at P.O. Wild Rose. He provided then that he suffered from a disease of the kidneys.
{US 1890; ROV; WCMR v.1, p.90, #380}

SCOTT, George F. - Pvt., Co. F, 25th Regt., Maine Vol. Inf.
George was listed as a musician assigned to the above company in the veteran section of the 1885, 1895 and 1905 Wisconsin State census at P.O. Oshkosh. He was listed in 1905 as retired and residing at 21 Powers Avenue in the city of Oshkosh. John C. Scott was also listed at that address.
{WC-V 1885, 1895, 1905; B-1905}

SCOTT, Henry Courtney - Pvt., Co. B, 21st Regt., Wis. Vol. Inf.
Henry was born on Oct. 4, 1843 (his marker shows Apr. 17) at Greenfield, Saratoga County, New York. He was a son of Henry and Nancy (Bell) Scott, both of Scottish

SCOTT, Henry Courtney (cont.)
descent. The father came to Wisconsin with his family in 1849 and settled on a farm in the town of Vinland. He died on Oct. 29, 1855 at age 45 years and 4 months while on a land-purchasing trip to Minnesota. Nancy was listed in the 1860 federal census as residing on a farm in the town of Vinland. She was born circa 1814 at Connecticut. Listed with her were the following children: Henry; Mary, born circa 1844; Jane, born circa 1847; Charles, born circa 1849; Frank, born circa 1851; and Julia Emogene, born circa 1854. The census lists Frank as born in Wisconsin which conflicts with the printed biographical sketches. The older children were all born in New York. Nancy died on July 26, 1876/8 at age 61 years. After the death of his father, Henry hired out on a farm for seven years. He enlisted at Vinland on Aug. 9, 1862 and was assigned as above. He was taken prisoner at Chickamauga, Georgia. Henry was first confined at Atlanta, Georgia and was then transferred to Libby Prison at Richmond, Virginia. After a few weeks he was again transferred, this time to Danville Prison in Virginia. In Mar. 1864 he was taken to Andersonville Prison in Georgia and on Sept. 20, 1864 he was again transferred to Savannah, Georgia. Henry was taken to Charleston and Florence Prisons, both in South Carolina. In October 1864 he attempted to escape from Florence with Charles A. Peterson, the subject of a previous sketch. They were captured within two weeks at Georgetown, S.C. and were returned to Florence. Henry then obtained a Confederate uniform and eventually escaped through a tunnel. He adopted the name John W. Jenkins and the unit designation of Private, Co. E, 21st S.C. Regt., C.S.A. After a long and adventurous trek, he emerged behind the Union lines at Knoxville, Tennessee. After travelling as an escort to Lexington he was given eighteen months pay and a 30-day furlough. He returned home and his visit was then extended to 70 days. When he returned to his unit, then just 26 miles from Raleigh, N.C., Henry found that most of his comrades had been killed, wounded or taken prisoner and had been replaced by new soldiers. The regiment returned to Milwaukee, Wisconsin on June 8, 1865 and was mustered out there. Henry returned to his home in the town of Vinland. He was married in 1866 to Mary A. Rogers, who was born in 1846 at Spring Prairie, Walworth County, Wisconsin and was a daughter of Elias and Thankful Rogers. She died in Butte des Morts on July 25, 1881. Henry and Mary had the following children: Almeda, born on Sept. 17, 1868; Charles H., born on Jan. 12, 1867, died of typhoid fever at Valparaiso, Indiana on Feb. 1, 1889; Amy, born circa 1872, married Dell Livingston, died circa 1888 at Omro; Harold, born on July 27, 1874, died in Jan. 1877; Harry, born on Feb. 7, 1876, died on Aug. 28, 1877; Russell, twin of Harry, died on Aug. 24, 1926; and Susan, born in 1878, married David Kirkpatrick, he died in Pines, Colorado, married second to J.C. Nudigate of Denver, Colorado. Mary and son Charles are buried in the town of Winneconne at Bell Cemetery. Henry was listed in the veteran section of the 1885 Wisconsin State census at P.O. Butte des Morts. He was listed in the 1890 federal census as residing in the village of Omro. He was married again in 1892 to Carrie Larzelere. Henry was listed in the veteran section of the 1895 state census at P.O. Omro. He then owned a large saw and shingle mill at Omro and he was also principal owner of a boat-building company located at Omro. His prison comrade, Charles Peterson, was working for him in the sawmill in 1895. Henry owned the family farm of his father and over 2,000 acres in northern Wisconsin. He was again listed in the veteran section of the 1905 state census at P.O. Omro. He was listed then as residing at 200 Park Street in the village of Omro. Henry died on June 28, 1912. He is buried with a simple military marker at Omro Cemetery, Pelton's Addition, Section A, plot 16.

SCOTT, Henry Courtney (cont.)
His parents are buried on that same plot.
{US 1860, 1890; WC-V 1885, 1895, 1905; ROV; CBR-FRV p.1151-5; B-1905; GRI}
{Cem. records}

SCOTT, Henry K. - Pvt., Co. C, 10th Regt., Wis. Vol. Inf.
Henry resided at Menasha and enlisted there on Sept. 12, 1861. He was assigned as above and was detailed as the regimental bugler. Henry was mustered out Nov. 3, 1864.
{ROV; Lawson p.812}

SCOTT, James - Pvt., Co. I, 3rd Regt., Wis. Cav.
James was born on Mar. 4, 1808. He enlisted on Jan. 3, 1862 and was assigned as above. He was discharged on May 29, 1862. James died on Jan. 30, 1877. He is buried in Oshkosh at Riverside Cemetery, GAR Plot, east row, #16 from the south.
{Cem. records}

SCOTT, James H. - Pvt., Co. G, 3rd Regt., Wis. Vol. Inf.
James was born circa 1841 at New Hampshire. He was a son of George and Pliny Scott. The father was born circa 1805 at New Hampshire and the mother was born circa 1813 at Massachusetts. George was listed in the 1860 federal census as a blacksmith residing in the village of Neenah. Listed with him were his wife and the following children: Cora, born circa 1832; Oscar, born circa 1839; James; Ermina, born circa 1843; Sarah, born circa 1846; Ella, born circa 1848; Charles, born circa 1850 at Massachusetts; and Edward, born circa 1856 at Wisconsin. The older children were all born in New Hampshire. James enlisted at Neenah on June 1, 1861. He was assigned as above and was taken prisoner on May 24, 1862. James was transferred to the 2nd Battery of the Veteran Reserve Corps on Jan. 20, 1864.
{US 1860; ROV; Lawson p.809}

SCOTT, John H. - Cpl., Co. G, 9th Regt., New York Art.
Harriet A., formerly the widow of John, was listed in the 1890 federal census as residing in the village of Omro. She provided his unit designation as above and his service dates as having been from Jan. 20, 1863 to July 24, 1865. John is buried with a simple military marker in the town of Poygan at Forest Hill Cemetery. The marker lists his unit designation as 95th Regt., N.Y. Hvy. Art.
{US 1890; Cem. records}

SCOTT, John W. - Col., 3rd Regt., Wis. Vol. Inf.
John was born circa 1824 at Pennsylvania. He was married on May 1, 1850 to Henrietta Wright. She was born circa 1830 at New York. John was listed in the 1860 federal census as a jeweler residing in the fifth ward of the city of Oshkosh. Residing with him were his wife and the following children: Eva, born circa 1852 at Wisconsin; and Nettie, born circa 1855 at Wisconsin. John enlisted at Oshkosh on Apr. 21, 1861. He was commissioned as Captain of Co. B, 3rd Regt., Wis. Vol. Inf. two days later and was promoted to Major in that regiment on June 1, 1862. John was promoted to Lieutenant Colonel on Mar. 10, 1863 and was wounded at Cedar Mountain. He was killed in action on May 1, 1863 at Chancellorsville, Virginia. His marriage was recorded in Winnebago County in July 1863. Mrs. J.W. Scott was listed in 1868 as residing at 11 Elm Street in Oshkosh. Henrietta Crane, formerly the widow of John, was listed in the 1890 federal

SCOTT, John W. (cont.)
census as residing in the town of Oshkosh at P.O. Oshkosh.
{US 1860, 1890; ROV; T-1868; WCMR v.1, p.242, #1382}

SCOTT, Norman H. - Cpl., Co. B, 21st Regt., Wis. Vol. Inf.
Norman resided at Vinland and enlisted there on Aug. 11, 1862. He was assigned as above and was promoted to Corporal in that company. Norman was taken prisoner at Chickamauga, Georgia and was then mustered out on June 8, 1865.
{ROV}

SCOTT, Thomas - Pvt., Co. E, 5th Regt., Wis. Vol. Inf.?
Thomas was listed as above in the veteran section of the 1895 Wisconsin State census at P.O. Oshkosh. He was not found in the records of that company.
{WC-V 1895}

SCOTT, Thomas D. - Sgt., Co. D, 41st Regt., Wis. Vol. Inf.
Thomas was born circa 1836 at Canada. He was listed in the 1860 federal census as a mill laborer residing with the family of John Lajest in the first ward of the village of Menasha. Thomas enlisted at Menasha on May 2, 1864. He was assigned as above and was promoted to Sergeant in that company. Thomas was mustered out on Sept. 23, 1864 at the end of his term of enlistment. He was listed in the veteran section of the 1895 and 1905 Wisconsin State census at P.O. Menasha. Thomas was listed in the 1890 federal census as residing in the city of Menasha. He was listed in 1905 as residing at 429 First Street in Menasha. Bessie H. and Marcelitte Scott were also listed at that address.
{US 1860, 1890; WC-V 1895, 1905; B-1905; ROV}

SCOTT, William W. - Civil War Veteran?
William was a son of William Williams and Clarissa Scott. Both parents were natives of New York, the father born there circa 1800 and the mother born circa 1805. They were listed in the 1860 federal census as residing on a farm in the town of Algoma. Then listed with them was daughter Martha, who was born circa 1840 at New York. Residing on an adjoining farm was son Solomon and his family. The father died on Nov. 3, 1878 at age 78 years and 8 months. Clarissa died on Feb. 15, 1888 at age 83 years, 5 months and 5 days. William was listed in 1868 as boarding at 48 Nebraska Street in Oshkosh. He died at age 25 years and 6 months. A GAR marker is placed at his grave. William is buried with his parents in the town of Algoma at Ellenwood Cemetery, Section A.
{US 1860; T-1868; Cem. records}

SCOVILLE, Henry - Pvt., Co. E, 2nd Regt., Wis. Vol. Inf.
Henry was born circa 1840 at Pennsylvania. He was a son of Ganem and Anna Scoville. The parents were both natives of Connecticut, the father born there circa 1801 and the mother born circa 1804. They were listed (Scovel) in the 1860 federal census as residing on a farm in the town of Algoma. Listed with them then were sons George and Henry. George was born circa 1837 at Pennsylvania. Henry listed his residence as Oshkosh when he enlisted on May 18, 1861 and was assigned as above. He contracted a disease and died at Washington, D.C. on Apr. 10, 1862 at age 22 years, 3 months and 9 days. He is buried with his parents and a brother in the town of Algoma at Ellenwood Cemetery, Section B. The marker for his father lists him as Caleb T. Scoville.
{US 1860; ROV; Cem. records}

SCRITSMIER, Christian - Pvt., Co. C, 1st Regt., Wis. Hvy. Art.
Christian resided at Neenah and enlisted there on Sept. 8, 1863. He was assigned as above and was mustered out on Sept. 21, 1865. Christian was married in Winnebago County on Oct. 18, 1868 to Bertha Spies.
{ROV; WCMR v.1, p.382, #2351}

SCRITSMIER, Peter L. - Pvt., Co. G, 3rd Regt., Wis. Vol. Inf.
Peter resided at Winchester and enlisted there on May 1, 1861. He was assigned as above and he was wounded and taken prisoner on May 25, 1862 at Chancellorsville, Virginia. Peter was mustered out on July 14, 1864 at the end of his term of enlistment. He was married in Winnebago County on Nov. 16, 1865 to Mary Spies.
{ROV; WCMR v.1, p.286, #1731; Lawson p.809}

SCRITSMIER, Rasmus - Pvt., Co. C, 1st Regt., Wis. Hvy. Art.
Rasmus resided at Vinland and enlisted there on Aug. 11, 1863. He was assigned as above and was mustered out on Sept. 21, 1865.
{ROV}

SCRYMIGER, James - Pvt., Co. B, 52nd Regt., Wis. Vol. Inf.
James resided at Hartford, Washington County and enlisted there on Mar. 22, 1865. He was assigned as above and was then mustered out on July 28, 1865. James was listed (Schruneger) in the veteran section of the 1885 Wisconsin State census at P.O. Winneconne. He was listed (Schrynnger) in the 1890 federal census as residing in the village of Winneconne. Ann, his widow, was listed in 1905 as residing on Olive Street in Winneconne.
{US 1890; WC-V 1885; ROV; B-1905}

SEAMERS, Oscar - Pvt., Co. G, 3rd (reorg.) Regt., Wis. Cav.
Oscar resided at Vinland and enlisted there on Feb. 26, 1864. He was assigned as a saddler with the above company and was mustered out on Oct. 27, 1865.
{ROV}

SEARLES, James M. - Lt., Co. A, 38th Regt., Wis. Vol. Inf.
James was a brother of W.H. Searles from a following sketch. He resided at Oshkosh and enlisted there on Aug. 13, 1862. He was assigned as Private, Co. C, 21st Regt., Wis. Vol. Inf. He was commissioned as 2nd Lieutenant of Co. A, 38th Regt., Wis. Vol. Inf. on Mar. 8, 1864. He was Assistant Quartermaster of that regiment from May 3, 1864 to Sept. 27, 1864. James was commissioned as Captain of Co. A on July 11, 1865 but was not mustered at that rank. He was mustered out on July 26, 1865. James was residing in Cedar Rapids, Iowa when he returned to Oshkosh in July 1884 to visit his brother.
{ROV; OWN 31 Jul 1884}

SEARLES, W.H. - Pvt., 43rd Regt., Wis. Vol. Inf.?
W.H. was a brother of James from a previous sketch. He was listed as above in the veteran section of the 1885 Wisconsin State census at P.O. Oshkosh. He was not found in the records of that regiment.
{WC-V}

SEARS, William H. - Pvt., Co. K, 14th Regt., Wis. Vol. Inf.
William resided at Fond du Lac, Fond du Lac County and enlisted there on Feb. 8, 1862. He was assigned as above and was mustered out on Feb. 6, 1865. William was listed in the 1890 federal census as residing in the city of Oshkosh. He provided his unit designation as Co. A in the above regiment. William was listed in 1905 as an employee at the Paine Lumber Co. and residing at 169 Ninth Street in Oshkosh.
{US 1890; ROV; B-1905}

SECOR, James D. - Pvt., Co. K, 11th Regt., Wis. Vol. Inf.
James resided at Clayton and enlisted there on Sept. 28, 1861. He was assigned as above. James contracted a disease and died on Jan. 1, 1863 at VanBuren, Missouri.
{ROV}

SEDGWICK, George H. - Cpl., Co. K, 7th Regt., Wis. Vol. Inf.
George resided at Neenah and enlisted on Aug. 16, 1861. He was assigned as above and was promoted to Corporal in that company. He was wounded in the battle at Antietam, Maryland. George died of those wounds on Sept. 19, 1862 at Boonesboro, Maryland.
{ROV}

SEELEY, Allen - Pvt., Co. F, 3rd (reorg.) Regt., Wis. Cav.
Allen resided at Oshkosh and enlisted there on Jan. 5, 1864. He was assigned as above and was mustered out on May 23, 1865.
{ROV}

SEELEY, David - Pvt., Co. H, 19th Regt., Wis. Vol. Inf.
David resided at Oshkosh and enlisted there on Jan. 18, 1862. He was assigned as above and was discharged on June 27, 1862 due to a disability.
{ROV}

SEELEY, Eli - Pvt., Co. D, 32nd Regt., Wis. Vol. Inf.
Eli was born on June 1, 1822 at Deerfield, Tioga County, Pennsylvania. He was a son of Eleazer and Mary (Conant) Seeley. Eleazer was born at Litchfield, Connecticut and was a veteran of the War of 1812. His father was a veteran of the American Revolution. Mary was still living at age 86 years in the town of Deerfield in 1887. Eli was married to Sarah Curtis on Dec. 25, 1842. She was born on Mar. 11, 1828 at New York and was a daughter of Daniel and Sarah (Sanderson) Curtis of New Hampshire. Eli was educated in the common schools of Pennsylvania and, being raised on a farm, he learned that occupation. Eli also attended the Alfred Academy at Alfred, Allegany County, New York. He was a mechanic and a skilled carpenter. He came to Wisconsin in May 1855 and settled at Oshkosh, where he resided on a farm north of town and was there engaged until the outbreak of the Civil War. Eli and Sarah were listed in the 1860 federal census as residing on a farm in the town of Clayton at P.O. Neenah. Listed with them were the following children: Eurenetta, born circa 1846; Sarah, born circa 1847; and Sophia, born circa 1850. All three daughters were born in Pennsylvania. Eli enlisted at Vinland on Aug. 20, 1862. He was assigned as above and was discharged by a surgeon's certificate on Feb. 9, 1863 at Memphis, Tennessee due to a disability. He had been a patient in the hospitals at both Oxford, Mississippi and Memphis. Eli returned to Oshkosh and recovered his health. He was then engaged in business as a carpenter and was listed as such in 1868 with his residence being at 21 W. Polk Street in Oshkosh. He increased the

SEELEY, Eli (cont.)
size of his business and was then a contractor and builder, having in 1888 constructed 90 buildings in the city of Oshkosh and another 50 nearby. He was listed in that year as a member of GAR Post #241 at Oshkosh. Eli was listed in the veteran section of the 1885, 1895 and 1905 Wisconsin State census at P.O. Oshkosh. He was listed in the 1890 federal census as residing in Oshkosh and suffering from partial paralysis. Eli died on Jan. 8, 1917 at Oshkosh. Sarah died on Nov. 19, 1897. Both are buried in the city of Oshkosh at Riverside Cemetery. Sophia, a daughter, was born on July 21, 1849 at Steuben County, New York. She was married first to Augustus Haight, the subject of a previous sketch. She was then married to a Professor Hall of the University of Minnesota. Sophia died on July 15, 1891.
{US 1860; WC-V 1885, 1895, 1905; SCA 1:604-5; OWN 16 July 1891; T-1868; ROV} {Cem. records}

SEELEY, James - Pvt., Co. E, 43rd Regt., Wis. Vol. Inf.
James resided at Neenah and enlisted there on Aug. 31, 1864. He was assigned as above and was mustered out on June 24, 1865.
{ROV}

SEIDMORE, Thomas - Pvt., unassigned, 3rd Regt., Wis. Cav.
Thomas resided at Oshkosh and enlisted there on Jan. 16, 1864. He was not found in the records of any company within that regiment.
{ROV}

SEILER, John - Pvt., Co. G, 3rd (reorg.) Regt., Wis. Cav.
John resided at Oshkosh and enlisted on Nov. 6, 1863. He was assigned as above and was mustered out on Oct. 27, 1865. John was listed in the 1890 federal census as residing in the town of Dupont, Waupaca County. He was listed as partially deaf.
{US 1890; ROV}

SELLMER, Gustavus - Sgt., Co. H, 21st Regt., Wis. Vol. Inf.
Gustavus resided at Oshkosh and enlisted there on Aug. 15, 1862. He was assigned as above and was promoted to Corporal and then Sergeant in that company. Gustavus was mustered out on June 8, 1865. He was listed in 1868 as a mill man boarding at 13 Twelfth Street in the city of Oshkosh.
{ROV; T-1868}

SELPOLE, Joseph - Pvt., Co. G, 3rd Regt., Wis. Vol. Inf.
Joseph resided at Clayton and enlisted there on Jan. 30, 1864. He was assigned as above and was mustered out on July 18, 1865.
{ROV}

SENTANCE, Thomas - Pvt., Co. G, 51st Regt., Wis. Vol. Inf.
Thomas and Ann, his wife, were both born in 1821. Thomas resided at Beaver Dam, Dodge County and enlisted there on Mar. 15, 1865. He was assigned as above and was then mustered out at Milwaukee, Wisconsin on May 6, 1865. Thomas was listed in the 1890 federal census as residing in the town of Vinland at P.O. Clemansville. He listed then that he had suffered from a rupture. Thomas died in 1895. Ann was listed in 1905

SENTANCE, Thomas (cont.)
as residing in the town of Vinland. She died in 1907. Both are buried in the town of Vinland at Brooks Cemetery.
{US 1890; ROV; B-1905; Cem. records}

SERVICE, David A. - Pvt., Co. B, 21st Regt., Wis. Vol. Inf.
David was born circa 1842 at New York. He was a son of Charles H. and Nancy A. Service. Charles was born circa 1819/27 at New York and Nancy was born circa 1821 in that same state. All three were listed in the 1850 federal census as residing with William E. Ford in the town of Vinland. Charles and Nancy were listed in the 1860 federal census as residing on a farm in the town of Vinland. Listed with them were the following children: David; Aurelia, born circa 1849; Lydia, born circa 1850; Ameline, born circa 1852; Celia, born circa 1854; and Cornelia, born circa 1857. The two elder children were born in New York and the others were born in Wisconsin. David enlisted at Vinland on Aug. 14, 1862. He was assigned as above and was then mustered out on June 8, 1865. David was listed in the veteran section of the 1885 Wisconsin State census at P.O. Oshkosh. He was married to Hester Ann, daughter of E. and H.C. Boulden. Hester was born on July 27, 1849 and died on Jan. 10, 1875. David was listed in 1888 as a member of GAR Post #10 at Oshkosh. He was listed in 1905 as residing at the Wisconsin Veterans' Home at King. He was listed in the 1910 federal census as a widower residing at King. He had been married for five years. David was still residing at King in 1920. He is buried with a simple military marker next to his wife in the town of Winneconne at Bell Cemetery.
{US 1850, 1860, 1910; WC-V 1885; Cem. records; ROV; 21-33rd; GAR 40th}

SEVERSON, Ole - Pvt., Co. H, 36th Regt., Wis. Vol. Inf.
Ole resided at Utica and enlisted there on Feb. 29, 1864. He was assigned as above and was wounded at Petersburg, Virginia on June 18, 1864. Ole was transferred to the Veteran Reserve Corps on Apr. 28, 1865 and was then discharged on July 31, 1865 due to a disability.
{ROV}

SEXTON, James H. - Pvt., Co. I, 21st Regt., Wis. Vol. Inf.
James was born circa 1830 at Massachusetts. He was listed in the 1860 federal census as a sailor residing with the family of Charles Shoemaker in the village of Neenah. James enlisted at Neenah on Aug. 13, 1862. He was assigned as above and was taken prisoner at Perryville, Kentucky on Oct. 10, 1862. He was been paroled on the field and was sent to Camp Lew Wallace near Columbus, Ohio where he still awaited exchange in Oct. 1862. James was transferred to the Veteran Reserve Corps on Jan. 28, 1865 and was mustered out on June 28, 1865.
{US 1860; ROV; Lawson p.833; OWN 29 Oct 1862}

SEYMOUR, David - Pvt., Co. B, 21st Regt., Wis. Vol. Inf.
David was born on Oct. 8, 1822. He resided at Rushford and enlisted there on Aug. 15, 1862. He was assigned as above and was transferred to the Veteran Reserve Corps on Sept. 1, 1863. David was listed in the veteran section of the 1885 Wisconsin State census at P.O. Waukau. Carrie E., daughter of David and Mary Seymour, died May 18, 1874 at age 11 years, 7 months and 18 days. Ellen, another daughter, was born on Apr. 29, 1844 and died on Mar. 13, 1889. David died on Mar. 18, 1888. Mary, widow of David,

SEYMOUR, David (cont.)
was listed in the 1890 federal census as residing in the town of Nepeuskun at P.O. Waukau. She died on Apr. 19, 1891 at age 68 years, 6 months and 18 days. David is buried with his wife and both daughters in the town of Rushford at Waukau Cemetery.
{US 1890; WC-V 1885; ROV; Cem. records}

SHAMBAUGH, Henry - Sgt., Co. A, 47th Regt., Wis. Vol. Inf.
Henry was born circa 1828 at Ohio. Margaret, his wife, was born circa 1832, also at Ohio. They were listed in the 1860 federal census as residing on a farm in the town of Winchester. Listed with them were the following children: Sarah, born circa 1854 at Ohio; William, born circa 1855 at Ohio; Mary, born circa 1857 at Wisconsin; and Nancy, born circa 1859 at Wisconsin. Henry enlisted at Winchester on Feb. 11, 1865. He was assigned as above and was promoted to 1st Sergeant of that company. He was then mustered out on Sept. 15, 1865.
{US 1860; ROV}

SHANNON, Sylvester S. - Pvt., Co. K, 46th Regt., Wis. Vol. Inf.
Sylvester resided at Winchester and enlisted there on Feb. 23, 1865. He was assigned as above and was mustered out on Sept. 27, 1865. Sylvester was listed in the veteran section of the 1885 and 1895 Wisconsin State census at P.O. Winchester. He was listed in the 1890 federal census as residing in the town of Winchester at P.O. Winchester. Sylvester was listed in 1905 as residing on Cedar Street in the village of Winneconne. He died at Oshkosh and was buried in Winneconne on Mar. 21, 1910.
{US 1890; WC-V 1885, 1895; ROV; B-1905}

SHANNON, William F. - Pvt., Co. D, 50th Regt., Wis. Vol. Inf.?
William was listed in the 1890 federal census as residing in the town of Dayton, Waupaca County at P.O. Rural. He then listed his unit designation as above and provided his service dates as having been from Feb. 13, 1865 to June 12, 1865. William added that he suffered from rheumatism. He was listed (W.F.) in the veteran section of the 1905 Wisconsin State census at P.O. Oshkosh, then as a veteran of Co. D, 50th Regt., N.Y. Vol. Inf.
{US 1890; WC-V 1905}

SHARER, Henry - Pvt., Unassigned, 3rd Regt., Wis. Cav.
Henry resided at Oshkosh and enlisted there on Feb. 23, 1864. He was assigned to the 3rd Regt., Wis. Cav. but not to any company within that regiment.
{ROV}

SHARP, James H. - Sgt., Co. L, 1st Regt., Wis. Cav.
James was born circa 1842 at New York, a son of Abram and Ruth Sharp. Abram was born circa 1799 at Vermont and Ruth was born circa 1815 at New York. They were listed in the 1860 federal census as residing on a farm in the town of Utica at P.O. Welaunee. James enlisted on Oct. 30, 1861 and was assigned as above. He was promoted to Corporal and then 1st Sergeant in that company. He was mustered out on Jan. 8, 1865 at the end of his term of enlistment. James was listed in the veteran section of the 1885 Wisconsin State census at P.O. Pickett. He was listed in 1888 as a member of GAR Post #241 at Oshkosh. He was listed in the veteran section of the 1895 and 1905 state census at P.O. Omro. He was listed in 1905 as a dealer in general merchandise

SHARP, James H. (cont.)
residing at 614 W. Division Street in the village of Omro. James died on Mar. 6, 1911. He is buried in the town of Utica at Liberty Prairie Cemetery.
{US 1860; WC-V 1885, 1895, 1905; ROV; GRI; B-1905}

SHARPE, Walter B. - Pvt., Co. B, 21st Regt., Wis. Vol. Inf.
Walter was born circa 1837 at Pennsylvania. He was listed in the 1860 federal census as residing with the family of Charles Wilson in the second ward of the city of Oshkosh. Walter enlisted at Oshkosh on Aug. 13, 1862. He was assigned as above and was mustered out on June 8, 1865. Walter was listed in the veteran section of the 1885 and 1905 Wisconsin State census at P.O. Oshkosh. He was listed in 1905 as a laborer boarding at 105 High Street in Oshkosh.
{US 1860; WC-V 1885, 1905; ROV; B-1905}

SHARPE, William - Lt., Co. B, 3rd Regt., Wis. Cav.
William was born circa 1821 at England. Elizabeth, his wife, was born circa 1828, also at England. William was listed in the 1860 federal census as a carpenter residing in the fourth ward of the city of Oshkosh. Listed with him were his wife and the following children: Elizabeth, born circa 1849 at England; and Charles, born circa 1857 at Wisconsin. William enlisted at Oshkosh on Nov. 23, 1861. He was assigned as above and was promoted to 1st Sergeant in that company. William was commissioned as 1st Lieutenant of Co. B, 3rd (reorg.) Regt., Wis. Cav. on Mar. 9, 1865. He was promoted to Major of that regiment on Sept. 15, 1865 but was not mustered at that rank. William was mustered out on Sept. 8, 1865. He was listed in the veteran section of the 1885 Wisconsin State census at P.O. Oshkosh. He was listed in 1888 as a member of GAR Post #241 at Oshkosh. William was listed in the 1890 federal census as residing at 25 Jefferson Avenue in Oshkosh. He was listed in 1905 as residing at 9 Jefferson Avenue in Oshkosh.
{US 1860, 1890; WC-V 1885; ROV; B-1905}

SHATTUCK, James Henry - Pvt., Co. G, 26th Regt., Wis. Vol. Inf.
James was born in 1836. He resided at Jackson, Washington County and enlisted there on Aug. 12, 1862. He was assigned as above and was discharged on Apr. 9, 1863 due to a disability. James and Ellen had at least a son, Perley, who died on July 20, 18__ at age 21 years and 7 months. James was listed in the veteran section of the 1885, 1895 and 1905 Wisconsin State census at P.O. Omro. He was listed in the 1890 federal census as residing in the village of Omro. James was then suffering from a kidney affliction. Ellen died on Feb. 1, 1890 at age 47 years and 8 months. James was listed in 1905 as a grocer residing at the corner of High and Mill Streets in Omro. He died at Omro on Feb. 15, 1912 and was buried with his wife and son Perley at Omro Cemetery, Olin's Addition, Section B, plot 62.
{US 1890; WC-V 1885, 1895, 1905; ROV; B-1905; Cem. records}

SHATTUCK, Nathan W. - Pvt., Co. C, 21st Regt., Wis. Vol. Inf.
Nathan resided at Omro and enlisted there on Aug. 14, 1862. He was assigned as above and was reported as in the hospital at Louisville, Kentucky on Nov. 6, 1862. He was then suffering with rheumatism. Nathan had returned to his unit prior to Apr. 16, 1863. He was then mustered out on June 8, 1865. Nathan was listed in the veteran section of

SHATTUCK, Nathan W. (cont.)
the 1895 Wisconsin State census at P.O. Sprague, Barron County.
{WC-V 1895; ROV; OWN 13 Nov 1862; OWN 07 May 1863}

SHEARS, Ira - Pvt., Co. G, 1st Regt., Michigan Cav.
Ira was listed as above in the veteran section of the 1905 Wisconsin State census at P.O. Omro.
{WC-V 1905}

SHEEL, August - Pvt., Co. B, 3rd Regt., Wis. Cav.
August was born circa 1826 at Prussia. Wilhelmine, his wife, was born circa 1825, also at Prussia. August was listed (Scheel) in the 1860 federal census as a tailor residing in the first ward of the city of Oshkosh. Residing with him were his wife and the following children: Emilie, born circa 1851 at Prussia; Anna, born circa 1853 at Prussia; and Carl, born circa 1859 at Wisconsin. August enlisted at Oshkosh on Dec. 23, 1861. He was assigned as above and was transferred to the brigade band on Feb. 24, 1863. Mary, widow of August, was listed in the 1890 federal census as residing in Oshkosh.
{US 1890; ROV}

SHEERIN, Francis S. Jr. - Pvt., Co. I, 21st Regt., Wis. Vol. Inf.
Frank was born circa 1843 at New York, a son of Francis and Catherine Sheerin and a brother of Thaddeus from a following sketch. The father was born circa 1818 at Ireland and the mother was born circa 1823 at Vermont. Francis was listed in the 1860 federal census as a tailor residing in the village of Neenah. Listed with him were his wife and the following children: James, born circa 1842 at New York; Francis; Oscar, born circa 1845 at Ohio; Thaddeus; Henry, born circa 1851 at Wisconsin; Charles, born circa 1856 at Wisconsin; and Ellen, born circa 1859 at Wisconsin. Frank resided at Neenah and enlisted there on Aug. 14, 1862. He was assigned as above and was then mustered out on June 8, 1865. Frank was listed in 1920 as residing at Ladysmith, Rusk County.
{US 1860; ROV; 21-33rd}

SHEERIN, Thaddeus S. - Pvt., 8th Batt., Wis. Lt. Art.
Thaddeus was born on Apr. 13, 1846 at Akron, Ohio. He was a son of Francis and Catherine Sheerin and a brother of Francis from a previous sketch. The family removed to Wisconsin in 1849 and settled at Neenah. Thaddeus enlisted at Neenah on Mar. 25, 1862. He was assigned as above and was discharged Aug. 28, 1862 due to a disability. Thaddeus then re-enlisted on Aug. 17, 1864 and he was assigned to the Naval Gunboat Service. He was trained on the Great Lakes at Chicago and was then assigned to the gunboat "Juliet." After his discharge, Thaddeus returned to Neenah. He was married in 1870 to Fannie Coleman of Neenah. Thaddeus was listed in the veteran section of the 1885, 1895 and 1905 Wisconsin State census at P.O. Neenah. He was listed in the 1890 federal census as residing in the city of Neenah. In 1895 he was listed as having been a member of the crew of the "Paw Paw" in the U.S. Navy. He was listed in 1905 as an engineer at Gilbert Paper Company and residing at 302 Hewitt Street in Neenah. His son Clifford D. Sheerin was listed at that same address. Fannie died in 1923. Thaddeus was listed in 1927 as residing at Neenah. He was married on Sept. 17, 1927 to Mary Runde. Thaddeus died at his home in Neenah on June 7, 1939. He was survived by his second wife, son Clifford of Menasha, and half-brother William Sheerin of Hortonville.

SHEERIN, Thaddeus S. (cont.)
Thaddeus was buried in Neenah at Oak Hill Cemetery.
{US 1860, 1890; WC-V 1885, 1895, 1905; ROV; 21-40th; Lawson p.840-1; B-1905}
{ODN 08 Jun 1939}

SHELDON, Emmett Timothy - Pvt., Co. C, 41st Regt., Wis. Vol. Inf.
Emmett was born on Aug. 16, 1845 at New York. He was a son of Timothy and Sarah Sheldon. The father was born circa 1817 at New York and the mother was born circa 1828 at Vermont. They were listed in the 1860 federal census as residing on a farm in the town of Omro. Listed with them were Emmett and a daughter, Ella, who was born circa 1857 at Wisconsin. Also listed with them was George Sheldon, father of Timothy. He was born circa 1791 at New York. Emmett enlisted at Omro on June 4, 1864. He was assigned as above and was mustered out on Sept. 23, 1864 at the end of his term of enlistment. Emmett was married to Mary Elizabeth Hueston in Winnebago County on May 27, 1871. She was born on Sept. 30, 1848 at Wisconsin. They had a daughter, unnamed at registration, who was born in Omro on Sept. 15, 1877. They were listed in the 1880 federal census as residing in the town of Omro along with two of their children: Harry H., born circa 1875; and Maude, born circa 1878. Emmett was listed in the veteran section of the 1885, 1895 and 1905 Wisconsin State census at P.O. Omro. He was listed in the 1890 federal census as residing in the town of Omro at P.O. Omro. He was listed in 1905 as a dealer in real estate and loans. He was then residing at 216 Water Street in the village of Omro. Mary died on June 16, 1888 at Omro and Emmett died on Mar. 8, 1927. Both are buried at Omro Cemetery, Hueston's Addition, plot 9.
{US 1860, 1880, 1890; WC-V 1885, 1895, 1905; WCMR v.1, p.498, #3278; B-1905}
{ROV; WCBR v.2, p.75, #181; Cem. records}

SHELDON, George S. - Cpl., Co. I, 21st Regt., Wis. Vol. Inf.
George was born circa 1840 at Vermont. He was a son of John and Lucina Sheldon. Both parents were also natives of Vermont, the father born there circa 1813 and the mother born circa 1815. They were listed in the 1860 federal census as residing on a farm in the town of Clayton at P.O. Neenah. Listed with them were the following children: George; Sanford, born circa 1844 at Vermont; Edith, born circa 1851 at Vermont; and Huldah, born circa 1857 at Ohio. George enlisted at Clayton on Aug. 12, 1862. He was assigned as above and was then promoted to Corporal in that company. George was discharged due to a disability on Jan. 25, 1863. Flora E., his daughter, was residing at Chilton in 1920. In August of that year she removed to the west coast in an attempt to recover her health.
{US 1860; ROV; 21-33rd}

SHELLEY, Simon - Pvt., Co. E, 21st Regt., Wis. Vol. Inf.
Simon resided at Brothertown, Calumet County and enlisted there on Aug. 13, 1862. He was assigned as above and was wounded at Dallas, Georgia. Simon was mustered out on May 25, 1865. A Henry F. Shelley was a member of that same company. Simon was listed in the 1890 federal census as residing at 34 Scott Street in the city of Oshkosh. He listed then that he had been shot in the jaw and the left shoulder during his military service. Simon was listed in the veteran section of the 1895 Wisconsin State census at P.O. Oshkosh. Cynthia, his widow, was listed in 1905 as residing at 34 Scott Street in Oshkosh.
{US 1890; WC-V 1895; ROV; B-1905}

SHELTON, Charles H. - Pvt., Co. D, 32nd Regt., Wis. Vol. Inf.
Charles was born on July 10, 1840 at Medina, Ohio. He was a son of Jeremiah and Clarissa (Mastin) Shelton. Jeremiah's father was a native of Germany and Clarissa's father was a veteran of the American Revolution. Clarissa was born circa 1806 at New York. Jeremiah removed to Wisconsin with his family circa 1845. Clarissa was listed in the 1860 federal census as residing in the town of Nekimi at P.O. Oshkosh. Listed with her were two sons, Charles and Edwin H. Shelton. Edwin was born circa 1846 at Wisconsin. Charles was married at Medina, Outagamie County, Wisconsin in March 1861 to Sophronia Rhoads. He resided at Nekimi and enlisted there on Nov. 17, 1863. He was assigned as above and was transferred to Co. D, 16th (reorg.) Regt., Wis. Vol. Inf. on June 4, 1865. Charles then mustered out at Louisville, Kentucky on July 12, 1865. He had provided his residence as Oshkosh at the time of his transfer. Charles contracted an illness which kept him confined for some time in the hospital at Marietta, Georgia. He was a member of GAR Post #7 at Omro and he removed with his family to Winneconne in 1881. Charles was listed in the veteran section of the 1885 Wisconsin State census at P.O. Winneconne. He was listed in the 1890 federal census as residing in the town of Winneconne at P.O. Winneconne.
{US 1860, 1890; WC-V 1885; ROV; SCA 1:421-2}

SHEPARD, Henry - Pvt., Co. A, 1st Regt., New York Mounted Rifles.
Henry was married in Winnebago County on Oct. 27, 1868 to M.L. Lansing. He was listed as above in the veteran section of the 1885 and 1895 Wisconsin State census at P.O. Neenah. He was listed in 1905 as residing at the Wisconsin Veterans' Home at King. Mary L., his wife, was residing there with him. Henry was credited with 36 months of service.
{WC-V 1885, 1895; GAR 40th; WCMR v.1, p.406, #2542}

SHEPARD, James R. - Cpl., Co. D, 41st Regt., Wis. Vol. Inf.
James was born circa 1844 at Massachusetts. He was a son of Lysander and Ethelinda Shepard and a brother of Joseph from a following sketch. Lysander was born circa 1807 at Massachusetts and Ethelinda was born circa 1813 at Connecticut. They were listed (Shepherd) in the 1860 federal census as residing on a farm in the town of Menasha. Listed with them were the following children: Joseph; Alice, born circa 1841; James; and Laura, born circa 1854. All of the children were born in Massachusetts. James enlisted at Menasha on May 2, 1864. He was assigned as above and was promoted to Corporal in that company. James was mustered out on Sept. 23, 1864 at the end of his term of enlistment. He died in 1905.
{US 1860; ROV; Lawson p.840}

SHEPARD, Joseph P. - Lt., Co. G, 3rd Regt., Wis. Vol. Inf.
Joseph was born circa 1838 at Massachusetts. He was a son of Lysander and Ethelinda Shepard and a brother of James from a previous sketch. Joseph was listed in the 1860 federal census as a carpenter residing with his parents in the town of Menasha. He listed his residence as Neenah when he enlisted on May 1, 1861. He was assigned as above and was promoted to Sergeant in that company. Joseph was commissioned as 2nd Lieutenant of that company on June 27, 1861 and was promoted to 1st Lieutenant on Nov. 11, 1861. He was wounded at Antietam, Maryland on Sept. 17, 1862 and he died of those wounds on Nov. 10, 1862.
{US 1860; ROV; HN 1878 p.123}

SHEPARD, Oliver W. - Pvt., Co. D, 146th Regt., Illinois Vol. Inf.
Oliver was listed in the 1890 federal census as residing at 89 E. Polk Street in the city of Oshkosh. He then provided his unit designation as above and his service dates as having been from Sept. 3, 1864 to July 8, 1865. Oliver listed that he suffered from a hernia. He was listed as a musician in the above company in the veteran section of the 1895 and 1905 Wisconsin State census at P.O. Oshkosh. Oliver was listed in 1905 as a painter and sign writer residing at 25 Boyd Street in Oshkosh.
{US 1890; WC-V 1895, 1905; B-1905}

SHEPARDSON, Albert J. - Pvt., Co. F, 18th Regt., Wis. Vol. Inf.
Albert resided at Omro and enlisted there on Dec. 17, 1861. He was assigned as above and was wounded at Vicksburg, Mississippi. Albert was mustered out on June 2, 1865. He was married in Winnebago County on July 4, 1874 to Martha Terrell.
{ROV; WCMR v.5, p.8, #48}

SHEPARDSON, Moody - Pvt., Co. G, 51st Regt., Wis. Vol. Inf.
Moody was born circa 1847 at Wisconsin, a son of Albert and Adaline Shepardson. Albert was born circa 1816 at Vermont and Adaline was born circa 1816 at New Hampshire. They were listed in the 1860 federal census as residing on a farm in the town of Winneconne. Listed with them were the following children: Electa, born circa 1837; Jonah, born circa 1839; Victoria, born circa 1841; Martha, born circa 1844; Moody; Albion, born circa 1849; Orville, born circa 1852; and Robert, born circa 1856. The four youngest children were born in Wisconsin and Electa was born in New York. The other children were born in Ohio. Moody listed his residence as Rushford when he enlisted on Mar. 13, 1865. He was assigned as above and was then mustered out at Milwaukee, Wisconsin on May 6, 1865.
{US 1860; ROV}

SHEPHERD, Sewell - Sgt., Co. H, 1st Regt., Wis. Hvy. Art.
Sewell resided at Algoma and enlisted there on Aug. 31, 1864. He was assigned as above and was promoted to Corporal and then Sergeant in that company. Sewell was mustered out on June 26, 1865.
{ROV}

SHERRY, Benjamin - Pvt., Co. G, 3rd Regt., Wis. Vol. Inf.
Benjamin was born circa 1835 at Pennsylvania. He was a son of Hugh and Caroline Sherry (Shary) who were both born at Pennsylvania. Hugh was born circa 1807/9 and Caroline was born circa 1813/5. They were listed in the 1850 federal census as residing in the town of Neenah. Listed with them were the following children: Benjamin; Henry, born circa 1837 at New York; and Isabella, born circa 1848 at Wisconsin. Hugh was listed in the 1860 federal census as a miller residing in the village of Neenah. Listed with him were his wife and the above-named children. Also listed was Barbara Slick. She was born circa 1789 at Pennsylvania and she was probably the mother of Caroline. Benjamin was listed as engaged in daugerrien arts. He enlisted at Neenah on Apr. 20, 1861. He was assigned as above and was wounded at Resaca, Georgia. Benjamin was mustered out on June 29, 1864 at the end of his term of enlistment.
{US 1850, 1860; ROV}

SHERRY, James A. - Pvt., Co. A, 1st Regt., Wis. Cav.
James enlisted on Aug. 15, 1861 and was assigned as above. He was mustered out on Sept. 1, 1864 at the end of his term of enlistment. He was listed in 1868 as a filer boarding at 107 Pearl Street in the city of Oshkosh. James was listed in the veteran section of the 1885 and 1895 Wisconsin State census at P.O. Neenah. He was listed in the 1890 federal census as residing in the town of Menasha at P.O. Menasha.
{US 1890; WC-V 1885, 1895; ROV; T-1868}

SHERRY, Thomas - Pvt., Co. A, 1st Regt., Wis. Cav.
Thomas was born circa 1843 at New York. He was a son of Peter and Ariminta Sherry. The mother was born circa 1808 at Maryland and the father was born about that same year at Pennsylvania. Peter was a brother of Hugh Sherry, father of Benjamin from a previous sketch. He and Ariminta were listed in the 1860 federal census as residing in the village of Neenah. Listed with them were the following children: Mary, born circa 1840; Thomas; and Isabella, born circa 1847. All three children were born at New York. Thomas enlisted on Aug. 22, 1861 and was assigned as above. He was discharged on Sept. 30, 1862. He was listed in 1868 as a cooper boarding at 23 Division Street in the city of Oshkosh. Thomas was listed in the veteran section of the 1885 and 1895 Wisconsin State census at P.O. Neenah. He was listed in the 1890 federal census as residing in the city of Neenah. Thomas then listed that he suffered from protruding piles.
{US 1860, 1890; WC-V 1885, 1895; T-1868; ROV}

SHERWOOD, Andrew - Pvt., Co. D, 31st Regt., Wis. Vol. Inf.
Andrew resided at Utica and enlisted there on Aug. 15, 1862. He was assigned as above and was mustered out on June 20, 1865.
{ROV}

SHERWOOD, Gilbert - Pvt., Co. H, 19th Regt., Wis. Vol. Inf.
Gilbert was born in 1797. He was married in 1818 to Cynthia Webster. She was born in 1801 at Rutland, Vermont. They began married life in New York City, where Gilbert was a dry goods merchant. After several years they removed to Ft. Niagara, New York. They then moved to Buffalo, New York where a sister of Cynthia was married to a cousin of President Fillmore. Gilbert and Cynthia again moved west and located in Wisconsin, settling at Oshkosh in 1854. They had five sons and one daughter, including: Gleason F., born in 1830, died on Mar. 8, 1855; Daniel, born in 1832, died in 1858; Eliphalet, born in 1836, died in a railroad accident in 1859; and Mrs. E.T. Ellsworth. Gilbert resided at Oshkosh and enlisted there on Jan. 20, 1862 at age 65 years. He was assigned as above and was discharged on Oct. 4, 1864 due to a disability. Gilbert died on May 30, 1865 and Cynthia died on May 10, 1887. Both are buried with members of their family in Oshkosh at Riverside Cemetery.
{ROV; OWN 19 May 1887; Cem. records}

SHERWOOD, Norman - Pvt., Co. D, 31st Regt., Wis. Vol. Inf.
Norman resided at Utica and enlisted there on Aug. 15, 1862. He was assigned as above. Norman was killed in action on Aug. 1, 1864 at Atlanta, Georgia.
{ROV}

SHERWOOD, Ogden - Pvt., Co. B, 32nd Regt., Wis. Vol. Inf.
Ogden was born circa 1810 at Vermont. He was listed in the 1860 federal census as a grocer residing in the first ward of the city of Oshkosh. No family was listed with him. Ogden listed his residence as Omro when he enlisted on Aug. 21, 1862. He was assigned as above. Ogden contracted a disease and died at Memphis, Tennessee on July 2, 1863. He is listed as having been buried there at the Mississippi River Cemetery.
{US 1860; ROV; GRI}

SHINEY, Franklin - Pvt., Co. C, 32nd Regt., Wis. Vol. Inf.
Franklin resided at Oshkosh and enlisted there on Dec. 29, 1863. He was assigned as above and was wounded at Bentonsville, N.C. on Mar. 21, 1865. He was transferred to Co. G, 16th (reorg.) Regt., Wis. Vol. Inf. on June 4, 1865 and was then mustered out on July 12, 1865.
{ROV}

SHINEY, Lewis - Pvt., Co. F, 18th Regt., Wis. Vol. Inf.
Lewis was born circa 1828 at Canada. Narcissa, his wife, was born circa 1829 at Canada. They were listed in the 1860 federal census as residing on a farm in the town of Omro. Then listed with them were the following children: Mary, born circa 1847; Elisabeth, born circa 1849; Augustus, born circa 1851; and Edward, born circa 1853. All of the children were born in Vermont. Lewis listed his residence as Oshkosh when he enlisted on Oct. 19, 1861. He was assigned as above and was taken prisoner at Shiloh, Tennessee. He was discharged on Jan. 16, 1863. Lewis then re-enlisted at Omro on Dec. 21, 1863 and was assigned as a Private to Co. C, 32nd Regt., Wis. Vol. Inf. He was wounded on Mar. 21, 1865 at Bentonsville, N.C. and was transferred to Co. G, 16th (reorg.) Regt., Wis. Vol. Inf. on June 4, 1865. He was mustered out on July 12, 1865.
{US 1860; ROV}

SHINNERS, John - Pvt., Co. I, 29th Regt., Wis. Vol. Inf.
John resided at Erin, Washington County and enlisted there on Aug. 20, 1862. He was assigned as above and was listed as having deserted on Oct. 12, 1862. John was listed in the veteran section of the 1885 Wisconsin State census at P.O. Menasha. He was listed in 1905 as an employee of the Menasha Woodenware Co. and residing at 357 Third Street in the city of Menasha.
{WC-V 1885; ROV; B-1905}

SHIPMAN, Ellet D. - Pvt., Co. D, 16th (reorg.) Regt., Wis. Vol. Inf.
Ellet was born on Apr. 14, 1839. He resided at Rosendale, Fond du Lac County and enlisted there on Aug. 27, 1864. He was assigned as above and was mustered out on June 2, 1865. Ellet was listed in the veteran section of the 1885 Wisconsin State census at P.O. Omro. He was listed in the 1890 federal census as residing in the village of Omro. Ellet reported then that he had first served as a Private in Co. I, 5th Regt., Wis. Vol. Inf. from May 10, 1861 to Nov. 12, 1861. He then reported a second enlistment as a Sergeant in the Wisconsin Light Artillery from Jan. 12, 1862 to June 12, 1862 before he enlisted in the 16th (reorg.) Regt., Wis. Vol. Inf. Ellet also added that he suffered from diarrhea due to exposure while in the service. He died on Apr. 6, 1895. Eliza Y., his widow, was listed in 1905 as residing on Quarter Street in Omro. She was born in 1840 and died in 1926. Ellet and Eliza are buried at Omro Cemetery, Olin's Addition,

SHIPMAN, Ellet D. (cont.)
Section C, plot 17.
{US 1890; WC-V 1885; ROV; B-1905; Cem. records}

SHIPMAN, Ira G. - Cpl., Co. B, 21st Regt., Wis. Vol. Inf.
Ira resided at Omro and enlisted there on Aug. 12, 1862. He was assigned as above and was promoted to Corporal in that company. Ira was mustered out on June 8, 1865. He was listed in the veteran section of the 1885 Wisconsin State census at Osseo, Trempeleau County.
{WC-V 1885; ROV}

SHOWERS, Elijah B. - Pvt., Co. B, 21st Regt., Wis. Vol. Inf.
Elijah resided at Wolf River and enlisted there on Aug. 15, 1862. He was assigned as above. Elijah was killed in action at Chaplin Hills, Kentucky on Oct. 8, 1862.
{ROV}

SHRADER, Herman - Cpl., Co. B, 3rd Regt., Wis. Cav.
Herman resided at Oshkosh and enlisted there on Dec. 26, 1861. He was assigned as above and was promoted to Corporal in that company. He was transferred to Co. B, 3rd (reorg.) Regt., Wis. Cav. on Feb. 1, 1865. He was mustered out on Sept. 8, 1865.
{ROV}

SHRIBE, John - Pvt., Co. G, 3rd Regt., Wis. Vol. Inf.
John resided at Neenah and enlisted there on Apr. 20, 1861. He was assigned as above. John was killed at Chancellorsville, Virginia on May 3, 1863.
{ROV}

SHUFELT, George - Pvt., Co. A, 48th Regt., Wis. Vol. Inf.
George resided at Algoma and enlisted there on Feb. 7, 1865. He was assigned as above and was mustered out on Dec. 30, 1865.
{ROV}

SHUFELT, George - Pvt., Co. C, 3rd Regt., Wis. Cav.
George G. Schufelt resided at Brandon, Fond du Lac County and he enlisted there on Feb. 18, 1862. He was assigned as above and was transferred to Co. H, 3rd (reorg.) Regt., Wis. Cav. on Mar. 23, 1865. He was then assigned as a bugler. George was mustered out on Sept. 29, 1865. Charlotte Buttrick, formerly widow of George, was listed in the 1890 federal census as residing in the city of Oshkosh. She then provided his unit designation as above and his service dates as having been from Mar. 24, 1864 to Sept. 29, 1865. She added that George had suffered a wound to his knee while in the military. In 1890 she was listed as the wife of Nathan A. Butrick, the subject of a previous sketch.
{US 1890; ROV}

SHUFELT, Orrin - Pvt., Co. D, 32nd Regt., Wis. Vol. Inf.
Orrin "Doc" Shufelt was born Aug. 27, 1845 at Berkshire, Franklin County, Vermont. He was the sixth son in the family of nine children of George and Alvira (Glover) Shufelt and a brother of Robert and Sheldon from following sketches. The father was born on Aug. 10, 1797 at New York (listed in 1860 as Canada) and he died on Sept. 3, 1860 in

SHUFELT, Orrin (cont.)
Poygan. Alvira was born on Sept. 20, 1804 in the province of Quebec, Canada and she died on Feb. 6, 1887. They removed to Wisconsin in 1854 and settled on a farm in the town of Poygan. They were listed in the 1860 federal census as residing the farm in the town of Poygan at P.O. Omro. Listed with them were the following children: Sheldon; Albert, born circa 1842 at Canada; Orrin; and Jane, born circa 1848 at Vermont. Orrin listed his residence as Omro when he enlisted on Aug. 21, 1862. He was assigned as above and was mustered out on June 12, 1865 after having participated in the Grand Review at Washington, D.C. Two of his brothers had served in Minnesota regiments and had also come home safely. While in service, Orrin sent home money to support his mother. She instead saved the money and paid off the mortgage on their farm. Orrin was married in Winnebago County on Jan. 1, 1867 to Sarah M. Hart. She was born on Oct. 2, 1850 and died on Oct. 12, 1867. He was then married in Winnebago County on Dec. 31, 1867 to Emily Wilber. Emily was born on Apr. 16, 1851 in Winnebago County and was a daughter of Ransom and Eliza (Martin) Wilber. Ransom was born in 1822 and died in 1907. His wife was born in 1822 and died on June 26, 1881. Orrin and Emily had four children: Frank W., born on Nov. 25, 1868; Edna, born on Apr. 10, 1876; Bernice, born Mar. 2, 1878; and Sarah, born in the town of Poygan on Feb. 12, 1881. Emily died on Aug. 17, 1893. Orrin was married third to Carrie I., who was born in 1857. Orrin was listed in the veteran section of the 1885 Wisconsin State census at P.O. Poygan. He was listed in that section of the 1895 and 1905 state census at P.O. Omro. Carrie died in 1927 and Orrin died in 1930. Both are buried, along with his first two wives in the town of Poygan at Oak Hill Cemetery. Ransom and Eliza Wilber are buried on one of his plots there.
{US 1860; WC-V 1885, 1895, 1905; WCBR v.3, p.12, #71; Randall p.50; ROV}
{WCMR v.1, p.316, #1972; Cem. records; ODN 10 Jul 1926}

SHUFELT, Robert A. - Pvt., Co. G, 5th (reorg.) Regt., Wis. Vol. Inf.
Robert was born circa 1826 at Canada. He was a son of George and Alvira (Glover) Shufelt and a brother of Orrin and Sheldon from other sketches. Robert was listed in the 1860 federal census as residing on a farm in the town of Poygan. Listed with him were his wife, Sarah, who was born on Apr. 18, 1833 at Canada, and a son, Homer, who was born circa 1852 at Vermont. Robert enlisted at Omro on Sept. 2, 1864 and was assigned as above. He was mustered out on June 12, 1865. Robert is buried with a simple military marker. Sarah died on Feb. 15, 1895. Both are buried in the town of Poygan at Oak Hill Cemetery.
{US 1860; ROV; Cem. records}

SHUFELT, Sheldon - Pvt., Co. H, 2nd Regt., Minnesota Cav.
Sheldon was born circa 1839 at Vermont. He was a son of George and Alvira Shufelt and a brother of Orrin and Robert from previous sketches. Sheldon was listed in the 1860 federal census as residing with his parents in the town of Poygan at P.O. Omro. He was listed as above in the veteran section of the 1885 Wisconsin State census at P.O. Poygan.
{US 1860; WC-V 1885}

SHUFELT, Sidney A. - Pvt., Co. D, 7th Regt., Wis. Vol. Inf.
Sidney was born on Apr. 19, 1824 at Franklin County, Vermont. He was a son of Frederick and Emily (Tallman) Shufelt. Frederick was born on Feb. 22, 1796 and Emily

SHUFELT, Sidney A. (cont.)
was born on July 14, 1802. They were married in Canada and soon thereafter removed to Vermont. In 1852 they removed with their family to Wisconsin and settled on a farm in the town of Poygan. Frederick died there on Jan. 16, 1868 and Emily died there on Dec. 11, 1870. Sidney was married on Jan. 12, 1848 to Mary Walker. She died in 1851 leaving two children. Sidney was then married on Feb. 1, 1853 to Mary Condon of Quebec, Canada. Mary was born on Feb. 25, 1833 in Canada. They came to Wisconsin with his parents and settled on a farm in the town of Poygan, where they were listed in the 1860 federal census. They were residing there when Sidney was drafted on Dec. 31, 1864. He was assigned as above and was mustered out on July 3, 1865. Sidney was listed in the veteran section of the 1885 and 1895 Wisconsin State census at P.O. Poygan. He was listed in the 1890 federal census as residing in the town of Poygan at P.O. Poygan. He was listed in the veteran section of the 1905 state census at P.O. Omro. Sidney was listed in 1905 as residing on 110 acres of section 26 in the town of Poygan. He died in 1910 and Mary died in 1916. Both are buried in the town of Poygan at Oak Hill Cemetery. His parents are buried in that same cemetery.
{US 1860, 1890; WC-V 1885, 1895, 1905; Lawson p.1143-5; Randall p.50; B-1905} {ROV; Cem. records}

SIEGER, Dominicus - Pvt., Co. D, 52nd Regt., Wis. Vol. Inf.
Dominicus was born circa 1833 at Germany. He was listed in the 1860 federal census as a farm laborer for Charles Boyson in the town of Orihula at P.O. Fremont. He listed his residence as Windsor, Dane County when he enlisted on Mar. 4, 1865. He was assigned as above and was mustered out on July 28, 1865. Dominicus was listed in the veteran section of the 1895 Wisconsin State census at P.O. Oshkosh.
{US 1860; WC-V 1895; ROV}

SIEGER, John B. - Pvt., Co. B, 37th Regt., Wis. Vol. Inf.
John was born in 1823 at Wurtemburg. Frederica, his wife, was born in 1832 at Bavaria. They were listed in the 1860 federal census as residing on a farm in the town of Orihula at P.O. Wolf River. Michael Sieger, a brother of John, was residing on a adjoining farm with his wife. John was drafted at Wolf River on Nov. 5, 1864. He was assigned as above and was mustered out on July 27, 1865. John and Frederica had at least the following children: John Jr., born in 1857 at Wisconsin, died in 1924; Henry J., born in 1862, died in 1883; Julius, born in 1865, died in 1867; and Joseph, born in 1871, died in 1959. John was listed in the 1890 federal census as residing in the town of Wolf River at P.O. Orihula. He listed that he suffered from rheumatism as a result of his military service. John was listed in the veteran section of the 1895 Wisconsin State census at P.O. Orihula. He died in 1904. Frederica was listed in 1905 as residing with the family of Joseph Sieger in section 29 of the town of Wolf River. She died in 1906. John and Frederica are buried with the four children listed above in the town of Wolf River at Wolf River Cemetery.
{US 1860, 1890; WC-V 1895; ROV; B-1905; Cem. records}

SILAS, Charles - Pvt., Co. G, 3rd (reorg.) Regt., Wis. Cav.
Charles resided at Oshkosh and enlisted there on Feb. 12, 1864. He was assigned as above and was mustered out on Oct. 27, 1865.
{ROV}

SILAS, John - Pvt., Co. G, 3rd (reorg.) Regt., Wis. Cav.
John resided at Oshkosh and enlisted there on Feb. 15, 1864. He was assigned as above and was mustered out on Oct. 27, 1865.
{ROV}

SILSBEE, Elias W. - Pvt., Co. D, 32nd Regt., Wis. Vol. Inf.
Elias was born circa 1833 at New York. He was listed in the 1860 federal census as a laborer residing in the town of Utica at P.O. Fisk's Corners. Charlotte, his wife, was born circa 1838 at New York. They had a son, George, who was born circa 1856 at Wisconsin. Elias listed his residence as Waukau when he enlisted on Nov. 20, 1863. He was assigned as above and was transferred to Co. D, 16th (reorg.) Regt., Wis. Vol. Inf. on June 4, 1865. Elias was mustered out on July 12, 1865. Charlotte, his wife, died on June 26, 1866 at age 28 years, 4 months and 15 days. She is buried in the town of Rushford at Waukau Cemetery. Elias was married second in Winnebago County on Apr. 4, 1867 to Sarah E. (Mallory) Hall. He was listed in the 1890 federal census as residing in the town of Union, Waupaca County at P.O. Symco. Elias then listed that he suffered from rheumatism.
{US 1860, 1890; ROV; WCMR v.1, p.322, #2019; Cem. records}

SILSBEE, G.W. - Pvt., Co. A, 1st Regt., Wis. Cav.
He is buried with a simple military marker in the town of Rushford at Waukau Cemetery.
{Cem. records}

SILVERNAIL, Ira A. - Pvt., Co. G, 128th Regt., New York Vol. Inf.
Ira was listed as above in the veteran section of the 1895 and 1905 Wisconsin State census at P.O. Oshkosh. He was listed in 1905 as a grocer residing at 343 New York Avenue in the city of Oshkosh. Ira J. Silvernail was also listed at that address.
{WC-V 1895, 1905; B-1905}

SILVERTHORN, John Newton - Pvt., Co. F, 18th Regt., Wis. Vol. Inf.
John was born circa 1841 at Pennsylvania. He was a son of Eli (Levi?) Silverthorn and a brother of Levi and Morgan from following sketches. The father's name was listed differently in several sources. Eli was born circa 1810 at Pennsylvania. He was listed in the 1860 federal census as residing on a farm in the town of Rushford at P.O. Waukau. Rebecca, his wife, was born circa 1821 at New York. Also listed with them were sons Morgan and Newton. John enlisted at Rushford on Feb. 22, 1864. He was assigned as above and was taken prisoner at Altoona, Alabama. John was then mustered out on July 12, 1865.
{US 1860; ROV}

SILVERTHORN, Levi J. - Pvt., Co. F, 1st Regt., Wis. Cav.
Levi was born on Aug. 29, 1843 at Fairview, Pennsylvania. He was a son of John and Caroline (Davis) Silverthorn. Levi removed to Wisconsin in 1860 and settled in Winnebago County. He enlisted there on Oct. 28, 1861 and was assigned as a saddler in the above company. Levi was taken prisoner at L'Anguille Ferry, Arkansas. He was mustered out on Oct. 31, 1864 at the end of his term of enlistment. A biography listed that he was with the unit that captured Jefferson Davis. Levi returned to Winnebago County and was married on Oct. 15, 1865 to Emily Ross. She was born on July 13, 1843

SILVERTHORN, Levi J. (cont.)
and was a daughter of Reuben and Eliza (Musgrave) Ross of Bramley, England. Levi and Emily had the following children: Byron, born on Sept. 2, 1867; Frank, born on July 27, 1869; Sherman, born on Oct. 28, 1882, died on Jan. 4, 1883; Mary, born on May 1, 1884; and Gracie, born on Jan. 29, 1886, died in 1906. Levi was listed in the veteran section of the 1885, 1895 and 1905 Wisconsin State census at P.O. Omro. He was listed in the 1890 federal census as residing in the town of Omro at P.O. Omro. Levi was then listed as suffering from diseased respiratory organs. In 1905, Levi and Emily were listed as residing on 138 acres of section 25 in the town of Rushford. Daughters Mary and Gracie were residing with them at that time. Levi and Emily both died in 1928. They are buried with children Sherman and Gracie at Omro Cemetery, Olin's Addition, Section A, plot 36.
{US 1890; WC-V 1885, 1895, 1905; Randall p.31; B-1905; Cem. records; ROV}

SILVERTHORN, Morgan - Pvt., Co. A, 48th Regt., Wis. Vol. Inf.
Morgan was born in 1846 at Pennsylvania. His father, Levi Silverthorn, was born on Jan. 30, 1809 and died on Dec. 23, 1884. Morgan resided at Rushford and enlisted there on Jan. 28, 1865. He was assigned as above and was mustered out on Dec. 30, 1865. Morgan had a son, Levi Edward, who was born in the town of Rushford on Sept. 2, 1877. Morgan was listed in the veteran section of the 1885, 1895 and 1905 Wisconsin State census at P.O. Omro. He was listed in the 1890 federal census as residing in the town of Rushford at P.O. Omro. He was listed in 1905, with his wife Emma and son Frank M., as residing on 107 acres of section 24 in the town of Rushford. Emma was born in 1856 and died in 1931. Morgan died in 1908. Both are buried, along with his father, at Omro Cemetery, Original Section, plot 1.
{US 1860, 1890; WC-V 1885, 1895, 1905; ROV; WCBR v.2, p.85, #211; B-1905}
{Cem. records}

SIMM, James - Pvt., Co. C, 53rd Regt., Wis. Vol. Inf.
James was born circa 1845 at England, a son of James and Sarah Simm. James Sr. was born in 1818 at Standish, England and Sarah was born circa 1818 at England. James Sr. removed to Liverpool, England in 1830 and worked in the office of his father for about two years. When the father died, James Sr. inherited the business. He was married in Liverpool in 1841 to Sarah Vessey. They emigrated to the United States in 1851 and settled on a farm in the town of Nekimi. They were listed in the 1860 federal census as residing on that farm at P.O. Oshkosh. Listed with them then were the following children: James; Alice, born circa 1853; Willie, born circa 1856; and Mary, born circa 1858. Other than James Jr., the children were born in Wisconsin. James enlisted at Nekimi on Mar. 28, 1865. He was assigned as above. Most of the men from that company were then transferred to Co. K, 51st Regt., Wis. Vol. Inf. under orders dated June 10, 1865. The transfer was completed on June 30, 1865 at Ft. Leavenworth, Kansas. The regiment returned to Madison, Wisconsin on Aug. 1, 1865 and was then mustered out by companies with the last company being mustered out on Aug. 30, 1865. James was mustered out on Aug. 21, 1865. He was married in Winnebago County on Dec. 8, 1867 to Ardilla Buck. James was listed in the 1890 federal census as residing in the town of Nekimi at P.O. Oshkosh. He was listed in the veteran section of the 1905 Wisconsin State census at P.O. Oshkosh. Ardilla, his wife, died on Oct. 28, 1868 at age 20 years, 6 months and 16 days. She is buried in the town of Omro at Omro Union Cemetery. James Sr. died at his home in Nekimi on July 30, 1894. He was survived by

SIMM, James (cont.)
Sarah, his widow, and six children: Mrs. M. DuBois of Oshkosh; James of Nekimi; Mrs. W. Morgan of Rosendale; Mr. W. Simm of Nekimi; Mrs. R. Pritchard of Fesington, Dakota; and Mrs. C. Cornish of Utica.
{US 1860; WC-V 1905; ROV; WCMR v.1, p.360, #2173*; OWN 04 Aug 1894} {OWN 11 Aug 1894}

SIMMONS, Isaac - Pvt., Co. A, 17th Regt., Wis. Vol. Inf.?
Isaac was listed as above in the veteran section of the 1895 Wisconsin State census. He was not found in the records of that company.
{WC-V 1895}

SIMMONS, Stephen - Pvt., Co. G, 16th (reorg.) Regt., Wis. Vol. Inf.
Stephen was born circa 1838 at New York. He was listed in the 1860 federal census as a laborer on the farm of E.M. Randall in the town of Nepeuskun. Stephen listed his residence as Berlin, Green Lake County when he enlisted on Nov. 19, 1863. His original unit assignment is not known but he was transferred to the above company on June 4, 1865 and was then mustered out on July 12, 1865.
{US 1860; ROV}

SIMMONS, Sumner - Civil War Veteran?
Sumner died on Mar. 24, 1873 at age 36 years, 11 months and 14 days. A GAR marker was placed at his grave but he was not found in any Wisconsin military records. Sumner may have served with a unit from another state. Hannah, his wife, died on July 15, 1872 at age 25 years, 10 months and 21 days. Alice, a daughter, died on Oct. 3, 1872 at age 2 months and 23 days. All three are buried at Omro Cemetery, Olin's Addition, Section A, plot 42. Mariette Townsend, first wife of Sumner, died on Apr. 3, 1863 at age 22 years. A son, Freddie William, died on Mar. 26, 1863 at age 2 years, 1 month and 22 days. Mariette and Freddie are buried in the town of Nepeuskun at Koro Cemetery on the Townsend plot.
{Cem. records; ROV}

SIMMS, Francis B. - Pvt., 9th Batt., Wis. Lt. Art.
Francis resided at Oshkosh and enlisted there on Oct. 19, 1861. He was assigned as above and was mustered out on Sept. 20, 1865.
{ROV}

SIMONDS, Austin A. - Pvt., Co. G, 3rd Regt., Wis. Vol. Inf.
Austin resided at Menasha and enlisted there on Apr. 20, 1861. He was assigned as above and was wounded on Sept. 17, 1862. Austin was killed at Chancellorsville, Virginia on May 3, 1863.
{ROV}

SIMONS, David E. - Pvt., Co. A, 4th Regt., Wis. Vol. Inf.
David resided at Whitewater, Walworth County and enlisted on Apr. 23, 1861. He was assigned as above and was discharged on Sept. 3, 1862 due to wounds. David was listed in the 1890 federal census as residing at 860 Main Street in the city of Oshkosh. He was listed in the veteran section of the 1885 Wisconsin State census at P.O. Oshkosh.
{US 1890; WC-V 1885; ROV}

SIMONS, Edward - Cpl., Co. C, 17th Regt., Wis. Vol. Inf.
Edward was born circa 1849. He listed his residence as Providence, Louisiana when he enlisted on Apr. 1, 1863. He was assigned as a cook to Co. C, 17th Regt., Wis. Vol. Inf. and was mustered out on July 14, 1865. He removed to Oshkosh about 1882. Edward was listed in 1883 at P.O. Oshkosh and receiving a pension of $4 per month for a wound to his right side. He was listed in the 1890 federal census as residing in the city of Oshkosh. Edward then provided his unit designation as above and his service dates as having been from Apr. 4, 1863 to June 14, 1865. He added that he suffered a gunshot wound to his right side while in the military. Edward, "a well known colored man," died at his home in Oshkosh on Oct. 13, 1893. He was survived by a wife and three children. He had been shot in his right side while at Atlanta, Georgia on Aug. 1, 1864. The shot exited the left side of his abdomen.
{US 1890; ROV; LOP-1883; OWN 14 Oct 1893}

SIMONSEN, Simon - Pvt., Co. B, 3rd Regt., Wis. Vol. Inf.
Simon resided at Oshkosh and enlisted there on Apr. 22, 1861. He was assigned as above and was wounded at Chancellorsville, Virginia. Simon died of those wounds on May 23, 1863 at Aquia Creek, Virginia.
{ROV}

SIMONSON, Peter A. - Pvt., Co. I, 49th Regt., Wis. Vol. Inf.
Peter resided at Utica and enlisted there on Feb. 8, 1865. He was assigned as above and was mustered out on Nov. 8, 1865.
{ROV}

SIMPSON, George - Pvt., Co. I, 21st Regt., Wis. Vol. Inf.
George resided at Menasha and enlisted there on Aug. 12, 1862. He was assigned as above and was wounded in the leg on Oct. 8, 1862 at Chaplin Hills, Kentucky. George died of those wounds on Oct. 20, 1862 at Perryville, Kentucky.
{ROV; Lawson p.835; OWN 16 Oct 1862}

SIMPSON, George - Lt., Co. A, 142nd Regt., New York Vol. Inf.
George was listed as above in the veteran section of the 1895 and 1905 Wisconsin State census at P.O. Oshkosh.
{WC-V 1895, 1905}

SIMPSON, John - Civil War Veteran?
John was born circa 1826 at New Brunswick, Canada. Phoebe, his wife, was born there circa 1830. They were listed in the 1860 federal census as residing on a farm in the town of Algoma. Listed with them were the following children: Douglas, born circa 1853; Joseph, born circa 1856; and George, born circa 1857. George was born in Wisconsin and the other boys were born at New Brunswick. John died on May 4, 1897 at age 71 years. A GAR marker has been placed on his grave. Phoebe, his widow, was listed in 1905 as residing at 205 Nebraska Street in the city of Oshkosh. She died on June 29, 1909 at age 79 years. Oscar H., a son, died on Mar. 11, 1867 at age 2 months and 4 days. All three are buried in the town of Algoma at Ellenwood Cemetery, Section A.
{US 1860; B-1905; Cem. records}

SINCLAIR, Duncan - Pvt., Co. H, 21st Regt., Wis. Vol. Inf.
Duncan resided at Oshkosh and enlisted there on Aug. 15, 1862. He was assigned as above and was transferred to the Mississippi Marine Brigade on Jan. 31, 1863.
{ROV}

SIPHER, Frederick P. - Pvt., Co. D, 8th Regt., Wis. Vol. Inf.
Frederick was born circa 1833 at New York. Lucy, his wife, was born circa 1835 at Vermont. They were listed in the 1860 federal census as residing on a farm in the town of Utica at P.O. Fisk's Corners. They then had a daughter, Dora, who was born circa 1856 at Wisconsin. Frederick enlisted at Utica on Mar. 19, 1864. He was assigned as above and was wounded at Nashville, Tennessee. Frederick was then mustered out on Sept. 5, 1865. He was listed in the 1890 federal census as residing in the town of Lind, Waupaca County at P.O. Weyauwega. Frederick then provided that he was a re-enlisted veteran and that one of his toes had been crushed by a wagon. He was residing with the former widow of Jacob Sipher, who had been a veteran of Co. F, 44th Regt., Wis. Vol. Inf. Jacob was listed as having died of dropsey.
{US 1860, 1890; ROV}

SITTIG, Constantine - Pvt., Co. F, 19th Regt., Wis. Vol. Inf.
Constantine was born circa 1821 at Prussia. Julie, his wife, was born circa 1821 at Saxony. Constantine was listed in the 1860 federal census as a laborer residing in the second ward of the city of Oshkosh. Herman, his brother, resided to one side with his family and Eleanor, his mother, resided on the other. She was born circa 1797 at Prussia. Constantine and Julie then had the following children: Charles, born circa 1848 at Prussia; Amalie, born circa 1850 at Denmark; Constantine, born circa 1853 at Wisconsin; Theodore, born circa 1854 at Wisconsin; and Clara, born circa 1858 at Wisconsin. Constantine enlisted at Oshkosh on Jan. 28, 1862. He was assigned as above and was mustered out on Apr. 29, 1865 at the end of his term of enlistment. He was listed in 1868 as a laborer residing at 81 River Street in Oshkosh.
{US 1860; ROV; T-1868}

SKINNER, Holland - Pvt., Co. B, 41st Regt., Wis. Vol. Inf.
Holland was born circa 1842 at New York, a son of Jeremiah and Anna Skinner. Both parents were natives of New York, the father born there in 1804 and the mother born in 1815. Jeremiah was listed in the 1860 federal census as a laborer residing in the second ward of the city of Oshkosh. Then residing with him were Anna and Holland. Holland enlisted at Oshkosh on June 8, 1864. He was assigned as above and was then mustered out on Sept. 23, 1864 at the end of his term of enlistment. Holland was listed in the veteran section of the 1885 Wisconsin State census at P.O. Winneconne as a veteran of Co. A, 8th Regt., Wis. Vol. Inf. Mary L., his widow, was listed in the 1890 federal census as residing in the village of Winneconne.
{US 1860, 1890; WC-V 1885; ROV}

SLAWSON, George F. - Pvt., Co. D, 41st Regt., Wis. Vol. Inf.
George resided at Menasha and enlisted there on May 11, 1864. He was assigned as above and was mustered out on Sept. 23, 1864 at the end of his term of enlistment.
{ROV}

SLOAN, Douglas E. - Cpl., Co. C, 21st Regt., Wis. Vol. Inf.
Douglas was born on July 1, 1844 at Erie County, New York. He was a son of William and Betsy (Cross) Sloan. William was born circa 1814 at New York and Betsy was born circa 1818 in Connecticut. William's parents removed to Wisconsin with their family when he was six years old. They settled at Winnebago County on a farm in the town of Algoma. William and Betsey were listed in the 1860 federal census as residing on a farm in the town of Omro. Listed with them were the following children: Douglas; Mary, born circa 1841 at New York; Julia, born circa 1846 at New York; and George, born circa 1852 at Wisconsin. Douglas was a farmer until he enlisted at Omro on Aug. 12, 1862. He was assigned as above and was promoted to Corporal in that company. He was severely wounded in his left shoulder by a rifle ball while engaged at Bentonsville, N.C. on Mar. 19, 1865. He was taken to Goldsboro for two weeks, then to Newbern, and finally to Willett's Point on Long Island. Douglas was mustered out on June 8, 1865. After about a month he was transferred to Prairie du Chien and then on to Milwaukee, where he was discharged on July 4, 1865. Douglas returned home to the town of Algoma and was employed there for three years as a brakeman on the Chicago & Northwestern Railroad. He worked at similar jobs between Wisconsin and Minnesota until 1870, when he took a trip to San Francisco, California and made a side trip into the mountains of the Sierra Nevada. On his return to the town of Algoma, Douglas was again employed by different railroads until 1884. He was listed in 1883 at P.O. Omro and receiving a pension of $18 per month for a wound to his left shoulder. He then removed to Omro and began operation of what was to become a popular and prosperous restaurant. Douglas was married in Omro on Sept. 8, 1884 to Sarah, a daughter of Patrick and Sarah (McMahon) Ryan. Her parents had come to America from Ireland in 1850. Douglas was listed in the veteran section of the 1885, 1895 and 1905 Wisconsin State census at P.O. Omro. He was listed in 1905 as a rural mail carrier residing at 115 Pearl Street in Omro. Georgina Sloan was also residing at that address. Douglas died May 20, 1915. He is buried at Omro Cemetery, Pelton's Addition, Section D, plot 22.
{US 1860; WC-V 1885, 1895, 1905; LOP-1883; SCA p.676-7; B-1905; ROV}
{Cem. records}

SLOATS, Andrew - Pvt., Co. K, 20th Regt., Wis. Vol. Inf.
Andrew resided at Nepeuskun and enlisted there on Aug. 14, 1862. He was assigned as above and was discharged on Apr. 8, 1863 due to a disability.
{ROV}

SLOVER, James - Sgt., Co. I, 43rd Regt., Wis. Vol. Inf.
James was born circa 1825 at New York. He was listed in the 1850 federal census as a farmer residing with George H. Slover and his family in the town of Clayton. James was listed in the 1860 federal census as residing on a farm in the town of Clayton at P.O. Neenah. Emma, his wife, was born circa 1832 at England. Thomas, their son, was born circa 1854 at Wisconsin and Juliet, their daughter, was born circa 1857 at Wisconsin. James listed his residence as Menasha when he enlisted on Sept. 5, 1864. He was assigned as above and was promoted to Sergeant in that company. He was mustered out on June 24, 1865. James was listed (Stover) in the veteran section of the 1885 Wisconsin State census at P.O. Neenah.
{US 1850, 1860; WC-V 1885; ROV}

SMAILES, Benjamin D. - Pvt., Co. H, 19th Regt., Wis. Vol. Inf.
Benjamin resided at Milwaukee, Milwaukee County and enlisted there on Dec. 26, 1861. He was assigned as above and was transferred to Co. E of that regiment on May 1, 1865. Benjamin was mustered out on Aug. 9, 1865. He was listed in the 1890 federal census as residing in the city of Neenah. Benjamin was listed in the veteran section of the 1895 Wisconsin State census at P.O. Neenah. He was listed in 1905 as a rural mail carrier residing at 312 Oak Street in Neenah. Mrs. Marion L. Smailes was also listed at that address.
{US 1890; WC-V 1895; ROV; B-1905}

SMALL, Robert - Pvt., Co. K, 11th Regt., Wis. Vol. Inf.
Robert was born in 1838 at England. He was listed in the 1860 federal census as a farm laborer for George Clark in the town of Vinland. Robert listed his residence as Vinland when he enlisted on Sept. 17, 1861. He was assigned as above and was mustered out on Nov. 18, 1864 at the end of his term of enlistment. Robert was married in Winnebago County on Nov. 2, 1865 to Elizabeth Clarke. She was born in 1844. Robert was listed in the veteran section of the 1885 Wisconsin State census at P.O. Vinland. He was listed in the 1890 federal census as residing in the town of Oshkosh at P.O. Clemansville. Robert died in 1904. Elizabeth was listed in 1905 as residing on 90 acres of section 26 in the town of Oshkosh. Mary and Elmer Small were residing with her. Elizabeth died in 1918. She is buried with Robert in the town of Vinland at Brooks Cemetery.
{US 1860, 1890; WC-V 1885; Cem. records; ROV; WCMR v.1, p.287, #1739; B-1905}

SMEDLEY, Abel B. - Col., 32nd Regt., Wis. Vol. Inf.
Abel was born circa 1826 at New York. Lydia, his wife, was born circa 1825, also at New York. Abel was listed in the 1860 federal census as a manufacturer residing in the first ward of the city of Oshkosh. He and Lydia then had one son, Clinton J., who was born circa 1852 at Wisconsin. Abel enlisted at Oshkosh and was assigned to the above unit. He was commissioned as Major of that regiment on Sept. 8, 1862 and was then promoted to Lieutenant Colonel on Apr. 2, 1863. He resigned his commission June 4, 1864. Abel re-enlisted in the 46th Regt., Wis. Vol. Inf. and was commissioned as Lieutenant Colonel of that regiment on Feb. 18, 1865. He was mustered out on Sept. 27, 1865. Abel was listed in 1868 as the owner of a stave and cheese box factory and residing at 6 Union Street in Oshkosh.
{US 1860; ROV; T-1868}

SMITH, Abner B. - Capt., Co. I, 21st Regt., Wis. Vol. Inf.
Abner was born circa 1830 at Ohio. Betsey, his wife, was born circa 1832, also at Ohio. They were listed in the 1860 federal census as residing in the village of Neenah. Carrie, their daughter, was born circa 1856 at Ohio and Hiram, their son, was born circa 1859 at Wisconsin. Abner enlisted at Neenah and was assigned to the above unit. He was commissioned as 1st Lieutenant of that company on Aug. 26, 1862. Abner was wounded at Perryville, Kentucky in October 1862 and he was promoted to Captain of the company on Apr. 25, 1863. He was discharged on Dec. 17, 1864 due to wounds. Abner was listed in 1868 as the Winnebago County Sheriff and residing at 42 Otter Street in the city of Oshkosh.
{US 1860; ROV; T-1868; OWN 16 Oct 1862}

SMITH, Abner S. - Pvt., 21st Regt., Wis. Vol. Inf.
Abner was born on July 15, 1802 at Vermont. Martha, his wife, was born circa 1805 at New Hampshire. They were listed in the 1860 federal census as residing with the family of Alpheus Stone in the town of Utica at P.O. Fisk's Corners. Abner enlisted on Aug. 14, 1862 at age 60 years and was assigned as the Principal Musician with the 21st Regt., Wis. Vol. Inf. He was discharged on Sept. 17, 1862. Abner died on Aug. 21, 1886. Martha, his wife, died on Dec. 29, 1868 at age 62 years, 7 months and 23 days. Both are buried in the town of Omro at Minckler Cemetery.
{US 1860; ROV; Cem. records}

SMITH, Absolom S. - Capt., Co. C, 14th Regt., Wis. Vol. Inf.
Absolom resided at Omro and enlisted there on Sept. 8, 1861. He was assigned as above and was commissioned as 2nd Lieutenant in that company on Oct. 1, 1861. Absolom was wounded at Shiloh, Tennessee and he was promoted to Captain of his company on Mar. 17, 1862. Absolom was commissioned as Colonel of the 6th Regt., Mississippi Colored Troops on Sept. 7, 1863. He eventually returned to Wisconsin and was named as a party in a civil suit at Omro in Aug. 1893.
{ROV}

SMITH, Alvin - Pvt., Co. G, 68th Regt., Pennsylvania Vol. Inf.
Alvin was listed as above in the veteran section of the 1885 Wisconsin State census at P.O. Neenah.
{WC-V 1885}

SMITH, Benjamin - Lt., Co. B, 5th (reorg.) Regt., Wis. Vol. Inf.
Benjamin listed his residence as Westford, Dodge County when he enlisted on Apr. 22, 1861. He was assigned as a Private in Co. B, 5th Regt., Wis. Vol. Inf. Benjamin was promoted to Corporal and Sergeant in that company. He was promoted to Commissary Sergeant of that company on Oct. 10, 1863 and was transferred to the 5th (reorg.) Regt., Wis. Vol. Inf. on July 13, 1864. Benjamin was promoted to Quartermaster Sergeant of that regiment on Nov. 1, 1864 and was reassigned to Co. B in that reorganized regiment. He was promoted to 1st Sergeant in that company and was then commissioned as 2nd Lieutenant of that company on Dec. 13, 1864. Benjamin was mustered out on June 20, 1865. He was listed in the 1890 federal census as residing in the city of Oshkosh. He was listed in the veteran section of the 1895 Wisconsin State census at P.O. Oshkosh. Emma, his widow, was listed in 1905 as boarding at 320 Ninth Street in Oshkosh.
{US 1890; WC-V 1895; ROV; B-1905}

SMITH, Benjamin F. - Pvt., Co. C, 14th Regt., Wis. Vol. Inf.
Benjamin resided at Omro and enlisted there on Nov. 4, 1861. He was assigned as above. Benjamin was wounded at Corinth and again at Vicksburg, Mississippi. He was discharged due to those wounds. Benjamin was married on July 6, 1873 in Winnebago County to Mary C. Ward. He was listed in 1888 as a member of GAR Post #10 at Oshkosh.
{ROV; WCMR v.1, p.583, #3964}

SMITH, Charles - Pvt., Co. B, 3rd Regt., Wis. Cav.
Charles resided at Oshkosh and enlisted there on Aug. 23, 1864. He was assigned as above and was transferred to Co. B, 3rd (reorg.) Regt., Wis. Cav. on Feb. 1, 1865.

SMITH, Charles (cont.)
Charles was mustered out on June 19, 1865.
{ROV}

SMITH, Charles H. - Sgt., Co. C, 14th Regt., Wis. Vol. Inf.
Charles resided at Omro and enlisted there on Sept. 8, 1861. He was assigned as above and was promoted to Sergeant in that company. While home on a furlough, Charles was married in Winnebago County on Feb. 28, 1864 to Anna Benedict. He returned to his unit and was mustered out on Oct. 9, 1865. He was listed in the veteran section of the 1885 Wisconsin State census at P.O. Bloomfield, Waushara County.
{WC-V 1885; ROV; WCMR v.1, p.252, #1457}

SMITH, Christian - Pvt., Co. I, 65th Regt., Illinois Vol. Inf.
Christian was listed as above in the veteran section of the 1885, 1895 and 1905 Wisconsin State census at P.O. Oshkosh. He was listed in the 1890 federal census as residing at 57 Lincoln Avenue in the city of Oshkosh. Christian then provided his unit designation as above and his service dates as having been from Apr. 22, 1862 to May 15, 1865. He added that he had been injured in the military by falling from a cliff.
{US 1890; WC-V 1885, 1895, 1905}

SMITH, Frederick - Cpl., Co. B, 37th Regt., Wis. Vol. Inf.
Frederick resided at Omro and enlisted there on Mar. 31, 1864. He was assigned as above and was promoted to Corporal in that company. He was wounded on Aug. 19, 1864 at Weldon R.R. and was mustered out on July 27, 1865.
{ROV}

SMITH, George E. - Sgt., Co. E, 2nd Regt., Wis. Vol. Inf.
George resided at Oshkosh and enlisted there on Apr. 21, 1861. He was assigned as above and was promoted to Corporal and then Sergeant in that company. George was mustered out on June 28, 1864 at the end of his term of enlistment. He was listed in an 1899 article by Col. Harshaw as residing at Racine, Racine County.
{ROV; ODN 07 May 1899}

SMITH, Gideon - Pvt., Co. D, 44th Regt., Wis. Vol. Inf.
Gideon was listed as Gilderoy when he enlisted at Larrabee, Fond du Lac County on Oct. 18, 1864. He was assigned as above and was then mustered out on Aug. 28, 1865. Gideon was listed in the 1890 federal census as residing in the town of Neenah at P.O. Neenah. He then reported that he suffered from "Army itch" skin disease.
{US 1890; ROV}

SMITH, Henry F. - Pvt., Co. I, 142nd Regt., Illinois Vol. Inf.
Henry was listed in the 1890 federal census as residing in the city of Neenah. No other information was provided. He was listed as above in the veteran section of the 1895 Wisconsin State census at P.O. Neenah. His widow was listed in 1905 as residing at 423 S. Commercial Street in the city of Neenah. Oscar W. Smith was also listed at that address.
{US 1890; WC-V 1895; B-1905}

SMITH, Henry G. - Pvt., Co. C, 3rd Regt., Wis. Cav.
Henry resided at Oshkosh and enlisted there on Feb. 15, 1864. He was assigned as above and was transferred to Co. H, 3rd (reorg.) Regt., Wis. Cav. on Mar. 23, 1865. Henry was mustered out on Sept. 29, 1865.
{ROV}

SMITH, Henry L. - Pvt., Co. C, 26th Regt., Massachusetts Vol. Inf.
Henry was listed as above in the veteran section of the 1885 Wisconsin State census at P.O. Eureka. He was listed in the 1890 federal census as residing in the town of Rushford at P.O. Eureka. Henry then provided his unit designation as above and his service dates as having been from Oct. 15, 1861 to Oct. 30, 1864. He was suffering from a lung complaint and deafness.
{US 1890; WC-V 1885}

SMITH, John - Pvt., Co. K, 11th Regt., Wis. Vol. Inf.
John resided at Neenah and enlisted there on Sept. 17, 1861. He was assigned as above and was discharged on Oct. 13, 1862 due to a disability.
{ROV}

SMITH, John - Pvt., Co. F, 19th Regt., Wis. Vol. Inf.
John resided at Oshkosh and enlisted there on Nov. 30, 1863. He was assigned as above and was transferred to Co. C of that regiment on May 1, 1865. John was mustered out on Aug. 9, 1865.
{ROV}

SMITH, John - Pvt., Co. G, 32nd Regt., Wis. Vol. Inf.
John resided at Winchester and enlisted there on Nov. 29, 1863. He was assigned as above and was wounded on Feb. 3, 1865 at River's Bridge, S.C. John was transferred to Co. H, 16th (reorg.) Regt., Wis. Vol. Inf. on June 4, 1865 and he was mustered out on June 9, 1865. He was listed in 1883 at P.O. Winchester and he was then receiving a pension of $6 per month for a wound to his right thigh. John was listed in the veteran section of the 1885 Wisconsin State census at P.O. Winchester. He was listed in the 1890 federal census as residing in the town of Winchester at P.O. Winchester. John then provided that he had suffered a gunshot wound to his right leg.
{US 1890; WC-V 1885; ROV; LOP-1883}

SMITH, John O. - Pvt., Co. H, 15th Regt., U.S. Army.
John was married in Winnebago County on June 10, 1863 to Frances (Bell) Wheeler. He was listed as above in the veteran section of the 1885 Wisconsin State census at P.O. Omro.
{WC-V 1885; WCMR v.1, p.242, #1377}

SMITH, Jonathan - Pvt., Co. I, 5th (reorg.) Regt., Wis. Vol. Inf.
Jonathan resided at Clayton and enlisted there on Sept. 30, 1864. He was assigned as above and was mustered out on June 20, 1865.
{ROV}

SMITH, Joseph - Pvt., Co. B, 37th Regt., Wis. Vol. Inf.
Joseph resided at Wolf River and was drafted there on Nov. 5, 1864. He was assigned

SMITH, Joseph (cont.)
as above and was mustered out on July 27, 1865. Joseph was listed (Schmidt) in the 1890 federal census as residing in the town of Wolf River at P.O. Orihula. He was suffering from rheumatism. He was listed (Schmidt) in the veteran section of the 1895 Wisconsin State census at P.O. Orihula.
{US 1890; WC-V 1895; ROV}

SMITH, Joseph M. - Pvt., Co. F, 3rd Regt., Wis. Cav.
Joseph resided at Oshkosh and enlisted there on Feb. 6, 1863. He was assigned as above and was listed as having deserted on Sept. 20, 1864.
{ROV}

SMITH, Joseph W. - Pvt., Co. E, 2nd Regt., Wis. Vol. Inf.
Joseph resided at Oshkosh and enlisted there on Dec. 1, 1861. He was assigned as above. Joseph was killed in action on Aug. 28, 1862 at Gainesville, Virginia.
{ROV}

SMITH, Junius A. - Pvt., Co. A, 1st (3 yr.) Regt., Wis. Vol. Inf.
Junius was born circa 1840 at Pennsylvania, a son of John and Lois (Harrington) Smith and a brother of Wallace from a following sketch. The father was born circa 1813 at Pennsylvania and Lois was born circa 1820 at New York. John was listed in the 1860 federal census as a farmer residing in the third ward of the city of Oshkosh. Residing with him were his wife and the following children: Julius; Wallace; Grace, born circa 1845; Rose, born circa 1850; Gilbert, born circa 1852; Fay, born circa 1854; Bess, born circa 1856; and Ellen, born circa 1858. All of the children except Junius were born in Wisconsin. John died at Oshkosh on May 7, 1883 at age 70 years, 8 months and 8 days. Lois died there on Sept. 5, 1912 at age 92 years, 9 months and 3 days. Junius enlisted at Oshkosh on Sept. 17, 1861. He was assigned as above. Junius was killed in action on Oct. 8, 1862 at Chaplin Hills, Kentucky at age 23 years. He is buried with his parents in the town of Algoma at Ellenwood Cemetery, Section B.
{US 1860; ROV; Cem. records}

SMITH, Lyman H. - Capt., Co. E, 2nd Regt., Wis. Vol. Inf.
Lyman was born circa 1826 at Vermont. He was listed in the 1860 federal census as a harness maker residing with the family of Albert Pride in the second ward of the city of Oshkosh. Lyman enlisted at Oshkosh on Apr. 21, 1861. He was assigned as above and was promoted to 1st Sergeant in that company. Lyman was then commissioned as 1st Lieutenant of that company on Oct. 15, 1861 and he was promoted to Captain of that company on Apr. 21, 1862. Lyman was wounded slightly in the thigh at Gainesville, Virginia on Aug. 28, 1862. He was discharged on Mar. 3, 1863 due to his wounds. Lyman was listed in an 1899 article by Col. Harshaw as residing near St. Albans, Vermont.
{US 1860; ODN 07 May 1899; OWN 11 Sep 1862; ROV}

SMITH, Noel B. - Pvt., Co. C, Hatch's Ind. Bn., Minnesota Cav.
Noel was listed in the 1890 federal census as residing in the town of Oshkosh at P.O. Oshkosh. He provided no other information. Noel was listed as above in the veteran section of the 1895 and 1905 Wisconsin State census at P.O. Oshkosh.
{US 1890; WC-V 1895, 1905}

SMITH, Norman W. - Cpl., Co. B, 38th Regt., Wis. Vol. Inf.
Norman resided at Omro and enlisted there on Mar. 30, 1864. He was assigned as above and was promoted to Corporal in that company. He was mustered out on July 26, 1865.
{ROV}

SMITH, Oatman - Pvt., Co. A, 3rd Regt., Wis. Cav.
Oatman resided at Oshkosh and enlisted there on Dec. 21, 1863. He was assigned as above and was transferred to Co. K, 3rd (reorg.) Regt., Wis. Cav. on Mar. 23, 1865. Oatman was mustered out on Sept. 29, 1865.
{ROV}

SMITH, Phillip - Pvt., Co. E, 2nd Regt., Wis. Vol. Inf.
Phillip resided at Oshkosh and enlisted there on Oct. 28, 1861. He was assigned as above and was wounded slightly at Gainesville, Virginia on Aug. 28, 1862. Phillip was again wounded in the battle at Wilderness, Virginia. He was transferred to Co. B, Ind. Bn., 2nd Regt., Wis. Vol. Inf. on June 10, 1864. Phillip was mustered out on Oct. 31, 1864 at the end of his term of enlistment. He was listed in 1868 as a partner in the firm of Smith & Ostrander, owners of a saloon and billiards hall in Oshkosh. He was then boarding at the Empire House. Phillip was listed in an 1899 article by Col. Harshaw as having died at Louisville, Kentucky.
{ROV; T-1868; ODN 07 May 1899; OWN 11 Sep 1862}

SMITH, Phillip B. - Pvt., Co. D, 32nd Regt., Wis. Vol. Inf.
Phillip resided at Oshkosh and enlisted there on Aug. 20, 1862. He was assigned as above and was discharged on Mar. 3, 1863 due to a disability.
{ROV}

SMITH, Richard - Sgt., Co. K, 23rd Regt., Wis. Vol. Inf.
Richard was born on May 4, 1838. He resided at Roxbury, Dane County and enlisted there on Aug. 11, 1862. Richard was assigned as above and was promoted to Sergeant in that company. He was mustered out on July 4, 1865. Richard died on Dec. 27, 1926. Sophia, his wife, was born on Dec. 21, 1848 and died on Feb. 12, 1927. Both are buried at Omro Cemetery, Olin's Addition, Section C, plot 65.
{ROV; Cem. records}

SMITH, Russell R. - Pvt., Co. B, 10th Regt., Michigan Cav.
Russell was born Aug. 15, 1840 at New York. He was a son of Hiel D. and Mary Smith. His mother died about 1845 and Russell went to Michigan while still young. He enlisted at Grand Rapids, Michigan in Sept. 1863 and was assigned as above. Russell was wounded in the battle at Strawberry Plains when he was struck in the left shoulder by a minnie ball. He carried that ball with him for the rest of his life. Russell received an honorable discharge at Memphis, Tennessee in Sept. 1866. After the war he went back to Grand Rapids and was married on Apr. 1, 1867 to Mary L. Lewis. They removed to Vermont. Russell returned to Michigan and then came to Wisconsin, settling at Winnebago County in the village of Omro. He removed to Shawano, Shawano County in 1876. Russell and Mary had seven children: William H., died in 1879; Hattie May, married Samuel Howard of Shawano; Clarissa A., married William Riley of Shawano; Francis N., a farmer in Dakota; Russell; Andrew G.; and Flora. Russell was still

SMITH, Russell R. (cont.)
residing at Shawano in 1888.
{SCA 1:513}

SMITH, Thomas T. - Pvt., Co. B, 3rd Regt., Wis. Cav.
Thomas was married in Winnebago County on Mar. 26, 1861 to Susan A. Miner. He resided at Oshkosh and enlisted there on Dec. 23, 1861. He was assigned as above and was transferred to Co. B, 3rd (reorg.) Regt., Wis. Cav. on Feb. 1, 1865. Thomas was listed as sick and in the hospital at Springfield, Missouri when that regiment was mustered out on Sept. 8, 1865. Susan, his wife, died on Oct. 6, 1875 at age 43 years, 8 months and 20 days. She is buried in the town of Vinland at Brooks Cemetery. Thomas was listed in the veteran section of the 1885 Wisconsin State census at P.O. Winneconne.
{WC-V 1885; ROV; Cem. records; WCMR v.1, p.212, #1144}

SMITH, Wallace - Sgt., Co. B, 3rd Regt., Wis. Vol. Inf.
Wallace was born circa 1840 at Pennsylvania, a son of John and Lois (Harrington) Smith and a brother of Junius from a previous sketch. Wallace was listed in the 1860 federal census as residing with his father's family in the third ward of the city of Oshkosh. He enlisted at Oshkosh on Apr. 19, 1861. He was assigned as above and was promoted to Corporal, Sergeant and then 1st Sergeant in that company. Wallace was mustered out on June 29, 1864 at the end of his term of enlistment. He was married in Winnebago County on Jan. 28, 1868 to Hannah Brennand.
{US 1860; ROV; WCMR v.1, p.370, #2259}

SMITH, William Henry - Sgt., Co. H, 2nd Regt., New York Vet. Cav.
William was born on Feb. 10, 1841 at Salmon River, Clinton County, New York. He was a son of Sidney and Julia (McKenney) Smith. Sidney was born on Sept. 20, 1820 and died on Aug. 1, 1898. He was a son of Alexander Smith, who was born on Aug. 4, 1796 and died on Jan. 16, 1882. William was raised in New York and was engaged there in farming until his enlistment. He enlisted at Plattsburg, New York on July 20, 1863 and was assigned as above. He was soon promoted to Corporal in that company and was promoted to Sergeant on Aug. 15, 1864. William was promoted to Commissary Sergeant and was then discharged on Nov. 8, 1865 at Talladegha, Alabama. He returned home to Plattsburg and, two weeks later, he removed to Wisconsin and settled in Winnebago County at Butte des Morts. He removed to the Black Hills in Dakota Territory in 1876 and mined for several months. William returned to Plattsburg for six weeks and then resettled at Butte des Morts, where he was engaged at farming in the summer and in lumbering in the winter. He continued this until 1881. He then removed to Antigo, Langlade County and established himself as a druggist there. William was still residing there in 1888. He had five uncles and a cousin who all fought in New York regiments during the Civil War. William died in 1900. Lois R., his wife, was born in 1845 and died in 1922. Both are buried with his father and grandfather in the town of Vinland at Allenville Cemetery.
{SCA 1:567-8; Cem. records}

SMITH, William W. - Cpl., Co. C, 21st Regt., Wis. Vol. Inf.
William resided at Oshkosh and enlisted there on Aug. 12, 1862. He was assigned as above and was promoted to Corporal in that company. William was wounded at

SMITH, William W. (cont.)
Chickamauga, Georgia. William was then mustered out on June 8, 1865.
{ROV}

SNELL, Austin W. - Pvt., Co. A, 1st (3 yr.) Regt., Wis. Vol. Inf.
Austin resided at Oshkosh and enlisted there on Sept. 16, 1861. He was assigned as above and was wounded at Chaplin Hills, Kentucky. Austin was discharged on Jan. 29, 1863 due to a disability. He was married on Sept. 6, 1866 in Winnebago County to Anna Lemon Bliss. She was born in 1845 at Louisville, Kentucky and removed to Oshkosh with her parents in 1861. Austin was listed in 1868 as residing at 46 Jackson Street in Oshkosh. He was then a part owner, along with Thomas J. Snell, of the Oshkosh Skating Rink. Thomas died in Lincoln, Kansas on July 2, 1890 after being kicked by a horse. Austin was listed in 1883 at P.O. Oshkosh and receiving a pension of $6 per month for the loss of his right thumb. He was listed in the veteran section of the 1885, 1895 and 1905 Wisconsin State census at P.O. Oshkosh. He was listed in 1888 as a member of GAR Post #10 at Oshkosh. Austin was listed in the 1890 federal census as residing at 140 Jefferson Avenue in Oshkosh. He then listed the loss of his right thumb and a wound to his left shoulder. Austin and Anna had two children, Arthur and Ethel. Anna died on May 11, 1896 after suffering for several weeks with a throat ailment. She was survived by her husband and both children. Son Arthur was then residing at Eau Claire, Eau Claire County. Austin was listed in 1905 as a clerk residing at that same address. Daughter Ethel M. was residing with him.
{US 1890; WC-V 1885, 1895, 1905; LOP-1883; T-1868; ODN 12 May 1896; ROV}
{B-1905; WCMR v.1, p.306, #1889*; OWN 10 Jul 1890}

SNELL, George W. - Lt., Co. A, 6th Regt., Massachusetts Vol. Inf.
George was born in Jan. 1828 at Maine. Both of his parents were natives of that state. George was listed in the 1890 federal census as residing in the city of Oshkosh. He provided no other information at that time. He was listed as above in the veteran section of the 1895 Wisconsin State census at P.O. Oshkosh. George was listed in the 1900 federal census as a widower residing at the Wisconsin Veterans' Home at King. He was listed at King in 1905 and was credited in the records of the home with 27 months of military service. George was again listed in the 1910 federal census at King. He then provided that he had been married for 60 years.
{US 1890, 1900, 1910; WC-V 1895; GAR 40th}

SNOVER, Theodore F. - Pvt., Co. C, 10th Regt., Wis. Vol. Inf.
Theodore resided at Menasha and enlisted there on Sept. 3, 1861. He was assigned as above and was wounded at Perryville, Kentucky. Theodore was then mustered out on Nov. 3, 1864. He died in 1903 at Oconto, Oconto County.
{ROV; Lawson p.811}

SNYDER, Charles M. - Pvt., Co. B, 16th Regt., Wis. Vol. Inf.
Charles was born on Sept. 21, 1848. He resided at Chester, Dodge County and enlisted there on Feb. 24, 1864. He was assigned as above and was mustered out on July 12, 1865. Charles was listed in the veteran section of the 1905 Wisconsin State census at P.O. Oshkosh. He was then listed as an employee of the Schmidt Bros. Trunk Co. and residing at 148 Evans Street in Oshkosh. Mathias Snyder was listed as retired and residing at that same address. Charles died on June 6, 1918 and is buried in Oshkosh

SNYDER, Charles M. (cont.)
at Riverside Cemetery, GAR Plot, west row, #16 from the south. He was survived by Dora, his widow.
{WC-V 1905; ROV; B-1905; Cem. records}

SNYDER, George W. - Pvt., Co. G, 1st Regt., Wis. Cav.
George was born in 1840 at New York. He was a son of Garrett P. and Delia Snyder. The father was of Mohawk Dutch descent and the mother was born in Connecticut. George was raised in New York until 8 years of age, when he removed to Wisconsin and worked as a day laborer at Oshkosh for three years. George enlisted on Nov. 4, 1861 and was assigned as above. He was mustered out at Louisville, Kentucky on Oct. 31, 1864 at the end of his term of enlistment. George returned to Wisconsin and was married on Dec. 14, 1864 to Anna E. Holderness. She was born in 1846 and was a daughter of John and Caroline Holderness. Her parents were both of English descent. George and Anna had at least one son, Ward K. Snyder, who was born on Mar. 25, 1888. George was listed in the veteran section of the 1885, 1895 and 1905 Wisconsin State census at P.O. Oshkosh. He was listed in the 1890 federal census as residing in the town of Algoma at P.O. Oshkosh. George was listed in 1905 as a fruit grower residing on 8 acres of section 35 in the town of Algoma. Son Ward K. was residing with him.
{US 1890; WC-V 1885, 1895, 1905; ROV; Randall p.17; B-1905}

SNYDER, Henry - Pvt., Co. G, 1st (3 yr.) Regt., Wis. Vol. Inf.
Henry resided at Oshkosh and enlisted there on Sept. 10, 1861. He was assigned as above and was wounded at Chickamauga, Georgia. Henry was then transferred to the Veteran Reserve Corps on Apr. 11, 1864.
{ROV}

SOMERSET, Peter - Pvt., Co. D, 21st Regt., Wis. Vol. Inf.
Peter resided at Menasha and enlisted there on Jan. 4, 1864. He was assigned as above. Peter died on Jan. 19, 1864 at Madison, Wisconsin.
{ROV}

SOMERSET, Pirie - Pvt., Co. H, 18th Regt., Wis. Vol. Inf.
Pirie resided at Oshkosh and enlisted there on Oct. 11, 1862. He was assigned as above and was discharged due to a disability on Aug. 6, 1863.
{ROV}

SOPER - see also Loper

SOPER, Peter H. - Sgt., Co. G, 5th Regt., Wis. Vol. Inf.
Peter enlisted on May 10, 1861 and was assigned as above, being promoted to Sergeant and then 1st Sergeant in that company. Peter was transferred to Co. B, Ind. Bn., Wis. Vol. Inf. on July 13, 1864. He was listed in 1883 at P.O. Oshkosh and receiving a pension of $4 per month since June 1881 for chronic rheumatism. He was listed in the veteran section of the 1885 Wisconsin State census at P.O. Oshkosh. Peter was listed in 1888 as a member of GAR Post #10 at Oshkosh. Peter and his wife then removed to Milwaukee. They were residing there when Fred E. Soper, a son, died in Sept. 1894. He had been born circa 1874 and died from the injuries received in an explosion.
{WC-V 1885; ROV; LOP-1883; OWN 22 Sep 1894}

SOPER, William W. - Pvt., Co. B, 4th Regt., Wis. Cav.
William was born in Sept. 1826 at Ohio. His father was a native of Vermont and his mother was born in Ohio. William resided at Omro and enlisted there on June 11, 1861. He was assigned as a musician in the above company and was listed as absent sick when that regiment was mustered out on May 28, 1866. William was listed in 1876 as a wheelright residing on the east side of Elm Street south of Vine Street in the city of Oshkosh. He was listed in the veteran section of the 1885 Wisconsin state census at P.O. Marion and in that section of the 1895 state census at P.O. Clintonville, both in Waupaca County. William was listed in the 1900 federal census as residing at the Wisconsin Veterans' Home at King. He had then been married for 5 years but his wife was not residing with him. William was listed in the veteran section 1905 state census at King.
{US 1900; WC-V 1885, 1895, 1905; GAR 40th; 1876 Oshkosh Directory; ROV}

SOUTH, Luther - Pvt., Co. G, 42nd Regt., Wis. Vol. Inf.
Luther resided at Nepeuskun and enlisted there on Aug. 31, 1864. He was assigned as above and was mustered out on June 11, 1865.
{ROV}

SPAULDING, Charles J. - Pvt., Co. K, 18th Regt., Wis. Vol. Inf.
Charles was born on Sept. 15, 1845 at Pennsylvania. He was a son of T.S. and Mary Spaulding and a brother of William H. Spaulding from a following sketch. The father was born circa 1811 at New York. Mary died on Sept. 9, 1856 at age 43 years. T.S. was listed in the 1860 federal census as residing on a farm in the town of Omro. Sarah, his second wife, was born circa 1815 at New York. Listed with them were the following children: Emily, born circa 1845; Charles, listed as born circa 1847; Martha, born circa 1850; Sarah, born circa 1852; and Caroline, born circa 1855. The three younger children were born in Wisconsin and the others were born in Pennsylvania. The father died on Jan. 10, 1890 at age 76 years. Charles resided at Omro and enlisted there on Mar. 17, 1862. He was assigned as above and was discharged on Aug. 5, 1862. Charles died on Aug. 11, 1862. He is buried with his parents in the town of Omro at Omro Union Cemetery. William H., his brother, is buried on that same plot.
{US 1860; ROV; Cem. records}

SPAULDING, Edward A. - Pvt., Co. G, 3rd Regt., Wis. Vol. Inf.
Edward resided at Neenah and enlisted there on Apr. 20, 1861. He was assigned as above and was mustered out on June 29, 1864 at the end of his term of enlistment. Edward was listed in the veteran section of the 1885 Wisconsin State census at P.O. Neenah as a veteran of the 32nd Regt., Wis. Vol. Inf.
{WC-V 1885; ROV}

SPAULDING, William H. - Pvt., Co. D, 13th Regt., Wis. Vol. Inf.
William was born circa 1836 at Pennsylvania. He was a son of T.S. and Mary Spaulding and a brother of Charles from a previous sketch. William was married in Winnebago County on Feb. 18, 1857 to Eliza Havens. Eliza was born circa 1839 at New York. William was listed in the 1860 federal census as residing with the family of Peter Snyder in the town of Omro. He was also listed that same year as residing with his parents in the town of Omro. Listed with him were his wife and Hulsea Havens, her sister, who was born circa 1833 at New York. William listed his residence as Magnolia, Rock

SPAULDING, William H. (cont.)
County when he enlisted on Sept. 26, 1861. He was assigned as above and was mustered out on Nov. 19, 1864 at the end of his term of enlistment according to some military records. His marker reads "killed at battle of Pleasant Hill, Louisiana - April 1864, aged 26 years." He was listed in the veterans grave registration file as a member of the above unit. William is buried in the town of Omro at Omro Union Cemetery. Eliza A. Havens, his wife, died on Nov. 11, 1865 at age 25 years. She is buried at his side.
{US 1860; GRI; ROV; WCMR v.1, p.99, #410*; Cem. records}

SPEAR, George W. - Pvt., Co. I, 21st Regt., Wis. Vol. Inf.
George resided at Menasha and enlisted there on Aug. 18, 1862. He was assigned as above and was wounded at Resaca, Georgia. George was transferred to the Veteran Reserve Corps on Jan. 10, 1865 and was mustered out in July 1865.
{ROV}

SPEAR, Valentine - Pvt., Co. L, 3rd (reorg.) Regt., Wis. Cav.
Valentine resided at Nepeuskun and enlisted there on Jan. 1, 1864. He was assigned as above and was mustered out on Oct. 31, 1865.
{ROV}

SPECHT, Franklin R. - Pvt., Co. K, 5th Regt., Pennsylvania Hvy. Art.
Franklin was born on Jan. 15, 1847/8 at Somerset County, Pennsylvania. He enlisted there and was assigned as a Private in the above company on Aug. 26, 1864. He was then mustered in at Pittsburg on Sept. 1, 1864. The muster roll lists him as age 18 years and a farmer by occupation. He was discharged on June 30, 1865 at Vienna, Virginia. Frank was married on Jan. 24, 1867 in Somerset County to Mary Rebecca Miller. They had six children: Annie E.; Florence R., died young; Charles E.; James N.; Jennie; and Cora Mahilday, died young. Mary died in March 1901 at Somerset County. Frank left Pennsylvania in early 1902 and removed to Wisconsin, settling at Oshkosh. He was married again on Apr. 17, 1902 at Menominee, Michigan to Mary Currier (Parsons) Forsythe. She had been married to Amos Forsythe on Dec. 15, 1897 and was divorced from him at Oshkosh on Oct. 6, 1900. Frank and Mary had a daughter, Erna Florence, who was born on Aug. 18, 1905. Frank was listed in the veteran section of the 1905 Wisconsin State census at P.O. Oshkosh. He was then listed as a commercial traveler residing at 132 Forest Avenue in the city of Oshkosh. On a Declaration for Pension filed at Oshkosh on Dec. 18, 1913, Frank listed that he had been a patient at Mt. Pleasant Hospital in fall of 1864 during his military service. He had contracted bilious fever which was followed by diarrhea, piles, rheumatism and a disease of the heart and stomache. Frank then listed his address as 301 Forest Avenue in Oshkosh and he was receiving pension #186,332. Mary died in June 1920 and Frank died on Oct. 9, 1920 at Oshkosh. He is buried there in the GAR Section at Riverside Cemetery. Frank was survived by his daughter Florence and a sister who resided at Canton, Pennsylvania.
{WC-V 1905; USDI-BP; Cem. records; ODN 09 Oct 1920}

SPECHT, Joseph - Civil War Veteran?
Joseph is buried at Oshkosh in Riverside Cemetery, GAR Plot, east row, #1 from the south. No other information was available from the cemetery records. Joseph was not listed in the 1905 county directory.
{Cem. records; B-1905}

SPENCER, Abner A. - Sgt., Co. A, 9th Regt., Minnesota Vol. Inf.
Abner was listed in 1868 as a lumberman boarding at 127 Algoma Street in the city of Oshkosh. He had a son, unnamed at registration, who was born in Oshkosh on Nov. 24, 1880/1. Abner was listed as above in the veteran section of the 1885 and 1895 Wisconsin State census at P.O. Oshkosh. He was listed in the 1890 federal census as residing at 421 Jefferson Avenue in Oshkosh. Abner then provided his unit designation as above and his service dates as having been from Aug. 14, 1862 to May 30, 1865. He added that he had been discharged from a hospital. Abner was listed in 1905 as residing at 23 Baldwin Avenue in Oshkosh. Amy C., T. Mabel and W. Bert Spencer were also residing at that address.
{US 1890; WC-V 1885, 1895; T-1868; B-1905; WCBR v.3, p.46, #272}

SPENCER, Charles - Pvt., Co. H, 18th Regt., Wis. Vol. Inf.
Charles resided at Poy Sippi, Waushara County and enlisted there on Dec. 9, 1861. He was assigned as above and was taken prisoner at Shiloh, Tennessee. Charles was then mustered out on Mar. 14, 1865 at the end of his term of enlistment. He was listed in the 1890 federal census as residing at Poy Sippi.
{US 1890; ROV}

SPENCER, Henry C. - Lt., Co. B, 3rd Regt., Wis. Vol. Inf.
Henry was born circa 1827 at New York. He was married to Elizabeth Reed on Oct. 13, 1853 in Winnebago County. She was born circa 1827, also at New York. Henry was listed in the 1860 federal census as a shoe dealer residing in the third ward of the city of Oshkosh. He enlisted at Oshkosh on Apr. 21, 1861. He was assigned as above and was promoted to 1st Sergeant in that company. He was commissioned as 2nd Lieutenant of that company on Apr. 12, 1862 and was taken prisoner on May 25, 1862. Henry died on July 3, 1862 in the rebel prison at Salisbury, N.C.
{US 1860; ROV; WCMR v.1, p.147, #623}

SPENCER, James - Cpl., Co. E, 2nd Regt., Wis. Vol. Inf.
James resided at Oshkosh and enlisted there on Apr. 21, 1861. He was assigned as above and was promoted to Corporal in that company. James was taken prisoner at Morrisville, Virginia on Nov. 7, 1863 and was mustered out on June 28, 1864 at the end of his term of enlistment. James had been wounded in Jan. 1862 by the bursting of a gun. He was listed in 1868 as a partner in the firm of Spencer & Caldwell. They were engaged in operating the Home Restaurant at 53 Main Street in the city of Oshkosh.
{ROV; OWN 24 Jan 1862; T-1868}

SPERRY, Frederick - Pvt., Co. B, 3rd Regt., Wis. Vol. Inf.
Frederick was born circa 1826 at New York. He was listed in the 1860 federal census as a sawyer residing with the family of Lovell Stow in the village of Neenah. Frederick enlisted at Neenah on Jan. 5, 1864. He was assigned as above and was transferred to Co. G of that regiment on Apr. 19, 1864. He was listed in Co. G as a musician and he was mustered out on July 18, 1865. At the time of his transfer Frederick listed his residence as Madison, Dane County.
{US 1860; ROV}

SPIEGELBERG, Frederick - Pvt., Co. C, 53rd Regt., Wis. Vol. Inf.
Friedrich was born on Mar. 25, 1822 at Prussia. He was a son of Frederick Spiegelberg.

SPIEGELBERG, Frederick (cont.)
The father was born circa 1793 at Prussia. Friedrich was married in Winnebago County on Apr. 18, 1856 to Juliana Bohlman. She was born on June 14, 1837, also at Prussia. Frederick was listed in the 1860 federal census as residing on a farm in the town of Winchester. Listed with him were his wife, his father and two children. Amelia was born circa 1858 at Wisconsin and Ernest was born circa 1859 at Wisconsin. Frederick listed his residence as Utica when he enlisted on Mar. 10, 1865. He was assigned as above. Most of that company was transferred to Co. K, 51st Regt., Wis. Vol. Inf. under orders dated June 10, 1865. The transfer was completed at Ft. Leavenworth, Kansas on June 30, 1865 and the regiment returned to Madison, Wisconsin on Aug. 1, 1865. The men were mustered out by companies with the last being mustered out on Aug. 30, 1865. Anna, widow of Frederick, was listed in the 1890 federal census as residing in the town of Wolf River at P.O. Zittau. She listed that he had died of cancer on Aug. 28, 1889. Julianna was listed in 1905 as residing with the family of Julius Spiegelberg in section 25 of the town of Wolf River. She died on Aug. 16, 1929. Adolph F., a son, was born in Wisconsin on Oct. 13, 1876 and died on Dec. 11, 1890. All three are buried in the town of Wolf River at Boom Bay Cemetery.
{US 1860, 1890; ROV; B-1905; Cem. records; WCMR v.1, p.164, #754}

SPIEGELBERG, Friedrich Wm. - Pvt., Co. F, 19th Regt., Wis. Vol. Inf.
Friedrich resided at Winchester and enlisted there on Feb. 3, 1862. He was assigned as above and was mustered out on Apr. 29, 1865. Fred was listed in 1883 at P.O. Winchester, where he had been receiving a pension of $6 per month since Jan. 1882 for partial deafness, intermittent fever and a disease of the spleen. He was listed in the 1890 federal census as residing in the town of Winchester at P.O. Winchester. Friedrich was listed in the veteran section of the 1895 Wisconsin State census at P.O. Winchester. Fred was listed in 1905 with Mollie, his wife, as a timber estimator residing on 2 acres of section 25 in the town of Wolf River.
{US 1890; WC-V 1895; ROV; LOP-1883; B-1905}

SPIEGELBERG, Wilhelm - Lt., Co. F, 19th Regt., Wis. Vol. Inf.
Wilhelm was born in 1824 at Prussia. Louise, his wife, was born circa 1820 at Prussia. They were listed in the 1860 federal census as residing on a farm in the town of Winchester. Agnes, their daughter, was born circa 1854 at Prussia and Charles, their son, was born circa 1857 at Prussia. William listed his residence as Bloomfield, Waushara County when he enlisted on Jan. 16, 1862. He was assigned as above and was commissioned as 2nd Lieutenant in that company on Mar. 27, 1862. Wilhelm was then promoted to 1st Lieutenant in that company and was wounded on Oct. 27, 1864 at Fair Oaks, Virginia. He had resigned his commission on Oct. 26, 1864. William was listed in 1883 at P.O. Zoar and receiving a pension of $4.25 per month for a wound to his right hand. Wilhelm was listed in the veteran section of the 1885, 1895 and 1905 Wisconsin State census at P.O. Oshkosh. He was listed in 1888 as a member of GAR Post #241 at Oshkosh. He had been listed in the 1890 federal census as residing in the town of Wolf River at P.O. Zittau. William then listed that he had suffered a gunshot wound and that he was then generally unhealthy. He was listed in 1905 as an insurance agent boarding at 238 Eighth Street in the city of Oshkosh. William died in 1908 and is buried in the town of Wolf River at Boom Bay Cemetery.
{US 1860, 1890; WC-V 1885, 1895, 1905; ROV; B-1905; Cem. records}

SPIKES, William - Sgt., Co. B, 3rd Regt., Wis. Cav.
William was born on Mar. 17, 1832 at Londonderry, Ireland. He was a son of James and Margaret (Campbell) Spikes. As a lad, William attended the Londerry Institute. He was then engaged on the sea for four years before emigrating to America in 1849. He landed at Boston and remained there for four years while learning the trade of a cabinet maker with Joseph Orr. William then removed to St. Johnsbury, Vermont and remained there for two years. He moved to Wisconsin and settled at Oshkosh in 1855. William was listed in the 1860 federal census as a cabinet maker residing in the third ward of the city of Oshkosh. William was residing there when he enlisted on Jan. 3, 1862. He was assigned as above and was promoted to Quartermaster Sergeant of that company in July 1862. He was promoted to Orderly Sergeant on Oct. 20, 1863. William was mustered out at Madison, Wisconsin on Feb. 14, 1865 at the end of his term of enlistment. He returned to Oshkosh and was engaged in the furniture business and as an undertaker. William was listed in 1868 as a partner in the firm of Soper & Spikes, furniture makers and undertakers. He was residing at 8 Thirteenth Street in Oshkosh. He later went into business for himself and owned three furniture stores in Oshkosh. William was married to Matilda Taggert. She was born circa 1825 at Ireland. They had one daughter, Eliza "Lizzie" Tucker Spikes. She was born circa 1851 at Massachusetts. William was married second on Oct. 26, 1887 to Mrs. Charles W. Griffin. She was born Lucy Wyman at Boston, Massachusetts in 1840 and came to Wisconsin in 1847 with her parents. Lucy died at Oshkosh on Feb. 8, 1888. She was survived by two daughters from her first marriage, Mrs. Cora Boomer of Beaver Dam and Mrs. A.D. Moulton. William's third wife was Eliza D. Spikes. She was born at Wilton, Maine in 1836. William was listed in the veteran section of the 1885 and 1895 Wisconsin State census at P.O. Oshkosh. He was listed in 1888 as a member of GAR Post #241 at Oshkosh. He was listed in the 1890 federal census as residing in the city of Oshkosh. In spring of 1899 he retired from his furniture business to devote his energies exclusively to undertaking. He died at his home in Oshkosh on Dec. 6, 1903 after an eleven week battle with heart disease. He was survived by his wife and a sister, Mrs. Elizabeth Rutherford of Waupaca. He was also survived by one granddaughter and one grandson. Eliza was listed in 1905 as his widow. She was residing at 129 Light Street in Oshkosh. Eliza died at Oshkosh on Oct. 27, 1924. She was survived by a daughter, Mrs. Ella Wheeler. Eliza was returned to McHenry, Illinois to be buried in the Wheeler plot at Woodland Cemetery.
{US 1860, 1890; WC-V 1885, 1895; ROV; SCA 1:642-3; T-1868; OWN 09 Feb 1888} {B-1905; OWN 12 Dec 1903; ODN 27 Oct 1924}

SPINDLER, Gottlieb - Pvt., Co. B, 3rd Regt., Wis. Vol. Inf.
Gottlieb was born circa 1830 at Prussia, a son of Gottlieb Spindler and a brother of Henry from a following sketch. Gottlieb was listed in the 1860 federal census as residing with his father and members of the family on a farm in the town of Orihula at P.O. Fremont. He had been married within the year to Rejita, who was born circa 1840 at Switzerland. Gottlieb resided at Wolf River and was drafted there on Nov. 4, 1864. He was assigned as above and was mustered out on July 18, 1865.
{US 1860; ROV}

SPINDLER, Henry - Pvt., Co. B, 21st Regt., Wis. Vol. Inf.
Henry was born in 1834 at Prussia, a son of Gottlieb and Johnanna Spindler and a brother of Gottlieb from a previous sketch. The father was born circa 1804 at Prussia

SPINDLER, Henry (cont.)
and the mother was born there circa 1808. Gottlieb Sr. was listed in the 1860 federal census as residing on a farm in the town of Orihula at P.O. Fremont. Listed with him were his wife and the following children: Gottlieb; Henry; Mary, born circa 1841; Anna, born circa 1843; and Herman, born circa 1847. The children were all born in Prussia. Henry resided at Wolf River and enlisted there on Aug. 15, 1862. He was assigned as above and was taken prisoner at Chickamauga, Georgia. Henry was mustered out on Aug. 11, 1865. He was listed in the 1890 federal census as residing at P.O. Fremont, Waupaca County. He was listed in the veteran section of the 1905 Wisconsin State census at P.O. Fisk. Henry was listed in that same year as residing with Amalia, his wife, on 70 acres of section 13 in the town of Utica. He died in 1911. Amalie was born in 1843 and died in 1916. Both are buried in the town of Wolf River at Wolf River Cemetery.
{US 1860, 1890; WC-V 1905; B-1905; Cem. records; ROV}

SPINK, Richard Angelo - Pvt., Co. A, 14th Regt., Wis. Vol. Inf.
Richard was born on Jan. 8, 1844 at Ennes Ellen, Ireland. He was a son of Richard Robert and Caroline (Bowyer) Spink. They were both natives of England. The father was born at Leeds, Yorkshire and was a graduate of Oxford University. Caroline was born in Macclesfield, Cheshire and taught art and music in a ladies seminery there. They were married at Macclesfield on Dec. 14, 1842 and they immediate left for Ireland. Richard Sr. was a civil engineer and, two months after the birth of Richard, he was assigned to Hamilton, Canada to work on the Welland Canal. After contracting rheumatism, the father resigned his position and emigrated to the United States, settling in Fond du Lac, Fond du Lac County in 1849. Richard Sr. died at Fond du Lac and Caroline later died at Indianapolis, Indiana at the home of a daughter. Richard was educated in the common schools at Fond du Lac and then at the Willoughby and Coolidge Academies in that place. He worked for his father in the merchandise business until he entered the service during the Civil War. Richard enlisted at Fond du Lac on Feb. 29, 1864. He was assigned as a musician in the above company and was detached to the Signal Corps. He was mustered out on Oct. 9, 1865 at Mobile, Alabama and returned to Fond du Lac on the 28th of that same month. He became interested in photography and engaged himself as a professional photographer. He was married at Fond du Lac in 1870 to Margarite Amanda Consaul. She was a daughter of Joseph J. and Lidia (Worthman) Consaul who were early settlers of Milwaukee. Shortly after their marriage, Richard and Margarite removed to Oshkosh. About 1878 Richard was one of the organizers of the old Arion Band and he continued with that organization for about 20 years. Richard was listed in 1888 as a member of GAR Post #241 at Oshkosh. He was listed in the 1890 federal census as residing at 488 Jackson Street in Oshkosh. He provided then that he had been wounded by a shell during his military service. Richard was listed in the veteran section of the 1895 and 1905 Wisconsin State census at P.O. Oshkosh. He was listed in 1905 as the Oshkosh City Treasurer. Richard was then residing at 438 Jackson Street in Oshkosh. Harry, Margarite, Robert and William Spink were also residing at that address. Margarite, his wife, died in 1919. Richard was re-elected as secretary-treasurer of the 14th Regiment Association in June 1920 and had held that position for altogether 44 consecutive years. Richard was married second in 1922 to Mrs. Minnie C. Shugart, widow of Dr. J.D. Shugart of Chicago. Richard was listed in 1927 as residing in Oshkosh. He died at his home in Oshkosh on May 10, 1935. He was the last local survivor from the 14th Regt., Wis. Vol. Inf. Richard was survived

SPINK, Richard Angelo (cont.)
by his second wife and five children: Mrs. Carrie Hale of St. Joseph, Michigan; Edward Lyman Spink of Chicago; Frank A. and Robert Spink of Oshkosh; and Mrs. Margurite Abbie Wolf of Rogers Park, Illinois. Richard was also survived by two sisters, Mrs. Lafayette Bishop of St. Croix Falls, Wisconsin and Mrs. William Spencer of Indianapolis, Indiana. He was buried in Oshkosh at Riverside Cemetery.
{US 1890; WC-V 1895, 1905; ROV; 21-40th; ODN 21 Jun 1920; ODN 07 Jan 1933} {ODN 11 May 1935; B-1905}

SPOER, Solomon C. - Cpl., Co. D, 32nd Regt., Wis. Vol. Inf.
Solomon was born circa 1840 at Ohio. He was a brother of Cyrus W. Spore from a following sketch. Lavina, wife of Solomon, was born circa 1838 at Ohio. Solomon was listed in the 1860 federal census as a jeweler residing in the fifth ward of the city of Oshkosh. Residing with him were his wife and a son, Charles, who was born circa 1858 at Ohio. Solomon enlisted at Oshkosh on Aug. 21, 1862. He was assigned as above and was promoted to Corporal in that company. He was discharged on Mar. 20, 1864 due to a disability. Solomon was listed in 1868 as a painter residing at 82 Washington Street in Oshkosh. He was listed in 1883 at P.O. Oshkosh and receiving a pension of $8 per month for ophthalmia. Solomon was listed in 1888 as a member of GAR Post #241 at Oshkosh. He was listed in the 1890 federal census as then residing at 40 W. Irving Street in Oshkosh. He listed then that he had lost the sight in his left eye and that vision in the other was impared. Solomon was listed in the veteran section of the 1895 and 1905 Wisconsin State census at P.O. Oshkosh. He was listed (Spore) in 1905 as a paper hanger residing at 72 Prospect Avenue in Oshkosh. Jessie M. Spore was also listed at that address.
{US 1860, 1890; WC-V 1895, 1905; ROV; LOP-1883; T-1868; B-1905}

SPOHR, Ernst - Pvt., Co. D, 51st Regt., Wis. Vol. Inf.
Ernst resided at Menasha and enlisted there on Mar. 6, 1865. He was assigned as above and was mustered out at Madison, Wisconsin on Aug. 29, 1865.
{ROV}

SPORE, Cyrus - Cpl., Co. E, 5th (reorg.) Regt., Wis. Vol. Inf.
Cyrus was a son of Lucy Spore and a brother of Solomon C. Spoer from a previous sketch. Each brother spelled their name differently. Lucy was born circa 1801. Cyrus resided at Oshkosh and enlisted there on Aug. 9, 1864. He was assigned as above and was promoted to Corporal in that company. He was mustered out on June 20, 1865. After the war Cyrus moved to Illinois and taught school for about six years. He then started a newspaper business at Astoria, Illinois. He was associated with various newspapers in that state until 1884, when he settled at Decatur and opened an office as a pension attorney. Cyrus died at Decatur, Illinois in July 1894. He was survived by his mother and Solomon. He was also survived by his wife and one daughter.
{ROV; OWN 28 Jul 1894}

SPORER, John - Pvt., Co. F, 19th Regt., Wis. Vol. Inf.
John resided at Oshkosh and enlisted there on Sept. 2, 1864. He was assigned as above and was wounded on Oct. 27, 1864 at Fair Oaks, Virginia. He was then transferred to Co. C of that same regiment on May 1, 1865 and was mustered out on July 21, 1865.
{ROV}

SPRAGUE, Ava - Pvt., Co. A, 31st Regt., Maine Vol. Inf.
Ava was listed in 1868 as a sawyer engaged by the firm of Spalding, Badger & Co. He was married in Winnebago County on Sept. 6, 1868 to Mary Baldwin. They had a daughter, unnamed at registration, who was born in Oshkosh on Feb. 6, 1879. Ava was listed in the 1890 federal census as residing at 334 Mt. Vernon Street in the city of Oshkosh. He then provided his unit designation as above and his dates of service as having been from Feb. 19, 1864 to July 15, 1865. Ava added that the sight in his right eye was destroyed while in the military. He was listed in the veteran section of the 1895 Wisconsin State census at P.O. Oshkosh. Ava was listed in 1905 as an oil inspector residing at 263 Main Street in Oshkosh.
{US 1890; WC-V 1895; WCBR v.2, p.135, #362; WCMR v.1, p.395, #2460; T-1868}
{B-1905}

SPRAGUE, John - Cpl., Co. B, 3rd Regt., Wis. Vol. Inf.
John resided at Alto, Fond du Lac County and enlisted there on Jan. 28, 1864. He was assigned as above and was promoted to Corporal in that company. He was mustered out on July 18, 1865. He was listed in 1868 as boarding at 31 River Street in the city of Oshkosh. John was listed in the veteran section of the 1885 Wisconsin State census at P.O. Oshkosh.
{WC-V 1885; ROV; T-1868}

SPRAGUE, John J. - Sgt., Co. E, 2nd Regt., Wis. Vol. Inf.
John was born circa 1838 at New York, a son of James G. and Susan D. Sprague. James was born circa 1811 at Vermont and Susan was born circa 1814 at New York. James was listed in the 1860 federal census as a crockery and glass merchant residing in the fourth ward of the city of Oshkosh. Listed with him were his wife and the following children: James, born circa 1834 at Canada, then a navy officer; Charles, born circa 1836 at New York, a telegraph operator; John, a clerk; Alida, born circa 1840 at New York; Henry, born circa 1845 at New York; and Rona, born at Wisconsin circa 1858. John enlisted at Oshkosh on Apr. 21, 1861. He was assigned as above and was promoted to Sergeant in that company. John was discharged on Aug. 19, 1861 due to a disability. He was married in Winnebago County on Oct. 11, 1864 to Hettie Maria Jenkins. She was born at Falmouth, Massachusetts on Oct. 29, 1839 and was a sister of James Jenkins from a previous sketch. In 1860 she came to Wisconsin and settled at Oshkosh with her parents, brother James and his wife. John and Hettie had three children: Mary; Howard; and Sidney. John was listed in 1868 as a dealer in crockery and residing at 15 Jefferson Avenue in Oshkosh. He was listed again in 1888 as a member of GAR Post #241 at Oshkosh. John was listed in the 1890 federal census as residing at 121 Washington Street in Oshkosh. He reported that he suffered from chronic diarrhea. While on a visit to Washington, D.C. with two of her children, Hettie suffered a cerebral hemmorhage and died on Feb. 1, 1893. She was returned to Oshkosh for services and burial. John was listed in the veteran section of the 1895 Wisconsin State census at P.O. Oshkosh. He was listed in an article by Col. Harshaw as having died at Oshkosh prior to May 1899.
{US 1860, 1890; WC-V 1895; ODN 07 May 1899; WCMR v.1, p.263, #1549*; ROV}
{T-1868; OWN 04 Feb 1893; OWN 11 Feb 1893}

SPRING, Fred - Pvt., 2nd Regt., Wis. Vol. Inf.
Fred resided at Menasha and enlisted there on June 6, 1861. He was discharged by

SPRING, Fred (cont.)
order on Nov. 15, 1861.
{ROV}

SPURGEON, Jeremiah - Pvt., Co. K, 11th Regt., Wis. Vol. Inf.
Jeremiah resided at Neenah and enlisted there on Mar. 2, 1864. He was assigned as above and was mustered out on Sept. 4, 1865. Jerry was listed in the 1890 federal census as residing in the town of Royalton, Waupaca County at P.O. Weyauwega.
{US 1890; ROV}

SPURGEON, John H. - Pvt., Co. E, 52nd Regt., Wis. Vol. Inf.
John resided at Winchester and enlisted there on Mar. 14, 1865. He was assigned as above and was mustered out on July 28, 1865.
{ROV}

STACY, Dwight - Pvt., Co. B, 21st Regt., Wis. Vol. Inf.
Dwight was born circa 1848 at New York. He was listed in the 1860 federal census as residing with the family of Thomas Roach in the town of Winneconne. Thomas is the subject of a previous sketch. Dwight enlisted at Winneconne on Feb. 1, 1864. He was assigned as above. Dwight contracted a disease and died on June 24, 1864 near Atlanta, Georgia.
{US 1860; ROV}

STADTMULLER, Joseph - Pvt., Co. C, 53rd Regt., Wis. Vol. Inf.
Joseph resided at Menasha and enlisted there on Mar. 10, 1865. He was assigned as above. Most of that company was transferred to Co. K, 51st Regt., Wis. Vol. Inf. under orders dated June 10, 1865. The transfer was completed at Ft. Leavenworth, Kansas on June 30, 1865 and the regiment returned to Madison, Wisconsin on Aug. 1, 1865. The men were mustered out by companies with the last being mustered out on Aug. 30, 1865. Joseph was mustered out on Aug. 21, 1865. He was listed in the veteran section of the 1885 Wisconsin State census at P.O. Nekimi. He was listed in the 1890 federal census as residing in the town of Nekimi at P.O. Oshkosh. Joseph was listed in that section of the 1895 and 1905 state census at P.O. Oshkosh. He was listed in 1905 as retired and residing at 281 Fourteenth Street in the city of Oshkosh.
{US 1890; WC-V 1885, 1895, 1905; ROV; B-1905}

STALEY, Stephen R. - Pvt., Co. A, 48th Regt., Wis. Vol. Inf.
Stephen was born circa 1830 at England. He was married June 12, 1856 in Winnebago County to Emma Eliza Elliott. She was born circa 1835 at England and was a daughter of John and Mary Elliott. Both of her parents were natives of England, the father born there circa 1793 and the mother born circa 1795. John and Mary were listed in the 1860 federal census as residing in the town of Omro. Their son Josiah is the subject of a previous sketch. Stephen and Mary were listed in the 1860 federal census as residing on a farm near her parents in the town of Omro. Listed with them were two children, both born in Wisconsin. Mary was born circa 1857 and John was born circa 1859. Stephen listed his residence as Oconomowoc, Waukesha County and he enlisted there on Feb. 3, 1865. He was assigned as above and was mustered out on Dec. 30, 1865. Eliza died on July 12, 1882. Stephen was listed in the veteran section of the 1885 and 1895 Wisconsin State census at P.O. Oshkosh. He was listed in 1888 as a member of GAR Post #10 at

STALEY, Stephen R. (cont.)
Oshkosh. Stephen was listed in the 1890 federal census as residing in the city of Oshkosh. There is only a concrete base and a GAR marker left to designate the grave of Stephen at Omro Cemetery, Olin's Addition, Section B, plot 25.
{US 1890; WC-V 1885, 1895; ROV; WCMR v.1, p.95, #394; Cem. records}

STALKER, Martin H. - Sgt., Co. B, 3rd Regt., Wis. Cav.
Martin resided at Oshkosh and he enlisted there on Dec. 2, 1861. He was assigned as above and was promoted to Sergeant in that company. Martin was then discharged on Nov. 27, 1862 due to a disability.
{ROV}

STAMMER, William R. - Pvt., Co. C, 21st Regt., Wis. Vol. Inf.
William resided at Oshkosh and enlisted there on Aug. 14, 1862. He was assigned as above and was wounded in the chest during October 1862 at Chaplin Hills, Kentucky. William was then transferred to the Veteran Reserve Corps on Mar. 7, 1864 and was mustered out on July 5, 1865. He was listed in 1883 at P.O. May, Outagamie County and receiving a pension of $8 per month for a wound to his right shoulder. William was listed in 1920 as residing at Appleton, Outagamie County.
{ROV; LOP-1883; 21-33rd; OWN 16 Oct 1862; OWN 07 May 1863}

STANFORD, Joseph - Pvt., Co. I, 4th Regt., Ohio Vol. Inf.
Joseph was listed as above in the veteran section of the 1885 Wisconsin State census at P.O. Neenah.
{WC-V 1885}

STANFORD, Robert - Pvt., Co. K, 33rd Regt., Ohio Vol. Inf.
Robert was listed as above in the veteran section of the 1885 Wisconsin State census at P.O. Neenah.
{WC-V 1885}

STANFORD, Thomas - Pvt., Co. I, 21st Regt., Wis. Vol. Inf.
Thomas was born circa 1828. He was a son of Richard Stanford. The father was born circa 1784 at England. Thomas was listed in the 1850 federal census as residing on a farm in the town of Vinland and as having been born in England. Others of his family were listed then as having been born in Canada. They are probably his brothers and sisters. Thomas was listed in the 1860 federal census as residing in the village of Neenah and as having been born in England. Tabitha, his wife, was born circa 1832 at England. Listed with them then were the following children: Matilda, born circa 1850 at England; Eliza, born circa 1853 at Ohio; Charles, born circa 1855 at Ohio; Mary, born circa 1858 at Wisconsin; and Alonzo, born in 1859 at Wisconsin. Listed with them was Richard, father of Thomas. Also listed was Jeremiah Stanford, a brother of Thomas. Thomas enlisted at Neenah on Aug. 14, 1862. He was assigned as above and was discharged on Apr. 24, 1863 due to a disability. Joseph and Robert Stanford of previous sketches are probably brothers of Thomas.
{US 1850, 1860; ROV}

STANGE, Frederick - Pvt., Co. C, 53rd Regt., Wis. Vol. Inf.
Frederick resided at Utica and enlisted there on Mar. 8, 1865. He was assigned as

STANGE, Frederick (cont.)
above. Most of that company was transferred to Co. K, 51st Regt., Wis. Vol. Inf. under orders dated June 10, 1865. The transfer was completed at Ft. Leavenworth, Kansas on June 30, 1865 and the regiment returned to Madison, Wisconsin on Aug. 1, 1865. The men were mustered out by companies with the last having been mustered out on Aug. 30, 1865.
{ROV}

STANLEY, Darius - Pvt., Co. D, 1st (3 yr.) Regt., Wis. Vol. Inf.
Darius was born circa 1836 at New York. He was listed in the 1860 federal census as a farm laborer for John R. Padelford in the town of Omro. Darius listed his residence as Vinland when he enlisted on Sept. 17, 1861. He was assigned as above and he was wounded in Sept. 1863. Darius was then transferred to the Veteran Reserve Corps on Apr. 30, 1864. He was married in Winnebago County on Nov. 3, 1868 to Clara Thirza Dilley.
{US 1860; ROV; WCMR v.1, p.397, #2475}

STANLEY, John E. - Pvt., Co. C, 46th Regt., Wis. Vol. Inf.
John resided at Oshkosh and enlisted there on Feb. 7, 1865. He was assigned as above and was mustered out on Sept. 27, 1865.
{ROV}

STANNARD, William C. - Sgt., Co. E, 5th (reorg.) Regt., Wis. Vol. Inf.
William was born on Dec. 25, 1844 at Cleveland, Ohio. He was a son of Abner and Orpha Stannard. Abner was born circa 1820 at Ohio and Orpha was born circa 1822 at Canada East. They were listed in the 1860 federal census as residing on a farm in the town of Clayton at P.O. Neenah. Listed with them were the following children: Julia, born circa 1842 at Ohio; William; Ransom, born circa 1847 at Illinois; Willard, born circa 1850 at Illinois, and Ida, born in 1859 at Wisconsin. William listed his residence as Oshkosh when he enlisted on Sept. 1, 1864. He was assigned as above and was then promoted to Sergeant in that company. William was mustered out on June 20, 1865. He was married in Winnebago County on Apr. 26, 1866 to Althea J. Brown. William was engaged as a timber estimater and as a lumberman. He was at one time considered wealthy while owning much timberland and other properties. He lost most of these assets in his later years. William was listed in the 1890 federal census as residing in the city of Oshkosh. He was listed in the veteran section of the 1895 Wisconsin State census at P.O. Oshkosh. William died of typhoid pneumonia in Oshkosh at the home of his sister, Mrs. James Hursh, on May 8, 1903. Althea, his wife, was born in 1845 and died in 1898. Both are buried in Oshkosh at Riverside Cemetery. William was survived by his mother, Mrs. Orpha Stannard of Butte des Morts, two brothers, William and Ransom Stannard, also of Butte des Morts, his sister, Mrs. Hursh of Oshkosh, daughters Adelaide Stannard of Chicago and Maude Stannard of Oshkosh, and sons Harry and Jesse Stannard, also of Oshkosh.
{US 1860, 1890; WC-V 1895; ROV; Cem. records; WCMR v.1, p.298, #1825}
{OWN 16 May 1903}

STANTON, James M. - Pvt., Co. F, 18th Regt., Wis. Vol. Inf.
James was born circa 1838 at New York. He was a son of Erastus and Sarah Stanton and a brother of John Emery Stanton from a following sketch. Both of his parents were

STANTON, James M. (cont.)
natives of Connecticut, the father born there circa 1806 and the mother born circa 1816. They were listed in the 1860 federal census as residing in the town of Rushford at P.O. Eureka. Listed with them were the following children: James; Mary, born circa 1842; Emery; and Charles, born circa 1849. All of the children were shown as having been born in New York. James enlisted at Rushford on Feb. 6, 1862. He was assigned as above and was wounded at Shiloh, Tennessee. James was discharged on July 14, 1862 due to his wounds. He was married in Winnebago County on May 15, 1867 to Mary C. Williams. He was listed in 1883 at P.O. Eureka and receiving a pension of $6 per month for a wound to his right foot. James was listed in the veteran section of the 1885 and 1895 Wisconsin State census at P.O. Eureka. He was listed in the 1890 federal census as residing in the town of Rushford at P.O. Eureka. Mary, his widow, was listed in 1905 as residing in the village of Eureka. James is buried with a simple military marker in the town of Rushford at Eureka Cemetery. Also buried on that plot are Mary C. Stanton and Erastus Stanton, his father. Mary was born on July 21, 1848 and died on Mar. 24, 1924. Erastus died on Aug. 26, 1861.
{US 1860, 1890; WC-V 1885, 1895; LOP-1883; WCMR v.1, p.324, #2036; ROV}
{B-1905; Cem. records}

STANTON, James S. - Pvt., Co. C, 1st Regt., Missouri Eng.
James was born circa 1835 at New York. His father was born in Massachusetts and his mother was a native of Germany. James was listed in the 1890 federal census as residing in the city of Neenah. He then provided his unit designation as Cpl., Co. I, 1st Regt., U.S. Engineers. He also provided his service dates as having been from Sept. 15, 1861 to July 15, 1865. He was listed in 1890 as having a lame back. James was listed as above in the veteran section of the 1895 Wisconsin State census at P.O. Neenah. He was listed in 1905 as residing at the Wisconsin Veterans' Home at King. His wife was then residing at 419 Sherry Street in the city of Neenah. Claude and Genie C. Stanton were also listed at that address. James was listed in the 1910 federal census at King. He had been married three times, the last for 31 years. Ada A., his wife, was then residing with him. She was born circa 1855 at Canada and came to this country in 1868.
{US 1890, 1910; WC-V 1895; B-1905; GAR 40th}

STANTON, John E. - Pvt., Co. A, 50th Regt., Wis. Vol. Inf.
John resided at Rushford and enlisted there on Feb. 6, 1865. He was assigned as above and was mustered out on June 12, 1866 at the end of his term of enlistment.
{ROV}

STANTON, William - Pvt., Co. G, 3rd Regt., Wis. Vol. Inf.
William resided at Neenah and enlisted there on Apr. 20, 1861. He was assigned as above and was discharged on Nov. 19, 1862 due to a disability.
{ROV}

STARK, David - Pvt., Co. E, 3rd Regt., Wis. Vol. Inf.
David resided at Christiana, Dane County and enlisted there on Jan. 21, 1864. He was assigned as above and was mustered out on July 13, 1865 with a disability. David was listed in the veteran section of the 1885 Wisconsin State census at P.O. Utica.
{WC-V 1885; ROV}

STARKS, George R. - Pvt., Co. B, 49th Regt., Wis. Vol. Inf.
George resided at Utica and enlisted there on Feb. 10, 1865. He was assigned as above and was mustered out on Nov. 1, 1865.
{ROV}

STARKWEATHER, Asher - Pvt., Co. C, 46th Regt., Wis. Vol. Inf.
Asher was married in Winnebago County on Mar. 22, 1864 to Eleanor L. Ambrose. He resided at Omro and enlisted there on Jan. 31, 1865. Asher was assigned as above and was mustered out on Sept. 27, 1865.
{ROV; WCMR v.1, p.252, #1462}

STARKWEATHER, Charles R. - Sgt., Co. F, 46th Regt., Wis. Vol. Inf.
Charles resided at Oshkosh and enlisted there in Feb. 1865. He was assigned as above and was promoted to Sergeant in that company. He was mustered out on Sept. 27, 1865.
{ROV}

STARLING, Samuel - Pvt., Co. D, 41st Regt., Wis. Vol. Inf.
Samuel resided at Menasha and enlisted there on May 19, 1864. He was assigned as above and was mustered out on Sept. 23, 1864 at the end of his term of enlistment. There were members of the Starling family residing in Waupaca County.
{ROV}

STATLER, Burns - Cpl., Co. C, 14th Regt., Wis. Vol. Inf.
Burns was born circa 1840 at Illinois. He was a son of Jonathan "John" Statler and a brother of Erastus, Solomon, James and Stephen Statler from following sketches. Burns was listed in the 1860 federal census as a laborer residing in the town of Omro. Also listed there were his father and the brothers named above. Burns enlisted at Omro on Sept. 8, 1861. He was assigned as above and was then promoted to Corporal in that company. Burns was discharged on May 2, 1862 due to a disability. He re-enlisted on Mar. 10, 1864 and was assigned to that same company. He was then mustered out on Oct. 9, 1865. Burns was listed in the veteran section of the 1905 Wisconsin State census at P.O. Mountain, Oconto County.
{US 1860; WC-V 1905; ROV}

STATLER, Erastus - Pvt., Co. C, 14th Regt., Wis. Vol. Inf.
Erastus was born circa 1835 at Ohio. He was a son of Jonathan Statler and a brother of James, Solomon, Burns and Stephen Statler from other sketches. Erastus was listed in the 1860 federal census as residing with his father and brothers in the town of Omro. He enlisted at Omro on Sept. 8, 1861. He was assigned as above and was wounded on June 27, 1864. Erastus contracted a disease and died on Feb. 22, 1865 at Vicksburg, Mississippi.
{US 1860; ROV}

STATLER, James L. - Pvt., Co. C, 14th Regt., Wis. Vol. Inf.
James was born circa 1830 at Ohio. He was a son of Jonathan Statler and a brother of Erastus, Solomon, Burns and Stephen Statler from other sketches. James was listed in the 1860 federal census as a laborer residing in the town of Omro. Phoebe, his wife, was born circa 1838 at New York. Eliza, their daughter, was born circa 1856 at Wisconsin. Also listed there were his father and brothers. James enlisted at Omro on Sept. 8, 1861.

STATLER, James L. (cont.)
He was assigned as above and was wounded at Shiloh, Tennessee. He was discharged on Aug. 14, 1862 due to a disability. James re-enlisted at Omro on Sept. 15, 1863 and was assigned as a Private to Co. C, 1st Regt., Wis. Hvy. Art. He was then discharged on June 9, 1865 due to a disability.
{US 1860; ROV}

STATLER, Jonathan - Pvt., Co. C, 14th Regt., Wis. Vol. Inf.?
Jonathan was born circa 1805 at Ohio. He was the father of James, Erastus, Burns and Stephen Statler of other sketches. Jonathan was listed on the cemetery roster of GAR Post #7 at Omro. He was not found in the records of any of the Wisconsin military organizations. Jonathan is buried with a simple military marker at Omro Cemetery, Original Section, plot 235.
{US 1860; Cem. records}

STATLER, Solomon - Pvt., Co. C, 14th Regt., Wis. Vol. Inf.
Solomon was born circa 1838 at Ohio. He was a son of Jonathan Statler and a brother of James, Erastus, Burns and Stephen Statler from other sketches. Solomon resided at Omro and enlisted there on Sept. 8, 1861. He was assigned as above and was wounded at Shiloh, Tennessee. While home on furlough to recover from his wounds, Solomon was married in Winnebago County on Feb. 15, 1864 to Louisa Weston. He contracted a disease and died at Omro on Feb. 26, 1865. Solomon is buried with a simple military marker at Omro Cemetery, Original Section, plot 235.
{US 1860; ROV; WCMR v.1, p.251, #1456*; Cem. records}

STATLER, Stephen C. - Pvt., Co. B, 4th Regt., Wis. Cav.
Stephen was born circa 1842 at Ohio. He was a son of Jonathan Statler and a brother of James, Erastus, Solomon and Burns Statler from previous sketches. Stephen resided at Omro and enlisted there on June 1, 1861. He was assigned as above and was then discharged by order of the War Dept. on Nov. 20, 1862.
{US 1860; ROV}

STATTON, Richard - Pvt., Co. I, 21st Regt., Wis. Vol. Inf.
Richard resided at Menasha and enlisted there on Aug. 11, 1862. He was assigned as above and was taken prisoner on Dec. 30, 1862. Richard was discharged on Apr. 13, 1863 due to a disability.
{ROV}

STATTON, William - Cpl., Co. H, 37th Regt., Wis. Vol. Inf.
William resided at Neenah and was drafted there on Nov. 23, 1863. He was assigned as above and was then promoted to Corporal in that company. William was wounded on June 17, 1864 at Petersburg, Virginia. He was then discharged due to a disability on Mar. 25, 1865. There was a William Statton residing at the Wisconsin Veterans' Home at King in 1900 but it has not been proven to be the same person.
{ROV}

STAUDENRAUS, Joseph - Lt., Co. F, 19th Regt., Wis. Vol. Inf.
Joseph was born at Laupheim, Germany. He was a son of Ignatz and Magdalena (Aich) Staudenraus. They were natives of Germany and both died there. Joseph emigrated to

STAUDENRAUS, Joseph (cont.)
America in May 1854 at age 20 years. He landed at New York and travelled to Toledo, Ohio, where he was engaged as a shoe maker. Joseph removed to Wisconsin on June 26, 1854 and settled at Oshkosh. He went to St. Louis and enlisted on Apr. 15, 1861. Joseph was assigned as a Private to Co. C, 2nd Regt., Missouri Vol. Inf. He was mustered in as a Sergeant in that company. He was then discharged on Aug. 31, 1861 at the end of his term of enlistment. Joseph returned to Oshkosh, where he enlisted on Jan. 29, 1862. He was assigned as above and was then promoted to Orderly Sergeant when the regiment was organized. Joseph was commissioned as 2nd Lieutenant of that company while stationed at Chapin's Farm on July 1, 1864. He was promoted to 1st Lieutenant on Nov. 28, 1864 but was not mustered at that rank. He was mustered out on Apr. 29, 1865. Joseph returned to Oshkosh and then went back to his native land. He was married there on Aug. 26, 1865 to Mary Denzel. She was born on Oct. 6, 1841 at Lauphein, Germany. Joseph returned to Oshkosh in fall of 1865 and was engaged in the hotel business, being the owner of the Tremont. He was listed in 1868 as operating a saloon and residing at 81 Waugoo Street in Oshkosh. A Jacob Staudenraus was also residing in Oshkosh at that time. Joseph was listed in the veteran section of the 1885 Wisconsin State census at P.O. Oshkosh. He was leasing the Tremont and had retired by 1888, when he was listed as a member of GAR Post #241 at Oshkosh. Joseph and Mary had four children: Lena; Albert A.; Bertha J.; and Emma Staudenraus. Roman S., a brother of Joseph, also resided at Oshkosh. Another brother, Jacob, resided in the Dakota Territory in 1888. Joseph was listed in the 1890 federal census as residing in the town of Oshkosh at P.O. Oshkosh. Marie, widow of Joseph, died in Oshkosh at the Tremont House on July 31, 1903. She had been residing there for five weeks after having removed from her home on High Street. She was planning to erect a new home and was staying temporarily with K.C. Frey of the Tremont, her son-in-law. Joseph had died about a year and one half earlier. Emma, his daughter, was listed in 1905 as residing at the Tremont House.
{US 1890; WC-V 1885; ROV; SCA 1:510-1; T-1868; B-1905; OWN 01 Aug 1903}

STEADMAN, Joseph - Pvt., Co. F, 19th Regt., Wis. Vol. Inf.?
Joseph was listed as above in the veteran section of the 1895 Wisconsin State census at P.O. Oshkosh. He was not found in the records of that company and was not found in the index to the Roster of Wisconsin Volunteers.
{WC-V 1895; ROV}

STEARNS, Gardner - Pvt., Co A, 31st Regt., Wis. Vol. Inf.
Gardner resided at Utica and enlisted there on Aug. 9, 1862. He was assigned as above and was wounded at Goldsboro, N.C. He was then listed as absent wounded when the regiment was mustered out on June 20, 1865.
{ROV}

STEARNS, John B. - Pvt., Co. F, 4th Regt., Wis. Cav.?
John was listed as above in the veteran section of the 1885 Wisconsin State census at P.O. Oshkosh. He was not found in the records of that company.
{WC-V 1885}

STEARNS, John R. - Pvt., Co. F, 1st Regt., Maine Cav.
John was listed as above in the veteran section of the 1895 Wisconsin State census at

STEARNS, John R. (cont.)
P.O. Oshkosh.
{WC-V 1895}

STEELE, Joseph - Seaman, "Juliet V," Gunboat Service, U.S. Navy.
Joseph was listed as above in the veteran section of the 1885 and 1905 Wisconsin State census at P.O. Oshkosh. He died about May 1, 1890 at Berlin, Green Lake County, where he had been residing with a son. Joseph was returned to Oshkosh for burial in Riverside Cemetery. Eliza, his widow, was listed in 1905 as residing at 747 High Street in the city of Oshkosh. Florence B. and Joseph D. Steele were also listed at that address.
{WC-V 1885, 1905; B-1905; OWN 08 May 1890}

STEELE, William G. - Pvt., Co. I, 32nd Regt., Wis. Vol. Inf.
William resided at Oshkosh and enlisted there on Aug. 15, 1862. He was assigned as above and was mustered out on June 12, 1865.
{ROV}

STEFFINS, Joseph J. - Pvt., Co. E, 5th (reorg.) Regt., Wis. Vol. Inf.
Joseph resided at Algoma and enlisted there on Sept. 1, 1864. He was assigned as above and was mustered out on June 20, 1865.
{ROV}

STEIGER, John S. - Civil War Veteran?
John died on Aug. 5, 1869 at age 52 years, 6 months and 10 days. He is buried in the town of Wolf River at Wolf River Cemetery. A GAR marker has been placed at his grave.
{Cem. records}

STEIGMAN, John - Cpl., Co. B, 3rd Regt., Wis. Vol. Inf.
John resided at Utica and enlisted there on Apr. 22, 1861. He was assigned as above and was then promoted to Corporal in that company. John contracted a disease and died on Oct. 28, 1861 at Frederick, Maryland.
{ROV}

STEIN, Charles - Pvt., Co. D, 3rd Regt., Wis. Cav.
Charles resided at Utica and enlisted there on Dec. 8, 1861. He was assigned as above and was listed as having deserted on Feb. 6, 1862. Charles was listed in 1868 as a clerk boarding at the Revere House in Oshkosh.
{ROV; T-1868}

STENGEL, August - Pvt., Co. E, 26th Regt., Wis. Vol. Inf.
August was born in Aug. 1830 at Maryland. His parents were both natives of France. August resided at Fond du Lac, Fond du Lac County and he enlisted there on Aug. 21, 1862. He was assigned as above and was transferred to the Veteran Reserve Corps on Oct. 12, 1863. He was mustered out on June 29, 1865. August was listed as above in the veteran section of the 1885 Wisconsin State census at P.O. Menasha. He was listed in the 1890 federal census as residing in the town of Menasha at P.O. Menasha. August was listed in the 1900 federal census as residing at the Wisconsin Veterans' Home at King. Sophia, his wife of 34 years, was residing there with him. She was born in May

STENGEL, August (cont.)
1845 at Germany and came to this country in 1860. August and Sophia had nine children, six then living.
{US 1890, 1900; WC-V 1885; ROV}

STEPHENSON, Septimus - Sgt., Co. H, 3rd (reorg.) Regt., Wis. Cav.
Septimus was born circa 1840 at New York. He was listed in the 1860 federal census as a farm laborer for Asher Hubbard in the town of Oshkosh. Septimus enlisted at Oshkosh on Nov. 24, 1863. He was assigned as a Private to Co. C, 3rd Regt., Wis. Cav. Septimus was transferred to Co. H, 3rd (reorg.) Regt., Wis. Cav. and was promoted to Quartermaster Sergeant in that company. He was mustered out on Sept. 29, 1865. Septimus was married in Winnebago County on Apr. 30, 1868 to Ellen L. Thompson.
{US 1860; ROV; WCMR v.1, p.375, #2299}

STEVENS, Edward P. - Pvt., Co. B, 3rd Regt., Wis. Cav.
Edward was born circa 1844 at Maine. He was a son of Hiram Stevens and a brother of William, both subjects of following sketches. Edward was listed in the 1860 federal census as residing with his parents and their family in the fourth ward of the city of Oshkosh. He enlisted at Oshkosh on Aug. 11, 1862. He was assigned as above and was transferred to Co. B, 3rd (reorg.) Regt., Wis. Cav. on Feb. 1, 1865. Edward was then mustered out on June 19, 1865. He was listed in 1868 as a mason boarding at 8 Alley Street in Oshkosh. Edward's wife, name not listed, had a stillborn daughter at Oshkosh on June 30, 1881. Edward was listed in 1888 as a member of GAR Post #10 at Oshkosh. He was listed in the veteran section of the 1885 and 1895 Wisconsin State census at P.O. Oshkosh. Edward was listed in the 1890 federal census as residing in Oshkosh. He listed that he suffered from defective eyesight. Nellie, his widow, was listed in 1905 as residing at 38 Mt. Vernon Street in Oshkosh.
{US 1860, 1890; WC-V 1885, 1895; ROV; WCBR v.3, p.41, #244; T-1868; B-1905}

STEVENS, Gaylord - Pvt., Co. H, 30th Regt., Wis. Vol. Inf.
Gaylord was born on Nov. 18, 1818 at New York. He was listed in the 1860 federal census as residing in the town of Aurora, Waushara County. Listed with him were Katherine, his wife, and the following children: W.H., born circa 1846 at New York; Ellen, born circa 1847 at New York; Alice, born circa 1850 at New York; and Jane, born circa 1856 at Wisconsin. Gaylord resided at Auroraville and enlisted there on Aug. 21, 1862. He was assigned as above and was mustered out on June 22, 1865. Gaylord died on Dec. 10, 1875. Katherine, his widow, was listed in the 1890 federal census as residing in the village of Omro. Katherine died on Sept. 22, 1898 at age 71 years. Both are buried at Omro Cemetery, Pelton's Addition, Section B, plot 32. Other members of their family are buried on that same plot.
{US 1860, 1890; ROV; Cem. records}

STEVENS, Hiram - Pvt., Co. B, 3rd Regt., Wis. Cav.
Hiram was born circa 1812 at Maine. Rosalie, his wife, was born circa 1816 in that same state. They were the parents of Edward from a previous sketch and William from a following sketch. Hiram was listed in the 1860 federal census as a mason residing in the fourth ward of the city of Oshkosh. Residing with him were his wife and the following children: William; Edward; Adelaide, born circa 1848 at Maine; Aldoras, born circa 1851 at Maine; Lillie, born circa 1855 at Wisconsin; Charles, born circa 1857 at

STEVENS, Hiram (cont.)
Wisconsin; and George, born circa 1859 at Wisconsin. Hiram enlisted at Oshkosh on Nov. 27, 1861. He was assigned as above and was discharged on Nov. 27, 1862 due to a disability.
{US 1860; ROV}

STEVENS, Hiram Z. - Pvt., Co. A, 2nd Regt., Ohio Cav.
Hiram was listed as above in the veteran section of the 1885 Wisconsin State census at P.O. Omro. He was listed in the 1890 federal census as residing in the town of Omro at P.O. Omro. Hiram then provided his unit designation as above and his service dates as having been from June 27, 1864 to Sept. 11, 1865. He was listed in the veteran section of the 1895 state census at P.O. Oshkosh and in that part of the 1905 state census at P.O. Leeman, Outagamie County.
{US 1890; WC-V 1885, 1895, 1905}

STEVENS, James H. - Pvt., Co. A, 31st Regt., Wis. Vol. Inf.
James resided at Utica and enlisted there on Dec. 10, 1862. He was assigned to the above company on Dec. 25, 1862 and was transferred to Co. K of that same regiment on June 20, 1865.
{ROV}

STEVENS, Julius A. - Sgt., Co. C, 14th Regt., Wis. Vol. Inf.
Julius was born on Jan. 28, 1823 at Vermont. He was listed in the 1860 federal census as residing on a farm in the town of Omro. Caroline, his wife, was born circa 1827 at Massachusetts. Listed with them were the following children: Julia, born circa 1846; Augusta, born circa 1852; Benjamin Franklin, born circa 1854; and Charles, born circa 1855. Julius enlisted at Omro on Sept. 8, 1861. He was assigned as above and was promoted to Sergeant and then 1st Sergeant in that company. He was discharged on Aug. 31, 1862. Julius re-enlisted at Winneconne on Sept. 13, 1864 and was assigned as a Private to Co. E, 1st Regt., Wis. Cav. He was listed as absent sick when that regiment was mustered out on July 19, 1865. Julius and Caroline had at least one other son, Willie, who was born circa 1861. Caroline died on Apr. 18, 1865 at age 38 years. Julius was then married to Mrs. Elizabeth Wagner. She was born circa 1835 at Prussia. Julius and Elizabeth were listed in the 1880 federal census as residing with his sons in the town of Omro. Julius died on Mar. 23, 1882. He is buried with wife Caroline at Omro Cemetery, Original Section, plot 121.
{US 1860, 1880; ROV; Cem. records}

STEVENS, Reuben - Pvt., Co. I, 3rd (reorg.) Regt., Wis. Cav.
Reuben resided at Nepeuskun and enlisted there on Jan. 5, 1864. He was assigned as above and was mustered out on Sept. 29, 1865.
{ROV}

STEVENS, William O. - Pvt., Co. B, 3rd Regt., Wis. Cav.
William was born circa 1841 at Maine. He was a son of Hiram Stevens and a brother of Edward, both subjects of previous sketches. He was listed in the 1860 federal census as a mason residing with his parents and their family in the fourth ward of the city of Oshkosh. William enlisted at Oshkosh on Dec. 27, 1861. He was assigned as above and was mustered out on Feb. 14, 1865 at the end of his term of enlistment. William was

STEVENS, William O. (cont.)
listed in 1868 as a mill man residing at 81 Merritt Street in Oshkosh. He was listed in 1888 as a member of GAR Post #10 at Oshkosh. William was listed in the veteran section of the 1885 Wisconsin State census at P.O. Oshkosh.
{US 1860; WC-V 1885; ROV; T-1868}

STEVER, George Henry - Pvt., Co. C, 46th Regt., Wis. Vol. Inf.
George was born on May 24, 1831 at Fleming, New York. He was a son on Jacob and Harriet (Henry) Stever and a brother of John, William, Wells and Robinson Stever from following sketches. Jacob was born circa 1807 at New York and Harriet was born circa 1814 at Pennsylvania. They were listed in the 1860 federal census as residing on a farm in the town of Algoma. Listed with them then were the following children: William; Robinson; Howard; Wells; Molovas, born circa 1848 at Ohio; Celestia, born circa 1849 at Ohio; Delbert, born circa 1851 at Wisconsin; and Charles, born circa 1853 at Wisconsin. George was married to Martha Hewitt in Winnebago County on Oct. 3, 1858. She was born circa 1835 at New York and was a daughter of Amos and Sallie Hewitt. Both of her parents were natives of New York, the father born there circa 1805 and the mother born circa 1808. George and Martha were listed in the 1860 federal census as residing with her parents and their family in the town of Omro at P.O. Oshkosh. George listed his residence as Algoma when he enlisted on Feb. 4, 1865. He was assigned as above and was mustered out on Sept. 27, 1865 at Nashville, Tennessee. He was listed on his discharge as being 5'9", dark complexion, hazel eyes and black hair. He was listed in 1888 as a member of GAR Post #241 at Oshkosh. George was listed in the veteran section of the 1885, 1895 and 1905 Wisconsin State census at P.O. Oshkosh. He was listed in the 1890 federal census as residing in the town of Algoma at P.O. Oshkosh. George was listed in 1905, with his wife Martha, as residing on 10 acres of section 29 in the town of Algoma. Martha was born on Oct. 21, 1834. George died on Nov. 16, 1907 and Martha died on June 21, 1924. They are buried in the town of Omro at Omro Union Cemetery.
{US 1860, 1890; WC-V 1885, 1895, 1905; B-1905; WCMR v.1, p.191, #971}
{ROV; Cem. records; Discharge cert.}

STEVER, John Howard - Pvt., Co. F, 18th Regt., Wis. Vol. Inf.
John was born on Apr. 1, 1843 at Farmington, Trumbull County, Ohio. He was a son of Jacob and Harriet (Henry) Stever and a brother of Robinson, George H., William R. and Robert Wells Stever from other sketches. Jacob was a native of New York and was a descendant of the Mohawk Dutch. Harriet was the daughter of a veteran of the War of 1812. Jacob and Harriet brought their family to Wisconsin in 1850 and settled on a farm in the town of Algoma. Harriet was listed in 1883 at P.O. Waukau and receiving a mother's pension of $8 per month. John was engaged in farming at the onset of the Civil War. He had been listed in the 1860 federal census as a farm laborer residing with his parents and also as a farm laborer residing with Orson Angell in the town of Algoma. He listed his residence as Oshkosh when he enlisted on Oct. 25, 1861 and was assigned as above. He was taken prisoner at Shiloh, Tennessee and was confined at Montgomery, Alabama for seven weeks before being transferred to Macon, Georgia. He was paroled from prison and was discharged due to a disability at Alexandria, Virginia on Dec. 9, 1862. John re-enlisted on May 17, 1863 and was assigned as a Private in Co. C, 41st Regt., Wis. Vol. Inf. He was mustered out at Milwaukee, Wisconsin on Sept. 23, 1864 at the end of that term of enlistment. John again re-enlisted at Oshkosh on Feb. 4, 1865

STEVER, John Howard (cont.)
and was then assigned as a Private to Co. I, 47th Regt., Wis. Vol. Inf. He was promoted to Corporal in that company and received his final discharge at Nashville, Tennessee on Sept. 4, 1865. John was married in Winnebago County on Feb. 19, 1865 to Eliza Jane Coley. She was born on Mar. 3, 1848. They had three children: George H.; Bessie I.; and Jennie L., who died on May 27, 1867. John was listed in 1868 as a lumberman residing at 97 Ceape Street in the city of Oshkosh. He was listed in 1888 as a member of GAR Post #241 at Oshkosh. He was listed in the 1890 federal census as residing in the town of Omro at P.O. Oshkosh. He was listed in the veteran section of the 1895 state census at P.O. Zion. John died at home on Apr. 4, 1911 and Eliza died there on Mar. 7, 1922. Both are buried in the town of Omro at Minckler Cemetery. John had five brothers who served in various units of the Union Army, four of whom are named above.
{US 1860, 1890; WC-V 1885, 1895; SCA p.479-80; WCMR v.1, p.270, #1606; ROV}
{LOP-1883; T-1868; Cem. records}

STEVER, Robinson - Pvt., Co. E, 2nd Regt., Wis. Vol. Inf.
Robinson was born circa 1841 at Ohio. He was a son of Jacob and Harriet Stever and a brother of William, John, Wells and George Stever of other sketches. Robinson was listed in the 1860 federal census as residing with his parents in the town of Algoma. He was listed as Robert and listed his residence as Oshkosh when he enlisted on May 18, 1861. He was assigned as above and was wounded and taken prisoner at Gainesville, Virginia. Robert was then transferred to the 4th Regt., U.S. Hvy. Art. on Jan. 6, 1863.
{US 1860; ROV}

STEVER, Robert Wells - Pvt., Co. E, 2nd Regt., Wis. Vol. Inf.
Robert was born circa 1846 at Ohio. He was a son of Jacob and Harriet Stever and a brother of William, Robinson, Wells and George Stever from other sketches. Robert enlisted at Oshkosh on June 15, 1861. He was assigned as above and was wounded and taken prisoner at Gainesville, Virginia. Robert died on Sept. 30, 1862 at Georgetown, D.C. of his wounds.
{US 1860; ROV; OWN 11 Sep 1862}

STEVER, Washington - Lt., Co. K, 7th Regt., Wis. Vol. Inf.
Washington was born on Feb. 3, 1832. He listed his residence as Allen's Grove, Walworth County when he enlisted on Sept. 9, 1861. He was assigned as a Private in the above company and was promoted to Corporal, Sergeant and then 1st Sergeant in that company. Washington was wounded in the 2nd battle at Fredericksburg, Maryland. He was commissioned 1st Lieutenant of his company on Dec. 29, 1864. He was mustered out on July 3, 1865. Washington was listed in 1883 at P.O. Menasha, where he had been receiving a pension of $4 per month since Aug. 1881 for a wound to the head and a disease of the eyes. He was listed in the veteran section of the 1885 Wisconsin State census at P.O. Menasha. He was listed in the 1890 federal census as residing in the city of Menasha. Washington was listed in the veteran section of the 1895 state census at P.O. Oshkosh and in that part of the 1905 state census at P.O. Omro. He was listed in 1905 as a machinist residing at 612 Delhi Road in Omro. Washington died on July 12, 1914 and he is buried in the town of Neenah at Oak Hill Cemetery, First Addition, lot 73. He may be a brother to the Stevers from other sketches.
{US 1890; WC-V 1885, 1895, 1905; ROV; GRI; LOP-1883; B-1905}

STEVER, William R. - Pvt., Co. C, 21st Regt., Wis. Vol. Inf.
William was born circa 1835 at New York. He was a son of Jacob and Harriet Stever and a brother of Robinson, John, George and Wells Stever from other sketches. William was listed in the 1860 federal census as residing with his parents in the town of Algoma. He was listed in that same census as residing with the family of Levens Curtis in the town of Omro. William enlisted at Algoma on Aug. 13, 1862 and was assigned as above. William died on May 23, 1864 at Chattanooga, Tennessee.
{US 1860; ROV}

STEWARD, John P. - Pvt., Co. K, 5th (reorg.) Regt., Wis. Vol. Inf.
John was born circa 1839 at New York. Elmira, his mother, was born circa 1806 at Connecticut. She was listed in the 1860 federal census as residing on a farm in the town of Rushford at P.O. Eureka. Listed with her were the following children: Robert, born circa 1837 at New York; John; and James, born circa 1851 at Wisconsin. John enlisted at Rushford on Aug. 30, 1864. He was assigned as above and he was mustered out on June 20, 1865. John may have removed to the town of Dayton, Waupaca County.
{US 1860; ROV}

STEWART, Alvin N. - Pvt., Co. B, 1st Regt., Vermont Cav.
Alvin was listed as above in the veteran section of the 1905 Wisconsin State census at P.O. Fisk.
{WC-V 1905}

STICKLES, Cyrenus R. - Pvt., Co. I, 1st Regt., New York Vol. Inf.
He was listed as above in the veteran section of the 1885 and 1895 Wisconsin State census at P.O. Winneconne. Cyrenus was listed in the 1890 federal census as residing in the town of Winneconne at P.O. Winneconne. No other information was provided.
{US 1890; WC-V 1885, 1895}

STICKLES, Emery - Pvt., Co. K, 11th Regt., Wis. Vol. Inf.
Emery resided at Neenah and enlisted there on Mar. 4, 1864. He was assigned as above and was discharged due to a disability on Nov. 18, 1864.
{ROV}

STIER, Charles - Pvt., Co. E, 26th Regt., Wis. Vol. Inf.
Charles resided at Fond du Lac, Fond du Lac County and enlisted there on Aug. 21, 1862. He was assigned as above and was wounded at Gettysburg, Pennsylvania. Charles was mustered out on June 13, 1865. He was listed in 1883 at P.O. Oshkosh, where he was receiving a pension of $4 per month for a wound to his left foot. Charles was listed in the 1890 federal census as residing in the city of Oshkosh. He was listed in the veteran section of the 1895 Wisconsin State census at P.O. Oshkosh. Charles was listed in 1905 as a harness maker residing at 121 Sixth Street in Oshkosh. Alfred Stier was listed at that same address.
{US 1890; WC-V 1895; ROV; LOP-1883; B-1905}

STIFFELS, John - Pvt., Co. B, 3rd Regt., Wis. Vol. Inf.
John resided at Oshkosh and enlisted there on Apr. 22, 1861. He was assigned as above and was discharged on Sept. 12, 1863 due to a disability.
{ROV}

STILES, Charles - Pvt., Co. K, 25th Regt., Wis. Vol. Inf.
Charles listed his residence as Big Flats, Adams County when he enlisted on Aug. 15, 1862. He was assigned as above and was discharged on May 29, 1863 due to a disability. Charles died in Nov. 1868. His wife died on Nov. 8, 1868. Both are buried at Omro Cemetery, Original Section, plot 215. Both markers are badly weather-damaged.
{ROV; Cem. records}

STILES, Joseph Mason - Pvt., Co. I, 21st Regt., Wis. Vol. Inf.
Joseph was born circa 1834 at Vermont. Rachel, his mother, was born circa 1800 in New Hampshire. Joseph was married in Winnebago County on July 3, 1860 to Emily R. Shufelt. She was born circa 1834 at Vermont. Joseph was listed in the 1860 federal census as a carpenter residing in the village of Neenah. Listed with him were his wife and his mother. Joseph enlisted at Neenah on Aug. 11, 1862. He was assigned as above and was wounded in the hip on Oct. 8, 1862 at Chaplin Hills, Kentucky. Joseph was discharged due to his wounds on Mar. 11, 1863. He had a son, Joseph Frederick, who was born in the city of Neenah on Apr. 15, 1877. He also had a daughter, Grace Darling, who was born in Neenah on Feb. 7, 1879. Joseph was listed in 1883 at P.O. Neenah and receiving a pension of $6 per month for a wound to his left hip. He was listed in the veteran section of the 1885 and 1895 Wisconsin State census at P.O. Neenah. Joseph was listed in the 1890 federal census as residing in the city of Neenah. He then provided that he had received a gunshot wound to his left hip.
{US 1860, 1890; WC-V 1885, 1895; WCMR v.1, p.203, #1067; LOP-1883; ROV}
{WCBR v.2, p.83, #207; WCBR v.2, p.173, #486; OWN 16 Oct 1862}

STILES, Melvin - Pvt., unassigned, 14th Regt., Wis. Vol. Inf.
Melvin resided at Oshkosh and enlisted there on Apr. 19, 1864. He was not found in the records as having been assigned to any company within that regiment.
{ROV}

STILLMAN, Benjamin H. - Cpl., Co. D, 7th Regt., Wis. Vol. Inf.
Benjamin resided at Utica and enlisted there on Aug. 10, 1861. He was assigned as above and was then promoted to Corporal in that company. Benjamin was detached to Battery B, 4th Regt., U.S. Hvy. Art. from Nov. 28, 1861 until Aug. 1864. He was also detached to Hart's N.Y. Battery until Oct. 1864. Benjamin was then mustered out on July 3, 1865.
{ROV}

STILLWELL, Lewis Delos - Pvt., Co. D, 52nd Regt., Wis. Vol. Inf.
Lewis was born on Nov. 17, 1845. He listed his residence as the town of Black Wolf when he enlisted on Mar. 24, 1865. He was assigned as above and was listed as having deserted on Apr. 18, 1865. Lewis was married to Sarah Jane, a daughter of Richard H. Runcorn of Plainfield, Waushara County, Wisconsin. She was born on Oct. 28, 1851. They had at least four children: Ida J., born on Feb. 24, 1871, died on Feb. 17, 1874; Ward B., born on July 15, 1874, died on Sept. 11, 1923; Ada, born on Jan. 4, 1877, married Milton W. Hall, died on Jan. 30, 1914; and Nettie B., born on Oct. 25, 1880, died on July 1, 1881. Delos was managing his father's farm at Plainfield in 1888. He was listed in the 1890 federal census as residing in the town of Plainfield. Lewis then provided that he had been discharged on July 29, 1865. He was suffering from kidney and bladder problems and catarrh. Sarah died Jan. 20, 1905 and Lewis died Aug. 11,

STILLWELL, Lewis Delos (cont.)
1911. They are buried with several of their children in the town of Plainfield at Plainfield Cemetery.
{US 1890; ROV; SCA 1:709-10; Cem. records}

STINSON, Joseph - Pvt., Co. E, 5th (reorg.) Regt., Wis. Vol. Inf.
Joseph resided at Oshkosh and enlisted there on Aug. 27, 1864. He was assigned as above and was mustered out on June 20, 1865. Joseph was married on Sept. 26, 1867 in Winnebago County to Jennie E. Courtney.
{ROV; WCMR v.1, p. 350, #2099}

STOKES, George - Chaplain, 18th Regt., Wis. Vol. Inf.
George was born circa 1814 at England. He emigrated to this country and settled at Omro in 1846, where he was a Methodist minister. He was also a mason and builder. Delany, his wife, was born circa 1815 at New York. They were listed in the 1860 federal census as residing on a farm in the town of Omro at P.O. Oshkosh. Listed with them were the following children: Margaret, born circa 1837; Celia, born circa 1839; Betsey, born circa 1842; William, subject of a following sketch; Mary, born circa 1848; Emma, born circa 1852; and Harriet, born circa 1854. The three youngest children were born in Wisconsin and the others were born in New York. George enlisted at Oshkosh on Dec. 20, 1861. He was commissioned as 1st Lieutenant of the above company and was promoted to Regimental Chaplain on Nov. 19, 1862. George was then mustered out on July 18, 1865. After the war he removed to Idaho with his family. From there he moved to Utah and then to Minnesota. George died in Minnesota on Oct. 27, 1885. His obituary shows that he was the father-in-law of Thomas Bailey and a cousin of Dr. Forbes, both of Omro.
{US 1860; ROV; OWN 26 Nov 1885}

STOKES, William - Sgt., Co. D, 8th Regt., Wis. Vol. Inf.
William was born circa 1843 at New York, a son of George Stokes from a previous sketch. William was listed in the 1860 federal census as residing with his parents on a farm in the town of Omro at P.O. Oshkosh. He enlisted at Omro on Oct. 1, 1861. He was assigned as above and was promoted to Corporal and then Sergeant in that company. William was mustered out on Sept. 5, 1865.
{US 1860; ROV}

STOLKE, William - Pvt., Co. B, 37th Regt., Wis. Vol. Inf.
William resided at Janesville, Rock County and enlisted there on Mar. 25, 1864. He was assigned as above and was mustered out on July 27, 1865. William was listed in 1888 as a member of GAR Post #10 at Oshkosh. He was listed (Stulke) in the 1890 federal census as residing at 154 Central Avenue in the city of Oshkosh. He was listed in the veteran section of the 1895 Wisconsin State census at P.O. Oshkosh.
{US 1890; WC-V 1895; ROV}

STOLL, Charles - Pvt., Co. C, 53rd Regt., Wis. Vol. Inf.
Charles was married in Winnebago County on Nov. 24, 1864 to Emily Kalbus. He listed his residence as Utica when he enlisted on Mar. 10, 1865. He was assigned as above. Most members of that company were transferred to Co. K, 51st Regt., Wis. Vol. Inf. under orders dated June 10, 1865. The transfer was completed on June 30, 1865 at Ft.

STOLL, Charles (cont.)
Leavenworth, Kansas and the regiment returned to Madison, Wisconsin on Aug. 1, 1865. Charles had been mustered out on June 29, 1865. He was listed (Stahl) in the veteran section of the 1885 Wisconsin State census at P.O. Nekimi. Carl was listed in the 1890 federal census as residing in the town of Nekimi at P.O. Oshkosh. He provided that he suffered from esysypilas. Carl was born in 1821 and died on Aug. 27, 1892. He is buried in the town of Algoma at Peace Lutheran Cemetery. Carl was survived by his wife and one child.
{US 1890; WC-V 1885; WCMR v.1, p.267, #1577; OWN 03 Sept 1892; Cem. records}
{ROV}

STONE, Benjamin H. - Pvt., Co. A, 50th Regt., Wis. Vol. Inf.
Benjamin resided at Rushford and enlisted there on Feb. 21, 1865. He was assigned as above and was mustered out on June 12, 1866 at the end of his term of enlistment.
{ROV}

STONE, Dwight E. - Cpl., Co. A, 50th Regt., Wis. Vol. Inf.
Dwight resided at Rushford and enlisted there on Feb. 22, 1865. He was assigned as above and was promoted to Corporal in that company. Dwight was mustered out on June 12, 1866 at the end of his term of enlistment. He was listed in the veteran section of the 1885 Wisconsin State census at P.O. Omro. Dwight was listed in the 1890 federal census as residing in the village of Omro. He provided then that he suffered from rheumatism and scurvy. Dwight died on Apr. 16, 1894 at age 53 years. Mary H., his wife, died on Apr. 24, 1874 at age 37 years, 6 months and 1 day. Mary E., his second wife, was listed in 1905 as residing on Water Street in Omro. Dwight is buried with his first wife at Omro Cemetery, Pelton's Addition, Section B, plot 6. He was survived by his second wife and "a family of grown up children scattered through the west."
{US 1890; WC-V 1885; ROV; Cem. records; B-1905; OWN 21 Apr 1894}

STONE, Herman A. - Pvt., Co. D, 1st Regt., Wis. Cav.
Herman was born circa 1846 at Wisconsin. He was a son of Dudley and Matilda Stone. The father was born circa 1818 at Canada and the mother was born circa 1820 at Vermont. They were listed in the 1860 federal census as residing on a farm in the town of Rushford at P.O. Eureka. Herman enlisted at Rushford on Dec. 7, 1863. He was assigned as above and was mustered out on July 19, 1865. Herman was residing at Bethel, Iowa in 1870 when he received his share of the bounty for the capture of Jefferson Davis.
{US 1860; ROV; Lawson p.843}

STONE, John N. - Capt., Co. G, 19th Regt., Wis. Vol. Inf.
John resided at Chilton, Calumet County. He was commissioned as Captain of the above company on Feb. 5, 1862. He then resigned his commission on June 1, 1863. John established the Neenah News on Oct. 15, 1875. He was listed in the 1890 federal census as residing in the city of Neenah. He was listed in the veteran section of the 1895 and 1905 Wisconsin State census at P.O. Neenah.
{US 1890; WC-V 1895, 1905; ROV; HN 1878 p.107}

STONE, John W. - Pvt., Co. C, 14th Regt., Wis. Vol. Inf.
John was born circa 1828 at Canada. He was married to Sarah Packard on Oct. 24,

STONE, John W. (cont.)
1857. She was born circa 1842 at New York. They were listed in the 1860 federal census as residing on a farm in the town of Nepeuskun at P.O. Waukau. Jesse, their son, was born circa 1858 at Wisconsin. John enlisted at Nepeuskun on Oct. 18, 1861. He was assigned as above. John contracted a disease and died on May 19, 1862 at Pittsburg Landing, Tennessee. His marriage was recorded in Winnebago County in early 1863. Sarah, his widow, was listed in the 1890 federal census as residing in the town of Nepeuskun at P.O. Waukau.
{US 1860, 1890; ROV; WCMR v.1, p.236, #1336}

STONE, Seth - Pvt., Co. G, 14th Regt., Wis. Vol. Inf.?
Seth was listed in the 1890 federal census as residing in the city of Oshkosh. He provided his unit designation as above and his service dates as having been Sept. 8, 1862 to July 13, 1865. Seth was listed in the veteran section of the 1895 Wisconsin State census at P.O. Oshkosh. He was not found in the records of that company and was not found in the index to the Roster of Wisconsin Volunteers. Seth was listed in 1905 as a blacksmith residing at 1 Frederick Avenue in Oshkosh.
{US 1890; WC-V 1895; ROV; B-1905}

STORKE, Charles A. - Pvt., Co. G, 36th Regt., Wis. Vol. Inf.
Charles resided at Oshkosh and enlisted there on Feb. 28, 1864. He was assigned as above and was taken prisoner at Cold Harbor, Virginia on June 1, 1864. Charles was mustered out on May 24, 1865.
{ROV}

STORM, John - Pvt., Co. G, 45th Regt., Wis. Vol. Inf.
John (Sturm) resided at Merrill, Lincoln County and enlisted there on Mar. 6, 1865. He was assigned as above and was mustered out on July 17, 1865. He was listed (Storm) in the 1890 federal census as residing in the town of Menasha at P.O. Appleton.
{US 1890; ROV}

STOWE, Franklin M. - Pvt., Co. D, 21st Regt., Wis. Vol. Inf.
Franklin was born on Mar. 11, 1844 at Caledonia County, Vermont. He was a son of Joseph and Priscilla (Page) Stowe. Franklin was seven months old when his parents removed to Wisconsin and settled at Milwaukee. They removed to Fond du Lac after a year and remained in that place for 12 years. The family then removed to Appleton, Outagamie County. Franklin listed Appleton as his residence when he enlisted there on Aug. 15, 1862. He was assigned as above and was wounded by accident at Louisville, Kentucky. Franklin suffered from heat exhaustion during the seige of Atlanta and was assigned to the hospital in Murfreesboro, Tennessee. He was discharged from there on July 22, 1864 due to a disability. He returned to his family at Appleton and was married on Sept. 30, 1866 to Carrie A.W. Ashby. They had two daughters, Phebe and Jessie. Jessie was married to Julius Ulrich Jr. of Winneconne. His father is the subject of a following sketch. Franklin removed to Winneconne in 1869. He was listed in 1883 at P.O. Winneconne and receiving a pension of $6 per month for a disease of the heart. He was listed in the veteran section of the 1885, 1895 and 1905 Wisconsin State census at P.O. Winneconne. Franklin was listed in the 1890 federal census as residing in the village of Winneconne. He was listed in 1905 as a veterinary surgeon residing on William Street in Winneconne. Franklin died at Winneconne and was buried there on

STOWE, Franklin M. (cont.)
Feb. 1, 1919. Carrie, his widow, was listed in June 1920 as residing at Winneconne.
{US 1890; WC-V 1885, 1895, 1905; ROV; LOP-1883; SCA 1:493-4; 21-33rd; B-1905}
{WCMR v.1, p.308, #1905*}

STOWE, George F. - Pvt., Co. G, 3rd (reorg.) Regt., Wis. Cav.
George resided at Vinland and enlisted there on Feb. 12, 1864. He was assigned as above and was mustered out on Oct. 27, 1865. He was married in Winnebago County on Feb. 9, 1868 to Ella T. Hurd. George was listed (Grover) in the 1890 federal census as residing in the town of Menasha at P.O. Menasha. He was listed in 1905 as a laborer residing at 649 Broad Street in the city of Menasha. George A. and Simeon Stowe were also listed at that address.
{US 1890; ROV; WCMR v.1, p.368, #2239; B-1905}

STOWE, Henry H. - Pvt., 8th Batt., Wis. Lt. Art.
Henry resided at Neenah and enlisted there on Feb. 10, 1862. He was assigned as above and was transferred to the Veteran Reserve Corps on Sept. 30, 1863. Henry was then mustered out on Mar. 23, 1865 at the end of his term of enlistment.
{ROV}

STOWE, Levi C. - Pvt., 8th Batt., Wis. Lt. Art.
Levi resided at Menasha and enlisted there on Jan. 1, 1864. He was assigned as above and was discharged on Apr. 12, 1865 due to a disability.
{ROV}

STOWE, William I. - Chaplain, 27th Regt., Wis. Vol. Inf.
William listed his residence as Sheboygan Falls, Sheboygan County when he was commissioned as Chaplain of the above regiment on Oct. 23, 1862. He resigned that commission on Aug. 24, 1863. William was listed in the veteran section of the 1895 Wisconsin State census at P.O. Oshkosh.
{WC-V 1895; ROV}

STOWE, William J. - Pvt., Co. G, 3rd (reorg.) Regt., Wis. Cav.
William resided at Winchester and enlisted there on Feb. 12, 1864. He was assigned as above and was mustered out on Oct. 27, 1865.
{ROV}

STRASSER, John - Cpl., Co. B, 3rd Regt., Wis. Vol. Inf.
John was born circa 1832 at Bavaria. Margaret, his wife, was born circa 1826 at Prussia. John was listed in the 1860 federal census as a laborer residing in the third ward of the city of Oshkosh. Residing with him were his wife and a daughter, Emma, who was born circa 1857 at Wisconsin. John enlisted at Oshkosh on Apr. 22, 1861. He was assigned as above and was promoted to Corporal in that company. John was then mustered out on June 29, 1864 at the end of his term of enlistment. He was listed in 1868 as the operator of a boarding house at 3 Tenth Street in Oshkosh. John was listed in the veteran section of the 1885, 1895 and 1905 Wisconsin State census at P.O. Oshkosh. He was listed in 1888 as a member of GAR Post #241 at Oshkosh. John was listed in the 1890 federal census as residing in Oshkosh. He was listed in 1905 as an

STRASSER, John (cont.)
employee of the Foster-Lothman Mills and residing at 192 Fifth Street in Oshkosh.
{US 1860, 1890; WC-V 1885, 1895, 1905; ROV; T-1868; B-1905}

STRATE, Squire Levi - Pvt., 3rd Regt., Wis. Cav.
Levi was born circa 1836 at New York. He was a son of Lothrip and Elizabeth Strate. The father was born circa 1813 at Pennsylvania and the mother was born circa 1817 at New York. Lothrip was listed in the 1860 federal census as a shoemaker residing in the town of Oshkosh. Listed with him were his wife and the following children: Levy; Paula, born circa 1839; Helen, born circa 1843; and Squire, born circa 1847. All of the children were born in New York. Levi was married to Eunice Reynolds on May 5, 1861 in Winnebago County. She was born on Apr. 12, 1840 at Wisconsin and was a daughter of Nelson and Sarah Reynolds. Both of her parents were natives of New York, Nelson born circa 1806 and Sarah born circa 1808. They were listed in the 1860 federal census as residing in the town of Oshkosh. Levi listed his residence as Omro when he enlisted on Apr. 6, 1864. He was assigned to the above regiment but was not assigned to a company. Squire Levy died on Apr. 13, 1864 at Madison, Wisconsin. His wife was listed in 1876 as a weaver residing at 51 Tenth Street in the city of Oshkosh. She was listed in 1905 as residing at 257 Tenth Street in Oshkosh. Eunice died on Apr. 21, 1912. Sarah E., a daughter, died on Feb. 17, 1865 at age 11 months and 23 days. Eunice and Sarah are buried in the town of Vinland at Brooks Cemetery.
{US 1860; B-1905; WCMR v.1, p.214, #1159; 1876 Oshkosh Directory; Cem. records} {ROV}

STRAUCH, John G. - Pvt., Co. C, 53rd Regt., Wis. Vol. Inf.
John resided at Black Wolf and enlisted there on Mar. 7, 1865. He was assigned as above. Most of that company was transferred to Co. K, 51st Regt., Wis. Vol. Inf. under orders dated June 10, 1865. The transfer was completed at Ft. Leavenworth, Kansas on June 30, 1865 and the regiment returned to Madison, Wisconsin on Aug. 1, 1865. The men were then mustered out by companies with the last having been mustered out on Aug. 30, 1865.
{ROV}

STREETER, John F. - Pvt., Unassigned, 18th Regt., Wis. Vol. Inf.
John resided at Theresa and enlisted there on Apr. 6, 1865. He was assigned to the above regiment but not to any company within that regiment. He was mustered out on Aug. 7, 1865. John was listed in 1888 as a member of GAR Post #241 at Oshkosh. He was listed in the veteran section of the 1895 and 1905 Wisconsin State census at P.O. Oshkosh and as a veteran of Co. C, 51st Regt., Wis. Vol. Inf. John was listed in 1905 as an employee of the Morgan Company and residing at 173 Tenth Street in the city of Oshkosh.
{WC-V 1885, 1895; ROV; B-1905}

STREETER, Theron A. - Pvt., Co. C, 14th Regt., Wis. Vol. Inf.
Theron was born circa 1844 at New Hampshire. He was a son of Ira and Priscilla Streeter. Both parents were natives of New Hampshire, the father born there circa 1825 and the mother born circa 1826. Ira was listed in the 1860 federal census as a laborer residing in the town of Omro. Listed with him were his wife, son Theron, and a daughter, Juliette, who was born circa 1847 at New Hampshire. Theron enlisted at

STREETER, Theron A. (cont.)
Omro on Dec. 22, 1861. He was assigned as above and was listed as having deserted on Aug. 3, 1862.
{US 1860; ROV}

STREVER, John - Pvt., Co. D, 8th Regt., Wis. Vol. Inf.
John resided at Oshkosh and enlisted there on Jan. 8, 1864. He was assigned as above and was mustered out on June 10, 1865.
{ROV}

STRICKLAND, William - Pvt., Co. E, 2nd Regt., Wis. Vol. Inf.
William resided at Oshkosh and enlisted there on Dec. 1, 1861. He was assigned as above and was discharged due to a disability on Nov. 26, 1862.
{ROV}

STROETZ, John N. - Pvt., Co. F, 29th Regt., Wis. Vol. Inf.
John resided at Jefferson and enlisted there on Aug. 21, 1862. He was assigned as above and was mustered out on June 22, 1865. John was listed in the veteran section of the 1885 Wisconsin State census at P.O. Menasha. He was listed in the 1890 federal census as residing in the city of Menasha. John was not found in the 1905 county directory.
{US 1890; WC-V 1885; ROV; B-1905}

STRONG, Amos Norton, Jr. - Pvt., Co. E, 6th Regt., Wis. Vol. Inf.
Amos was born on Mar. 8, 1841. He resided at Omro and enlisted there on June 16, 1861. Amos was assigned as above. He was wounded at Antietam, Maryland and again at Fitzhugh's Crossing. Amos was mustered out on July 15, 1864 at the end of his term of enlistment. He was married to Henrietta (Hall) Clement in Winnebago County on Mar. 12, 1867. Amos was listed in the veteran section of the 1885 and 1895 Wisconsin State census at P.O. Winneconne. He was listed in the 1890 federal census as residing in the village of Winneconne. He was listed in that section of the 1905 state census at P.O. Omro. Amos and Henrietta were listed in 1905 as residing on 80 acres of section 29 in the town of Winneconne at P.O. Omro. Residing with them at that time were May and Harry Strong. Amos died at home on Aug. 7, 1926. He is buried at Winneconne Cemetery, Block 2, lot 33.
{US 1890; WC-V 1885, 1895, 1905; ROV; WCMR v.1, p.317, #1983; GRI}
{B-1905}

STRONG, Dewitt C. - Pvt., Co. B, 4th Regt., Wis. Cav.
Dewitt resided at Omro and enlisted on June 6, 1861. He was assigned as above. Dewitt was wounded and he died of his wounds on June 14, 1863 at Port Hudson, Louisiana.
{ROV}

STRONG, William H. - Pvt., Co. C, 1st Regt., Wis. Cav.
William was born on Apr. 8, 1842 at Guilford, Chenango County, New York. He was a son of Bela and Lucia (Bishop) Strong. Bela was born at New Berlin, New York on Feb. 16, 1805. Lucia was born at Louisville, Otsego County, New York in 1813. Bela removed with his family to Otsego County shortly after the birth of William. They removed to Wisconsin in 1854 and settled on a farm at Metomen, Green Lake County. Bela remained there for a year and then moved to a farm in the town of Lanark, Portage

STRONG, William H. (cont.)
Portage County. He retired in 1865 and returned to live with a son at Belmont, Portage County where he died in 1868. Lucia died in Feb. 1878 at Stevens Point, Portage County. William was married on Jan. 2, 1863 in Portage County to Abbey Curtis. He listed his residence as Eden, Fond du Lac County when he enlisted on Oct. 29, 1864. He was assigned as above and was mustered out at Nashville, Tennessee. William returned to Wisconsin, where he was discharged on July 19, 1865. Abbey died at Waukau on Aug. 30, 1879. She left six children: Russell H.; Lucy M.; Ella D.; Clara M.; Elmer M.; and Clinton. William was then married to Mrs. Frances E. (Kelsey) Hunt, the widow of William H. Hunt. Frances was born in Otsego, New York and was a daughter of Philo and Mary M. (Traver) Kelsey. William and Frances had two children, Anna M. and Charles W. Strong. Anna was married prior to 1888 to George W. Little. William resided at Stevens Point in 1888.
{ROV; SCA 1:299}

STRONISKY, Anthony - Pvt., Co. K, 5th (reorg.) Regt., Wis. Vol. Inf.
Anthony resided at Nepeuskun and enlisted there on Aug. 30, 1864. He was assigned as above and was mustered out on June 20, 1865.
{ROV}

STROUD, Horace - Pvt., Co. E, 2nd Regt., Wis. Vol. Inf.
Horace was born on Jan. 16, 1841 at New York. He was a son of William D. and Laura Stroud. William was born on July 10, 1808 at Essex County, New York and Laura was born circa 1815 at Vermont. They were married on Jan. 22, 1832 and they came to Winnebago County in 1851. William was listed in the 1860 federal census as a farmer residing in the third ward of the city of Oshkosh. Residing with him were his wife and the following children: Laura, born circa 1835 at New York, married a Thompson; Horace; Albert E., born circa 1844 at Vermont; James N., born circa 1845 at New York; Irene M., born circa 1852 at Wisconsin, married a Blyman; and Charles T., born circa 1858 at Wisconsin. They also had two sons, William L. Stroud and George F. Stroud, and a daughter, Amanda (Stroud) Harney. Horace enlisted at Oshkosh on Apr. 21, 1861. He was assigned as above and was wounded in the first battle at Bull Run, Virginia. He was discharged on Oct. 27, 1862 due to a disability. Horace was listed in 1868 as boarding at 32 Frankfort Street in Oshkosh, that being the residence of William D. Stroud, his father. William died at his home in Oshkosh on June 19, 1895. He was survived by his wife, a sister, Mrs. Zilpha Norton and eight children. Horace had a son, unnamed at registration, who was born in Oshkosh on Jan. 23, 1881. Horace was listed in the veteran section of the 1885, 1895 and 1905 Wisconsin State census at P.O. Oshkosh. He was listed in 1888 as a member of GAR Post #10 at Oshkosh. He was listed in the 1890 federal census as residing at 118 Frederick Avenue in Oshkosh. Horace provided that he suffer a shell wound, rheumatism, sunstroke, chronic diarrhea and scurvy. He also added that he had been held prisoner during his military service. Matilda, his wife, was born on Dec. 25, 1843 and died on June 7, 1888. Laura Irene (Stroud) Flye, a daughter, died from pneumonia at her home in Barker, Dunn County on Feb. 19, 1894. Horace also had a daughter Ella who resided in Chicago and a son Frank. Horace was listed in 1905 as an insurance agent residing at 41 Pleasant Avenue in Oshkosh. He died there on Mar. 2, 1922. Both are buried in the town of Algoma at

STROUD, Horace (cont.)
Ellenwood Cemetery, Section B.
{US 1860, 1890; WC-V 1885, 1895, 1905; B-1905; WCBR v.3, p.40, #238; ROV}
{T-1868; Cem. records; OWN 24 Feb 1894; ODT 20 Jun 1895}

STUART, James E. - Capt., Co. B, 21st Regt., Wis. Vol. Inf.
James resided at Oshkosh and enlisted there on Aug. 4, 1862. He was assigned as above and was promoted to 1st Sergeant in that company. James was commissioned as 2nd Lieutenant of that company on Feb. 4, 1863 and was then promoted to 1st Lieutenant on Dec. 23, 1863. He was promoted to Captain of that company on Aug. 31, 1864 and was mustered out on June 8, 1865. James was listed in 1868 as a mail agent boarding at 26 Church Street in the city of Oshkosh. That was the residence of James Stuart, probably his father. James was listed in 1920 and again in 1927 and 1928 as residing at Chicago, Illinois.
{ROV; T-1868; 21-33rd; 21-40th; ODN 22 Jun 1928}

STUNKARD, Matthew - Cpl., Co. H, 36th Regt., Wis. Vol. Inf.
Matthew resided at Utica and enlisted there on Feb. 29, 1864. He was assigned as above and was then promoted to Corporal in that company. Matthew was mustered out on July 12, 1865.
{ROV}

STUNTZ, George E. - Pvt., Co. C, 14th Regt., Wis. Vol. Inf.
George resided at Omro and enlisted there on Sept. 8, 1861. He was assigned as above and was wounded at Shiloh, Tennessee. George was discharged on Oct. 15, 1862 due to a disability.
{ROV}

STURTEVANT, Henry H. - Pvt., Co. A, 1st (3 yr.) Regt., Wis. Vol. Inf.
Henry was born circa 1830 at New York. He was listed in the 1860 federal census as a lumberman residing in the fifth ward of the city of Oshkosh. Several of his brothers and a sister were also residing there. Henry enlisted at Oshkosh on Oct. 9, 1861. He was assigned as above and was wounded at Chaplin Hills, Kentucky. Henry was discharged on Jan. 29, 1863 due to a disability.
{US 1860; ROV}

STUTZMAN, Michael - Pvt., Co. F, 50th Regt., Wis. Vol. Inf.
Michael was born on July 2, 1839 in New York City. His parents were natives of France and they emigrated to America in 1833. They settled at New York and remained there for 12 years. They then removed with their family of seven children to Wisconsin in 1845 and settled at Germantown, Washington County. Michael listed his residence as Oshkosh when he enlisted on Mar. 2, 1865. He was assigned as above and was mustered out at Madison, Wisconsin on June 14, 1866 at the end of his term of enlistment. Michael suffered a disability as the result of drinking ice water after a fatiguing march. That caused inflammation of the stomach which remained with him until his death at Black Creek, Outagamie County on Feb. 28, 1882. He had been married on Feb. 18, 1867 to Wilhelmina Lemke. They had six children: Michael; William; George; Caroline; Wilhelmina; and Elvira, died at age 5 years. Wilhelmina's parents were natives of

STUTZMAN, Michael (cont.)
Stettin, Pomerania, Germany. After the death of Michael, she was married to John Endlich of Black Creek.
{ROV; SCA 1:408}

STUTZMAN, William - Pvt., Co. A, 88th Regt., Ohio Vol. Inf.
William was born on July 17, 1847. His wife was born on May 4, 1852. William was listed as above in the veteran section of the 1885 Wisconsin State census at P.O. Winneconne. He was listed in the 1890 federal census as residing in the town of Winneconne at P.O. Winneconne. William then provided his unit designation as above and his service dates as having been from May 1862 to Sept. 1862. He was listed in the veteran section of the 1895 and 1905 state census at P.O. Butte des Morts. William was listed in 1905 as residing on 158 acres of section 13 in the town of Winneconne at P.O. Butte des Morts. Lizzie, Valentine, William and Belle Stutzman were also residing there. William died on Jan. 30, 1907 and his wife died on May 16, 1901. Son Willie was born on Dec. 27, 1879 and died on Feb. 15, 1880. Son Valentine was born on Sept. 28, 1886 and died on Oct. 15, 1905. All four are buried in the town of Winneconne at Bell Cemetery.
{US 1890; WC-V 1885, 1895, 1905; B-1905; Cem. records}

STYLES, Josiah S. - Sgt. Maj., 32nd Regt., Wis. Vol. Inf.
Josiah resided at Utica and enlisted there on Aug. 20, 1862. He was assigned as a Private to Co. D of the above regiment. He was promoted to Sergeant and transferred to Co. I of the same regiment. Josiah was promoted to Sergeant Major of the regiment on Aug. 3, 1864 and was promoted to Adjutant on Aug. 31, 1864. He was then mustered out on June 12, 1865.
{ROV}

SULLIVAN, C.G. - Civil War Veteran?
He was listed in 1888 as the Commander of GAR Post #129 at Neenah. He was not found in any military census for this area.
{SCA}

SULLIVAN, Dennis Joseph - Pvt., Co. G, 1st (3 yr.) Regt., Wis. Vol. Inf.
Dennis was born circa 1844 at Massachusetts, a son of John and Catherine Sullivan. Catherine was born circa 1819 at Ireland and John was born circa 1815, also at Ireland. The father was listed in the 1860 federal census as a carpenter residing in the fifth ward of the city of Oshkosh. Listed with him were his wife and the following children: Dennis; John, born circa 1850 at Massachusetts; and Edward, born circa 1859 at Wisconsin. Dennis enlisted at Oshkosh on Sept. 7, 1861. He was assigned as a musician in the above company and was mustered out on Oct. 14, 1864 at the end of his term of enlistment. Dennis was married to Mary Melissa Vance in Winnebago County on Nov. 2, 1867. He was listed in 1868 as a carpenter boarding at 35 Vinland Road in Oshkosh. That was the residence of John J. Sullivan, his father.
{US 1860; T-1868; WCMR v.1, p.361, #2182; ROV}

SULLIVAN, Jeremiah - Pvt., Co. K, 46th Regt., Wis. Vol. Inf.
Jeremiah was an early settler of Winnebago County. He was born circa 1830 at Ireland. Alice, his wife, was also born circa 1830 at Ireland. They were listed in the 1860 federal

SULLIVAN, Jeremiah (cont.)
census as residing on a farm in the town of Poygan. Listed with them were the following children: Honora, born circa 1855; Thomas, born circa 1858; and Mary, born circa 1859. All three children were born in Wisconsin. Jeremiah listed his residence as Winneconne when he enlisted on Feb. 11, 1865. He was assigned as above and was mustered out on Sept. 27, 1865. He was listed in 1868 as a laborer boarding at 15 Blackhawk Street in the city of Oshkosh. Jerry was listed in the 1890 federal census as residing in the town of Rushford at P.O. Waukau. He then provided the information that he had fallen by accident and had hurt his side and head during his military service. Jeremiah was listed in the veteran section of the 1895 Wisconsin State census at P.O. Waukau. He contracted pneumonia and, after an illness of just three days, he died on Jan. 3, 1903 at age 85 years. The Rev. J. Madden of Chicago, a nephew of Jeremiah, conducted his funeral service at St. Thomas Catholic Church in Poygan. Alice, his widow, was listed in 1905 as residing at 90 Wisconsin Avenue in the city of Oshkosh. Daughters Eliza and Esther were residing with her. Alice died in Oshkosh on Feb. 8, 1908 at age 76 years. She was survived by three sons and four daughters, including: Thomas Sullivan of Omro; Mrs. T. Lennon of Washington; Mrs. Edward Crane of Boyd, Chippewa County; John and Will Sullivan of Fairbanks, Alaska; and Esther and Eliza Sullivan, both of Oshkosh. Jerry and his wife are buried in the town of Poygan at St. Thomas Cemetery.
{US 1860, 1890; WC-V 1895; T-1868; B-1905; OmJ 08 Jan 1903; Cem. records; ROV}
{OmJ 13 Feb 1908}

SULLIVAN, John - Pvt., Co. C, 1st Regt., Wis. Hvy. Art.
John resided at Neenah and enlisted there on Aug. 31, 1863. He was assigned as above and was listed as having deserted from the 16th Regt., Wis. Vol. Inf. John returned to his original regiment on Oct. 15, 1863.
{ROV}

SULLIVAN, Michael - Pvt., Co. F, 18th Regt., Wis. Vol. Inf.
Michael was born circa 1844 at Ireland. He was listed in the 1860 federal census as a farm laborer for Henry Rogers in the town of Vinland. Michael listed his residence as Oshkosh when he enlisted on Nov. 15, 1861. He was assigned as above and was listed as having deserted on July 1, 1862. Michael was possibly a brother of Patrick from a following sketch.
{US 1860; ROV}

SULLIVAN, Patrick - Pvt., Co. F, 18th Regt., Wis. Vol. Inf.
Patrick was born circa 1842 at Ireland. He was possibly a brother of Michael from a previous sketch. Patrick was listed in the 1860 federal census as a farm laborer for Thomas Knott in the town of Vinland. He listed his residence as Oshkosh when he enlisted on Jan. 2, 1862. He was assigned as above and was transferred to the Veteran Reserve Corps on Oct. 21, 1863. Patrick died on Nov. 15, 1863 at Memphis, Tennessee.
{US 1860; ROV}

SULLIVAN, William - Pvt., unassigned, 1st Regt., Wis. Hvy. Art.
William resided at Utica and enlisted there on Oct. 17, 1864. He was assigned as above and was not assigned to a company within that regiment.
{ROV}

SUMNER, Zenas M. - Pvt., Co. A, 48th Regt., Wis. Vol. Inf.
Zenas was born circa 1824 at Vermont. He was a son of John and Clara Sumner. Both parents were natives of Vermont and both were born circa 1804. They were listed in the 1860 federal census as residing on a farm in the town of Winneconne. Listed with them were two other sons, Lawrence and Charles. Lawrence was born circa 1830 at Vermont and Charles was born there circa 1841. Also listed were Zenas and Juliette, his wife. She was born circa 1832 at Vermont. Clara, their daughter, was born circa 1857 at Wisconsin. Arthur, a son, was born circa 1859 at Wisconsin and died on Nov. 27, 1912 at Winneconne. Zenas enlisted at Winneconne on Feb. 7, 1865. He was assigned as above and was mustered out on Dec. 30, 1865. Zenas was listed in the veteran section of the 1885 and 1895 Wisconsin State census at P.O. Winneconne. He was listed in the 1890 federal census as residing in the town of Winneconne at P.O. Winneconne. Julia, his widow, was listed in 1905 as residing with the family of Arthur Sumner in section 30 of the town of Winneconne.
{US 1860, 1890; WC-V 1885, 1895; B-1905; ROV}

SURNS, John - Pvt., Co. B, 44th Regt., Wis. Vol. Inf.
John was born circa 1836 at Denmark. He was listed (Searns) in the 1860 federal census as residing with the family of Charles J. Root in the town of Nekimi. John listed his residence as Wayne, Washington County when he enlisted on Sept. 28, 1864 and was assigned as above. He was mustered out on July 2, 1865. Rosanna, his wife, died on Feb. 20, 1865 at age 23 years, 5 months and 25 days. Isabel, their daughter, died on Feb. 19, 1897 at age 33 years, 10 months and 11 days. Rosa, another daughter, died on June 3, 1865 at the age of 3 months. John was married second in Winnebago County on Nov. 5, 1866 to Sarah, widow of William P. Williams. John died on Mar. 22, 1869 at age 33 years, 5 months and 23 days. He is buried with Rosanna and their daughters in the town of Omro at Omro Union Cemetery. Sarah was listed in the 1890 federal census as residing in the town of Nekimi at P.O. Nekimi.
{US 1860, 1890; ROV; WCMR v.1, p.309, #1918; Cem. records}

SUTSCHUTZ, John - Pvt., Co. D, 21st Regt., Wis. Vol. Inf.
John resided at Menasha and enlisted there on Jan. 4, 1864. He was assigned as above and was transferred to the 3rd Regt., Wis. Vol. Inf. on June 8, 1865. John was then mustered out on July 18, 1865.
{ROV}

SUTTON, Arton F. - Pvt., Co. H, 132nd Regt., New York Vol. Inf.
Arton was listed as above in the veteran section of the 1885, 1895 and 1905 Wisconsin State census at P.O. Oshkosh. He was listed in the 1890 federal census as residing at 51 E. Irving Street in Oshkosh. Arton then provided his unit designation as above and his service dates as having been from Sept. 3, 1864 to June 29, 1865. He reported suffering from chronic diarrhea. Arton P. Sutton, a son of Arton, was kicked in the head by a horse and died as a result some four years later, in Apr. 1894 at the age of 19 years. Arton was listed in 1905 as a rural mail carrier residing 51 E. Irving Street in Oshkosh.
{US 1890; WC-V 1885, 1895, 1905; B-1905; OWN 14 Apr 1894}

SUTTON, M. - Seaman, "Juliet," Gunboat Service, U.S. Navy.
He enlisted on Aug. 17, 1864 and was assigned to the Naval Gunboat Service. He was

SUTTON, M. (cont.)
trained on the Great Lakes at Chicago and was assigned to the Gunboat "Juliet."
{Lawson p.840-1}

SVENSON, Soren - Pvt., Co. C, 46th Regt., Wis. Vol. Inf.
Soren resided at Winchester and enlisted there on Feb. 8, 1865. He was assigned as above and was mustered out on Sept. 27, 1865. Soren was listed in the 1890 federal census as residing in the village of Winneconne.
{US 1890; ROV}

SWAIN, Frederick K. - Pvt., Co. D, 41st Regt., Wis. Vol. Inf.
Frederick resided at Neenah and enlisted there on May 10, 1864. He was assigned as above and was mustered out on Sept. 23, 1864 at the end of his term of enlistment.
{ROV}

SWAMP, Joseph - Pvt., Co. G, 3rd (reorg.) Regt., Wis. Cav.
Joseph resided at Oshkosh and enlisted there on Feb. 12, 1864. He was assigned as above and was mustered out on Oct. 27, 1865.
{ROV}

SWAN, Henry C. - Pvt., Co. A, 6th Regt., Michigan Vol. Inf.
Henry was listed as above in the veteran section of the 1885 Wisconsin State census at P.O. Oshkosh. He was listed as "husband of Christie Swan, now absent" in the 1890 federal census for the city of Oshkosh. At that time his unit designation was provided as Co. A, 11th Regt., Mich. Vol. Inf. Henry was listed in 1905 as a commercial traveler residing at 328 Central Avenue in Oshkosh. Fannie L. and Nellie C. Swan were also listed at that address.
{US 1890; WC-V 1885; B-1905}

SWAN, John W. - Pvt., Co. E, 16th Regt., Wis. Vol. Inf.
John resided at Belmont, Portage County and enlisted there on Nov. 21, 1863. He was transferred as a Private to Co. E, 16th Regt., Wis. Vol. Inf. on June 4, 1865 and was mustered out on July 12, 1865. John provided his residence as Oshkosh at the time of his transfer.
{ROV}

SWAN, Timothy - Capt., Co. H, 7th Regt., Maine Vol. Inf.
Timothy was born circa 1843 at Maine. He was listed in 1868 as a tinsmith boarding at 53 Algoma Street in the city of Oshkosh. He was listed in 1888 as a member of GAR Post #10 at Oshkosh. Timothy was listed in the 1890 federal census as residing in the town of Algoma at P.O. Oshkosh. He then provided his unit designation as above and his service dates as having been from June 3, 1861 through Mar. 18, 1865. Timothy was listed as above in the veteran section of the 1895 and 1905 Wisconsin State census at P.O. Oshkosh. He was listed in 1905 with Emma, his wife, as residing on 120 acres of section 18 in the town of Algoma. Timothy Jr., Susie L. and Marion I. Swan were also listed as residing there. Timothy was also listed in 1905 as residing at the Wisconsin Veterans' Home at King. He was listed in the 1910 federal census as residing at King. He had been married once for 29 years. Although he was not listed as a widower, his

SWAN, Timothy (cont.)
wife was not residing with him.
{US 1890, 1910; WC-V 1895, 1905; T-1868; B-1905; GAR 40th}

SWART, William - Pvt., Co. B, 3rd Regt., Wis. Vol. Inf.
William resided at Oshkosh and enlisted there on Apr. 22, 1861. He was assigned as above and was taken prisoner at Winchester, Virginia. William was mustered out on June 29, 1864 at the end of his term of enlistment.
{ROV}

SWENSON, Alfred - Seaman, U.S. Navy.
Alfred was listed as above in the veteran section of the 1895 Wisconsin State census at P.O. Winchester.
{WC-V 1895}

SWIFT, Heman F. - Cpl., Co. F, 92nd Regt., New York Vol. Inf.
Heman was listed in 1868 as a carpenter and joiner residing at 48 Broad Street in the city of Oshkosh. He was listed as above in the veteran section of the 1885 Wisconsin State census at P.O. Oshkosh. Heman was listed in the 1890 federal census as residing at 291 Broad Street in Oshkosh. He then provided his unit designation as above and his service dates as having been Nov. 22, 1861 to Feb. 7, 1863. Heman also reported that he was suffering from a liver complaint, a light stroke of palsey and nervous prostration. He died at Oshkosh on Jan. 24, 1894 at the age of 70 years. Anna F., his widow, was listed in 1905 as residing at 370 Broad Street in Oshkosh.
{US 1890; WC-V 1885; T-1868; B-1905; OWN 27 Jan 1894}

SWIFT, Jackson F. - Pvt., Co. K, 1st (3 yr.) Regt., Wis. Vol. Inf.
Jackson was born circa 1843 at New York. He was a son of Jackson and Ruth Swift. The father was born circa 1791 at Vermont and the mother was born circa 1792 at Massachusetts. They were listed in the 1860 federal census as residing on a farm in the town of Black Wolf. Also listed with them was a Betsey Perry. She was born circa 1782 at Massachusetts. Jackson F. resided at Black Wolf and enlisted there on Sept. 5, 1861. He was assigned as above and was discharged due to a disability on Apr. 13, 1862.
{US 1860; ROV}

TAIT, Henry C. - Sgt., Co. G, 3rd Regt., Wis. Vol. Inf.
Henry was born in 1816 at England. Charlotte, his wife, was born in 1815 and died on Aug. 15, 1849. Henry was listed in the 1860 federal census as a tailor residing in the village of Neenah. Christain, his second wife, was born circa 1823 at Holland. Listed with them were the following children: Martha, born circa 1840 at Vermont; Jane, born circa 1847 at Scotland; John, born circa 1849 at Scotland; James, born circa 1851 at Wisconsin; and Henrietta, born circa 1859 at Wisconsin. Henry listed his residence as Oshkosh when he enlisted on Apr. 20, 1861. He was assigned as above and was then promoted to Sergeant in that company. Henry was wounded on Sept. 17, 1862. He died of his wounds on Oct. 22, 1862 at Antietam, Maryland. Henry and Charlotte are buried in the town of Menasha section of Oak Hill Cemetery. Martha A. and Julia Tait are buried on the same plot.
{US 1860; ROV; Cem. records}

TALLMAN, Nelson A. - Pvt., Co. A, 31st Regt., Wis. Vol. Inf.
Nelson resided at Utica and enlisted there on Aug. 13, 1862. He was assigned as above and was transferred to Co. K of that same regiment on Dec. 23, 1862. His transfer was rejected and he was returned to Co. A on Jan. 1, 1863. Nelson was then mustered out on June 20, 1865.
{ROV}

TANCRE, Louis - Pvt., Co. F, 19th Regt., Wis. Vol. Inf.
Louis was born circa 1797 at Prussia. He was married to Theresa Lenz on Dec. 15, 1857 in Winnebago County. She was at least his second wife and she was born circa 1815 at Austria. They were listed in the 1860 federal census as residing on a farm in the town of Winchester at P.O. Rat River. Listed with them were the following children: Charles, born circa 1847; Bertha, born circa 1850; and William, born circa 1859. All of the children were born in Wisconsin. Louis enlisted at Winchester on Mar. 14, 1862. He was assigned as above and was discharged on Sept. 6, 1862 due to a disability.
{US 1860; ROV; WCMR v.1, p.121, #499}

TANNER, John J. - Sgt., Co. D, 41st Regt., Wis. Vol. Inf.
John resided at Menasha and enlisted there on May 6, 1864. He was assigned as above and was promoted to 1st Sergeant in that company. John was then mustered out on Sept. 23, 1864 at the end of his term of enlistment.
{ROV}

TANNER, William A. - Lt., Co. D, 32nd Regt., Wis. Vol. Inf.
William resided at Oshkosh and enlisted in the above company. He was commissioned as 2nd Lieutenant of that company on Sept. 2, 1862. William was detailed as acting Assistant Inspector General on June 8, 1863. He was assigned as a conductor for the U.S. Military Railroad on Oct. 14, 1864 and remained in that position for the remainder of his military service. William was promoted to 1st Lieutenant on Oct. 28, 1864 but was not mustered at that rank. He was mustered out on July 5, 1865. William was listed in 1868 as residing at 78 Sterling Street in the city of Oshkosh. Priscilla, his widow, was listed in 1905 as residing at 395 Otter Street in Oshkosh.
{ROV; T-1868; B-1905}

TAPLIN, Osman B. - Pvt., Co. E, 2nd Regt., Wis. Vol. Inf.
Osman resided at Oshkosh and enlisted there on Apr. 21, 1861. He was assigned as above and was wounded severely in the side at Antietam, Maryland on Sept. 17, 1862. Osman died of his wounds on Sept. 24, 1862.
{ROV; OWN 02 Oct 1862}

TARR, Johnson - Pvt., Co. B, 36th Regt., Wis. Vol. Inf.
Johnson resided at Poygan and enlisted there on Feb. 26, 1864. He was assigned as above and was wounded on June 1, 1864 at Cold Harbor, Virginia. Johnson was then discharged due to his wounds on Sept. 30, 1864.
{ROV}

TARR, Leroy S. - Pvt., Co. K, 29th Regt., Maine Vol. Inf.
Leroy was married to Clara J. Wilson. They had a daughter, unnamed at registration, who was born in Oshkosh on Dec. 17, 1879. Harriet Jeanette, another daughter, was

TARR, Leroy S. (cont.)
born in Oshkosh on Oct. 14, 1882. Leroy was listed in 1888 as a member of GAR Post #10 at Oshkosh. He was listed as above in the veteran section of the 1905 Wisconsin State census at P.O. Oshkosh. He was then listed as an employee of the McMillen Lumber Company. Leroy was residing at 1 McMillen Avenue in Oshkosh. Frank H. Tarr was listed at that same address.
{WC-V 1905; B-1905; WCBR v.2, p.169, #473; WCBR v.3, p.62, #372}

TAUNT, Stephen - Pvt., Co. K, 32nd Regt., Wis. Vol. Inf.
Stephen resided at Oshkosh and enlisted there on Jan. 4, 1864. He was assigned as above. Stephen was killed on Aug. 19, 1864 at Atlanta, Georgia.
{ROV}

TAYLOR, Abram - Pvt., Co. I, 21st Regt., Wis. Vol. Inf.
Abram was born circa 1833 at England. He was listed in the 1860 federal census as a laborer residing in the village of Neenah. Hannah, his wife, was born circa 1835 at England. Listed with them were the following children: Elizabeth, born circa 1854 at Ohio; Rosetta, born circa 1856 at Wisconsin; and Flora, born circa 1858 at Wisconsin. Abram enlisted at Neenah on Aug. 12, 1862. He was assigned as above and was listed as having deserted on Oct. 21, 1862.
{US 1860; ROV}

TAYLOR, Albert - Pvt., Co. C, 14th Regt., Wis. Vol. Inf.
Albert resided at Nepeuskun and enlisted there on Mar. 8, 1864. He was assigned as above and was mustered out on Oct. 9, 1865.
{ROV}

TAYLOR, Charles H. - Pvt., Co. D, 41st Regt., Wis. Vol. Inf.
Charles resided at Menasha and enlisted there on May 5, 1864. He was assigned as above and was mustered out on Sept. 23, 1864 at the end of his term of enlistment. Charles died circa 1871.
{ROV; Lawson p.840}

TAYLOR, James P. - Pvt., 9th Batt., Wis. Lt. Art.
James resided at Hudson, St. Croix County and enlisted there on Feb. 6, 1864. He was assigned as above and was mustered out on Sept. 30, 1865. James was listed in the veteran section of the 1895 Wisconsin State census at P.O. Omro.
{WC-V 1895; ROV}

TAYLOR, Truman R. - Pvt., Co. C, 14th Regt., Wis. Vol. Inf.
Truman was born in Feb. 1838 at New York. His parents were both natives of Vermont. Truman was married in Winnebago County on Jan. 18, 1860 to Hannah M. Pingry. She was born circa 1841 at Illinois. They were listed in the 1860 federal census as residing on a farm in the town of Omro. Truman enlisted at Omro on Nov. 27, 1863. He was assigned as above and was mustered out on Oct. 9, 1865. Truman was listed in the veteran section of the 1885 and 1895 Wisconsin State census at P.O. Omro. He was listed in the 1890 federal census as residing in the village of Omro. Truman then provided that he had suffered a rupture during his military service. He was listed in the 1900 federal census as residing at the Wisconsin Veterans' Home at King. Truman then

TAYLOR, Truman R. (cont.)
provided that he had been married for one year. His wife was not listed there with him. Truman was listed in the veteran section of the 1905 state census at King. Hannah was listed in 1905 as residing with and working for Mulberry Whitemarsh in the town of Omro.
{US 1860, 1890, 1900; WC-V 1885, 1895, 1905; WCMR v.1, p.197, #1020; ROV} {B-1905; GAR 40th}

TAYLOR, William P. - Pvt., Co. E, 2nd Regt., Wis. Vol. Inf.
William was born in 1831 at Fredrickton, New Brunswick, Canada. He enlisted at Oshkosh on May 18, 1861. He was assigned as a fifer in the above company and was taken prisoner in the 1st battle at Bull Run, Virginia. William was then mustered out on June 28, 1864 at the end of his term of enlistment. During the great Oshkosh fire on July 1874, while helping a widow remove a heavy chest from a second floor apartment before the flames reached there, he suddenly dropped the chest and sat down in great pain. He was eventually taken back to his room at the Adams House by a doctor, where he died that same evening. Although single, William left a great legacy in this area. He was generous to a fault and helped anyone who truly needed it whenever he could. As a testament to his friendship, mourners numbering in the thousands attended the solemn procession.
{ROV; OWN 18 Jul 1874; OWN 23 Jul 1874; ODN 07 May 1899}

TEAL, Peter - Pvt., Co. B, 1st (3 mo.) Regt., Wis. Vol. Inf.
Peter resided at Oshkosh and enlisted there on Apr. 22, 1861. He was assigned as above and was mustered out on Aug. 21, 1861.
{ROV}

TEAL, Phillip J. - Lt., Co. B, 14th Regt., Wis. Vol. Inf.?
Phillip was listed in the 1890 federal census as residing at 162 Main Street in the city of Oshkosh. He provided his unit designation as above and added that "the roster of Adj. Gen. of State does not give his name." Phillip was suffering from a kidney disease and was reported by the census canvasser as "inebriated." Only George W. and Peter Teal were listed as members of the above company. George was listed in the 1890 federal census at P.O. Weyauwega, Waupaca County.
{US 1890; ROV}

TEGTMIER, Frederick Jr. - Pvt., Co. B, 9th (reorg) Regt., Wis. Vol. Inf.
Frederick H. Tegtmier was born on Sept. 4, 1829 at Hanover, Germany. He was a son of Friedrich and Frederica (Brockman) Tegtmier. The father was born in Germany in 1801 and died in 1866 at Oconto County, Wis. Fred Jr. became a sailor at the age of 15 years and made voyages between European and American ports. He emigrated to America in 1849 and settled at Sheboygan County. Fred was married there in 1857 to Wilhelmine Besant. She was born on Jan. 8, 1835 in Germany and was a daughter of Frederick and Caroline (Housman) Besant. Fred and Wilhelmine had the following children: Annie; Louisa; Henry; Willie; Mary, died on Feb. 15, 1880 at age 13 years, 9 months and 28 days; Helen, died on Aug. 30, 1868 at age 10 days; and Frederick. Fred removed with his family to Oconto County in 1861. He resided at Marinette and enlisted there on Sept. 16, 1864. Fred was assigned as above and was mustered out on June 3, 1865. At the close of the war he brought his family to Winnebago County and settled

TEGTMIER, Frederick Jr. (cont.)
on a farm in the town of Poygan. Fred was listed in the veteran section of the 1885 Wisconsin State census at Poygan. He was listed in the 1890 federal census as residing in the town of Poygan at P.O. Omro. Fred then listed that he had lost an eye during a skirmish at Little Rock, Arkansas. He was listed in the veteran section of the 1895 and 1905 state census at P.O. Omro. Fred is buried with a simple military marker. Wilhelmine died on Feb. 18, 1893. Both are buried in the town of Poygan at Oak Hill Cemetery.
{US 1890; WC-V 1885, 1895, 1905; ROV; Randall p.50; Cem. records}

TENANT - see also Tennant

TENANT, Robert - Pvt., Co. F, 18th Regt., Wis. Vol. Inf.
Robert was born on Mar. 18, 1843 at New York. He was listed in the 1860 federal census as residing with L.M. Parsons in the town of Rushford at P.O. Waukau. The Tennants of following sketches were listed then as residing on the next farm. Robert enlisted at Rushford on Jan. 5, 1864. He was later transferred to the Veteran Reserve Corps. Robert was listed in the 1890 federal census as residing in the town of Matteson, Waupaca County at P.O. Embarrass. He died on Oct. 28, 1903. Julia, his widow, was listed in 1905 as residing on Lincoln Street in the village of Omro. Florence and D.S., widow of George Tenant, were also residing at that address. Julia was born on June 27, 1842 and died on May 20, 1905. Jason R., a son, died on July 2, 1873 at age 4 years, 3 months and 19 days. He is buried with Robert and Julia in the town of Aurora, Waushara County at Shead Island Cemetery.
{US 1860, 1890; ROV; B-1905; Cem. records}

TENNANT, Charles E. - Pvt., Co. D, 32nd Regt., Wis. Vol. Inf.
Charles was born circa 1846 at New York. He was listed in the 1860 federal census as residing with the family of Matthew Porter in the town of Nepeuskun at P.O. Koro. Charles was probably a brother to James and Robert from other sketches. Charles resided at Rushford and enlisted there on Oct. 21, 1863. He was assigned as above and was transferred to Co. D, 16th (reorg.) Regt., Wis. Vol. Inf. on June 4, 1865. Charles was then mustered out on July 12, 1865.
{US 1860; ROV}

TENNANT, James - Pvt., Co. D, 32nd Regt., Wis. Vol. Inf.
James was born circa 1848 at New York. He was a son of John and Martha Tennant and he was probably a brother of Robert and Charles from previous sketches. John was born circa 1806 at Ireland and Martha was born circa 1819 at New York. They were listed in the 1860 federal census as residing in the town of Rushford at P.O. Waukau. Listed with them were the following children: James; Hiram, born circa 1850; Jerome, born circa 1854; and Julia, born circa 1857. Julia was born in Wisconsin and the other children were born in New York. James enlisted at Rushford on Oct. 21, 1863. He was assigned as above. James died on Apr. 24, 1864 at Decatur, Alabama.
{US 1860; ROV}

TERWILLAGER, John W. - Pvt., Co. G, 3rd Regt., Wis. Vol. Inf.
John resided at Neenah and enlisted there on Apr. 20, 1861. He was assigned as above and was discharged May 29, 1862 due to a disability. John then re-enlisted in that same

TERWILLAGER, John W. (cont.)
company on Dec. 24, 1863. He was again discharged due to a disability on Nov. 28, 1864.
{ROV}

TESCH, Gustav Adolph - Pvt., Co. B, 3rd Regt., Wis. Vol. Inf.
Gustav was born on Oct. 1, 1840 near Brandenberg, Germany. He emigrated to this country with friends in 1860 and came directly to Oshkosh. While new here and hardly able to speak or understand the language, Gustav enlisted at Oshkosh on Apr. 22, 1861. He was assigned as above and was wounded at Antietam, Maryland and again on two other occasions. Gustav was mustered out on Apr. 22, 1864 at the end of his term of enlistment. He was married in Winnebago County on Sept. 5, 1865 to Emilie Beck. He was in a partnership with his father-in-law and then went into business for himself. Gustav was listed in 1868 as a grocer residing on Waugoo Street in Oshkosh. He died in Oshkosh on Sept. 7, 1880 and is buried there in the Masonic Section of Riverside Cemetery. Gustav was survived by his wife and four children. Emilie, his widow, was listed in 1905 as residing at 692 High Street in Oshkosh.
{WCMR v.1, p.280, #1683; T-1868; B-1905; OWN 16 Sep 1880; WiT 10 Sep 1880}
{ROV}

TEUBNER, Augustus - Pvt., Co. B, 3rd Regt., Wis. Cav.
Augustus was born circa 1842 at Bavaria. He was a son of Charles and Anna Teubner. Anna and Charles were both born circa 1824 at Bavaria. Charles was listed in the 1860 federal census as a teamster residing in the fourth ward of the city of Oshkosh. Residing with him were his wife and the following children: August; Dorothea, born circa 1848 at Bremen, Germany; Charles, born circa 1850; Alfred, born circa 1855; Julius, born circa 1857; and Edwin, born circa 1859. The last four were born in Wisconsin. Augustus enlisted at Oshkosh on Dec. 7, 1861. He was assigned as above and re-enlisted in that same company at the end of his term. Augustus contracted a disease and died on Sept. 28, 1864 at Little Rock, Arkansas.
{US 1860; ROV}

THACKERY, George W. - Pvt., Co. K, 31st Regt., Wis. Vol. Inf.
George resided at Utica and enlisted there on Aug. 15, 1862. He was assigned as a Private to Co. D, 31st Regt., Wis. Vol. Inf. George was transferred to Co. K of that same regiment on Nov. 6, 1862. He was mustered out on June 20, 1865.
{ROV}

THATCHER, Norman - Capt., Co. G, 10th Regt., Wis. Vol. Inf.
Norman was born on Nov. 22, 1823 at Pomfret, Vermont. He removed to Wisconsin in 1857 and settled at Menasha. Norman was listed in the 1860 federal census as a mason residing in the second ward of the village of Menasha. Mary, his wife, was born circa 1827 at Vermont. Then listed with them were the following children: Emma, born circa 1847; Ella, born circa 1849; Truman, born circa 1851; and Frederick, born circa 1859. Frederick was born in Wisconsin and the other children were born in Vermont. Norman enlisted at Menasha on Sept. 30, 1861. He was assigned as a Private to Co. C, 10th Regt., Wis. Vol. Inf. and was promoted to 1st Sergeant in that company. Norman was commissioned as 2nd Lieutenant of Co. E in that regiment on Aug. 12, 1862 and was promoted to 1st Lieutenant on Nov. 19, 1862. He was promoted to Captain of Co. G of

THATCHER, Norman (cont.)
that regiment on Aug. 25, 1863 and was then mustered out on Nov. 3, 1864. Norman was listed in the veteran section of the 1885 Wisconsin State census at P.O. Menasha. He died at his home in Menasha on July 29, 1888. He was still listed in the 1890 federal census as residing in the city of Menasha.
{US 1860, 1890; WC-V 1885; ROV; Lawson p.810; OWN 02 Aug 1888}

THEBE, George H. - Pvt., Co. E, 10th Regt., Missouri Vol. Inf.
George was listed as above in the veteran section of the 1885 Wisconsin State census at P.O. Neenah. He was listed in the 1890 federal census as residing in the city of Neenah. George then provided his designation as Capt., Co. B, 2nd Regt., Missouri Vol. Inf. He added that his service dates had been from Apr. 10, 1861 to July 18, 1861 and that he had suffered sunstroke during that service. He was listed in the veteran section of the 1895 state census at P.O. Neenah and as being a veteran of Co. D, 14th Regt., Kentucky Vol. Inf.
{US 1890; WC-V 1885, 1895}

THIERMAN, George - Pvt., Co. E, 32nd Regt., Wis. Vol. Inf.
George resided at Oshkosh and enlisted there as a Veteran Recruit on Dec. 25, 1863. He was assigned as above and was transferred to Co. E, 16th Regt., Wis. Vol. Inf. on June 4, 1865. George was mustered out on July 12, 1865. Julius, a son of George H. and M.A. Thierman, died on Aug. 14, 1862 at age 11 years. Lincoln, another son, died on Jan. 14, 1866 at age 4 years and 7 months. Both sons are buried in the town of Weyauwega, Waupaca County at Evanswood Cemetery.
{ROV; Cem. records}

THILKA, Charles A. - Pvt., Co. I, 3rd Regt., Wis. Vol. Inf.
Charles resided at Nekimi and enlisted there on Aug. 31, 1864. He was assigned as above and was mustered out on June 9, 1865.
{ROV}

THOM, Gustav - Pvt., Co. B, 3rd Regt., Wis. Vol. Inf.
Gustav was born circa 1840 at Prussia. He was a son of Casimer and Wilhelmine Thom. Wilhelmine was born circa 1824 at Prussia and Casimir was born circa 1810 in that same country. Casimir was listed in the 1860 federal census as a laborer residing in the third ward of the city of Oshkosh. Listed with him were his wife and the following children: Gustav; Mathilde, born circa 1842; Richard, born circa 1844; Emma, born circa 1846; and Hannchen, born circa 1854. All of the children were born in Prussia. Gustav enlisted at Oshkosh on May 21, 1861. He was assigned as above and was discharged by orders dated Oct. 25, 1862. Gustav was married in Winnebago County on Sept. 1, 1864 to Augusta Magalowsky. She was a daughter of Frederick Maglowski from a previous sketch. Gustav contracted dropsy which caused his limbs to swell and affected his heart. He died from that illness at his home in Oshkosh on Apr. 28, 1883
{US 1860; WCMR v.1, p.261, #1534; ODN 30 Apr 1883; WiT 04 May 1883; ROV}

THOMAS, Alanson - Lt., Co. E, 2nd Regt., Wis. Vol. Inf.
Alanson resided at Oshkosh and enlisted there on Apr. 21, 1861. He was assigned as above and was promoted to Corporal, Sergeant and then 1st Sergeant in that company. Alanson was commissioned 2nd Lieutenant of that company on Oct. 15, 1861 and he

THOMAS, Alanson (cont.)
resigned his commission on Dec. 28, 1862. Alanson was listed in an 1899 article by Col. Harshaw as residing in Maine.
{ROV; ODN 07 May 1899}

THOMAS, David W. - Pvt., Co. K, 8th Regt., Wis. Vol. Inf.
David resided at Racine, Racine County and he enlisted there on Sept. 5, 1861. He was assigned as above and was mustered out on Sept. 5, 1865. David was listed in the 1890 federal census as residing at 9 Myrtle Street in the city of Oshkosh. He then provided that he had been shot in the foot and the ear during his military service. David was listed in the veteran section of the 1895 Wisconsin State census at P.O. Oshkosh. Ann, his widow, was listed in 1905 as residing at 347 Mt. Vernon Street in Oshkosh. David H. and Olive M. Thomas were also listed at that address.
{US 1890; WC-V 1895; ROV; B-1905}

THOMAS, John - Pvt., Co. B, 3rd Regt., Wis. Cav.
John resided at Vinland and enlisted there on Dec. 27, 1861. He was assigned as above and was transferred to Co. B, 3rd (reorg.) Regt., Wis. Cav. on Feb. 1, 1865. John was mustered out on Sept. 8, 1865.
{ROV}

THOMAS, John H. - Pvt., Co. F, 1st Regt., Wis. Hvy. Art.
John resided at Utica and enlisted there on Sept. 5, 1864. He was assigned as above and was mustered out on July 6, 1865. John was listed in the 1890 federal census as residing in the town of Aurora, Waushara County at P.O. Berlin.
{US 1890; ROV}

THOMAS, Owen N. - Pvt., Co. I, 32nd Regt., Wis. Vol. Inf.
Owen resided at Neenah and enlisted there on Nov. 1, 1863. He was assigned as above and was transferred to Co. C, 16th Regt., Wis. Vol. Inf. on June 4, 1865. Owen was mustered out on July 24, 1865. He was married in Winnebago County on Sept. 19, 1867 to Hattie Royce.
{ROV; WCMR v.1, p.356, #2145}

THOMBS, Melzar T. - Pvt., Co. D, 41st Regt., Wis. Vol. Inf.
Melzar resided at Menasha and enlisted there on May 26, 1864. He was assigned as above and was mustered out on Sept. 23, 1864 at the end of his term of enlistment. Melzar died prior to 1908.
{ROV; Lawson p.840}

THOMPSON, Albert L. - Pvt., Co. G, 1st (3 yr.) Regt., Wis. Vol. Inf.
Albert resided at Oshkosh and he was drafted there on Nov. 23, 1861. He was assigned as above and was then transferred to Co. E, 21st Regt., Wis. Vol. Inf. on Sept. 20, 1864. Albert was transferred to Co. F, 3rd Regt., Wis. Vol. Inf. June 8, 1865 and was mustered out on July 18, 1865.
{ROV}

THOMPSON, Archibald - Sgt., Co. D, 8th Regt., Wis. Vol. Inf.
Archibald was born circa 1833 at New Brunswick, Canada. He was a son of William S.

THOMPSON, Archibald (cont.)
and Almi Thompson and a brother of John B. from a following sketch. Almi was born circa 1813 at New Brunswick and William was born circa 1807 at Maine. William was listed in the 1860 federal census as a carpenter residing in the first ward of the city of Oshkosh. Residing with him were his wife and the following children: Archibald; Laura E., born circa 1836 at new Brunswick; John B.; Anna A., born circa 1841 at Maine; William Wallace, born circa 1843 at Maine; and Emma A., born circa 1850 at Maine. Archibald was also listed in that year as a farm laborer for Charles Libby in the town of Vinland. He enlisted at Oshkosh on Oct. 1, 1861. He was assigned as above and was promoted to Commissary Sergeant of that regiment on July 26, 1862. Archibald then contracted a disease and he died on May 19, 1863 at Grand Gulf, Mississippi.
{US 1860; ROV}

THOMPSON, C.S. - Pvt., Co. K, 11th Regt., Wis. Vol. Inf.
He resided at Winneconne and enlisted there on Mar. 29, 1864. C.S. was assigned as above. He contracted a disease and died on Apr. 12, 1864 at Camp Randall, Madison, Wisconsin.
{ROV}

THOMPSON, Charles - Pvt., Co. H, 18th Regt., Wis. Vol. Inf.
Charles resided at Oshkosh and enlisted there on Jan. 8, 1862. He was assigned as above and was not found again in the Wisconsin records.
{ROV}

THOMPSON, Charles G. - Pvt., Co. A, 48th Regt., Wis. Vol. Inf.
Charles was born circa 1831 at Massachusetts. His parents were natives of that state. Charles resided at Mukwanago, Waukesha County and enlisted there on Feb. 2, 1865. He was assigned as above and was listed as having deserted on Sept. 15, 1865. Charles was listed in the 1880 federal census as residing in the town of Omro. Sarah M., his wife, was born circa 1835 at New York. Her parents were natives of Pennsylvania. Charles and Sarah then had a son, Ellis A., a photographer, who was born circa 1854 at New York. Charles was listed in the veteran section of the 1885 Wisconsin State census at P.O. Omro. He was listed in the 1890 federal census as residing in the village of Omro. Charles was listed in 1905 as residing on Oshkosh Road in Omro.
{US 1880, 1890; WC-V 1885; ROV; B-1905}

THOMPSON, Christian O. - Pvt., Co. K, 11th Regt., Wis. Vol. Inf.
Christian resided at Winneconne and enlisted there on Sept. 17, 1861. He was assigned as a wagoner in the above company. Christian contracted a disease and died on Feb. 13, 1863 at St. Louis, Missouri.
{ROV}

THOMPSON, Duane - Pvt., 8th Batt., Wis. Lt. Art.
Duane resided at Menasha and enlisted there on Feb. 26, 1864. He was assigned as above and was mustered out on Aug. 10, 1865.
{ROV}

THOMPSON, Edwin - Sgt., Co. A, 31st Regt., Wis. Vol. Inf.
Edwin resided at Utica and enlisted there on Aug. 9, 1862. He was assigned as above

THOMPSON, Edwin (cont.)
and was promoted to Corporal and then Sergeant in that company. Edwin was wounded at Goldsboro, N.C. and was mustered out on July 14, 1865.
{ROV}

THOMPSON, George F. - Pvt., Co. I, 21st Regt., Wis. Vol. Inf.
George was born circa 1842 at New York. He was listed in the 1860 federal census as a hostler residing at the hotel of Sanford Babcock in the village of Neenah. George enlisted at Neenah on Aug. 14, 1862. He was assigned as above and was discharged on Feb. 26, 1863 due to a disability. He re-enlisted on Aug. 17, 1864 and was assigned to the Naval Gunboat Service. George received his training on the Great Lakes at Chicago and he was then assigned to the Gunboat "Juliet." He was wounded at Sunny Side, Arkansas and was hospitalized at Memphis, Tennessee. George was married on Jan. 26, 1868 in Winnebago County to Eliza A. Richards. He was listed in 1883 at P.O. Neenah, where he had been receiving pension #1,321 of $4 per month since October 1869 for a wound to his right leg. He was listed in the veteran section of the 1885, 1895 and 1905 Wisconsin State census at P.O. Neenah. George was listed in the 1890 federal census as residing in Neenah. He then provided that he had suffered a gunshot wound to his right knee while in the service. George was listed in 1905 as retired and residing at 148 Lake Street in Neenah. Pearl S. and Sam G. Thompson were also listed at that address.
{US 1860; 1890; WC-V 1885, 1895, 1905; Lawson p.841-2; WCMR v.1, p.367, #2230}
{ROV; B-1905}

THOMPSON, George Henry - Pvt., Co. K, 5th (reorg.) Regt., Wis. Vol. Inf.
George resided at Rushford and enlisted there on Sept. 3, 1864. He was assigned as above and was mustered out on June 20, 1865. George was married on Dec. 10, 1867 in Winnebago County to Celia Ann Whitney. He was listed in the veteran section of the 1895 and 1905 Wisconsin State census at P.O. Oshkosh. He was listed in 1905 as an employee of the Paine Lumber Company and residing at 107 Division Street in the city of Oshkosh. Gertrude E. Thompson was also listed at that address.
{WC-V 1895, 1905; ROV; B-1905}

THOMPSON, John - Civil War Veteran?
John was listed as above in the veteran section of the 1885 Wisconsin State census at P.O. Winneconne. No other information was provided.
{WC-V 1885}

THOMPSON, John B. - Sgt., Co. E, 2nd Regt., Wis. Vol. Inf.
John was born circa 1838 at Maine. He was a son of William S. and Almi Thompson and a brother of Archibald from a previous sketch. John was listed in 1860 as a clerk residing with his parents and their family in the first ward of the city of Oshkosh. He was listed again in that same census as residing with the family of Francis L. Billings in the first ward of the city of Oshkosh. He enlisted at Oshkosh on Apr. 21, 1861. He was assigned as above and was promoted to Sergeant in that company. John was promoted to Commissary Sergeant of that regiment on July 1, 1862. He was then mustered out on July 2, 1864 at the end of his term of enlistment. In an 1899 article by Col. Harshaw, John was listed as residing at Longmont, Colorado.
{US 1860; ROV; ODN 07 May 1899}

THOMPSON, John C. - Pvt., Co. I, 11th Regt., Indiana Vol. Inf.
He was listed as above in the veteran section of the 1905 Wisconsin State census at P.O. Oshkosh. John was then listed as an attorney residing at 125 Elm Street in the city of Oshkosh.
{WC-V 1905; B-1905}

THOMPSON, Joseph - Pvt., Co. D, 32nd Regt., Wis. Vol. Inf.
Joseph resided at Menasha and enlisted there on Dec. 16, 1863. He was assigned as above and was transferred to the 3rd Regt., Wis. Vol. Inf. on June 8, 1865. Joseph was mustered out on July 18, 1865.
{ROV}

THOMPSON, Loring F. - Pvt., Co. G, 11th Regt., Vermont Vol. Inf.
Loring was listed as above in the veteran section of the 1885 and 1895 Wisconsin State census at P.O. Oshkosh. He was also listed in 1888 as a member of GAR Post #10 at Oshkosh. He was listed in the 1890 federal census as residing in the city of Oshkosh. Loring then provided his unit designation as above and his service dates as having been from Aug. 5, 1862 to June 24, 1865.
{US 1890; WC-V 1885, 1895}

THOMPSON, Peter - Pvt., Co. H, 36th Regt., Wis. Vol. Inf.
Peter resided at Utica and enlisted there on Feb. 28, 1864. He was assigned as above and was wounded on June 7, 1864 at Cold Harbor, Virginia. He was taken prisoner at Ream's Station. Peter died in the rebel prison at Salisbury, N.C. on Nov. 30, 1864.
{ROV}

THOMPSON, Robert Sims - Pvt., 2nd Regt., Wis. Vol. Inf.
Robert was born on Apr. 7, 1828 at Antwerp, Jefferson County, New York. He was a son of Isaac and Lydia (Simms) Thompson. Isaac was a native of Connecticut and was a veteran of the War of 1812. Lydia was born in Scotland. Robert was married to Minerva C. Monroe on Oct. 30, 1848. She was born circa 1832 at New York and was a daughter of John Smith and Sarah (Chapman) Monroe. John was a native of Russia and he died when Minerva was five years old. He had been a veteran of the War of 1812. Robert removed from New York in 1853 and settled in Wisconsin at Green Bay, Brown County. He was engaged as an employee in a woolen mill and later learned the skills of a carpenter. Robert followed that trade at Green Bay, Oconto and then Menasha. He was listed in the 1860 federal census as residing in the first ward of the village of Menasha. Listed with him were his wife and two sons. Ambrose was born circa 1850 and Erwin was born circa 1855, both in Wisconsin. Robert left his family in Menasha when he enlisted on June 6, 1861. He was assigned to the regimental band as a tuba player at a pay scale of $34 per month. When the General Order was issued to discontinue regimental bands he was paid for his time as a common soldier. Robert was discharged under that order on Nov. 15, 1861. He returned to Neenah after his service and followed his trade there until fall of 1883. He then removed to Antigo, Langlade County. Robert and Minerva had six children, four of whom died young. A brother of Robert was Lieutenant Colonel of the 3rd Penn. Reserve Corps. He resigned that position to accept one as the Chief Engineer of the captured rebel steamer "Atlanta." He had been a veteran of the Mexican War and was killed at Charleston, S.C. as a torpedo burst while he was examining it. Robert still resided at Antigo in 1888 and he

THOMPSON, Robert Sims (cont.)
was a member of GAR Post #78. He was listed in the 1900 federal census as divorced and residing at the Wisconsin Veterans' Home at King. Minerva, his widow, was listed in 1905 as residing at 420 Second Street in Menasha.
{US 1860, 1900; ROV; SCA 1:155-6; B-1905}

THOMPSON, Thomas - Cpl., Co. H, 15th Regt., Wis. Vol. Inf.
Thomas resided at Utica and enlisted there on Oct. 28, 1861. He was assigned as above and was promoted to Corporal in that company. Thomas was wounded at Stone River. He was discharged due to his wounds on June 9, 1863.
{ROV}

THOMPSON, William Edwin - Pvt., Co. K, 5th (reorg.) Regt., Wis. Vol. Inf.
William E. Thompson was born circa 1847 at Vermont. His parents were also natives of that state. William resided at Rushford and enlisted there on Sept. 3, 1864. He was assigned as above and was mustered out on June 20, 1865. William was married to Louisa Beauprey(?). They had a daughter, unnamed at registration, who was born in the village of Omro on Nov. 13, 1878. William was listed in the 1880 federal census as a farmer residing in the town of Omro. Listed with him was his wife, Louisa, who was born circa 1844 in Wisconsin. Listed with them were daughters Agnes, born circa 1875; and Isabelle, born circa 1879. William was listed in the veteran section of the 1885 Wisconsin State census at P.O. Omro.
{US 1880; WC-V 1885; ROV; WCBR v.2, p.125, #331}

THOMPSON, William P. - Pvt., 2nd Regt., New Hampshire Vol. Inf.
William was listed as above in the veteran section of the 1895 Wisconsin State census at P.O. Oshkosh.
{WC-V 1895}

THORN, Henry H. - Pvt., Co. G, 3rd (reorg.) Regt., Wis. Vol. Inf.
Henry resided at Oshkosh and enlisted there on Nov. 27, 1863. He was assigned as a farrier in the above company and was mustered out on Oct. 27, 1865.
{ROV}

THORNTON, Joseph P. - Pvt., Co. K, 19th Regt., Wis. Vol. Inf.
Joseph was born on Oct. 14, 1833 at Erie County, Pennsylvania. His parents removed to Ohio when he was five years old and then moved again to Lake County, Illinois in 1848. They removed to Wisconsin in 1850 and settled in Racine County. Joseph was engaged as a miller until he enrolled in service. He was married to Charlotte Dibble on Jan. 9, 1853. She was born in England and was a daughter of Richard and Charlotte Dibble. Joseph listed his residence as Racine, Racine County when he enlisted there on Apr. 14, 1862. He was assigned as above. Joseph was ill with chronic bowel disease and he suffered from sore eyes. He spent a long time in the hospital at Hampton, Virginia. In Sept. 1864 he was detailed to dress wounds for the patients. Several hundred soldiers had been wounded at Dutch Gap and had been left on the field for three days. Many suffered gangrene before being brought to Hampton. Joseph absorbed poison from a wound and his hand began to turn black, yet he was back serving with his regiment in Oct. 1864. Joseph was mustered out on Apr. 29, 1865. After returning to Wisconsin he was employed in a mill until the disease in his eyes became so troublesome that he

THORNTON, Joseph P. (cont.)
could no longer work there. Joseph and Charlotte had three children: Henry A., resided in Waukesha County; Ellen, died in 1880; and Allie D., resided at Grand Rapids, Michigan. Charlotte died and Joseph was then married on July 4, 1873 to her sister Amelia. Joseph and Amelia had seven children, including: Sarah E.; Charles E.; Clarence A.; Ellen M.; and Arthur J. Thornton. Joseph had a brother, Henry, who served in Co. E of the same regiment. Henry died at New London, Waupaca County in 1876. He had lost three sons in the war: William R., 26th Regt., N.Y. Vol. Inf., died at Alexandria, Virginia; Francis, served with the 101st Regt., N.Y. Vol. Inf., died at Salisbury Prison; and Charles, who died at Madison, Wisconsin. Another brother, Leonard, is the subject of a following sketch. Joseph was listed in 1883 at P.O. Neenah. He was then receiving a pension of $18 per month for an injury to his right hand and an inflammation of his eyes. Joseph was listed in the veteran section of the 1885 Wisconsin State census at P.O. Neenah. He was listed in the 1890 federal census as residing in the town of Neenah at P.O. Neenah. Joseph was then reported as suffering from the effects of "diarrhea, blindness, consumption, crippled hand, etc., etc." Amelia, his widow, was listed in 1905 as residing at 549 Chestnut Street in the city of Neenah. Clarence and Ezra Thornton were also listed at that address.
{US 1890; WC-V 1885; ROV; LOP-1883; SCA 1:562-3; B-1905}

THORNTON, Leonard - Pvt., Co. F, 50th Regt., Wis. Vol. Inf.
Leonard was a brother of Joseph from a previous sketch. Leonard resided at Racine, Racine County and enlisted there on Mar. 6, 1865. He was assigned as above and was mustered out on May 16, 1865. Leonard was listed in the veteran section of the 1885 Wisconsin State census at P.O. Menasha. He was residing at Antigo, Langlade County in 1888.
{WC-V 1885; ROV; SCA 1:562-3}

THORNTON, William L. - Pvt., Co. D, 1st Regt., Wis. Hvy. Art.
William resided at Clayton and enlisted there on Sept. 5, 1864. He was assigned as above and was mustered out on June 30, 1865. William was listed in the 1890 federal census as residing in the town of Menasha at P.O. Menasha.
{US 1890; ROV}

THORP, William G. - Cpl., Co. D, 7th Regt., Wis. Cav.?
William was listed as above in the 1890 federal census as residing in the village of Winneconne. He then provided his service dates as having been from June 5, 1861 to Aug. 27, 1862. There was no 7th Regt., Wis. Cav. William also provided that he had re-enlisted in the 21st Regt., Wis. Vol. Inf. There was no Thorp found in the records of the 21st Regt., Wis. Vol. Inf.
{US 1890; ROV}

THRALL, Horace R. - Pvt., Co. F, 18th Regt., Wis. Vol. Inf.
Horace was born on Nov. 1, 1841 at Brockville, Canada. He was a son of Friend and Betsey (Parsons) Thrall. Friend was born circa 1815 at Kingsboro, Montgomery County, New York. His father Isaac was a native of Connecticut. Betsey was born circa 1817 at Gouverneur, St. Lawrence County, New York. Israel R. Parsons, the father of Betsey, was born in Connecticut and was a veteran of the War of 1812. Friend removed to Wisconsin when Horace was twelve years old and settled first at Berlin, Green Lake

THRALL, Horace R. (cont.)
County. The family then removed to Oshkosh. Horace was educated in the common schools at his several homes and was trained for the career of an engineer. Friend was listed in the 1860 federal census as residing in the second ward of the city of Oshkosh. With him were his wife and the following children: Horace; Preston, born circa 1844 at Canada, later resided at Green Bay; Charles, born circa 1847 at New York, later resided in California; Stella, born circa 1854 at New York; and Frederick, born circa 1857 at Wisconsin, later resided in Kaukauna. Betsey died at their home on Pearl Street in Oshkosh on Aug. 11, 1888. Her obituary showed that she was also survived by a son Herbert, then residing in California. Horace enlisted at Oshkosh on Nov. 24, 1861. He was assigned as above. After the successful siege of Vicksburg, Mississippi Horace was transferred to the military railroad service of the army. He was an engineer on the run from Vicksburg to the Big Black. He was then mustered out at Madison, Wisconsin on Mar. 14, 1865 at the end of his term of enlistment. Horace was listed in 1868 as an engineer boarding at 58 Pearl Street in Oshkosh. That was the residence of his father, who was then listed as a furrier. Horace was engaged as the Chief Engineer of the Green Bay and Ft. Howard water works. He was married on Apr. 14, 1873 to Amy Thrall. She was the adopted daughter of Alfred Thrall, a relative of Horace. Amy was born in New York and her mother died when she was three years old. Her father was a soldier from a Wisconsin regiment during the civil war. Horace and Amy had a daughter, Stella C. Thrall. Horace was residing at Green Bay in 1888.
{US 1860; ROV; T-1868; SCA 1:373-4; OWN 16 Aug 1888}

THRALL, Willis Edward - Cpl., Co. A, 48th Regt., Wis. Vol. Inf.
Willis was born on June 6, 1842 at New York. He was a son of William and Phoebe (Whitlock) Thrall, both natives of Connecticut. William was born there circa 1805 and Phoebe was born circa 1810. Willis remained at New York with his parents until the family removed to Wisconsin in 1848 and settled on a farm in the town of Omro. They were listed in the 1860 federal census as residing on that farm. Listed with them were the following children: Edward; Frances, born circa 1846 at New York; Narcissa, born circa 1848 at New York; and Emily, born circa 1849 at Wisconsin. William and Phoebe are buried in the town of Omro at Omro Union Cemetery. Only their names are on their markers. William died on Sept. 13, 1881. Willis went back to New York for a time but then returned to Omro. He enlisted there on Feb. 6, 1865 and was assigned as above. He was promoted to Corporal in that company and was listed as having deserted on Sept. 10, 1865. Willis was married in Winnebago County on Apr. 18, 1872 (records say Apr. 24) to Marian Amos. She was born in 1851 and was a daughter of William and Louisa Amos. Willis and Marian had one son, Edward W. Thrall. Marian died on Mar. 4, 1873. Willis was again married in Winnebago County on Aug. 1, 1875 to Tasia Coats. She was born on May 15, 1848 and was a daughter of Avery and Lucy Coats. Willis was listed in the veteran section of the 1885 and 1895 Wisconsin State census at P.O. Omro. He was listed in the 1890 federal census as residing in the town of Omro at P.O. Omro. He was listed in 1905 as residing on 80 acres of section 15 in the town of Omro. Willis died on Jan. 30, 1912 and is buried at the side of his first wife in the town of Omro at Omro Union Cemetery.
{US 1860, 1890; WC-V 1885, 1895; Randall p.31; WCMR v.1, p.532, #3550; ROV}
{Cem. records; B-1905; ODN 17 Sep 1881}

THROOP, E.B. - Civil War Veteran?
He was listed as a veteran from a Michigan unit on the cemetery roster of GAR Post #7 as having been buried at Omro Cemetery. He was not listed in the veteran section of any Wisconsin State census and was not found in the records of Omro Cemetery.
{Cem. records}

THURSTON, Myron S. - Pvt., Co. F, 5th (reorg.) Regt., Wis. Vol. Inf.
Myron resided at Menasha and enlisted there on Sept. 17, 1864. He was assigned as above and was mustered out on June 20, 1865.
{ROV}

TIBBETS, George W. - Sgt., Co. K, 51st Regt., Wis. Vol. Inf.
George was born circa 1841 at Maine. He was a son of Tilly Tibbets. She was born circa 1807 at Maine and was listed in the 1860 federal census as residing on a farm in the town of Nekimi at P.O. Oshkosh. Listed with her were George and Ebenezer, his brother. Ebenezer was born circa 1829 at Maine. Also listed were Ebenezer's wife and three of their children. George listed his residence as Oshkosh when he enlisted there on Mar. 7, 1865. He was assigned as a Private to Co. C, 53rd Regt., Wis. Vol. Inf. Most of that company was transferred to Co. K, 51st Regt., Wis. Vol. Inf. under orders dated June 10, 1865. The transfer was completed on June 30, 1865 at Ft. Leavenworth, Kansas and George was promoted to 1st Sergeant. The regiment returned to Madison, Wisconsin on Aug. 1, 1865 and the men were mustered out by companies. The last company was mustered out on Aug. 30, 1865.
{US 1860; ROV}

TICE, Aaron Bartholomew - Pvt., Co. C, 10th Regt., Iowa Vol. Inf.
Aaron was born on June 14, 1845 at Youngstown, Trumbull County, Ohio. His parents were natives of Pennsylvania. William, the father, was born on July 4, 1819 and died on Sept. 10, 1851 near Youngstown, Ohio. He was married to Sarah (Tourney) Fox. Frederick, father of William, was born circa 1796 at Canada. He was listed in the 1860 federal census as residing with the family of Josiah Goodwin in the town of Utica at P.O. Oshkosh. Nelson Henry Tice, a son of Frederick, is the father of Jesse Tice from a following sketch. Aaron was married in Winnebago County on May 6, 1866 to Jennie Stevens. She was born circa 1848 in England and both of her parents were natives of that place. Aaron was listed in the 1880 federal census as operating a meat market in the village of Omro. Listed also were their children: Fred, born circa 1872, later a doctor residing at Chicago; Lewis Francis, born circa 1874, died at Omro in 1903; and Rosa, born circa 1876, died on Apr. 4, 1893 at Omro. Jennie died in 1888. Aaron was then married second on Aug. 10, 1889 to Mrs. Elizabeth A. (Hoskins) Gadbaw. She was born on Jan. 17, 1857 at French Canada and was a daughter of George and Surviva E. (Holt) Hoskins. Aaron and Eliza had the following children: Harvey Aaron, born on Nov. 7, 1890 at Omro, married Vera Baker, resided at Huron, S.D., died on May 18, 1967; Charles William, born on Aug. 26, 1896, died of pneumonia on Dec. 31, 1896; and Roy William, born July 29, 1898, married Evelyn Anderson, died in Oshkosh Dec. 19, 1923. Aaron was listed in the veteran section of the 1885 and 1895 Wisconsin State census at Omro. Omro and as a veteran of the above company. He was listed in the 1890 federal census as residing in the village of Omro. Aaron provided his unit designation as above and his service dates as having been from July 31, 1861 to Sept. 28, 1864. He listed that he suffered from kidney disease due to exposure. Aaron also listed then that

TICE, Aaron Bartholomew (cont.)
he had re-enlisted as a Private in Co. A, 36th Regt., Ill. Vol. Inf. on Mar. 1, 1865 and had served until Oct. 8, 1865. He was listed in 1905 as residing on Quarter Street in the village of Omro. Ethel, widow of Lewis Tice, was also listed at that address. Aaron died on Aug. 6, 1937. He was the last surviving Civil War veteran from the Omro area. He is buried with a simple military marker. Eliza A., his second wife, died on Apr. 20, 1947. Both are buried with others of their family at Omro Cemetery, Pelton's Addition, Section A, plot 1.
{US 1860, 1880, 1890; WC-V 1885, 1895; B-1905; WCMR v.1, p.297, #1819}
{ODN 30 Jul 1937; ODN 07 Aug 1937; research of Pamela Crane; Cem. records}
{OWN 08 Apr 1893}

TICE, Jesse - Cpl., Co. B, 38th Regt., Wis. Vol. Inf.
Jesse was born on Aug. 28, 1844 at Mercer County, Pennsylvania. He was a son of Nelson Henry and Sarah H. (Thompson) Tice. Nelson was born in 1816 at Pennsylvania and died on Oct. 9, 1899 at Waukau. He was survived by his wife and several children. Sarah was born circa 1815 at Massachusetts and died on May 3, 1902 at Waukau. Both are buried in the town of Omro at Tice Cemetery. They had a family of five sons and three daughters. Nelson was a son of Frederick Tice. William, his brother, was the father of Aaron Tice from a previous sketch. Emeline Sophia Chaffee, wife of Jesse, was born in 1842 at Vermont. Jesse resided at Omro and enlisted there on Mar. 30, 1864. He was assigned as above and was promoted to Corporal in that company. He was then mustered out on July 26, 1865. Jesse and Emeline were listed in the 1880 federal census as residing in the village of Waukau. Listed with them were the following children: Winnie, born circa 1869, married a Fancher, died before her father; Clinton A., born circa 1872; Frank, born circa 1873; and Maggie, born circa 1876, married Fred Hotchkiss of Waukau. All four children were born in Wisconsin. Jesse was listed in the veteran section of the 1885, 1895 and 1905 Wisconsin State census at P.O. Waukau. He was listed in the 1890 federal census as residing in the town of Rushford at P.O. Waukau and suffering from rheumatism. He was listed in 1905 as a U.S. Mail carrier residing in the village of Waukau. Jesse died in Waukau on July 8, 1934. He was the last surviving Civil War veteran in the town of Rushford. Emeline died in 1921. Nellie, a daughter, was born in 1871 and died in 1925. All three are buried in the town of Rushford at Waukau Cemetery.
{US 1880, 1890; WC-V 1885, 1895, 1905; ROV; OWN 14 Oct 1899; Cem. records}
{B-1905; ODN 09 Jul 1934; research of Pamela Crane}

TIPLER, John - Pvt., Co. B, 21st Regt., Wis. Vol. Inf.
John was born circa 1843 at England. He was a son of George and Sarah Tipler and was probably a cousin of William Tipler from a following sketch. George was born circa 1798 at England and Sarah was born there circa 1799. John was listed in the 1860 federal census as residing with his parents on a farm in the town of Vinland. Edward, a brother, was born circa 1846 at England and was also residing there. John enlisted at Vinland on Aug. 14, 1862. He was assigned as above and was then taken prisoner on Dec. 30, 1862. John died on Feb. 6, 1863 at Camp Chase, Ohio.
{US 1860; ROV; WCMR v.1, p.193, #991}

TIPLER, William Jr. - Pvt., Co. D, 49th Regt., Wis. Vol. Inf.
William was born circa 1822 at England. William, his father, was born there circa 1793.

TIPLER, William Jr. (cont.)
William was married in Winnebago County on Oct. 13, 1850 to Sarah Ann Benedict. She was born circa 1831 at Ohio. They were listed in the 1860 federal census as residing on a farm in the town of Clayton at P.O. Neenah. Listed with them were the following children: Ann, born circa 1853; Helen, born circa 1854; and Susan, born circa 1858. Listed with them was William Sr. Residing on a nearby farm was Isaac Tipler and his family. Isaac was a brother of William Jr. William listed his residence as Winneconne when he enlisted on Feb. 16, 1865. He was assigned as above and was mustered out on Nov. 1, 1865.
{US 1860; ROV; WCMR v.1, p.40, #172}

TIPPENS, Frederick - Pvt., Co. I, 21st Regt., Wis. Vol. Inf.
Frederick was born circa 1841 at Canada West. He was a son of John (Tippin) who was born circa 1803 at England. John was listed in the 1860 federal census as a shoemaker residing in the village of Neenah. Mary Ann, his wife, was born circa 1825 at England. Listed with them were Frederick and a daughter, Charlotte, who was born circa 1853 at New York. Frederick enlisted at Neenah on Aug. 14, 1862. He was assigned as above and was wounded at Resaca, Georgia on May 14, 1864. Frederick was listed as being absent wounded when that regiment was mustered out on June 8, 1865. He was listed in 1883 at P.O. Neenah, where he had been receiving a pension of $2 per month since June 1882 for a wound to his left ankle. Frederick was listed (Tipkens) in the veteran section of the 1885 Wisconsin State census at P.O. Neenah. Dorethe, his widow, was listed in the 1890 federal census as residing in the city of Neenah.
{US 1860, 1890; WC-V 1885; ROV; LOP-1883; Lawson p.834}

TISCH, - Civil War Veteran?
Emily, his widow, was listed in the 1890 federal census as residing in the city of Oshkosh. She provided no other information.
{US 1890}

TITTEMORE, Nelson - Cpl., Co. F, 18th Regt., Wis. Vol. Inf.
Nelson resided at Oshkosh and enlisted there on Nov. 26, 1861. He was assigned as above and was promoted to Corporal in that company. Nelson was then discharged on Oct. 19, 1862. He was married in Winnebago County on May 16, 1863 to Margaret Crowley. She was born on Aug. 24, 1841 at Chatham, New Brunswick, Canada and came to Wisconsin with her parents in 1855. They settled on a farm in the town of Poysippi, Waushara County. Margaret died at the home farm in Poygan, then in the posession of her son J.N. Tittemore on Mar. 17, 1917. Her obituary listed that Nelson had been engaged in the lumbering business, first as a sawyer with Paine Lumber Company in Oshkosh and later in that same business at Wausau. He died in an accident some 40 years prior to the death of Margaret. Nelson and Margaret had six children, three of whom survived the mother: Mrs. Mary Ely and Mrs. Helen Hughes, both of Chicago, and J.N. Tittemore of Poygan. She was also survived by an adopted son, Louis Tittemore of Poygan.
{ROV; WCMR v.1, p.242, #1384*; ODN 17 Mar 1917}

TOBIN, William H. - Pvt., Co. E, 48th Regt., Wis. Vol. Inf.
William resided at Oshkosh and enlisted there on Feb. 27, 1865. He was assigned as

TOBIN, William H. (cont.)
above. William contracted a disease and died on Sept. 11, 1865 at Ft. Leavenworth, Kansas.
{ROV}

TODD, Henry - Pvt., Co. H, 7th Regt., Wis. Vol. Inf.
Henry resided at Hampton, Columbia County and enlisted there on Feb. 6, 1864. He was assigned as above and was transferred to the Veteran Reserve Corps on Apr. 28, 1865. Henry was listed in the veteran section of the 1895 Wisconsin State census at P.O. Omro.
{WC-V 1895; ROV}

TODD, Henry - Cpl., Co. F, 18th Regt., Wis. Vol. Inf.
Henry was born circa 1845 at England. He was a son of Jabez C. and Lydia Todd and a brother of Joseph H. from a following sketch. Jabez was born circa 1808 at England and died on Sept. 16, 1864 at age 56 years, 6 months and 5 days. Lydia was born in England on Feb. 15, 1809 and died on Feb. 24, 1897. Both were listed in the 1850 federal census as residing in the town of Winnebago. Listed with them then were the following children: Charles, born circa 1841; Joseph; Henry; and Hannah, born circa 1847. All of the children were born in England. They were listed again in the 1860 federal census as residing on a farm in the town of Nekimi at P.O. Oshkosh. In addition to Joseph, Henry and Anna, son Emerson was born circa 1855 at Wisconsin. Henry resided at Oshkosh and enlisted there on Mar. 10, 1862. He was assigned as above and was then promoted to Corporal in that company. Henry was taken prisoner at Shiloh, Tennessee and was confined at Montgomery Prison in Alabama. He was captured again at Allatoona, Georgia and was taken to the Florence Military Prison. He was sent to Annapolis, Maryland for his discharge, which occurred at Wheeling, West Virginia. He died at Wheeling, W.V. on Mar. 7, 1865 at age 20 years. Henry is buried with his parents and brother Charles in the town of Algoma at Ellenwood Cemetery, Section A.
{US 1850, 1860; ROV; Cem. records}

TODD, Joseph H. - Pvt., 9th Batt., Wis. Lt. Art.
Joseph was born circa 1843 at England. He was a son of Jabez C. and Lydia Todd and a brother of Henry of a previous sketch. Joseph was listed in the 1860 federal census as residing with his parents on a farm in the town of Nekimi at P.O. Oshkosh. He resided at Oshkosh and enlisted there on Nov. 1, 1861. He was assigned as above and was mustered out on Sept. 30, 1865. He was listed in 1868 as a carpenter residing at 118 Ohio Street in the city of Oshkosh. That was the residence of his mother Lydia. Joseph was listed in the veteran section of the 1885 and 1895 Wisconsin State census at P.O. Oshkosh. He was listed in the 1890 federal census as residing at 386 Ohio Street in Oshkosh. Wilhelmina, widow of John?, was listed in 1905 as residing at that address with her son George Todd.
{US 1850, 1860, 1890; WC-V 1885, 1895; ROV; T-1868; B-1905}

TOLLEFSON, Gunder - Pvt., Co. F, 19th Regt., Wis. Vol. Inf.
Gunder resided at Winchester and enlisted there on Mar. 31, 1864. He was assigned as above and was transferred to Co. C of that same regiment on May 1, 1865. Gunder was then mustered out on Aug. 9, 1865.
{ROV}

TOLLIVER, William H. - Pvt., 8th Batt., Wis. Lt. Art.
William resided at Menasha and enlisted there on Feb. 19, 1864. He was assigned as above and was mustered out on Aug. 10, 1865.
{ROV}

TONNTZ, Fred - Pvt., Co. F, 19th Regt., Wis. Vol. Inf.?
Fred was listed as above in the veteran section of the 1895 Wisconsin State census at P.O. Winneconne. He was not found in the records of that company and was not found in the index to Roster of Wisconsin Volunteers.
{WC-V 1895; ROV}

TOOTHMAN, Ratliff B. - Pvt., Co. H, 1st Regt., Wis. Cav.
Ratliff resided at Clayton and enlisted there on Feb. 3, 1862. He re-enlisted at the end of his term and was assigned as a blacksmith in that same company. Ratliff was then mustered out on July 19, 1865.
{ROV}

TOPLIFF, George F. - Lt., Co. F, 18th Regt., Wis. Vol. Inf.
George resided at Eureka and enlisted in the above company. He was commissioned as 2nd Lieutenant of that company on Dec. 20, 1861. George resigned his commission on July 14, 1862.
{ROV}

TORKELSON, Ole - Pvt., Co. A, 47th Regt., Wis. Vol. Inf.
Ole resided at Winchester and enlisted there on Feb. 10, 1865. He was assigned as above and was mustered out on Sept. 4, 1865. Ole was listed in the veteran section of the 1885 Wisconsin State census at P.O. Winchester.
{WC-V 1885; ROV}

TORRENCE, Elmer - Pvt., Co. E, 2nd Regt., Wis. Vol. Inf.
Elmer resided at Oshkosh and enlisted there on Oct. 28, 1861. He wa assigned as above and was detached to the Western Gunboat Service in Feb. 1862. Elmer was killed by the explosion of the gunboat "Mound City."
{ROV}

TORRENCE, Wilber E. - Pvt., Co. K, 11th Regt., Wis. Vol. Inf.
Wilber resided at Vinland and enlisted there on Sept. 17, 1861. He was assigned as above. Wilber contracted a disease and died on Dec. 3, 1862 at St. Louis, Missouri.
{ROV}

TORREY, Benjamin R. - Pvt., Co. D, 16th Regt., Wis. Vol. Inf.
Benjamin resided at Neenah and enlisted there on Dec. 10, 1861. He was assigned as above. Benjamin was transferred to the 15th Regt., Mich. Vol. Inf. on May 20, 1862.
{ROV}

TORREY, Ira A. - Surg., 14th Regt., Wis. Vol. Inf.
Ira resided at Neenah. He was commissioned as 2nd Asst. Surgeon of the 16th Regt., Wis. Vol. Inf. on Nov. 13, 1861 and was promoted to 1st Asst. Surgeon on Feb. 1, 1862. Ira was then commissioned as Surgeon of the 14th Regt., Wis. Vol. Inf. on Oct. 13,

TORREY, Ira A. (cont.)
1862. He died on Sept. 16, 1863 at Neenah, Wisconsin.
{ROV}

TORREY, Wilder B.M. - Sgt., Co. I, 21st Regt., Wis. Vol. Inf.
Wilder was born circa 1831 at Ohio. He was listed in the 1860 federal census as a druggist residing in the village of Neenah. Margaret, his wife, was born circa 1830 at Connecticut. Frank, their son, was born circa 1858 at Wisconsin. Wilder enlisted at Neenah on Aug. 11, 1861. He was assigned as above and was promoted to Sergeant in that company. Wilder was transferred to the Veteran Reserve Corps on Sept. 30, 1863. He was listed (Walter) in the veteran section of the 1885 and 1895 Wisconsin State census at P.O. Neenah.
{US 1860; WC-V 1885, 1895; ROV}

TORREYSON, John N.R. - Fireman, "Cincinnati," U.S. Navy.
John was listed in the 1890 federal census as residing in the town of Oshkosh at P.O. Oshkosh. He provided his unit designation as above and his service dates as having been from Aug. 1864 to Feb. 1866. John was listed in the veteran section of the 1895 Wisconsin State census at P.O. Oshkosh. He was listed as having been the assistant engineer on that vessel. John was born in 1837 and died in 1896. Ida, his widow, was listed in 1905 as residing at 104 Prospect Avenue in the city of Oshkosh. Son Louis was also listed at that address. Ida was born in 1858 and died in 1922. Both are buried in Oshkosh at Riverside Cemetery.
{US 1890; WC-V 1895; Cem. records; B-1905}

TOURTELLOTTE, Abraham J. - Civil War Veteran?
Abraham resided at Algoma and enlisted on Feb. 22, 1864. He was assigned as above and was mustered out on Sept. 29, 1865. Mary M., his widow, was listed in the 1890 federal census as residing in the village of Omro. She provided no other information.
{US 1890; ROV}

TOWER, Cornelius P. - Pvt., Co. I, 6th Regt., Wis. Vol. Inf.
Cornelius resided at Utica and was drafted there on Oct. 29, 1861. He was assigned as above and was wounded at Hatcher's Run, Virginia. Cornelius was then mustered out on July 14, 1865.
{ROV}

TOWLE, Charles H. - Pvt., 8th Batt., Wis. Lt. Art.
Charles was born circa 1832 at New York. He was listed in the 1860 federal census as a sailor residing with the family of Charles Shoemaker in the village of Neenah. Charles listed his residence as Menasha when he enlisted on Jan. 4, 1864. He was assigned as above and was then transferred to the Mississippi Marine Brigade. Charles was assigned as a boatswain on the steam ram "Vindicator." He was then promoted to purser.
{ROV; Lawson p.841; HN 1878 p.152}

TOWLE, James I. - Sgt., Co. E, 5th (reorg.) Regt., Wis. Vol. Inf.
James resided at Oshkosh and enlisted on Aug. 8, 1864. He was assigned as above and was promoted to Sergeant in that company. James was mustered out on June 20, 1865.
{ROV}

TOWN, John - Pvt., Co. I, 21st Regt., Wis. Vol. Inf.
John was born circa 1839 at New York, a son of Randall and Mary Town. Both parents were natives of New York, the father born there circa 1800 and the mother born circa 1801. They were listed in the 1860 federal census as residing with members of their family on a farm in the town of Oshkosh. John resided at Vinland and enlisted there on Aug. 14, 1862. He was assigned as above and was wounded at Chaplin Hills, Kentucky. John was discharged on Jan. 24, 1863 due to his wounds.
{US 1860; ROV}

TOWNE, Ephraim P. - Pvt., Co. E, 5th (reorg.) Regt., Wis. Vol. Inf.
Ephraim resided at Oshkosh and enlisted there on Aug. 25, 1864. He was assigned as above and was mustered out on June 20, 1865.
{ROV}

TOWNSEND, Charles Carroll - Sgt., Co. C, 1st Regt., Wis. Cav.
Charles was born on Aug. 11, 1842 at Alexander, Genesee County, New York. He was a son of Chester C. and Carolina (DeMarie) Townsend. The father was born circa 1810 at Maine and Caroline was born circa 1821 at New York. Chester removed with his family about 1848 and settled first at Chicago, Illinois. He moved to Beloit and then to Janesville, Rock County, Wisconsin where he was the first Register of Deeds. Chester later removed to Winnebago County and settled at Neenah. There he was a cashier at a bank, a Justice of the Peace and also the City Treasurer. Chester was listed in the 1860 federal census as a banker residing in the village of Neenah. Listed with him were his wife and son Carroll. Also listed was another son, George, who was born circa 1847 at Wisconsin. Charles was educated at Neenah and then attended Lawrence University at Appleton, Outagamie County. He went to Ripon and enlisted on Sept. 1, 1861, when he was assigned as above. Charles was promoted to Corporal at the formation of the company and he was promoted to Duty Sergeant at Benton Barracks, Missouri in spring 1862. In Sept. 1863 he was promoted to Orderly Sergeant. Charles was commissioned as 1st Lieutenant of his company for bravery in the battle at Anderson's Gap, Georgia and for saving the life of Colonel LaGrange. He was detached at the time and was never mustered at that rank. Charles was captured at Dandridge, Tennessee and spent nearly a year in rebel prisons. He was mustered out on Apr. 10, 1865 and was discharged in July 1865 at Madison, Wisconsin. Charles had also received minor injuries twice while in the service but neither caused the loss of a duty day. He returned to Neenah to begin recruiting his health. Charles went to Colorado in 1866 and spent the summer travelling in the western territories. He returned to Neenah in good health and opened a grocery enterprise there. In 1871 Charles removed to Rockford, Illinois where he managed a flour and feed mill. He was married to May A. Reynolds on Oct. 15, 1872. She was a daughter of G.W. Reynolds of Rockford. Charles returned to Wisconsin and settled for a while at Fond du Lac, Fond du Lac County. There he became interested in the manufacturing of pumps. He removed to Merrill, Lincoln County in 1881. Charles and May had six children: Harvey; G. Ray; Charles Carroll; William B.; Harold; and Esther May. Charles was still residing at Merrill in 1888.
{US 1860; ROV; SCA 1:149-50}

TOWNSEND, John Harrison - Pvt., Co. E, 1st Regt., Wis. Cav.
John was born on Apr. 4, 1840 at New York, a son of John and Clara Townsend. John was born on Oct. 18, 1803 at New York and died on Jan. 12, 1886. Clara was born on

TOWNSEND, John Harrison (cont.)
Apr. 29, 1812 at Vermont and died on Oct. 27, 1888. They were listed in the 1860 federal census as residing on a farm in the town of Rushford at P.O. Ripon. John was then residing with them. They also had a daughter, Mary, who was born circa 1847 at New York. John enlisted at Nepeuskun on Nov. 21, 1863. He was assigned as above and was mustered out on July 19, 1865. John was listed in the 1890 federal census as residing in the town of Nepeuskun at P.O. Rush Lake. He was listed in the veteran section of the 1905 Wisconsin State census at P.O. Rush Lake. He was listed then with Eliza, his wife, as residing on 120 acres of section 28 in the town of Nepeuskun. Daughter Gertrude was residing there also. John died on Nov. 12, 1907. He is buried with his parents in the town of Nepeuskun at Koro Cemetery.
{US 1860, 1890; WC-V 1905; ROV; Cem. records; B-1905}

TOWNSEND, William - Pvt., Co. G, 3rd Regt., Wis. Inf.
William was born on June 2, 1839 at Manchester, Lancashire, England. He emigrated to America about 1860. William came to Wisconsin and resided several places until he enlisted at Neenah on Feb. 29, 1864. He was assigned as above. William was wounded at Averysboro on Mar. 16, 1865. A minnie ball entered his head at the corner of his right eye and came out below his left ear. He was listed as absent wounded when that regiment was mustered out on July 18, 1865. William was taken to the hospital at Madison, Wisconsin. He was discharged on Aug. 22, 1865. He then returned to Neenah and was married there on July 27, 1866 to Alice L. Jones. She was from the town of Winchester. They removed to Minnesota in 1870 but returned to Wisconsin and settled in Waupaca County in 1881. They finally settled at Clintonville, Waupaca County, where William was still residing in 1888. He and Alice had three sons and one daughter. William was listed in the 1890 federal census as residing in the town of Larrabee, Waupaca County at P.O. Clintonville.
{US 1890; ROV; SCA 1:332; WCMR v.1, p.303, #1865}

TOYCEN, Swen - Pvt., Co. A, 47th Regt., Wis. Vol. Inf.
Swen resided at Winchester and enlisted there on Feb. 10, 1865. He was assigned as above and was mustered out on Sept. 4, 1865.
{ROV}

TRACEY, Charles - Cpl., Co. B, 16th (reorg.) Regt., Wis. Vol. Inf.
Charles was born circa 1828 at New Hampshire. He was listed in the 1860 federal census as residing on a farm in the town of Black Wolf. Maria, his wife, was born circa 1836 at New Brunswick, Canada. They then had two daughters. Julia M. was born circa 1858 and Effie J. was born in 1859, both in Wisconsin. Charles listed his residence as Nekimi when he enlisted on Mar. 9, 1864. He was assigned as above and was then promoted to Corporal in that company. Charles was mustered out on July 12, 1865. He was listed in the 1890 federal census as residing in the town of Wautoma, Waushara County. Charles then reported that he was suffering from diabetes.
{US 1860, 1890; ROV}

TRACEY, David S. - Pvt., Co. C, 14th Regt., Wis. Vol. Inf.
David was born circa 1836 at New York. He was listed in the 1860 federal census as a farmer residing with the family of Edward S. Winchester in the town of Rushford at P.O. Omro. David enlisted at Omro on Sept. 8, 1861. He was assigned as above and

TRACEY, David S. (cont.)
was discharged on May 2, 1862 due to a disability. David re-enlisted on Aug. 14, 1862 and was assigned as a Private to Co. F, 21st Regt., Wis. Vol. Inf. He was listed as absent sick when that regiment was mustered out on June 8, 1865.
{US 1860; ROV}

TRACEY, George E. - Pvt., Co. D, 32nd Regt., Wis. Vol. Inf.
George resided at Oshkosh and enlisted there on Nov. 18, 1863. He was assigned as above and was transferred to Co. D, 16th (reorg.) Regt., Wis. Vol. Inf. on June 4, 1865. George was mustered out on July 12, 1865.
{ROV}

TRACEY, John F. - Pvt., Co. D, 32nd Regt., Wis. Vol. Inf.
John resided at Oshkosh and enlisted there on Dec. 28, 1863. He was assigned as above and was taken prisoner on Sept. 1, 1864 at Atlanta, Georgia. John was transferred to Co. D, 16th (reorg.) Regt., Wis. Vol. Inf. on June 4, 1865 and was then mustered out on July 12, 1865.
{ROV}

TRACEY, John R. - Pvt., Co. I, 2nd Regt., Wis. Cav.
John resided at Oshkosh and enlisted there on Aug. 19, 1864. He was assigned as above and was mustered out on May 28, 1865.
{ROV}

TREFETHEN, C. - Pvt., Co. F, 52nd Regt., Illinois Vol. Inf.
He was listed as above in the veteran section of the 1905 Wisconsin State census at P.O. Winneconne.
{WC-V 1905}

TREFETHEN, Hubbard - Pvt., Co. I, 75th Regt., Illinois Vol. Inf.
Hubbard was born on Aug. 2, 1836 at Rye, Rockingham County, New Hampshire. He was a son of Sebastian and Elizabeth Trefethen. Hubbard had little recollection of his parents as his mother died while he was young and his father went west and was not heard from again. Hubbard was raised in New Hampshire and he attended the common school at Rye. He was trained as an engineer and a blacksmith. Hubbard followed those trades until his enlistment. He was in Illinois during the first months of the war and he enlisted there at Fulton on Aug. 8, 1862. He became ill at Tullahoma, Tennessee and was sent to the hospital. While a patient, Hubbard was stung in his left eye by a scorpion, causing intense suffering and finally the loss of that eye. He was also in the hospital at Mound City, Illinois. Hubbard rejoined his regiment after the battle at Chickamauga but before the action at Resaca, Georgia. He was transferred to the Pioneer service and was discharged on June 22, 1865 at Quincy, Illinois. Hubbard removed to Wisconsin and settled for a time at Fond du Lac, Fond du Lac County. He then removed to Winnebago County and settled at Winneconne. Hubbard was married there to Teah Olson. They had one daughter, Bessie Trefethen. Hubbard was listed in the 1890 federal census as residing in the village of Winneconne. He was listed in the veteran section of the 1895 and 1905 Wisconsin State census at P.O. Winneconne. Hubbard died at Winneconne and was buried there on May 23, 1913.
{US 1890; WC-V 1895, 1905; SCA 1:526-7}

TRETTEN, August - Cpl., Co. L, 3rd (reorg.) Regt., Wis. Cav.
August enlisted at Oshkosh on Dec. 4, 1863. He was assigned as above and was then promoted to Corporal in that company. August was mustered out on Oct. 23, 1865.
{ROV}

TRITT, William Lloyd G. - Pvt., Co. F, 21st Regt., Wis. Vol. Inf.
William Lloyd Garrison Tritt was born on June 15, 1819 at Newville, Cumberland County, Pennsylvania. He was a son of Christian and Elizabeth (Vanderbilt) Tritt. Christian was a native of Germany. William removed with his parents to Ohio in 1822. His father died about that same time and he was orphaned there at age 15 years when his mother died. William was married on July 2, 1842 at Deerfield, Portage County, Ohio to Julissa Hubbard. She was born Mar. 11, 1826 at Deerfield and was a daughter of Alexander Kidd and Eliza (Borton) Hubbard. Her father was born on May 7, 1787 at Schoharie County, New York. Her mother was born on June 2, 1799 at Burlington County, N.C. William came to Wisconsin in 1850, accompanied by his brother-in-law Euclid Hubbard. For $200, William purchased the squatter's rights of George Rossin. William resided on that same farm until 1904, when he moved to and adjoining farm which he also owned. William and Julissa had the following children: Zenas C., subject of a following sketch; Frederica M., born on May 6, 1848 at Ohio, died on Feb. 26, 1905; William Lloyd, born on Dec. 17, 1849 at Ohio, died Mar. 16, 1927; Ida Eliza, born on Feb. 26, 1852 at Wisconsin; Hiram B., born in 1854, died in 1936; Sarah A., born circa 1856 at Wisconsin; Euclid H., born on Nov. 25, 1857, married Adelbert Safford, the subject of a pevious sketch; Mialma Ida, born Apr. 15, 1860; Julissa I., born on Mar. 8, 1862 at Poygan; and Florence M., married George Wilkinson. William resided at Poygan when he enlisted on Aug. 14, 1862. He was assigned as above and was taken prisoner at Chickamauga, Georgia. William was confined to prisons at Richmond, Andersonville, Florence and Goldsborough. During his months in confinement William maintained a diary of his prison life. A copy of his narrative is on file at the Oshkosh Public Library. After his release, William was sent to the hospital at St. Louis, Missouri. He was transferred from there to Benton Barracks and finally to the Marine Hospital, where he was then mustered out with an honorable discharged on June 13, 1865. William was listed in the veteran section of the 1885 Wisconsin State census at P.O. Poygan. He was listed in the 1890 federal census as residing in the town of Poygan at P.O. Omro. William then reported that he suffered from dyspepsia. He was listed in the veteran section of the 1895 and 1905 state census at P.O. Omro. William was listed in 1905 as residing on 567 acres, mainly in section 26 of the town of Poygan. Soon thereafter, he divided his farm and presented portions to his children, retaining 310 acres for himself. William fell from a stack of barley and struck his head. He died on that same day, Aug. 5, 1909, at age 90 years. Julissa died in 1917. Both are buried in the town of Poygan at Oak Hill Cemetery.
{US 1860, 1890; WC-V 1885, 1895, 1905; Lawson p.1170-1; Randall p.51; ROV}
{B-1905; Cem. records}

TRITT, Zenas C. - Sgt., Co. A, 37th Regt., Wis. Vol. Inf.
Zenas was born on July 25, 1846 in Portage County, Ohio. He was a son of William L.G. Tritt, the subject of a previous sketch. Zenas resided at Poygan and enlisted there on Mar. 17, 1864. He was assigned as above and was promoted to Corporal and then Sergeant in that company. Zenas was wounded on July 30, 1864 and was mustered out on July 27, 1865. He was married in Winnebago County on July 4, 1867 to Hannah

TRITT, Zenas C. (cont.)
Amelia Disbrow. After the war, Zenas resided in Kansas and died there on Sept. 27, 1918. Hannah A., his wife, was born in 1849 and died in 1947. Both are buried with his parents in the town of Poygan at Oak Hill Cemetery.
{US 1860; ROV; Cem. records; WCMR v.1, p.345, #2057}

TROXELL, Anthony W. - Pvt., Co. C, 46th Regt., Wis. Vol. Inf.
Anthony resided at Oshkosh and enlisted there on Feb. 14, 1865. He was assigned as above and was mustered out on Sept. 27, 1865. Anthony was listed in 1868 as a match maker residing at 13 Irving Street in the city of Oshkosh.
{ROV; T-1868}

TROXELL, Joseph - Sgt., Co. B, 21st Regt., Wis. Vol. Inf.
Joseph resided at Oshkosh and enlisted there on Aug. 12, 1862. He was assigned as above and was promoted to Corporal and then Sergeant in that company. Joseph was mustered out on June 8, 1865.
{ROV}

TROXELL, Richard - Cpl., Co. F, 18th Regt., Wis. Vol. Inf.
Richard resided at Oshkosh and enlisted there on Feb. 8, 1862. He was assigned as above and was promoted to Corporal in that company. Richard was taken prisoner at Shiloh, Tennessee and again at Altoona, Alabama. He was mustered out July 18, 1865. Richard was married in Winnebago County on Sept. 20, 1865 to Ellen Hayes. He was listed in the 1890 federal census as residing in the town of Warren, Waushara County at P.O. Spring Lake. Richard then provided that he had suffered from chronic piles and a disease of the stomach and liver since being discharge.
{US 1890; ROV; WCMR v.1, p.280, #1685}

TROY, Martin - Pvt., Co. D, 53rd Regt., Wis. Vol. Inf.
Martin resided at Oshkosh and enlisted there on Mar. 2, 1865. He was assigned as above. Most of that company was transferred to Co. K, 51st Regt., Wis. Vol. Inf. under orders dated June 10, 1865. The transfer was completed at Ft. Leavenworth, Kansas on June 30, 1865 and the regiment returned to Madison, Wisconsin on Aug. 1, 1865. The men were then mustered out by companies with the last company being mustered out on Aug. 30, 1865.
{ROV}

TRUDELL, James - Sgt., Co. I, 21st Regt., Wis. Vol. Inf.
James resided at Neenah and enlisted there on Aug. 13, 1862. He was assigned as above and was promoted to Corporal in that company. James was promoted to Sergeant on Nov. 1, 1862. He was taken prisoner at Stony River, Tennessee on Dec. 30, 1862. He was promoted to 1st Sergeant of that company on Apr. 25, 1863. James contracted a disease and died on Sept. 24, 1863 at Stevenson, Alabama.
{ROV; Lawson p.831, 835}

TRUDELL, Oliver F. - Pvt., Co. I, 21st Regt., Wis. Vol. Inf.
Oliver resided at Neenah and enlisted there on Aug. 18, 1862. He was assigned as above and was mustered out on May 11, 1865.
{ROV}

TUCKER, Edward L. - Lt., Co. F, 4th Regt., Michigan Cav.
Dr. Edward L. Tucker served in the above unit and was killed in action at Chattanooga, Tennessee. Frank T., a son, was born on June 11, 1861. He came to Wisconsin with his mother in 1866 and settled at Omro. Mary F., widow of Edward, was listed in 1883 at P.O. Omro. She was then receiving a widow's pension of $17 per month. She was listed in the 1890 federal census as residing in the town of Omro at P.O. Omro. Mary provided his unit designation as above and his enlistment date as Oct. 2, 1863. She added that Edward had been shot through the left lung and that he had died in service on Oct. 5, 1863.
{US 1890; LOP-1883; ODN 12 Sep 1896}

TUNKS, William - Pvt., Co. C, 14th Regt., Wis. Vol. Inf.
William resided at Nepeuskun and enlisted there on Mar. 8, 1864. He was assigned as above and was mustered out on Oct. 9, 1865.
{ROV}

TURCK, Albert - Pvt., Co. I, 18th Regt., Wis. Vol. Inf.
Albert resided at Fall River, Columbia County and enlisted there on Nov. 27, 1861. He was discharged. Albert was listed in 1883 at P.O. Oshkosh. He was then receiving a pension of $3 per month for a wound to his right arm. Albert was listed in the veteran section of the 1885 and 1895 Wisconsin State census at P.O. Oshkosh. He was listed in 1888 as a member of GAR Post #10 at Oshkosh. He was listed in the 1890 federal census as residing at 164 Jefferson Avenue in the city of Oshkosh. Albert then provided the information that he had re-enlisted in the 3rd Batt., Wis. Lt. Art. He enlisted in that unit on Nov. 25, 1863 and was then mustered out on July 3, 1865.
{US 1890; WC-V 1885, 1895; ROV; LOP-1883}

TURK, Samuel M. - Pvt., Co. A, 43rd Regt., Wis. Vol. Inf.
Samuel resided at Utica and enlisted there on Aug. 22, 1864. He was assigned as above and was mustered out on June 24, 1865.
{ROV}

TURNCLIFFE, William W. - Pvt., Co. L, 1st Regt., Ohio Cav.
William was listed as above in the veteran section of the 1895 Wisconsin State census at P.O. Menasha. He was listed in 1905 (Tunnicliffe) as a foreman working at the Menasha Woodenware Company and residing at 353 First Street in the city of Menasha. Richard M., his son, was also listed at that address.
{WC-V 1895; B-1905}

TURNELL, William - Pvt., Co. I, 21st Regt., Wis. Vol. Inf.
William resided at Neenah and enlisted there on Aug. 11, 1862. He was assigned as above and was taken prisoner at Chickamauga, Georgia on Sept. 20, 1863. William was listed as absent and still a prisoner when the regiment was mustered out on June 8, 1865.
{ROV; Lawson p.834}

TURNER, Albert H. - Pvt., Co. F, 101st Regt., Ohio Vol. Inf.
Albert was listed in 1868 as a laborer residing at 17 Bay Street in the city of Oshkosh. Harriet, widow of Albert, was listed in the 1890 federal census as residing at 59 Peck Court in Oshkosh. She then provided his unit designation as above and that he had

TURNER, Albert H. (cont.)
enlisted as such on Aug. 5, 1862.
{US 1890; T-1868}

TURNER, Andrew - Pvt., Co. C, 14th Regt., Wis. Vol. Inf.
Andrew was born circa 1832 at Scotland. He was listed in the 1860 federal census as residing on a farm in the town of Utica at P.O. Welaunee. Rachel Chaffee, his wife, was born circa 1839 at Canada. They had at least the following children: Elisabeth, born circa 1855; Mary, born circa 1857; and Frank, born in 1860. All three children were born in Wisconsin. Elisabeth Chaffee, mother of Rachel, was also listed as residing with them. She was born circa 1805 at Canada. Andrew enlisted at Utica on Nov. 11, 1861. He was assigned as above and was transferred to the Veteran Reserve Corps on Apr. 1, 1865. Andrew was then mustered out on Oct. 16, 1865.
{US 1860; ROV}

TURNER, Charles Granville - Pvt., Co. E, 3rd Regt., Wis. Cav.
Charles resided at Magnolia, Rock County and enlisted there on Feb. 20, 1862. He was assigned as above and was then transferred to Co. C, 3rd (reorg.) Regt., Wis. Cav. on Feb. 1, 1865. Charles was mustered out on Mar. 5, 1865 at the end of his term of enlistment. He was listed in the veteran section of the 1895 Wisconsin State census at P.O. Oshkosh.
{WC-V 1895; ROV}

TURNER, Charles H. - Pvt., Co. C, 21st Regt., Wis. Vol. Inf.
Charles was born circa 1835 at New York. He was married in Winnebago County on Sept. 11, 1858 to Louisa J. Whitemarsh. She was born in 1834, also at New York. They were listed in the 1860 federal census as residing on a farm in the town of Omro at P.O. Oshkosh. Charles enlisted at Omro on Aug. 12, 1862, when he was assigned as above. He was wounded in the arm at Chaplin Hills, Kentucky in Oct. 1862. He contracted a disease and died on Dec. 1, 1862 at Bowling Green, Kentucky. Louisa died in 1877. She is buried in the town of Omro on the Whitemarsh plot at Omro Junction Cemetery.
{US 1860; ROV; WCMR v.1, p.175; #844; Cem. records; OWN 16 Oct 1862}

TURNER, John W. - Sgt., Co. L, 3rd (reorg.) Regt., Wis. Vol. Inf.
John resided at Nepeuskun and enlisted there on Jan. 4, 1864. He was assigned as above and was promoted to Commissary Sergeant in that company. John was mustered out on Oct. 23, 1865.
{ROV}

TURNER, Stephen A. - Sgt., Co. L, 3rd (reorg.) Regt., Wis. Cav.
Stephen resided at Oshkosh and enlisted there on Dec. 28, 1863. He was assigned as above and was promoted to 1st Sergeant in that company. Stephen was mustered out on July 17, 1865. He was last known to be residing at Soldiers' Home at Leavenworth, Kansas in an 1899 article by Col. Harshaw.
{ROV; ODN 07 May 1899}

TURNER, Stephen W. - Cpl., Co. H, 20th Regt., Wis. Vol. Inf.
Stephen was born in Dec. 1831 at New York. His mother was a native of that state and his father was born in Maine. Stephen resided at Omro and enlisted there on Aug. 6,

TURNER, Stephen W. (cont.)
1862. He was assigned as above and was promoted to Corporal in that company. Stephen was discharged under orders dated Feb. 19, 1863. He was listed in the veteran section of the 1885 Wisconsin State census at P.O. Omro. Stephen was listed in the 1890 federal census as residing at 282 Main Street in the city of Oshkosh. Stephen then listed that he was a veteran of Co. D, 1st Regt., Wis. Cav. He provided his service dates as having been from Feb. 19, 1863 to Aug. 29, 1864 and that he had also served with the Mississippi Marine Brigade. He added that he suffered from bronchitis and chronic diarrhea. Stephen was not found in the records of the 1st Regt., Wis. Cav. He was listed in the veteran section of the 1895 state census at P.O. Oshkosh. Stephen was listed in the 1900 federal census as residing at the Wisconsin Veterans' Home at King. Frances, his wife of 7 years, was residing there with him. She was born in March 1844 at New York. They had no children.
{US 1890, 1900; WC-V 1885, 1895; ROV}

TURNEY, Ira J.J. - Pvt., Co. L, 3rd (reorg.) Regt., Wis. Cav.
Ira was a brother of James C. Turney from a following sketch. Ira resided at Algoma and enlisted there on Feb. 22, 1864. He was assigned as above and was mustered out on Oct. 23, 1865. Ira was listed in the 1890 federal census as residing at P.O. New London, Waupaca County.
{US 1890; ROV; SCA 1:290-1}

TURNEY, James C. - Sgt., Co. L, 3rd (reorg.) Regt., Wis. Cav.
James was born on Mar. 4, 1828 at Cool Springs, Mercer Co., Pennsylvania. He was a son of Joseph and Mary (Wilson) Turney. Mary's father was a native of Scotland. Joseph was a native of Westmoreland County, Pennsylvania. He was a poor man with six children. Each was allowed to attend a three-month term at school in order. As such, James received one term of school every six years. He removed to Wisconsin in 1846 and settled in Winnebago County at Oshkosh. The city was then little more than an Indian trading post and a post office. James was engaged as a surveyor and an estimator of land values. He was married on Feb. 3, 1851 to Emily Rogers. Their marriage was recorded as having occurred on Mar. 20, 1851. She died in 1859, leaving a daughter Emma, who was later married to William Struck. James was residing at Liberty, Outagamie County when he enlisted on Nov. 29, 1863. He was assigned as above and was promoted to Sergeant in that company. James was then mustered out on Oct. 23, 1865. He was married on Dec. 25, 1867 to Frances Dexter. James and Frances had three children: J.C.; Maud; and Dell. In 1888 James was residing at New London, Waupaca County, where he was a member of GAR Post #46. He was listed in the 1890 federal census as residing at P.O. New London and suffering the effects of chronic diarrhea. Four of his brothers served in Wisconsin regiments. Samuel was a member of Co. D, 21st Regt., Wis. Vol. Inf. He was taken prisoner during the battle at Chickamauga, Georgia and died of scorbutus on June 18, 1864 while in the rebel prison at Andersonville, Georgia. He was buried there in grave #2,148. Benjamin L., youngest of the five, was a member of that same company. He was killed on Dec. 30, 1862 at Stone River, Tennessee. Ira is the subject of a previous sketch. John M. was a member of Co. L, 3rd (reorg.) Regt., Wis. Cav. He was listed in the 1890 federal census as residing in Waupaca County. Ripley J. Richards, a brother-in-law, was a member of Co. E, 2nd Regt., Wis. Vol. Inf. John R. Nickels, another brother-in-law, is the subject of a previous sketch. Eleazor Dexter, a brother of Frances, was a veteran of the

TURNEY, James C. (cont.)
Mexican War and served as a Corporal in Co. I, 44th Regt., Wis. Vol. Inf.
{US 1890; ROV; SCA 1:290-1; WCMR v.1, p.33, #141}

TUTTLE, Amos C. - Cpl., Co. B, 3rd Regt., Wis. Cav.
Amos was a son of Solomon and Mary Tuttle. Mary died on Apr. 2, 1874 at age 77 years, 6 months and 8 days. Amos resided at Algoma and enlisted there on Dec. 27, 1861. He was assigned as above and was promoted to Corporal in that company. Amos was transferred to Co. B, 3rd (reorg.) Regt., Wis. Vol. Inf. on Feb. 1, 1865 and was mustered out on Sept. 8, 1865. He died on Mar. 12, 1869 at age 26 years, 11 months and 22 days. He is buried with his mother and brother Sylvester W. in the town of Algoma at Ellenwood Cemetery, Section B.
{ROV; Cem. records}

TUTTLE, Burton A. - Pvt., Co. G, 148th Regt., New York Vol. Inf.
Burton was born circa 1845 at New York. He was married to Sarah Hough on May 23, 1868 in Winnebago County. Burton was listed in 1883 at P.O. Menasha, where he was receiving a pension of $4 per month for the loss of his right thumb. He was listed in the veteran section of the 1885, 1895 and 1905 Wisconsin State census at P.O. Menasha. Burton was listed in the 1890 federal census as residing in the town of Menasha at P.O. Menasha. He was listed in 1905 as a painter at the Pulley Works and residing at 202 Chute Street in the city of Menasha. Burton was listed in the 1910 federal census as a widower residing at the Wisconsin Veterans' Home at King. He had been married for 14 years.
{US 1890, 1910; WC-V 1885, 1895, 1905; WCMR v.1, p.387, #2394; B-1905}
{LOP-1883}

TUTTLE, Wilmar - Pvt., Co. I, 57th Regt., ? Vol. Inf.
Wilmar was born on Sept. 12, 1844 at Vermont. He was a son of Milo and Mary Tuttle. Both parents were natives of Vermont, the father born there circa 1822 and the mother born on Jan. 24, 1820. They were listed in the 1860 federal census as residing on a farm in the town of Nepeuskun at P.O. Koro. Listed with them were the following children: Mariette, born circa 1842; Wilmar; Loranc, born circa 1846; Ervin, born circa 1848; Angelia, born circa 1851; Arthur, born circa 1854; and Adelaide, born circa 1856. The three youngest children were born in Wisconsin and the others were born in Vermont. Wilmar died in the hospital at Corinth, Mississippi on June 10, 1863. Mary A., his mother, died on Sept. 18, 1910. She was listed in 1905 as the widow of Milo Tuttle and residing in the village of Waukau. Mary is buried with Wilmar in the town of Rushford at Waukau Cemetery.
{US 1860; B-1905; Cem. records}

TWEEDY, Ephraim - Pvt., Co. A, 1st (3 yr.) Regt., Wis. Vol. Inf.
Ephraim was born circa 1834 at Canada. He was listed in the 1860 federal census as a lumberman residing with William R. Garrick in the third ward of the city of Oshkosh. Ephraim enlisted at Oshkosh on Oct. 5, 1861. He was assigned as above and was taken prisoner at Jefferson, Tennessee. Ephraim was mustered out on Oct. 13, 1864 at the end of his term of enlistment.
{US 1860; ROV}

TWING, William A. - Pvt., unassigned, 6th Regt., Wis. Vol. Inf.
William resided at Clayton and was drafted there on Mar. 20, 1865. He was assigned as above but did not appear on the rolls of any company within that regiment.
{ROV}

TWINING, David M. - Pvt., Co. D, 31st Regt., Wis. Vol. Inf.
David resided at Utica and enlisted there on Aug. 15, 1862. He was assigned as above and was mustered out on June 20, 1865.
{ROV}

TWINING, George R. - Cpl., Co. C, 6th Regt., Wis. Vol. Inf.
George resided at Utica and enlisted on Jan. 2, 1864. He was assigned as above and was promoted to Corporal in that company. George was mustered out on July 14, 1865.
{ROV}

TWINING, Henry L. - Pvt., Co. G, 31st Regt., Wis. Vol. Inf.
Henry resided at Utica and enlisted there on Aug. 14, 1862. He was assigned as a musician in the above company and was promoted to regimental Principal Musician on Nov. 1, 1863. This promotion was rejected and he was then transferred to Co. G of that regiment on Nov. 11, 1864. Henry was again promoted to Principal Musician of the regiment on Jan. 1, 1865. He was mustered out on June 20, 1865.
{ROV}

TYLER, Delancey H. - Pvt., Co. K, 11th Regt., Wis. Vol. Inf.
Delancey resided at Clayton and enlisted there on Oct. 17, 1861. He was assigned as above and was mustered out on Sept. 4, 1865.
{ROV}

TYLER, VanRansselear Fitch - Pvt., Co. C, 20th Regt., Iowa Vol. Inf.
Van and his wife came to Oshkosh from Lone Rock, Richland County about 1871/2. They opened a restaurant which was not successful. Van then returned to his profession as a painter. His wife eloped with Mr. Hammond of Fond du Lac soon after she arrived in Oshkosh. Van was then married to Emma Hall. They had a son who was born circa 1880. Emma died soon after her son was born and Van was married third about 1883 to Emma Swallow. Her parents were residing at Van Dyne. Van was listed as above in the veteran section of the 1885 Wisconsin State census at P.O. Oshkosh. He and his wife moved to Minneapolis about 1888. On Oct. 14, 1893 he shot his wife and then killed himself in Minneapolis, Minnesota.
{WC-V 1885; OWN 21 Oct 1893}

Continued in Volume Three

www.ingramcontent.com/pod-product-compliance
Lightning Source LLC
Chambersburg PA
CBHW051626230426
43669CB00013B/2194